ANNUAL 1996-7

Published by Invincible Press, an imprint of HarperCollins*Publishers*, 77-85 Fulham Palace Road, Hammersmith, London W6 8JB.

First published 1887

Editorial compilation by Hayters, Humatt House, 146-148 Clerkenwell Road, London EC1R 5DP

Typesetting by Letterpart Limited, Reigate, Surrey

Printed and bound in Great Britain

Distributed by The Magazine Marketing Company, Octagon House, White Hart Meadows, Ripley, Woking, Surrey GU23 6HR. Telephone (01483) 211222

ISBN 0 00 218737 X

FRONT COVER

HISTORIC MOMENT: ERIC CANTONA, Footballer of the Year, lifts the F.A. Cup. It's a record second Double for Manchester United.

(Photograph by *Empics*)

CONTENTS

A YEAR TO REMEMBER

By Albert Sewell

On the back of England's successful staging of the European Championship, and following an unprecedented second Double for Manchester United, the new season faces a daunting challenge in terms of presentation and achievement.

In semi-final overtime, **England** came within a coat of goalpost paint of reaching the Final of the Euro 96. So near, so far, but by the end of his 2½-year reign that amounted to just five competitive matches, **Terry Venables** had restored pride to our game with a team that played like England again. He leaves his successor the basis of a decent, rejuvenated side.

In contrast to Venables' long wait for the real thing, **Glenn Hoddle** goes straight into World Cup action away to Moldova on September 1, with Italy, Poland and Georgia lurking in the group.

He will take to Eastern Europe the nucleus of a team only recently hardened to the needs of competitive International play. In waiting for World Cup 98 there are already outstanding young talents like Gareth Southgate, Jamie Redknapp, the Neville brothers, Robbie Fowler and Steve McManaman (who, suggests no less an eminence than Pele, might find a free role in the middle his most potent position up front).

Stuart Pearce, now retired from the International battlefield, will not be the only member of the Euro 96 squad who has played his last game for England.

It will be fascinating to see how Hoddle builds on the foundations he inherits, and among those awaiting with special interest the naming of his early squads are David Beckham, Ugo Ehiogu, Jason Wilcox – and Matthew Le Tissier. His talents have been largely mistrusted by two England team bosses, in the way that Hoddle was himself frustrated in the early part of an International career that ultimately reached 53 caps. At 27, Le Tissier can be remotivated by the arrival of Graeme Souness at Southampton, to England's as well as his own advantage.

Hoddle and the F.A. need to draw up a new off-the-field code of conduct for England's players. This was highlighted by the Far East trip that preceded Euro 96. Whatever happened – or did not happen, according to the party line – on the plane bringing them home from Hong Kong, it does the country no credit for their footballers to be seen as a slovenly lot travelling the world on England's behalf.

In this context, a story from Bobby Charlton's England days is not inappropriate. Before a summer tour, he was delegated to ask Alf Ramsey on behalf of the squad: "Would you think about allowing the players to travel in casual gear?" Alf responded: "I'll think about it . . . I've thought about it . . . we'll travel in blazers and flannels."

Wembley in June will be remembered as much for the atmosphere off the field as for the drama on it – painted faces, stirring patriotism with the waving of the flag of St. George by thousands, the hearty singing of the National Anthem and the tournament's theme song, Football's Coming Home. A festival of football indeed. Can there, realistically, be any other venue than Wembley for the new national stadium, when the decision is announced this autumn?

The other seven excellently appointed grounds provided pitches remarkably recovered from a season's wear, which will not have escaped those who favour summer football. And without a fence in sight, the matches were kept hooligan-free; reward for vast pre-tournament preparation by police and organisers.

The Tartan Army again did Scotland proud, and if Craig Brown can solve a long-term scoring problem, they could be travelling in force to France 98.

The draw for Euro 96 brought England and Scotland together again after seven years. It was trouble-free, other than in Trafalgar Square that night, and revived hopes that the oldest International fixture in the calendar might be played regularly again.

How best to resolve major cup-ties that are deadlocked after 90 minutes remains a subject for debate across the world. In the last three World Cups, three of the quarter-finals in 1986, both semi-finals in 1990 and the Final itself in 1994 went to penalties. At Euro 96, the newly-introduced "golden goal" rule failed to decide two quarter-finals and both semi-finals, but **did** settle the Final five minutes into overtime.

The penalty shoot-out becomes increasingly unsatisfactory. A goalkeeper who may have played heroically through normal and extra time, is suddenly the fall guy, while there is no hiding place for the unfortunate individual who ultimately makes **THE** miss from the spot.

FIFA are looking again at the shoot-out and "golden goal" system. Why not play until a winner is scored, be it one minute or two hours into overtime – never mind the TV schedules? Alternatively, if scores are still level after regulation extra time, the winners to be the side with the better disciplinary record over the competition, i.e. a reward for fair play?

If such a card-count had applied in the Euro 96 semi-finals, England and France would have gone through. Instead, the Final was between the countries with the worst disciplinary figures in the tournament. And, as so often in the past, Germany go on winning the important matches. Alan Hansen summed up their qualities in six words: "Technical ability, strong minds, good system."

The **transfer market** went quiet during Euro 96 and flared into multi-million pound action afterwards. With its ever-growing assembly of foreign stars, English club football has become what one Italian commentator describes as the "new Eldorado of world soccer."

The arrival this summer of Vialli, Ravanelli, Di Matteo, Leboeuf, Futre and Raducioiu – doubtless with others on the way before kick-off in August – is evidence of the pay appeal to which the Premier League of Nations has been elevated by vast injections of TV money and merchandising.

But can **Middlesbrough** really afford to pay Fabrizio Ravanelli a reported £42,000 a week – this the club that had the bailiffs in ten years ago?

Gordon Taylor, the PFA's chief executive, warns of the influx of foreign players: "The North-east used to be a regular breeding ground, with players like Alan Shearer, Paul Gascoigne and Peter Beardsley coming through. Now Newcastle and Middlesbrough are turning to seasoned Internationals from abroad.

"That might be good from the spectators' point of view, but clubs need to be reminded of their responsibilities, to strike a balance and put more resources into youth development."

Manchester United spent nothing on their first team while doing the Double for the second time in three years. In the season between, remember, they were one goal short of the Championship, and lost the Cup by another.

Alex Ferguson had said of that double miss: "The Cantona situation cost us everything." Last October the player came back from his 8-month suspension saying: "I have lots of things to prove this season." He did exactly that as United's top scorer in 1995-6 – their General de Goals – as Footballer of the Year, as the Cup-winning goalscorer and captain.

Newcastle started the season with nine wins in the first ten Premiership games, and when they led the field by 12 points in January, betting on the Championship was suspended.

But the signing of Faustino Asprilla from Parma in February was not, it turned out, the last piece in Kevin Keegan's jigsaw. For whatever reason, Les Ferdinand's goalscoring lost its edge – 24 in 31 games before the arrival of the Colombian International, only 5 in 14 afterwards.

So Newcastle had to settle for second place to the only opponents who took 6 points off them. If the last two seasons have taught them that they need a defence, too, the Championship that faithful Geordies have dreamed of since 1927 may not be delayed much longer.

As Manchester United celebrated another Double, **Manchester City** were relegated for a third time in 13 years. They paid the penalty for an abysmal start that brought only 2 points out of the first 33.

Not often does **Anfield** start a season in debt to its supporters, but they are owed something after a Cup Final performance that just wasn't "Liverpool." Neither were the cream designer suits in which they paraded at Wembley. The Liverpool teams of Shankly and Paisley turned up for work in their boiler-suits. Wembley on Cup Final day is no place for dandies. Neither is Anfield.

It was another excellent season at the turnstiles, and if the combined attendance total for Premiership and Football League matches was fractionally down, that was explained by the reduction of the Premier League to 20 clubs, several of whose capacities were affected by redevelopment.

With Paul Gascoigne voted Scotland's Player of the Year twice over, **Rangers** did the Double for a 14th. Time and set a new Scottish points record (87). Though Celtic showed overdue signs of a re-awakening, the odds are that their record of nine titles in a row, from 1966-74, will be matched in 1997.

The **Bosman Affair**, which is outlined on other pages, brought a landmark ruling to a transfer system that had evolved for more than 100 years. There may be loopholes to close, and the full implications will become apparent only in the course of time.

Keeping up with the continuing expansion of the game, the **News of the World Annual**, in its 110th. Edition, has grown by 48 pages. The Records Section in particular appreciates the increase, just as I appreciate help from so many directions in the production of the Annual. Especially David Barber, of the Football Association, Chris Hull at the Football League, David Thomson of the Scottish League and, at the hub of it all, **Trevor Simmons** and **Simon Wheeler**, of Hayters staff.

HODDLE'S ENGLAND TASK

By Alex Montgomery

News of the World Chief Football Reporter

GLENN HODDLE officially took over as England coach with what can only be called indecent haste. One out, one in. Goodbye Terry Venables, welcome Glenn. Less than 36 hours after England's Euro 96 semi-final defeat by Germany, Hoddle was holding his first Press conference in the job.

There wasn't time for Venables to clear his desk at the F.A.'s Lancaster Gate headquarters before the new man was being asked to outline his England Plans.

It was an unnecessarily insensitive act in what had been a bizarre business from the moment Venables felt that the F.A.'s decision, in refusing to offer him what they quite happily offered Hoddle, a new contract for the World Cup, would be final.

Having waited three months possibly to persuade Venables to change his mind – a move which would have been greeted with public acclaim – they outrageously refused to offer him the two-year contract which would have clinched it.

Instead they appointed Hoddle for four years at twice the money. It is called rubbing your nose in it, and the deal was completed just as Venables began final preparations for what he believed would be a highly successful European Championship campaign.

If the timing was distracting for him, he made it clear he would offer all possible help to his successor, but understandably refused him daily access to training.

Limited by Code

There was no animosity between them, but the professional code meant Hoddle was limited to one training visit with the players and one lunch-time meeting with the man he would replace.

It was not the way it should have been for either of them, certainly not how they would have wanted the takeover to be completed, but it tells you a lot about how an important few at the F.A. still see the job of England coach.

Despite the determined efforts being made to update their image, a strong "them and us" attitude remains obvious in football's corridors of power.

One high-ranking official was heard to say at Euro 96 how much better it would be when Venables left, the remark coming after he had produced the best series of performances from an England team since Sir Alf Ramsey's side during the Mexico World Cup in 1970. Hoddle has been warned.

He takes the seat of office with assistant John Gorman very much unproven at this highest and most difficult coaching level.

Hoddle has many qualities, and the most significant will be his vast experience of International football. It will allow him to demand of his players nothing that he couldn't do better himself.

In his first managerial role he steered Swindon into the top division, and he was respectably successful with Chelsea. What he has, and should be able, to do is maintain the progress England made under Venables.

Hoddle will want to see his England produce good football, winning football. There will be changes, and how far-reaching these can be will become known as the season unfolds and the early World Cup qualifying matches are played out.

Hoddle will almost certainly play the sweeper system he used at Swindon and Chelsea, and my guess is that he will find a place for Matthew Le Tissier, who failed to win Venables' confidence.

These are exciting times. England came out of Euro 96 on a high, and the country will expect from Hoddle nothing less than qualification for the World Cup finals in France two years from now.

GLENN HODDLE FACT-FILE

Born: Hayes, Middlesex, October 27, 1957.

Clubs: Tottenham 1974-87; AS Monaco 1987-90; Swindon (player-manager) 1991-93; Chelsea (player-manager) 1993-96.

Transfers: Tottenham to Monaco, June 1987 (£800,000), Monaco to Swindon, April 1991 (free), Swindon to Chelsea, June 1993 (£75,000).

HONOURS:

England: Caps 53, goals 8; Youth, "B" and U-21 Int. (12 caps).

PFA Young Player of the Year: 1980.

Tottenham: FA Cup 1981, 1982.

Monaco: French League Champions 1988.

Swindon: Promotion to Premier League via First Division play-offs 1993.

FOOTBALLER OF THE YEAR

(Original award by the Football Writers' Association to the "player who, by precept and example, on the field and off, shall be considered to have done most for football")

1948 Stanley Matthews (Blackpool); **1949** Johnny Carey (Man. Utd.); **1950** Joe Mercer (Arsenal); **1951** Harry Johnston (Blackpool); **1952** Billy Wright (Wolves); **1953** Nat Lofthouse (Bolton); **1954** Tom Finney (Preston); **1955** Don Revie (Man. City); **1956** Bert Trautmann (Man. City); **1957** Tom Finney (Preston); **1958** Danny Blanchflower (Tottenham); **1959** Syd Owen (Luton); **1960** Bill Slater (Wolves); **1961** Danny Blanchflower (Tottenham); **1962** Jimmy Adamson (Burnley); **1963** Stanley Matthews (Stoke); **1964** Bobby Moore (West Ham); **1965** Bobby Collins (Leeds); **1966** Bobby Charlton (Man. Utd.); **1967** Jack Charlton (Leeds); **1968** George Best (Man. Utd.); **1969** Tony Book (Man. City) & Dave Mackay (Derby) – shared; **1970** Billy Bremner (Leeds); **1971** Frank McLintock (Arsenal); **1972** Gordon Banks (Stoke); **1973** Pat Jennings (Tottenham); **1974** Ian Callaghan (Liverpool); **1975** Alan Mullery (Fulham); **1976** Kevin Keegan (Liverpool); **1977** Emlyn Hughes (Liverpool); **1978** Kenny Burns (Nott'm F.); **1979** Kenny Dalglish (Liverpool); **1980** Terry McDermott (Liverpool); **1981** Frans Thijssen (Ipswich); **1982** Steve Perryman (Tottenham); **1983** Kenny Dalglish (Liverpool); **1984** Ian Rush (Liverpool); **1985** Neville Southall (Everton); **1986** Gary Lineker (Everton); **1987** Clive Allen (Tottenham); **1988** John Barnes (Liverpool); **1989** Steve Nicol (Liverpool); Special award to the Liverpool players for the compassion shown to bereaved families after the Hillsborough Disaster; **1990** John Barnes (Liverpool); **1991** Gordon Strachan (Leeds); **1992** Gary Lineker (Tottenham); **1993** Chris Waddle (Sheff. Wed.); **1994** Alan Shearer (Blackburn); **1995** Jurgen Klinsmann (Tottenham); **1996** Eric Cantona (Man. Utd.).

P.F.A. AWARDS

Player of the Year: 1974 Norman Hunter (Leeds); **1975** Colin Todd (Derby); **1976** Pat Jennings (Tottenham); **1977** Andy Gray (Aston Villa); **1978** Peter Shilton (Nott'm F.); **1979** Liam Brady (Arsenal); **1980** Terry McDermott (Liverpool); **1981** John Wark (Ipswich); **1982** Kevin Keegan (Southampton); **1983** Kenny Dalglish (Liverpool); **1984** Ian Rush (Liverpool); **1985** Peter Reid (Everton); **1986** Gary Lineker (Everton); **1987** Clive Allen (Tottenham); **1988** John Barnes (Liverpool); **1989** Mark Hughes (Man. Utd.); **1990** David Platt (Aston Villa); **1991** Mark Hughes (Man. Utd.); **1992** Gary Pallister (Man. Utd.); **1993** Paul McGrath (Aston Villa); **1994** Eric Cantona (Man. Utd.); **1995** Alan Shearer (Blackburn); **1996** Les Ferdinand (Newcastle).

Young Player of the Year: 1974 Kevin Beattie (Ipswich); **1975** Mervyn Day (West Ham); **1976** Peter Barnes (Man. City); **1977** Andy Gray (Aston Villa); **1978** Tony Woodcock (Nott'm F.); **1979** Cyrille Regis (W.B.A.); **1980** Glenn Hoddle (Tottenham); **1981** Gary Shaw (Aston Villa); **1982** Steve Moran (Southampton); **1983** Ian Rush (Liverpool); **1984** Paul Walsh (Luton); **1985** Mark Hughes (Man. Utd.); **1986** Tony Cottee (West Ham); **1987** Tony Adams (Arsenal); **1988** Paul Gascoigne (Newcastle); **1989** Paul Merson (Arsenal); **1990** Matthew Le Tissier (Southampton); **1991** Lee Sharpe (Man. Utd.); **1992** Ryan Giggs (Man. Utd.); **1993** Ryan Giggs (Man. Utd.); **1994** Andy Cole (Newcastle); **1995** Robbie Fowler (Liverpool); **1996** Robbie Fowler (Liverpool).

Merit Awards: 1974 Bobby Charlton & Cliff Lloyd; **1975** Denis Law; **1976** George Eastham; **1977** Jack Taylor; **1978** Bill Shankly; **1979** Tom Finney; **1980** Sir Matt Busby; **1981** John Trollope; **1982** Joe Mercer; **1983** Bob Paisley; **1984** Bill Nicholson; **1985** Ron Greenwood; **1986** England 1966 World Cup-winning team; **1987** Sir Stanley Matthews; **1988** Billy Bonds; **1989** Nat Lofthouse; **1990** Peter Shilton; **1991** Tommy Hutchison; **1992** Brian Clough; **1993** Man. Utd., 1968 European Champions; Eusebio (Benfica & Portugal); **1994** Billy Bingham; **1995** Gordon Strachan; **1996** Pele.

MANAGER OF THE YEAR (1)

1966 Jock Stein (Celtic); **1967** Jock Stein (Celtic); **1968** Matt Busby (Man. Utd.); **1969** Don Revie (Leeds); **1970** Don Revie (Leeds); **1971** Bertie Mee (Arsenal); **1972** Don Revie (Leeds); **1973** Bill Shankly (Liverpool); **1974** Jack Charlton (Middlesbrough); **1975** Ron Saunders (Aston Villa); **1976** Bob Paisley (Liverpool); **1977** Bob Paisley (Liverpool); **1978** Brian Clough (Nott'm F.); **1979** Bob Paisley (Liverpool); **1980** Bob Paisley (Liverpool); **1981** Ron Saunders (Aston Villa); **1982** Bob Paisley (Liverpool); **1983** Bob Paisley (Liverpool); **1984** Joe Fagan (Liverpool); **1985** Howard Kendall (Everton); **1986** Kenny Dalglish (Liverpool); **1987** Howard Kendall (Everton); **1988** Kenny Dalglish (Liverpool); **1989** George Graham (Arsenal); **1990** Kenny Dalglish (Liverpool); **1991** George Graham (Arsenal); **1992** Howard Wilkinson (Leeds); **1993** Alex Ferguson (Man. Utd.); **1994** Alex Ferguson (Man. Utd.); **1995** Kenny Dalglish (Blackburn); **1996** Alex Ferguson (Man. Utd.).

MANAGER OF THE YEAR (2)

(As chosen by the League Managers' Association and awarded to "the manager who has made best use of the resources available to him")

1993 Dave Bassett (Sheff. United); **1994** Joe Kinnear (Wimbledon); **1995** Frank Clark (Nott'm. Forest); **1996** Peter Reid (Sunderland).

SCOTTISH FOOTBALL WRITERS' ASSOCIATION

Player of the Year: 1965 Billy McNeill (Celtic); **1966** John Greig (Rangers); **1967** Ronnie Simpson (Celtic); **1968** Gordon Wallace (Raith); **1969** Bobby Murdoch (Celtic); **1970** Pat Stanton (Hibernian); **1971** Martin Buchan (Aberdeen); **1972** David Smith (Rangers); **1973** George Connelly (Celtic); **1974** World Cup Squad; **1975** Sandy Jardine (Rangers); **1976** John Greig (Rangers); **1977** Danny McGrain (Celtic); **1978** Derek Johnstone (Rangers); **1979** Andy Ritchie (Morton); **1980** Gordon Strachan (Aberdeen); **1981** Alan Rough (Partick Thistle); **1982** Paul Sturrock (Dundee Utd.); **1983** Charlie Nicholas (Celtic); **1984** Willie Miller (Aberdeen); **1985** Hamish McAlpine (Dundee Utd.); **1986** Sandy Jardine (Hearts); **1987** Brian McClair (Celtic); **1988** Paul McStay (Celtic); **1989** Richard Gough (Rangers); **1990** Alex McLeish (Aberdeen); **1991** Maurice Malpas (Dundee Utd.); **1992** Ally McCoist (Rangers); **1993** Andy Goram (Rangers); **1994** Mark Hateley (Rangers); **1995** Brian Laudrup (Rangers); **1996** Paul Gascoigne (Rangers).

SCOTTISH P.F.A. AWARDS

Player of the Year: 1978 Derek Johnstone (Rangers); **1979** Paul Hegarty (Dundee Utd.); **1980** Davie Provan (Celtic); **1981** Mark McGee (Aberdeen); **1982** Sandy Clarke (Airdrieonians); **1983** Charlie Nicholas (Celtic); **1984** Willie Miller (Aberdeen); **1985** Jim Duffy (Morton); **1986** Richard Gough (Dundee Utd.); **1987** Brian McClair (Celtic); **1988** Paul McStay (Celtic); **1989** Theo Snelders (Aberdeen); **1990** Jim Bett (Aberdeen); **1991** Paul Elliott (Celtic); **1992** Ally McCoist (Rangers); **1993** Andy Goram (Rangers); **1994** Mark Hateley (Rangers); **1995** Brian Laudrup (Rangers); **1996** Paul Gascoigne (Rangers).

Young Player of Year: 1978 Graeme Payne (Dundee Utd.); **1979** Ray Stewart (Dundee Utd.); **1980** John McDonald (Rangers); **1981** Charlie Nicholas (Celtic); **1982** Frank McAvennie (St. Mirren); **1983** Paul McStay (Celtic); **1984** John Robertson (Hearts); **1985** Craig Levein (Hearts); **1986** Craig Levein (Hearts); **1987** Robert Fleck (Rangers); **1988** John Collins (Hibernian); **1989** Billy McKinlay (Dundee Utd.); **1990** Scott Crabbe (Hearts); **1991** Eoin Jess (Aberdeen); **1992** Philip O'Donnell (Motherwell); **1993** Eoin Jess (Aberdeen); **1994** Phil O'Donnell (Motherwell); **1995** Charlie Miller (Rangers); **1996** Jackie McNamara (Celtic).

SCOTTISH MANAGER OF THE YEAR

1987 Jim McLean (Dundee Utd.); **1988** Billy McNeill (Celtic); **1989** Graeme Souness (Rangers); **1990** Andy Roxburgh (Scotland); **1991** Alex Totten (St. Johnstone); **1992** Walter Smith (Rangers); **1993** Walter Smith (Rangers); **1994** Walter Smith (Rangers); **1995** Jimmy Nicholl (Raith); **1996** Walter Smith (Rangers).

EUROPEAN FOOTBALLER OF THE YEAR

(Poll conducted by *France Football*)

1956 Stanley Matthews (Blackpool); **1957** Alfredo di Stefano (Real Madrid); **1958** Raymond Kopa (Real Madrid); **1959** Alfredo di Stefano (Real Madrid); **1960** Luis Suarez (Barcelona); **1961** Omar Sivori (Juventus); **1962** Josef Masopust (Dukla Prague); **1963** Lev Yashin (Moscow Dynamo); **1964** Denis Law (Man. Utd.); **1965** Eusebio (Benfica); **1966** Bobby Charlton (Man. Utd.); **1967** Florian Albert (Ferencvaros); **1968** George Best (Man. Utd.); **1969** Gianni Rivera (AC Milan); **1970** Gerd Muller (Bayern Munich); **1971** Johan Cruyff (Ajax); **1972** Franz Beckenbauer (Bayern Munich); **1973** Johan Cruyff (Barcelona); **1974** Johan Cruyff (Barcelona); **1975** Oleg Blokhin (Dynamo Kiev); **1976** Franz Beckenbauer (Bayern Munich); **1977** Allan Simonsen (Borussia Moenchengladbach); **1978** Kevin Keegan (SV Hamburg); **1979** Kevin Keegan (SV Hamburg); **1980** Karl-Heinz Rummenigge (Bayern Munich); **1981** Karl-Heinz Rummenigge (Bayern Munich); **1982** Paolo Rossi (Juventus); **1983** Michel Platini (Juventus); **1984** Michel Platini (Juventus); **1985** Michel Platini (Juventus); **1986** Igor Belanov (Dynamo Kiev); **1987** Ruud Gullit (AC Milan); **1988** Marco Van Basten (AC Milan); **1989** Marco Van Basten (AC Milan); **1990** Lothar Matthaus (Inter Milan); **1991** Jean-Pierre Papin (Marseille); **1992** Marco Van Basten (AC Milan); **1993** Roberto Baggio (Juventus); **1994** Hristo Stoichkov (Barcelona); **1995** George Weah (AC Milan).

QUOTE-UNQUOTE

SIR BOBBY CHARLTON, 58, Man. United director and England's all-time record goalscorer: "I have all my cartilages, I've no arthritis and I'm as busy as I've ever been."

ALEX FERGUSON on an incident in Man. United's F.A. Cup semi-final against Chelsea: "You know Dennis Wise – he could start a row in an empty house."

CLIVE TYLDESLEY (BBC TV) on another Liverpool goal by Robbie Fowler: "He just has the incredible habit of scoring with magnificent monotony."

Crewe manager **DARIO GRADI**'s reminder in his office: "All you have to do to be successful is work half days – the first 12 hours or the second."

JOE ROYLE, after Everton's victory in the Merseyside derby: "A lot of dummies came flying out of the pram last night."

BOBBY ROBSON: "Where are the great English passers of the ball, like those I worked with from Haynes to Hoddle? Very few now seem to be able to pass, caressingly and accurately, from A to B, let alone to C."

GRAHAM TAYLOR: "You never play as badly when you lose as people say. You never play as well when you win as people say."

JACK CHARLTON: "I've been very lucky because I've had three careers in football – one as a player, one as a club manager and one as an International manager. It may have taken me 50 years to do it, but I've enjoyed every minute."

ALAN HANSEN on BBC TV after Man. United began last season with a 3-1 defeat away to Aston Villa: "You just can't win anything with kids."

LEAGUE CLUB MANAGERS

Figure in brackets = number of managerial changes at club since war.
Date present manager took over shown on right.

F.A. CARLING PREMIERSHIP

Arsenal (10)	Bruce Rioch	June 1995
Aston Villa (15)	Brian Little	November 1994
Blackburn Rovers (18)	Ray Harford	June 1995
Chelsea (16)	Ruud Gullit (player-manager)	May 1996
Coventry City (20)	Ron Atkinson	February 1995
Derby County (14)	Jim Smith	June 1995
Everton (13)	Joe Royle	November 1994
Leeds United (15)	Howard Wilkinson	October 1988
Leicester City (15)	Martin O'Neill	December 1995
Liverpool (9)	Roy Evans	January 1994
Manchester United (8)	Alex Ferguson	November 1986
Middlesbrough (15)	Bryan Robson (player-manager)	May 1994
Newcastle United (15)	Kevin Keegan	February 1992
Nottingham Forest (8)	Frank Clark	May 1993
Sheffield Wednesday (15)	David Pleat	June 1995
Southampton (10)	Graeme Souness	July 1996
Sunderland (17)	Peter Reid	March 1995
Tottenham Hotspur (13)	Gerry Francis	November 1994
West Ham United (7)	Harry Redknapp	August 1994
Wimbledon (7)	Joe Kinnear	March 1992

(Wimbledon manager changes total since elected to Football League, 1977).

NATIONWIDE LEAGUE – FIRST DIVISION

Barnsley (11)	Danny Wilson (player-manager)	June 1994
Birmingham City (20)	Trevor Francis	May 1996
Bolton Wanderers (16)	Colin Todd	January 1996
Bradford City (22)	Chris Kamara	November 1995
Charlton Athletic (12)	Alan Curbishley	July 1991
Crystal Palace (22)	Dave Bassett	February 1996
Grimsby Town (21)	Brian Laws (player-manager)	November 1994
Huddersfield Town (16)	Brian Horton	June 1995
Ipswich Town (11)	George Burley	December 1994
Manchester City (20)	Alan Ball	July 1995
Norwich City (18)	Mike Walker	June 1996
Oldham Athletic (15)	Graeme Sharp (player-manager)	November 1994
Oxford United (11)	Denis Smith	September 1993
Portsmouth (16)	Terry Fenwick (player-manager)	February 1995
Port Vale (16)	John Rudge	March 1984
Q.P.R. (17)	Ray Wilkins (player-manager)	November 1994
Reading (12)	Mick Gooding/Jimmy Quinn (joint player-managers)	January 1995
Sheffield United (14)	Howard Kendall	December 1995
Southend United (20)	Ronnie Whelan (player-manager)	July 1995
Stoke City (13)	Lou Macari	September 1994
Swindon Town (15)	Steve McMahon (player-manager)	November 1994
Tranmere Rovers (13)	John Aldridge (player-manager)	April 1996
W.B.A. (21)	Alan Buckley	October 1994
Wolverhampton W. (16)	Mark McGhee	December 1995

SECOND DIVISION

Blackpool (19)	Gary Megson	July 1996
Bournemouth (17)	Mel Machin	September 1994
Brentford (18)	David Webb	May 1993
Bristol City (14)	Joe Jordan	November 1994
Bristol Rovers (16)	Ian Holloway (player-manager)	May 1996
Burnley (17)	Adrian Heath	March 1996
Bury (19)	Stan Ternent	September 1995
Chesterfield (13)	John Duncan	February 1993
Crewe Alexandra (17)	Dario Gradi	June 1983
Gillingham (15)	Tony Pulis	July 1995
Luton Town (15)	Lennie Lawrence	December 1995
Millwall (17)	Jimmy Nicholl	February 1996
Notts County (21)	Steve Thompson	June 1995
Peterborough United (20)	Barry Fry (owner-manager)	May 1996
Plymouth Argyle (22)	Neil Warnock	June 1995
Preston North End (19)	Gary Peters	December 1994
Rotherham United (16)	Archie Gemmill/John McGovern (joint managers)	September 1994
Shrewsbury Town (14)	Fred Davies	May 1993
Stockport County (26)	Dave Jones	March 1995
Walsall (24)	Chris Nicholl	September 1994
Watford (20)	Kenny Jackett	May 1996
Wrexham (16)	Brian Flynn	November 1989
Wycombe Wanderers (1)	Alan Smith	June 1995
York City (16)	Alan Little	March 1993

(Peterborough manager changes total since elected to Football League, 1960; Wycombe since elected 1993).

THIRD DIVISION

Barnet (3)	Ray Clemence	January 1994
Brighton & H.A. (18)	Jimmy Case	November 1995
Cambridge United (10)	Tommy Taylor	April 1995
Cardiff City (19)	Phil Neal	January 1996
Carlisle United (22)	Mervyn Day	January 1996
Colchester United (17)	Steve Wignall	January 1995
Darlington (25)	Jim Platt	December 1995
Doncaster Rovers (24)	Sammy Chung	July 1994
Exeter City (21)	Peter Fox (player-manager)	June 1995
Fulham (18)	Micky Adams (player-manager)	February 1996
Hartlepool United (23)	Keith Houchen (player-manager)	April 1995
Hereford United (22)	Graham Turner	August 1995
Hull City (16)	Terry Dolan	January 1991
Leyton Orient (17)	Pat Holland	April 1995
Lincoln City (18)	John Beck	October 1995
Mansfield Town (18)	Andy King	November 1993
Northampton Town (20)	Ian Atkins	January 1995
Rochdale (23)	Graham Barrow	May 1996
Scarborough (8)	Mick Wadsworth	June 1996
Scunthorpe United (20)	Mick Buxton	March 1996
Swansea City (19)	Jan Molby (player-manager)	February 1996
Torquay United (24)	Kevin Hodges (player-coach)	June 1996
Wigan Athletic (11)	John Deehan	October 1995

(Cambridge manager changes total since elected to Football League, 1970; Hereford since elected 1972; Scarborough since elected 1987; Wigan since elected 1978; Barnet since elected 1991).

THE BOSMAN RULING

After five years of legal wrangling, a 30-year-old midfield player Jean-Marc Bosman, little known outside Belgium when the case began, won a ruling in the European Court of Justice (Dec. 15, 1995) that shook the football world.

It gave out-of-contract players within the EC the right to become free agents, bringing footballers into line with other EU workers, and became effective this summer. Bosman, the rebel with a cause, said of the ruling: "It is very positive. It is superb."

But there were warnings. Martin Edwards, chairman of Manchester United, commercially Britain's most successful club, said: "I think the new regulations will make it a paradise for stars and their agents. We might lose an expensively-signed player for nothing; we can bring in a new man for nothing, as well. It must be a serious concern for football that a lot less money will circulate. It will affect the smaller, selling clubs and their schools of excellence in producing players."

As a further sequel to the Bosman ruling, UEFA was required (Feb. 1996) to scrap its restriction on the "3 plus 2" system which limited a club, domestically or in European competition, to fielding three foreign players and two "assimilated players" in any one side.

Manchester United will be among the first to benefit as they enter the Champions' League this season. Managers and coaches will no longer have to juggle their teams in Europe and leave out some of their best players. If they wish, a club can now field an entirely foreign eleven.

The first British player to take advantage of the Bosman verdict was Scottish International John Collins who, at the end of his contract with Celtic, joined Monaco with effect July 1. He agreed a 3-year deal with the French club, reportedly worth £20,000 a week (plus signing-on fee), while Celtic received nothing.

This is how the Bosman affair unfolded:

JUNE 1990: Jean-Marc Bosman, a midfield player with RFC Liege, wants to move to Dunkirk after Liege cut his wages by 60 per cent. They demand £533,000 which Dunkirk refuse to pay. Liege subsequently deny Bosman a free transfer before suspending him.

AUG 1990: Bosman takes his club and the Belgian Football Union to court in Liege to seek damages.

MAY 1991: Liege Appeals Court confirms verdict of lower court that Bosman can move freely to new club. Appeals Court later asks Court of Justice as to how EU rules on workers' free movement should be interpreted.

MARCH 1995: Belgium's highest court reject new appeal by UEFA, Belgian Football Union and RFC Liege.

JUNE 1995: In European Court of Justice in Luxembourg, Bosman asks for damages of £600,000+.

SEPT 20, 1995: Advocate General advises the Court to rule that football's system of transfers and its limits on foreign players are illegal.

NOV 24, 1995: FIFA back UEFA and express concern that ruling in favour of Bosman will leave EU countries out of step with rest of world.

DEC 15, 1995: Court rule in favour of Bosman. No appeal is possible.

THE OUTCOME: The judgment will affect only players whose contracts are at an end. Players who are still under contract may be transferred as normal for whatever fee the clubs agree.

However, when a player gets to the end of his contract, his club must negotiate with him as the equal of any other club that is interested.

The implications for the smaller clubs, who survive by selling, could be serious as they will be deprived of vital transfer income. The top clubs with strong squads and effective commercial operations could expect to become stronger.

In February 1996, UEFA were obliged to capitulate to the demands of the Bosman ruling and scrap the restriction on foreign players appearing in its competitions.

They confirmed to the European Commission that "the transfer system for out-of-contract players moving across frontiers in the European Economic Area is no longer applicable and will not be enforced."

SUMMER DECISIONS 1996

FA Summer Meeting (London, July 11-12): **Sir Bert Millichip** (81) retired after 15 years as chairman of the Football Association. His successor is 51-year-old **Keith Wiseman**.

Wiseman, a solicitor and vice-chairman of Southampton FC, was one of four candidates for the post. He defeated Geoff Thompson in a third ballot by 49 votes to 37.

Premiership match squads this season will be increased from 14 to 16 players, with clubs able to use 3 of the 5 named substitutes.

With effect from July 1, **linesmen** to be known as **referees' assistants**, a FIFA decision to reflect the game's growing number of women officials.

League club managers are to be allowed **greater freedom** in 1996-7. During matches they can stand in a designated area near the dugout.

In the **Coca-Cola Cup**, the Football League have given Man. United, Aston Villa, Newcastle, Arsenal and Liverpool byes to the 3rd. Round, to assist their start in the European competitions.

Blank dates: Because of World Cup qualifying round fixtures, there will be 4 blank week-ends in the Premier League this season: Aug. 31-Sept. 1, Oct. 5–6, Nov. 9-10 and Apr. 26-27.

UEFA confirmed (May 23) that, following the Bosman ruling, clubs in Europe can field an **unlimited number of foreign players**, starting this season.

From season 1997-8, the **European Champions' League** is due to be **expanded** from 16 to **24 clubs**.

FIFA's membership grew to 198 with the addition (July 4) of Andorra, Anguilla, Bosnia-Herzegovina, British Virgin Islands, Guam and Montserrat. Palestine is a provisional member.

QUOTE-UNQUOTE

MICK McCARTHY, succeeding Jack Charlton as Rep. of Ireland manager: "It would be much wiser becoming the manager who replaces the manager who replaces Jack, don't you think? I'll be happy with 50 per cent of the success he achieved in the job."

JOHNNY GILES: "There is no such thing as the long ball or the short ball. Only the right ball."

SOCCER HITS NEW TV JACKPOT

The explosion of wealth brought to English football over the last five years – via sponsorship, merchandising and particularly television – was fuelled to new heights on June 6 when Premier League chairmen, meeting at a Coventry hotel, completed a deal worth £743m. over four seasons, commencing 1997-98.

In a record TV deal for British sport, the Premier League will receive £670m. from **Sky** for exclusive live match coverage until the year 2001, while **BBC TV** will pay £73m. to show recorded highlights over the same period.

Screenwise, but at vastly increased cost, it is the same Sky/BBC arrangement that completes the fifth season on its existing contract in 1996-97. It means that until the next century Premier League football will be shown live only on satellite TV.

For terrestrial viewers, the BBC beat off strong competition from ITV to preserve *Match of the Day* (born August 1964) in highlights form until 2001.

But from season 1997-98, BBC TV will lose live coverage of the F.A. Cup, dating back to 1938. They were priced out by **ITV** on November 30 when the Football Association agreed a £130m. four-year package with Sky (£55m.), ITV (£60m.) and BBC (£15m.).

Sky will screen F.A. Cup matches, including replays, live from first round to semi-finals. ITV will show the Final exclusively live from 1998 after earlier-round live coverage on Sunday afternoons and replay highlights in midweek. BBC will preserve their Road to Wembley with Saturday night highlights through the rounds.

England matches will continue to be shown live on Sky, with ITV annexing England highlights from BBC, starting season 1997-98.

Sky's take-over of live football is further demonstrated by the £125m. deal which the Football League completed with them on November 28. In the five-year contract beginning this season, up to 60 matches from Divisions 1, 2 and 3, plus Coca-Cola Cup-ties and all three end-of-season play-off finals, will be screened live on BSkyB.

When the new TV double deal is fully in place in 1997-98, Premier League and Football League clubs will benefit by some £200m. a year.

Meanwhile, season 1995-96 is the fourth in football's current biggest TV deal – a £304m. contract between the F.A. Premier League and BSkyB/BBC from 1992-93 to 1996-97 inclusive.

Sky's investment was reckoned at £190m. and the BBC's £22.5m., with the package topped up to £304m. by £50m. in sponsorship deals and £40m. from foreign TV rights. Each Premier League club was guaranteed a minimum £1.5m. per season, increased according to the number of live TV appearances.

In a separate 5-year deal with the Football Association, also starting in 1992-93, Sky and BBC agreed a £72m. contract for exclusive coverage of the F.A. Cup and England home matches.

This is how football on TV has developed since the first live transmission of the Cup Final in 1938:

1964 First Match of the Day (BBC2, Liverpool 3, Arsenal 2).

1968 First Cup Final live in colour.

1979 BBC nearly lose Match of the Day, win High Court appeal against ITV's originally-accepted £5m. offer for 3-year exclusive contract for football coverage on TV. The BBC/ITV "cartel" continues with £9.2m. deal (for highlights) over 4 years.

1983 First contract for *live* TV coverage of League football (5 matches on BBC, Friday nights; 5 Sunday afternoon games on ITV). Cost of £5.2m. for 2-year deal split equally between TV companies.

1985 Soccer and TV in deadlock over new contract. Coverage blacked out from start of season until January 1986. Football then accepts £1.3m. for second half of season, including 11 live matches in League and Cups.

1986 BBC and ITV agree 2-year, £6.2m. contract (split equally) – each company to show 7 live League matches per season, plus League Cup semi-finals and Final.

1988 Satellite TV enters the bidding . . . end of BBC/ITV cartel. ITV sign League/League Cup contract (£44m. over 4 years, 21 live matches per season) . . . BBC/BSkyB deal is with the F.A. (£30m. over 5 years for F.A. Cup and England matches, live and recorded).

1992* Sky's the limit as new Premier League completes £304m. deal with BSkyB and BBC for next 5 seasons. ITV agree 4-year, £24m. contract with the newly-formed Football League for League and League Cup coverage, live and recorded. Channel 4 brings Italian football to British screens (Sunday live).

1995 Sky begin £10.5m., 4-year deal to screen Scottish league matches live in midweek – 17 per season, starting with Rangers v Celtic (1-1) on Jan. 4.

* Sky cover up to 60 **Premier League** matches per season live on Sunday afternoons/Monday nights. BBC show League match highlights on Match of the Day (Saturday) and Sportsnight (Wednesday).

F.A. Cup: BBC show Sunday match live from 3rd. Round to semi-final inclusive; otherwise highlights Saturday/Monday/Wednesday. Cup Final exclusively live on BBC. Sky cover at least one match live from 1st Round to semi-finals.

European club competitions: Season-by-season contracts, live coverage in selected rounds since 1991: **1991-92** BBC – UEFA Cup (plus E.Cup Final); ITV – European Cup, Cup-Winners' Cup; **1992-93** BBC – CWC; ITV – EC, UEFA Cup; **1993-94** BBC – UEFA Cup; ITV – EC, CWC; **1994-95** BBC – UEFA Cup; ITV – EC, CWC; **1995-96** BBC – UEFA Cup; ITV –EC.

LIVE ON SKY

F.A. CARLING PREMIERSHIP

Sun, Aug 18: Southampton v Chelsea. **Mon, 19**: Liverpool v Arsenal. **Sun, 25**: Man. Utd. v Blackburn. **Mon, 26**: Leeds v Wimbledon. **Mon, Sept 2**: Sheff. Wed. v Leicester. **Sun, 8**: Sunderland v West Ham. **Mon, 9**: Blackburn v Derby. **Sun, 15**: Chelsea v Aston Villa. **Mon, 16**: Arsenal v Sheff. Wed. **Sun, 22**: Tottenham v Leicester. **Mon, 23**: Wimbledon v Southampton. **Sun, 29**: Man. Utd. v Tottenham. **Mon, 30**: Newcastle v Aston Villa.

Sat, Oct 12: Man. Utd. v Liverpool (11.15am). **Sun, 13**: Coventry v Southampton. **Mon, 14**: Sunderland v Middlesbrough. **Sun, 20**: Newcastle v Man. Utd. **Sun, 27**: Liverpool v Derby. **Mon, 28**: Nottm. Forest v Everton. **Sun, Nov 3**: Newcastle v Middlesbrough. **Mon, 4**: Everton v Coventry. **Sun, 17**: Derby v Middlesbrough. **Mon, 18**: Sheff. Wed. v Nottm. Forest. **Sun, 24**: Arsenal v Tottenham.

Sun, Dec 1: Leeds v Chelsea. **Mon, 2**: Tottenham v Liverpool. **Sun, 8**: West Ham v Man. Utd. **Mon, 9**: Nottm. Forest v Newcastle. **Sun, 15**: Sunderland v Chelsea. **Sun, 22**: Aston Villa v Wimbledon. **Mon, 23**: Newcastle v Liverpool. **Thur, 26**: Sheff. Wed. v Arsenal. **Wed, Jan 1**: Everton v Blackburn; Man. Utd. v Aston Villa.

NATIONWIDE FOOTBALL LEAGUE

Fri, Aug 16: Man. City v Ipswich. **Sun, 18**: Birmingham v Crystal Palace. **Tues, 20**: Swindon v Wolves (Coca Cola Cup). **Fri, 23**: Portsmouth v QPR. **Sun, 25**: Barnsley v Huddersfield. **Fri, 30**: West Brom v Sheff. United. **Sun, Sept 1**: QPR v Bolton. **Fri, 6**: Wolves v Charlton. **Sun, 8**: Reading v Oxford. **Fri, 13**: Huddersfield v Oldham. **Sun, 15**: West Brom v Wolves. **Fri, 20**: Ipswich v Charlton. **Sun, 22**: Stoke v Huddersfield. **Fri, 27**: Swindon v Wolves. **Sun, 29**: Port Vale v Bradford.

Fri, Oct 4: Stoke v Norwich. **Sun, 6**: Crystal Palace v Sheff. United. **Fri, 11**: Norwich v Ipswich. **Sun, 13**: Southend v Wolves. **Fri, 18**: Oxford v Birmingham. **Sun, 20**: Tranmere v QPR. **Fri, 25**: Barnsley v Bolton. **Sun, 27**: Man. City v Wolves.

Sun, Nov 3: Grimsby v Sheff. United. **Fri, 8**: Huddersfield v Bradford. **Sun, 10**: Crystal Palace v QPR. **Fri, Dec 13**: Preston v Blackpool. **Sun, 15**: Bristol City v Bristol Rovers.

FERGUSON SUPREME

Alex Ferguson is the most successful Anglo-Scottish football manager the game has known. Six days after taking Manchester United to their third Championship triumph in four seasons last May, he made history as the first manager to complete the English Double twice.

In his ten seasons at Old Trafford (appointed Nov. 1986), he has won 8 major prizes for the club. It took him four years to win the first – the F.A. Cup in 1990 – since when the silverware has piled up: Cup-Winners' Cup in 1991, League Cup 1992, Premier League in 1993, Championship and F.A. Cup 1994, Premiership title and F.A. Cup in 1996 after the previous year's near miss as Double runners-up. He has been voted England's Manager of the Year 3 times in the last 4 seasons.

Before all this, Ferguson broke the Rangers-Celtic domination in Scotland by winning 9 trophies in 8½ years with Aberdeen: 3 Championships, 4 Scottish Cups (including hat-trick), the Cup-Winners' Cup and Scottish League Cup.

He is the only manager since the war to win both English and Scottish F.A. Cups.

For his services to football, he received the OBE in 1984 and the CBE in 1995. New target for Alex Ferguson: the European Cup in 1996-97.

ALEX FERGUSON FACT-FILE

Born: Govan, Glasgow, December 31, 1941.

PLAYING CAREER

Clubs: Queen's Park 1957-60, St. Johnstone 1960-64, Dunfermline 1964-67, Rangers 1967-1970, Falkirk 1970-73, Ayr United 1973-74.

Transfers: Queen's Park to St. Johnstone, July 1960, St. Johnstone to Dunfermline, June 1964 (£25,000), Dunfermline to Rangers, July 1967 (£65,000), Rangers to Falkirk, November 1969 (£20,000), Falkirk to Ayr, September 1973.

HONOURS: Falkirk – Second Division Champions 1970.

MANAGERIAL CAREER

July 1974: Appointed East Stirling manager.
Oct. 1974: Appointed St. Mirren manager.
May 1978: Appointed Aberdeen manager.
May 1986: Appointed Scotland caretaker manager for 1986 World Cup Finals following Jock Stein's death.
Nov. 1986: Appointed Manchester United manager.

HONOURS

St. Mirren: First Division Champions 1977.
Aberdeen: Scottish Champions 1980, 1984, 1985; Scottish Cup 1982, 1983, 1984, 1986; Scottish League Cup 1986; European Cup-Winners' Cup 1983.
Man. Utd: Champions 1993, 1994, 1996; FA Cup 1990, 1994, 1996; League Cup 1992; European Cup-Winners' Cup 1991; European Super Cup 1992.
Manager of Year: 1993, 1994, 1996.

IN QUEST OF THE 'DOUBLE'

Manchester United may have completed the League Championship and F.A. Cup double twice in the last three seasons, but it has still been achieved only six times in the history of English football: Preston (1889), Tottenham (1961), Arsenal (1971), Liverpool (1986), Man. United (1994, 1996).

Liverpool have been denied a further place in this particular Hall of Fame no fewer than six times from 1977. Here are details of failed "double" attempts, in two cases failed bids for the "treble," since 1972:

1995: A year after their first "double," Manchester United came to the last week of the season with it in their sights again. But in the final Premiership match, they were held 1-1 at West Ham – if they had won, Blackburn would have been denied the title – and six days later United lost the Cup to Everton (1-0). Instead of a second successive "double," they were double runners-up. But they made up for it in 1996.

1991: Arsenal, chasing their second 'double', beaten 3-1 by Tottenham in FA Cup semi-final at Wembley three weeks before clinching League title.

1990: Liverpool, cruising to record 18th Championship, beaten 4-3 by Crystal Palace in FA Cup semi-final at Villa Park. It is the third successive season in which Liverpool go close to the 'double'.

1989: Liverpool, already FA Cup winners and needing to avoid 2-0 home defeat by Championship rivals Arsenal in last game to clinch 'double', concede a second goal in injury-time; instead, Arsenal take their first League title since 1971 'double' triumph.

1988: Liverpool, runaway League Champions, beaten 1-0 by unfashionable Wimbledon in one of Wembley's biggest FA Cup Final shocks.

1985: Everton beaten 1-0 by Man. United in FA Cup Final, the last leg of a unique 'treble' attempt. Everton had won the League Championship and European Cup-Winners' Cup in previous fortnight.

1980: Liverpool lose marathon FA Cup semi-final to Arsenal in third replay 48 hours before clinching Championship.

1979: Liverpool lose FA Cup semi-final replay to Man. United in season they win Championship with best-ever defensive record, conceding only 16 goals.

1977: Liverpool, chasing 'treble' of League, FA Cup and European Cup, beaten 2-1 by Man. United in FA Cup Final. They were crowned League Champions before the Cup Final and won the European Cup in Rome for first time four days after their Wembley defeat.

1972: Leeds United's 2-1 defeat away to Wolves in final League game two days after beating Arsenal in FA Cup Final handed Championship to Derby County, who by then were on holiday in Majorca.

RISING PRICE OF SOCCER

A **Manchester United** season-ticket priced £108 for 21 home League games in 1990-91 cost £304 for 19 matches in 1995-96.

BIG PENNY

A one-penny programme for the **1889 Cup Final**, in which Preston beat Wolves to complete the first Double, sold for £7,130 at Bonhams in London last August.

TEN-GOAL WONDERS

In the history of the League football in England, beginning in 1888, there have been 61 instances of a club scoring **TEN** goals or more in a match. The old Second Division produced 20 of these double-figure scores (but only three of them since 1919).

There have been none in the past eight seasons, and none so far in the Premiership:

Date	Div.	Result			
Nov. 7, 1987	2	Manchester City	10	Huddersfield Town	1
Sept. 5, 1987	3	Gillingham	10	Chesterfield	0
Jan. 25, 1964	4	Doncaster Rovers	10	Darlington	0
Dec. 26, 1963	1	Fulham	10	Ipswich Town	1
Dec. 26, 1962	4	Oldham Athletic	11	Southport	0
Mar. 3, 1962	4	Wrexham	10	Hartlepools United	1
Nov. 14, 1959	2	Aston Villa	11	Charlton Athletic	1
Apr. 4, 1959	4	Hartlepools United	10	Barrow	1
Oct. 11, 1958	1	Tottenham Hotspur	10	Everton	4
Jan. 19, 1952	3N	Oldham Athletic	11	Chester	2
Sept. 29, 1951	3N	Lincoln City	11	Crewe Alexandra	1
Jan. 15, 1949	3S	Notts County	11	Newport County	1
Oct. 5, 1946	2	* Newcastle United	13	Newport County	0
Sept. 4, 1946	3S	Reading	10	Crystal Palace	2
Jan. 14, 1939	3N	Hull City	11	Carlisle United	1
Apr. 15, 1938	1	Wolves	10	Leicester City	1
Jan. 13, 1938	3N	Hull City	10	Southport	1
Feb. 4, 1937	1	Stoke City	10	W.B.A.	3
Apr. 13, 1936	3S	Luton Town	12	Bristol Rovers	0
Feb. 1, 1936	3N	Chester	12	York City	0
Dec. 26, 1935	3N	† Tranmere Rovers	13	Oldham Athletic	4
May 5, 1934	3N	Barrow	12	Gateshead	1
Jan. 6, 1934	3N	* Stockport County	13	Halifax Town	0
Nov. 18, 1933	1	Middlesbrough	10	Sheffield United	3
Sept. 2, 1933	3S	Luton Town	10	Torquay United	2
Sept. 7, 1931	3S	Fulham	10	Torquay United	2
Dec. 26, 1930	3N	Hull City	10	Halifax Town	0
Dec. 13, 1930	1	Huddersfield Town	10	Blackpool	1
Apr. 10, 1930	3S	Newport County	10	Merthyr Tydfil	0
Mar. 15, 1930	3S	Norwich City	10	Coventry City	2
Mar. 6, 1929	3N	South Shields	10	Rotherham United	1
Jan. 19, 1929	1	Sheffield United	10	Burnley	0
Oct. 20, 1928	1	Leicester City	10	Portsmouth	0
Aug. 25, 1928	3N	Bradford City	11	Rotherham United	1
Jan. 7, 1928	3N	Tranmere Rovers	11	Durham City	1
Nov. 5, 1927	3S	Northampton Town	10	Walsall	0
Jan. 1, 1926	1	Sheffield United	11	Cardiff City	2
Aug. 29, 1925	1	Aston Villa	10	Burnley	0
Dec. 27, 1919	2	Hull City	10	Wolves	3
Jan. 6, 1915	2	Birmingham	11	Glossop	1
Oct. 5, 1912	1	Aston Villa	10	Sheffield Wednesday	0
Apr. 21, 1909	1	Nottingham Forest	12	Leicester Fosse	0
Apr. 11, 1903	2	Small Heath	12	Doncaster Rovers	0
Jan. 17, 1903	2	Chesterfield	10	Glossop	0
Mar. 2, 1901	2	Small Heath	10	Blackpool	1
Mar. 12, 1900	2	Woolwich Arsenal	12	Loughborough Town	0
Apr. 1, 1899	2	Loughborough Town	10	Darwen	0
Mar. 4, 1899	2	Walsall	10	Darwen	2
Feb. 18, 1899	2	Manchester City	10	Darwen	0
Dec. 26, 1896	2	Darwen	12	Walsall	0

Feb. 18, 1896	2	Liverpool	10	Rotherham Town	1
Jan. 13, 1896	2	Darwen	10	Rotherham Town	2
Mar. 23, 1895	2	Manchester City	11	Lincoln City	3
Feb. 26, 1895	2	Notts County	10	Burslem Port Vale	0
Mar. 17, 1894	2	Small Heath	10	Ardwick	2
Dec. 17, 1892	2	Small Heath	12	Walsall Town Swifts	0
Dec. 10, 1892	2	Burslem Port Vale	0	Sheffield United	10
Oct. 15, 1892	1	Newton Heath	10	Wolves	1
Apr. 4, 1892	1	W.B.A.	12	Darwen	0
Mar. 12, 1892	1	Aston Villa	12	Accrington	2
Sept. 14, 1889	1	Preston North End	10	Stoke	0

*Joint record Football League win (13-0)
†Highest Football League aggregate (17 goals)

(Small Heath later became Birmingham, Ardwick became Man. City, Newton Heath became Man. United)

Continuing the story of our . . . NEW HOMES OF SOCCER

Sunderland and Derby County, both promoted to the Premier League this season, have major re-location plans in hand. **Sunderland** are to leave Roker Park, their home since 1898, for a 40,000 all-seater super stadium to be built on the site of the old Wearmouth Colliery. It is scheduled to be ready in 1997.

Derby, who have played at the Baseball Ground since 1895, plan to move to a 30,000 all-seater ground in the Pride Park area at the start of season 1997-98. Difficulties over the redevelopment of their present home led to the club seeking City Council approval for the new stadium.

Reading are to leave Elm Park and move to a 25,000 all-seat stadium on a 66-acre site in the Smallmead area of the town. The new development, costing £30m., is to be completed for the start of season 1997-98. It will include community sports facilities and parking space for 3,000 cars.

Plymouth Argyle are teaming up with their local council in the construction of Central Park, a £25m. multi-sports complex close to Home Park. In addition to the 23,000 all-seater football arena – scheduled to be ready in 1999 – the development will cater adjacently for a standing capacity of over 30,000 at pop band and other outdoor concerts.

Oxford United signed a £15.3m. agreement (Feb. 1996) with Taylor Woodrow to build a 15,000 all-seat stadium in the Minchery Farm area, for the start of season 1997-98.

Huddersfield Town are extending the capacity of the Alfred McAlpine Stadium to 30,000 with an additional 5,000 seats this season. There are plans for a ten-screen cinema to be built adjoining the ground, profits from which will fund development of a fourth stand, swimming pool and dance studio.

Blackpool are to leave Bloomfield Road, where they have played since 1899. They have council-approved plans for a £50m. development at Whyndyke, with completion due by the end of 1997.

Leyton Orient's ground will be 3-sided this season, work having begun to turn Brisbane Road into a 16,000 all-seater stadium by the summer of 1997. The £8m. development will include new stands, a theatre, cinema, health centre and sports complex.

Under the Football League Achievement Awards portfolio, relating to improved facilities for spectators, **Peterborough United** and **Preston North End** have received the "design and innovation" award for their ground developments. **Barnsley** and **Scarborough** were recognised in the "most progress" category for outstanding stadium improvements.

F.A. CARLING PREMIERSHIP RESULTS 1995-96

	Arsenal	Aston Villa	Blackburn Rovers	Bolton Wanderers	Chelsea	Coventry City	Everton	Leeds United	Liverpool	Manchester City	Manchester Utd.	Middlesbrough	Newcastle Utd.	Nott'm Forest
Arsenal	–	2-0	0-0	2-1	1-1	1-1	1-2	2-1	0-0	3-1	1-0	1-1	2-0	1-1
Aston Villa	1-1	–	2-0	1-0	0-1	4-1	1-0	3-0	0-2	0-1	3-1	0-0	1-1	1-1
Blackburn Rovers	1-1	1-1	–	3-1	3-0	5-1	0-3	1-0	2-3	2-0	1-2	1-0	2-1	7-0
Bolton Wanderers	1-0	0-2	2-1	–	2-1	1-2	1-1	0-2	0-1	1-1	0-6	1-1	1-3	1-1
Chelsea	1-0	1-2	2-3	3-2	–	2-2	0-0	4-1	2-2	1-1	1-4	5-0	1-0	1-0
Coventry City	0-0	0-3	5-0	0-2	1-0	–	2-1	0-0	1-0	2-1	0-4	0-0	0-1	1-1
Everton	0-2	1-0	1-0	3-0	1-1	2-2	–	2-0	1-1	2-0	2-3	4-0	1-3	3-0
Leeds United	0-3	2-0	0-0	0-1	1-0	3-1	2-2	–	1-0	0-1	3-1	0-1	0-1	1-3
Liverpool	3-1	3-0	3-0	5-2	2-0	0-0	1-2	5-0	–	6-0	2-0	1-0	4-3	4-2
Manchester City	0-1	1-0	1-1	1-0	0-1	1-1	0-2	0-0	2-2	–	2-3	0-1	3-3	1-1
Manchester Utd.	1-0	0-0	1-0	3-0	1-1	1-0	2-0	1-0	2-2	1-0	–	2-0	2-0	5-0
Middlesbrough	2-3	0-2	2-0	1-4	2-0	2-1	0-2	1-1	2-1	4-1	0-3	–	1-2	1-1
Newcastle Utd.	2-0	1-0	1-0	2-1	2-0	3-0	1-0	2-1	2-1	3-1	0-1	1-0	–	3-1
Nott'm Forest	0-1	1-1	1-5	3-2	0-0	0-0	3-2	2-1	1-0	3-0	1-1	1-0	1-1	–
Q.P.R.	1-1	1-0	0-1	2-1	1-2	1-1	3-1	1-2	1-2	1-0	1-1	1-1	2-3	1-1
Sheffield Wed.	1-0	2-0	2-1	4-2	0-0	4-3	2-5	6-2	1-1	1-1	0-0	0-1	0-2	1-3
Southampton	0-0	0-1	1-0	1-0	2-3	1-0	2-2	1-1	1-3	1-1	3-1	2-1	1-0	3-4
Tottenham H.	2-1	0-1	2-3	2-2	1-1	3-1	0-0	2-1	1-3	1-0	4-1	1-1	1-1	0-1
West Ham Utd.	0-1	1-4	1-1	1-0	1-3	3-2	2-1	1-2	0-0	4-2	0-1	2-0	2-0	1-0
Wimbledon	0-3	3-3	1-1	3-2	1-1	0-2	2-3	2-4	1-0	3-0	2-4	0-0	3-3	1-0

Read across for home results, down for away

Q.P.R.	Sheffield Wed.	Southampton	Tottenham H.	West Ham Utd.	Wimbledon	
3-0	4-2	4-2	0-0	1-0	1-3	Arsenal
4-2	3-2	3-0	2-1	1-1	2-0	Aston Villa
1-0	3-0	2-1	2-1	4-2	3-2	Blackburn Rovers
0-1	2-1	0-1	2-3	0-3	1-0	Bolton Wanderes
1-1	0-0	3-0	0-0	1-2	1-2	Chelsea
1-0	0-1	1-1	2-3	2-2	3-3	Coventry City
2-0	2-2	2-0	1-1	3-0	2-4	Everton
1-3	2-0	1-0	1-3	2-0	1-1	Leeds United
1-0	1-0	1-1	0-0	2-0	2-2	Liverpool
2-0	1-0	2-1	1-1	2-1	1-0	Manchester City
2-1	2-2	4-1	1-0	2-1	3-1	Manchester Utd.
1-0	3-1	0-0	0-1	4-2	1-2	Middlesbrough
2-1	2-0	1-0	1-1	3-0	6-1	Newcastle Utd.
3-0	1-0	1-0	2-1	1-1	4-1	Nott'm Forest
–	0-3	3-0	2-3	3-0	0-3	Q.P.R.
1-3	–	2-2	1-3	0-1	2-1	Sheffield Wed.
2-0	0-1	–	0-0	0-0	0-0	Southampton
1-0	1-0	1-0	–	0-1	3-1	Tottenham H.
1-0	1-1	2-1	1-1	–	1-1	West Ham Utd.
2-1	2-2	1-2	0-1	0-1	–	Wimbledon

ENDSLEIGH INSURANCE LEAGUE RESULTS 1995-96

FIRST DIVISION

	Barnsley	Birmingham City	Charlton Athletic	Crystal Palace	Derby County	Grimsby Town	Huddersfield Town	Ipswich Town	Leicester City	Luton Town	Millwall	Norwich City	Oldham Athletic	Portsmouth
Barnsley	–	0-5	1-2	1-1	2-0	1-1	3-0	3-3	2-2	1-0	3-1	2-2	2-1	0-0
Birmingham City	0-0	–	3-4	0-0	1-4	3-1	2-0	3-1	2-2	4-0	2-2	3-1	0-0	2-0
Charlton Athletic	1-1	3-1	–	0-0	0-0	0-1	2-1	0-2	0-1	1-1	2-0	1-1	1-1	2-1
Crystal Palace	4-3	3-2	1-1	–	0-0	5-0	0-0	1-1	0-1	2-0	1-2	0-1	2-2	0-0
Derby County	4-1	1-1	2-0	2-1	–	1-1	3-2	1-1	0-1	1-1	2-2	2-1	2-1	3-2
Grimsby Town	3-1	2-1	1-2	0-2	1-1	–	1-1	3-1	2-2	0-0	1-2	2-2	1-1	2-1
Huddersfield Town	3-0	4-2	2-2	3-0	0-1	1-3	–	2-1	3-1	1-0	3-0	3-2	0-0	0-1
Ipswich Town	2-2	2-0	1-5	1-0	1-0	2-2	2-1	–	4-2	0-1	0-0	2-1	2-1	3-2
Leicester City	2-2	3-0	1-1	2-3	0-0	2-1	2-1	0-2	–	1-1	2-1	3-2	2-0	4-2
Luton Town	1-3	0-0	0-1	0-0	1-2	3-2	2-2	1-2	1-1	–	1-0	1-3	1-1	3-1
Millwall	0-1	2-0	0-2	1-4	0-1	2-1	0-0	2-1	1-1	1-0	–	2-1	0-1	1-1
Norwich City	3-1	1-1	0-1	1-0	1-0	2-2	2-0	2-1	0-1	0-1	0-0	–	2-1	1-1
Oldham Athletic	0-1	4-0	1-1	3-1	0-1	1-0	3-0	1-1	3-1	1-0	2-2	2-0	–	1-1
Portsmouth	0-0	0-1	2-1	2-3	2-2	3-1	1-1	0-1	2-1	4-0	0-1	1-0	2-1	–
Port Vale	3-0	1-2	1-3	1-2	1-1	1-0	1-0	2-1	0-2	1-0	0-1	1-0	1-3	0-2
Reading	0-0	0-1	0-0	0-2	3-2	0-2	3-1	1-4	1-1	3-1	1-2	0-3	2-0	0-1
Sheffield Utd.	1-0	1-1	2-0	2-3	0-2	1-2	0-2	2-2	1-3	1-0	2-0	2-1	2-1	4-1
Southend Utd.	0-0	3-1	1-1	1-1	1-2	1-0	0-0	2-1	2-1	0-1	2-0	1-1	1-1	2-1
Stoke City	2-0	1-0	1-0	1-2	1-1	1-2	1-1	3-1	1-0	5-0	1-0	1-1	0-1	2-1
Sunderland	2-1	3-0	0-0	1-0	3-0	1-0	3-2	1-0	1-2	1-0	6-0	0-1	1-0	1-1
Tranmere Rovers	1-3	2-2	0-0	2-3	5-1	0-1	3-1	5-2	1-1	1-0	2-2	1-1	2-0	1-2
Watford	2-3	1-1	1-2	0-0	0-0	6-3	0-1	2-3	0-1	1-1	0-1	0-2	2-1	1-2
W.B.A.	2-1	1-0	1-0	2-3	3-2	3-1	1-2	0-0	2-3	0-2	1-0	1-4	1-0	2-1
Wolves	2-2	3-2	0-0	0-2	3-0	4-1	0-0	2-2	2-3	0-0	1-1	0-2	1-3	2-2

Read across for home results, down for away

	Port Vale	Reading	Sheffield Utd.	Southend Utd.	Stoke City	Sunderland	Tranmere Rovers	Watford	W.B.A.	Wolves
Barnsley	1-1	0-1	2-2	1-1	3-1	0-1	2-1	2-1	1-1	1-0
Birmingham City	3-1	1-2	0-1	2-0	1-1	0-2	1-0	1-0	1-1	2-0
Charlton Athletic	2-2	2-1	1-1	0-3	2-1	1-1	0-0	2-1	4-1	1-1
Crystal Palace	2-2	0-2	0-0	2-0	1-1	0-1	2-1	4-0	1-0	3-2
Derby County	0-0	3-0	4-2	1-0	3-1	3-1	6-2	1-1	3-0	0-0
Grimsby Town	1-0	0-0	0-2	1-1	1-0	0-4	1-1	0-0	1-0	3-0
Huddersfield Town	0-2	3-1	1-2	3-1	1-1	1-1	1-0	1-0	4-1	2-1
Ipswich Town	5-1	1-2	1-1	1-1	4-1	3-0	1-2	4-2	2-1	1-2
LeicesterCity	1-1	1-1	0-2	1-3	2-3	0-0	0-1	1-0	1-2	1-0
Luton Town	3-2	1-2	1-0	3-1	1-2	0-2	3-2	0-0	1-2	2-3
Millwall	1-2	1-1	1-0	0-0	2-3	1-2	2-2	1-2	2-1	0-1
Norwich City	2-1	3-3	0-0	0-1	0-1	0-0	1-1	1-2	2-2	2-3
Oldham Athletic	2-2	2-1	2-1	0-1	2-0	1-2	1-2	0-0	1-2	0-0
Portsmouth	1-2	0-0	1-2	4-2	3-3	2-2	0-2	4-2	0-2	0-2
Port Vale	–	3-2	2-3	2-1	1-0	1-1	1-1	1-1	3-1	2-2
Reading	2-2	–	0-3	3-3	1-0	1-1	1-0	0-0	3-1	3-0
Sheffield Utd.	1-1	0-0	–	3-0	0-0	0-0	0-2	1-1	1-2	2-1
Southend Utd.	2-1	0-0	2-1	–	2-4	0-2	2-0	1-1	2-1	2-1
Stoke City	0-1	1-1	2-2	1-0	–	1-0	0-0	2-0	2-1	2-0
Sunderland	0-0	2-2	2-0	1-0	0-0	–	0-0	1-1	0-0	2-0
Tranmere Rovers	2-1	2-1	1-1	3-0	0-0	2-0	–	2-3	2-2	2-2
Watford	5-2	4-2	2-1	2-2	3-0	3-3	3-0	–	1-1	1-1
W.B.A.	1-1	2-0	3-1	3-1	0-1	0-1	1-1	4-4	–	0-0
Wolves	0-1	1-1	1-0	2-0	1-4	3-0	2-1	3-0	1-1	–

SECOND DIVISION

	Blackpool	Bournemouth	Bradford City	Brentford	Brighton & H.A.	Bristol City	Bristol Rovers	Burnley	Carlisle United	Chesterfield	Crewe Alexandra	Hull City	Notts County	Oxford United
Blackpool	–	2-1	4-1	1-0	2-1	3-0	3-0	3-1	3-1	0-0	2-1	1-1	1-0	1-1
Bournemouth	1-0	–	3-1	1-0	3-1	1-1	2-1	0-2	2-0	2-0	0-4	2-0	0-2	0-1
Bradford City	2-1	1-0	–	2-1	1-3	3-0	2-3	2-2	3-1	2-1	2-1	1-1	1-0	1-0
Brentford	1-2	2-0	2-1	–	0-1	2-2	0-0	1-0	1-1	1-2	2-1	1-0	0-0	1-0
Brighton & H.A.	1-2	2-0	0-0	0-0	–	0-2	2-0	1-0	1-0	0-2	2-2	4-0	1-0	1-2
Bristol City	1-1	3-0	2-1	0-0	0-1	–	0-2	0-1	1-1	2-1	3-2	4-0	0-2	0-2
Bristol Rovers	1-1	0-2	1-0	2-0	1-0	2-4	–	1-0	1-1	1-0	1-2	2-1	0-3	2-0
Burnley	0-1	0-0	2-3	1-0	3-0	0-0	0-1	–	2-0	2-2	0-1	2-1	3-4	0-2
Carlisle United	1-2	4-0	2-2	2-1	1-0	2-1	1-2	2-0	–	1-1	1-0	2-0	0-0	1-2
Chesterfield	1-0	3-0	2-1	2-2	1-0	1-1	2-1	4-2	3-0	–	1-2	0-0	1-0	1-0
Crewe Alexandra	1-2	2-0	1-2	3-1	3-1	4-2	1-2	3-1	2-1	3-0	–	1-0	2-2	1-2
Hull City	2-1	1-1	2-3	0-1	0-0	2-3	1-3	3-0	2-5	0-0	1-2	–	0-0	0-0
Notts County	1-1	2-0	0-2	4-0	2-1	2-2	4-2	1-1	3-1	4-1	0-1	1-0	–	1-1
Oxford United	1-0	2-0	2-0	2-1	1-1	2-0	1-2	5-0	4-0	1-0	1-0	2-0	1-1	–
Peterborough Utd.	0-0	4-5	3-1	0-1	3-1	1-1	0-0	0-2	6-1	0-1	3-1	3-1	0-1	1-1
Rotherham United	2-1	1-0	2-0	1-0	1-0	2-3	1-0	1-0	2-2	0-1	2-2	1-1	2-0	1-0
Shrewsbury Town	0-2	1-2	1-1	2-1	2-1	4-1	1-1	3-0	1-1	0-0	2-3	1-1	0-1	2-0
Stockport County	1-1	3-1	1-2	1-1	3-1	0-0	2-0	0-0	2-0	0-1	1-1	0-0	2-0	4-2
Swansea City	0-2	1-1	2-0	2-1	2-1	2-1	2-2	2-4	1-1	3-2	2-1	0-0	0-0	1-1
Swindon Town	1-1	2-2	4-1	2-2	3-2	2-0	2-1	0-0	2-1	1-1	2-1	3-0	1-0	1-1
Walsall	1-1	0-0	2-1	0-1	2-1	2-1	1-1	3-1	2-1	3-0	3-2	3-0	0-0	2-2
Wrexham	1-1	5-0	1-2	2-2	1-1	0-0	3-2	0-2	3-2	3-0	2-3	5-0	1-1	2-1
Wycombe W.	0-1	1-2	5-2	2-1	0-2	1-1	1-1	4-1	4-0	1-0	1-1	2-2	1-1	0-3
York City	0-2	3-1	0-3	2-2	3-1	0-1	0-1	1-1	1-1	0-1	2-3	0-1	1-3	1-0

Read across for home results, down for away

Peterborough Utd.	Rotherham United	Shrewsbury Town	Stockport County	Swansea City	Swindon Town	Walsall	Wrexham	Wycombe W.	York City	
2-1	1-2	2-1	0-1	4-0	1-1	1-2	2-0	1-1	1-3	Blackpool
3-0	2-1	0-2	3-2	3-1	0-0	0-0	1-1	2-3	2-2	Bournemouth
2-1	2-0	3-1	0-1	5-1	1-1	1-0	2-0	0-4	2-2	Bradford City
3-0	1-1	0-2	1-0	0-0	0-2	1-0	1-0	1-0	2-0	Brentford
1-2	1-1	2-2	1-1	0-2	1-3	0-3	2-2	1-2	1-3	Brighton & H.A.
0-1	4-3	2-0	1-0	1-0	0-0	0-2	3-1	0-0	1-1	Bristol City
1-1	1-0	2-1	1-3	2-2	1-4	2-0	1-2	2-1	1-0	Bristol Rovers
2-1	2-1	2-1	4-3	3-0	0-0	1-1	2-2	1-1	3-3	Burnley
1-1	2-0	1-1	0-1	3-0	0-1	1-1	1-2	4-2	2-0	Carlisle United
1-1	3-0	1-0	1-2	3-2	1-3	1-1	1-1	3-1	2-1	Chesterfield
2-1	0-2	3-0	0-1	4-1	0-2	1-0	0-0	2-0	1-1	Crewe Alexandra
2-3	1-4	2-3	1-1	0-0	0-1	1-0	1-1	4-2	0-3	Hull City
1-0	2-1	1-1	1-0	4-0	1-3	2-1	1-0	2-0	2-2	Notts County
4-0	1-1	6-0	2-1	5-1	3-0	3-2	0-0	1-4	2-0	Oxford United
–	1-0	2-2	0-1	1-1	0-2	2-3	1-0	3-0	6-1	Peterborough Utd.
5-1	–	2-2	2-0	1-1	0-2	0-1	0-1	0-0	2-2	Rotherham United
1-1	3-1	–	1-2	1-2	1-2	0-2	2-2	1-1	2-1	Shrewsbury Town
0-1	1-1	0-2	–	2-0	1-1	0-1	2-3	1-1	3-0	Stockport County
0-0	0-0	3-1	0-3	–	0-1	2-1	1-3	1-2	0-1	Swansea City
2-0	1-0	0-1	0-0	3-0	–	1-1	1-1	0-0	3-0	Swindon Town
1-1	3-1	3-0	0-2	4-1	0-0	–	1-2	0-1	2-0	Walsall
1-0	7-0	1-1	2-3	1-0	4-3	3-0	–	1-0	2-3	Wrexham
1-1	1-1	2-0	4-1	0-1	1-2	1-0	1-1	–	2-1	Wycombe W.
3-1	2-2	1-2	2-2	0-0	2-0	1-0	1-0	2-1	–	York City

THIRD DIVISION

	Barnet	Bury	Cambridge United	Cardiff City	Chester City	Colchester United	Darlington	Doncaster Rovers	Exeter City	Fulham	Gillingham	Hartlepool United	Hereford United	Leyton Orient
Barnet	–	0-0	2-0	1-0	1-1	1-1	1-1	1-1	3-2	3-0	0-2	5-1	1-3	3-0
Bury	0-0	–	1-2	3-0	1-1	0-0	0-0	4-1	2-0	3-0	1-0	0-3	2-0	2-1
Cambridge United	1-1	2-4	–	4-2	1-1	3-1	0-1	2-2	1-1	0-0	0-0	0-1	2-2	2-0
Cardiff City	1-1	0-1	1-1	–	0-0	1-2	0-2	3-2	0-1	1-4	2-0	2-0	3-2	0-0
Chester City	0-2	1-1	1-1	4-0	–	1-1	4-1	0-3	2-2	1-1	1-1	2-0	2-1	1-1
Colchester United	3-2	1-0	2-1	1-0	1-2	–	1-1	1-0	1-1	2-2	1-1	4-1	2-0	0-0
Darlington	1-1	4-0	0-0	0-1	3-1	2-2	–	1-2	1-0	1-1	1-0	1-0	1-0	2-0
Doncaster Rovers	1-0	0-1	2-1	0-0	1-2	3-2	1-2	–	2-0	0-2	0-1	1-0	0-0	4-1
Exeter City	1-0	1-1	1-0	2-0	1-2	2-2	0-1	1-0	–	2-1	0-0	1-0	0-2	2-2
Fulham	1-1	0-0	0-2	4-2	2-0	1-1	2-2	3-1	2-1	–	0-0	2-2	0-0	2-1
Gillingham	1-0	3-0	3-0	1-0	3-1	0-1	0-0	4-0	1-0	1-0	–	2-0	1-1	1-1
Hartlepool United	0-0	1-2	1-2	2-1	2-1	2-1	1-1	0-1	0-0	1-0	1-1	–	0-1	4-1
Hereford United	4-1	3-4	5-2	1-3	1-0	1-1	0-1	1-0	2-2	1-0	0-0	4-1	–	3-2
Leyton Orient	3-3	0-2	3-1	4-1	0-2	0-1	1-1	3-1	0-3	1-0	0-1	4-1	0-1	–
Lincoln City	1-2	2-2	1-3	0-1	0-0	0-0	0-2	4-0	0-1	4-0	0-3	1-1	2-1	1-0
Mansfield Town	2-1	1-5	2-1	1-1	3-4	1-2	2-2	0-0	1-1	1-0	0-1	0-3	1-2	0-0
Northampton Town	0-2	4-1	3-0	1-0	1-0	2-1	1-1	3-3	0-0	2-0	1-1	0-0	1-1	1-2
Plymouth Argyle	1-1	1-0	1-0	0-0	4-2	1-1	0-1	3-1	2-2	3-0	1-0	3-0	0-1	1-1
Preston North End	0-1	0-0	3-3	5-0	2-0	2-0	1-1	1-0	2-0	1-1	0-0	3-0	2-2	4-0
Rochdale	0-4	1-1	3-1	3-3	1-3	1-1	1-2	1-0	4-2	1-1	2-0	4-0	0-0	1-0
Scarborough	1-1	0-2	2-0	1-0	0-0	0-0	1-2	0-2	0-0	2-2	0-2	1-2	2-2	2-1
Scunthorpe United	2-0	1-2	1-2	1-1	0-2	1-0	3-3	2-2	4-0	3-1	1-1	2-1	0-1	2-0
Torquay United	1-1	0-2	0-3	0-0	1-1	2-3	0-1	1-2	0-2	2-1	0-0	0-0	1-1	2-1
Wigan Athletic	1-0	1-2	3-1	3-1	2-1	2-0	1-1	2-0	1-0	1-1	2-1	1-0	2-1	1-0

Read across for home results, down for away

Lincoln City	Mansfield Town	Northampton Town	Plymouth Argyle	Preston North End	Rochdale	Scarborough	Scunthorpe United	Torquay United	Wigan Athletic	
3-1	0-0	2-0	1-2	1-0	0-4	1-0	1-0	4-0	5-0	Barnet
7-1	0-2	0-1	0-5	0-0	1-1	0-2	3-0	1-0	2-1	Bury
2-1	0-2	0-1	2-3	2-1	2-1	4-1	1-2	1-1	2-1	Cambridge United
1-1	3-0	0-1	0-1	0-1	1-0	2-1	0-1	0-0	3-0	Cardiff City
5-1	2-1	1-0	3-1	1-1	1-2	5-0	3-0	4-1	0-0	Chester City
3-0	1-3	1-0	2-1	2-2	1-0	1-1	2-1	3-1	1-2	Colchester United
3-2	1-1	1-2	2-0	1-2	0-1	1-2	0-0	1-2	2-1	Darlington
1-1	0-0	1-0	0-0	2-2	0-3	1-0	2-0	1-0	2-1	Doncaster Rovers
1-1	2-2	1-2	1-1	1-1	2-0	2-0	1-0	0-0	0-4	Exeter City
1-2	4-2	1-3	4-0	2-2	1-1	1-0	1-3	4-0	1-0	Fulham
2-0	2-0	0-0	1-0	1-1	1-0	1-0	0-0	2-0	2-1	Gillingham
3-0	1-1	2-1	2-2	0-2	1-1	1-1	2-0	2-2	1-2	Hartlepool United
1-0	0-1	1-0	3-0	0-1	2-0	0-0	3-0	2-1	2-2	Hereford United
2-0	1-0	2-0	0-1	0-2	2-0	1-0	0-0	1-0	1-1	Leyton Orient
–	2-1	1-0	0-0	0-0	1-2	3-1	2-2	5-0	2-4	Lincoln City
1-2	–	0-0	1-1	0-0	2-2	2-0	1-1	2-0	1-0	Mansfield Town
1-1	3-3	–	1-0	1-2	2-1	2-0	1-2	1-1	0-0	Northampton Town
3-0	1-0	1-0	–	0-2	2-0	5-1	1-3	4-3	3-1	Plymouth Argyle
1-2	6-0	0-3	3-2	–	1-2	3-2	2-2	1-0	1-1	Preston North End
3-3	1-1	1-2	0-1	0-3	–	0-2	1-1	3-0	0-2	Rochdale
0-0	1-1	2-1	2-2	1-2	1-1	–	1-4	2-1	0-0	Scarborough
2-3	1-1	0-0	1-1	1-2	1-3	3-3	–	1-0	3-1	Scunthorpe United
0-2	1-1	3-0	0-2	0-4	1-0	0-0	1-8	–	1-1	Torquay United
1-1	2-6	1-2	0-1	0-1	2-0	2-0	2-1	3-0	–	Wigan Athletic

FINAL TABLES 1995-96

F.A. CARLING PREMIERSHIP

		HOME					AWAY						
	P	W	D	L	F	A	W	D	L	F	A	Pts	GD
1 Man. Utd.	38	15	4	0	36	9	10	3	6	37	26	82	+38
2 Newcastle Utd.	38	17	1	1	38	9	7	5	7	28	28	78	+29
3 Liverpool	38	14	4	1	46	13	6	7	6	24	21	71	+36
4 Aston Villa	38	11	5	3	32	15	7	4	8	20	20	63	+17
5 Arsenal	38	10	7	2	30	16	7	5	7	19	16	63	+17
6 Everton	38	10	5	4	35	19	7	5	7	29	25	61	+20
7 Blackburn Rov.	38	14	2	3	44	19	4	5	10	17	28	61	+14
8 Tottenham H	38	9	5	5	26	19	7	8	4	24	19	61	+12
9 Nott'm Forest	38	11	6	2	29	17	4	7	8	21	37	58	–4
10 West Ham Utd.	38	9	5	5	25	21	5	4	10	18	31	51	–9
11 Chelsea	38	7	7	5	30	22	5	7	7	16	22	50	+2
12 Middlesbrough	38	8	3	8	27	27	3	7	9	8	23	43	–15
13 Leeds Utd.	38	8	3	8	21	21	4	4	11	19	36	43	–17
14 Wimbledon	38	5	6	8	27	33	5	5	9	28	37	41	–15
15 Sheffield Wed.	38	7	5	7	30	31	3	5	11	18	30	40	–13
16 Coventry City	38	6	7	6	21	23	2	7	10	21	37	38	–18
17 Southampton	38	7	7	5	21	18	2	4	13	13	34	38	–18
18 Man. City	38	7	7	5	21	19	2	4	13	12	39	38	–25
19 Q.P.R.	38	6	5	8	25	26	3	1	15	13	31	33	–19
20 Bolton Wand.	38	5	4	10	16	31	3	1	15	23	40	29	–32

(Positions of clubs level on points decided on goal diff; if still level, on goals scored)

Prize Money: **1** £983,300; **2** £934,125; **3** £884,970; **4** £835,805; **5** £786,640; **6** £737,575; **7** £688,310; **8** £639,145; **9** £589,980; **10** £540,815; **11** £491,650; **12** £442,485; **13** £393,320; **14** £344,155; **15** £294,990; **16** £245,825; **17** £196,660; **18** £147,495; **19** £98,330; **20** £49,165.

Biggest Win: Blackburn 7, Nott'm Forest 0.
Highest Attendance: 53,926 (Man. Utd. v Nott'm Forest).
Lowest Attendance: 6,352 (Wimbledon v Sheff. Wed.).
Top League Scorer: 31 Alan Shearer (Blackburn).
Top Scorer, all Competitions: 37 Alan Shearer (Blackburn).
Carling Manager of Year (£7,500): Alex Ferguson (Man. Utd.).
Carling Player of Year (£2,500): Peter Schmeichel (Man. Utd.).
Football Writers' Footballer of Year: Eric Cantona (Man. Utd.).
PFA Player of Year: Les Ferdinand (Newcastle).
PFA Young Player of Year: Robbie Fowler (Liverpool).
PFA Divisional Team of Season: James (Liverpool); G. Neville (Man. Utd.), Adams (Arsenal), Ehiogu (Aston V.), Wright (Aston V.), Ginola (Newcastle), Lee (Newcastle), Stone (Nott'm Forest), Gullit (Chelsea), Ferdinand (Newcastle), Shearer (Blackburn).
Community Club of Year: Manchester City.
Wilkinson Sword Groundsman of Year (all divisions): Dave Braddock (Arsenal).

ENDSLEIGH INSURANCE LEAGUE
FIRST DIVISION

		HOME					AWAY						
	P	W	D	L	F	A	W	D	L	F	A	Pts	Gls
1 Sunderland	46	13	8	2	32	10	9	9	5	27	23	83	59
2 Derby Co.	46	14	8	1	48	22	7	8	8	23	29	79	71
3 Crystal Palace	46	9	9	5	34	22	11	6	6	33	26	75	67
4 Stoke City	46	13	6	4	32	15	7	7	9	28	34	73	60
5 *Leicester City	46	9	7	7	32	29	10	7	6	34	31	71	66
6 Charlton Ath.	46	8	11	4	28	23	9	9	5	29	22	71	57
7 Ipswich Town	46	13	5	5	45	30	6	7	10	34	39	69	79
8 Huddersfield T.	46	14	4	5	42	23	3	8	12	19	35	63	61
9 Sheff. Utd.	46	9	7	7	29	25	7	7	9	28	29	62	57
10 Barnsley	46	9	10	4	34	28	5	8	10	26	38	60	60
11 West Brom.	46	11	5	7	34	29	5	7	11	26	39	60	60
12 Port Vale	46	10	5	8	30	29	5	10	8	29	37	60	59
13 Tranmere Rov.	46	9	9	5	42	29	5	8	10	22	31	59	64
14 Southend Utd.	46	11	8	4	30	22	4	6	13	22	39	59	52
15 Birmingham City ..	46	11	7	5	37	23	4	6	13	24	41	58	61
16 Norwich City	46	7	9	7	26	24	7	6	10	33	31	57	59
17 Grimsby Town	46	8	10	5	27	25	6	4	13	28	44	56	55
18 Oldham Ath.	46	10	7	6	33	20	4	7	12	21	30	56	54
19 Reading	46	8	7	8	28	30	5	10	8	26	33	56	54
20 Wolves	46	8	9	6	34	28	5	7	11	22	34	55	56
21 Portsmouth	46	8	6	9	34	32	5	7	11	27	37	52	61
22 Millwall	46	7	6	10	23	28	6	7	10	20	35	52	43
23 Watford	46	7	8	8	40	33	3	10	10	22	37	48	62
24 Luton Town	46	7	6	10	30	34	4	6	13	10	30	45	40

(*Also promoted via play-offs)
(Positions of clubs level on points decided on goals scored)

Prize Money – Champions: Sunderland £50,000; runners-up: Derby £25,000.
Biggest Win: Sunderland 6, Millwall 0.
Highest Attendance: 27,381 (Wolves v Leicester).
Lowest Attendance: 3,993 (Grimsby v Watford).
Top League Scorer: 27 John Aldridge (Tranmere).
Top Scorer, all Competitions: 29 John Aldridge (Tranmere).
First Division Manager of Year: Peter Reid (Sunderland).
PFA Divisional Team of Season: A. Kelly (Sheff. U.); Kubicki (Sunderland), Richards (Wolves), Rufus (Charlton), Gordon (Crystal P.), Bowyer (Charlton), Rae (Millwall), M. Gray (Sunderland), Parker (Leicester), Strurridge (Derby), Claridge (Leicester).
Football League First Division Achievements Award (ground development): Barnsley.
Community Club of Year: Sunderland.
Wilkinson Sword Div. 1 Groundsman of Year: David Saltman (Wolves).

SECOND DIVISION

	HOME					AWAY						
	P	W	D	L	F	A	W	D	L	F	A	Pts	Gls
1 Swindon Town	46	12	10	1	37	16	13	7	3	34	18	92	71
2 Oxford Utd.	46	17	4	2	52	14	7	7	9	24	25	83	76
3 Blackpool	46	14	5	4	41	20	9	8	6	26	20	82	67
4 Notts Co.	46	14	6	3	42	21	7	9	7	21	18	78	63
5 Crewe Alex.	46	13	3	7	40	24	9	4	10	37	36	73	77
6 *Bradford City	46	15	4	4	41	25	7	3	13	30	44	73	71
7 Chesterfield	46	14	6	3	39	21	6	6	11	17	30	72	56
8 Wrexham	46	12	6	5	51	27	6	10	7	25	28	70	76
9 Stockport Co.	46	8	9	6	30	20	11	4	8	31	27	70	61
10 Bristol Rovers	46	12	4	7	29	28	8	6	9	28	32	70	57
11 Walsall	46	12	7	4	38	20	7	5	11	22	25	69	60
12 Wycombe Wand.	46	9	8	6	36	26	6	7	10	27	33	60	63
13 Bristol City	46	10	6	7	28	22	5	9	9	27	38	60	55
14 Bournemouth	46	12	5	6	33	25	4	5	14	18	45	58	51
15 Brentford	46	12	6	5	24	15	3	7	13	19	34	58	43
16 Rotherham Utd.	46	11	7	5	31	20	3	7	13	23	42	56	54
17 Burnley	46	9	8	6	35	28	5	5	13	21	40	55	56
18 Shrewsbury T.	46	7	8	8	32	29	6	6	11	26	41	53	58
19 Peterborough Utd.	46	9	6	8	40	27	4	7	12	19	39	52	59
20 York City	46	8	6	9	28	29	5	7	11	30	44	52	58
21 Carlisle Utd.	46	11	6	6	35	20	1	7	15	22	52	49	57
22 Swansea City	46	8	8	7	27	29	3	6	14	16	50	47	43
23 Brighton & H.A.	46	6	7	10	25	31	4	3	16	21	38	40	46
24 Hull City	46	4	8	11	26	37	1	8	14	10	41	31	36

(*Also promoted via play-offs)
(Positions of clubs level on points decided on goals scored)

Prize Money – Champions: Swindon £25,000; runners-up: Oxford £10,000.
Biggest Win: Wrexham 7, Rotherham 0.
Highest Attendance: 20,007 (Bristol C. v Bristol R.).
Lowest Attendance: 1,788 (Swansea v Rotherham).
Top League Scorer: 21 Marcus Stewart (Bristol R.); Gary Martindale (15 Peterborough, 6 Notts Co.).
Top Scorer, all Competitions: 30 Marcus Stewart (Bristol R.).
Second Division Manager of Year: Steve McMahon (Swindon).
PFA Divisional Team of Season: Ward (Notts Co.); Wilder (Notts Co.), Taylor (Swindon), Culverhouse (Swindon), Bodin (Swindon), Lennon (ex-Crewe), Mellon (Blackpool), O'Connor (Walsall), Connolly (Wrexham), Stewart (Bristol R.), Nogan (Burnley).
Football League Second Division Achievements Award (ground development): Peterborough.
Community Club of Year: Walsall.
Wilkinson Sword Div. 2 Groundsman of Year: Jim Gardner (Wycombe).

THIRD DIVISION

		HOME					AWAY						
	P	W	D	L	F	A	W	D	L	F	A	Pts	Gls
1 Preston N.E.	46	11	8	4	44	22	12	9	2	34	16	86	78
2 Gillingham	46	16	6	1	33	6	6	11	6	16	14	83	49
3 Bury	46	11	6	6	33	21	11	7	5	33	27	79	66
4 *Plymouth Arg.	46	14	5	4	41	20	8	7	8	27	29	78	68
5 Darlington	46	10	6	7	30	21	10	12	1	30	21	78	60
6 Hereford Utd.	46	13	5	5	40	22	7	9	7	25	25	74	65
7 Colchester Utd.	46	13	7	3	37	22	5	11	7	24	29	72	61
8 Chester City	46	11	9	3	45	22	7	7	9	27	31	70	72
9 Barnet	46	13	6	4	40	19	5	10	8	25	26	70	65
10 Wigan Ath.	46	15	3	5	36	21	5	7	11	26	35	70	62
11 Northampton T.	46	9	10	4	32	22	9	3	11	19	22	67	51
12 Scunthorpe Utd. ..	46	8	8	7	36	30	7	7	9	31	31	60	67
13 Doncaster Rov.	46	11	6	6	25	19	5	5	13	24	41	59	49
14 Exeter City	46	9	9	5	25	22	4	9	10	21	31	57	46
15 Rochdale	46	7	8	8	32	33	7	5	11	25	28	55	57
16 Cambridge Utd.	46	8	8	7	34	30	6	4	13	27	41	54	61
17 Fulham	46	10	9	4	39	26	2	8	13	18	37	53	57
18 Lincoln City	46	8	7	8	32	26	5	7	11	25	47	53	57
19 Mansfield Town	46	6	10	7	25	29	5	10	8	29	35	53	54
20 Hartlepool Utd.	46	8	9	6	30	24	4	4	15	17	43	49	47
21 Leyton Orient	46	11	4	8	29	22	1	7	15	15	41	47	44
22 Cardiff City	46	8	6	9	24	22	3	6	14	17	42	45	41
23 Scarborough	46	5	11	7	22	28	3	5	15	17	41	40	39
24 Torquay Utd.	46	4	9	10	17	36	1	5	17	13	48	29	30

(*Also promoted via play-offs)
(Positions of clubs level on points decided on goals scored)
(Torquay not relegated to Football Conference)

Prize Money – Champions: Preston £25,000; runners-up: Gillingham £10,000; third-place Bury £5,000.
Biggest Win: Torquay 1, Scunthorpe 8.
Highest Attendance: 18,700 (Preston v Exeter).
Lowest Attendance: 1,198 (Hartlepool v Fulham).
Top League Scorer: 29 Andy Saville (Preston); Steve White (Hereford).
Top Scorer, all Competitions: 33 Steve White (Hereford).
Third Division Manager of Year: Tony Pullis (Gillingham).
PFA Divisional Team of Season: Stannard (Gillingham); Jupp (Fulham), Heathcote (Plymouth), Wilcox (Preston), Williams (Plymouth), Davey (Preston), Bryson (Preston), Martinez (Wigan), Kinsella (Colchester), Saville (Preston), Dale (Cardiff).
Football League Third Division Achievements Award (ground development): Scarborough and Preston.
Community Clubs of Year: Leyton Orient and Fulham.
Wilkinson Sword Div. 3 Groundsman of Year: David Pinch (Wigan).

ENDSLEIGH INSURANCE LEAGUE PLAY-OFFS 1996

When **Dave Bassett** was appointed **Crystal Palace** manager in February, they were 16th. in the First Division, but a storming run took them to third in the final table, four points clear of Leicester City. But in a dramatic finish to the play-off Final, **Leicester**, from a goal down, beat them with a shot by Steve Claridge in the last moments of extra time. In anticipation of a penalty shoot-out, City had sent on 6ft. 7in. Australian goalkeeper Zeljko Kalac for the last 30 seconds.

So under new manager **Martin O'Neill** – a Wembley play-off winner with Wycombe in 1994 – Leicester returned to the Premier League a year after leaving it. But promotion from this division should be accompanied by a health warning: the last three clubs to achieve it were all relegated a year later.

The Second Division produced one of the unluckiest stories in play-off history. **Blackpool**, having missed second-place promotion by a point, finished 9 points ahead of **Bradford City** (6th). Then, in the semi-final first leg, Blackpool won 2-0 at Bradford, only to lose the home leg 3-0, and first-season manager **Chris Kamara's** City clinched promotion at Wembley (2-0 v Notts County). It was the biggest day the club had known since they won the Cup in 1911.

For **Sam Allardyce**, giving Blackpool their best season for 19 years counted for nothing without promotion. He was sacked. Yet another example of the cruelty of the play-off system.

Plymouth Argyle finished third in Div.3, then made up for that near miss by beating **Darlington** in the play-off Final to earn promotion a year after being relegated. The crowd of 43,431 was Wembley's highest for a bottom-division play-off and nearly 10,000 more than saw any of England's pre-Euro 96 matches there last season. Plymouth's success confirmed manager **Neil Warnock** as King of the Play-offs. It was his fourth such promotion in seven seasons, after two with Notts County and a third with Huddersfield in 1995.

But there was tragedy, too, to Plymouth's day. In a fight involving two of their supporters outside the stadium before the match, one man died.

SEMI-FINALS

(1st legs Sunday, May 12; 2nd legs Wednesday, May 15)

Div. 1: Charlton 1, Crystal Palace 2; Crystal Palace 1, Charlton 0 (**Palace** won 3-1 on agg.).
Leicester 0, Stoke 0; Stoke 0, Leicester 1 (Leicester won 1-0 on agg.).

Div. 2: Bradford C. 0, Blackpool 2; Blackpool 0, Bradford C. 3 (**Bradford C.** won 3-2 on agg.).
Crewe 2, Notts Co. 2; Notts Co. 1, Crewe 0 (Notts Co. won 3-2 on agg.).

Div. 3: Colchester 1, Plymouth 0; Plymouth 3, Colchester 1 (**Plymouth** won 3-2 on agg.).
Hereford 1, Darlington 2; Darlington 2, Hereford 1 (Darlington won 4-2 on agg.).

FINALS – AT WEMBLEY

Div. 3: Sat., May 25 – **Darlington 0**, **Plymouth 1** (Mauge 65). **Att**: 43,431.
Darlington: Newell; Brumwell, Crosby, Appleby, Gregan, Barnard, Gaughan (Carmichael 85), Carss, Bannister, Painter, Blake. Subs not used: Twynham, Mattison. **Manager**: Jim Platt.
Plymouth: Cherry; Patterson, Heathcote, Logan, Curran, Williams, Barlow, Mauge, Leadbitter, Littlejohn, Evans. Subs not used: Billy, Baird, Corazzin. **Manager**: Neil Warnock.
Referee: W. Burns (Scarborough). **Half-time**: 0-0.

Div. 2: Sun., May 26 – **Bradford City 2** (Hamilton 8, Stallard 75), **Notts Co. 0**. **Att**: 39,972.
Bradford C: Gould; Huxford, Mohan, Youds, Jacobs, Hamilton (Ormondroyd 71), Mitchell, Duxbury, Kiwomya (Wright 77), Stallard, Shutt. Sub not used: Tolson (gk). **Manager**: Chris Kamara.
Notts Co: Ward; Derry, Murphy, Strodder, Baraclough, Finnan, Rogers, Richardson, Agana, Battersby (Jones 82), Martindale. Subs not used: Hogg, Pollitt (gk). **Team Manager**: Steve Thompson.
Referee: G. Singh (Wolverhampton). **Half-time**: 1-0.

Div. 1: Mon., May 27 – **Crystal Palace 1** (Roberts 13), **Leicester City 2** (Parker 76 pen, Claridge 120), after extra time. **Att**: 73,573.
Crystal Palace: Martyn; Tuttle (Rodger 101), Roberts, Quinn, Edworthy, Hopkin (Veart 70), Pitcher, Houghton, Brown, Freedman (Dyer 99), Ndah. **Manager**: Dave Bassett
Leicester: Poole (Kalac 119); Grayson, Watts, Walsh (Hill 119), Whitlow, Izzet, Parker, Lennon, Heskey, Taylor (Robins 100), Claridge. **Manager**: Martin O'Neill.
Referee: D. Allison (Lancaster). **Half-time**: 1-0. **90 Mins**: 1-1.

PLAY-OFF FINALS – HOME & AWAY

1987 **Divs 1/2**: **Charlton** beat Leeds 2-1 in replay (Birmingham) after 1-1 agg (1-0h, 0-1a). Charlton remained in Div.1. Losing semi-finalists: Ipswich and Oldham.
Divs 2/3: **Swindon** beat Gillingham 2-0 in replay (Crystal P.) after 2-2 agg (0-1a, 2-1h). Swindon promoted to Div.2. Losing semi-finalists: Sunderland and Wigan; Sunderland relegated to Div.3.
Divs 3/4: **Aldershot** beat Wolves 3-0 on agg (2-0h, 1-0a) and promoted to Div.3. Losing semi-finalists: Bolton and Colchester; Bolton relegated to Div.4.

1988 **Divs 1/2**: **Middlesbrough** beat Chelsea 2-1 on agg (2-0h, 0-1a) and promoted to Div.1; Chelsea relegated to Div.2. Losing semi-finalists: Blackburn and Bradford C.
Divs 2/3: **Walsall** beat Bristol City 4-0 in replay (h) after 3-3 agg (3-1a, 0-2h) and promoted to Div.2. Losing semi-finalists: Sheff. Utd. and Notts Co; Sheff. Utd. relegated to Div.3.
Divs 3/4: **Swansea** beat Torquay 5-4 on agg (2-1h, 3-3a) and promoted to Div.3. Losing semi-finalists: Rotherham and Scunthorpe; Rotherham relegated to Div.4.

1989 **Div.2**: **Crystal Palace** beat Blackburn 4-3 on agg (1-3a, 3-0h). Losing semi-finalists: Watford and Swindon.
Div.3: **Port Vale** beat Bristol R. 2-1 on agg (1-1a, 1-0h). Losing semi-finalists: Fulham and Preston.
Div.4: **Leyton O.** beat Wrexham 2-1 on agg (0-0a, 2-1h). Losing semi-finalists: Scarborough and Scunthorpe.

PLAY-OFF FINALS AT WEMBLEY

1990 **Div.2**: **Swindon** 1, Sunderland 0 (att: 72,873). Swindon promoted, then demoted for financial irregularities; Sunderland promoted. Losing semi-finalists: Blackburn and Newcastle.
Div.3: **Notts Co.** 2, Tranmere 0 (att: 29,252). Losing semi-finalists: Bolton and Bury.
Div.4: **Cambridge Utd.** 1, Chesterfield 0 (att: 26,404). Losing semi-finalists: Maidstone and Stockport.

1991 **Div.2**: **Notts Co.** 3, Brighton 1 (att: 59,940). Losing semi-finalists: Middlesbrough and Millwall.
Div.3: **Tranmere** 1, Bolton 0 (att: 30,217). Losing semi-finalists: Brentford and Bury.

Div.4: **Torquay** 2, Blackpool 2 – Torquay won 5-4 on pens (att: 21,615). Losing semi-finalists: Burnley and Scunthorpe.

1992 **Div.2**: **Blackburn** 1, Leicester 0 (att: 68,147). Losing semi-finalists: Derby and Cambridge Utd.

Div.3: **Peterborough** 2, Stockport 1 (att: 35,087). Losing semi-finalists: Huddersfield and Stoke.

Div.4: **Blackpool** 1, Scunthorpe 1 – Blackpool won 4-3 on pens (att: 22,741). Losing semi-finalists: Barnet and Crewe.

1993 **Div.1**; **Swindon** 4, Leicester 3 (att: 73,802). Losing semi-finalists: Portsmouth and Tranmere.

Div.2: **W.B.A.** 3, Port Vale 0 (att: 53,471). Losing semi-finalists: Stockport and Swansea.

Div.3: **York** 1, Crewe 1 – York won 5-3 on pens (att: 22,416). Losing semi-finalists: Bury and Walsall.

1994 **Div.1**: **Leicester** 2, Derby 1 (att: 73,671). Losing semi-finalists: Millwall and Tranmere.

Div.2: **Burnley** 2, Stockport 1 (att: 44,806). Losing semi-finalists: Plymouth and York.

Div.3: **Wycombe** 4, Preston 2 (att: 40,109). Losing semi-finalists: Carlisle and Torquay.

1995 **Div.1**: **Bolton** 4, Reading 3 (att: 64,107). Losing semi-finalists: Tranmere and Wolves.

Div.2: **Huddersfield** 2, Bristol R. 1 (att: 59,175). Losing semi-finalists: Brentford and Crewe.

Div.3: **Chesterfield** 2, Bury 0 (att: 22,814). Losing semi-finalists: Mansfield and Preston.

1996 **Div.1**: **Leicester** 2, Crystal Palace 1, aet (att: 73,573). Losing semi-finalists: Charlton and Stoke.

Div.2: **Bradford City** 2, Notts County 0 (att: 39,972). Losing semi-finalists: Blackpool and Crewe.

Div.3: **Plymouth** 1, Darlington 0 (att: 43,431). Losing semi-finalists: Colchester and Hereford.

HISTORY OF THE PLAY-OFFS

There's really nothing new. The introduction of play-off matches by the Football League to decide final promotion and relegation issues at the end of season 1986-87 certainly wasn't.

A similar series styled "Test Matches" had operated between Divisions 1 and 2 for six seasons from 1893-98, and was abolished when both divisions were increased from 16 to 18 clubs.

Eighty-eight years later, the play-offs were back in vogue. In the first three seasons (1987-88-89), the Finals were played home-and-away, and since they were made one-off matches in 1990, they have featured regularly in Wembley's spring calendar.

Through the years, these have been the ups and downs of the play-offs:

1987 Initially, the 12 clubs involved comprised the one that finished directly above those relegated in Divisions 1, 2 and 3 and the three who followed the sides automatically promoted in each section. Two of the home-and-away Finals went to neutral-ground replays, in which **Charlton** clung to First Division status by denying Leeds promotion while **Swindon** beat Gillingham to complete their climb from Fourth Division to Second in successive seasons. Via the play-offs, **Sunderland** fell into Div.3 and **Bolton** into Div.4, both for the first time. **Aldershot** went up after finishing only sixth in Div.4; in their Final, they beat Wolves, who had finished nine points higher and missed automatic promotion by one point.

1988 Chelsea were relegated from the First Division after losing on aggregate to Middlesbrough, who had finished third in Div.2. So Boro', managed by Bruce Rioch, completed the rise from Third Division to First in successive seasons, only two years after their very existence had been threatened by the bailiffs. Also promoted via the play-offs were **Walsall** from Div.3 and **Swansea** from Div.4. Relegated, besides Chelsea, were **Sheffield United** (to Div.3) and **Rotherham** to Div.4.

1989 After two seasons of promotion-relegation play-offs, the system was changed to involve the four clubs who had just missed automatic promotion in Divs. 2, 3 and 4. That format has remained. Steve Coppell's **Crystal Palace**, third in Div.2, returned to the top flight after eight years, beating Blackburn 4-3 on aggregate after extra time. Similarly, **Port Vale** confirmed third place in Div.3 with promotion via the play-offs. For **Leyton Orient**, promotion seemed out of the question in Div.4 when they stood 15th. on March 1. But eight wins and a draw in the last nine home games swept them to sixth in the final table, and two more home victories in the play-offs completed their season in triumph.

1990 The play-off Finals now moved to Wembley over three days of Spring Holiday week-end. On successive afternoons, **Cambridge United** won promotion from Div.4 and **Notts County** from Div.3. Then, on Bank Holiday Monday, the biggest crowd for years at a Football League fixture (72,873) saw Ossie Ardiles' **Swindon Town** beat Sunderland 1-0 to reach the First Division for the first time. A few weeks later, however, Wembley losers **Sunderland** were promoted instead, by default; Swindon were found guilty of "financial irregularities" and stayed in Div.2.

1991 Again, the season's biggest League crowd (59,940) gathered at Wembley for the First Division Final in which **Notts County** (having missed promotion by one point) still fulfilled their ambition, beating Brighton 3-1. In successive years, County had climbed from Third Division to First via the play-offs – the first club to achieve double promotion by this route. Bolton were denied automatic promotion in Div.3 on goal difference, and lost at Wembley to an extra-time goal by **Tranmere**. The Fourth Division Final made history, with Blackpool beaten 5-4 on penalties by **Torquay** – first instance of promotion being decided by a shoot-out. In the table, Blackpool had finished seven points ahead of Torquay.

1992 Wembley that Spring Bank Holiday was the turning point in the history of **Blackburn Rovers**. Bolstered by Kenny Dalglish's return to management and owner Jack Walker's millions, they beat Leicester 1-0 by Mike Newell's 45th-minute penalty to achieve their objective – a place in the new Premier League. Newell, who also missed a second-half penalty, had recovered from a broken leg just in time for the play-offs. In the Div.4 Final **Blackpool** (denied by penalties the previous year) this time won a shoot-out 4-3 against Scunthorpe, who were unlucky in the play-offs for the fourth time in five years. **Peterborough** climbed out of the Third Division for the first time, beating Stockport 2-1 at Wembley.

1993 The crowd of 73,802 at Wembley to see **Swindon** beat Leicester 4-3 in the First Division Final was 11,000 bigger than that for the F.A. Cup Final replay between Arsenal and Sheffield Wednesday. Leicester rallied from three down to 3-3 before Paul Bodin's late penalty wiped away Swindon's bitter memories of three years earlier, when they were denied promotion after winning at Wembley. In the Third Division Final, **York** beat Crewe 5-3 in a shoot-out after a 1-1 draw, and in the Div.2 decider, **West Bromwich Albion** beat Port Vale 3-0. That was tough on Vale, who had finished third in the table with 89 points – the highest total never to earn promotion in any division. They had beaten Albion twice in the League, too.

1994 Wembley's record turn-out of 158,586 spectators at the three Finals started with a crowd of 40,109 to see Martin O'Neill's **Wycombe Wanderers** beat Preston 4-2. They thus climbed from Conference to Second Division with successive promotions. **Burnley's** 2-1 victory in the Second Division Final was marred by the sending-off of two Stockport players, and in the First Division decider **Leicester** came from behind to beat Derby and end the worst Wembley record of any club. They had lost on all six previous appearances there – four times in the F.A. Cup Final and in the play-offs of 1992 and 1993.

1995 Two months after losing the Coca-Cola Cup Final to Liverpool, Bruce Rioch's **Bolton** were back at Wembley for the First Division play-off Final. From two goals down to Reading in front of a crowd of 64,107, they returned to the top company after 15 years, winning 4-3 with two extra-time goals. **Huddersfield** ended the first season at their new £15m. home with promotion to the First Division via a 2-1 victory against Bristol Rovers – manager Neil Warnock's third play-off success (after two with Notts County). Of the three clubs who missed automatic promotion by one place, only **Chesterfield** achieved it in the play-offs, comfortably beating Bury 2-0.

1996 See start of Play-off Section.

RECORDS OF ALL CLUBS IN PLAY-OFFS

In the ten seasons of modern play-offs, no fewer than 62 clubs have participated in them.

Here are the play-off records of all the clubs who have been involved (W = Final winners; L = Final losers):

Aldershot 1 1987 (W)

Barnet 1 1992
Blackburn 4 1988, 89 (L), 90, 92 (W)
Blackpool 3 1991 (L), 92 (W), 96
Bolton 4 1987, 90, 91 (L), 95 (W)
Bradford C. 2 1988, 96 (W)
Brentford 2 1991, 95
Brighton 1 1991 (L)
Bristol C. 1 1988 (L)
Bristol R. 2 1989 (L), 95
Burnley 2 1991, 94 (W)
Bury 4 1990, 91, 93 ,95 (L)

Cambridge U. 2 1990 (W), 92
Carlisle 1 1994
Charlton 2 1987 (W), 96
Chelsea 1 1988 (L)
Chesterfield 2 1990 (L), 95 (W)
Colchester 2 1987, 96
Crewe 4 1992, 93 (L), 95, 96
Crystal P. 2 1989 (W), 96 (L)

Darlington 1 1996 (L)
Derby 2 1992, 94 (L)

Fulham 1 1989

Gillingham 1 1987 (L)

Hereford 1 1996
Huddersfield 2 1992, 95 (W)

Ipswich 1 1987

Leeds 1 1987 (L)
Leicester 4 1992 (L), 93 (L), 94 (W), 96 (W)
Leyton O. 1 1989 (W)

Maidstone 1 1990
Mansfield 1 1995
Mid'bro' 2 1988 (W), 91
Millwall 2 1991, 94

Newcastle 1 1990
Notts Co. 4 1988, 90 (W), 91 (W), 96 (L)

Oldham 1 1987

Peterborough 1 1992 (W)
Plymouth 2 1994, 96 (W)
Portsmouth 1 1993
Port Vale 2 1989 (W), 93 (L)
Preston 3 1989, 94 (L), 95

Reading 1 1995 (L)
Rotherham 1 1988

Scarborough 1 1989
Scunthorpe 4 1988, 89, 91, 92 (L)
Sheff. Utd. 1 1988

Stockport	4 1990, 92 (L), 93, 94 (L)	Walsall	2 1988 (W), 93
		Watford	1 1989
Stoke	2 1992, 96	W.B.A.	1 1993 (W)
Sunderland	2 1987, 90 (L)	Wigan	1 1987
Swansea	2 1988 (W), 93	Wolves	2 1987 (L), 95
Swindon	4 1987 (W), 89, 90 (W), 93 (W)	Wrexham	1 1989 (L)
		Wycombe	1 1994 (W)
Torquay	3 1988 (L), 91 (W), 94	York	2 1993 (W), 94
Tranmere	5 1990 (L), 91 (W), 93, 94, 95		

PLAY-OFF CROWDS YEAR BY YEAR

The rights and wrongs of the play-offs have been argued ever since they were introduced, but their popularity is beyond question.

Clubs have frequently reported season-best crowds at the home-and-away semi-finals, and over ten seasons the 162 play-off matches have been watched by 2,924,314 spectators.

Of that number, some 978,000 have watched the Finals in the seven seasons they have been staged at Wembley, including a record 158,586 at the three matches there in May 1994.

Year	Matches	Agg. Att.
1987	20	310,000
1988	19	305,817
1989	18	234,393
1990	15	291,428
1991	15	266,442
1992	15	277,684
1993	15	319,907
1994	15	314,817
1995	15	295,317
1996	15	308,515
	162	2,924,314

QUOTE-UNQUOTE

SIR STANLEY MATTHEWS, on modern player behaviour: "They pay you not only for what you do on the field but for how you conduct yourself off it. I don't blame players for getting as much money as they can, but something important has gone. A player can now get drunk publicly, he can find himself in jail – and when he comes out he is given a standing ovation."

HOSPITAL RADIO COMMENTATOR at Barnsley-Birmingham match: "Bullock breaks free on the left and cuts inside and . . . and . . . will you sit down – I can't see a thing."

EDDIE BISHOP, injured Chester striker, watching match from beside the Tannoy announcer and grabbing the mike when Chester were denied a penalty: "Come on, ref – open your eyes, man."

ALAN HARDAKER, secretary of the Football League, quoted in 1979: "If we don't watch out, football will be played on Sundays, there will be advertising on players' shirts and matches in the summer."

ATTENDANCES 1995-96

(Official Figures)

For the fifth successive season **League attendances** (Premiership and Football League) exceeded 20 million in 1995-96. The total of 21,844,416 was just short of the previous figure (down by 11,807), and the appeal of the Great Game, in terms of spectator presence, shows no sign of wavering.

While many modern-day star players can be seen as mercenaries, the fans stay loyal despite ever-escalating admission prices and growing commercial exploitation.

In a **Premier League** reduced to 20 clubs, crowds totalling 10,469,107 were down by 744,264, but the average was up by more than 2,000 at 27,550. **Football League** attendances increased by 732,457 at an aggregate of 11,375,309.

The League's **Coca-Cola Cup** competition was also played to gates increased by some 265,000 at a total of 1,765,821.

F.A. Cup attendances, from first round to Final, totalled 2,045,961 compared with 2,015,261 the previous season.

The **ten best-supported clubs** in the **Premier League** were: 1 Man. United, average 41,700; 2 Liverpool 39,553; 3 Arsenal 37,568; 4 Newcastle 36,507; 5 Everton 35,435; 6 Aston Villa 32,614; 7 Leeds 32,580; 8 Tottenham 30,510; 9 Middlesbrough 29,283; 10 Man. City 27,869.

Top average attendance in **Div.1** was Wolves' 24,786; in **Div.2** Swindon's 10,602; and in **Div.3** Preston's 10,012.

LEAGUE CROWDS SINCE 1980

	Total	**Div. One**	**Div. Two**	**Div. Three**	**Div. Four**
1980-81	21,907,569	11,392,894	5,175,442	3,637,854	1,701,379
1981-82	20,006,961	10,420,793	4,750,463	2,836,915	1,998,790
1982-83	18,766,158	9,295,613	4,974,937	2,943,568	1,552,040
1983-84	18,358,631	8,711,448	5,359,757	2,729,942	1,557,484
1984-85	17,849,835	9,761,404	4,030,823	2,667,008	1,390,600
1985-86	16,498,868	9,037,854	3,555,343	2,495,991	1,409,680
1986-87	17,383,032	9,144,676	4,168,131	2,354,784	1,715,441
1987-88	17,968,887	8,094,571	5,350,754	2,751,275	1,772,287
1988-89	18,477,565	7,809,993	5,827,805	3,048,700	1,791,067
1989-90	19,466,826	7,887,658	6,884,439	2,803,551	1,891,178
1990-91	19,541,341	8,618,709	6,297,733	2,847,813	1,777,086
1991-92	20,487,273	9,989,160	5,809,787	2,993 352	1,694,974
New format	**Total**	**Premier Lge.**	**Div. One**	**Div. Two**	**Div. Three**
1992-93	20,657,327	9,759,809	5,874,017	3,483,073	1,540,428
1993-94	21,693,889	10,655,059	6,487,104	2,972,702	1,579,024
1994-95	21,856,223	11,213,371	6,044,293	3,037,752	1,560,807
1995-96	21,844,416	10,469,107	6,566,349	2,843,652	1,965,308

Note: All-time record Football League attendance aggregate: 41,271,414 in season 1948-49 (88 clubs).

BIGGEST CLUB GROUND

Old Trafford, with its capacity now 55,000, is the biggest club stadium in Britain. Rangers' capacity at Ibrox is fixed at 51,000.

OTHER COMPETITIONS 1995-96

ANGLO-ITALIAN CUP FINAL

PORT VALE 2, GENOA 5

Wembley (12,663), Sunday, March 17, 1996

Port Vale: Musselwhite; Hill, Griffiths, Aspin, Stokes (Walker 37), McCarthy, Porter (Capt.), Bogie, Guppy (Talbot 85), Foyle, L. Glover (Naylor 59). **Scorer**: Foyle (68, 82). **Booked**: Hill, Foyle.

Genoa: Pastine (Spagnulo 75); Carri, Cavallo, Galante, Magoni, Ruotolo (Capt.), Bortolazzi, Onorati (Torrente 45), Nicola (Van't Schip 50), Montella, Nappi. **Scorers**: Ruotolo (13, 54, 65), Galante (22), Montella (39). **Booked**: Nicola, Magoni, Bortolazzi.

Referee: I. Koho (Finland). **Half-time:** 0-3.

Guest of Honour: Enzo Bearzot.

FINALS – RESULTS
(* Home club)

1970 *Napoli 0, Swindon Town 3.
1971 *Bologna 1, Blackpool 2 (aet).
1972 *AS Roma 3, Blackpool 1.
1973 *Fiorentina 1, Newcastle United 2.
1993 Derby County 1, Cremonese 3 (at Wembley).
1994 Notts County 0, Brescia 1 (at Wembley).
1995 Ascoli 1, Notts County 2 (at Wembley).

AUTO WINDSCREENS SHIELD FINAL

ROTHERHAM UNITED 2, SHREWSBURY TOWN 1

Wembley (35,235), Sunday, April 14, 1996

Rotherham: Clarke (Capt.); Blades, Hurst, Garner, Richardson, Breckin, Jemson, Goodwin, Berry, Goater, Roscoe. **Subs not used**: Bowyer, Hayward, McGlashan. **Scorer**: Jemson (20, 58). **Booked**: Breckin.

Shrewsbury: Edwards; Kay, Withe, Taylor (Capt.), Whiston, Scott, Robinson (Lynch 75), Stevens, Spink (Anthrobus 45), Walton, Berkley. **Sub not used**: Clarke (gk). **Scorer**: Taylor (81). **Booked**: Withe, Scott.

Referee: D. Allison (Lancaster). **Half-time:** 1-0.

Guest of Honour: Geoff Hurst.

FINALS – RESULTS

Associated Members' Cup
1984 (Hull) Bournemouth 2, Hull City 1.
Freight Rover Trophy
1985 (Wembley) Wigan Athletic 3, Brentford 1.
1986 (Wembley) Bristol City 3, Bolton Wanderers 0.
1987 (Wembley) Mansfield Town 1, Bristol City 1 (aet; Mansfield won 5-4 on pens.).

Sherpa Van Trophy
1988 (Wembley) Wolverhampton Wanderers 2, Burnley 0.
1989 (Wembley) Bolton Wanderers 4, Torquay United 1.
Leyland Daf Cup
1990 (Wembley) Tranmere Rovers 2, Bristol Rovers 1.
1991 (Wembley) Birmingham City 3, Tranmere Rovers 2.
Autoglass Trophy
1992 (Wembley) Stoke City 1, Stockport County 0.
1993 (Wembley) Port Vale 2, Stockport County 1.
1994 (Wembley) Huddersfield Town 1, Swansea City 1 (aet; Swansea won 3-1 on pens.).
Auto Windscreens Shield
1995 (Wembley) Birmingham City 1, Carlisle United 0 (Birmingham won in sudden-death overtime).

ADDITIONAL LEAGUE CLUBS' CUP COMPETITIONS

(Discontinued after 1992)

FINALS – AT WEMBLEY

Full Members' Cup
1985-86 Chelsea 5, Manchester City 4.
1986-87 Blackburn Rovers 1, Charlton Athletic 0.
Simod Cup
1987-88 Reading 4, Luton Town 1.
1988-89 Nottingham Forest 4, Everton 3.
Zenith Data Systems Cup
1989-90 Chelsea 1, Middlesbrough 0.
1990-91 Crystal Palace 4, Everton 1.
1991-92 Nottingham Forest 3, Southampton 2.

F.A. CHALLENGE VASE FINALS (At Wembley)

1975 Hoddesdon Town 2, Epsom & Ewell 1
1976 Billericay Town 1, Stamford 0*
1977 Billericay Town 2, Sheffield 1 (replay Nottingham, after a 1-1 draw at Wembley)
1978 Blue Star 2, Barton Rovers 1
1979 Billericay Town 4, Almondsbury Greenway 1
1980 Stamford 2, Guisborough Town 0
1981 Whickham 3, Willenhall Town 2*
1982 Forest Green Rovers 3, Rainworth Miners' Welfare 0
1983 V.S. Rugby 1, Halesowen Town 0
1984 Stansted 3, Stamford 2
1985 Halesowen Town 3, Fleetwood Town 1
1986 Halesowen Town 3, Southall 0
1987 St. Helens Town 3, Warrington Town 2
1988 Colne Dynamoes 1, Emley 0*
1989 Tamworth 3, Sudbury Town 0 (replay Peterborough, after a 1-1 draw at Wembley)
1990 Yeading 1, Bridlington 0 (replay Leeds, after 0-0 draw at Wembley)
1991 Guiseley 3, Gresley Rovers 1 (replay Bramall Lane, Sheffield, after a 4-4 draw at Wembley)
1992 Wimborne Town 5, Guiseley 3
1993 Bridlington Town 1, Tiverton Town 0

1994 Diss Town 2, Taunton Town 1*
1995 Arlesey Town 2, Oxford City 1 (Sponsors: Carlsberg)
1996 Brigg Town 3, Clitheroe 0 (Sponsors: Carlsberg)

(* After extra time)

F.A. CHALLENGE TROPHY FINALS (At Wembley)

1970 Macclesfield Town 2, Telford United 0
1971 Telford United 3, Hillingdon Borough 2
1972 Stafford Rangers 3, Barnet 0
1973 Scarborough 2, Wigan Athletic 1*
1974 Morecambe 2, Dartford 1
1975 Matlock Town 4, Scarborough 0
1976 Scarborough 3, Stafford Rangers 2*
1977 Scarborough 2, Dagenham 1
1978 Altrincham 3, Leatherhead 1
1979 Stafford Rangers 2, Kettering Town 0
1980 Dagenham 2, Mossley 1
1981 Bishop's Stortford 1, Sutton United 0
1982 Enfield 1, Altrincham 0*
1983 Telford United 2, Northwich Victoria 1
1984 Northwich Victoria 2, Bangor City 1 (replay Stoke, after a 1-1 draw at Wembley)
1985 Wealdstone 2, Boston United 1
1986 Altrincham 1, Runcorn 0
1987 Kidderminster Harriers 2, Burton Albion 1 (replay W.B.A., after a 0-0 draw at Wembley)
1988 Enfield 3, Telford United 2 (replay W.B.A., after a 0-0 draw at Wembley)
1989 Telford United 1, Macclesfield Town 0*
1990 Barrow 3, Leek Town 0
1991 Wycombe Wanderers 2, Kidderminster Harriers 1
1992 Colchester United 3, Witton Albion 1
1993 Wycombe Wanderers 4, Runcorn 1
1994 Woking 2, Runcorn 1
1995 Woking 2, Kidderminster 1 (Sponsors: Umbro)
1996 Macclesfield Town 3, Northwich Victoria 1 (Sponsors: Umbro)

(* After extra time)

F.A. YOUTH CUP WINNERS

Year	Winners	Runners-up	Aggregate
1953	Manchester United	Wolves	9-3
1954	Manchester United	Wolves	5-4
1955	Manchester United	W.B.A.	7-1
1956	Manchester United	Chesterfield	4-3
1957	Manchester United	West Ham United	8-2
1958	Wolves	Chelsea	7-6
1959	Blackburn Rovers	West Ham United	2-1
1960	Chelsea	Preston North End	5-2
1961	Chelsea	Everton	5-3
1962	Newcastle United	Wolves	2-1
1963	West Ham United	Liverpool	6-5
1964	Manchester United	Swindon Town	5-2
1965	Everton	Arsenal	3-2
1966	Arsenal	Sunderland	5-3

1967	Sunderland	Birmingham City	2-0
1968	Burnley	Coventry City	3-2
1969	Sunderland	W.B.A.	6-3
1970	Tottenham Hotspur	Coventry City	4-3
1971	Arsenal	Cardiff City	2-0
1972	Aston Villa	Liverpool	5-2
1973	Ipswich Town	Bristol City	4-1
1974	Tottenham Hotspur	Huddersfield Town	2-1
1975	Ipswich Town	West Ham United	5-1
1976	W.B.A.	Wolves	5-0
1977	Crystal Palace	Everton	1-0
1978	Crystal Palace	Aston Villa	*1-0
1979	Millwall	Manchester City	2-0
1980	Aston Villa	Manchester City	3-2
1981	West Ham United	Tottenham Hotspur	2-1
1982	Watford	Manchester United	7-6
1983	Norwich City	Everton	6-5
1984	Everton	Stoke City	4-2
1985	Newcastle United	Watford	4-1
1986	Manchester City	Manchester United	3-1
1987	Coventry City	Charlton Athletic	2-1
1988	Arsenal	Doncaster Rovers	6-1
1989	Watford	Manchester City	2-1
1990	Tottenham Hotspur	Middlesbrough	3-2
1991	Millwall	Sheffield Wednesday	3-0
1992	Manchester United	Crystal Palace	6-3
1993	Leeds United	Manchester United	4-1
1994	Arsenal	Millwall	5-3
1995	Manchester United	Tottenham	†2-2
1996	Liverpool	West Ham United	4-1

(* One match only; † Man. U. won 4-3 on pens.)

F.A. SUNDAY CUP FINAL

May 5 (at Northampton): St. Joseph's (Luton) 2, Croxteth & Gilmoss RBL 1.

WELSH CUP FINAL

May 19 (at National Stadium, Cardiff):
Llansantffraid 3, Barry Town 3 (aet, 2-2 at 90 mins,
Llansantffraid won 3-2 on pens).

SCOTTISH B & Q CUP FINALS

(For clubs outside Premier Division)

1990-91 Dundee 3, Ayr United 2 (at Motherwell)
1991-92 Hamilton Academical 1, Ayr United 0 (at Motherwell)
1992-93 Hamilton Academical 3, Morton 2 (at St. Mirren)
1993-94 Falkirk 3, St. Mirren 0 (at Motherwell)
1994-95 Airdrieonians 3, Dundee 2 (at McDiarmid Park, Perth)

SCOTTISH LEAGUE CHALLENGE CUP FINAL

1995-96 Dundee United 0, Stenhousemuir 0 (aet); Stenhousemuir won 5-4 on pens (at McDiarmid Park, Perth).

F.A. CHARITY SHIELD
(SPONSORS: LITTLEWOODS POOLS)

BLACKBURN ROVERS 0, EVERTON 1

Wembley (40,149), Sunday, August 13, 1995

Blackburn (blue and white shirts): Flowers; Kenna (Atkins 31), Pearce, Sutton, Le Saux, Ripley (Makel 68), Batty, Sherwood (Capt.), Gallacher (Marker 80), Newell, Shearer. **Subs not used**: Mimms, Tallon. **Booked**: Gallacher, Sherwood, Le Saux.

Everton (white shirts): Southall; Barrett, Ablett, Unsworth, Hinchcliffe, Grant (Watson 45), Parkinson, Horne (Capt.), Limpar, Samways, Rideout. **Scorer**: Samways (57). **Subs not used**: Kearton, Amokachi, Ebbrell, Jackson. **Booked**: Samways.

Referee: D. Gallagher (Banbury). **Half-time**: 0-0.

Kick-off: 4pm (Sky live, BBC TV highlights).

Man of Match: Barry Horne (Everton).

• F.A. Cup-winning captain Dave Watson collected Everton's second Wembley prize in three months. He replaced Grant at half-time, and took the armband from acting skipper Horne. Vinny Samways won a poor match with a cross-shot in off the far post. The attendance of 40,149 was the lowest for the Charity Shield since the fixture moved to Wembley in 1974.

• On their last six appearances in the Charity Shield, Everton have won five and drawn the other.

SHIELD HISTORY: The Charity Shield fixture began in 1908, and has been played every year since, except in war-time. It has mostly featured League Champions against F.A. Cup winners, and has taken place at Wembley since 1974.

CHARITY SHIELD RESULTS

(Played at Wembley since 1974)

Year	Winners	Runners-up	Score
1908	Manchester United	Q.P.R.	4-0 (after 1-1- draw)
1909	Newcastle United	Northampton Town	2-0
1910	Brighton & H.A.	Aston Villa	1-0
1911	Manchester United	Swindon Town	8-4
1912	Blackburn Rovers	Q.P.R.	2-1
1913	Professionals	Amateurs	7-2
1920	West Bromwich Albion	Tottenham Hotspur	2-0
1921	Tottenham Hotspur	Burnley	2-0
1922	Huddersfield Town	Liverpool	1-0
1923	Professionals	Amateurs	2-0
1924	Professionals	Amateurs	3-1
1925	Amateurs	Professionals	6-1
1926	Amateurs	Professionals	6-3
1927	Cardiff City	Corinthians	2-1
1928	Everton	Blackburn Rovers	2-1
1929	Professionals	Amateurs	3-0
1930	Arsenal	Sheffield Wednesday	2-1
1931	Arsenal	West Bromwich Albion	1-0

1932	Everton	Newcastle United	5-3
1933	Arsenal	Everton	3-0
1934	Arsenal	Manchester City	4-0
1935	Sheffield Wednesday	Arsenal	1-0
1936	Sunderland	Arsenal	2-1
1937	Manchester City	Sunderland	2-0
1938	Arsenal	Preston North End	2-1
1948	Arsenal	Manchester United	4-3
1949	Portsmouth	Wolverhampton W.	*1-1
1950	England World Cup XI	F.A. Canadian Tour Team	4-2
1951	Tottenham Hotspur	Newcastle United	2-1
1952	Manchester United	Newcastle United	4-2
1953	Arsenal	Blackpool	3-1
1954	Wolverhampton W.	West Bromwich Albion	*4-4
1955	Chelsea	Newcastle United	3-0
1956	Manchester United	Manchester City	1-0
1957	Manchester United	Aston Villa	4-0
1958	Bolton Wanderers	Wolverhampton W.	4-1
1959	Wolverhampton W.	Nottingham Forest	3-1
1960	Burnley	Wolverhampton W.	*2-2
1961	Tottenham Hotspur	F.A. XI	3-2
1962	Tottenham Hotspur	Ipswich Town	5-1
1963	Everton	Manchester United	4-0
1964	Liverpool	West Ham United	*2-2
1965	Manchester United	Liverpool	*2-2
1966	Liverpool	Everton	1-0
1967	Manchester United	Tottenham Hotspur	*3-3
1968	Manchester City	West Bromwich Albion	6-1
1969	Leeds United	Manchester City	2-1
1970	Everton	Chelsea	2-1
1971	Leicester City	Liverpool	1-0
1972	Manchester City	Aston Villa	1-0
1973	Burnley	Manchester City	1-0
1974	Liverpool	Leeds United	1-1
	(Liverpool won 6-5 on penalties)		
1975	Derby County	West Ham United	2-0
1976	Liverpool	Southampton	1-0
1977	Liverpool	Manchester United	*0-0
1978	Nottingham Forest	Ipswich Town	5-0
1979	Liverpool	Arsenal	3-1
1980	Liverpool	West Ham United	1-0
1981	Aston Villa	Tottenham Hotspur	*2-2
1982	Liverpool	Tottenham Hotspur	1-0
1983	Manchester United	Liverpool	2-0
1984	Everton	Liverpool	1-0
1985	Everton	Manchester United	2-0
1986	Everton	Liverpool	*1-1
1987	Everton	Coventry City	1-0
1988	Liverpool	Wimbledon	2-1
1989	Liverpool	Arsenal	1-0
1990	Liverpool	Manchester United	*1-1
1991	Arsenal	Tottenham Hotspur	*0-0
1992	Leeds United	Liverpool	4-3
1993	Manchester United	Arsenal	1-1
	(Man. United won 5-4 on penalties)		
1994	Manchester United	Blackburn Rovers	2-0
1995	Everton	Blackburn Rovers	1-0

(* Trophy shared)

HONOURS LIST

F.A. PREMIER LEAGUE

	First	Pts.	Second	Pts.	Third	Pts.
1992-3*a*	Man. Utd.	84	Aston Villa	74	Norwich	72
1993-4*a*	Man. Utd.	92	Blackburn	84	Newcastle	77
1994-5*a*	Blackburn	89	Man. Utd.	88	Nott'm Forest	77
1995-6*b*	Man. Utd.	82	Newcastle	78	Liverpool	71

Maximum points: *a*, 126; *b*, 114.

FOOTBALL LEAGUE FIRST DIVISION (NEW)

	First	Pts.	Second	Pts.	Third	Pts.
1992-3	Newcastle	96	West Ham	88	††Portsmouth	88
1993-4	Crystal Palace	90	Nott'm Forest	83	††Millwall	74
1994-5	Middlesbrough	82	††Reading	79	Bolton	77
1995-6	Sunderland	83	Derby	79	††Crystal Palace	75

Maximum points: 138. ††Not promoted after play-offs.

SECOND DIVISION (NEW)

	First	Pts.	Second	Pts.	Third	Pts.
1992-3	Stoke	93	Bolton	90	††Port Vale	89
1993-4	Reading	89	Port Vale	88	††Plymouth	85
1994-5	Birmingham	89	††Brentford	85	††Crewe	83
1995-6	Swindon	92	Oxford Utd.	83	††Blackpool	82

Maximum points: 138. †† Not promoted after play-offs.

THIRD DIVISION (NEW)

	First	Pts.	Second	Pts.	Third	Pts.
1992-3*a*	Cardiff	83	Wrexham	80	Barnet	79
1993-4*a*	Shrewsbury	79	Chester	74	Crewe	73
1994-5*a*	Carlisle	91	Walsall	83	Chesterfield	81
1995-6*b*	Preston	86	Gillingham	83	Bury	79

Maximum points: *a*, 126; *b*, 138.

FOOTBALL LEAGUE

	First	Pts.	Second	Pts.	Third	Pts.
1888-89*a*	Preston	40	Aston Villa	29	Wolves	28
1889-90*a*	Preston	33	Everton	31	Blackburn	27
1890-1*a*	Everton	29	Preston	27	Notts County	26
1891-2*b*	Sunderland	42	Preston	37	Bolton	36

FIRST DIVISION (ORIGINAL)

	First	Pts.	Second	Pts.	Third	Pts.
1892-3*c*	Sunderland	48	Preston	37	Everton	36
1893-4*c*	Aston Villa	44	Sunderland	38	Derby	36
1894-5*c*	Sunderland	47	Everton	42	Aston Villa	39
1895-6*c*	Aston Villa	45	Derby	41	Everton	39
1896-7*c*	Aston Villa	47	Sheff. Utd.	36	Derby	36
1897-8*c*	Sheff. Utd.	42	Sunderland	39	Wolves	35

Season	First	Second	Third
1898-9*d*	Aston Villa 45	Liverpool 43	Burnley 39
1899-1900*d*	Aston Villa 50	Sheff. Utd. 48	Sunderland 41
1900-1*d*	Liverpool 45	Sunderland 43	Notts County 40
1901-2*d*	Sunderland 44	Everton 41	Newcastle 37
1902-3*d*	The Wednesday .. 42	Aston Villa 41	Sunderland 41
1903-4*d*	The Wednesday .. 47	Man. City 44	Everton 43
1904-5*d*	Newcastle 48	Everton 47	Man. City 46
1905-6*e*	Liverpool 51	Preston 47	The Wednesday .. 44
1906-7*e*	Newcastle 51	Bristol City 48	Everton 45
1907-8*e*	Man. Utd. 52	Aston Villa 43	Man. City 43
1908-9*e*	Newcastle 53	Everton 46	Sunderland 44
1909-10*e*	Aston Villa 53	Liverpool 48	Blackburn 45
1910-11*e*	Man. Utd. 52	Aston Villa 51	Sunderland 45
1911-12*e*	Blackburn 49	Everton 46	Newcastle 44
1912-13*e*	Sunderland 54	Aston Villa 50	Sheff. Wed. 49
1913-14*e*	Blackburn 51	Aston Villa 44	Middlesbrough 43
1914-15*e*	Everton 46	Oldham 45	Blackburn 43
1919-20*f*	W.B.A. 60	Burnley 51	Chelsea 49
1920-1*f*	Burnley 59	Man. City 54	Bolton 52
1921-2*f*	Liverpool 57	Tottenham 51	Burnley 49
1922-3*f*	Liverpool 60	Sunderland 54	Huddersfield 53
1923-4*f*	*Huddersfield 57	Cardiff 57	Sunderland 53
1924-5*f*	Huddersfield 58	W.B.A. 56	Bolton 55
1925-6*f*	Huddersfield 57	Arsenal 52	Sunderland 48
1926-7*f*	Newcastle 56	Huddersfield 51	Sunderland 49
1927-8*f*	Everton 53	Huddersfield 51	Leicester City 48
1928-9*f*	Sheff. Wed. 52	Leicester City 51	Aston Villa 50
1929-30*f*	Sheff. Wed. 60	Derby 50	Man. City 47
1930-1*f*	Arsenal 66	Aston Villa 59	Sheff. Wed. 52
1931-2*f*	Everton 56	Arsenal 54	Sheff. Wed. 50
1932-3*f*	Arsenal 58	Aston Villa 54	Sheff. Wed. 51
1933-4*f*	Arsenal 59	Huddersfield 56	Tottenham 49
1934-5*f*	Arsenal 58	Sunderland 54	Sheff. Wed. 49
1935-6*f*	Sunderland 56	Derby 48	Huddersfield 48
1936-7*f*	Man. City 57	Charlton 54	Arsenal 52
1937-8*f*	Arsenal 52	Wolves 51	Preston 49
1938-9*f*	Everton 59	Wolves 55	Charlton 50
1946-7*f*	Liverpool 57	Man. Utd. 56	Wolves 56
1947-8*f*	Arsenal 59	Man. Utd. 52	Burnley 52
1948-9*f*	Portsmouth 58	Man. Utd. 53	Derby 53
1949-50*f*	*Portsmouth 53	Wolves 53	Sunderland 52
1950-1*f*	Tottenham 60	Man. Utd. 56	Blackpool 50
1951-2*f*	Man. Utd. 57	Tottenham 53	Arsenal 53
1952-3*f*	*Arsenal 54	Preston 54	Wolves 51
1953-4*f*	Wolves 57	W.B.A. 53	Huddersfield 51
1954-5*f*	Chelsea 52	Wolves 48	Portsmouth 48
1955-6*f*	Man. Utd. 60	Blackpool 49	Wolves 49
1956-7*f*	Man. Utd. 64	Tottenham 56	Preston 56
1957-8*f*	Wolves 64	Preston 59	Tottenham 51
1958-9*f*	Wolves 61	Man. Utd. 55	Arsenal 50
1959-60*f*	Burnley 55	Wolves 54	Tottenham 53
1960-1*f*	Tottenham 66	Sheff. Wed. 58	Wolves 57
1961-2*f*	Ipswich 56	Burnley 53	Tottenham 52
1962-3*f*	Everton 61	Tottenham 55	Burnley 54
1963-4*f*	Liverpool 57	Man. Utd. 53	Everton 52
1964-5*f*	*Man. Utd. 61	Leeds 61	Chelsea 56
1965-6*f*	Liverpool 61	Leeds 55	Burnley 55
1966-7*f*	Man. Utd. 60	Nott'm Forest 56	Tottenham 56
1967-8*f*	Man. City 58	Man. Utd. 56	Liverpool 55
1968-9*f*	Leeds 67	Liverpool 61	Everton 57
1969-70*f*	Everton 66	Leeds 57	Chelsea 55

1970-1*f*	Arsenal	65	Leeds	64	Tottenham	52
1971-2*f*	Derby	58	Leeds	57	Liverpool	57
1972-3*f*	Liverpool	60	Arsenal	57	Leeds	53
1973-4*f*	Leeds	62	Liverpool	57	Derby	48
1974-5*f*	Derby	53	Liverpool	51	Ipswich	51
1975-6*f*	Liverpool	60	Q.P.R.	59	Man. Utd.	56
1976-7*f*	Liverpool	57	Man. City	56	Ipswich	52
1977-8*f*	Nott'm Forest	64	Liverpool	57	Everton	55
1978-9*f*	Liverpool	68	Nott'm Forest	60	W.B.A.	59
1979-80*f*	Liverpool	60	Man. Utd.	58	Ipswich	53
1980-1*f*	Aston Villa	60	Ipswich	56	Arsenal	53
1981-2*g*	Liverpool	87	Ipswich	83	Man. Utd.	78
1982-3*g*	Liverpool	82	Watford	71	Man. Utd.	70
1983-4*g*	Liverpool	80	Southampton	77	Nott'm Forest	74
1984-5*g*	Everton	90	Liverpool	77	Tottenham	77
1985-6*g*	Liverpool	88	Everton	86	West Ham	84
1986-7*g*	Everton	86	Liverpool	77	Tottenham	71
1987-8*h*	Liverpool	90	Man. Utd.	81	Nott'm Forest	73
1988-9*j*	†Arsenal	76	Liverpool	76	Nott'm Forest	64
1989-90*j*	Liverpool	79	Aston Villa	70	Tottenham	63
1990-1*j*	Arsenal	83	Liverpool	76	Crystal Palace	69
1991-2*g*	Leeds.	82	Man. Utd.	78	Sheff. Wed.	75

Maximum points: *a*, 44; *b*, 52; *c*, 60; *d*, 68; *e*, 76; *f*, 84; *g*, 126; *h*, 120; *j*, 114.
*Won on goal average. †Won on goal diff. No comp. 1915-19 – 1939-46 (war-time)

SECOND DIVISION (ORIGINAL)

	First	Pts.	Second	Pts.	Third	Pts.
1892-3*a*	Small Heath	36	Sheff. Utd.	35	Darwen	30
1893-4*b*	Liverpool	50	Small Heath	42	Notts County	39
1894-5*c*	Bury	48	Notts County	39	Newton Heath	38
1895-6*c*	*Liverpool	46	Man. City	46	Grimsby	42
1896-7*c*	Notts County	42	Newton Heath	39	Grimsby	38
1897-8*c*	Burnley	48	Newcastle	45	Man. City	39
1898-9*d*	Man. City	52	Glossop	46	Leicester Fosse	45
1899-1900*d*	The Wednesday	54	Bolton	52	Small Heath	46
1900-1*d*	Grimsby	49	Small Heath	48	Burnley	44
1901-2*d*	W.B.A.	55	Middlesbrough	51	Preston	42
1902-3*d*	Man. City	54	Small Heath	51	Woolwich Arsenal	48
1903-4*d*	Preston	50	Woolwich Arsenal	49	Man. Utd.	48
1904-5*d*	Liverpool	58	Bolton	56	Man. Utd.	53
1905-6*e*	Bristol City	66	Man. Utd.	62	Chelsea	53
1906-7*e*	Nott'm Forest	60	Chelsea	57	Leicester Fosse	48
1907-8*e*	Bradford City	54	Leicester Fosse	52	Oldham	50
1908-9*e*	Bolton	52	Tottenham	51	W.B.A.	51
1909-10*e*	Man. City	54	Oldham	53	Hull	53
1910-11*e*	W.B.A.	53	Bolton	51	Chelsea	49
1911-12*e*	*Derby	54	Chelsea	54	Burnley	52
1912-13*e*	Preston	53	Burnley	50	Birmingham	46
1913-14*e*	Notts County	53	Bradford P.A.	49	Woolwich Arsenal	49
1914-15*e*	Derby	53	Preston	50	Barnsley	47
1919-20*f*	Tottenham	70	Huddersfield	64	Birmingham	56
1920-1*f*	*Birmingham	58	Cardiff	58	Bristol City	51
1921-2*f*	Nott'm Forest	56	Stoke	52	Barnsley	52
1922-3*f*	Notts County	53	West Ham	51	Leicester City	51
1923-4*f*	Leeds	54	Bury	51	Derby	51
1924-5*f*	Leicester City	59	Man. Utd.	57	Derby	55
1925-6*f*	Sheff. Wed.	60	Derby	57	Chelsea	52

1926-7*f*	Middlesbrough 62	Portsmouth 54	Man. City 54
1927-8*f*	Man. City 59	Leeds 57	Chelsea 54
1928-9*f*	Middlesbrough 55	Grimsby 53	Bradford City 48
1929-30*f*	Blackpool 58	Chelsea 55	Oldham 53
1930-1*f*	Everton 61	W.B.A. 54	Tottenham 51
1931-2*f*	Wolves 56	Leeds 54	Stoke 52
1932-3*f*	Stoke 56	Tottenham 55	Fulham 50
1933-4*f*	Grimsby 59	Preston 52	Bolton 51
1934-5*f*	Brentford 61	Bolton 56	West Ham 56
1935-6*f*	Man. Utd. 56	Charlton 55	Sheff. Utd. 52
1936-7*f*	Leicester City 56	Blackpool 55	Bury 52
1937-8*f*	Aston Villa 57	Man. Utd. 53	Sheff. Utd. 53
1938-9*f*	Blackburn 55	Sheff. Utd. 54	Sheff. Wed. 53
1946-7*f*	Man. City 62	Burnley 58	Birmingham 55
1947-8*f*	Birmingham 59	Newcastle 56	Southampton 52
1948-9*f*	Fulham 57	W.B.A. 56	Southampton 55
1949-50*f*	Tottenham 61	Sheff. Wed. 52	Sheff. Utd. 52
1950-1*f*	Preston 57	Man. City 52	Cardiff 50
1951-2*f*	Sheff. Wed. 53	Cardiff 51	Birmingham 51
1952-3*f*	Sheff. Utd. 60	Huddersfield 58	Luton 52
1953-4*f*	*Leicester City 56	Everton 56	Blackburn 55
1954-5*f*	*Birmingham 54	Luton 54	Rotherham 54
1955-6*f*	Sheff. Wed. 55	Leeds 52	Liverpool 48
1956-7*f*	Leicester City 61	Nott'm Forest 54	Liverpool 53
1957-8*f*	West Ham 57	Blackburn 56	Charlton 55
1958-9*f*	Sheff. Wed. 62	Fulham 60	Sheff. Utd. 53
1959-60*f*	Aston Villa 59	Cardiff 58	Liverpool 50
1960-1*f*	Ipswich 59	Sheff. Utd. 58	Liverpool 52
1961-2*f*	Liverpool 62	Leyton Orient 54	Sunderland 53
1962-3*f*	Stoke 53	Chelsea 52	Sunderland 52
1963-4*f*	Leeds 63	Sunderland 61	Preston 56
1964-5*f*	Newcastle 57	Northampton 56	Bolton 50
1965-6*f*	Man. City 59	Southampton 54	Coventry 53
1966-7*f*	Coventry 59	Wolves 58	Carlisle 52
1967-8*f*	Ipswich 59	Q.P.R. 58	Blackpool 58
1968-9*f*	Derby 63	Crystal Palace 56	Charlton 50
1969-70*f*	Huddersfield 60	Blackpool 53	Leicester City 51
1970-1*f*	Leicester City 59	Sheff. Utd. 56	Cardiff 53
1971-2*f*	Norwich 57	Birmingham 56	Millwall 55
1972-3*f*	Burnley 62	Q.P.R. 61	Aston Villa 60
1973-4*f*	Middlesbrough 65	Luton 50	Carlisle 49
1974-5*f*	Man. Utd. 61	Aston Villa 58	Norwich 53
1975-6*f*	Sunderland 56	Bristol City 53	W.B.A. 53
1976-7*f*	Wolves 57	Chelsea 55	Nott'm Forest 52
1977-8*f*	Bolton 58	Southampton 57	Tottenham 56
1978-9*f*	Crystal Palace 57	Brighton 56	Stoke 56
1979-80*f*	Leicester City 55	Sunderland 54	Birmingham 53
1980-1*f*	West Ham 66	Notts County 53	Swansea 50
1981-2*g*	Luton 88	Watford 80	Norwich 71
1982-3*g*	Q.P.R. 85	Wolves 75	Leicester City 70
1983-4*g*	†Chelsea 88	Sheff. Wed. 88	Newcastle 80
1984-5*g*	Oxford 84	Birmingham 82	Man. City 74
1985-6*g*	Norwich 84	Charlton 77	Wimbledon 76
1986-7*g*	Derby 84	Portsmouth 78	†† Oldham 75
1987-8*h*	Millwall 82	Aston Villa 78	Middlesbrough 78
1988-9*j*	Chelsea 99	Man. City 82	Crystal Palace 81
1989-90*j*	†Leeds 85	Sheff. Utd. 85	†† Newcastle 80
1990-1*j*	Oldham 88	West Ham 87	Sheff. Wed. 82
1991-2*j*	Ipswich 84	Middlesbrough 80	†† Derby 78

Maximum points: *a*, 44; *b*, 56; *c*, 60; *d*, 68; *e*, 76; *f*, 84; *g*, 126; *h*, 132; *j*, 138.
* Won on goal average. † Won on goal difference. †† Not promoted after play-offs.

THIRD DIVISION (1958-92)

	First	Pts.	Second	Pts.	Third	Pts.
1958-9	Plymouth	62	Hull	61	Brentford	57
1959-60	Southampton	61	Norwich	59	Shrewsbury	52
1960-1	Bury	68	Walsall	62	Q.P.R.	60
1961-2	Portsmouth	65	Grimsby	62	Bournemouth	59
1962-3	Northampton	62	Swindon	58	Port Vale	54
1963-4	*Coventry	60	Crystal Palace	60	Watford	58
1964-5	Carlisle	60	Bristol City	59	Mansfield	59
1965-6	Hull	69	Millwall	65	Q.P.R.	57
1966-7	Q.P.R.	67	Middlesbrough	55	Watford	54
1967-8	Oxford	57	Bury	56	Shrewsbury	55
1968-9	*Watford	64	Swindon	64	Luton	61
1969-70	Orient	62	Luton	60	Bristol Rovers	56
1970-1	Preston	61	Fulham	60	Halifax	56
1971-2	Aston Villa	70	Brighton	65	Bournemouth	62
1972-3	Bolton	61	Notts County	57	Blackburn	55
1973-4	Oldham	62	Bristol Rovers	61	York	61
1974-5	Blackburn	60	Plymouth	59	Charlton	55
1975-6	Hereford	63	Cardiff	57	Millwall	56
1976-7	Mansfield	64	Brighton	61	Crystal Palace	59
1977-8	Wrexham	61	Cambridge	58	Preston	56
1978-9	Shrewsbury	61	Watford	60	Swansea	60
1979-80	Grimsby	62	Blackburn	59	Sheff. Wed.	58
1980-1	Rotherham	61	Barnsley	59	Charlton	59
†1981-2	*Burnley	80	Carlisle	80	Fulham	78
†1982-3	Portsmouth	91	Cardiff	86	Huddersfield	82
†1983-4	Oxford	95	Wimbledon	87	Sheff. Utd.	83
†1984-5	Bradford City	94	Millwall	90	Hull	87
†1985-6	Reading	94	Plymouth	87	Derby	84
†1986-7	Bournemouth	97	Middlesbrough	94	Swindon	87
†1987-8	Sunderland	93	Brighton	84	Walsall	82
†1988-9	Wolves	92	Sheff. Utd.	84	Port Vale	84
†1989-90	Bristol Rovers	93	Bristol City	91	Notts County	87
†1990-1	Cambridge	86	Southend	85	Grimsby	83
† 1991-2	Brentford	82	Birmingham	81	†† Huddersfield	78

* Won on goal average. † Maximum points 138 (previously 92).
†† Not promoted after play-offs.

FOURTH DIVISION (1958-92)

	First	Pts.	Second	Pts.	Third	Pts.	Fourth	Pts.
1958-9	Port Vale	64	Coventry	60	York	60	Shrewsbury	58
1959-60	Walsall	65	Notts County	60	Torquay	60	Watford	57
1960-1	Peterborough	66	Crystal Palace	64	Northampton	60	Bradford P.A.	60
1961-2	Millwall	56	Colchester	55	Wrexham	53	Carlisle	52
1962-3	Brentford	62	Oldham	59	Crewe	59	Mansfield	57
1963-4	*Gillingham	60	Carlisle	60	Workington	59	Exeter	58
1964-5	Brighton	63	Millwall	62	York	62	Oxford	61
1965-6	*Doncaster	59	Darlington	59	Torquay	58	Colchester	56
1966-7	Stockport	64	Southport	59	Barrow	59	Tranmere	58
1967-8	Luton	66	Barnsley	61	Hartlepool	60	Crewe	58
1968-9	Doncaster	59	Halifax	57	Rochdale	56	Bradford City	56
1969-70	Chesterfield	64	Wrexham	61	Swansea	60	Port Vale	59
1970-1	Notts County	69	Bournemouth	60	Oldham	59	York	56
1971-2	Grimsby	63	Southend	60	Brentford	59	Scunthorpe	57
1972-3	Southport	62	Hereford	58	Cambridge	57	Aldershot	56
1973-4	Peterborough	65	Gillingham	62	Colchester	60	Bury	59
1974-5	Mansfield	68	Shrewsbury	62	Rotherham	58	Chester	57
1975-6	Lincoln	74	Northampton	68	Reading	60	Tranmere	58

1976-7	Cambridge	65	Exeter	62	Colchester	59	Bradford City	59
1977-8	Watford	71	Southend	60	Swansea	56	Brentford	59
1978-9	Reading	65	Grimsby	61	Wimbledon	61	Barnsley	61
1979-80	Huddersfield	66	Walsall	64	Newport	61	Portsmouth	60
1980-1	Southend	67	Lincoln	65	Doncaster	56	Wimbledon	55
†1981-2	Sheff. Utd.	96	Bradford City	91	Wigan	91	Bournemouth	88
†1982-3	Wimbledon	98	Hull	90	Port Vale	88	Scunthorpe	83
†1983-4	York	101	Doncaster	85	Reading	82	Bristol City	82
†1984-5	Chesterfield	91	Blackpool	86	Darlington	85	Bury	84
†1985-6	Swindon	102	Chester	84	Mansfield	81	Port Vale	79
†1986-7	Northampton	99	Preston	90	Southend	80	††Wolves	79
†1987-8	Wolves	90	Cardiff	85	Bolton	78	††Scunthorpe	77
†1988-9	Rotherham	82	Tranmere	80	Crewe	78	††Scunthorpe	77
†1989-90	Exeter	89	Grimsby	79	Southend	75	††Stockport	74
†1990-1	Darlington	83	Stockport	82	Hartlepool	82	Peterborough	80
1991-2*a*	Burnley	83	Rotherham	77	Mansfield	77	Blackpool	76

* Won on goal average. Maximum points: †, 138; *a*, 126.
†† Not promoted after play-offs.

THIRD DIVISION – SOUTH (1920-58)

	First	Pts.	Second	Pts.	Third	Pts.
1920-1*a*	Crystal Palace	59	Southampton	54	Q.P.R.	53
1921-2*a*	*Southampton	61	Plymouth	61	Portsmouth	53
1922-3*a*	Bristol City	59	Plymouth	53	Swansea	53
1923-4*a*	Portsmouth	59	Plymouth	55	Millwall	54
1924-5*a*	Swansea	57	Plymouth	56	Bristol City	53
1925-6*a*	Reading	57	Plymouth	56	Millwall	53
1926-7*a*	Bristol City	62	Plymouth	60	Millwall	56
1927-8*a*	Millwall	65	Northampton	55	Plymouth	53
1928-9*a*	*Charlton	54	Crystal Palace	54	Northampton	52
1929-30*a*	Plymouth	68	Brentford	61	Q.P.R.	51
1930-31*a*	Notts County	59	Crystal Palace	51	Brentford	50
1931-2*a*	Fulham	57	Reading	55	Southend	53
1932-3*a*	Brentford	62	Exeter	58	Norwich	57
1933-4*a*	Norwich	61	Coventry	54	Reading	54
1934-5*a*	Charlton	61	Reading	53	Coventry	51
1935-6*a*	Coventry	57	Luton	56	Reading	54
1936-7*a*	Luton	58	Notts County	56	Brighton	53
1937-8*a*	Millwall	56	Bristol City	55	Q.P.R.	53
1938-9*a*	Newport	55	Crystal Palace	52	Brighton	49
1946-7*a*	Cardiff	66	Q.P.R.	57	Bristol City	51
1947-8*a*	Q.P.R.	61	Bournemouth	57	Walsall	51
1948-9*a*	Swansea	62	Reading	55	Bournemouth	52
1949-50*a*	Notts County	58	Northampton	51	Southend	51
1950-1*d*	Nott'm Forest	70	Norwich	64	Reading	57
1951-2*d*	Plymouth	66	Reading	61	Norwich	61
1952-3*d*	Bristol Rovers	64	Millwall	62	Northampton	62
1953-4*d*	Ipswich	64	Brighton	61	Bristol City	56
1954-5*d*	Bristol City	70	Leyton Orient	61	Southampton	59
1955-6*d*	Leyton Orient	66	Brighton	65	Ipswich	64
1956-7*d*	*Ipswich	59	Torquay	59	Colchester	58
1957-8*d*	Brighton	60	Brentford	58	Plymouth	58

THIRD DIVISION – NORTH (1921-58)

	First	Pts.	Second	Pts.	Third	Pts.
1921-2*b*	Stockport	56	Darlington	50	Grimsby	50
1922-3*b*	Nelson	51	Bradford P.A.	47	Walsall	46
1923-4*a*	Wolves	63	Rochdale	62	Chesterfield	54

1924-5*a*	Darlington	58	Nelson	53	New Brighton	53
1925-6*a*	Grimsby	61	Bradford P.A.	60	Rochdale	59
1926-7*a*	Stoke	63	Rochdale	58	Bradford P.A.	57
1927-8*a*	Bradford P.A.	63	Lincoln	55	Stockport	54
1928-9*a*	Bradford City	63	Stockport	62	Wrexham	52
1929-30*a*	Port Vale	67	Stockport	63	Darlington	50
1930-1*a*	Chesterfield	58	Lincoln	57	Wrexham	54
1931-2*c*	*Lincoln	57	Gateshead	57	Chester	50
1932-3*a*	Hull	59	Wrexham	57	Stockport	54
1933-4*a*	Barnsley	62	Chesterfield	61	Stockport	59
1934-5*a*	Doncaster	57	Halifax	55	Chester	54
1935-6*a*	Chesterfield	60	Chester	55	Tranmere	54
1936-7*a*	Stockport	60	Lincoln	57	Chester	53
1937-8*a*	Tranmere	56	Doncaster	54	Hull	53
1938-9*a*	Barnsley	67	Doncaster	56	Bradford City	52
1946-7*a*	Doncaster	72	Rotherham	64	Chester	56
1947-8*a*	Lincoln	60	Rotherham	59	Wrexham	50
1948-9*a*	Hull	65	Rotherham	62	Doncaster	50
1949-50*a*	Doncaster	55	Gateshead	53	Rochdale	51
1950-1*d*	Rotherham	71	Mansfield	64	Carlisle	62
1951-2*d*	Lincoln	69	Grimsby	66	Stockport	59
1952-3*d*	Oldham	59	Port Vale	58	Wrexham	56
1953-4*d*	Port Vale	69	Barnsley	58	Scunthorpe	57
1954-5*d*	Barnsley	65	Accrington	61	Scunthorpe	58
1955-6*d*	Grimsby	68	Derby	63	Accrington	59
1956-7*d*	Derby	63	Hartlepool	59	Accrington	58
1957-8*d*	Scunthorpe	66	Accrington	59	Bradford City	57

Maximum points: *a*, 84; *b*, 76; *c*, 80; *d*, 92. * Won on goal average.

CHAMPIONSHIP WINNERS

F.A. PREMIER LEAGUE

Man. Utd. 3
Blackburn 1

FOOTBALL LEAGUE DIV.1 (NEW)

Crystal Palace 1
Middlesbrough 1
Newcastle 1
Sunderland 1

DIV.1 (ORIGINAL)

Liverpool 18
Arsenal 10
Everton 9
Aston Villa 7
Man. Utd. 7
Sunderland 6
Newcastle 4
Sheff. Wed. 4
Huddersfield 3
Leeds 3
Wolves 3
Blackburn 2
Burnley 2
Derby 2
Man. City 2
Portsmouth 2
Preston 2
Tottenham 2
Chelsea 1
Ipswich 1
Nott'm Forest 1
Sheff. Utd. 1
W.B.A. 1

DIV.2 (NEW)

Birmingham 1
Reading 1
Stoke 1
Swindon 1

DIV.2 (ORIGINAL)

Leicester City 6
Man. City 6
Sheff. Wed. 5
Birmingham 4
Derby 4
Liverpool 4
Ipswich 3
Leeds 3
Middlesbrough 3
Notts County 3
Preston 3
Aston Villa 2
Bolton 2
Burnley 2
Chelsea 2
Grimsby 2
Man. Utd. 2
Norwich 2
Nott'm Forest 2
Stoke 2
Tottenham 2
W.B.A. 2
West Ham 2
Wolves 2
Blackburn 1
Blackpool 1
Bradford City 1
Brentford 1
Bristol City 1
Bury 1
Coventry 1
Crystal Palace 1
Everton 1
Fulham 1
Huddersfield 1
Luton 1
Millwall 1
Newcastle 1
Oldham 1
Oxford 1
Q.P.R. 1
Sheff. Utd. 1
Sunderland 1

APPLICATIONS FOR RE-ELECTION

(System discontinued 1987)

14 Hartlepool	5 Gillingham	2 Aberdare	2 Watford
12 Halifax	5 Lincoln	2 Ashington	1 Blackpool
11 Barrow	5 New Brighton	2 Bournemouth	1 Brighton
11 Southport	4 Bradford P.A.	2 Brentford	1 Bristol Rovers
10 Crewe	4 Northampton	2 Colchester	1 Cambridge
10 Newport	4 Norwich	2 Durham C.	1 Cardiff
10 Rochdale	3 Aldershot	2 Gateshead	1 Carlisle
8 Darlington	3 Bradford City	2 Grimsby	1 Charlton
8 Exeter	3 Crystal Palace	2 Millwall	1 Mansfield
7 Chester	3 Doncaster	2 Nelson	1 Port Vale
7 Walsall	3 Hereford	2 Oldham	1 Preston
7 Workington	3 Merthyr Tyd.	2 Q.P.R.	1 Shrewsbury
7 York	3 Swindon	2 Rotherham	1 Swansea
6 Stockport	3 Torquay	2 Scunthorpe	1 Thames
5 Accrington	3 Tranmere	2 Southend	1 Wrexham

RELEGATED CLUBS (To 1992)

1892-3 In Test matches, Darwen and Sheff. Utd. won promotion in place of Accrington and Notts County.
1893-4 Tests, Liverpool and Small Heath won promotion. Darwen and Newton Heath relegated.
1894-5 After Tests, Bury promoted, Liverpool relegated.
1895-6 After Tests, Liverpool promoted, Small Heath relegated.
1896-7 After Tests, Notts County promoted, Burnley relegated.
1897-8 Test system abolished after success of Burnley and Stoke, League extended. Blackburn and Newcastle elected to First Division. Automatic promotion and relegation introduced.

FIRST DIVISION TO SECOND DIVISION

1898-9 Bolton, Sheff. Wed.
1899-1900 Burnley, Glossop
1900-1 Preston, W.B.A.
1901-2 Small Heath, Man. City
1902-3 Grimsby, Bolton
1903-4 Liverpool, W.B.A.
1904-5 League extended. Bury and Notts County, two bottom clubs in First Division, re-elected.
1905-6 Nott'm Forest, Wolves
1906-7 Derby, Stoke
1907-8 Bolton, Birmingham
1908-9 Man. City, Leicester Fosse
1909-10 Bolton, Chelsea
1910-11 Bristol City, Nott'm Forest
1911-12 Preston, Bury
1912-13 Notts County, Woolwich Arsenal
1913-14 Preston, Derby
1914-15 Tottenham, *Chelsea
1919-20 Notts County, Sheff. Wed.
1920-1 Derby, Bradford P.A.
1921-2 Bradford City, Man. Utd.
1922-3 Stoke, Oldham
1923-4 Chelsea, Middlesbrough
1924-5 Preston, Nott'm Forest
1925-6 Man. City, Notts County
1926-7 Leeds, W.B.A.
1927-8 Tottenham, Middlesbrough
1928-9 Bury, Cardiff
1929-30 Burnley, Everton
1930-1 Leeds, Man. Utd.
1931-2 Grimsby, West Ham
1932-3 Bolton, Blackpool
1933-4 Newcastle, Sheff. Utd.
1934-5 Leicester City, Tottenham
1935-6 Aston Villa, Blackburn
1936-7 Man. Utd., Sheff. Wed.
1937-8 Man. City, W.B.A.
1938-9 Birmingham, Leicester City
1946-7 Brentford, Leeds
1947-8 Blackburn, Grimsby
1948-9 Preston, Sheff. Utd.
1949-50 Man. City, Birmingham
1950-1 Sheff. Wed., Everton
1951-2 Huddersfield, Fulham
1952-3 Stoke, Derby
1953-4 Middlesbrough, Liverpool
1954-5 Leicester City, Sheff. Wed.

1955-6	Huddersfield, Sheff. Utd.	1978-9	Q.P.R., Birmingham, Chelsea
1956-7	Charlton, Cardiff	1979-80	Bristol City, Derby, Bolton
1957-8	Sheff. Wed., Sunderland	1980-1	Norwich, Leicester City, Crystal Palace
1958-9	Portsmouth, Aston Villa	1981-2	Leeds, Wolves, Middlesbrough
1959-60	Luton, Leeds	1982-3	Man. City, Swansea, Brighton
1960-61	Preston, Newcastle	1983-4	Birmingham, Notts County, Wolves
1961-2	Chelsea, Cardiff	1984-5	Norwich, Sunderland, Stoke
1962-3	Man. City, Leyton Orient	1985-6	Ipswich, Birmingham, W.B.A.
1963-4	Bolton, Ipswich	1986-7	Leicester City, Man. City, Aston Villa
1964-5	Wolves, Birmingham	1987-8	Chelsea**, Portsmouth, Watford, Oxford
1965-6	Northampton, Blackburn	1988-9	Middlesbrough, West Ham, Newcastle
1966-7	Aston Villa, Blackpool	1989-90	Sheff. Wed., Charlton, Millwall
1967-8	Fulham, Sheff. Utd.	1990-1	Sunderland, Derby
1968-9	Leicester City, Q.P.R.	1991-2	Luton, Notts County, West Ham
1969-70	Sheff. Wed., Sunderland		
1970-1	Burnley, Blackpool		
1971-2	Nott'm Forest, Huddersfield		
1972-3	W.B.A., Crystal Palace		
1973-4	Norwich, Man. Utd., Southampton		
1974-5	Chelsea, Luton, Carlisle		
1975-6	Sheff. Utd., Burnley, Wolves		
1976-7	Tottenham, Stoke, Sunderland		
1977-8	Leicester City, West Ham, Newcastle		

* Subsequently re-elected to First Division when League extended after the war.
** Relegated after play-offs.

SECOND DIVISION TO THIRD DIVISION

1920-1	Stockport	1955-6	Plymouth, Hull
1921-2	Bradford City, Bristol City	1956-7	Port Vale, Bury
1922-3	Rotherham, Wolves	1957-8	Doncaster, Notts County
1923-4	Nelson, Bristol City	1958-9	Barnsley, Grimsby
1924-5	Crystal Palace, Coventry	1959-60	Bristol City, Hull
1925-6	Stoke, Stockport	1960-1	Lincoln, Portsmouth
1926-7	Darlington, Bradford City	1961-2	Brighton, Bristol Rovers
1927-8	Fulham, South Shields	1962-3	Walsall, Luton
1928-9	Port Vale, Clapton Orient	1963-4	Grimsby, Scunthorpe
1929-30	Hull, Notts County	1964-5	Swindon, Swansea
1930-1	Reading, Cardiff	1965-6	Middlesbrough, Leyton Orient
1931-2	Barnsley, Bristol City	1966-7	Northampton, Bury
1932-3	Chesterfield, Charlton	1967-8	Plymouth, Rotherham
1933-4	Millwall, Lincoln	1968-9	Fulham, Bury
1934-5	Oldham, Notts County	1969-70	Preston, Aston Villa
1935-6	Port Vale, Hull	1970-1	Blackburn, Bolton
1936-7	Doncaster, Bradford City	1971-2	Charlton, Watford
1937-8	Barnsley, Stockport	1972-3	Huddersfield, Brighton
1938-9	Norwich, Tranmere	1973-4	Crystal Palace, Preston, Swindon
1946-7	Swansea, Newport	1974-5	Millwall, Cardiff, Sheff. Wed.
1947-8	Doncaster, Millwall	1975-6	Portsmouth, Oxford, York
1948-9	Nott'm Forest, Lincoln	1976-7	Carlisle, Plymouth, Hereford
1949-50	Plymouth, Bradford P.A.	1977-8	Hull, Mansfield, Blackpool
1950-1	Grimsby, Chesterfield		
1951-2	Coventry, Q.P.R.		
1952-3	Southampton, Barnsley		
1953-4	Brentford, Oldham		
1954-5	Ipswich, Derby		

1978-9	Sheff. Utd., Millwall, Blackburn	1986-7	Sunderland**, Grimsby, Brighton
1979-80	Fulham, Burnley, Charlton	1987-8	Sheff. Utd.**, Reading, Huddersfield
1980-1	Preston, Bristol City, Bristol Rovers	1988-9	Shrewsbury, Birmingham, Walsall
1981-2	Cardiff, Wrexham, Orient	1989-90	Bournemouth, Bradford City, Stoke
1982-3	Rotherham, Burnley, Bolton	1990-1	W.B.A., Hull
1983-4	Derby, Swansea, Cambridge	1991-2	Plymouth, Brighton, Port Vale
1984-5	Notts County, Cardiff, Wolves		
1985-6	Carlisle, Middlesbrough, Fulham		

** Relegated after play-offs.

THIRD DIVISION TO FOURTH DIVISION

1958-9	Rochdale, Notts County, Doncaster, Stockport	1975-6	Aldershot, Colchester, Southend, Halifax
1959-60	Accrington, Wrexham, Mansfield, York	1976-7	Reading, Northampton, Grimsby, York
1960-1	Chesterfield, Colchester, Bradford City, Tranmere	1977-8	Port Vale, Bradford City, Hereford, Portsmouth
1961-2	Newport, Brentford, Lincoln, Torquay	1978-9	Peterborough, Walsall, Tranmere, Lincoln
1962-3	Bradford P.A., Brighton, Carlisle, Halifax	1979-80	Bury, Southend, Mansfield, Wimbledon
1963-4	Millwall, Crewe, Wrexham, Notts County	1980-1	Sheff. Utd., Colchester, Blackpool, Hull
1964-5	Luton, Port Vale, Colchester, Barnsley	1981-2	Wimbledon, Swindon, Bristol City, Chester
1965-6	Southend, Exeter, Brentford, York	1982-3	Reading, Wrexham, Doncaster, Chesterfield
1966-7	Doncaster, Workington, Darlington, Swansea	1983-4	Scunthorpe, Southend, Port Vale, Exeter
1967-8	Scunthorpe, Colchester, Grimsby, Peterborough (demoted)	1984-5	Burnley, Orient, Preston, Cambridge
1968-9	Oldham, Crewe, Hartlepool, Northampton	1985-6	Lincoln, Cardiff, Wolves, Swansea
1969-70	Bournemouth, Southport, Barrow, Stockport	1986-7	Bolton**, Carlisle, Darlington, Newport
1970-1	Gillingham, Doncaster, Bury, Reading	1987-8	Doncaster, York, Grimsby, Rotherham**
1971-2	Mansfield, Barnsley, Torquay, Bradford City	1988-9	Southend, Chesterfield, Gillingham, Aldershot
1972-3	Scunthorpe, Swansea, Brentford, Rotherham	1989-90	Cardiff, Northampton, Blackpool, Walsall
1973-4	Cambridge, Shrewsbury, Rochdale, Southport	1990-1	Crewe, Rotherham, Mansfield
1974-5	Bournemouth, Watford, Tranmere, Huddersfield	1991-2	Bury, Shrewsbury, Torquay, Darlington

** Relegated after plays-offs.

DEMOTED FROM FOURTH DIVISION TO GM VAUXHALL CONFERENCE

1987	Lincoln	1990	Colchester
1988	Newport	1991	No demotion
1989	Darlington	1992	No demotion

DEMOTED FROM THIRD DIVISION TO GM VAUXHALL CONFERENCE

1993	Halifax	1995	No demotion
1994	No demotion	1996	No demotion

RELEGATED CLUBS (Since 1993)

1993

Premier League to Div. 1: Crystal Palace, Middlesbrough, Nott'm Forest
Div. 1 to Div. 2: Brentford, Cambridge, Bristol Rovers
Div. 2 to Div. 3: Preston, Mansfield, Wigan, Chester

1994

Premier League to Div. 1: Sheffield Utd., Oldham, Swindon
Div. 1 to Div. 2: Birmingham, Oxford, Peterborough
Div. 2 to Div. 3: Fulham, Exeter, Hartlepool, Barnet

1995

Premier League to Div. 1: Crystal Palace, Norwich, Leicester, Ipswich
Div. 1 to Div. 2: Swindon, Burnley, Bristol City, Notts Co.
Div. 2 to Div. 3: Cambridge, Plymouth, Cardiff, Chester, Leyton Orient

1996

Premier League to Div. 1: Manchester City, Q.P.R., Bolton
Div. 1 to Div. 2: Millwall, Watford, Luton
Div. 2 to Div. 3: Carlisle, Swansea, Brighton, Hull

QUOTE-UNQUOTE

ROY EVANS, Liverpool manager, on Eric Cantona's triumphant return for Man. United last season after his 8-month suspension: "He has come back with a different head on."

KENNY DALGLISH on why he took a back seat at Blackburn: "Management is a seven-days-a-week job. The intensity of it takes its toll on your health. Some people want to go on for ever, and I obviously don't. I saw Alan Hansen playing golf three times a week, and it got me thinking."

BARRY FRY, then Birmingham manager, asked whom he would like to date: "My missus, because I never see her now."

BARRY FRY's answerphone after he was sacked by Birmingham at the end of last season: "Kristine (his wife) has gone shopping and I'm at the job centre, looking for employment. Funny old game, isn't it!"

STUART HALL (Radio 5): "Barmby stood out like a Pamela Anderson in a sea of Claire Rayners."

GLENN HODDLE, England coach-in-waiting, after being appointed to succeed Terry Venables: "This is a great job – until a ball is kicked."

JOCK STEIN: "The secret of being a manager is to keep the six players who hate you away from the five who are undecided."

MANCHESTER UNITED'S RECORD 9TH F.A. CUP AND SECOND 'DOUBLE'

THIRD ROUND (January 6)	FOURTH ROUND (January 27)	FIFTH ROUND (February 17)	SIXTH ROUND (March 9)	SEMI-FINALS (March 31)	FINAL (May 11)
***Liverpool** 7	**Liverpool** 4	***Liverpool** 2	**Liverpool** 0:3	**Liverpool** 3	**Liverpool** 0
Rochdale 0					
Shrewsbury 1:2	*Shrewsbury 0				
*Fulham 1:1					
Brentford 2	Brentford 2	Charlton 1			
*Norwich 1					
*Charlton 2	*Charlton 3				
Sheff. Wed. 0					
*Bradford C. 0	*Bolton 0	*Leeds 0:2	*Leeds 0:0		
Bolton 3					
*Derby 2	Leeds 1				
Leeds 4					
Stockport 2:2	*Everton 2:1	Port Vale 0:1			
*Everton 2:3					
*Crystal Palace 0:†3	Port Vale 2:2				
Port Vale 0:4				(at Old Trafford)	
Aston Villa A3	Aston Villa 1	Aston Villa 3	Aston Villa 1	Aston Villa 0	
*Gravesend & N. 0					
Sheff. Utd. 1:1	*Sheff. Utd. 0				
*Arsenal 1:0					
Wigan 0	Walsall 0	*Ipswich 1			
*Walsall 1					
Blackburn 0:†0	*Ipswich 1				
*Ipswich 0:1					
Tottenham 1:5	*Tottenham 1:2	Tottenham C2:†1	*Nott'm Forest 0		
*Hereford 1:1					
Wolves 1:2	Wolves 1:0				
*Birmingham 1:1					
*Millwall 3:0	Oxford Utd. 1:0	*Nott'm Forest 2:1			
Oxford Utd. 3:1					
Nott'm Forest 1:2	*Nott'm Forest 1:3				
*Stoke 1:0					(at Wembley – Att: 79,007)

*Chelsea .... B1:†2	Chelsea 2				
Newcastle 1:2		Chelsea 0:4			
*Tranmere 0	*Q.P.R. 1				
Q.P.R. 2			*Chelsea 2:3		
*West Ham 2	*West Ham 1:0				
Southend 0		*Grimsby 0:1			
Luton 1	Grimsby 1:3				
*Grimsby 7				Chelsea 1	
*Notts County 1	*Middlesbrough .. 0:0				
Middlesbrough 2		Wimbledon 2:3			
Wimbledon 1:1	Wimbledon 0:1				
*Watford 1:0			Wimbledon 2:1		
*Peterborough 1	Peterborough 0				
Wrexham 0		*Huddersfield ... 2:1			
Blackpool 1	*Huddersfield 2				
*Huddersfield 2				(at Villa Park)	**Man. Utd** 1
Portsmouth 0	*Southampton .. 1:3				
*Southampton 3		Southampton 1:2			
*Crewe 4	Crewe 1:2				
W.B.A. 3			Southampton 0		
Oldham 0:2	Oldham 0				
*Barnsley 0:1		*Swindon 1:0			
Woking 0	*Swindon 2				
*Swindon 2				**Man. Utd.** 2	
*Leicester 0:0	Man. City 2:2				
Man. City 0:5		Man. City 1			
Coventry 3	*Coventry 2:1				
*Plymouth 1			***Man. Utd.** 2		
*Reading 3	*Reading 0				
Gillingham 1		***Man. Utd.** 2			
Sunderland 2:1	**Man. Utd.** 3				
***Man. Utd.** 2:2					

(* Drawn at home. †After extra time. A – Played at Aston Villa. B – Chelsea won 4-2 on pens. C – Nott'm Forest won 3-1 on pens. (original replay abandoned after 14 mins. due to snow). Dates shown as scheduled for main round – some variations for TV.)

F.A. CUP 1995-96

First Round – November 11

Altrincham v Crewe	0-2
Barnet v Woking	2-2
Barrow v Nuneaton	2-1
Blackpool v Chester	2-1
Bognor Regis v Ashford T.	1-1
Bournemouth v Bristol City	0-0
Bradford City v Burton	4-3
Brentford v Farnborough	1-1
Burnley v Walsall	1-3
Bury v Blyth Spartans	0-2
Canvey Island v Brighton	2-2
Carlisle v Preston	1-2
Cinderford v Bromsgrove	2-1
Exeter v Peterborough	0-1
Fulham v Swansea	7-0
Gravesend & N. v Colchester	2-0
Hartlepool v Darlington	2-4
Hereford v Stevenage	2-1
Hitchin v Bristol Rovers	2-1
Hull v Wrexham	0-0
Kidderminster v Sutton Utd.	2-2
Kingstonian v Wisbech	5-1
Mansfield v Doncaster	4-2
Newport I.O.W. v Enfield	1-1
Northampton v Hayes	1-0
Northwich v Scunthorpe	1-3
Oxford Utd. v Dorchester	9-0
Rochdale v Rotherham	5-3
Runcorn v Wigan	1-1
Rushden v Cardiff	1-3
Scarborough v Chesterfield	0-2
Shrewsbury v Marine	11-2
Slough v Plymouth	0-2
Spennymoor v Colwyn Bay	0-1
Stockport v Lincoln	5-0
Swindon v Cambridge Utd.	4-1
Telford v Witton	2-1
Torquay v Leyton Orient	1-0
Wycombe v Gillingham	1-1
York v Notts County	0-1

Replays

Ashford T. v Bognor Regis	0-1
Brighton v Canvey Island	4-1
Bristol City v Bournemouth	0-1
Enfield v Newport I.O.W.	2-1
Farnborough v Brentford	0-4
Gillingham v Wycombe	1-0
Sutton Utd. v Kidderminster	†1-1
(Sutton Utd. won 3-2 on pens.)	
Wigan v Runcorn	4-2
Woking v Barnet	†2-1
Wrexham v Hull	†0-0
(Wrexham won 3-1 on pens.)	

Second Round – December 2

Barrow v Wigan	0-4
Blackpool v Colwyn Bay	2-0
Bournemouth v Brentford	0-1
Bradford City v Preston	2-1
Cinderford v Gravesend & N.	1-1
Crewe v Mansfield	2-0
Enfield v Woking	1-1
Fulham v Brighton	0-0
Gillingham v Hitchin	3-0
Hereford v Sutton Utd.	2-0
Kingstonian v Plymouth	1-2
Oxford Utd. v Northampton	2-0
Peterborough v Bognor Regis	4-0
Rochdale v Darlington	2-2
Scunthorpe v Shrewsbury	1-1
Stockport v Blyth Spartans	2-0
Swindon v Cardiff	2-0
Telford v Notts County	0-2
Torquay v Walsall	1-1
Wrexham v Chesterfield	3-2

Replays

Brighton v Fulham	†0-0
(Fulham won 4-1 on pens.)	
Darlington v Rochdale	0-1
Gravesend & N. v Cinderford	3-0
Shrewsbury v Scunthorpe	2-1
Walsall v Torquay	†8-4
Woking v Enfield	2-1
(at Wycombe)	

(† After extra time.)

FOG ON THE TYNE

The turnstiles at St. James's Park clicked more than 120,000 times when the holders **Newcastle United** played Swansea in the F.A. Cup 3rd. Round in January 1953. With 63,000 packed in at the start, thick fog swirled in from the Tyne, and the match was abandoned without score after 8 minutes. It was re-staged 4 days later, and 61,000 paid again to see Newcastle win 3-0. Gate receipts for the 2 games totalled . . . £17,000.

F.A. CUP FINAL TEAMS 1900-96

1900 **BURY** – Thompson; Darrock, Davidson, Pray, Leeming, Ross, Richards, Wood, McLuckie, Sagar, Plant.
SOUTHAMPTON – Robinson; Meehan, Durber, Meston, Chadwick, Petrie, Turner, Yates, Farrell, Wood, Milward.
Scorers: Bury – McLuckie 2, Wood, Plant.

1901 **TOTTENHAM HOTSPUR** – Clawley; Erentz, Tait, Norris, Hughes, Jones, Smith, Cameron, Brown, Copeland, Kirwan.
SHEFFIELD UNITED – Foulke; Thickett, Boyle, Johnson, Morren, Needham, Bennett, Field, Hedley, Priest, Lipsham.
Scorers: (first match) Tottenham – Brown 2, Sheff. Utd. – Bennett, Priest.
Scorers: (second match) Tottenham – Cameron, Smith, Brown, Sheff. Utd. – Priest.

1902 **SHEFFIELD UNITED** – Foulke; Thickett, Boyle, Needham, Wilkinson, Johnson, Barnes, Common, Hedley, Priest, Lipsham. (Bennett injured in first match and Barnes took his place in the replay).
SOUTHAMPTON – Robinson; C. B. Fry, Molyneux, Bowman, Lee, A. Turner, Wood, Brown, Chadwick, J. Turner, Metson.
Scorers: (first match) Sheff. Utd. – Common, Southampton – Wood.
Scorers: (second match) Sheff. Utd. – Hedley, Barnes, Southampton – Brown.

1903 **BURY** – Monteith; Lindsey, McEwan, Johnson, Thorpe, Ross, Richards, Wood, Sagar, Leeming, Plant.
DERBY COUNTY – Fryer; Methven, Morris, Warren, Goodall (A.), May, Warrington, York, Boag, Richards, Davis.
Scorers: Bury – Ross, Sagar, Leeming 2, Wood, Plant.

1904 **MANCHESTER CITY** – Hillman; McMahon, Burgess, Frost, Hynde, S. B. Ashworth, Meredith, Livingstone, Gillespie, Turnbull (A.), Booth.
BOLTON WANDERERS – D. Davies; Brown, Struthers, Clifford, Greenhalgh, Freebairn, Stokes, Marsh, Yenson, White, Taylor.
Scorer: Man. City – Meredith.

1905 **ASTON VILLA** – George; Spencer, Miles, Pearson, Leake, Windmill, Brawn, Garratty, Hampton, Bache, Hall.
NEWCASTLE UNITED – Lawrence; McCombie, Carr, Gardner, Aitken, McWilliam, Rutherford, Howie, Appleyard, Veitch, Gosnell.
Scorer: Aston Villa – Hampton 2.

1906 **EVERTON** – Scott; Balmer (W.), Crelly, Makepeace, Taylor, Abbott, Sharp, Bolton, Young, Settle, H. P. Hardman.
NEWCASTLE UNITED – Lawrence; McCombie, Carr, Gardner, Aitken, McWilliam, Rutherford, Howie, Veitch, Orr, Gosnell.
Scorer: Everton – Young.

1907 **SHEFFIELD WEDNESDAY** – Lyall; Layton, Burton, Brittleton, Crawshaw, Bartlett, Chapman, Bradshaw, Wilson, Stewart, Simpson.
EVERTON – Scott; Balmer (W.), Balmer (R.), Makepeace, Taylor, Abbott, Sharp, Bolton, Young, Settle, H. P. Hardman.
Scorers: Sheff. Wed. – Stewart, Simpson, Everton – Sharp.

1908 **WOLVERHAMPTON WANDERERS** – Lunn; Jones, Collins, Rev. K. R. G. Hunt, Wooldridge, Bishop, Harrison, Shelton, Hedley, Radford, Pedley.
NEWCASTLE UNITED – Lawrence; McCracken, Pudan, Gardner, Veitch, McWilliam, Rutherford, Howie, Appleyard, Speedle, Wilson.
Scorers: Wolves – Rev. K. R. G. Hunt, Hedley, Harrison, Newcastle – Howie.

1909 **MANCHESTER UNITED** – Moger; Stacey, Hayes, Duckworth, Roberts, Bell, Meredith, Halse, Turnbull (J.), Turnbull (A.), Wall.

BRISTOL CITY – Clay; Annan, Cottle, Hanlin, Wedlock, Spear, Staniforth, Hardy, Gilligan, Burton, Hilton.
Scorer: Man. Utd. – Turnbull (A.).

1910 **NEWCASTLE UNITED** – Lawrence; McCracken, Carr, Veitch, Low, McWilliam, Rutherford, Howie, Shepherd, Higgins, Wilson. (Whitson was injured in first match and Carr took his place in the replay).
BARNSLEY – Mearns; Downs, Ness, Glendinning, Boyle, Utley, Bartrop, Gadsby, Lillycrop, Tufnell, Forman.
Scorers: (first match) Newcastle – Rutherford, Barnsley – Tufnell.
Scorer: (second match) Newcastle – Shepherd 2 (1 pen.).

1911 **BRADFORD CITY** – Mellors; Campbell, Taylor, Robinson, Torrance, McDonald, Logan, Spiers, O'Rourke, Devine, Thompson. (Gildea played centre half in the first match).
NEWCASTLE UNITED – Lawrence; McCracken, Whitson, Veitch, Low, Willis, Rutherford, Jobey, Stewart, Higgins, Wilson.
Scorer: Bradford – Spiers.

1912 **BARNSLEY** – Cooper; Downs, Taylor, Glendinning, Bratley, Utley, Bartrop, Tufnell, Lillycrop, Travers, Moore.
WEST BROMWICH ALBION – Pearson; Cook, Pennington, Baddeley, Buck, McNeal, Jephcott, Wright, Pailor, Bower, Shearman.
Scorer: Barnsley – Tufnell.

1913 **ASTON VILLA** – Hardy; Lyons, Weston, Barber, Harrop, Leach, Wallace, Halse, Hampton, Stephenson (C.), Bache.
SUNDERLAND – Butler; Gladwin, Ness, Cuggy, Thompson, Low, Mordue, Buchan, Richardson, Holley, Martin.
Scorer: Aston Villa – Barber.

1914 **BURNLEY** – Sewell; Bamford, Taylor, Halley, Boyle, Watson, Nesbit, Lindley, Freeman, Hodgson, Mosscrop.
LIVERPOOL – Campbell; Longworth, Pursell, Fairfoul, Ferguson, McKinlay, Sheldon, Metcalfe, Miller, Lacey, Nicholl.
Scorer: Burnley – Freeman.

1915 **SHEFFIELD UNITED** – Gough; Cook, English, Sturgess, Brelsford, Utley, Simmons, Fazackerley, Kitchen, Masterman, Evans.
CHELSEA – Molyneux; Bettridge, Harrow, Taylor, Logan, Walker, Ford, Halse, Thompson, Croal, McNeil.
Scorers: Sheff. Utd. – Simmons, Fazackerley, Kitchen.

1920 **ASTON VILLA** – Hardy; Smart, Weston, Ducat, Barson, Moss, Wallace, Kirton, Walker, Stephenson (C.), Dorrell.
HUDDERSFIELD TOWN – Mutch; Wood, Bullock, Slade, Wilson, Watson, Richardson, Mann, Taylor, Swan, Islip.
Scorer: Aston VIlla – Kirton.

1921 **TOTTENHAM HOTSPUR** – Hunter; Clay, McDonald, Smith, Walters, Grimsdell; Banks, Seed, Cantrell, Bliss, Dimmock.
WOLVERHAMPTON WANDERERS – George; Woodward, Marshall, Gregory, Hodnett, Riley, Lea, Burrill, Edmonds, Potts, Brooks.
Scorer: Tottenham – Dimmock.

1922 **HUDDERSFIELD TOWN** – Mutch; Wood, Wadsworth, Slade, Wilson, Watson, Richardson, Mann, Islip, Stephenson, Smith (W.H.).
PRESTON NORTH END – J. F. Mitchell; Hamilton, Doolan, Duxbury, McCall, Williamson, Rawlings, Jefferis, Roberts, Woodhouse, Quinn.
Scorer: Huddersfield – Smith (pen.).

1923 **BOLTON WANDERERS** – Pym; Hawarth, Finney, Nuttall, Seddon, Jennings, Butler, Jack, Smith (J. R.), Smith (J.), Vizard.
WEST HAM UNITED – Hufton; Henderson, Young, Bishop, Kay, Tresadern, Richards, Brown, Watson (V.), Moore, Ruffell.
Scorers: Bolton – Jack, Smith (J. R.).

1924 **NEWCASTLE UNITED** – Bradley; Hampson, Hudspeth, Mooney, Spencer, Gibson, Low, Cowan, Harris, McDonald, Seymour.

ASTON VILLA – Jackson; Smart, Mort, Moss, Dr. V. E. Milne, Blackburn, York, Kirton, Capewell, Walker, Dorrell.
Scorers: Newcastle – Harris, Seymour.

1925 **SHEFFIELD UNITED** – Sutcliffe; Cook, Milton, Pantling, King, Green, Mercer, Boyle, Johnson, Gillespie, Tunstall.
CARDIFF CITY – Farquharson; Nelson, Blair, Wake, Keenor, Hardy, Davies (W.), Gill, Nicholson, Beadles, Evans (J.).
Scorer: Sheff. Utd. – Tunstall.

1926 **BOLTON WANDERERS** – Pym; Haworth, Greenhalgh, Nuttall, Seddon, Jennings, Butler, Jack, Smith (J. R.), Smith (J.), Vizard.
MANCHESTER CITY – Goodchild; Cookson, McCloy, Pringle, Cowan, McMullan, Austin, Browell, Roberts, Johnson, Hicks.
Scorer: Bolton – Jack.

1927 **CARDIFF CITY** – Farquharson; Nelson, Watson, Keenor, Sloan, Hardy, Curtis, Irving, Ferguson, Davies (L.), McLachlan.
ARSENAL – Lewis; Parker, Kennedy, Baker, Butler, John, Hulme, Buchan, Brain, Blyth, Hoar.
Scorer: Cardiff – Ferguson.

1928 **BLACKBURN ROVERS** – Crawford; Hutton, Jones, Healless, Rankin, Campbell, Thornwell, Puddefoot, Roscamp, McLean, Rigby.
HUDDERSFIELD TOWN – Mercer; Goodall, Barkas, Redfern, Wilson, Steele, Jackson (A.), Kelly, Brown, Stephenson, Smith (W.H.).
Scorers: Blackburn – Roscamp 2, McLean, Huddersfield – Jackson.

1929 **BOLTON WANDERERS** – Pym; Hawarth, Finney, Kean, Seddon, Nuttall, Butler, McClelland, Blackmore, Gibson, Cook (W.).
PORTSMOUTH – Gilfillan; Mackie, Bell, Nichol, McIlwaine, Thackeray, Forward, Smith (J.), Weddle, Watson, Cook (F.).
Scorers: Bolton – Butler, Blackmore.

1930 **ARSENAL** – Preedy; Parker, Hapgood, Baker, Seddon, John, Hulme, Jack, Lambert, James, Bastin.
HUDDERSFIELD TOWN – Turner; Goodall, Spence, Naylor, Wilson, Campbell, Jackson (A.), Kelly, Davies, Raw, Smith (W. H.).
Scorers: Arsenal – James, Lambert.

1931 **WEST BROMWICH ALBION** – Pearson; Shaw, Trentham, Magee, Richardson (W.), Edwards, Glidden, Carter, Richardson (W. G.), Sandford, Wood.
BIRMINGHAM – Hibbs; Liddell, Barkas, Cringan, Morrall, Leslie, Briggs, Crosbie, Bradford, Gregg, Curtis.
Scorers: W.B.A. – Richardson (W. G.) 2, Birmingham – Bradford.

1932 **NEWCASTLE UNITED** – McInroy; Nelson, Fairhurst, McKenzie, Davidson, Weaver, Boyd, Richardson, Allen, McMenemy, Lang.
ARSENAL – Moss; Parker, Hapgood, Jones (C.), Roberts, Male, Hulme, Jack, Lambert, Bastin, John.
Scorers: Newcastle – Allen 2, Arsenal – John.

1933 **EVERTON** – Sagar; Cook, Cresswell, Britton, White, Thomson, Geldard, Dunn, Dean, Johnson, Stein.
MANCHESTER CITY – Langford; Cann, Dale, Busby, Cowan, Bray, Toseland, Marshall, Herd, McMullan, Brook.
Scorers: Everton – Stein, Dean, Dunn.

1934 **MANCHESTER CITY** – Swift; Barnett, Dale, Busby, Cowan, Bray, Toseland, Marshall, Tilson, Herd, Brook.
PORTSMOUTH – Gilfillan; Mackie, Smith (W.), Nichol, Allen, Thackeray, Worrall, Smith (J.), Weddle, Easson, Rutherford.
Scorers: Man. City – Tilson 2, Portsmouth – Rutherford.

1935 **SHEFFIELD WEDNESDAY** – Brown; Nibloe, Catlin, Sharp, Millership, Burrows, Hooper, Surtees, Palethorpe, Starling, Rimmer.
WEST BROMWICH ALBION – Pearson; Shaw, Trentham, Murphy, Richardson (W.), Edwards, Glidden, Carter, Richardson (W. G.), Sandford, Boyes.

Scorers: Sheff. Wed. – Rimmer 2, Palethorpe, Hooper, W.B.A. – Boyes, Sandford.

1936 **ARSENAL** – Wilson; Male, Hapgood, Crayston, Roberts, Copping, Hulme, Bowden, Drake, James, Bastin.
SHEFFIELD UNITED – Smith; Hooper, Wilkinson, Jackson, Johnson, McPherson, Barton, Barclay, Dodds, Pickering, Williams.
Scorer: Arsenal – Drake.

1937 **SUNDERLAND** – Mapson; Gorman, Hall, Thompson, Johnston, McNab, Duns, Carter, Gurney, Gallacher, Burbanks.
PRESTON NORTH END – Burns; Gallimore, Beattie (A.), Shankly, Tremelling, Milne, Dougal, Beresford, O'Donnell (F.), Fagan, O'Donnell (H).
Scorers: Sunderland – Gurney, Carter, Burbanks, Preston – O'Donnell (F.).

1938 **PRESTON NORTH END** – Holdcroft; Gallimore, Beattie (A.), Shankly, Smith, Batey, Watmough, Mutch, Maxwell, Beattie (R.), O'Donnell (H.).
HUDDERSFIELD TOWN – Hesford; Craig, Mountford, Willingham, Young, Boot, Hulme, Isaac, McFadyen, Barclay, Beasley.
Scorer: Preston – Mutch (pen.).

1939 **PORTSMOUTH** – Walker; Morgan, Rochford, Guthrie, Rowe, Wharton, Worrall, McAlinden, Anderson, Barlow, Parker.
WOLVERHAMPTON WANDERERS – Scott; Morris, Taylor, Galley, Cullis, Gardiner, Burton, McIntosh, Westcott, Dorsett, Maguire.
Scorers: Portsmouth – Parker 2, Barlow, Anderson, Wolves – Dorsett.

1946 **DERBY COUNTY** – Woodley; Nicholas, Howe, Bullions, Leuty, Musson, Harrison, Carter, Stamps, Doherty, Duncan.
CHARLTON ATHLETIC – Bartram; Phipps, Shreeve, Turner (H.), Oakes, Johnson, Fell, Brown, A. A. Turner, Welsh, Duffy.
Scorers: Derby – Turner (H.) (o.g.), Doherty, Stamps 2, Charlton – Turner (H.).

1947 **CHARLTON ATHLETIC** – Bartram; Croker (P.), Shreeve, Johnson, Phipps, Whittaker, Hurst, Dawson, Robinson (W.), Welsh, Duffy.
BURNLEY – Strong; Woodruff, Mather, Attwell, Brown, Bray, Chew, Morris, Harrison, Potts, F. P. Kippax.
Scorer: Charlton – Duffy.

1948 **MANCHESTER UNITED** – Crompton; Carey, Aston, Anderson, Chilton, Cockburn, Delaney, Morris, Rowley, Pearson, Mitten.
BLACKPOOL – Robinson; Shimwell, Crosland, Johnston, Hayward, Kelly, Matthews, Munro, Mortensen, Dick, Rickett.
Scorers: Man. Utd. – Rowley 2, Pearson, Anderson, Blackpool – Shimwell (pen.), Mortensen.

1949 **WOLVERHAMPTON WANDERERS** – Williams; Pritchard, Springthorpe, Crook (W.), Shorthouse, Wright, Hancocks, Smyth, Pye, Dunn, Mullen.
LEICESTER CITY – Bradley; Jelly, Scott, Harrison (W.), Plummer, King, Griffiths, Lee, Harrison (J.), Chisholm, Adam.
Scorers: Wolves – Pye 2, Smyth, Leicester – Griffiths.

1950 **ARSENAL** – Swindin; Scott, Barnes, Forbes, Compton (L.), Mercer, Cox, Logie, Goring, Lewis, Compton (D.).
LIVERPOOL – Sidlow; Lambert, Spicer, Taylor, Hughes, Jones, Payne, Baron, Stubbins, Fagan, Liddell.
Scorer: Arsenal – Lewis 2.

1951 **NEWCASTLE UNITED** – Fairbrother; Cowell, Corbett, Harvey, Brennan, Crowe, Walker, Taylor, Milburn, Robledo (G.), Mitchell.
BLACKPOOL – Farm; Shimwell, Garrett, Johnston, Hayward, Kelly, Matthews, Mudie, Mortensen, W. J. Slater, Perry.
Scorer: Newcastle – Milburn 2.

1952 **NEWCASTLE UNITED** – Simpson; Cowell, McMichael, Harvey, Brennan, Robledo (E.), Walker, Foulkes, Milburn, Robledo (G.), Mitchell.
ARSENAL – Swindin; Barnes, Smith (L.), Forbes, Daniel, Mercer, Cox, Logie, Holton, Lishman, Roper.
Scorer: Newcastle – Robledo (G.).

1953 **BLACKPOOL** – Farm; Shimwell, Garrett, Fenton, Johnston, Robinson, Matthews, Taylor, Mortensen, Mudie, Perry.
BOLTON WANDERERS – Hanson; Ball, Banks (R.), Wheeler, Barrass, Bell, Holden, Moir, Lofthouse, Hassall, Langton.
Scorers: Blackpool – Mortensen 3, Perry, Bolton – Lofthouse, Moir, Bell.

1954 **WEST BROMWICH ALBION** – Sanders; Kennedy, Millard, Dudley, Dugdale, Barlow, Griffin, Ryan, Allen, Nicholls, Lee.
PRESTON NORTH END – Thompson; Cunningham, Walton, Docherty, Marston, Forbes, Finney, Foster, Wayman, Baxter, Morrison.
Scorers: W.B.A. – Allen 2 (1 pen.), Griffin, Preston – Morrison, Wayman.

1955 **NEWCASTLE UNITED** – Simpson; Cowell, Batty, Scoular, Stokoe, Casey, White, Milburn, Keeble, Hannah, Mitchell.
MANCHESTER CITY – Trautmann; Meadows, Little, Barnes, Ewing, Paul, Spurdle, Hayes, Revie, Johnstone, Fagan.
Scorers: Newcastle – Milburn, Mitchell, Hannah, Man. City – Johnstone.

1956 **MANCHESTER CITY** – Trautmann; Leivers, Little, Barnes, Ewing, Paul, Johnstone, Hayes, Revie, Dyson, Clarke.
BIRMINGHAM CITY – Merrick; Hall, Green, Newman, Smith, Boyd, Astall, Kinsey, Brown, Murphy, Govan.
Scorers: Man. City – Hayes, Dyson, Johnstone, Birmingham – Kinsey.

1957 **ASTON VILLA** – Sims; Lynn, Aldis, Crowther, Dugdale, Saward, Smith, Sewell, Myerscough, Dixon, McParland.
MANCHESTER UNITED – Wood; Foulkes, Byrne, Colman, Blanchflower, Edwards, Berry, Whelan, Taylor (T.), Charlton, Pegg.
Scorers: Aston Villa – McParland 2, Man. Utd. – Taylor.

1958 **BOLTON WANDERERS** – Hopkinson; Hartle, Banks (T.), Hennin, Higgins, Edwards, Birch, Stevens, Lofthouse, Parry, Holden.
MANCHESTER UNITED – Gregg; Foulkes, Greaves, Goodwin, Cope, Crowther, Dawson, Taylor (E.), Charlton, Viollet, Webster.
Scorer: Bolton – Lofthouse 2.

1959 **NOTTINGHAM FOREST** – Thomson; Whare, McDonald, Whitefoot, McKinlay, Burkitt, Dwight, Quigley, Wilson, Gray, Imlach.
LUTON TOWN – Baynham; McNally, Hawkes, Groves, Owen, Pacey, Bingham, Brown, Morton, Cummins, Gregory.
Scorers: Nott'm. Forest – Dwight, Wilson, Luton – Pacey.

1960 **WOLVERHAMPTON WANDERERS** – Finlayson; Showell, Harris, Clamp, Slater, Flowers, Deeley, Stobart, Murray, Broadbent, Horne.
BLACKBURN ROVERS – Leyland; Bray, Whelan, Clayton, Woods, McGrath, Bimpson, Dobing, Dougan, Douglas, MacLeod.
Scorers: Wolves – McGrath (o.g.), Deeley 2.

1961 **TOTTENHAM HOTSPUR** – Brown; Baker, Henry, Blanchflower, Norman, Mackay, Jones, White, Smith, Allen, Dyson.
LEICESTER CITY – Banks; Chalmers, Norman, McLintock, King, Appleton, Riley, Walsh, McIlmoyle, Keyworth, Cheesebrough.
Scorers: Tottenham – Smith, Dyson.

1962 **TOTTENHAM HOTSPUR** – Brown; Baker, Henry, Blanchflower, Norman, Mackay, Medwin, White, Smith, Greaves, Jones.

BURNLEY – Blacklaw; Angus, Elder, Adamson, Cummings, Miller, Connelly, McIlroy, Pointer, Robson, Harris.
Scorers: Tottenham – Greaves, Smith, Blanchflower (pen.), Burnley – Robson.

1963 **MANCHESTER UNITED** – Gaskell; Dunne, Cantwell, Crerand, Foulkes, Setters, Giles, Quixall, Herd, Law, Charlton.
LEICESTER CITY – Banks; Sjoberg, Norman, McLintock, King, Appleton, Riley, Cross, Keyworth, Gibson, Stringfellow.
Scorers: Man. Utd. – Law, Herd 2, Leicester – Keyworth.

1964 **WEST HAM UNITED** – Standen; Bond, Burkett, Bovington, Brown, Moore, Brabrook, Boyce, Byrne, Hurst, Sissons.
PRESTON NORTH END – Kelly; Ross, Smith, Lawton, Singleton, Kendall, Wilson, Ashworth, Dawson, Spavin, Holden.
Scorers: West Ham – Sissons, Hurst, Boyce, Preston – Holden, Dawson.

1965 **LIVERPOOL** – Lawrence; Lawler, Byrne, Strong, Yeats, Stevenson, Callaghan, Hunt, St. John, Smith, Thompson.
LEEDS UNITED – Sprake; Reaney, Bell, Bremner, Charlton, Hunter, Giles, Storrie, Peacock, Collins, Johanneson.
Scorers: Liverpool – Hunt, St. John, Leeds – Bremner.

1966 **EVERTON** – West; Wright, Wilson, Gabriel, Labone, Harris, Scott, Trebilcock, Young, Harvey, Temple.
SHEFFIELD WEDNESDAY – Springett; Smith, Megson, Eustace, Ellis, Young, Pugh, Fantham, McCalliog, Ford, Quinn.
Scorers: Everton – Trebilcock 2, Temple, Sheff. Wed. – McCalliog, Ford.

1967 **TOTTENHAM HOTSPUR** – Jennings; Kinnear, Knowles, Mullery, England, Mackay, Robertson, Greaves, Gilzean, Venables, Saul.
CHELSEA – Bonetti; Harris (A.), McCreadie, Hollins, Hinton, Harris (R.), Cooke, Baldwin, Hateley, Tambling, Boyle.
Scorers: Tottenham – Robertson, Saul, Chelsea – Tambling.

1968 **WEST BROMWICH ALBION** – Osborne; Fraser, Williams, Brown, Talbut, Kaye (Clarke), Lovett, Collard, Astle, Hope, Clark.
EVERTON – West; Wright, Wilson, Kendall, Labone, Harvey, Husband, Ball, Royle, Hurst, Morrissey.
Scorer: W.B.A. – Astle.

1969 **MANCHESTER CITY** – Dowd; Book, Pardoe, Doyle, Booth, Oakes, Summerbee, Bell, Lee, Young, Coleman.
LEICESTER CITY – Shilton; Rodrigues, Nish, Roberts, Woollett, Cross, Fern, Gibson, Lochhead, Clarke, Glover (Manley).
Scorer: Man. City – Young.

1970 **CHELSEA** – Bonetti; Webb, McCreadie, Hollins, Dempsey, Harris (R.) (Hinton), Baldwin, Houseman, Osgood, Hutchinson, Cooke.
LEEDS UNITED – Sprake; Madeley, Cooper, Bremner, Charlton, Hunter, Lorimer, Clarke, Jones, Giles, Gray.
Scorers: Chelsea – Houseman, Hutchinson, Leeds – Charlton, Jones.
Replay: CHELSEA – Bonetti; Harris (R.), McCreadie, Hollins, Dempsey, Webb, Baldwin, Cooke, Osgood (Hinton), Hutchinson, Houseman.
LEEDS UNITED – Harvey; Madeley, Cooper, Bremner, Charlton, Hunter, Lorimer, Clarke, Jones, Giles, Gray.
Scorers: Chelsea – Osgood, Webb, Leeds – Jones.

1971 **ARSENAL** – Wilson; Rice, McNab, Storey (Kelly), McLintock, Simpson, Armstrong, Graham, Radford, Kennedy, George.
LIVERPOOL – Clemence; Lawler, Lindsay, Smith, Lloyd, Hughes, Callaghan, Evans (Thompson), Heighway, Toshack, Hall.
Scorers: Arsenal – Kelly, George, Liverpool – Heighway.

1972 **LEEDS UNITED** – Harvey; Reaney, Madeley, Bremner, Charlton, Hunter, Lorimer, Clarke, Jones, Giles, Gray.

ARSENAL – Barnett; Rice, McNab, Storey, McLintock, Simpson, Armstrong, Ball, Radford (Kennedy), George, Graham.
Scorer: Leeds – Clarke.

1973 **SUNDERLAND** – Montgomery; Malone, Guthrie, Horswill, Watson, Pitt, Kerr, Hughes, Halom, Porterfield, Tueart.
LEEDS UNITED – Harvey; Reaney, Cherry, Bremner, Madeley, Hunter, Lorimer, Clarke, Jones, Giles, Gray (Yorath).
Scorer: Sunderland – Porterfield.

1974 **LIVERPOOL** – Clemence; Smith, Lindsay, Thompson, Cormack, Hughes, Keegan, Hall, Heighway, Toshack, Callaghan.
NEWCASTLE UNITED – McFaul; Clark, Kennedy, McDermott, Howard, Moncur, Smith (Gibb), Cassidy, Macdonald, Tudor, Hibbitt.
Scorers: Liverpool – Keegan (2), Heighway.

1975 **WEST HAM UNITED** – Day; McDowell, Lampard, Bonds, Taylor (T.), Lock, Jennings, Paddon, Taylor (A.), Brooking, Holland.
FULHAM – Mellor; Cutbush, Fraser, Mullery, Lacy, Moore, Mitchell, Conway, Busby, Slough, Barrett.
Scorer: West Ham – Taylor (A.) 2.

1976 **SOUTHAMPTON** – Turner; Rodrigues, Peach, Holmes, Blyth, Steele, Gilchrist, Channon, Osgood, McCalliog, Stokes.
MANCHESTER UNITED – Stepney; Forsyth, Houston, Daly, Greenhoff (B.), Buchan, Coppell, McIlroy, Pearson, Macari, Hill (McCreery).
Scorer: Southampton – Stokes.

1977 **MANCHESTER UNITED** – Stepney; Nicholl, Albiston, McIlroy, Greenhoff (B.), Buchan, Coppell, Greenhoff (J.), Pearson, Macari, Hill (McCreery).
LIVERPOOL – Clemence; Neal, Jones, Smith, Kennedy, Hughes, Keegan, Case, Heighway, McDermott, Johnson (Callaghan).
Scorers: Man. Utd. – Pearson, Greenhoff (J.), Liverpool – Case.

1978 **IPSWICH TOWN** – Cooper; Burley, Mills, Talbot, Hunter, Beattie, Osborne (Lambert), Wark, Mariner, Geddis, Woods.
ARSENAL – Jennings; Rice, Nelson, Price, O'Leary, Young, Brady (Rix), Sunderland, Macdonald, Stapleton, Hudson.
Scorer: Ipswich – Osborne.

1979 **ARSENAL** – Jennings; Rice, Nelson, Talbot, O'Leary, Young, Brady, Sunderland, Stapleton, Price (Walford), Rix.
MANCHESTER UNITED – Bailey; Nicholl, Albiston, McIlroy, McQueen, Buchan, Coppell, Greenhoff (J.), Jordan, Macari, Thomas.
Scorers: Arsenal – Talbot, Stapleton, Sunderland, Man. Utd. – McQueen, McIlroy.

1980 **WEST HAM UNITED** – Parkes; Stewart, Lampard, Bonds, Martin, Devonshire, Allen, Pearson, Cross, Brooking, Pike.
ARSENAL – Jennings; Rice, Devine (Nelson), Talbot, O'Leary, Young, Brady, Sunderland, Stapleton, Price, Rix.
Scorer: West Ham – Brooking.

1981 **TOTTENHAM HOTSPUR** – Aleksic; Hughton, Miller, Roberts, Perryman, Villa (Brooke), Ardiles, Archibald, Galvin, Hoddle, Crooks.
MANCHESTER CITY – Corrigan; Ranson, McDonald, Reid, Power, Caton, Bennett, Gow, Mackenzie, Hutchison (Henry), Reeves.
Scorer: Tottenham – Hutchison (o.g.), Man. City – Hutchison.
Replay: TOTTENHAM HOTSPUR – Aleksic; Hughton, Miller, Roberts, Perryman, Villa, Ardiles, Archibald, Galvin, Hoddle, Crooks.
MANCHESTER CITY – Corrigan; Ranson, McDonald (Tueart), Reid, Power, Caton, Bennett, Gow, Mackenzie, Hutchison, Reeves.
Scorers: Tottenham – Villa 2, Crooks, Man. City – Mackenzie, Reeves (pen.).

1982 **TOTTENHAM HOTSPUR** – Clemence; Hughton, Miller, Price, Hazard (Brooke), Perryman, Roberts, Archibald, Galvin, Hoddle, Crooks.

QUEENS PARK RANGERS – Hucker; Fenwick, Gillard, Waddock, Hazell, Roeder, Currie, Flanagan, Allen (Micklewhite), Stainrod, Gregory.

Scorers: Tottenham – Hoddle, Q.P.R. – Fenwick.

Replay: TOTTENHAM HOTSPUR – Clemence; Hughton, Miller, Price, Hazard (Brooke), Perryman, Roberts, Archibald, Galvin, Hoddle, Crooks.

QUEENS PARK RANGERS – Hucker; Fenwick, Gillard, Waddock, Hazell, Neill, Currie, Flanagan, Micklewhite (Burke), Stainrod, Gregory.

Scorer: Tottenham – Hoddle (pen.).

1983 **MANCHESTER UNITED** – Bailey; Duxbury, Albiston, Wilkins, Moran, McQueen, Robson, Muhren, Stapleton, Whiteside, Davies.

BRIGHTON & HOVE ALBION – Moseley; Ramsey (Ryan), Pearce, Grealish, Gatting, Stevens, Case, Howlett, Robinson, Smith, Smillie.

Scorers: Man. Utd. – Stapleton, Wilkins, Brighton – Smith, Stevens.

Replay: MANCHESTER UNITED – Bailey; Duxbury, Albiston, Wilkins, Moran, McQueen, Robson, Muhren, Stapleton, Whiteside, Davies.

BRIGHTON & HOVE ALBION – Moseley; Gatting, Pearce, Grealish, Foster, Stevens, Case, Howlett (Ryan), Robinson, Smith, Smillie.

Scorers: Man. Utd. – Robson 2, Whiteside, Muhren (pen.).

1984 **EVERTON** – Southall; Stevens, Bailey, Ratcliffe, Mountfield, Reid, Steven, Heath, Sharp, Gray, Richardson.

WATFORD – Sherwood; Bardsley, Price (Atkinson), Taylor, Terry, Sinnott, Callaghan, Johnston, Reilly, Jackett, Barnes.

Scorers: Everton – Sharp, Gray.

1985 **MANCHESTER UNITED** – Bailey; Gidman, Albiston (Duxbury), Whiteside, McGrath, Moran, Robson, Strachan, Hughes, Stapleton, Olsen.

EVERTON – Southall; Stevens, Van den Hauwe, Ratcliffe, Mountfield, Reid, Steven, Sharp, Gray, Bracewell, Sheedy.

Scorer: Man. Utd. – Whiteside.

Sent off: Moran.

1986 **LIVERPOOL** – Grobbelaar; Lawrenson, Beglin, Nicol, Whelan, Hansen, Dalglish, Johnston, Rush, Molby, MacDonald.

EVERTON – Mimms; Stevens (Heath), Van den Hauwe, Ratcliffe, Mountfield, Reid, Steven, Lineker, Sharp, Bracewell, Sheedy.

Scorers: Liverpool – Rush 2, Johnston, Everton – Lineker.

1987 **COVENTRY CITY** – Ogrizovic; Phillips, Downs, McGrath, Kilcline (Rodger), Peake, Bennett, Gynn, Regis, Houchen, Pickering.

TOTTENHAM HOTSPUR – Clemence; Hughton (Claesen), Thomas (M.), Hodge, Gough, Mabbutt, Allen (C.), Allen (P.), Waddle, Hoddle, Ardiles (Stevens).

Scorers: Coventry – Bennett, Houchen, Mabbutt (o.g.), Tottenham – Allen (C.), Mabbutt.

1988 **WIMBLEDON** – Beasant; Goodyear, Phelan, Jones, Young, Thorn, Gibson (Scales), Cork (Cunningham), Fashanu, Sanchez, Wise.

LIVERPOOL – Grobbelaar; Gillespie, Ablett, Nicol, Spackman (Molby), Hansen, Beardsley, Aldridge (Johnston), Houghton, Barnes, McMahon.

Scorer: Wimbledon – Sanchez.

1989 **LIVERPOOL** – Grobbelaar; Ablett, Staunton (Venison), Nicol, Whelan, Hansen, Beardsley, Aldridge (Rush), Houghton, Barnes, McMahon.

EVERTON – Southall; McDonald, Van den Hauwe, Ratcliffe, Watson, Bracewell (McCall), Nevin, Steven, Sharp, Cottee, Sheedy (Wilson).
Scorers: Liverpool – Aldridge, Rush 2, Everton – McCall 2.

1990 **MANCHESTER UNITED** – Leighton; Ince, Martin (Blackmore), Bruce, Phelan, Pallister (Robins), Robson, Webb, McClair, Hughes, Wallace.
CRYSTAL PALACE – Martyn; Pemberton, Shaw, Gray (Madden), O'Reilly, Thorn, Barber (Wright), Thomas, Bright, Salako, Pardew.
Scorers: Man. Utd. – Robson, Hughes 2, Crystal Palace – O'Reilly, Wright 2.
Replay: MANCHESTER UNITED – Sealey; Ince, Martin, Bruce, Phelan, Pallister, Robson, Webb, McClair, Hughes, Wallace.
CRYSTAL PALACE – Martyn; Pemberton, Shaw, Gray, O'Reilly, Thorn, Barber (Wright), Thomas, Bright, Salako (Madden), Pardew.
Scorer: Man. Utd. – Martin.

1991 **TOTTENHAM HOTSPUR** – Thorstvedt; Edinburgh, Van den Hauwe, Sedgley, Howells, Mabbutt, Stewart, Gascoigne (Nayim), Samways (Walsh), Lineker, Allen.
NOTTINGHAM FOREST – Crossley; Charles, Pearce, Walker, Chettle, Keane, Crosby, Parker, Clough, Glover (Laws), Woan (Hodge).
Scorers: Tottenham – Stewart, Walker (o.g.), Nott'm. Forest – Pearce.

1992 **LIVERPOOL** – Grobbelaar; Jones (R.), Burrows, Nicol, Molby, Wright, Saunders, Houghton, Rush (I.), McManaman, Thomas.
SUNDERLAND – Norman; Owers, Ball, Bennett, Rogan, Rush (D.) (Hardyman), Bracewell, Davenport, Armstrong (Hawke), Byrne, Atkinson.
Scorers: Liverpool – Thomas, Rush (I.).

1993 **ARSENAL** – Seaman; Dixon, Winterburn, Linighan, Adams, Parlour (Smith), Davis, Merson, Jensen, Wright (O'Leary), Campbell.
SHEFFIELD WEDNESDAY – Woods; Nilsson, Worthington, Palmer, Hirst, Anderson (Hyde), Waddle (Bart-Williams), Warhurst, Bright, Sheridan, Harkes.
Scorers: Arsenal – Wright, Sheff. Wed. – Hirst.
Replay:ARSENAL – Seaman; Dixon, Winterburn, Linighan, Adams, Davis, Jensen, Merson, Smith, Wright (O'Leary), Campbell.
SHEFFIELD WEDNESDAY – Woods; Nilsson (Bart-Williams), Worthington, Palmer, Hirst, Wilson (Hyde), Waddle, Warhurst, Bright, Sheridan, Harkes.
Scorers: Arsenal – Wright, Linighan, Sheff. Wed. – Waddle.

1994 **MANCHESTER UNITED** – Schmeichel; Parker, Bruce, Pallister, Irwin (Sharpe), Kanchelskis (McClair), Keane, Ince, Giggs, Cantona, Hughes.
CHELSEA – Kharine; Clarke, Johnsen, Kjeldbjerg, Sinclair, Burley (Hoddle), Newton, Wise, Peacock, Stein (Cascarino), Spencer.
Scorers: Man. Utd. – Cantona 2 (2 pens.), Hughes, McClair.

1995 **EVERTON** – Southall; Jackson, Watson, Unsworth, Ablett, Horne, Parkinson, Hinchcliffe, Stuart, Limpar (Amokachi), Rideout (Ferguson).
MANCHESTER UNITED – Schmeichel; Neville (G.), Bruce (Giggs), Pallister, Irwin, Butt, Keane, Ince, Sharpe (Scholes), McClair, Hughes.
Scorer: Everton – Rideout.

1996 **MANCHESTER UNITED** – Schmeichel; Irwin, May, Pallister, Neville (P.), Beckham (Neville, G.), Keane, Butt, Giggs, Cantona, Cole (Scholes).
LIVERPOOL – James; McAteer, Scales, Wright, Babb, Jones (Thomas), McManaman, Redknapp, Barnes, Collymore (Rush), Fowler.
Scorer: Man. Utd. – Cantona.

F.A. CUP FINALS – COMPLETE RESULTS

AT KENNINGTON OVAL

1872 The Wanderers beat Royal Engineers (1-0)

AT LILLIE BRIDGE, LONDON

1873 The Wanderers beat Oxford University (2-1)

AT KENNINGTON OVAL

1874 Oxford University beat Royal Engineers (2-0)
1875 Royal Engineers beat Old Etonians (2-0 after a 1-1 draw)
1876 The Wanderers beat Old Etonians (3-0 after a 0-0 draw)
1877†† The Wanderers beat Oxford University (2-1)
1878* The Wanderers beat Royal Engineers (3-1)
1879 Old Etonians beat Clapham Rovers (1-0)
1880 Clapham Rovers beat Oxford University (1-0)
1881 Old Carthusians beat Old Etonians (3-0)
1882 Old Etonians beat Blackburn Rovers (1-0)
1883†† Blackburn Olympic beat Old Etonians (2-1)
1884 Blackburn Rovers beat Queen's Park (Glasgow) (2-1)
1885 Blackburn Rovers beat Queen's Park (Glasgow) (2-0)
1886†*a* Blackburn Rovers beat West Bromwich Albion (2-0 after a 0-0 draw)
1887 Aston Villa beat West Bromwich Albion (2-0)
1888 West Bromwich Albion beat Preston North End (2-1)
1889 Preston North End beat Wolverhampton Wanderers (3-0)
1890 Blackburn Rovers beat Sheffield Wednesday (6-1)
1891 Blackburn Rovers beat Notts County (3-1)
1892 West Bromwich Albion beat Aston Villa (3-0)

AT FALLOWFIELD, MANCHESTER

1893 Wolverhampton Wanderers beat Everton (1-0)

AT GOODISON PARK, LIVERPOOL

1894 Notts County beat Bolton Wanderers (4-1)

AT CRYSTAL PALACE

1895 Aston Villa beat West Bromwich Albion (1-0)
1896 Sheffield Wednesday beat Wolverhampton Wanderers (2-1)
1897 Aston Villa beat Everton (3-2)
1898 Nottingham Forest beat Derby County (3-1)
1899 Sheffield United beat Derby County (4-1)
1900 Bury beat Southampton (4-0)
1901††† Tottenham Hotspur beat Sheffield United (3-1 after a 2-2 draw)
1902 Sheffield United beat Southampton (2-1 after a 1-1 draw)
1903 Bury beat Derby County (6-0)
1904 Manchester City beat Bolton Wanderers (1-0)
1905 Aston Villa beat Newcastle United (2-0)
1906 Everton beat Newcastle United (1-0)
1907 Sheffield Wednesday beat Everton (2-1)
1908 Wolverhampton Wanderers beat Newcastle United (3-1)
1909 Manchester United beat Bristol City (1-0)

1910** Newcastle United beat Barnsley (2-0 after a 1-1 draw)
1911*b* Bradford City beat Newcastle United (1-0 after a 0-0 draw)
1912*c* Barnsley beat West Bromwich Albion (1-0 after a 0-0 draw)
1913 Aston Villa beat Sunderland (1-0)
1914 Burnley beat Liverpool (1-0)

AT OLD TRAFFORD, MANCHESTER

1915 Sheffield United beat Chelsea (3-0)

AT STAMFORD BRIDGE, LONDON

1920†† Aston Villa beat Huddersfield Town (1-0)
1921 Tottenham Hotspur beat Wolverhampton Wanderers (1-0)
1922 Huddersfield Town beat Preston North End (1-0)

AT WEMBLEY

1923 Bolton Wanderers beat West Ham United (2-0)
1924 Newcastle United beat Aston Villa (2-0)
1925 Sheffield United beat Cardiff City (1-0)
1926 Bolton Wanderers beat Manchester City (1-0)
1927 Cardiff City beat Arsenal (1-0)
1928 Blackburn Rovers beat Huddersfield Town (3-1)
1929 Bolton Wanderers beat Portsmouth (2-0)
1930 Arsenal beat Huddersfield Town (2-0)
1931 West Bromwich Albion beat Birmingham (2-1)
1932 Newcastle United beat Arsenal (2-1)
1933 Everton beat Manchester City (3-0)
1934 Manchester City beat Portsmouth (2-1)
1935 Sheffield Wednesday beat West Bromwich Albion (4-2)
1936 Arsenal beat Sheffield United (1-0)
1937 Sunderland beat Preston North End (3-1)
1938†† Preston North End beat Huddersfield Town (1-0)
1939 Portsmouth beat Wolverhampton Wanderers (4-1)
1946†† Derby County beat Charlton Athletic (4-1)
1947†† Charlton Athletic beat Burnley (1-0)
1948 Manchester United beat Blackpool (4-2)
1949 Wolverhampton Wanderers beat Leicester City (3-1)
1950 Arsenal beat Liverpool (2-0)
1951 Newcastle United beat Blackpool (2-0)
1952 Newcastle United beat Arsenal (1-0)
1953 Blackpool beat Bolton Wanderers (4-3)
1954 West Bromwich Albion beat Preston North End (3-2)
1955 Newcastle United beat Manchester City (3-1)
1956 Manchester City beat Birmingham City (3-1)
1957 Aston Villa beat Manchester United (2-1)
1958 Bolton Wanderers beat Manchester United (2-0)
1959 Nottingham Forest beat Luton Town (2-1)
1960 Wolverhampton Wanderers beat Blackburn Rovers (3-0)
1961 Tottenham Hotspur beat Leicester City (2-0)
1962 Tottenham Hotspur beat Burnley (3-1)
1963 Manchester United beat Leicester City (3-1)
1964 West Ham United beat Preston North End (3-2)
1965†† Liverpool beat Leeds United (2-1)
1966 Everton beat Sheffield Wednesday (3-2)
1967 Tottenham Hotspur beat Chelsea (2-1)
1968†† West Bromwich Albion beat Everton (1-0)
1969 Manchester City beat Leicester City (1-0)
1970††• Chelsea beat Leeds United (2-1 after a 2-2 draw)
1971†† Arsenal beat Liverpool (2-1)

1972	Leeds United beat Arsenal (1-0)
1973	Sunderland beat Leeds United (1-0)
1974	Liverpool beat Newcastle United (3-0)
1975	West Ham United beat Fulham (2-0)
1976	Southampton beat Manchester United (1-0)
1977	Manchester United beat Liverpool (2-1)
1978	Ipswich Town beat Arsenal (1-0)
1979	Arsenal beat Manchester United (3-2)
1980	West Ham United beat Arsenal (1-0)
1981	Tottenham Hotspur beat Manchester City (3-2 after a 1-1 draw)
1982	Tottenham Hotspur beat Queens Park Rangers (1-0 after a 1-1 draw)
1983	Manchester United beat Brighton & H.A. (4-0 after a 2-2 draw)
1984	Everton beat Watford (2-0)
1985††	Manchester United beat Everton (1-0)
1986	Liverpool beat Everton (3-1)
1987††	Coventry City beat Tottenham Hotspur (3-2)
1988	Wimbledon beat Liverpool (1-0)
1989††	Liverpool beat Everton (3-2)
1990	Manchester United beat Crystal Palace (1-0 after a 3-3 draw)
1991††	Tottenham Hotspur beat Nottingham Forest (2-1)
1992	Liverpool beat Sunderland (2-0)
1993††	Arsenal beat Sheffield Wednesday (2-1 after a 1-1 draw)
1994	Manchester United beat Chelsea (4-0)
1995	Everton beat Manchester United (1-0)
1996	Manchester United beat Liverpool (1-0)

†† After extra time. * Won outright but restored to the Association. *a* Replayed at Baseball Ground, Derby. † A special trophy was awarded for the third consecutive win. ††† Replayed at Burnden Park, Bolton. ** Replayed at Goodison Park, Liverpool. *b* Replayed at Old Trafford, Manchester, new trophy provided. *c* Replayed at Bramall Lane, Sheffield. ● Replayed at Old Trafford.
(All replays since 1981 played at Wembley.)

1996 F.A. CUP FINAL

MANCHESTER UNITED 1 (Cantona 85), LIVERPOOL 0

(Competition sponsored by Littlewoods)

Wembley, Saturday, May 11. **Attendance**, 79,007. **Receipts**, (est. £2,400,000).

Man. Utd. (red shirts): Schmeichel; Irwin, May, Pallister, P. Neville, Beckham (G. Neville 89), Keane, Butt, Giggs, Cantona (Capt.), Cole (Scholes 65). Sub not used: Sharpe. **Booked**: P. Neville. **Manager**: Alex Ferguson.

Liverpool (green and white shirts): James; McAteer, Scales, Wright, Babb, Jones (Thomas 85), McManaman, Redknapp, Barnes, Collymore (Rush 74), Fowler. Sub not used: Warner (gk). **Booked**: Babb, Redknapp. **Manager**: Roy Evans.

Man of Match: Roy Keane.

Referee: D. Gallagher (Banbury). **Half-time**: 0-0. **Kick-off**: 3.0 (BBC TV).

Guests of Honour: The Duke and Duchess of Kent.

Conditions: Dry, sunny spells. Pitch immaculate.

With their second F.A. Cup triumph in three seasons, Manchester United became the first club to complete the English Double twice, and claimed further distinction by winning the game's oldest competition for a record ninth time. Playing in the Final for a third successive year, they reproduced Wembley's most frequent score for this event as the Cup was won 1-0 there for the 20th time.

Once again, the hype of modern Finals far exceeded the product, but with the prospect of an extra half-hour looming, the occasion was rescued by Eric Cantona's goal five minutes from time. Beckham's corner was cleared by James only to the edge of the box, where Cantona struck an awkward ball that dropped almost under his feet past three defenders.

A year before, the suspended Cantona probably cost United a second successive Double. Now, as captain (Steve Bruce did not make the 14), he led his team up football's most famous steps to receive the Cup from the Duchess of Kent.

On the day, United never allowed the opposition to shape their game. Liverpool had not beaten United in the Cup for 75 years, and now bowed to them for the sixth time running in a series of nine meetings in the competition.

Colour clash: Man. United won the toss to wear their normal red. Liverpool were the first side to wear green in the Cup Final (green and white shirts, green shorts, green and white socks).

Cup Final betting: Never closer, with both clubs quoted at odds on (5-6). This had happened only once before (Man. United v Everton in 1985).

Tickets: The Finalists each received 25,500. Prices: Except in the Olympic Gallery, the same as in 1995: £17-25-30-35-40-45-60. Gallery tickets went up from £90-100 to £100-115.

Cup Final programme: £6 (previously £5).

The referee's fee was increased to £325 (from £300), linesmen each £135. They also received medals.

Mistimed: Because a dancing-girls display over-ran, the teams entered the arena while the crowd were still singing Abide With Me.

In the **Legends' Penalty Contest** before the match, Man. United beat Liverpool 5-4.

HOW THEY REACHED THE FINAL

MANCHESTER UNITED

3rd Round: D 2-2 home to Sunderland (Butt, Cantona).
Replay: W 2-1 away to Sunderland (Scholes, Cole).
4th Round: W 3-0 away to Reading (Giggs, Parker, Cantona).
5th Round: W 2-1 home to Man. City (Cantona pen., Sharpe).
6th Round: W 2-0 home to Southampton (Cantona, Sharpe).
Semi-final (Villa Park): W 2-1 v Chelsea (Cole, Beckham).

LIVERPOOL

3rd Round: W 7-0 home to Rochdale (Collymore 3, Fowler, Rush, McAteer, Opponent og).
4th Round: W 4-0 away to Shrewsbury (Collymore, Fowler, McAteer, Opponent og).
5th Round: W 2-1 home to Charlton (Fowler, Collymore).
6th Round: D 0-0 away to Leeds
Replay: W 3-0 home to Leeds (McManaman 2, Fowler).
Semi-final (Old Trafford): W 3-0 v Aston Villa (Fowler 2, McAteer).

SUMMARY OF F.A. CUP WINS

Manchester United 9
Tottenham Hotspur 8
Aston Villa 7
Arsenal 6
Blackburn Rovers 6
Newcastle United 6
Everton 5
Liverpool 5
The Wandererers 5
W.B.A 5
Bolton Wanderers 4
Manchester City 4

Sheffield United 4	Blackburn Olympic 1	Huddersfield Town 1
Wolves 4	Blackpool 1	Ipswich Town 1
Sheffield Wednesday . 3	Bradford City 1	Leeds United 1
West Ham United 3	Burnley 1	Notts County 1
Bury 2	Cardiff City 1	Old Carthusians 1
Nottingham Forest 2	Charlton Athletic 1	Oxford University 1
Old Etonians 2	Chelsea 1	Portsmouth 1
Preston North End 2	Clapham Rovers 1	Royal Engineers 1
Sunderland 2	Coventry City 1	Southampton 1
Barnsley 1	Derby County 1	Wimbledon 1

APPEARANCES IN FINALS

(Figures do not include replays)

Manchester United . 14	Chelsea 4	Clapham Rovers 2
Arsenal 12	Derby County 4	Notts County 2
Everton 12	Leeds United 4	Queen's Park (Glas.) . 2
Liverpool 11	Leicester City 4	*Blackburn Olympic 1
Newcastle United 11	Oxford University 4	*Bradford City 1
W.B.A. 10	Royal Engineers 4	Brighton & H.A. 1
Aston Villa 9	Sunderland 4	Bristol City 1
Tottenham Hotspur ... 9	West Ham United 4	*Coventry City 1
Blackburn Rovers 8	Blackpool 3	Crystal Palace 1
Manchester City 8	Burnley 3	Fulham 1
Wolves 8	Nottingham Forest 3	*Ipswich Town 1
Bolton Wanderers 7	Portsmouth 3	Luton Town 1
Preston North End 7	Southampton 3	*Old Carthusians 1
Old Etonians 6	Barnsley 2	Queens Park Rangers 1
Sheffield United 6	Birmingham City 2	Watford 1
Sheffield Wednesday . 6	*Bury 2	*Wimbledon 1
Huddersfield Town 5	Cardiff City 2	
*The Wanderers 5	Charlton Athletic 2	(* Denotes undefeated)

APPEARANCES IN SEMI-FINALS

(Figures do not include replays)

Everton 23, Man. Utd. 21, Liverpool 20, W.B.A. 19, Arsenal 18, Aston Villa 18, Blackburn Rovers 16, Sheffield Wed. 16, Tottenham H. 15, Derby Co. 13, Newcastle Utd. 13, Wolves 13, Bolton W. 12, Chelsea 12, Nott'm Forest 12, Sheffield Utd. 11, Sunderland 11, Man. City 10, Preston N.E. 10, Southampton 10, Birmingham City 9, Burnley 8, Leeds Utd. 8, Huddersfield Town 7, Leicester City 7, Old Etonians 6, Oxford University 6, West Ham United 6, Fulham 5, Notts County 5, Portsmouth 5, The Wanderers 5, Luton Town 4, Queen's Park (Glasgow) 4, Royal Engineers 4, Blackpool 3, Cardiff City 3, Clapham Rovers 3, *Crystal Palace 3, Ipswich Town 3, Millwall 3, Norwich City 3, Old Carthusians 3, Oldham Athletic 3, Stoke City 3, The Swifts 3, Watford 3, Barnsley 2, Blackburn Olympic 2, Bristol City 2, Bury 2, Charlton Athletic 2, Grimsby Town 2, Swansea Town 2, Swindon Town 2, Bradford City 1, Brighton & H.A. 1, Cambridge University 1, Coventry City 1, Crewe Alexandra 1, Darwen 1, Derby Junction 1, Hull City 1, Marlow 1, Old Harrovians 1, Orient 1, Plymouth Argyle 1, Port Vale 1, Q.P.R. 1, Rangers (Glasgow) 1, Reading 1, Shropshire Wanderers 1, Wimbledon 1, York City 1.

*(*A previous and different Crystal Palace club also reached the semi-final in season 1871-72)*

WEMBLEY'S F.A. CUP FINALS – THE TOP MEN

Year	Winners	Manager	Captain	Referee
1923	Bolton Wanderers	Charles Foweraker	Joe Smith	D.H. Asson (West Bromwich)
1924	Newcastle United	No manager	Frank Hudspeth	W.E. Russell (Swindon)
1925	Sheffield United	John Nicholson	Billy Gillespie	G.N. Watson (Nottingham)
1926	Bolton Wanderers	Charles Foweraker	Joe Smith	I. Baker (Crewe)
1927	Cardiff City	Fred Stewart	Fred Keenor	W.F. Bunnell (Preston)
1928	Blackburn Rovers	Bob Crompton	Harry Healless	T.G. Bryan (Willenhall)
1929	Bolton Wanderers	Charles Foweraker	Jimmy Seddon	A. Josephs (South Shields)
1930	Arsenal	Herbert Chapman	Tom Parker	T. Crew (Leicester)
1931	West Bromwich Albion	Fred Everiss	Tommy Glidden	A.H. Kingscott (Long Eaton)
1932	Newcastle United	Andy Cunningham	Jimmy Nelson	W.P. Harper (Stourbridge)
1933	Everton	No manager	W.R. ('Dixie') Dean	E. Wood (Sheffield)
1934	Manchester City	Wilf Wild	Sam Cowan	S.F. Rous (Watford)
1935	Sheffield Wednesday	Billy Walker	Ronnie Starling	A.E. Fogg (Bolton)
1936	Arsenal	George Allison	Alex James	H. Nattrass (Seaham, Co. Durham)
1937	Sunderland	Johnny Cochrane	Raich Carter	G. Rudd (Kenton, Middlesex)
1938	Preston North End	No manager	Tom Smith	A.J. Jewell (London)
1939	Portsmouth	Jack Tinn	Jimmy Guthrie	T. Thompson (Lemington-on-Tyne)
1946	Derby County	Stuart McMillan	Jack Nicholas	E.D. Smith (Whitehaven)
1947	Charlton Athletic	Jimmy Seed	Don Welsh	J.M. Wiltshire (Sherborne)
1948	Manchester United	Matt Busby	Johnny Carey	C.J. Barrick (Northampton)
1949	Wolves	Stan Cullis	Billy Wright	R.A. Mortimer (Huddersfield)
1950	Arsenal	Tom Whittaker	Joe Mercer	H. Pearce (Luton)
1951	Newcastle United	Stan Seymour (Snr.)	Joe Harvey	W. Ling (Stapleford, Cambs.)

continued overleaf

Year	Winners	Manager	Captain	Referee
1952	Newcastle United	Stan Seymour (Snr.)	Joe Harvey	A.E. Ellis (Halifax)
1953	Blackpool	Joe Smith	Harry Johnston	B.M. Griffiths (Newport, Mon.)
1954	West Bromwich Albion	Vic Buckingham	Len Millard	A.W. Luty (Leeds)
1955	Newcastle United	Dugald Livingstone	Jimmy Scoular	R.J. Leafe (Nottingham)
1956	Manchester City	Les McDowall	Roy Paul	A. Bond (Fulham)
1957	Aston Villa	Eric Houghton	Johnny Dixon	F. Coultas (Hull)
1958	Bolton Wanderers	Bill Ridding	Nat Lofthouse	J. Sherlock (Sheffield)
1959	Nottingham Forest	Billy Walker	Jack Burkitt	J.H. Clough (Bolton)
1960	Wolves	Stan Cullis	Bill Slater	K. Howley (Middlesbrough)
1961	Tottenham Hotspur	Bill Nicholson	Danny Blanchflower	J. Kelly (Chorley)
1962	Tottenham Hotspur	Bill Nicholson	Danny Blanchflower	J. Finney (Hereford)
1963	Manchester United	Matt Busby	Noel Cantwell	K.G. Aston (Ilford, Essex)
1964	West Ham United	Ron Greenwood	Bobby Moore	A. Holland (Barnsley)
1965	Liverpool	Bill Shankly	Ron Yeats	W. Clements (West Bromwich)
1966	Everton	Harry Catterick	Brian Labone	J.F. Taylor (Wolverhampton)
1967	Tottenham Hotspur	Bill Nicholson	Dave Mackay	K. Dagnall (Bolton)
1968	West Bromwich Albion	Alan Ashman	Graham Williams	L. Callaghan (Merthyr Tydfil)
1969	Manchester City	Joe Mercer	Tony Book	G. McCabe (Sheffield)
1970	Chelsea (Rep. Old Trafford)	Dave Sexton	Ron Harris	E. Jennings (Stourbridge)
1971	Arsenal	Bertie Mee	Frank McLintock	N. Burtenshaw (Gt. Yarmouth)
1972	Leeds United	Don Revie	Billy Bremner	D. Smith (Gloucester)
1973	Sunderland	Bob Stokoe	Bobby Kerr	K. Burns (Stourbridge)
1974	Liverpool	Bill Shankly	Emlyn Hughes	C.G. Kew (Amersham)
1975	West Ham United	John Lyall	Billy Bonds	P. Partridge (Durham)
1976	Southampton	Lawrie McMenemy	Peter Rodrigues	C. Thomas (Treorchy)

1977	Manchester United	Tommy Docherty	Martin Buchan	R. Matthewson (Bolton)
1978	Ipswich Town	Bobby Robson	Mick Mills	D.R.G. Nippard (Bournemouth)
1979	Arsenal	Terry Neill	Pat Rice	R. Challis (Tonbridge)
1980	West Ham United	John Lyall	Billy Bonds	G. Courtney (Spennymoor)
1981	Tottenham Hotspur	Keith Burkinshaw	Steve Perryman	K. Hackett (Sheffield)
1982	Tottenham Hotspur	Keith Burkinshaw	Steve Perryman	C. White (Harrow)
1983	Manchester United	Ron Atkinson	Bryan Robson	A. Grey (Gt. Yarmouth)
1984	Everton	Howard Kendall	Kevin Ratcliffe	J. Hunting (Leicester)
1985	Manchester United	Ron Atkinson	Bryan Robson	P. Willis (Co. Durham)
1986	Liverpool	Kenny Dalglish	Alan Hansen	A. Robinson (Waterlooville)
1987	Coventry City	John Sillett (Coach)	Brian Kilcline	N. Midgley (Salford)
1988	Wimbledon	Bobby Gould	Dave Beasant	B. Hill (Kettering)
1989	Liverpool	Kenny Dalglish	Ronnie Whelan	J. Worrall (Warrington)
1990	Manchester United	Alex Ferguson	Bryan Robson	A. Gunn (Sussex)
1991	Tottenham Hotspur	Terry Venables	Gary Mabbutt	R. Milford (Bristol)
1992	Liverpool	Graeme Souness	Mark Wright	P. Don (Middlesex)
1993	Arsenal	George Graham	Tony Adams	K. Barratt (Coventry)
1994	Manchester United	Alex Ferguson	Steve Bruce	D. Elleray (Harrow)
1995	Everton	Joe Royle	Dave Watson	G. Ashby (Worcester)
1996	Manchester United	Alex Ferguson	Eric Cantona	D. Gallagher (Banbury)

COCA-COLA CUP: ASTON VILLA'S FIFTH TRIUMPH EQUALS RECORD

SECOND ROUND	THIRD ROUND	FOURTH ROUND	FIFTH ROUND	SEMI-FINALS	FINAL
***Aston Villa** 6:1	***Aston Villa** 2	***Aston Villa** 1	***Aston Villa** 1	**Aston Villa** . D2:†0	**Aston Villa** 3
Peterborough 0:1					
*Stockport .... 1:†2	Stockport 0				
Ipswich 1:1					
York 3:1	York 1	Q.P.R. 0			
*Man. Utd. 0:3					
*Oxford Utd. ...... 1:†1	*Q.P.R. 3				
Q.P.R. 1:2					
*Wimbledon ...... 4:†3	Charlton .... 0:†1	*Wolves 2	Wolves 0		
Charlton 5:3					
Fulham 0:1	*Wolves 0:2				
*Wolves 2:5					
Chester 0:1	Tottenham 2	Coventry 1			
*Tottenham 4:3					
Hull 0:0	*Coventry 3				
*Coventry 2:1					
*Hartlepool 0:0	Arsenal 3	*Arsenal 2	*Arsenal 2	Arsenal 2:0	
Arsenal 3:5					
Barnsley 0:4	*Barnsley 0				
*Huddersfield 2:0					
Everton .... 0:†2	*Millwall 0	Sheff. Wed. 1			
*Millwall 0:4					
*Crewe 2:2	Sheff. Wed. 2				
Sheff. Wed. 2:5					
*Liverpool 2:1	*Liverpool 4	*Liverpool 0	Newcastle 0		
Sunderland 0:0					
Man. City 0:4	Man. City 0				
*Wycombe 0:0					
Chelsea 0:0	*Stoke 0	Newcastle 1			(at Wembley – Sunday, March 24. Att: 77,056)
*Stoke 0:1					
Newcastle 5:3	Newcastle 4				
*Bristol City 0:1					

*Birmingham 3:1
Grimsby 1:1
Oldham 0:1
*Tranmere 1:3
Crystal Palace ... 2:2
*Southend 2:0
Rotherham 1:0
*Middlesbrough .. 2:1
Nott'm Forest 2:2
*Bradford C. 3:2
*Norwich 6:3
Torquay 1:2
*Leicester 2:2
Burnley 0:0
Brentford 0:2
*Bolton 1:3
W.B.A. 1:2
*Reading 1:4
Bury 1:4
*Sheff. Utd. 2:2
West Ham 1:3
*Bristol Rovers ... 0:0
*Cardiff 0:1
Southampton 3:2
*Swindon 2:0
Blackburn 3:2
*Watford .... A1:†1
Bournemouth 1:1
Derby 3:1
*Shrewsbury 1:1
Notts County 0:2
***Leeds** 0:3

*Birmingham ... 1:†3
Tranmere 1:1
*Crystal Palace 2:0
Middlesbrough . 2:2
Bradford C. .... 0:†3
*Norwich 0:5
Leicester 0:2
*Bolton 0:3
*Reading B2
Bury 1
West Ham 1
*Southampton 2
Blackburn 2
*Watford 1
*Derby 0
Leeds 1

Birmingham 0:2
*Middlesbrough 0:0
*Norwich ...... C0:†0
Bolton 0:0
*Reading 2
Southampton 1
Blackburn 1
***Leeds** 2

Birmingham 1:2
*Norwich 1:1
Reading 1
***Leeds** 2

*Birmingham 1:0
Leeds 2:3

Leeds 0

(* Drawn at home: in 2nd round and semi-finals; team drawn at home in first leg. † After extra time. A – Watford won 6-5 on pens. B – Original match abandoned after 28 mins due to rain. C – Norwich won 3-2 on pens. D – Aston Villa won on away goals.)

COCA-COLA CUP 1995-96

First Round (Two Legs)

Birmingham 3 Plymouth 1 (1-0h, 2-1a); Bournemouth 3 Luton 2† (2-1h, 1-1a); Bradford 5 Blackpool 3 (2-1h, 3-2a); Brentford 5 Walsall 4 (3-2h, 2-2a).

Bristol City 3 Colchester 3† (2-1h, 1-2a, Bristol City won 5-3 on pens.); Bristol Rovers 5 Gillingham 3 (4-2h, 1-1a); Burnley 4 Mansfield 1 (3-1h, 1-0a); Bury 3 Chesterfield 1 (2-1h, 1-0a).

Cardiff 3 Portsmouth 0 (1-0h, 2-0a); Charlton 2 Barnet 0 (2-0h, 0-0a); Chester 7 Wigan 2 (4-1h, 3-1a); Crewe 5 Darlington 1 (4-0h, 1-1a).

Fulham 5 Brighton 0 (3-0h, 2-0a); Hartlepool 1 Scarborough 1† (1-0h, 0-1a, Hartlepool won 7-6 on pens.); Huddersfield 4 Port Vale 3 (1-2h, 3-1a); Hull 5 Carlisle 4 (1-2h, 4-2a).

Notts County 4 Lincoln 0 (2-0h, 2-0a); Oxford 5 Hereford 2 (3-2h, 2-0a); Peterborough 4 Swansea 4† (3-0h, 1-4a, Peterborough won on away goals); Rotherham 6 Scunthorpe 4† (5-0h, 1-4a).

Shrewsbury 1 Doncaster 1† (0-0h, 1-1a, Shrewsbury won on away goals); Stockport 3 Wrexham 2 (1-0h, 2-2a); Sunderland 4 Preston 3 (3-2h, 1-1a); Swindon 3 Cambridge 2 (2-0h, 1-2a).

Torquay 1 Exeter 1† (0-0h, 1-1a, Torquay won on away goals); W.B.A. 5 Northampton 3 (1-1h, 4-2a); Wycombe 3 Leyton Orient 2 (3-0h, 0-2a); York 6 Rochdale 3 (5-1h, 1-2a).

(† After extra time)

LEAGUE CUP FINALS

1961*	Aston Villa beat Rotherham United 3-2 on agg. (0-2a, 3-0h)
1962	Norwich City beat Rochdale 4-0 on agg. (3-0a, 1-0h)
1963	Birmingham City beat Aston Villa 3-1 on agg. (3-1h, 0-0a)
1964	Leicester City beat Stoke City 4-3 on agg. (1-1a, 3-2h)
1965	Chelsea beat Leicester City 3-2 on agg. (3-2h, 0-0a)
1966	West Bromwich Albion beat West Ham United 5-3 on agg. (1-2a, 4-1h)

AT WEMBLEY

1967	Queens Park Rangers beat West Bromwich Albion (3-2)
1968	Leeds United beat Arsenal (1-0)
1969*	Swindon Town beat Arsenal (3-1)
1970*	Manchester City beat West Bromwich Albion (2-1)
1971	Tottenham Hotspur beat Aston Villa (2-0)
1972	Stoke City beat Chelsea (2-1)
1973	Tottenham Hotspur beat Norwich City (1-0)
1974	Wolverhampton Wanderers beat Manchester City (2-1)
1975	Aston Villa beat Norwich City (1-0)
1976	Manchester City beat Newcastle United (2-1)
1977†*	Aston Villa beat Everton (3-2 after 0-0 and 1-1 draws)
1978††	Nottingham Forest beat Liverpool (1-0 after 0-0 draw)
1979	Nottingham Forest beat Southampton (3-2)
1980	Wolverhampton Wanderers beat Nottingham Forest (1-0)
1981†††	Liverpool beat West Ham United (2-1 after 1-1 draw)

MILK CUP

1982*	Liverpool beat Tottenham Hotspur (3-1)
1983*	Liverpool beat Manchester United (2-1)
1984**	Liverpool beat Everton (1-0 after *0-0 draw)
1985	Norwich City beat Sunderland (1-0)
1986	Oxford United beat Queens Park Rangers (3-0)

LITTLEWOODS CUP

1987 Arsenal beat Liverpool (2-1)
1988 Luton Town beat Arsenal (3-2)
1989 Nottingham Forest beat Luton Town (3-1)
1990 Nottingham Forest beat Oldham Athletic (1-0)

RUMBELOWS CUP

1991 Sheffield Wednesday beat Manchester United (1-0)
1992 Manchester United beat Nottingham Forest (1-0)

COCA-COLA CUP

1993 Arsenal beat Sheffield Wednesday (2-1)
1994 Aston Villa beat Manchester United (3-1)
1995 Liverpool beat Bolton Wanderers (2-1)
1996 Aston Villa beat Leeds United (3-0)

* After extra time. † First replay at Hillsborough, second replay at Old Trafford. †† Replayed at Old Trafford. ††† Replayed at Villa Park. ** Replayed at Maine Road.

COCA-COLA (LEAGUE) CUP FINAL

ASTON VILLA 3 (Milosevic 21, Taylor 55, Yorke 90), **LEEDS UNITED 0**

Wembley (77,056), Sunday, March 24, 1996. Kick-off: 5.0 (ITV live)

Aston Villa (maroon/blue): Bosnich; Ehiogu, McGrath, Southgate, Charles, Draper, Taylor, Townsend (Capt.), Wright, Milosevic, Yorke. **Subs not used**: Staunton, Johnson, Oakes (gk). **Booked**: McGrath, Southgate. **Manager**: Brian Little.

Leeds (all white): Lukic; Wetherall, Pemberton, Radebe (Brolin 65), Kelly, Ford (Deane 45), McAllister (Capt.), Palmer, Speed, Gray, Yeboah. **Sub not used**: Worthington. **Booked**: Wetherall, Ford. **Manager**: Howard Wilkinson.

Referee: Robbie Hart (Darlington). **Weather**: Grey, cold.

Guest of Honour: Virginia Bottomley (Secretary of State, National Heritage).

Man of the Match – Alan Hardaker Trophy: Andy Townsend (Villa captain).

Receipts: £2,500,000. **Prize money**: Aston Villa £100,000, Leeds £50,000.

A year after avoiding relegation by one place, Aston Villa were back in the silverware business and, with their fifth victory in 11 Finals, joined Liverpool at the head of the League Cup-winners' list (5 each). Each club received 34,000 tickets for the "people's Final."

You would have got long odds against Brian Little's men for the Coca-Cola Cup when they trailed 2-0 away to Arsenal in the semi-final but, having survived then, their day was never in doubt at Wembley from the 21st. minute, when £3.5m. striker Savo Milosevic's left foot shot them ahead from 25 yards.

After waiting 23 years for a Cup Final, Leeds supporters were totally let down. In what was Howard Wilkinson's first Final in a long career in management, he chose to leave £7.2m. of talent on the bench in Brian Deane and Tomas Brolin and there was never the suggestion of recovery as Tommy Johnson and Dwight Yorke added the second-half goals that put Villa's domination in true perspective.

"Being booed by our fans on the way off hurt," said Wilkinson. "But we were a massive disappointment, and just didn't perform." Some consolation came in the display of 18-year-old Andy Gray, son of Frank. In only his fourth start, he showed the wing pedigree of his uncle Eddie. One for the future if ever there was.

SUMMARY OF LEAGUE CUP WINNERS

Aston Villa	5	Wolverhampton W.	2	Oxford United	1
Liverpool	5	Birmingham City	1	Queens Park Rangers	1
Nottingham Forest	4	Chelsea	1	Sheffield Wednesday	1
Arsenal	2	Leeds United	1	Stoke City	1
Manchester City	2	Leicester City	1	Swindon Town	1
Norwich City	2	Luton Town	1	West Bromwich Albion	1
Tottenham Hotspur	2	Manchester United	1		

LEAGUE CUP FINAL APPEARANCES

(Figures do not include replays)

7 Aston Villa, Liverpool; **6** Nott'm. F.; **5** Arsenal; **4** Man. Utd., Norwich; **3** Man. C., Tottenham, W.B.A.; **2** Chelsea, Everton, Leeds, Leicester, Luton, Q.P.R., Sheff. Wed., Stoke, West Ham, Wolves; **1** Birmingham, Bolton, Newcastle, Oldham, Oxford, Rochdale, Rotherham, Southampton, Sunderland, Swindon.

LEAGUE CUP SEMI-FINAL APPEARANCES

(Figures do not include replays)

10 Aston Villa; **9** Liverpool; **8** Arsenal, Tottenham; **7** Man. Utd., West Ham; **6** Nott'm. F.; **5** Chelsea, Leeds, Man C., Norwich; **4** W.B.A.; **3** Birmingham, Burnley, Everton, Q.P.R., Sheff. Wed., Swindon, Wolves; **2** Blackburn, Bolton, Bristol C., Coventry, Crystal P., Ipswich, Leicester, Luton, Mid'bro', Oxford, Plymouth, Southampton, Stoke, Sunderland; **1** Blackpool, Bury, Cardiff, Carlisle, Chester, Derby, Huddersfield, Newcastle, Oldham, Peterboro', Rochdale, Rotherham, Shrewsbury, Tranmere, Walsall, Watford.

COCA-COLA CUP FIRST ROUND DRAW

The Football League's decision to give England's five European candidates – Manchester United, Liverpool, Arsenal, Aston Villa and Newcastle – exemption from the 1996-97 Coca-Cola Cup until Round 3 meant that more First Division clubs than previously went into the first round draw. Only six were exempt until the second stage.

First round, first leg matches to be played in the week commencing August 19, second legs in week commencing September 2:

Carlisle v Chester
Darlington v Rotherham
Doncaster v York
Hartlepool v Lincoln
Huddersfield v Wrexham
Hull v Scarborough
Mansfield v Burnley
Notts County v Bury
Oldham v Grimsby
Port Vale v Crewe
Rochdale v Barnsley
Scunthorpe v Blackpool
Sheff. United v Bradford C.
Shrewsbury v Tranmere
Stockport v Chesterfield
Wigan v Preston

Brentford v Plymouth
Brighton v Birmingham
Bristol Rovers v Luton
Cardiff v Northampton
Colchester v W.B.A.
Exeter v Barnet
Hereford v Cambridge
Ipswich v Bournemouth
Millwall v Peterborough
Oxford Utd. v Norwich
Portsmouth v Leyton Orient
Reading v Wycombe
Southend v Fulham
Swansea v Gillingham
Swindon v Wolves
Torquay v Bristol City
Walsall v Watford

DOWN WEMBLEY'S MEMORY LANE

April 1923	Wembley's first Cup Final (Bolton 2, West Ham 0). The new stadium's capacity is officially 126,000 but more than 200,000 get in.
April 1938	Preston's George Mutch sends a penalty in off the underside of the crossbar in the last seconds of extra time – the only goal of the Cup Final against Huddersfield.
May 1953	"The Matthews Final," plus a hat-trick by Stan Mortensen in Blackpool's 4-3 win against Bolton.
May 1961	Tottenham (2-0 v Leicester) do more than win the Cup – they complete the first Double this century.
April 1961	England's record victory over Scotland (9-3), their tally topped by a hat-trick from Jimmy Greaves.
July 1966	Alf Ramsey's England win the World Cup, dramatically beating West Germany 4-2 in extra time. The Queen presents football's greatest prize to Bobby Moore, and there's a knighthood for Alf.
May 1968	Matt Busby's dream comes true: Manchester United 4, Benfica 1 in the European Cup Final.
May 1973	Second Division Sunderland shock Leeds in the Cup Final. Has Wembley seen a greater save than Jim Montgomery's that keeps out a "certain" goal by Peter Lorimer?
June 1977	Scotland beat England 2-1 in the Home Championship and their fans go wild, invading the field, pulling down the goalposts and tearing up the pitch.
May 1996	Manchester United beat Liverpool for a record ninth F.A. Cup triumph and become the first English club to do the Double twice.
June 1996	England are one short of reaching the European Championship Final – beaten 6-5 on penalties by Germany.
June 1996	Germany are Kings of Europe for the third time, beating the Czech Republic by the first sudden death goal to decide a major tournament.

QUOTE-UNQUOTE

LAWRIE McMENEMY, Director of Football at The Dell: "Southampton is a very well-run outfit from Monday to Friday. It's Saturday we've got a problem with."

FRANK CLARK, Nott'm. Forest manager, after the 1-1 draw in May that virtually ended Newcastle's Championship chance: "Me feel sorry for Kevin Keegan? When he's got Asprilla and Barton and Clark on the bench?"

HOWARD WILKINSON (Leeds) on life as a manager: "The appeal of the job is being out there on the edge. Sometimes you fall off, but sometimes you see over that edge, and that's what makes it worthwhile."

TV's MRS. MERTON to George Best: "Do you think if you hadn't played as much football you wouldn't have been so thirsty?"

BARRY DAVIES on BBC TV: "It's got to be 15 yards if it's a day."

JOE KINNEAR, Wimbledon manager, at the end of last season: "Each season we're criticised from here to kingdom come, but we're still good enough to ruffle a few feathers and we're in the Premiership for another year."

TONY ADAMS, England captain, after the 1-1 draw in the friendly against Portugal at Wembley last December: "At least we got a point."

BELL'S SCOTTISH LEAGUE FINAL TABLES 1995-96

PREMIER DIVISION

		HOME					AWAY						
	P	W	D	L	F	A	W	D	L	F	A	Pts	GD
1 Rangers	36	13	3	2	47	16	14	3	1	38	9	87	+60
2 Celtic	36	12	5	1	40	12	12	6	0	34	13	83	+49
3 Aberdeen	36	11	1	6	31	17	5	6	7	21	28	55	+7
4 Hearts	36	10	2	6	33	26	6	5	7	22	27	55	+2
5 Hibernian	36	7	5	6	25	26	4	5	9	18	31	43	–14
6 Raith Rovers	36	7	5	6	23	21	5	2	11	18	36	43	–16
7 Kilmarnock	36	8	4	6	25	21	3	4	11	14	33	41	–15
8 Motherwell	36	6	6	6	15	16	3	6	9	13	23	39	–11
9 *Partick Thistle	36	3	5	10	12	28	5	1	12	17	34	30	–33
10 Falkirk	36	4	4	10	17	26	2	2	14	14	34	24	–29

(* Relegated after losing play-off v Dundee Utd., 1-1h, 1-2a, 2-3 agg.)

FIRST DIVISION

		HOME					AWAY						
	P	W	D	L	F	A	W	D	L	F	A	Pts	GD
1 Dunfermline Ath.	36	11	4	3	40	23	10	4	4	33	18	71	+32
2 *Dundee United	36	11	3	4	47	18	8	7	3	26	19	67	+36
3 Greenock Morton	36	10	4	4	32	16	10	3	5	25	23	67	+18
4 St. Johnstone	36	11	5	2	33	14	8	3	7	27	22	65	+24
5 Dundee	36	5	8	5	24	20	10	4	4	29	20	57	+13
6 St. Mirren	36	6	2	10	23	30	7	6	5	23	21	47	–5
7 Clydebank	36	6	4	8	20	24	4	6	8	19	34	40	–19
8 Airdrie	36	4	7	7	24	25	5	4	9	19	29	38	–11
9 Hamilton Acad.	36	5	3	10	22	26	5	3	10	18	31	36	–17
10 Dumbarton	36	2	1	15	10	36	1	1	16	13	58	11	–71

(* Promoted after winning play-off v Partick Thistle, 1-1a, 2-1h, 3-2 agg.)

SECOND DIVISION

		HOME					AWAY						
	P	W	D	L	F	A	W	D	L	F	A	Pts	GD
1 Stirling Albion	36	12	4	2	36	15	12	5	1	47	15	81	+53
2 East Fife	36	8	6	4	27	17	11	4	3	23	12	67	+21
3 Berwick Rangers	36	10	4	4	32	18	8	2	8	32	29	60	+17
4 Stenhousemuir	36	8	3	7	26	21	6	4	8	25	28	49	+2
5 Clyde	36	7	4	7	28	23	4	8	6	19	22	45	+2
6 Ayr United	36	7	6	5	26	18	4	6	8	14	22	45	0
7 Queen of South	36	6	6	6	27	38	5	4	9	27	29	43	–13
8 Stranraer	36	6	10	2	21	14	2	8	8	17	29	42	–5
9 Forfar Athletic	36	8	3	7	21	32	3	4	11	16	29	40	–24
10 Montrose	36	3	2	13	18	39	2	3	13	15	47	20	–53

THIRD DIVISION

		HOME					AWAY						
	P	W	D	L	F	A	W	D	L	F	A	Pts	GD
1 Livingston	36	8	5	5	21	14	13	4	1	30	10	72	+27
2 Brechin City	36	10	3	5	25	9	8	6	4	16	12	63	+20
3 Caledonian Th.	36	5	8	5	28	23	10	4	4	36	15	57	+26
4 Ross County	36	6	9	3	30	20	6	8	4	26	19	53	+17
5 Arbroath	36	6	7	5	22	21	7	6	5	19	20	52	0
6 Queen's Park	36	6	8	4	21	15	6	4	8	19	28	48	–3
7 East Stirling	36	6	3	9	26	32	5	8	5	32	30	44	–4
8 Cowdenbeath	36	7	5	6	26	23	3	3	12	19	36	38	–14
9 Alloa	36	5	3	10	18	37	1	8	9	8	21	29	–32
10 Albion Rovers	36	5	4	9	20	28	2	4	12	17	46	29	–37

SCOTTISH HONOURS LIST

PREMIER DIVISION

	First	Pts.	Second	Pts.	Third	Pts.
1975-6	Rangers	54	Celtic	48	Hibernian	43
1976-7	Celtic	55	Rangers	46	Aberdeen	43
1977-8	Rangers	55	Aberdeen	53	Dundee Utd	40
1978-9	Celtic	48	Rangers	45	Dundee Utd	44
1979-80	Aberdeen	48	Celtic	47	St. Mirren	42
1980-81	Celtic	56	Aberdeen	49	Rangers	44
1981-2	Celtic	55	Aberdeen	53	Rangers	43
1982-3	Dundee Utd	56	Celtic	55	Aberdeen	55
1983-4	Aberdeen	57	Celtic	50	Dundee Utd	47
1984-5	Aberdeen	59	Celtic	52	Dundee Utd	47
1985-6	*Celtic	50	Hearts	50	Dundee Utd	47
1986-7	Rangers	69	Celtic	63	Dundee Utd.	60
1987-8	Celtic	72	Hearts	62	Rangers	60
1988-9	Rangers	56	Aberdeen	50	Celtic	46
1989-90	Rangers	51	Aberdeen	44	Hearts	44
1990-1	Rangers	55	Aberdeen	53	Celtic	41
1991-2	Rangers	72	Hearts	63	Celtic	62
1992-3	Rangers	73	Aberdeen	64	Celtic	60
1993-4	Rangers	58	Aberdeen	55	Motherwell	54
1994-5	Rangers	69	Motherwell	54	Hibernian	53
1995-6	Rangers	87	Celtic	83	Aberdeen	55

Maximum points: 72 except 1986-8, 1991-4 (88) and 1994-6 (108).
* Won on goal difference.

FIRST DIVISION
(Scottish Championship until 1975-76)

	First	Pts.	Second	Pts.	Third	Pts.
1890-1*a*	††Dumbarton	29	Rangers	29	Celtic	24
1891-2*b*	Dumbarton	37	Celtic	35	Hearts	30
1892-3*a*	Celtic	29	Rangers	28	St Mirren	23
1893-4*a*	Celtic	29	Hearts	26	St Bernard's	22
1894-5*a*	Hearts	31	Celtic	26	Rangers	21
1895-6*a*	Celtic	30	Rangers	26	Hibernian	24

1896-7*a*	Hearts 28	Hibernian 26	Rangers 25
1897-8*a*	Celtic 33	Rangers 29	Hibernian 22
1898-9*a*	Rangers 36	Hearts 26	Celtic 24
1899-1900*a*	Rangers 32	Celtic 25	Hibernian 24
1900-1*c*	Rangers 35	Celtic 29	Hibernian 25
1901-2*a*	Rangers 28	Celtic 26	Hearts 22
1902-3*b*	Hibernian 37	Dundee 31	Rangers 29
1903-4*d*	Third Lanark 43	Hearts 39	Rangers 38
1904-5*a*	†Celtic 41	Rangers 41	Third Lanark 35
1905-6*a*	Celtic 46	Hearts 39	Rangers 38
1906-7*f*	Celtic 55	Dundee 48	Rangers 45
1907-8*f*	Celtic 55	Falkirk 51	Rangers 50
1908-9*f*	Celtic 51	Dundee 50	Clyde 48
1909-10*f*	Celtic 54	Falkirk 52	Rangers 49
1910-11*f*	Rangers 52	Aberdeen 48	Falkirk 44
1911-12*f*	Rangers 51	Celtic 45	Clyde 42
1912-13*f*	Rangers 53	Celtic 49	Hearts 41
1913-14*g*	Celtic 65	Rangers 59	Hearts 54
1914-15*g*	Celtic 65	Hearts 61	Rangers 50
1915-16*g*	Celtic 67	Rangers 56	Morton 51
1916-17*g*	Celtic 64	Morton 54	Rangers 53
1917-18*f*	Rangers 56	Celtic 55	Kilmarnock 43
1918-19*f*	Celtic 58	Rangers 57	Morton 47
1919-20*h*	Rangers 71	Celtic 68	Motherwell 57
1920-1*h*	Rangers 76	Celtic 66	Hearts 56
1921-2*h*	Celtic 67	Rangers 66	Raith 56
1922-3*g*	Rangers 55	Airdrieonians 50	Celtic 40
1923-4*g*	Rangers 59	Airdrieonians 50	Celtic 41
1924-5*g*	Rangers 60	Airdrieonians 57	Hibernian 52
1925-6*g*	Celtic 58	Airdrieonians 50	Hearts 50
1926-7*g*	Rangers 56	Motherwell 51	Celtic 49
1927-8*g*	Rangers 60	Celtic 55	Motherwell 55
1928-9*g*	Rangers 67	Celtic 51	Motherwell 50
1929-30*g*	Rangers 60	Motherwell 55	Aberdeen 53
1930-1*g*	Rangers 60	Celtic 58	Motherwell 56
1931-2*g*	Motherwell 66	Rangers 61	Celtic 48
1932-3*g*	Rangers 62	Motherwell 59	Hearts 50
1933-4*g*	Rangers 66	Motherwell 62	Celtic 47
1934-5*g*	Rangers 55	Celtic 52	Hearts 50
1935-6*g*	Celtic 68	Rangers 61	Aberdeen 61
1936-7*g*	Rangers 61	Aberdeen 54	Celtic 52
1937-8*g*	Celtic 61	Hearts 58	Rangers 49
1938-9*f*	Rangers 59	Celtic 48	Aberdeen 46
1946-7*f*	Rangers 46	Hibernian 44	Aberdeen 39
1947-8*g*	Hibernian 48	Rangers 46	Partick 46
1948-9*i*	Rangers 46	Dundee 45	Hibernian 39
1949-50*i*	Rangers 50	Hibernian 49	Hearts 43
1950-1*i*	Hibernian 48	Rangers 38	Dundee 38
1951-2*i*	Hibernian 45	Rangers 41	East Fife 37
1952-3*i*	*Rangers 43	Hibernian 43	East Fife 39
1953-4*i*	Celtic 43	Hearts 38	Partick 35
1954-5*f*	Aberdeen 49	Celtic 46	Rangers 41
1955-6*f*	Rangers 52	Aberdeen 46	Hearts 45
1956-7*f*	Rangers 55	Hearts 53	Kilmarnock 42
1957-8*f*	Hearts 62	Rangers 49	Celtic 46
1958-9*f*	Rangers 50	Hearts 48	Motherwell 44
1959-60*f*	Hearts 54	Kilmarnock 50	Rangers 42
1960-1*f*	Rangers 51	Kilmarnock 50	Third Lanark 42
1961-2*f*	Dundee 54	Rangers 51	Celtic 46
1962-3*f*	Rangers 57	Kilmarnock 48	Partick 46
1963-4*f*	Rangers 55	Kilmarnock 49	Celtic 47

1964-5*f*	*Kilmarnock 50	Hearts 50	Dunfermline 49
1965-6*f*	Celtic 57	Rangers 55	Kilmarnock 45
1966-7*f*	Celtic 58	Rangers 55	Clyde 46
1967-8*f*	Celtic 63	Rangers 61	Hibernian 45
1968-9*f*	Celtic 54	Rangers 49	Dunfermline 45
1969-70*f*	Celtic 57	Rangers 45	Hibernian 44
1970-1*f*	Celtic 56	Aberdeen 54	St Johnstone 44
1971-2*f*	Celtic 60	Aberdeen 50	Rangers 44
1972-3*f*	Celtic 57	Rangers 56	Hibernian 45
1973-4*f*	Celtic 53	Hibernian 49	Rangers 48
1974-5*f*	Rangers 56	Hibernian 49	Celtic 45

* Won on goal average. †Won on deciding match. ††Title shared.
Competition suspended 1940-46 (Second World War).

SCOTTISH CHAMPIONSHIP WINS

Rangers	*46	Hibernian	4	Kilmarnock	1
Celtic	35	Dumbarton	*2	Motherwell	1
Aberdeen	4	Dundee	1	Third Lanark	1
Hearts	4	Dundee Utd.	1	(* Incl. 1 shared)	

FIRST DIVISION
(Since formation of Premier Division)

	First .... Pts.	Second .... Pts.	Third .... Pts.
1975-6*d*	Partick 41	Kilmarnock 35	Montrose 30
1976-7*j*	St. Mirren 62	Clydebank 58	Dundee 51
1977-8*j*	*Morton 58	Hearts 58	Dundee 57
1978-9*j*	Dundee 55	Kilmarnock 54	Clydebank 54
1979-80*j*	Hearts 53	Airdrieonians 51	Ayr 44
1980-1*j*	Hibernian 57	Dundee 52	St. Johnstone 51
1981-2*j*	Motherwell 61	Kilmarnock 51	Hearts 50
1982-3*j*	St. Johnstone 55	Hearts 54	Clydebank 50
1983-4*j*	Morton 54	Dumbarton 51	Partick 46
1984-5*j*	Motherwell 50	Clydebank 48	Falkirk 45
1985-6*j*	Hamilton 56	Falkirk 45	Kilmarnock 44
1986-7*k*	Morton 57	Dunfermline 56	Dumbarton 53
1987-8*k*	Hamilton 56	Meadowbank 52	Clydebank 49
1988-9*j*	Dunfermline 54	Falkirk 52	Clydebank 48
1989-90*j*	St. Johnstone 58	Airdrieonians 54	Clydebank 44
1990-1*j*	Falkirk 54	Airdrieonians 53	Dundee 52
1991-2*k*	Dundee 58	Partick 57	Hamilton 57
1992-3k	Raith 65	Kilmarnock 54	Dunfermline 52
1993-4*k*	Falkirk 66	Dunfermline 65	Airdrieonians 54
1994-5*l*	Raith 69	Dunfermline 68	Dundee 68
1995-6*l*	Dunfermline 71	Dundee Utd. 67	Greenock Morton .. 67

Maximum points: a, 36; *b*, 44; *c*, 40; *d*, 52; *e*, 60; *f*, 68; *g*, 76; *h*, 84; *i*, 60; *j*, 78; *k*, 88; *l*, 108. * Won on goal difference.

SECOND DIVISION

	First .... Pts.	Second .... Pts.	Third .... Pts.
1921-2*a*	Alloa 60	Cowdenbeath 47	Armadale 45
1922-3*a*	Queen's Park 57	Clydebank 52	St. Johnstone 50
1923-4*a*	St. Johnstone 56	Cowdenbeath 55	Bathgate 44
1924-5*a*	Dundee Utd. 50	Clydebank 48	Clyde 47
1925-6*a*	Dunfermline 59	Clyde 53	Ayr 52

1926-7*a*	Bo'ness	56	Raith	49	Clydebank	45
1927-8*a*	Ayr	54	Third Lanark	45	King's Park	44
1928-9*b*	Dundee Utd.	51	Morton	50	Arbroath	47
1929-30*a*	*Leith Athletic	57	East Fife	57	Albion	54
1930-1*a*	Third Lanark	61	Dundee Utd.	50	Dunfermline	47
1931-2*a*	*East Stirling	55	St. Johnstone	55	Stenhousemuir	46
1932-3*c*	Hibernian	55	Queen of South	49	Dunfermline	47
1933-4*c*	Albion	45	Dunfermline	44	Arbroath	44
1934-5*c*	Third Lanark	52	Arbroath	50	St. Bernard's	47
1935-6*c*	Falkirk	59	St. Mirren	52	Morton	48
1936-7*c*	Ayr	54	Morton	51	St. Bernard's	48
1937-8*c*	Raith	59	Albion	48	Airdrieonians	47
1938-9*c*	Cowdenbeath	60	Alloa	48	East Fife	48
1946-7*d*	Dundee Utd.	45	Airdrieonians	42	East Fife	31
1947-8*e*	East Fife	53	Albion	42	Hamilton	40
1948-9*e*	*Raith	42	Stirling	42	Airdrieonians	41
1949-50*e*	Morton	47	Airdrieonians	44	St. Johnstone	36
1950-1*e*	*Queen of South	45	Stirling	45	Ayr	36
1951-2*e*	Clyde	44	Falkirk	43	Ayr	39
1952-3*e*	Stirling	44	Hamilton	43	Queen's Park	37
1953-4*e*	Motherwell	45	Kilmarnock	42	Third Lanark	36
1954-5*e*	Airdrieonians	46	Dunfermline	42	Hamilton	39
1955-6*b*	Queen's Park	54	Ayr	51	St. Johnstone	49
1956-7*b*	Clyde	64	Third Lanark	51	Cowdenbeath	45
1957-8*b*	Stirling	55	Dunfermline	53	Arbroath	47
1958-9*b*	Ayr	60	Arbroath	51	Stenhousemuir	46
1959-60*b*	St. Johnstone	53	Dundee Utd.	50	Queen of South	49
1960-1*b*	Stirling	55	Falkirk	54	Stenhousemuir	50
1961-2*b*	Clyde	54	Queen of South	53	Morton	44
1962-3*b*	St. Johnstone	55	East Stirling	49	Morton	48
1963-4*b*	Morton	67	Clyde	53	Arbroath	46
1964-5*b*	Stirling	59	Hamilton	50	Queen of South	45
1965-6*b*	Ayr	53	Airdrieonians	50	Queen of South	47
1966-7*b*	Morton	69	Raith	58	Arbroath	57
1967-8*b*	St. Mirren	62	Arbroath	53	East Fife	49
1968-9*b*	Motherwell	64	Ayr	53	East Fife	48
1969-70*b*	Falkirk	56	Cowdenbeath	55	Queen of South	50
1970-1*b*	Partick	56	East Fife	51	Arbroath	46
1971-2*b*	*Dumbarton	52	Arbroath	52	Stirling	50
1972-3*b*	Clyde	56	Dunfermline	52	Raith	47
1973-4*b*	Airdrieonians	60	Kilmarnock	58	Hamilton	55
1974-5*b*	Falkirk	54	Queen of South	53	Montrose	53

SECOND DIVISION (Modern)

	First	Pts.	Second	Pts.	Third	Pts.
1975-6*d*	*Clydebank	40	Raith	40	Alloa	35
1976-7*f*	Stirling	55	Alloa	51	Dunfermline	50
1977-8*f*	*Clyde	53	Raith	53	Dunfermline	48
1978-9*f*	Berwick	54	Dunfermline	52	Falkirk	50
1979-80*f*	Falkirk	50	East Stirling	49	Forfar	46
1980-1*f*	Queen's Park	50	Queen of South	46	Cowdenbeath	45
1981-2*f*	Clyde	59	Alloa	50	Arbroath	50
1982-3*f*	Brechin	55	Meadowbank	54	Arbroath	49
1983-4*f*	Forfar	63	East Fife	47	Berwick	43
1984-5*f*	Montrose	53	Alloa	50	Dunfermline	49
1985-6*f*	Dunfermline	57	Queen of South	55	Meadowbank	49
1986-7*f*	Meadowbank	55	Raith	52	Stirling	52
1987-8*f*	Ayr	61	St. Johnstone	59	Queen's Park	51
1988-9*f*	Albion	50	Alloa	45	Brechin	43
1989-90*f*	Brechin	49	Kilmarnock	48	Stirling	47

1990-1*f*	Stirling 54	Montrose 46	Cowdenbeath 45
1991-2*f*	Dumbarton 52	Cowdenbeath 51	Alloa 50
1992-3*f*	Clyde 54	Brechin 53	Stranraer 53
1993-4*f*	Stranraer 56	Berwick 48	Stenhousemuir 47
1994-5*g*	Greenock Morton .. 64	Dumbarton 60	Stirling 58
1995-6*g*	Stirling 81	East Fife 67	Berwick 60

Maximum points: *a*, 76; *b*, 72; *c*, 68; *d*, 52; *e*, 60; *f*, 78; *g*, 108.
* Won on goal average.

THIRD DIVISION (Modern)

	First .... Pts.	Second .... Pts.	Third .... Pts.
1994-5	Forfar 80	Montrose 67	Ross County 60
1995-6	Livingston 72	Brechin 63	Caledonian Th. 57

Maximum points: 108.

RELEGATED FROM PREMIER DIVISION

1975-6	Dundee, St. Johnstone	1986-7	Clydebank, Hamilton
1976-7	Kilmarnock, Hearts	1987-8	Falkirk, Dunfermline, Morton
1977-8	Ayr, Clydebank	1988-9	Hamilton
1978-9	Hearts, Motherwell	1989-90	Dundee
1979-80	Dundee, Hibernian	1990-1	No relegation
1980-1	Kilmarnock, Hearts	1991-2	St. Mirren, Dunfermline
1981-2	Partick, Airdrieonians	1992-3	Falkirk, Airdrieonians
1982-3	Morton, Kilmarnock	1993-4	St. J'stone, Raith, Dundee
1983-4	St. Johnstone, Motherwell	1994-5	Dundee Utd.
1984-5	Dumbarton, Morton	1995-6	Falkirk, Partick Thistle
1985-6	No relegation		

RELEGATED FROM FIRST DIVISION

1975-6	Dunfermline, Clyde	1986-7	Brechin, Montrose
1976-7	Raith, Falkirk	1987-8	East Fife, Dumbarton
1977-8	Alloa, East Fife	1988-9	Kilmarnock, Queen of South
1978-9	Montrose, Queen of South	1989-90	Albion, Alloa
1979-80	Arbroath, Clyde	1990-1	Clyde, Brechin
1980-1	Stirling, Berwick	1991-2	Montrose, Forfar
1981-2	East Stirling, Queen of South	1992-3	Meadowbank, Cowdenbeath
1982-3	Dunfermline, Queen's Park	1993-4	Dumbarton, Stirling Alb., Clyde, Morton, Brechin
1983-4	Raith, Alloa	1994-5	Ayr, Stranraer
1984-5	Meadowbank, St. Johnstone	1995-6	Hamilton, Dumbarton
1985-6	Ayr, Alloa		

RELEGATED FROM SECOND DIVISION

1993-4	Alloa, Forfar, E. Stirling, Montrose, Queen's Park, Arbroath, Albion, Cowdenbeath	1994-5	Meadowbank, Brechin
		1995-6	Forfar, Montrose

BELL'S SCOTTISH LEAGUE RESULTS 1995-96

PREMIER DIVISION

	Aberdeen	Celtic	Falkirk	Hearts	Hibernian	Kilmarnock	Motherwell	Partick Thistle	Raith Rovers	Rangers
Aberdeen	–	2-3	3-1	1-2	1-2	4-1	1-0	3-0	3-0	0-1
	–	1-2	2-1	1-1	2-1	3-0	2-1	1-0	1-0	0-1
Celtic	2-0	–	1-0	3-1	2-2	4-2	1-1	2-1	0-0	0-2
	5-0	–	4-0	4-0	2-1	1-1	1-0	4-0	4-1	0-0
Falkirk	2-3	0-1	–	2-0	2-0	0-2	0-0	0-1	2-1	0-2
	1-1	0-0	–	0-2	1-1	4-2	0-1	1-2	2-3	0-4
Hearts	1-2	0-4	4-1	–	2-1	2-1	1-1	3-0	4-2	0-2
	1-3	1-2	2-1	–	1-1	1-0	4-0	2-5	2-0	2-0
Hibernian	1-1	0-4	2-1	2-2	–	2-0	4-2	3-0	1-2	1-4
	1-2	1-2	2-1	2-1	–	1-1	0-0	1-0	1-1	0-2
Kilmarnock	1-2	0-0	4-0	3-1	0-3	–	1-1	2-1	5-1	0-2
	1-1	0-0	1-0	0-2	3-2	–	0-1	2-1	2-0	0-3
Motherwell	2-1	0-2	1-1	0-0	0-2	3-0	–	1-1	0-2	0-0
	1-0	0-0	1-0	1-1	3-0	0-1	–	0-2	1-0	1-3
Partick Thistle	1-0	1-2	1-1	2-0	1-1	1-1	1-0	–	0-2	0-4
	1-1	2-4	0-3	0-1	0-0	0-1	0-2	–	0-3	1-2
Raith Rovers	1-0	0-1	0-1	1-1	3-0	2-0	0-0	3-1	–	2-2
	2-2	1-3	1-0	1-3	1-0	1-1	2-0	0-2	–	2-4
Rangers	1-1	3-3	2-0	4-1	0-1	1-0	2-1	1-0	4-0	–
	3-1	1-1	3-2	0-3	7-0	3-0	3-2	5-0	4-0	–

(Play-off: Partick Thistle 1, Dundee Utd. 1; Dundee Utd. 2, Partick Thistle 1. After extra time; Dundee Utd. win 3-2 on agg., Partick Thistle relegated to Div. 1).

Read across for home results, down for away

FIRST DIVISION

	Airdrieonians	Clydebank	Dumbarton	Dundee	Dundee United	Dunfermline Ath.	Greenock Morton	Hamilton Acad.	St. Johnstone	St. Mirren
Airdrieonians	–	1-1	2-1	2-3	1-1	0-1	3-2	0-0	1-1	1-2
	–	1-1	5-1	0-0	1-1	1-2	0-2	3-0	1-3	1-3
Clydebank	1-1	–	2-1	1-1	1-2	0-4	1-0	2-0	2-0	1-1
	2-1	–	1-0	0-1	1-1	2-3	0-1	1-3	1-2	1-2
Dumbarton	1-2	1-2	–	1-5	1-0	0-4	0-2	1-0	1-3	0-0
	1-2	0-1	–	1-2	1-3	0-3	0-1	1-2	0-3	0-1
Dundee	1-1	1-1	1-1	–	2-3	2-4	0-0	1-1	0-1	3-1
	2-0	3-0	3-0	–	0-2	1-1	1-1	2-1	0-0	1-2
Dundee United	1-2	3-0	8-0	2-3	–	3-1	1-1	2-1	2-1	1-0
	2-2	6-0	6-1	2-0	–	0-1	4-0	1-1	1-3	2-1
Dunfermline Ath.	2-0	2-1	3-1	0-1	3-0	–	0-2	4-0	2-1	1-1
	2-1	4-3	4-1	1-1	2-2	–	4-1	1-3	3-2	2-2
Greenock Morton	2-1	3-0	1-2	2-2	1-2	2-0	–	2-0	4-0	0-3
	3-0	0-0	2-0	1-0	2-2	1-1	–	4-1	1-0	1-2
Hamilton Acad.	1-2	0-2	3-0	1-2	0-1	1-3	2-3	–	0-3	2-2
	4-1	1-1	2-1	0-1	0-2	0-0	0-1	–	2-1	3-0
St. Johnstone	1-0	2-2	4-1	0-2	0-0	1-0	0-2	2-0	–	0-0
	0-0	3-1	3-0	3-2	1-0	2-2	6-1	4-1	–	1-0
St. Mirren	1-2	2-1	3-2	1-2	1-1	0-2	1-4	0-3	0-0	–
	2-1	1-2	5-0	2-1	1-3	2-1	0-1	0-1	1-3	–

(Play-off: Partick Thistle 1, Dundee Utd. 1; Dundee Utd. 2, Partick Thistle 1. After extra time; Dundee Utd. win 3-2 on agg., promoted to Premier Division).

Read across for home results, down for away

SECOND DIVISION

	Ayr United	Berwick Rangers	Clyde	East Fife	Forfar Athletic	Montrose	Queen of South	Stenhousemuir	Stirling Albion	Stranraer
Ayr United	–	1-4	1-1	0-1	1-3	2-0	2-0	1-2	1-2	0-0
	–	5-0	2-1	1-0	1-1	2-0	3-0	1-1	2-2	0-0
Berwick Rangers	2-2	–	0-0	0-1	1-0	2-2	0-0	3-1	3-0	4-0
	2-1	–	2-3	1-2	1-0	4-1	4-1	2-1	0-3	1-0
Clyde	1-2	3-1	–	0-1	1-2	3-0	2-1	0-1	1-2	1-1
	2-0	2-1	–	2-2	3-1	1-3	0-0	3-0	1-3	2-2
East Fife	1-0	1-0	0-0	–	1-1	3-0	2-1	0-2	0-3	3-3
	1-1	0-0	1-1	–	1-0	7-0	1-2	3-1	0-1	2-1
Forfar Athletic	2-1	1-4	1-0	0-2	–	0-0	2-1	1-0	0-6	0-0
	1-0	1-3	4-2	0-2	–	2-1	0-3	3-1	1-4	2-2
Montrose	0-1	1-3	0-0	1-2	1-0	–	1-4	1-4	2-2	4-2
	0-1	1-2	2-3	0-1	3-1	–	0-6	1-3	0-3	0-1
Queen of South	0-0	1-4	0-3	0-2	1-1	4-2	–	2-2	1-5	0-3
	2-2	3-0	2-1	1-0	4-1	1-1	–	3-3	0-7	2-1
Stenhousemuir	1-1	4-1	0-1	0-1	3-1	3-1	2-1	–	1-1	3-0
	0-1	0-3	1-0	2-2	0-2	3-1	1-3	–	0-1	2-0
Stirling Albion	2-0	1-0	1-1	0-2	4-1	3-0	2-2	2-1	–	1-1
	2-0	4-3	3-0	2-2	1-0	2-0	4-1	0-1	–	2-0
Stranraer	2-0	0-0	0-0	2-0	1-1	4-1	0-0	2-1	0-0	–
	1-1	0-3	2-2	0-0	1-0	1-2	3-1	0-0	2-2	–

Read across for home results, down for away

THIRD DIVISION

	Albion Rovers	Alloa	Arbroath	Brechin City	Caledonian Th.	Cowdenbeath	East Stirling	Livingston	Queen's Park	Ross County
Albion Rovers	–	2-1	0-2	1-0	2-2	2-3	1-2	0-2	3-1	3-4
	–	1-0	1-1	0-0	0-2	2-0	2-2	0-1	0-2	0-3
Alloa	3-2	–	0-2	3-2	0-5	2-3	1-3	0-2	0-0	1-0
	3-1	–	0-3	0-3	0-2	2-1	2-2	1-1	0-1	0-4
Arbroath	2-0	1-1	–	1-1	2-1	2-1	2-2	1-3	1-1	1-2
	2-1	1-0	–	0-1	1-2	0-0	2-1	1-2	1-1	1-1
Brechin City	0-1	0-1	1-1	–	0-0	2-0	3-1	2-0	1-0	2-1
	1-0	3-0	0-1	–	0-1	2-0	4-1	0-1	4-0	0-0
Caledonian Th.	6-1	1-1	5-1	1-2	–	3-2	1-1	0-3	3-1	1-1
	1-1	0-0	1-1	0-1	–	2-0	0-3	1-2	1-1	1-1
Cowdenbeath	4-1	1-0	1-1	0-1	0-0	–	4-2	0-1	3-2	2-0
	1-1	3-0	1-2	0-0	2-1	–	1-4	0-3	2-3	1-1
East Stirling	5-1	2-2	0-1	2-0	0-5	3-1	–	1-2	1-2	1-2
	1-1	1-0	1-0	3-0	1-5	1-1	–	0-3	1-2	2-4
Livingston	2-1	2-0	0-1	0-0	0-2	0-1	1-1	–	2-0	0-0
	0-1	1-0	3-0	0-1	2-2	2-1	1-1	–	3-1	2-1
Queen's Park	4-1	0-0	2-0	0-2	0-3	3-1	1-0	0-1	–	1-1
	5-1	0-0	0-0	0-0	1-2	2-1	2-2	0-0	–	0-0
Ross County	5-1	2-2	4-2	0-0	2-0	2-2	1-1	1-1	2-0	–
	1-1	0-0	0-0	1-2	2-1	4-1	1-3	2-2	0-1	–

Read across for home results, down for away

SCOTTISH CUP RETURNS TO IBROX: RANGERS' 14TH 'DOUBLE'

THIRD ROUND	FOURTH ROUND	FIFTH ROUND	SEMI-FINALS	FINAL
***Hearts** 1	**Hearts** 2			
Partick 0		**Hearts** 2		
*Hibernian 0	*Kilmarnock 1			
Kilmarnock 2			**Hearts** 2	
Montrose 1:3	Montrose 0			
*Gr. Morton 1:2		*St. Johnstone 1		
*Hamilton 0	*St. Johnstone 3			
St. Johnstone 1			(at Hampden Park, Glasgow)	**Hearts** 1
Stirling 1	*Stirling 0			
*Clydebank 0		*Aberdeen 2		
*Motherwell 0	Aberdeen 2			
Aberdeen 2			Aberdeen 1	
*Ross County 0	Forfar .... D2:†0			
Forfar 3		Airdrie 1		
*Dumbarton 1	*Airdrie 2:0			
Airdrie 3				(At Hampden Park – Saturday, May 18)
Celtic A3	*Celtic 2			
*Whitehill Welf. 0		*Celtic 2		
*Raith 3	Raith 0			
Queen's Park 0			Celtic 1	

Dundee Utd. .... 2 *Berwick 1	*Dundee Utd. 1	Dundee Utd. 1	(at Hampden Park, Glasgow)	**Rangers** 5
*Dunfermline .... 3 St. Mirren 0	Dunfermline 0			
*Caledonian ... B1:†1 East Fife 1:1	Caledonian Th. 1	*Caledonian Th. . E0	**Rangers** 2	
*Falkirk .... 0 Stenhousemuir 2	*Stenhousemuir .. 0			
*Clyde .... 3 Dundee 1	*Clyde 1	**Rangers** 3		
*Keith .... C1 **Rangers** 10	**Rangers** 4			

FIRST ROUND: Albion 0, Deveronvale 2; Glasgow Univ. 0, Spartans 1; Stenhousemuir 2, Arbroath 2; Stranraer 0, Livingston 3. **Replay**: Arbroath 0, Stenhousemuir 1.
SECOND ROUND: Ayr 0, Ross County 2; Berwick 3, Annan 3; Caledonian Th. 3, Livingston 2; Clyde 2, Brechin 2; Deveronvale 0, Keith 0; East Stirling 0, Stenhousemuir 1; Forfar 3, Lossiemouth 1; Montrose 2, Cowdenbeath 1; Queen of the South 2, Queen's Park 4; Spartans 0, East Fife 0; Stirling 3, Alloa 1; Whitehill Welf. 2, Fraserburgh 2. **Replays**: Annan 1, Berwick 2; Brechin 1, Clyde 2†; East Fife 2, Spartans 1; Fraserburgh 1, Whitehill Welf 2; Keith 2, Deveronvale 0.
(* Drawn at home. † After extra time. A – Played at Hibernian. B – Caledonian Th. won 3-1 on pens. C – Played at Aberdeen. D – Airdrie won 4-2 on pens. E – Played at Dundee Utd.).

TENNENTS SCOTTISH F.A. CUP FINAL

HEARTS 1 (Colquhoun 76), **RANGERS 5** (Laudrup 37, 49, Durie 65, 80, 86)
Hampden Park (37,730), Saturday, May 18, 1996

Hearts: Rousset; McPherson, McManus, Bruno (Robertson 58), Ritchie, Locke (Capt.) (Lawrence 7), Mackay, Fulton, Pointon, Colquhoun, Johnston. **Sub not used**: Hogarth. **Booked**: Ritchie. **Manager**: Jim Jefferies.

Rangers: Goram; McLaren, Gough (Capt.), Brown, Cleland, Ferguson (Durrant 87), Gascoigne, McCall, Robertson, Laudrup, Durie. **Subs not used**: Petric, Andersen. **Booked**: Cleland, Ferguson. **Manager**: Walter Smith.

Referee: H. Dallas (Motherwell). **Half-time**: 0-1. **Guest of Honour**: Michael Forsyth.

- Gordon Durie's hat-trick was the first in the Scottish Cup Final since Dixie Dean helped Celtic beat Hibernian 6-1 in 1972.

SCOTTISH F.A. CUP FINALS

1874	Queen's Park beat Clydesdale (2-0)
1875	Queen's Park beat Renton (3-0)
1876	Queen's Park beat Third Lanark (2-0 after 1-1 draw)
1877	Vale of Leven beat Rangers (3-2 after 0-0, 1-1 draws)
1878	Vale of Leven beat Third Lanark (1-0)
1879	Vale of Leven awarded Cup (Rangers withdrew after 1-1 draw)
1880	Queen's Park beat Thornlibank (3-0)
1881	Queen's Park beat Dumbarton (3-1)
1882	Queen's Park beat Dumbarton (4-1 after 2-2 draw)
1883	Dumbarton beat Vale of Leven (2-1 after 2-2 draw)
1884	Queen's Park awarded Cup (Vale of Leven withdrew from Final)
1885	Renton beat Vale of Leven (3-1 after 0-0 draw)
1886	Queen's Park beat Renton (3-1)
1887	Hibernian beat Dumbarton (2-1)
1888	Renton beat Cambuslang (6-1)
1889	Third Lanark beat Celtic (2-1)
1890	Queen's Park beat Vale of Leven (2-1 after 1-1 draw)
1891	Hearts beat Dumbarton (1-0)
1892	Celtic beat Queen's Park (5-1)
1893	Queen's Park beat Celtic (2-1)
1894	Rangers beat Celtic (3-1)
1895	St. Bernard's beat Renton (2-1)
1896	Hearts beat Hibernian (3-1)
1897	Rangers beat Dumbarton (5-1)
1898	Rangers beat Kilmarnock (2-0)
1899	Celtic beat Rangers (2-0)
1900	Celtic beat Queen's Park (4-3)
1901	Hearts beat Celtic (4-3)
1902	Hibernian beat Celtic (1-0)
1903	Rangers beat Hearts (2-0 after 0-0, 1-1 draws)
1904	Celtic beat Rangers (3-2)
1905	Third Lanark beat Rangers (3-1 after 0-0 draw)
1906	Hearts beat Third Lanark (1-0)
1907	Celtic beat Hearts (3-0)
1908	Celtic beat St. Mirren (5-1)
1909	Cup withheld because of riot after two drawn games in Final between Celtic and Rangers (2-2, 1-1)
1910	Dundee beat Clyde (2-1 after 2-2, 0-0 draws)
1911	Celtic beat Hamilton Academical (2-0 after 0-0 draw)
1912	Celtic beat Clyde (2-0)
1913	Falkirk beat Raith Rovers (2-0)
1914	Celtic beat Hibernian (4-1 after 0-0 draw)
1915-19	No competition (World War 1)
1920	Kilmarnock beat Albion Rovers (3-2)
1921	Partick Thistle beat Rangers (1-0)
1922	Morton beat Rangers (1-0)
1923	Celtic beat Hibernian (1-0)
1924	Airdrieonians beat Hibernian (2-0)
1925	Celtic beat Dundee (2-1)
1926	St. Mirren beat Celtic (2-0)
1927	Celtic beat East Fife (3-1)
1928	Rangers beat Celtic (4-0)
1929	Kilmarnock beat Rangers (2-0)
1930	Rangers beat Partick Thistle (2-1 after 0-0 draw)
1931	Celtic beat Motherwell (4-2 after 2-2 draw)
1932	Rangers beat Kilmarnock (3-0 after 1-1 draw)
1933	Celtic beat Motherwell (1-0)
1934	Rangers beat St. Mirren (5-0)
1935	Rangers beat Hamilton Academical (2-1)
1936	Rangers beat Third Lanark (1-0)

1937	Celtic beat Aberdeen (2-1)
1938	East Fife beat Kilmarnock (4-2 after 1-1 draw)
1939	Clyde beat Motherwell (4-0)
1940-6	No competition (World War 2)
1947	Aberdeen beat Hibernian (2-1)
1948†	Rangers beat Morton (1-0 after 1-1 draw)
1949	Rangers beat Clyde (4-1)
1950	Rangers beat East Fife (3-0)
1951	Celtic beat Motherwell (1-0)
1952	Motherwell beat Dundee (4-0)
1953	Rangers beat Aberdeen (1-0 after 1-1 draw)
1954	Celtic beat Aberdeen (2-1)
1955	Clyde beat Celtic (1-0 after 1-1 draw)
1956	Hearts beat Celtic (3-1)
1957†	Falkirk beat Kilmarnock (2-1 after 1-1 draw)
1958	Clyde beat Hibernian (1-0)
1959	St. Mirren beat Aberdeen (3-1)
1960	Rangers beat Kilmarnock (2-0)
1961	Dunfermline Athletic beat Celtic (2-0 after 0-0 draw)
1962	Rangers beat St. Mirren (2-0)
1963	Rangers beat Celtic (3-0 after 1-1 draw)
1964	Rangers beat Dundee (3-1)
1965	Celtic beat Dunfermline Athletic (3-2)
1966	Rangers beat Celtic (1-0 after 0-0 draw)
1967	Celtic beat Aberdeen (2-0)
1968	Dunfermline Athletic beat Hearts (3-1)
1969	Celtic beat Rangers (4-0)
1970	Aberdeen beat Celtic (3-1)
1971	Celtic beat Rangers (2-1 after 1-1 draw)
1972	Celtic beat Hibernian (6-1)
1973	Rangers beat Celtic (3-2)
1974	Celtic beat Dundee United (3-0)
1975	Celtic beat Airdrieonians (3-1)
1976	Rangers beat Hearts (3-1)
1977	Celtic beat Rangers (1-0)
1978	Rangers beat Aberdeen (2-1)
1979†	Rangers beat Hibernian (3-2 after two 0-0 draws)
1980†	Celtic beat Rangers (1-0)
1981	Rangers beat Dundee United (4-1 after 0-0 draw)
1982†	Aberdeen beat Rangers (4-1)
1983†	Aberdeen beat Rangers (1-0)
1984†	Aberdeen beat Celtic (2-1)
1985	Celtic beat Dundee United (2-1)
1986	Aberdeen beat Hearts (3-0)
1987†	St. Mirren beat Dundee United (1-0)
1988	Celtic beat Dundee United (2-1)
1989	Celtic beat Rangers (1-0)
1990†	Aberdeen beat Celtic (9-8 on pens. after 0-0 draw) – Tennents Cup
1991†	Motherwell beat Dundee United (4-3) – Tennents Cup
1992	Rangers beat Airdrieonians (2-1) – Tennents Cup
1993	Rangers beat Aberdeen (2-1) – Tennents Cup
1994	Dundee United beat Rangers (1-0) – Tennents Cup
1995	Celtic beat Airdrieonians (1-0) – Tennents Cup
1996	Rangers beat Hearts (5-1) – Tennents Cup

(† After extra time)

SUMMARY OF SCOTTISH F.A. CUP WINNERS

Celtic 30, Rangers 27, Queen's Park 10, Aberdeen 7, Hearts 5, Clyde 3, St. Mirren 3, Vale of Leven 3, Dunfermline Ath. 2, Falkirk 2, Hibernian 2, Kilmarnock 2, Motherwell 2, Renton 2, Third Lanark 2, Airdrieonians 1, Dumbarton 1, Dundee 1, Dundee United 1, East Fife 1, Morton 1, Partick Thistle 1, St. Bernard's 1.

ROY AITKEN LIFTS DONS TO SCOTTISH COCA-COLA CUP TRIUMPH

SECOND ROUND	THIRD ROUND	FOURTH ROUND	SEMI-FINALS	FINAL
***Aberdeen** 3	**Aberdeen** 4			
St. Mirren 1		**Aberdeen** .... †2		
*Queen of South ... 0	*Falkirk 1			
Falkirk 2			**Aberdeen** 2	
*Clydebank .... A†1	Motherwell 2			
Motherwell 1		*Motherwell 1		
*Cowdenbeath 0	*Dundee Utd. 1			
Dundee Utd. 4			(at Hampden Park, Glasgow)	**Aberdeen** 2
*Rangers 3	*Rangers 3			
Gr. Morton 0		Rangers 1		
Hamilton 0	Stirling 2			
*Stirling 2			Rangers 1	
*Raith 2	Raith 1			
Arbroath 1		*Celtic 0		
Ayr 0	*Celtic 2			
Celtic 3				(at Hampden Park – Sunday, November 26)
Partick 7	Partick C2			
*Berwick 0		Partick .... D†1		
*St. Johnstone .. B†1	*Livingston 1			
Livingston 1			Airdrie 1	
*East Fife 2	*Airdrie 2			
Airdrie 3		*Airdrie 1		

Stenhousemuir ...... 1 *Hibernian 3	Hibernian 0			**Dundee** 0
*Dunfermline .... 3 Stranraer 0	Dunfermline 1	Hearts .... E†4	(at McDiarmid Park, Perth)	
Alloa .... 0 *Hearts 3	*Hearts 2			
*Kilmarnock .... †1 Dumbarton 0	Kilmarnock 1	***Dundee** 4	**Dundee** 2	
*East Stirling .... 0 **Dundee** 6	***Dundee** 3			

FIRST ROUND: Albion 0, Cowdenbeath 1; Alloa 2, Forfar 1; Berwick 1, Caledonian Th. 1† (Berwick won 5-3 on pens.); Brechin 2, East Fife 3†; Clyde 1, East Stirling 2; Montrose 0, Livingston 2, Queen of the South 3, Queen's Park 1; Ross County 0, Arbroath 2.

(* Drawn at home. † After extra time. A – Motherwell won 4-1 on pens. B – Livingston won 4-2 on pens. C – at Meadowbank Stadium. D – Airdrie won 3-2 on pens. E – Dundee won 5-4 on pens.).

SCOTTISH LEAGUE (COCA-COLA) CUP FINAL

ABERDEEN 2 (Dodds 33, Shearer 46), **DUNDEE 0**

Hampden Park (33,096), Sunday, November 26, 1995

Aberdeen: Watt; Grant, Irvine, Smith, McKimmie (Capt.), Miller (Robertson 80), Jess, Bernard (Hetherston 84), Glass, Shearer, Dodds. **Sub not used**: Stillie (gk). **Manager**: Roy Aitken.

Dundee: Pageaud; J. Duffy, McQueen, Manley, Wieghorst, N. Duffy (Capt.), Shaw, Vrto (Farningham 60), Tosh (Britton 50), Hamilton, McCann (Anderson 75). **Booked**: Vrto, Hamilton **Player-manager**: James Duffy.

Referee: L. Mottram (Forth). **Half-time**: 1-0.

- This was Aberdeen's first triumph in six seasons – six months after they narrowly avoided relegation to the First Division.

COCA-COLA SCOTTISH LEAGUE CUP 1996-97

1st Round – Sat., Aug. 3

Clyde v Inverness Caledonian Thistle
Ayr v Livingston
Cowdenbeath v Forfar
Stranraer v Queen of the South
Brechin v Montrose
Queen's Park v Ross County
East Stirling v Alloa
Albion Rovers v Arbroath

2nd Round – Tues, Wed., Aug. 13-14

Partick v Cowdenbeath or Forfar
Queen's Park or Ross County v Aberdeen
Greenock Morton v Hamilton
Airdrie v Raith Rovers
St. Mirren v Berwick
East Fife v St. Johnstone
Dundee v Dumbarton
Stranraer or Queen of the South v Dunfermline
Kilmarnock v Ayr or Livingston
Stirling Albion v Dundee Utd.
Motherwell v E. Stirling or Alloa
Clyde or Inverness Caledonian Thistle v Celtic
Falkirk v Albion Rovers or Arbroath
Brechin or Montrose v Hibernian
Hearts v Stenhousemuir
Clydebank v Rangers

Dates of other rounds – see inside-back cover.

PROMOTION SPECIALIST

When new club **Livingston** clinched the Scottish Third Division title last season, it was no new experience for manager **Jim Leishman**. He had climbed through the divisions with Dunfermline, and with Livingston was managing a club to a championship for the third time.

GROWING THISTLE

Starting this season, Scottish League club Caledonian Thistle will be known as **Inverness Caledonian Thistle**.

QUOTE-UNQUOTE

ALAN HANSEN, on Chelsea signing 31-year-old Gianluca Vialli this summer: "It worries me that the majority of the star-name foreigners being imported to the Premiership are the elder brigade. There are very few coming here at their peak, around the age of 26 or 27."

MARK HATELEY, Q.P.R. and former England striker: "I've played in great stadiums all over the world, but for me they are simply the places where I do my work. My actual favourite is the front garden, playing with my four kids."

DESMOND LYNAM (Match of the Day) over picture of 91-year-old Alice Sachs, a Man. United fan for 86 years, celebrating their win v Middlesbrough last October: "Football's a game for all ages, and after all this time Alice is still in Wonderland."

BRIAN SAUNDERS, Southampton fan, frustrated by departures from The Dell down the years: "What is Southampton FC anyway, but a transport cafe on the soccer highway?"

RUUD GULLIT (Chelsea) on managing in the Premiership: "It's like a fast game of chess, trying to out-think the opposition."

SCOTTISH LEAGUE CUP FINALS

1946	Aberdeen beat Rangers (3-2)
1947	Rangers beat Aberdeen (4-0)
1948	East Fife beat Falkirk (4-1 after 0-0 draw)
1949	Rangers beat Raith Rovers (2-0)
1950	East Fife beat Dunfermline Athletic (3-0)
1951	Motherwell beat Hibernian (3-0)
1952	Dundee beat Rangers (3-2)
1953	Dundee beat Kilmarnock (2-0)
1954	East Fife beat Partick Thistle (3-2)
1955	Hearts beat Motherwell (4-2)
1956	Aberdeen beat St. Mirren (2-1)
1957	Celtic beat Partick Thistle (3-0 after 0-0 draw)
1958	Celtic beat Rangers (7-1)
1959	Hearts beat Partick Thistle (5-1)
1960	Hearts beat Third Lanark (2-1)
1961	Rangers beat Kilmarnock (2-0)
1962	Rangers beat Hearts (3-1 after 1-1 draw)
1963	Hearts beat Kilmarnock (1-0)
1964	Rangers beat Morton (5-0)
1965	Rangers beat Celtic (2-1)
1966	Celtic beat Rangers (2-1)
1967	Celtic beat Rangers (1-0)
1968	Celtic beat Dundee (5-3)
1969	Celtic beat Hibernian (6-2)
1970	Celtic beat St. Johnstone (1-0)
1971	Rangers beat Celtic (1-0)
1972	Partick Thistle beat Celtic (4-1)
1973	Hibernian beat Celtic (2-1)
1974	Dundee beat Celtic (1-0)
1975	Celtic beat Hibernian (6-3)
1976	Rangers beat Celtic (1-0)
1977†	Aberdeen beat Celtic (2-1)
1978†	Rangers beat Celtic (2-1)
1979	Rangers beat Aberdeen (2-1)
1980	Dundee United beat Aberdeen (3-0 after 0-0 draw)
1981	Dundee United beat Dundee (3-0)
1982	Rangers beat Dundee United (2-1)
1983	Celtic beat Rangers (2-1)
1984†	Rangers beat Celtic (3-2)
1985	Rangers beat Dundee United (1-0) – Skol Cup
1986	Aberdeen beat Hibernian (3-0) – Skol Cup
1987	Rangers beat Celtic (2-1) – Skol Cup
1988†	Rangers beat Aberdeen (5-3 on pens. after 3-3 draw) – Skol Cup
1989	Rangers beat Aberdeen (3-2) – Skol Cup
1990†	Aberdeen beat Rangers (2-1) – Skol Cup
1991†	Rangers beat Celtic (2-1) – Skol Cup
1992	Hibernian beat Dunfermline Athletic (2-0) – Skol Cup
1993†	Rangers beat Aberdeen (2-1) – Skol Cup
1994	Rangers beat Hibernian (2-1)
1995	Raith Rovers beat Celtic (6-5 on pens. after 2-2 draw) – Coca-Cola Cup
1996	Aberdeen beat Dundee (2-0) – Coca-Cola Cup

(† After extra time)

SUMMARY OF SCOTTISH LEAGUE CUP WINNERS

Rangers	19	Dundee	3	Motherwell	1
Celtic	9	East Fife	3	Partick Thistle	1
Aberdeen	6	Dundee United	2	Raith Rovers	1
Hearts	4	Hibernian	2		

WELSH CUP FINALS 1878-1996

1878 **Wrexham 1** Druids 0
1879 **Newtown 2** Wrexham 1
1880 **Druids 2** Ruthin 1
1881 **Druids 2** Newtown 0
1882 **Druids 2** Northwich 1
1883 **Wrexham 1** Druids 0
1884 **Oswestry 3** Druids 2
1885 **Druids 2** Oswestry 0
1886 **Druids 5** Newtown 2
1887 **Chirk 4** Davenham 2
1888 **Chirk 5** Newtown 0
1889 **Bangor 2** Northwich 1
1890 **Chirk 1** Wrexham 0
1891 **Shrewsbury 5** Wrexham 2
1892 **Chirk 2** Westminster 1
1893 **Wrexham 2** Chirk 1
1894 **Chirk 2** Westminster 0
1895 **Newtown 3** Wrexham 2
1896 **Bangor 3** Wrexham 1
1897 **Wrexham 2** Newtown 0
1898 **Druids 2** Wrexham 1
1899 **Druids 1** Wrexham 0
1900 **Aberwystwyth 3** Druids 0
1901 **Oswestry 1** Druids 0
1902 **Wellington 1** Wrexham 0
1903 **Wrexham 8** Aberaman 0
1904 **Druids 3** Aberdare 2
1905 **Wrexham 3** Aberdare 0
1906 **Wellington 3** Whitchurch 2
1907 **Oswestry 2** Whitchurch 0
1908 **Chester 3** Connah's Quay 1
1909 **Wrexham 1** Chester 0
1910 **Wrexham 2** Chester 0
1911 **Wrexham 6** Connah's Quay 1
1912 **Cardiff City 3** Pontypridd 0
1913 **Swansea 1** Pontypridd 0
1914 **Wrexham 3** Llanelli 0
1915 **Wrexham 1** Swansea 0
1920 **Cardiff City 2** Wrexham 1
1921 **Wrexham 3** Pontypridd 1
1922 **Cardiff City 2** Ton Pentre 0
1923 **Cardiff City 3** Aberdare 2
1924 **Wrexham 1** Merthyr 0
1925 **Wrexham 3** Flint 1
1926 **Ebbw Vale 3** Swansea 2
1927 **Cardiff City 2** Rhyl 0
1928 **Cardiff City 2** Bangor 0
1929 **Connah's Quay 3** Cardiff City 0
1930 **Cardiff City 4** Rhyl 2
1931 **Wrexham 7** Shrewsbury 0
1932 **Swansea 2** Wrexham 0
1933 **Chester 2** Wrexham 0
1934 **Bristol City 3** Tranmere 0
1935 **Tranmere 1** Chester 0
1936 **Crewe 2** Chester 0
1937 **Crewe 3** Rhyl 1
1938 **Shrewsbury 2** Swansea 1
1939 **South Liverpool 2** Cardiff City 1
1940 **Wellington 4** Swansea 0
1947 **Chester 5** Merthyr 1
1948 **Lovells 3** Shrewsbury 0
1949 **Merthyr 2** Swansea 0
1950 **Swansea 4** Wrexham 1
1951 **Merthyr 3** Cardiff City 2
1952 **Rhyl 4** Merthyr 3
1953 **Rhyl 2** Chester 1
1954 **Flint 2** Chester 1
1955 **Barry 4** Chester 3
1956 **Cardiff City 3** Swansea 2
1957 **Wrexham 2** Swansea 1
1958 **Wrexham 2** Chester 0
1959 **Cardiff City 2** Lovells 0
1960 **Wrexham 1** Cardiff City 0
1961 **Swansea 3** Bangor 1
1962 **Bangor 3** Wrexham 1
1963 **Borough** v Newport 2-1, 0-0
1964 **Cardiff City 2** Bangor 0
1965 **Cardiff City 3** Wrexham 0
1966 **Swansea 2** Chester 1
1967 **Cardiff City** v Wrexham 2-2, 2-1
1968 **Cardiff City** v Hereford 2-0, 4-1
1969 **Cardiff City** v Swansea 3-1, 2-0
1970 **Cardiff City** v Chester 1-0, 4-0
1971 **Cardiff City** v Wrexham 1-0, 3-1
1972 **Wrexham** v Cardiff City 2-1, 1-1
1973 **Cardiff City** v Bangor 0-1, 5-0
1974 **Cardiff City** v S'bridge 1-0, 1-0
1975 **Wrexham** v Cardiff City 2-1, 3-1
1976 **Cardiff City** v Hereford 3-3, 3-2
1977 **Shr'sbury** v Cardiff City 1-2, 3-0
1978 **Wrexham** v Bangor 2-1, 1-0
1979 **Shrewsbury** v Wrexham 1-1, 1-0
1980 **Newport Co.** v Shr'sbury 2-1, 3-0
1981 **Swansea** v Hereford 1-0, 1-1
1982 **Swansea** v Cardiff 0-0, 2-1
1983 **Swansea** v Wrexham 2-1, 2-0
1984 **Shrewsbury** v Wrexham 2-0, 0-0
1985 **Shrewsbury** v Bangor 3-1, 2-0
1986 **Wrexham 2** K'minster 1
1987 **Merthyr 1** Newport County 0
1988 **Cardiff City 2** Wrexham 0
1989 **Swansea 5** K'minster 0
1990 **Hereford 2** Wrexham 1
1991 **Swansea 2** Wrexham 0
1992 **Cardiff City 1**Hednesford 0
1993 **Cardiff City 5** Rhyl 0
1994 **Barry Town 2** Cardiff City 1
1995 **Wrexham 2** Cardiff City 1
1996 **Llansantffraid 3** Barry Town 3
(Llansantffraid won 3-2 on pens).

IRISH FOOTBALL 1995-96

BORD GAIS FAI NATIONAL LEAGUE

PREMIER DIVISION

	P	W	D	L	F	A	Pts
St. Patrick's Ath.	33	19	10	4	53	34	67
Bohemians	33	18	8	7	60	29	62
Sligo Rovers	33	16	7	10	45	38	55
Shelbourne	33	15	9	9	45	33	54
Shamrock Rovers	33	14	8	11	32	32	50
Derry City	33	11	13	9	50	38	46
Dundalk	33	11	9	13	38	39	42
U.C.D.	33	12	6	15	38	40	42
*Cork City	33	12	8	13	37	41	41
Athlone Town	33	8	7	18	38	59	31
Drogheda Utd.	33	7	9	17	39	51	30
Galway United	33	5	6	22	26	67	21

*Deducted 3 points for playing illegal players.

Top Scorer: 19 Stephen Geoghegan (Shelbourne); **Player of the Year:** Eddie Gormley (St. Patrick's Ath.); **Young Player of the Year:** Mick O'Byrne (U.C.D.); **Personality of the Year:** Brian Kerr (St. Patrick's Ath.).

FIRST DIVISION

	P	W	D	L	F	A	Pts
Bray Wanderers	27	16	7	4	53	21	55
Finn Harps	27	14	7	6	50	25	49
Home Farm/Everton	27	14	4	9	42	34	46
Cobh Ramblers	27	10	13	4	30	15	43
St. James's Gate	27	9	11	7	35	30	38
Limerick FC	27	10	6	11	37	34	36
Kilkenny City	27	9	8	10	33	38	35
Waterford Utd.	27	9	7	11	37	40	34
Longford Town	27	5	6	16	26	46	21
Monaghan Utd.	27	2	5	20	10	70	11

Top Scorer: 17 Jonathan Speak (Finn Harps); **Player of the Year:** Jonathan Speak (Finn Harps).

FAI HARP LAGER CUP FINAL

(Lansdowne Road, Dublin, May 5)

SHELBOURNE 1 (Sheridan), **ST. PATRICK'S ATHLETIC 1** (D. Campbell)

REPLAY

(Dalymount Park, Dublin, May 11)

SHELBOURNE 2 (Sheridan, S. Geoghegan), **ST. PATRICK'S ATHLETIC 1** (D. Campbell)

St. Patrick's Ath: Byrne; Burke, McDonnell (P. Campbell), D. Campbell, Carpenter, Osam (Reilly), Mernagh (Glynn), Gormley, Buckley, Morrisroe, O'Flaherty.

Shelbourne: Gough; Costello, Neville, Duffy, D. Geoghegan, Sheridan, Kelly (Rutherford), Flood, O'Rourke, Tilson, S. Geoghegan.

Referee: W. Wallace (Donegal).

BORD GAIS LEAGUE CUP FINAL

1st leg, The Showgrounds, October 30: Sligo Rovers 1 (Gilzean), **Shelbourne 0**; **2nd leg, Tolka Park, November 7: Shelbourne 2** (D. Geoghegan, S. Geoghegan), **Sligo Rovers 1** (Moran). (2-2 on aggregate. Shelbourne won 4-3 on penalties).

SMIRNOFF IRISH LEAGUE

PREMIER DIVISION

	P	W	D	L	F	A	Pts
Portadown	28	16	8	4	61	40	56
Crusaders	28	15	7	6	45	32	52
Glentoran	28	13	7	8	56	38	46
Glenavon	28	13	5	10	47	32	44
Linfield	28	11	8	9	34	35	41
Cliftonville	28	6	11	11	27	48	29
Ards	28	6	7	15	29	43	25
Bangor	28	3	5	20	23	54	14

Top Scorer: 20 Gary Haylock (Portadown); **Player of the Year:** Peter Kennedy (Portadown); **Young Player of the Year:** Glen Little (Glentoran); **Manager of the Year:** Ron McFall (Portadown).

FIRST DIVISION

	P	W	D	L	F	A	Pts
Coleraine	28	21	4	3	82	28	67
Ballymena	28	13	10	5	28	25	49
Omagh Town	28	12	7	9	50	43	43
Distillery	28	10	7	11	35	34	37
Ballyclare	28	10	3	15	29	48	33
Carrick Rangers	28	9	3	16	32	56	30
Larne	28	7	7	14	31	36	28
Newry Town	28	7	5	16	31	58	26

Top Scorer: 20 Shields (Coleraine).

BASS IRISH CUP FINAL

(Windsor Park, May 4)

GLENTORAN 1 (Little), **GLENAVON 0**

Glentoran: D. Devine; Nixon, Finlay, Walker, J. Devine, Parker, Smith, Little, Coyle, Batey, McBride.

Glenavon: Straney; Smyth, Glendenning, Murphy, Gauld, Smyth, Johnston, Shepherd, Ferguson, McBride (McCoy), Shipp.

Referee: A. Snoddy (Carryduff).

IRISH F.A. CUP WINNERS

1881	Moyola Park	1910	Distillery	1939	Linfield	1968	Crusaders
1882	Queen's Island	1911	Shelbourne	1940	Ballymena	1969	Ards
1883	Cliftonville	1912	Linfield	1941	Celtic	1970	Linfield
1884	Distillery	1913	Linfield	1942	Linfield	1971	Distillery
1885	Distillery	1914	Glentoran	1943	Celtic	1972	Coleraine
1886	Distillery	1915	Linfield	1944	Celtic	1973	Glentoran
1887	Ulster	1916	Linfield	1945	Linfield	1974	Ards
1888	Cliftonville	1917	Glentoran	1946	Linfield	1975	Coleraine
1889	Distillery	1918	Celtic	1947	Celtic	1976	Carrick Rgrs.
1890	Gordon H.	1919	Linfield	1948	Linfield	1977	Coleraine
1891	Linfield	1920	Shelbourne	1949	Derry City	1978	Linfield
1892	Linfield	1921	Glentoran	1950	Linfield	1979	Cliftonville
1893	Linfield	1922	Linfield	1951	Glentoran	1980	Linfield
1894	Distillery	1923	Linfield	1952	Ards	1981	Ballymena Utd.
1895	Linfield	1924	Queen's Island	1953	Linfield	1982	Linfield
1896	Distillery	1925	Distillery	1954	Derry City	1983	Glentoran
1897	Cliftonville	1926	Celtic	1955	Dundela	1984	Ballymena Utd.
1898	Linfield	1927	Ards	1956	Distillery	1985	Glentoran
1899	Linfield	1928	Willowfield	1957	Glenavon	1986	Glentoran
1900	Cliftonville	1929	Ballymena	1958	Ballymena	1987	Glentoran
1901	Cliftonville	1930	Linfield	1959	Glenavon	1988	Glentoran
1902	Linfield	1931	Linfield	1960	Linfield	1989	Ballymena Utd.
1903	Distillery	1932	Glentoran	1961	Glenavon	1990	Glentoran
1904	Linfield	1933	Glentoran	1962	Linfield	1991	Portadown
1905	Distillery	1934	Linfield	1963	Linfield	1992	Glenavon
1906	Shelbourne	1935	Glentoran	1964	Derry City	1993	Bangor
1907	Cliftonville	1936	Linfield	1965	Coleraine	1994	Linfield
1908	Bohemians	1937	Celtic	1966	Glentoran	1995	Linfield
1909	Cliftonville	1938	Celtic	1967	Crusaders	1996	Glentoran

IRISH LEAGUE CHAMPIONS

1891	Linfield
1892	Linfield
1893	Linfield
1894	Glentoran
1895	Linfield
1896	Distillery
1897	Glentoran
1898	Linfield
1899	Distillery
1900	Celtic
1901	Distillery
1902	Linfield
1903	Distillery
1904	Linfield
1905	Glentoran
1906	Cliftonville
	Distillery
1907	Linfield
1908	Linfield
1909	Linfield
1910	Cliftonville
1911	Linfield
1912	Glentoran
1913	Glentoran
1914	Linfield
1915	Celtic
1916	Celtic
1921	Glentoran
1922	Linfield
1923	Linfield
1924	Queen's Island
1925	Glentoran
1926	Celtic
1927	Celtic
1928	Celtic
1929	Celtic
1930	Linfield
1931	Glentoran
1932	Linfield
1933	Celtic
1934	Linfield
1935	Linfield
1936	Celtic
1937	Celtic
1938	Celtic
1939	Celtic
1940	Celtic
1948	Celtic
1949	Linfield
1950	Linfield
1951	Glentoran
1952	Glenavon
1953	Glentoran
1954	Linfield
1955	Linfield
1956	Linfield
1957	Glenavon
1958	Ards
1959	Linfield
1960	Glenavon
1961	Linfield
1962	Linfield
1963	Distillery
1964	Glentoran
1965	Derry City
1966	Linfield
1967	Glentoran
1968	Glentoran
1969	Linfield
1970	Glentoran
1971	Linfield
1972	Glentoran
1973	Crusaders
1974	Coleraine
1975	Linfield
1976	Crusaders
1977	Glentoran
1978	Linfield
1979	Linfield
1980	Linfield
1981	Glentoran
1982	Linfield
1983	Linfield
1984	Linfield
1985	Linfield
1986	Linfield
1987	Linfield
1988	Glentoran
1989	Linfield
1990	Portadown
1991	Portadown
1992	Glentoran
1993	Linfield
1994	Linfield
1995	Crusaders
1996	Portadown

REPUBLIC OF IRELAND: All-time Winners

Season	League	FAI Cup
1921-22	St.James' Gate	St.James' Gate
1922-23	Shamrock R.	Alton United
1923-24	Bohemians	Athlone Town
1924-25	Shamrock R.	Shamrock R.
1925-26	Shelbourne	Fordsons
1926-27	Shamrock R.	Drumcondra
1927-28	Bohemians	Bohemians
1928-29	Shelbourne	Shamrock R.
1929-30	Bohemians	Shamrock R.
1930-31	Shelbourne	Shamrock R.
1931-32	Shamrock R.	Shamrock R.
1932-33	Dundalk	Shamrock R.
1933-34	Bohemians	Cork
1934-35	Dolphin	Bohemians
1935-36	Bohemians	Shamrock R.
1936-37	Sligo Rovers	Waterford
1937-38	Shamrock R.	St.James' Gate
1938-39	Shamrock R.	Shelbourne
1939-40	St.James' Gate	Shamrock R.
1940-41	Cork United	Cork United
1941-42	Cork United	Dundalk
1942-43	Cork United	Drumcondra
1943-44	Shelbourne	Shamrock R.
1944-45	Cork United	Shamrock R.
1945-46	Cork United	Drumcondra
1946-47	Shelbourne	Cork United
1947-48	Drumcondra	Shamrock R.
1948-49	Drumcondra	Dundalk
1949-50	Cork Athletic	Transport
1950-51	Cork Athletic	Dundalk
1951-52	St.Patrick's Ath.	Dundalk
1952-53	Shelbourne	Cork Athletic
1953-54	Shamrock R.	Drumcondra
1954-55	St.Patrick's Ath.	Shamrock R.
1955-56	St.Patrick's Ath.	Shamrock R.
1956-57	Shamrock R.	Drumcondra
1957-58	Drumcondra	Dundalk
1958-59	Shamrock R.	St.Patrick's Ath.

Season	League	FAI Cup
1959-60	Limerick	Shelbourne
1960-61	Drumcondra	St.Patrick's Ath.
1961-62	Shelbourne	Shamrock R.
1962-63	Dundalk	Shelbourne
1963-64	Shamrock R.	Shamrock R.
1964-65	Drumcondra	Shamrock R.
1965-66	Waterford	Shamrock R.
1966-67	Dundalk	Shamrock R.
1967-68	Waterford	Shamrock R.
1968-69	Waterford	Shamrock R.
1969-70	Waterford	Bohemians
1970-71	Cork Hibs.	Limerick
1971-72	Waterford	Cork Hibs.
1972-73	Waterford	Cork Hibs.
1973-74	Cork Celtic	Finn Harps
1974-75	Bohemians	Home Farm
1975-76	Dundalk	Bohemians
1976-77	Sligo Rovers	Dundalk
1977-78	Bohemians	Shamrock R.
1978-79	Dundalk	Dundalk
1979-80	Limerick United	Waterford
1980-81	Athlone Town	Dundalk
1981-82	Dundalk	Limerick United
1982-83	Athlone Town	Sligo Rovers
1983-84	Shamrock R.	Univ. Cllge. Dublin
1984-85	Shamrock R.	Shamrock R.
1985-86	Shamrock R.	Shamrock R.
1986-87	Shamrock R.	Shamrock R.
1987-88	Dundalk	Dundalk
1988-89	Derry City	Derry City
1989-90	St.Patrick's Ath.	Bray Wanderers
1990-91	Dundalk	Galway United
1991-92	Shelbourne	Bohemians
1992-93	Cork City	Shelbourne
1993-94	Shamrock R.	Sligo Rovers
1994-95	Dundalk	Derry City
1995-96	St. Patrick's Ath.	Shelbourne

OTHER LEAGUES 1995-96

GM VAUXHALL CONFERENCE

	P	W	D	L	F	A	Pts
1 Stevenage Borough	42	27	10	5	101	44	91
2 Woking	42	25	8	9	83	54	83
3 Hednesford Town	42	23	7	12	71	46	75
4 Macclesfield Town	42	22	9	11	66	49	75
5 Gateshead	42	18	13	11	58	46	67
6 Southport	42	18	12	12	77	64	66
7 Kidderminster Harriers	42	18	10	14	78	66	64
8 Northwich Victoria	42	16	12	14	72	64	60
9 Morecambe	42	17	8	17	78	72	59
10 Farnborough Town	42	15	14	13	63	58	59
11 Bromsgrove Rovers	42	15	14	13	59	57	59
12 Altrincham	42	15	13	14	59	64	58
13 Telford United	42	15	10	17	51	56	55
14 Stalybridge Celtic	42	16	7	19	59	68	55
15 Halifax Town	42	13	13	16	49	63	52
16 Kettering Town	42	13	9	20	68	84	48
17 Slough Town	42	13	8	21	63	76	47
18 Bath City	42	13	7	22	45	66	46
19 Welling United	42	10	15	17	42	53	45
20 Dover Athletic	42	11	7	24	51	74	40
21 Runcorn	42	9	8	25	48	87	35
22 Dagenham & Redbridge	42	7	12	23	43	73	33

• Stevenage Borough not promoted to Football League – did not meet ground criteria (6,000 capacity, 1,000 seats) required by League on Dec. 31, 1995.

CONFERENCE AWARDS

Prize money – Champions: Stevenage Borough £10,000; Woking (runners-up) £5,000; Hednesford (third) £3,000.
Manager of Year: Paul Fairclough (Stevenage Borough).
Player of Year: Barry Hayles (Stevenage Borough).
Goalscorer of Year: Barry Hayles (Stevenage Borough), £1,000.

Relegated: Runcorn, Dagenham & Redbridge.
Promoted to Conference: Rushden & Diamonds (Beazer Homes) and Hayes (ICIS).

GM VAUXHALL CONFERENCE CHAMPIONS

1979-80	Altrincham
1980-81	Altrincham
1981-82	Runcorn
1982-83	Enfield
1983-84	Maidstone United
1984-85	Wealdstone
1985-86	Enfield
1986-87	* Scarborough
1987-88	* Lincoln City
1988-89	* Maidstone United
1989-90	* Darlington
1990-91	* Barnet
1991-92	* Colchester United
1992-93	* Wycombe Wanderers
1993-94	Kidderminster H.
1994-95	Macclesfield Town
1995-96	Stevenage Borough

(* Promoted to Football League)

Conference – Record Attendance: 9,432, Lincoln City v Wycombe, May 2, 1988.

PONTIN'S LEAGUE

DIVISION ONE

		P	W	D	L	F	A	Pts
1	Manchester United	34	22	5	7	71	35	71
2	Derby County	34	17	10	7	59	43	61
3	Stoke City	34	17	8	9	57	42	59
4	Leeds United	34	17	8	9	40	32	59
5	Liverpool	34	16	8	10	57	42	56
6	Tranmere Rovers	34	17	4	13	70	62	55
7	Everton	34	14	10	10	50	41	52
8	Oldham Athletic	34	12	11	11	55	54	47
9	Bolton Wanderers	34	12	9	13	51	52	45
10	Newcastle United	34	13	6	15	55	59	45
11	Birmingham City	34	13	5	16	57	64	44
12	Nottingham Forest	34	12	8	14	46	55	44
13	Sheffield Wednesday	34	11	8	15	66	63	41
14	Blackburn Rovers	34	9	13	12	48	44	40
15	Sheffield United	34	8	13	13	40	61	37
16	Wolverhampton Wanderers	34	10	5	19	42	48	35
17	Notts County	34	9	7	18	48	64	34
18	West Bromwich Albion	34	5	6	23	33	84	21

DIVISION TWO

		P	W	D	L	F	A	Pts
1	Middlesbrough	34	23	5	6	80	31	74
2	Huddersfield Town	34	19	7	8	62	34	64
3	Sunderland	34	18	9	7	62	37	63
4	Preston North End	34	17	11	6	51	34	62
5	Coventry City	34	17	7	10	67	52	58
6	Blackpool	34	15	9	10	55	40	54
7	Port Vale	34	14	11	9	69	50	53
8	Aston Villa	34	14	11	9	62	46	53
9	Leicester City	34	13	13	8	64	42	52
10	Manchester City	34	13	11	10	40	39	50
11	Barnsley	34	14	6	14	61	59	48
12	Burnley	34	11	10	13	62	68	43
13	Grimsby Town	34	10	9	15	59	68	39
14	Rotherham United	34	9	7	18	35	57	34
15	Bradford City	34	10	3	21	47	75	33
16	York City	34	8	9	17	38	66	33
17	Hull City	34	5	4	25	19	68	19
18	Mansfield Town	34	2	6	26	35	102	12

DIVISION THREE

	P	W	D	L	F	A	Pts
1 Wrexham	28	20	2	6	74	36	62
2 Carlisle United	28	18	7	3	53	15	61
3 Stockport County	28	18	5	5	69	36	59
4 Shrewsbury Town	28	12	9	7	58	39	45
5 Bury	28	13	5	10	46	37	44
6 Wigan Athletic	28	12	7	9	59	43	43
7 Chesterfield	28	12	6	10	49	43	42
8 Walsall	28	12	5	11	40	39	41
9 Rochdale	28	9	8	11	64	70	35
10 Doncaster Rovers	28	10	4	14	42	49	34
11 Lincoln City	28	9	6	13	33	45	33
12 Scarborough	28	9	5	14	27	51	32
13 Chester City	28	6	7	15	39	54	25
14 Darlington	28	5	5	18	28	55	20
15 Scunthorpe United	28	4	1	23	34	103	13

FOOTBALL COMBINATION
(Sponsors: Avon Insurance)

DIVISION ONE

	P	W	D	L	F	A	Pts
1 Q.P.R.	38	27	3	8	77	43	84
2 Tottenham Hotspur	38	26	4	8	33	47	82
3 Arsenal	38	22	10	6	82	37	76
4 Wimbledon	38	21	5	12	82	57	68
5 Norwich City	38	20	7	11	72	48	67
6 Crystal Palace	38	16	12	10	50	41	60
7 Luton Town	38	17	7	14	56	48	58
8 West Ham United	38	15	9	14	60	63	54
9 Chelsea	38	14	11	13	50	47	53
10 Southampton	38	13	11	14	48	56	50
11 Charlton Athletic	38	14	8	16	52	65	50
12 Ipswich Town	38	13	10	15	62	62	49
13 Bristol City	38	13	8	17	41	52	47
14 Portsmouth	38	12	10	16	47	57	46
15 Millwall	38	11	10	17	53	68	43
16 Brighton & Hove Albion	38	10	8	20	48	76	38
17 Oxford United	38	8	12	18	50	66	36
18 Bristol Rovers	38	9	6	23	47	79	33
19 Swindon Town	38	6	13	19	35	66	31
20 Watford	38	8	6	24	46	74	30

Div. 2 Champions: Bournemouth.

SOUTH-EAST COUNTIES LEAGUE

DIVISION ONE

		P	W	D	L	F	A	Pts
1	West Ham United	30	22	4	4	79	37	48
2	Tottenham Hotspur	30	21	2	7	88	37	44
3	Watford	30	19	6	5	70	34	44
4	Arsenal	30	19	5	6	64	27	43
5	Norwich City	30	16	6	8	56	30	38
6	Millwall	30	14	3	13	44	46	31
7	Gillingham	30	10	9	11	49	59	29
8	Charlton Athletic	30	10	8	12	50	51	28
9	Leyton Orient	30	12	4	14	40	49	28
10	Chelsea	30	10	7	13	57	50	27
11	Ipswich Town	30	10	6	14	51	57	26
12	Q.P.R.	30	8	6	16	46	58	22
13	Southend United	30	6	9	15	36	60	21
14	Portsmouth	30	6	8	16	28	55	20
15	Cambridge United	30	5	6	19	42	96	16
16	Fulham	30	5	5	20	26	80	15

Div. 2 Champions: Crystal Palace.

QUOTE-UNQUOTE

BRUCE RIOCH, Arsenal manager: "Respect – that's an important word that has gone out of our society. When I went to watch football, I didn't jeer Dave Mackay, George Eastham or Bobby Charlton. I went to admire them, to respect their talents."

HARRY REDKNAPP (West Ham): "I think the managers of the season are not those who win titles with loads of dough, but those who avoid relegation with none."

ALAN BALL on the large playing staff he inherited at Man. City: "I arrived at Maine Road just as they were returning from a training run. They were coming over the hill, and they kept coming and coming and coming. I now know how General Custer felt."

ALAN BALL after Man. City's 6-0 defeat at Anfield last October: "Daft as it may seem, I enjoyed the game, enjoyed Liverpool. They totally outclassed us, got the start they wanted. After that, I had to sit back and admire them."

JOHN RUDGE, Port Vale manager, looking up from the bottom of Div. 1 last December: "I give the players £20 for a round of drinks when they keep a clean sheet. I wish I was a couple of hundred quid worse off."

Message on answerphone of Wimbledon manager **JOE KINNEAR**: "I'm sorry I'm not here at the moment. If you are the president of AC Milan, Barcelona or Real Madrid, I'll get back to you."

THOMAS LELEUX, who has visited all 92 League grounds, just to buy the club scarves: "People think I'm potty, but I never get chilly."

BILL SHANKLY again: "A good football side is made up of some youngsters, old heads, a good captain, 100 per cent effort players and the odd marionette."

UNIBOND LEAGUE

PREMIER DIVISION

		P	W	D	L	F	A	Pts
1	Bamber Bridge	42	20	16	6	81	49	76
2	Boston United	42	23	6	13	86	59	75
3	Hyde United	42	21	11	10	86	51	74
4	Barrow	42	20	13	9	69	42	73
5	Gainsborough Trinity	42	20	13	9	60	41	73
6	Blyth Spartans	42	17	13	12	75	61	64
7	Accrington Stanley	42	17	14	11	62	54	62
8	Emley	42	17	10	15	57	53	61
9	Spennymoor United	42	14	18	10	67	61	60
10	Guiseley	42	15	14	13	62	57	59
11	Bishop Auckland	42	16	11	15	60	55	59
12	Marine	42	15	14	13	59	54	59
13	Witton Albion	42	17	8	17	60	62	59
14	Chorley	42	14	9	19	67	74	51
15	Knowsley United	42	14	6	22	61	89	48
16	Winsford United	42	10	16	16	56	79	46
17	Leek Town	42	10	15	17	52	55	45
18	Colwyn Bay	42	8	21	13	43	57	45
19	Frickley Athletic	42	11	14	17	63	87	44
20	Buxton	42	9	11	22	43	72	38
21	Droylsden	42	10	8	24	58	100	38
22	Matlock Town	42	8	11	23	71	86	35

First Div. – 1 Lancaster City; 2 Alfreton Town.

LEAGUE OF WALES

		P	W	D	L	F	A	Pts
1	Barry Town	40	30	7	3	92	23	97
2	Newtown	40	23	11	6	69	25	80
3	Conwy United	40	21	13	6	101	58	76
4	Bangor City	40	21	6	13	72	65	69
5	Flint Town United	40	19	9	12	76	57	66
6	Caernarfon Town	40	16	13	11	77	59	61
7	Cwmbran Town	40	14	15	11	58	49	57
8	Inter Cardiff	40	14	12	14	62	62	54
9	Caersws	40	15	9	16	81	97	54
10	Connah's Quay Nomads	40	13	14	13	68	63	53
11	Ebbw Vale	40	14	11	15	59	56	53
12	Llansantffraid	40	14	10	16	66	57	52
13	CPD Porthmadog	40	13	11	16	56	62	50
14	Aberystwyth Town	40	13	9	18	60	68	48
15	Cemaes Bay	40	13	7	20	63	80	46
16	Holywell Town	40	12	7	21	53	74	43
17	Briton Ferry Athletic	40	11	7	20	64	91	42
18	Rhyl	40	11	9	20	47	83	42
19	Ton Pentre	40	8	16	16	46	65	40
20	Afan Lido	40	9	9	22	33	71	36
21	Llanelli	40	8	9	23	50	88	33

FEDERATION BREWERY NORTHERN LEAGUE

DIVISION ONE

		P	W	D	L	F	A	Pts
1	Billingham Synthonia	38	24	8	6	78	34	80
2	Bedlington Terriers	38	22	12	4	90	37	78
3	Durham City	38	24	6	8	85	35	78
4	Tow Law Town	38	23	9	6	82	43	78
5	Whitby Town	38	21	7	10	100	59	70
6	Guisborough Town	38	20	8	10	80	54	68
7	Dunston FB	38	20	8	10	75	52	68
8	West Auckland Town	38	19	5	14	66	57	62
9	Crook Town	38	17	9	12	59	41	60
10	Consett	38	17	7	14	76	64	58
11	Stockton	38	16	8	14	88	71	56
12	Shildon	38	16	3	19	74	74	51
13	Seaham Red Star	38	13	11	14	62	66	50
14	Murton	38	12	11	15	57	53	47
15	RTM Newcastle	38	13	7	18	68	58	46
16	Chester-le-St-Town	38	11	9	18	72	78	42
17	Whickham	38	11	8	19	43	77	41
18	Peterlee	38	5	4	29	40	96	19
19	Eppleton CW	38	2	3	33	26	153	9
20	Ferryhill Athletic	38	0	5	33	27	146	5

Div. 2 – 1 Morpeth Town; 2 South Shields; 3 Easington.

CARLING NORTH WEST LEAGUE

DIVISION ONE

		P	W	D	L	F	A	Pts
1	Flixton	42	28	8	6	85	30	92
2	Newcastle Town	42	26	7	9	88	42	85
3	Trafford	42	26	5	11	89	45	83
4	Mossley	42	24	8	10	87	59	80
5	Burscough	42	23	8	11	77	40	77
6	Bootle	42	23	5	14	74	55	74
7	Clitheroe	42	20	12	10	63	44	72
8	St. Helens Town	42	19	13	10	71	53	70
9	Nantwich Town	42	20	7	15	64	59	67
10	Prescot Cables	42	17	11	14	70	66	62
11	Holker Old Boys	42	19	4	19	77	72	61
12	Glossop North End	42	15	15	12	55	48	60
13	Kidsgrove Athletic	42	15	9	18	61	64	54
14	Eastwood Hanley	42	12	15	15	60	57	51
15	Maine Road	42	12	14	16	60	71	50
16	Chadderton	42	14	8	20	52	69	50
17	Blackpool Rovers	42	11	9	22	49	74	42
18	Penrith	42	9	12	21	57	69	39
19	Darwen	42	9	10	23	57	77	37
20	Salford City	42	10	5	27	49	93	35
21	Rossendale United	42	6	10	26	32	114	28
22	Skelmersdale United	42	5	3	34	45	121	18

Div. 2 – 1 Vauxhall GM; 2 Atherton Collieries.

BEAZER HOMES LEAGUE

PREMIER DIVISION

		P	W	D	L	F	A	Pts
1	Rushden & Diamonds	42	29	7	6	99	41	94
2	Halesowen Town	42	27	11	4	70	36	92
3	Cheltenham Town	42	21	11	10	76	57	74
4	Gloucester City	42	21	8	13	65	47	71
5	Gresley Rovers	42	20	10	12	70	58	70
6	Worcester City	42	19	12	11	61	43	69
7	Merthyr Tydfil	42	19	6	17	67	59	63
8	Hastings Town	42	16	13	13	68	56	61
9	Crawley Town	42	15	13	14	57	56	58
10	Sudbury Town	42	15	10	17	69	71	55
11	Gravesend & Northfleet	42	15	10	17	60	62	55
12	Chelmsford City	42	13	16	13	46	53	55
13	Dorchester Town	42	15	8	19	62	57	53
14	Newport AFC	42	13	13	16	53	59	52
15	Salisbury City	42	14	10	18	57	69	52
16	Burton Albion	42	13	12	17	55	56	51
17	Atherstone United	42	12	12	18	58	75	48
18	Baldock Town	42	11	14	17	51	56	47
19	Cambridge City	42	12	10	20	56	68	46
20	Stafford Rangers	42	11	10	21	53	87	43
21	Ilkeston Town	42	11	4	27	58	90	37
22	VS Rugby	42	5	10	27	37	92	25

Midland Div. – 1 Nuneaton Borough; 2 King's Lynn.
Southern Div. – 1 Sittingbourne; 2 Ashford Town.

ICIS LEAGUE

PREMIER DIVISION

		P	W	D	L	F	A	Pts
1	Hayes	42	24	14	4	76	32	86
2	Enfield	42	26	8	8	78	35	86
3	Boreham Wood	42	24	11	7	69	29	83
4	Yeovil Town	42	23	11	8	83	51	80
5	Dulwich Hamlet	42	23	11	8	85	59	80
6	Carshalton Athletic	42	22	8	12	68	49	74
7	St. Albans City	42	20	12	10	70	41	72
8	Kingstonian	42	20	11	11	62	38	71
9	Harrow Borough	42	19	10	13	70	56	67
10	Sutton United	42	17	14	11	71	56	65
11	Aylesbury United	42	17	12	13	71	58	63
12	Bishop's Stortford	42	16	9	17	61	62	57
13	Yeading	42	11	14	17	48	60	47
14	Hendon	42	12	10	20	52	65	46
15	Chertsey Town	42	13	6	23	45	71	45
16	Purfleet	42	12	8	22	48	67	44
17	Grays Athletic	42	11	11	20	43	63	44
18	Hitchin Town	42	10	10	22	41	74	40
19	Bromley	42	10	7	25	52	91	37
20	Molesey	42	9	9	24	46	81	36
21	Walton & Hersham	42	9	7	26	42	79	34
22	Worthing	42	4	7	31	42	106	19

Div. 1 – 1 Oxford City; 2 Heybridge Swifts; 3 Staines Town.

JEWSON WESSEX LEAGUE

FIRST DIVISION

		P	W	D	L	F	A	Pts
1	Thatcham Town	40	28	8	4	73	27	92
2	Lymington AFC	40	28	7	5	100	31	91
3	Ryde	40	25	8	7	92	41	83
4	Eastleigh	40	21	13	6	83	50	76
5	Christchurch	40	21	8	11	66	49	71
6	Wimborne Town	40	20	6	14	85	61	66
7	Bournemouth	40	17	13	10	85	40	64
8	Bemerton HH	40	18	8	14	67	63	62
9	Andover	40	18	7	15	101	70	61
10	East Cowes Vics	40	17	8	15	60	60	59
11	Gosport Borough	40	16	9	15	59	58	57
12	Downton	40	16	6	18	65	73	54
13	Whitchurch United	40	12	13	15	66	76	49
14	Totton AFC	40	10	13	17	55	66	43
15	BAT	40	10	12	18	44	58	42
16	Cowes Sports	40	11	7	22	38	76	40
17	Portsmouth RN	40	10	8	22	52	84	38
18	Aerostructures	40	9	10	21	41	71	37
19	Brockenhurst	40	11	4	25	42	74	37
20	Petersfield Town	40	8	4	28	53	93	28
21	Swanage Town & H	40	6	4	30	32	138	22

JEWSON SOUTH WESTERN

FIRST DIVISION

		P	W	D	L	F	A	Pts
1	Truro City	34	26	4	4	99	27	82
2	Torpoint Athletic	34	23	8	3	81	32	77
3	Falmouth Town	34	22	4	8	89	37	70
4	Launceston	34	20	9	5	95	29	69
5	Bodmin Town	34	18	10	6	91	36	64
6	Penzance	34	18	5	11	64	43	59
7	Newquay	34	18	4	12	73	54	58
8	Holsworthy	34	17	5	12	58	43	56
9	Wadebridge Town	34	16	5	13	65	55	53
10	Saltash United	34	14	8	12	66	67	50
11	Porthleven	34	13	5	16	61	64	44
12	St. Austell	34	10	5	19	57	78	35
13	Millbrook	34	9	7	18	60	58	34
14	Liskeard Athletic	34	9	6	19	58	96	33
15	Appledore BAAC	34	7	7	20	43	80	28
16	Tavistock	34	6	6	22	55	99	24
17	St. Blazey	34	4	4	26	38	106	16
18	Okehampton	34	4	2	28	24	143	14

SCOTTISH HIGHLAND LEAGUE

		P	W	D	L	F	A	Pts
1	Huntly	30	27	0	3	103	34	81
2	Cove Rangers	30	20	5	5	74	35	65
3	Lossiemouth	30	18	3	9	54	37	57
4	Peterhead	30	16	7	7	74	51	55
5	Fraserburgh	30	14	9	7	85	46	51
6	Keith	30	14	6	10	59	40	48
7	Elgin City	30	15	3	12	59	55	48
8	Brora Rangers	30	12	5	13	40	50	41
9	Deveronvale	30	12	3	15	47	53	39
10	Wick Academy	30	11	5	14	42	63	38
11	Clachnacuddin	30	9	7	14	45	61	34
12	Buckie Thistle	30	8	8	14	45	61	32
13	Forres Mechanics	30	6	8	16	38	51	28
14	Fort William	30	8	2	20	27	71	26
15	Rothes	30	4	8	18	39	74	20
16	Nairn County	30	4	5	21	26	85	17

EAST OF SCOTLAND LEAGUE

PREMIER DIVISION

		P	W	D	L	F	A	Pts
1	Whitehill Welfare	18	16	0	2	71	14	48
2	Gala Fairydean	18	10	4	4	37	25	34
3	Annan Athletic	18	9	6	3	41	30	33
4	Spartans	18	8	2	8	24	32	26
5	Craigroyston	18	6	4	8	33	37	22
6	Pencaitland	18	5	6	7	25	28	21
7	Preston Athletic	18	4	7	7	29	42	19
8	Edinburgh University	18	3	6	9	18	31	15
9	Vale of Leithen	18	3	6	9	28	50	15
10	Civil Service Strollers	18	3	5	10	24	41	14

F.A. WOMEN'S PREMIER LEAGUE

NATIONAL DIVISION

		P	W	D	L	F	A	Pts
1	Croydon	18	13	5	0	58	17	44
2	Doncaster Belles	18	14	2	2	57	19	44
3	Arsenal	18	11	4	3	54	12	37
4	Everton	18	10	1	7	44	40	31
5	Liverpool	18	9	2	7	36	27	29
6	Wembley	18	7	5	6	43	21	26
7	Millwall Lionesses	18	5	3	10	20	32	18
8	Ilkeston Town	18	4	3	11	21	46	15
9	Villa Aztecs	18	4	1	13	22	51	13
10	Wolverhampton Wanderers	18	0	0	18	8	98	0

SOUTHERN DIVISION

		P	W	D	L	F	A	Pts
1	Southampton Saints	18	13	2	3	52	21	41
2	Berkhamsted Town	18	13	1	4	42	26	40
3	Wimbledon	18	12	1	5	53	36	37
4	Three Bridges	18	11	1	6	47	24	34
5	Ipswich Town	18	8	1	9	36	35	25
6	Brighton & Hove Albion	18	5	4	9	35	47	19
7	Town & County	18	6	1	11	27	48	19
8	*Leyton Orient	18	5	2	11	33	45	16
9	Oxford United	18	4	4	10	24	46	16
10	Brentford	18	3	3	12	29	50	12

** 1 point deducted.*

NORTHERN DIVISION

		P	W	D	L	F	A	Pts
1	Tranmere Rovers	16	14	2	0	73	11	44
2	Huddersfield Town	16	12	3	1	60	23	39
3	Garswood/St. Helens	16	9	4	3	51	23	31
4	Sheffield Wednesday	16	9	3	4	41	22	30
5	*Langford	16	6	2	8	27	44	17
6	RTM Newcastle Kestrels	16	3	4	9	21	43	13
7	Notts County	16	4	1	11	18	43	13
8	Kidderminster Harriers	16	4	1	11	27	53	13
9	Bronte	16	0	2	14	11	67	2

** 3 points deducted.*

UK LIVING F.A. WOMEN'S CUP FINAL

Sunday, April 28 (at Millwall – att: 2,500):
Croydon 1, Liverpool 1 (aet)
(Croydon won 4-2 on penalties)

EUROPEAN CUP FINALS

1956 Real Madrid 4, Rheims 3 (Paris)
1957 Real Madrid 2, Fiorentina 0 (Madrid)
1958† Real Madrid 3, AC Milan 2 (Brussels)
1959 Real Madrid 2, Rheims 0 (Stuttgart)
1960 Real Madrid 7, Eintracht Frankfurt 3 (Glasgow)
1961 Benfica 3, Barcelona 2 (Berne)
1962 Benfica 5, Real Madrid 3 (Amsterdam)
1963 AC Milan 2, Benfica 1 (Wembley)
1964 Inter Milan 3, Real Madrid 1 (Vienna)
1965 Inter Milan 1, Benfica 0 (Milan)
1966 Real Madrid 2, Partizan Belgrade 1 (Brussels)
1967 Celtic 2, Inter Milan 1 (Lisbon)
1968† Manchester United 4, Benfica 1 (Wembley)
1969 AC Milan 4, Ajax 1 (Madrid)
1970† Feyenoord 2, Celtic 1 (Milan)
1971 Ajax 2, Panathinaikos 0 (Wembley)
1972 Ajax 2, Inter Milan 0 (Rotterdam)
1973 Ajax 1, Juventus 0 (Belgrade)
1974 Bayern Munich 4, Atletico Madrid 0 (replay Brussels, after a 1-1 draw, Brussels)
1975 Bayern Munich 2, Leeds United 0 (Paris)
1976 Bayern Munich 1, St. Etienne 0 (Glasgow)
1977 Liverpool 3, Borussia Moenchengladbach 1 (Rome)
1978 Liverpool 1, Brugge 0 (Wembley)
1979 Nottingham Forest 1, Malmo 0 (Munich)
1980 Nottingham Forest 1, Hamburg 0 (Madrid)
1981 Liverpool 1, Real Madrid 0 (Paris)
1982 Aston Villa 1, Bayern Munich 0 (Rotterdam)
1983 SV Hamburg 1, Juventus 0 (Athens)
1984† Liverpool 1, AS Roma 1 (Liverpool won 4-2 on penalties) (Rome)
1985 Juventus 1, Liverpool 0 (Brussels)
1986† Steaua Bucharest 0, Barcelona 0 (Steaua won 2-0 on penalties) (Seville)
1987 Porto 2, Bayern Munich 1 (Vienna)
1988† PSV Eindhoven 0, Benfica 0 (PSV won 6-5 on penalties) (Stuttgart)
1989 AC Milan 4, Steaua Bucharest 0 (Barcelona)
1990 AC Milan 1, Benfica 0 (Vienna)
1991† Red Star Belgrade 0, Marseille 0 (Red Star won 5-3 on penalties) (Bari)
1992 Barcelona 1, Sampdoria 0 (Wembley)
1993 Marseille 1, AC Milan 0 (Munich)
1994 AC Milan 4, Barcelona 0 (Athens)
1995 Ajax 1, AC Milan 0 (Vienna)
1996† Juventus 1, Ajax 1 (Juventus won 4-2 on penalties) (Vienna)

(† After extra time)

EUROPEAN CUP FINAL

AJAX 1, JUVENTUS 1 (aet)
(Juventus won 4-2 on penalties)
Rome (67,000), Wednesday, May 22, 1996

Ajax: Van der Sar; Blind, F. de Boer (Scholten 66), Bogarde, R. de Boer, George, Davids, Musampa (Kluivert 45), Silooy, Kanu, Litmanen. **Scorer:** Litmanen (41).

Juventus: Peruzzi; Ferrara, Vierchowod, Pessotto, Torricelli, Sousa (Di Livio 58), Deschamps, Conte (Jugovic 43), Del Piero, Vialli, Ravanelli (Padovano 78). **Scorer:** Ravanelli (13).

Referee: M. Diaz Vega (Spain). **Half-time:** 1-1. **90 mins**: 1-1.

Penalty shoot-out (Ajax first): Davids (saved), Ferrara (0-1), Litmanen (1-1), Pessotto (1-2), Scholten (2-2), Padovano (2-3), Silooy (saved), Jugovic (2-4).

• Gianluca Vialli lifted the European Cup in his farewell match for Juventus before signing for Chelsea.

CUP-WINNERS' CUP FINALS

1961	Fiorentina beat Rangers 4-1 on agg. (Glasgow first leg. Florence second leg)
1962	Atletico Madrid beat Fiorentina 3-0 (replay Stuttgart, after a 1-1 draw, Glasgow)
1963	Tottenham Hotspur beat Atletico Madrid 5-1 (Rotterdam)
1964	Sporting Lisbon beat MTK Budapest 1-0 (replay Antwerp, after a 3-3 draw, Brussels)
1965	West Ham United beat Munich 1860 2-0 (Wembley)
1966†	Borussia Dortmund beat Liverpool 2-1 (Glasgow)
1967†	Bayern Munich beat Rangers 1-0 (Nuremberg)
1968	AC Milan beat SV Hamburg 2-0 (Rotterdam)
1969	Slovan Bratislava beat Barcelona 3-2 (Basle)
1970	Manchester City beat Gornik Zabrze 2-1 (Vienna)
1971†	Chelsea beat Real Madrid 2-1 (replay Athens, after a 1-1 draw, Athens)
1972	Rangers beat Moscow Dynamo 3-2 (Barcelona)
1973	AC Milan beat Leeds United 1-0 (Salonika)
1974	Magdeburg beat AC Milan 2-0 (Rotterdam)
1975	Dynamo Kiev beat Ferencvaros 3-0 (Basle)
1976	Anderlecht beat West Ham United 4-2 (Brussels)
1977	SV Hamburg beat Anderlecht 2-0 (Amsterdam)
1978	Anderlecht beat Austria WAC 4-0 (Paris)
1979†	Barcelona beat Fortuna Dusseldorf 4-3 (Basle)
1980†	Valencia beat Arsenal 5-4 on penalties after a 0-0 draw (Brussels)
1981	Dynamo Tbilisi beat Carl Zeiss Jena 2-1 (Dusseldorf)
1982	Barcelona beat Standard Liege 2-1 (Barcelona)
1983†	Aberdeen beat Real Madrid 2-1 (Gothenburg)
1984	Juventus beat Porto 2-1 (Basle)
1985	Everton beat Rapid Vienna 3-1 (Rotterdam)
1986	Dynamo Kiev beat Atletico Madrid 3-0 (Lyon)
1987	Ajax beat Lokomotiv Leipzig 1-0 (Athens)
1988	Mechelen beat Ajax 1-0 (Strasbourg)
1989	Barcelona beat Sampdoria 2-0 (Berne)
1990	Sampdoria beat Anderlecht 2-0 (Gothenburg)
1991	Manchester United beat Barcelona 2-1 (Rotterdam)
1992	Werder Bremen beat Monaco 2-0 (Lisbon)
1993	Parma beat Royal Antwerp 3-1 (Wembley)
1994	Arsenal beat Parma 1-0 (Copenhagen)
1995†	Real Zaragoza beat Arsenal 2-1 (Paris)
1996	Paris St. Germain beat Rapid Vienna 1-0 (Brussels)

(† After extra time)

CUP-WINNERS' CUP FINAL

PARIS ST. GERMAIN 1, RAPID VIENNA 0

Brussels (37,500), Wednesday, May 8, 1996

Paris St. Germain: Lama; Fournier, N'Gotty, Roche, Le Guen, Colleter, Bravo, Guerin, Djorkaeff, Rai (Valdes 12), Loko. **Scorer:** N'Gotty (29).

Rapid Vienna: Konsel; Hatz, Guggi, Ivanov, Schoettel, Stoeger, Stumpf, Marasek, Jancker, Kuehbauer, Heraf.

UEFA CUP FINALS

1972 Tottenham Hotspur beat Wolverhampton Wanderers 3-2 on agg. (2-1a, 1-1h)
1973 Liverpool beat Borussia Moenchengladbach 3-2 on agg. (3-0h, 0-2a)
1974 Feyenoord beat Tottenham Hotspur 4-2 on agg. (2-2a, 2-0h)
1975 Borussia Moenchengladbach beat Twente Enschede 5-1 on agg. (0-0h, 5-1a)
1976 Liverpool beat Brugge 4-3 on agg. (3-2h, 1-1a)
1977 Juventus beat Atletico Bilbao on away goals after 2-2 agg. (1-0h, 1-2a)
1978 PSV Eindhoven beat Bastia 3-0 on agg. (0-0a, 3-0h)
1979 Borussia Moenchengladbach beat Red Star Belgrade 2-1 on agg. (1-1a, 1-0h)
1980 Eintracht Frankfurt beat Borussia Moenchengladbach on away goals after 3-3 agg. (2-3a, 1-0h)
1981 Ipswich Town beat AZ 67 Alkmaar 5-4 on agg. (3-0h, 2-4a)
1982 IFK Gothenburg beat SV Hamburg 4-0 on agg. (1-0h, 3-0a)
1983 Anderlecht beat Benfica 2-1 on agg. (1-0h, 1-1a)
1984 Tottenham Hotspur beat Anderlecht 4-3 on penalties after 2-2 agg. (1-1a, 1-1h)
1985 Real Madrid beat Videoton 3-1 on agg. (3-0a, 0-1h)
1986 Real Madrid beat Cologne 5-3 on agg. (5-1h, 0-2a)
1987 IFK Gothenburg beat Dundee United 2-1 on agg. (1-0h, 1-1a)
1988 Bayer Leverkusen beat Espanol 3-2 on penalties after 3-3 agg. (0-3a, 3-0h)
1989 Napoli beat VfB Stuttgart 5-4 on agg. (2-1h, 3-3a)
1990 Juventus beat Fiorentina 3-1 on agg. (3-1h, 0-0a)
1991 Inter Milan beat AS Roma 2-1 on agg. (2-0h, 0-1a)
1992 Ajax beat Torino on away goals after 2-2 agg. (2-2a, 0-0h)
1993 Juventus beat Borussia Dortmund 6-1 on agg. (3-1a, 3-0h)
1994 Inter Milan beat Salzburg 2-0 on agg. (1-0a, 1-0h)
1995 Parma beat Juventus 2-1 on agg. (1-0h, 1-1a)
1996 Bayern Munich beat Bordeaux 5-1 on agg. (2-0h, 3-1a)

FAIRS CUP FINALS

(As UEFA Cup previously known)

1958 Barcelona beat London 8-2 on agg. (2-2a, 6-0h)
1960 Barcelona beat Birmingham 4-1 on agg. (0-0a, 4-1h)
1961 AS Roma beat Birmingham City 4-2 on agg. (2-2a, 2-0h)
1962 Valencia beat Barcelona 7-3 on agg. (6-2h, 1-1a)
1963 Valencia beat Dynamo Zagreb 4-1 on agg. (2-1a, 2-0h)
1964 Real Zaragoza beat Valencia 2-1 (Barcelona)
1965 Ferencvaros beat Juventus 1-0 (Turin)
1966 Barcelona beat Real Zaragoza 4-3 on agg. (0-1h, 4-2a)
1967 Dynamo Zagreb beat Leeds United 2-0 on agg. (2-0h, 0-0a)
1968 Leeds United beat Ferencvaros 1-0 on agg. (1-0h, 0-0a)
1969 Newcastle United beat Ujpest Dozsa 6-2 on agg. (3-0h, 3-2a)
1970 Arsenal beat Anderlecht 4-3 on agg. (1-3a, 3-0h)
1971 Leeds United beat Juventus on away goals after 3-3 agg. (2-2a, 1-1h)

UEFA CUP FINAL

First Leg, Wednesday, May 1, 1996

BAYERN MUNICH 2, BORDEAUX 0 (Att: 63,000)

Bayern Munich: Kahn; Helmer, Babbel, Kreutzer, Hamann, Sforza, Matthaus, (Frey 53), Scholl, Ziege, Klinsmann, Papin (Witeczek 68). **Scorers:** Helmer (35), Scholl (60).

Bordeaux: Huard; Friis-Hansen, Grenet, Dogon, Lizarazu, Lucas, Croci, Bancarel, Dutuel, Witschge, Tholot (Anselin 89).

Second Leg, Wednesday, May 15, 1996

BORDEAUX 1, BAYERN MUNICH 3 (Att: 36,000)

Bordeaux: Huard; Bancarel, Lizarazu (Anselin 32), Friis-Hansen, Dogon, Lucas (Grenet 79), Zidane, Croci (Dutuel 57), Tholot, Witschge, Dugarry. **Scorer:** Dutuel 75.

Bayern Munich: Kahn; Babbel, Ziege, Strunz, Helmer, Frey (Zickler 60), Scholl, Sforza, Klinsmann, Matthaus, Kostadinov (Witeczek 75). **Scorers:** Scholl 53, Kostadinov 66, Klinsmann 77.

• Winning their first European trophy for 20 years, Bayern became the fourth club to succeed in all 3 Euro competitions (after Ajax, Juventus and Barcelona). They won the Cup-Winners' Cup in 1967, and the European Cup in 1974-75-76.

Club president Franz Beckenbauer took charge of the team after Otto Rehhagel was sacked just before this Final, and now won a European prize as coach after doing so as a player.

Jurgen Klinsmann, with 15 goals for Bayern in the 1995-6 UEFA Cup, became the highest individual scorer in 1 season of European competition. Previous resord of 14 was shared by Jose Altafini (AC Milan 1962-3) and John Wark (Ipswich 1980-1).

BRITISH AND IRISH CLUBS IN EUROPE 1995-96

EUROPEAN CUP

Preliminary Round: Rangers beat Anorthosis Famagusta (Cyprus) 1-0 (1-0h, 0-0a).

Champions' League (Gp. B): **Blackburn** 0, Spartak Moscow 1; Rosenborg 2, **Blackburn** 1; Legia Warsaw 1, **Blackburn** 0; **Blackburn** 0, Legia Warsaw 0; Spartak Moscow 3, **Blackburn** 0; **Blackburn** 4, Rosenborg 1.

Champions' League (Gp. C): Steaua Bucharest 1, **Rangers** 0; **Rangers** 2, Borussia Dortmund 2; Juventus 4, **Rangers** 1; **Rangers** 0 Juventus 4; **Rangers** 1, Steaua Bucharest 1; Borussia Dortmund 2, **Rangers** 2.

CUP-WINNERS' CUP

Preliminary Round: Linfield lost to Shakytyor (Ukraine) 1-5 (0-1h, 1-4a); **Derry** lost to Lokomotiv Sofia (Bulgaria) 1-2 (1-0h, 0-2a); **Wrexham** lost to Petrolul Ploiestii (Romania) 0-1 (0-0h, 0-1a).

First Round: Celtic beat Dinamo Batumi (Georgia) 7-2 (4-0h, 3-2a); **Everton** beat KR Reykjavik (Iceland) 6-3 (3-1h, 3-2a).

Second Round: **Celtic** lost to Paris St. Germain (France) 0-4 (0-3h, 0-1a); **Everton** lost to Feyenoord (Holland) 0-1 (0-0h, 0-1a).

UEFA CUP

Preliminary Round: **Bangor City** (Wales) lost to Widzew Lodz (Poland) 0-5 (0-4h, 0-1a); **Motherwell** lost to MyPa-47 (Finland) on away goals (1-3h, 2-0a); **Crusaders** lost to Silkeborg (Denmark) 1-6 (1-2h, 0-4a); **Afan Lido** lost to RAF Riga (Latvia) 1-2 (1-2h, 0-0a); **Raith** beat Gotu Itrottarfelag (Faroe Islands) 6-2 (4-0h, 2-2a); **Dundalk** lost to Malmo (Sweden) 0-4 (0-2h, 0-2a); **Shelbourne** lost to Akranes (Iceland) 0-6 (0-3h, 0-3a); **Glenavon** beat Hafnarfjordur (Iceland) 1-0 (0-0h, 1-0a).

First Round: **Raith** beat Akranes 3-2 (3-1h, 0-1a); **Leeds** beat Monaco (France) 3-1 (0-1h, 3-0a); **Liverpool** beat Spartak Vladikavkaz (Russia) 2-1 (0-0h, 2-1a); **Man. United** lost to Rotor Volgograd (Russia) on away goals (2-2h, 0-0a); **Nott'm Forest** beat Malmo on away goal (1-0h, 1-2a); **Glenavon** lost to Werder Bremen (Germany) 0-7 (0-2h, 0-5a).

Second Round: **Raith** lost to Bayern Munich (Germany) 1-4 (0-2h, 1-2a); **Liverpool** lost to Brondby (Denmark) 0-1 (0-1h, 0-0a); **Nott'm Forest** beat Auxerre (France) 1-0 (0-0h, 1-0a); **Leeds** lost to PSV Eindhoven (Holland) 3-8 (3-5h, 0-3a).

Third Round: **Nott'm Forest** beat Lyon (France) 1-0 (1-0h, 0-0a).

Quarter-final: Nott'm Forest lost to Bayern Munich 2-7 (1-5h, 1-2a).

EUROPEAN TROPHY WINNERS – SUMMARY

European Cup (41 competitions, 20 different winners): **6** Real Madrid; **5** AC Milan; **4** Ajax Amsterdam, Liverpool; **3** Bayern Munich; **2** Benfica, Inter Milan, Juventus, Nott'm. Forest; **1** Aston Villa, Barcelona, Celtic, Feyenoord, Hamburg SV, Man. United, Marseille, PSV Eindhoven, FC Porto, Red Star Belgrade, Steaua Bucharest.

Cup-Winners' Cup (36 competitions, 31 different winners): **3** Barcelona; **2** Anderlecht, Dynamo Kiev, AC Milan; **1** Aberdeen, Ajax Amsterdam, Arsenal, Atletico Madrid, Bayern Munich, Borussia Dortmund, Chelsea, Dynamo Tbilisi, Everton, Fiorentina, Hamburg SV, Juventus, Magdeburg, Man. City, Man. United, Mechelen, Paris St. Germain, Parma, Rangers, Real Zaragoza, Sampdoria, Slovan Bratislava, Sporting Lisbon, Tottenham, Valencia, Werder Bremen, West Ham.

UEFA Cup (orig. Fairs Cup) (38 competitions, 26 different winners): **3** Barcelona, Juventus; **2** Borussia Moenchengladbach, IFK Gothenburg, Inter Milan, Leeds, Liverpool, Real Madrid, Tottenham, Valencia; **1** Ajax Amsterdam, Anderlecht, Arsenal, Bayer Leverkusen, Bayern Munich, Dynamo Zagreb, Eintracht Frankfurt, PSV Eindhoven, Ferencvaros, Feyenoord, Ipswich, Napoli, Newcastle, Parma, Real Zaragoza, AS Roma.

EUROPE'S TOP CLUBS 1995-96

(Source: *World Soccer*)

Country	Champions	P	W	D	L	F	A	Pts
Belgium	Club Bruges	34	25	6	3	83	30	81
Bulgaria	Slavia Sofia	30	20	7	3	51	14	67
Croatia	FC Croatia Zagreb	10	7	0	3	28	14	26*
Cyprus	Apoel Nicosia	26	19	7	0	65	21	64
Czech. Rep.	Slavia Prague	30	23	1	6	68	28	70
England	Manchester United	38	25	7	6	73	35	82
Finland	Haka Valkeakoski	26	18	5	3	56	17	59
France	Auxerre	38	22	6	10	66	30	72
Germany	Borussia Dortmund	34	19	11	4	76	38	68
Greece	Panathinaikos	34	26	5	3	72	22	83
Holland	Ajax	34	26	5	3	97	24	83
Italy	AC Milan	34	21	10	3	60	24	73
Luxembourg	Jeunesse D'Esch	22	15	3	4	59	19	48
N. Ireland	Portadown	28	16	8	4	61	41	56
Norway	Rosenborg	26	19	5	2	78	29	62
Portugal	FC Porto	34	26	6	2	84	20	84
Rep. of Ireland	St. Patrick's	33	19	10	4	53	34	67
Romania	Steaua Bucharest	34	23	8	3	72	25	77
Russia	Alania Vladikavkaz	30	23	4	3	64	21	73
Scotland	Rangers	36	27	6	3	85	25	87
Spain	Atletico Madrid	42	26	9	7	75	32	87
Sweden	IFK Gothenburg	26	12	10	4	43	20	46
Switzerland	Grasshopper	14	8	6	0	26	7	52†
Turkey	Fenerbahce	34	26	6	2	68	19	84
Yugoslavia	Partizan Belgrade	18	13	3	2	51	17	60*

Other Champions: **Albania**: FK Tirana; **Armenia**: Pyounik Erevan; **Estonia**: Flora Tallinn; **Georgia**: Dinamo Tbilisi; **Hungary**: Ferencvaros; **Israel**: Maccabi Tel Aviv; **Malta**: Sliema Wanderers; **Moldavia**: Zimbru Chisinau; **Poland**: Widzew Lodz; **Slovakia**: Slovan Bratislava; **Slovenia**: HIT Gorica; **Ukraine**: Dynamo Kiev; **Wales**: Barry Town.

† after play-offs
* Incl. bonus points.

QUOTE-UNQUOTE

MATTHEW LE TISSIER, when Graham Taylor resigned as England manager: "Whoever gets the job, I've got to have a better chance now of fulfilling my International ambitions."

COLIN MURPHY after Notts County were paired with Telford in last season's F.A. Cup second round: "A cup draw is like a woman. You should always want who you end up with."

KEVIN KEEGAN, at half-time, to the Newcastle players, losing 1-0 at home to Bristol City (Coca-Cola Cup 2nd. Round. 2nd leg): "If things don't improve, I'm going home." Newcastle won 3-1 (8-1 agg.).

OSSIE ARDILES, sacked last October after ten games as coach of Guadalajara, Mexico, and a year after his dismissal by Tottenham: "It's still a wonderful job from Monday morning until 3 o'clock on Saturday. After that it's purgatory."

MIKE INGHAM (BBC Radio 5) when Liverpool led Aston Villa 3-0 after eight minutes last March: "I imagine Villa would quite like to hear the final whistle now."

WORLD CLUB CUP 1995 FINAL

AJAX 0, GREMIO (Brazil) 0

After extra time; Ajax won 4-3 on pens.
Tokyo (60,000), Tuesday, November 28, 1995

Ajax: Van der Sar; Reiziger, Blind (Capt.), F. de Boer, George, Bogarde, R. de Boer, Davids, Litmanen (Reuser 95), Kluivert, Overmars (Kanu 69). **Coach**: Louis van Gaal.

Gremio: Danrlei; Francisco Arce, Rivarola, Adilson, Roger (Capt.), Goiano, Dinho, Arilson (Luciano 62), Carlos Miguel (Gelson 97), Paulo Nunes, Jardel (Magno 79). **Sent-off**: Rivarola (56). **Coach**: Luis Felipe.

Referee: D. Elleray (England).

COMPLETE RESULTS

(Played as a single match in Tokyo since 1980)

Year	Winners	Runners-up	Score
1960	Real Madrid (Spa.)	Penarol (Uru.)	0-0 5-1
1961	Penarol (Uru.)	Benfica (Por.)	0-1 2-1 5-0
1962	Santos (Bra.)	Benfica (Por.)	3-2 5-2
1963	Santos (Bra.)	AC Milan (Ita.)	2-4 4-2 1-0
1964	Inter Milan (Ita.)	Independiente (Arg.)	0-1 2-0 1-0
1965	Inter Milan (Ita.)	Independiente (Arg.)	3-0 0-0
1966	Penarol (Uru.)	Real Madrid (Spa.)	2-0 2-0
1967	Racing (Arg.)	Celtic (Sco.)	0-1 2-1 1-0
1968	Estudiantes (Arg.)	Manchester Utd. (Eng.)	1-0 1-1
1969	AC Milan (Ita.)	Estudiantes (Arg.)	3-0 1-2
1970	Feyenoord (Hol.)	Estudiantes (Arg.)	2-2 1-0
1971	Nacional (Uru.)	Panathanaikos (Gre.)*	1-1 2-1
1972	Ajax (Hol.)	Independiente (Arg.)	1-1 3-0
1973	Independiente (Arg.)	Juventus (Ita.)*	1-0
1974	Atletico Madrid (Spa.)*	Independiente (Arg.)	0-1 2-0
1975	Not played		
1976	Bayern Munich (W.Ger.)	Cruzeiro (Bra.)	2-0 0-0
1977	Boca Juniors (Arg.)	Borussia Mönchengladbach (W.Ger.)*	2-2 3-0
1978	Not played		
1979	Olimpia Asuncion (Par.)	Malmö (Swe.)*	1-0 2-1
1980	Nacional (Arg.)	Nottingham Forest (Eng.)	1-0
1981	Flamengo (Bra.)	Liverpool (Eng.)	3-0
1982	Penarol (Uru.)	Aston Villa (Eng.)	2-0
1983	Porto Alegre (Bra.)	SV Hamburg (W.Ger.)	2-1
1984	Independiente (Arg.)	Liverpool (Eng.)	1-0
1985	Juventus (Ita.)	Argentinos Juniors (Arg.)	2-2 (aet)
	(Juventus won 4-2 on penalties)		
1986	River Plate (Arg.)	Steaua Bucharest (Rum.)	1-0
1987	Porto (Por.)	Penarol (Uru.)	2-1 (aet)
1988	Nacional (Uru.)	PSV Eindhoven (Hol.)	1-1 (aet)
	(Nacional won 7-6 on penalties)		
1989	AC Milan (Ita.)	Nacional (Col.)	1-0 (aet)
1990	AC Milan (Ita.)	Olimpia Asuncion (Par.)	3-0
1991	Red Star (Yug.)	Colo Colo (Chi.)	3-0
1992	Sao Paulo (Bra.)	Barcelona (Spa.)	2-1
1993	Sao Paulo (Bra.)	AC Milan (Ita.)	3-2
1994	Velez Sarsfield (Arg.)	AC Milan (Ita.)	2-0
1995	Ajax (Hol.)	Gremio (Bra.)	0-0 (aet)
	(Ajax won 4-3 on penalties)		

* European Cup runners-up.

Summary: 34 contests; South America 20 wins, Europe 14 wins.

EURO 96: IT'S GERMANY AGAIN

In the highly successful presentation of the tenth European Championship, the Football Association achieved what they set out to do, while on the field England were so close to going all the way.

They started moderately against Switzerland, produced a convincing second-half display to beat Scotland, and outplayed Holland 4-1 to clinch the group.

Then they won a quarter-final shoot-out against Spain (4-2) and, in the semi-final, led five times against Germany in another contest from the spot. But Gareth Southgate, youngest member of the team and England's discovery of the season, saw his shot saved, David Seaman was unable to repeat earlier heroics and Terry Venables' reign was over one match too soon.

Scotland, under the genial guidance of Craig Brown, were denied a place in the quarter-finals only by Holland scoring late against England.

With 16 countries competing (from a record entry of 48) and 31 matches packed into 3 weeks, this was the biggest-ever European Championship – double in size compared with 8 qualifiers and 15 matches in Sweden in 1992.

Germany, the only country to win the competition more than once, ultimately justified favouritism to take the title for a third time, but the prospect of the 66-1 shots Czech Republic, in title a country barely 3 years old, meeting them in the Final was unthinkable when they lost their opening match to . . . Germany.

But in the final round of group matches, the Czechs scored a dramatic last-minute equaliser (3-3) against Russia, which put them into the quarter-finals at the expense of Italy.

The innovation of sudden death after 90 minutes failed to deliver a winner in 2 of the quarter-finals and both semi-finals. They all went to a penalty contest and England and France, successful from the spot in the "quarters", bowed out at the penultimate stage.

It was left to Germany to achieve the tournament's one result via the Golden Goal system – in the Final itself.

Official attendances exceeded 1¼ million in total, and all 6 matches at Wembley pulled crowds upwards of 73,000.

Excluding shoot-outs, the 31 matches produced no more than 64 goals, of which only 1 was scored direct from a free-kick (Hristo Stoitchkov for Bulgaria v France).

The most disappointing statistic was a total of 167 disciplinary cards (160 yellow) shown by referees, some of whom reached for their pockets far too zealously in response to UEFA's call for strict control.

As part of the **Football Comes Home** theme of the 1996 European Championship, the Royal Mail issued a set of **commemorative stamps** featuring 5 Football Legends: Dixie Dean, Bobby Moore, Duncan Edwards, Billy Wright and Danny Blanchflower.

ENGLAND SQUAD: 1 Seaman (Arsenal), 13 Flowers (Blackburn), 22 Walker (Tottenham); 2 G. Neville (Man. Utd.), 3 Pearce (Nott'm. Forest), 5 Adams (Arsenal, Captain), 6 Southgate (Aston Villa), *12 Howey (Newcastle), 16 Campbell (Tottenham), 19 P. Neville (Man. Utd.); 4 Ince (Inter Milan), 7 Platt (Arsenal), 8 Gascoigne (Rangers), 11 Anderton (Tottenham), 15 Redknapp (Liverpool), 17 McManaman (Liverpool), 20 Stone (Nott'm. Forest); 9 Shearer (Blackburn), 10 Sheringham (Tottenham), 14 Barmby (Middlesbrough), 18 Ferdinand (Newcastle), 21 Fowler (Liverpool). **Coach:** Terry Venables. (*Withdrew June 11, ankle injury).

SCOTLAND SQUAD: 1 Leighton (Hibernian), 12 Goram (Rangers), 22 Walker (Partick); 2 McKimmie (Aberdeen), 3 Boyd (Celtic), 4 Calderwood (Tottenham), 5 Hendry (Blackburn), 6 Whyte (Middlesbrough), 13 T. McKinlay (Celtic); 8 McCall (Rangers), 10 McAllister (Leeds, Captain), 11 Collins (Celtic), 15 Jess (Coventry), 16 Burley (Chelsea), 17 B. McKinlay (Blackburn), 21 Gemmill (Nott'm. Forest); 7 Spencer (Chelsea), 9 McCoist (Rangers), 14 Durie (Rangers), 18 Gallacher (Blackburn), 19 Jackson (Hibernian), 20 Booth (Aberdeen). **Manager:** Craig Brown.

EURO 96 – SUMMARIES

Match 1 – Saturday, June 8 (Wembley, 76,567)

ENGLAND 1, SWITZERLAND 1

England: Seaman; G. Neville, Adams, Southgate, Pearce, Anderton, Ince, Gascoigne (Platt 77), McManaman (Stone 67), Sheringham (Barmby 67), Shearer. **Scorer:** Shearer 23. **Booked:** G. Neville, Adams.

Switzerland: Pascolo; Geiger (Koller 69), Vogel, Henchoz, Jeanneret, Bonvin (Chapuisat 66), Sforza, Vega, Quentin, Grassi, Turkyilmaz. **Scorer:** Turkyilmaz 83 (pen.). **Booked:** Vogel, Quentin, Grassi, Vega. **Suspended:** Hottiger.

Referee: M. Vega (Spain). **Half-time:** 1-0.

Match 2 – Sunday, June 9 (Leeds, 24,006)

SPAIN 1, BULGARIA 1

Spain: Zubizaretta; Belsue, Alkorta, Abelardo, Sergi, Caminero (Donato 81), Amor (Alfonso 71), Hierro, Luis Enrique, Guerrero (Amavisca 52), Pizzi. **Scorer:** Alfonso 73. **Booked:** Caminero, Sergi, Amor, Abeladro. **Sent-off:** Pizzi. **Suspended:** Nadal.

Bulgaria: Mihaylov; Kischischev, Houbtchev, Ivanov, Kiriakov (Tzvetanov 71), Letchkov, Iankov, Balakov, Kostadinov (Iordanov 71), Stoitchkov, Penev (Borimirov 77). **Scorer:** Stoitchkov 65 (pen.). **Booked:** Stoitchkov, Kischischev, Iankov. **Sent-off:** Houbtchev.

Referee: P Ceccarini (Italy). **Half-time:** 0-0.

Match 3 – Sunday, June 9 (Old Trafford, 37,300)

CZECH REPUBLIC 0, GERMANY 2

Czech Republic: Kouba; Hornak, Kadlec, Suchoparek, Latal, Frydek (Berger 45), Bejbl, Nemec, Nedved, Poborsky (Drulak 45), Kuka. **Booked:** Bejbl, Nedved, Kadlec, Drulak.

Germany: Kopke; Sammer, Reuter, Kohler (Babbel 13), Helmer, Ziege, Hassler, Eilts, Moller, Bobic, Kuntz (Bierhoff 82). **Scorers:** Ziege 26, Moller 32. **Booked:** Ziege, Kuntz, Moller, Babbel, Reuter, Hassler. **Suspended:** Klinsmann, Freund.

Referee: D. Elleray (England). **Half-time:** 0-2.

Match 4 – Sunday, June 9 (Hillsborough, 34,993)

DENMARK 1, PORTUGAL 1

Denmark: Schmeichel; Hogh, Helveg, Rieper, Risager, B. Laudrup, Larsen (Vilfort 89), Thomsen (Piechnik 83), B. Nielson, M. Laudrup, Beck. **Scorer:** B. Laudrup 21. **Booked:** Helveg, Risager.

Portugal: Vitor Baia; Paulinho Santos, Couto, Helder, Dimas, Sa Pinto, Paulo Sousa (Tavares 79), Oceano (Folha 37), Figo (Domingos 62), Rui Costa, Joao Pinto. **Scorer:** Sa Pinto 52. **Booked:** Oceano, Paulinho Santos, Sa Pinto, Paulo Sousa, Joao Pinto.

Referee: M. Van der Ende (Holland). **Half-time:** 1-0.

Match 5 – Monday, June 10 (Villa Park, 34,363)

HOLLAND 0, SCOTLAND 0

Holland: Van der Sar; Reiziger, de Kock, Bogarde, R. de Boer (Winter 68), Davids, Seedorf, Witschge (Cocu 78), Taument (Kluivert 63), Bergkamp, Cruyff. **Booked:** Witschge, Taument. **Suspended:** Blind.

Scotland: Goram; McKimmie (Burley 85), Calderwood, Hendry, Boyd, Gallacher (B. McKinlay 56), McCall, McAllister, Collins, Durie, Booth (Spencer 45). **Booked:** Boyd, Gallacher.

Referee: L. Sundell (Sweden).

Match 6 – Monday, June 10 (Newcastle, 26,323)

ROMANIA 0, FRANCE 1

Romania: Stelea; Lupescu, Mihali, Belodedici, Petrescu (Filipescu 76), Hagi, Popescu, Selymes, Lacatus (Ilie 54), Munteanu, Raducioiu (Moldovan 45). **Booked:** Mihali, Selymes, Ilie. **Suspended:** Prodan.

France: Lama; Thuram, Blanc, Desailly, Di Meco (Lizarazu 66), Karembeu, Deschamps, Guerin, Djorkaeff, Zidane (Roche 79), Dugarry (Loko 66). **Scorer:** Dugarry 24. **Booked:** Di Meco.

Referee: H. Krug (Germany). **Half-time:** 0-1.

Match 7 – Tuesday, June 11 (Anfield, 35,120)

ITALY 2, RUSSIA 1

Italy: Peruzzi; Mussi, Costacurta, Apolloni, Maldini, Di Livio (Fuser 61), Albertini, Di Matteo, Del Piero (Donadoni 45), Casiraghi (Ravanelli 79), Zola. **Scorer:** Casiraghi 5,52. **Booked:** Albertini, Donadoni.

Russia: Cherchesov; Tetradze, Bushmanov (Yanovskii 45), Onopko, Kovtun, Kanchelskis, Radimov, Mostovoi, Tsymbalar (Dobrovolskii 70), Karpin (Kiriyakov 62), Kolyvanov. **Scorer:** Tsymbalar 20. **Booked:** Onopko, Kolyvanov, Kovtun. **Suspended:** Nikiforov.

Referee: L. Mottram (Scotland). **Half-time:** 1-1.

Match 8 – Tuesday, June 11 (City Ground, Nottingham, 22,406)

TURKEY 0, CROATIA 1

Turkey: Rustu; Alpay, Rahim, Vedat, Ogun, Tolunay (Saffet 89), Tugay, Abdullah, Arif (Hami 82), Sergen, Hakan. **Booked:** Tolunay.

Croatia: Ladic; Jerkan, Bilic, Stimac, Jarni, Stanic, Asanovic, Boban (Soldo 57), Prosinecki, Suker (Pavlicic 89), Boksic (Vlaovic 73). **Scorer:** Vlaovic 86. **Booked:** Asanovic, Boban, Soldo.

Referee: S. Muhmenthaler (Switzerland). **Half-time:** 0-0.

Match 9 – Thursday, June 13 (Newcastle, 19,107)

BULGARIA 1, ROMANIA 0

Bulgaria: Mihaylov; Kischischev, Ivanov, Iordanov, Tzvetanov, Letchkov

(Guentchev 90), Balakov, Iankov, Kostadinov (Borimirov 31), Penev (Sirakov 71), Stoitchkov. **Scorer:** Stoitchkov 3. **Booked:** Kischischev, Tzvetanov.

Romania: Stelea; Petrescu, Lupescu (Galca 45), Prodan, Belodedici, Selymes, Lacatus (Moldovan 28), Popescu (Ilie 77), Hagi, Munteanu, Raducioiu.

Referee: P. Mikkelsen (Denmark). **Half-time:** 1-0.

Match 10 – Thursday, June 13 (Villa Park, 36,800)

SWITZERLAND 0, HOLLAND 2

Switzerland: Pascolo; Jeanneret (Comisetti 68), Henchoz, Quentin, Vega, Hottiger, Vogel, Sforza, Chapuisat, Turkyilmaz, Grassi. **Booked:** Jeanneret, Chapuisat, Turkyilmaz, Grassi.

Holland: Van der Sar; Blind, Bogarde, Reiziger, Winter, Seedorf (de Kock 25), R. de Boer (Davids 78), Witschge, Cruyff (Kluivert 84), Hoekstra, Bergkamp. **Scorers:** Cruyff 65, Bergkamp 78. **Booked:** Seedorf.

Referee: A. Ouzounov (Bulgaria). **Half-time:** 0-0.

Match 11 – Friday, June 14 (City Ground, Nottingham, 22,670)

PORTUGAL 1, TURKEY 0

Portugal: Vitor Baia; Paulinho Santos, Couto, Helder, Dimas, Sa Pinto (Cadete 65), Paulo Sousa, Folha (Tavares 45), Figo, Rui Costa, Joao Pinto (Porfirio 77). **Scorer:** Couto 66. **Booked:** Paulinho Santos, Tavares, Figo.

Turkey: Rustu; Alpay, Recep, Vedat, Abdullah, Ogun (Rahim 45), Oguz (Arif 69), Tugay, Sergen, Hakan, Saffet (Tolunay 62). **Booked:** Abdullah, Vedat, Rahim, Tolunay.

Referee: S. Puhl (Hungary). **Half-time:** 0-0.

Match 12 – Friday, June 14 (Anfield, 37,320)

CZECH REPUBLIC 2, ITALY 1

Czech Republic: Kouba; Hornak, Kadlec, Suchoparek, Latal (Nemecek 87), Bejbl, Berger (Smicer 63), Nemec, Nedved, Kuka, Poborsky. **Scorers:** Nedved 4, Bejbl 35. **Booked:** Suchoparek, Latal, Kuka, Kadlec.

Italy: Peruzzi; Mussi, Costacurta, Apolloni, Maldini, Fuser, D. Baggio (Carboni 38), Albertini, Donadoni, Ravanelli (Casiraghi 57), Chiesa (Zola 77). **Scorer:** Chiesa 18. **Booked:** Fuser. **Sent-off:** Apolloni.

Referee: A. Lopez-Nieto (Spain). **Half-time:** 2-1.

Match 13 – Saturday, June 15 (Wembley, 76,864)

SCOTLAND 0, ENGLAND 2

Scotland: Goram; McKimmie, Calderwood, Hendry, Boyd, T. McKinlay (Burley 83), McCall, McAllister, Collins, Spencer (McCoist 67), Durie (Jess 87). **Booked:** Hendry, Spencer, Collins.

England: Seaman; G. Neville, Adams, Pearce (Redknapp 45, Campbell 85), Southgate, Ince (Stone 77), Gascoigne, Anderton, McManaman, Sheringham,

Shearer. **Scorers:** Shearer 53, Gascoigne 79. **Booked:** Ince, Shearer.

Referee: P. Pairetto (Italy). **Half-time:** 0-0.

Match 14 – Saturday, June 15 (Leeds, 35,626)

FRANCE 1, SPAIN 1

France: Lama; Blanc, Angloma (Roche 65), Desailly, Lizarazu, Karembeu, Deschamps, Guerin (Thuram 81), Zidane, Djorkaeff, Loko (Dugarry 74). **Scorer:** Djorkaeff 48. **Booked:** Blanc, Karembeu, Djorkaeff. **Suspended:** Pizzi.

Spain: Zubizaretta; Otero (Kiko 59), Lopez, Sergi, Amavisca, Alfonso (Salinas 83), Luis Enrique (Manjarin 55), Caminero, Abelardo, Hierro, Alkorta. **Scorer:** Caminero 85. **Booked:** Amavisca, Otero.

Referee: V. Zhuk (Belarus). **Half-time:** 0-0.

Match 15 – Sunday, June 16 (Old Trafford, 50,760)

RUSSIA 0, GERMANY 3

Russia: Kharine; Tetradze, Onopko, Kovtun, Nikiforov, Tsymbalar, Radimov (Karpin 45), Kanchelskis, Mostovoi, Kolyvanov, Khokhlov (Simutenkov 65). **Booked:** Kanchelskis, Onopko. **Sent-off:** Kovtun.

Germany: Kopke; Babbel, Sammer, Helmer, Reuter, Ziege, Moller (Strunz 86), Hassler (Freund 66), Eilts, Klinsmann, Bierhoff (Kuntz 85). **Scorers:** Sammer 56, Klinsmann 77,90.

Referee: K. Nielsen (Denmark). **Half-time:** 0-0.

Match 16 – Sunday, June 16 (Hillsborough, 33,671)

CROATIA 3, DENMARK 0

Croatia: Ladic; Stanic, Bilic, Jerkan, Stimac, Jarni, Asanovic, Prosinecki (Mladenovic 88), Boban (Soldo 81), Suker, Vlaovic (Jurcevic 81). **Scorers:** Suker 53 (pen.), 89, Boban 80. **Booked:** Stanic, Prosinecki, Vlaovic.

Denmark: Schmeichel; Helveg (Laursen 45), Rieper, Thomsen, Hogh, Schjonberg, Larsen (Tofting 68), Vilfort (Beck 58), M. Laudrup, B. Nielsen, B. Laudrup.

Referee: M. Batta (France). **Half-time:** 0-0.

Match 17 – Tuesday, June 18 (Newcastle, 26,976)

FRANCE 3, BULGARIA 1

France: Lama; Thuram, Blanc, Desailly, Lizarazu, Karembeu, Deschamps, Guerin, Djorkaeff, Zidane (Pedros 62), Dugarry (Loko 70). **Scorers:** Blanc 20, Penev 63 (og.), Loko 90. **Booked:** Desailly, Dugarry.

Bulgaria: Mihaylov; Kremenliev, Ivanov, Houbtchev, Tzvetanov, Letchkov, Iankov (Borimirov 79), Iordanov, Balakov (Donkov 82), Stoitchkov, Penev. **Scorer:** Stoitchkov 69. **Booked:** Ivanov, Kremenliev.

Referee: D. Gallagher (England) (P. Durkin, England, 28). **Half-time:** 1-0.

Match 18 – Tuesday, June 18 (Leeds, 32,719)

ROMANIA 1, SPAIN 2

Romania: Prunea; Dobos, Prodan (Lupescu 85), Selymes, Petrescu, Stinga, Popescu, Hagi, Galca, Raducioiu (Vladoiu 78), Ilie (Munteanu 66). **Scorer:** Raducioiu 29. **Booked:** Popescu, Hagi, Ilie, Galca.

Spain: Zubizarreta; Lopez, Abelardo (Amor 64), Alkorta, Sergi, Nadal, Hierro, Manjarin, Kiko, Amavisca (Guerrero 69), Pizzi (Alfonso 57). **Scorers:** Manjarin 11, Amor 85. **Booked:** Kiko, Nadal.

Referee: A. Cakar (Turkey). **Half-time:** 1-1.

Match 19 – Tuesday, June 18 (Villa Park, 34,926)

SCOTLAND 1, SWITZERLAND 0

Scotland: Goram; Calderwood, Hendry, Boyd, Burley, McCall, McAllister, Collins, T. McKinlay (Booth 60), Durie, McCoist (Spencer 85). **Scorer:** McCoist 37. **Booked:** Calderwood, McCall, Collins.

Switzerland: Pascolo; Hottiger, Vega, Henchoz, Quentin (Comisetti 81), Vogel, Sforza, Koller (Fournier 45), Bonvin (Wicky 45), Turkyilmaz, Chapuisat. **Booked:** Vega, Vogel, Wicky, Fournier. **Suspended:** Grassi.

Referee: V. Krondl (Czech Republic). **Half-time:** 1-0.

Match 20 – Tuesday, June 18 (Wembley, 76,798)

HOLLAND 1, ENGLAND 4

Holland: Van der Sar; Reiziger, Blind, Bogarde, Seedorf, R. de Boer (Cocu 73), Cruyff, Bergkamp, Witschge (de Kock 45), Winter, Hoekstra (Kluivert 72). **Scorer:** Kluivert 78. **Booked:** Winter, Blind, Bergkamp.

England: Seaman; G. Neville, Adams, Southgate, Pearce, McManaman, Ince (Platt 68), Gascoigne, Anderton, Shearer (Barmby 76), Sheringham (Fowler 76). **Scorers:** Shearer 23 (pen.), 57, Sheringham 51, 62. **Booked:** Sheringham, Ince, Southgate.

Referee: G. Grabher (Austria). **Half-time:** 0-1.

Match 21 – Wednesday, June 19
(City Ground, Nottingham, 20,484)

CROATIA 0, PORTUGAL 3

Croatia: Mrmic; Soldo, Jarni, Bilic, Jurcevic, Prosinecki (Boban 45), Pamic (Suker 45), Simic, Mladenovic (Asanovic 45), Vlaovic, Pavlicic. **Booked:** Pamic, Jarni, Pavlicic.

Portugal: Vitor Baia; Secretario, Couto, Sa Pinto (Domingos 45), Dimas, Oceano, Helder, Figo, Joao Pinto, Rui Costa (Pedro 61), Paulo Sousa (Tavares 70). **Scorers:** Figo 4, Joao Pinto 32, Dimingos 82. **Suspended:** Paulinho Santos.

Referee: B. Heynemann (Germany). **Half-time:** 0-2.

Match 22 – Wednesday, June 19 (Hillsborough, 28,951)

TURKEY 0, DENMARK 3

Turkey: Rustu; Recep (Saffet 68), Alpay, Ogun, Vedat, Hami, Tayfun, Tugay, Abdullah, Hakan (Arif 45), Orhan (Bulent 68). **Booked:** Tugay, Tayfun, Rustu. **Suspended:** Tolunay.

Denmark: Schmeichel; Rieper, Hogh, Thomsen, Helveg, A. Nielsen, B. Nielsen, M. Laudrup, Schjonberg (Larsen 45), E. Andersen (S. Andersen 88), B. Laudrup. **Scorers:** B. Laudrup 50, 84, A. Nielsen 70.

Referee: N. Levnikov (Russia). **Half-time:** 0-0.

Match 23 – Wednesday, June 19 (Anfield, 21,128)

RUSSIA 3, CZECH REPUBLIC 3

Russia: Cherchesov; Tetradze, Gorlukovich, Nikiforov, Yanovskii, Karpin, Radimov, Khokhlov, Tsymbalar (Shalimov 65), Simutenkov (Mostovoi 45), Kolyvanov (Beschastnykh 45). **Scorers:** Mostovoi 49, Tetradze 54, Beschastnykh 85. **Booked:** Nikiforov, Radimov, Tsymbalar, Yanovskii. **Suspended:** Onopko, Kovtun.

Czech Republic: Kouba; Hornak, Kubik, Suchoparek, Latal, Bejbl, Berger (Nemecek 45), Nemec, Nedved, Kuka (Smicer 67), Poborsky. **Scorers:** Suchoparek 6, Kuka 19, Smicer 89. **Booked:** Nedved, Nemec. **Suspended:** Kadlec.

Referee: A. Frisk (Sweden). **Half-time:** 0-2.

Match 24 – Wednesday, June 19 (Old Trafford, 53,740)

ITALY 0, GERMANY 0

Italy: Peruzzi; Costacurta, Maldini, Carboni (Torricelli 77), Mussi, Albertini, Donadoni, Di Matteo (Chiesa 67), Fuser (Di Livio 81), Zola, Casiraghi. **Booked:** Casiraghi. **Suspended:** Apolloni.

Germany: Kopke; Sammer, Strunz, Helmer, Eilts, Freund, Moller (Bode 89), Hassler, Ziege, Bobic, Klinsmann. **Sent-off:** Strunz. **Suspended:** Babbel.

Referee: G. Goethals (Belgium).

GROUP A – Final table

	P	W	D	L	F	A	Pts
1 England	3	2	1	0	7	2	7
2 Holland	3	1	1	1	3	4	4
3 Scotland	3	1	1	1	1	2	4
4 Switzerland	3	0	1	2	1	4	1

GROUP B – Final Table

	P	W	D	L	F	A	Pts
1 France	3	2	1	0	5	2	7
2 Spain	3	1	2	0	4	3	5
3 Bulgaria	3	1	1	1	3	4	4
4 Romania	3	0	0	3	1	4	0

GROUP C – Final table

	P	W	D	L	D	A	Pts
1 Germany	3	2	1	0	5	0	7
2 Czech Rep.	3	1	1	1	5	6	4
3 Italy	3	1	1	1	3	3	4
4 Russia	3	0	1	2	4	8	1

GROUP D – Final table

	P	W	D	L	F	A	Pts
1 Portugal	3	2	1	0	5	1	7
2 Croatia	3	2	0	1	4	3	6
3 Denmark	3	1	1	1	4	4	4
4 Turkey	3	0	0	3	0	5	0

QUARTER-FINALS

March 25 – Saturday, June 22 (Wembley, 75,447)

SPAIN 0, ENGLAND 0 (aet)
(England won 4-2 on penalties)

Spain: Zubizarreta; Belsue, Alkorta (Lopez 72), Abelardo, Hierro, Sergi, Kiko, Manjarin (Caminero 45), Amor, Salinas (Alfonso 45), Nadal. **Booked:** Abelardo, Belsue, Alfonso.

England: Seaman; G. Neville, Adams, Southgate, Pearce, Anderton (Stone 108), Gascoigne, Platt, McManaman (Barmby 108), Sheringham (Fowler 108), Shearer. **Booked:** G. Neville. **Suspended:** Ince.

Penalty Shoot-out (England first kick): Shearer (1-0), Hierro (hit bar), Platt (2-0), Amor (2-1), Pearce (3-1), Belsue (3-2), Gascoigne (4-2), Nadal (saved).

Referee: M. Batta (France).

Match 26 – Saturday, June 22 (Anfield, 37,465)

FRANCE 0, HOLLAND 0 (aet)
(France won 5-4 on penalties)

France: Lama; Thuram, Blanc, Desailly, Lizarazu, Karembeu, Deschamps, Guerin, Djorkaeff, Zidane, Loko (Dugarry 61, Pedros 80). **Booked:** Deschamps, Karembeu.

Holland: Van der Sar, Reiziger, Blind, de Kock, Bogarde, R. de Boer, Witschge (Mulder 80), Cruyff (Winter 69), Bergkamp (Seedorf 59), Cocu, Kluivert. **Booked:** de Kock, Kluivert, Bogarde.

Penalty Shoot-out (Holland first kick): de Kock (1-0), Zidane (1-1), de Boer (2-1), Djorkaeff (2-2), Kluivert (3-2), Lizarazu (3-3), Seedorf (saved), Guerin (3-4), Blind (4-4), Blanc (4-5).

Referee: A. Lopez-Nieto (Spain).

Match 27 – Sunday, June 23 (Old Trafford, 43,412)

GERMANY 2, CROATIA 1

Germany: Kopke; Sammer, Babbel, Eilts, Helmer, Reuter, Moller, Scholl (Hassler 88), Ziege, Bobic (Kuntz 45), Klinsmann (Freund 38). **Scorers:** Klinsmann 21 (pen.), Sammer 58. **Booked:** Sammer, Klinsmann. **Suspended:** Strunz.

Croatia: Ladic; Bilic, Jerkan, Stimac, Stanic, Jurcevic (Mladenovic 78), Asanovic, Boban, Jarni, Vlaovic, Suker. **Scorer:** Suker 51. **Sent-off:** Stimac.

Referee: L. Sundell (Sweden). **Half-time:** 1-0.

Match 28 – Sunday, June 23 (Villa Park, 26,832)

PORTUGAL 0, CZECH REPUBLIC 1

Portugal: Vitor Baia; Secretario, Couto, Helder, Dimas, Oceano (Folha 64), Paulo Sousa, Rui Costa, Figo (Cadete 82), Sa Pinto (Domingos 45), Joao Pinto. **Booked:** Helder, Sa Pinto, Secretario, Joao Pinto.

Czech Republic: Kouba; Hornak, Kadlec, Suchoparek, Latal, Bejbl, Nemec, Nemecek (Berger 90), Poborsky, Kuka, Smicer (Kubik 84). **Scorer:** Poborsky 53. **Booked:** Suchoparek, Smicer, Bejbl, Kuka. **Sent-off:** Latal. **Suspended:** Nedved.

Referee: H. Krug (Germany). **Half-time:** 0-0.

SEMI-FINALS

Match 29 – Wednesday, June 26 (Old Trafford, 43,877)

FRANCE 0, CZECH REPUBLIC 0 (aet)
(Czech Republic won 6-5 on penalties)

France: Lama; Thuram (Angloma 83), Blanc, Roche, Lizarazu, Lamouchi (Pedros 62), Desailly, Guerin, Zidane, Djorkaeff, Loko. **Booked:** Thuram, Roche. **Suspended:** Karembeu.

Czech Republic: Kouba; Hornak, Kadlec, Rada, Nedved, Nemecek, Nemec (Kubik 83), Novotni, Poborsky, Smicer (Berger 45), Drulak (Kotulek 70). **Booked:** Nedved, Nemecek, Kubik. **Suspended:** Suchoparek, Latal, Bejbl, Kuka.

Penalty Shoot-out (France first kick): Zidane (1-0), Kubik (1-1), Djorkaeff (2-1), Nedved (2-2), Lizarazu (3-2), Berger (3-3), Guerin (4-3), Poborsky (4-4), Blanc (5-4), Rada (5-5), Pedros (saved), Kadlec (5-6).

Referee: L. Mottram (Scotland).

Match 30 – Wednesday, June 26 (Wembley, 75,862)

GERMANY 1, ENGLAND 1 (aet)
(Germany won 6-5 on penalties)

Germany: Kopke; Sammer, Reuter, Babbel, Helmer (Bode 109), Ziege, Scholl (Hassler 76), Freund (Strunz 118), Moller, Eilts, Kuntz. **Scorer:** Kuntz 16. **Booked:** Reuter, Moller.

England: Seaman; Southgate, Adams, Pearce, Ince, Anderton, Platt, Gascoigne, McManaman, Sheringham, Shearer. **Scorer:** Shearer 3. **Booked:** Gascoigne. **Suspended:** G. Neville.

Penalty Shoot-out (England first kick): Shearer (1-0), Hassler (1-1), Platt (2-1), Strunz (2-2), Pearce (3-2), Reuter (3-3), Gascoigne (4-3), Ziege (4-4), Sheringham (5-4), Kuntz (5-5), Southgate (saved), Moller (5-6).

Referee: S. Puhl (Hungary).

- Germany won draw to wear first-choice white shirts; England in grey strip.

FINAL

Match 31 – Sunday, June 30 (Wembley, kick-off 7pm., 73,611)

CZECH REPUBLIC 1 GERMANY 2
(Golden Goal decider 95 mins)

Czech Republic (Red shirts, coach Dusan Urhin): 1 Kouba (Sparta Prague); 3 Suchoparek (Slavia Prague), 4 Nedved (Sparta Prague), 5 Kadlec, captain (Kaiserslautern), 7 Nemec (Schalke 04), 8 Poborsky (Slavia Prague) (17 Smicer, Slavia Prague, 87), 9 Kuka (Kaiserslautern), 13 Bejbl (Slavia Prague), 14 Berger (Borussia Dortmund), 15 Hornak (Sparta Prague), 19 Rada (Sigma Olomouc). **Scorer:** Berger 59 (pen.). **Booked:** Hornak. **Suspended:** Latal.

Germany (White shirts, coach Berti Vogts): 1 Kopke (Eintracht Frankfurt); 6 Sammer (Borussia Dortmund), 5 Helmer (Bayern Munich), 14 Babbel (Bayern Munich), 19 Strunz (Bayern Munich), 21 Eilts (Werder Bremen) (3 Bode, Werder Bremen, 45), 17 Ziege (Bayern Munich), 10 Hassler (Karlsruhe), 8 Scholl (Bayern Munich) (20 Bierhoff, Udinese, 69), 11 Kuntz (Besiktas), 18 Klinsmann, captain (Bayern Munich). **Scorer:** Bierhoff 72, 95. **Booked:** Sammer, Helmer, Ziege. **Suspended:** Reuter, Moller.

Referee: Pierluigi Pairetto (Italy). **Man of the Match:** Karel Poborsky (Czech Rep.)

Half-time: 0-0. **90 mins:** 1-1. **Weather:** Cloudy, fine. **TV coverage:** BBC/ITV live.

Guests of Honour: HM The Queen, Duke of Edinburgh, Duke of Kent (President FA), John Major (Prime Minister), Helmut Kohl (German Chancellor), Vaclav Havel (President Czech Republic).

Support at Final: Germany 11,000, Czech Republic 4,000.

Betting: 1-3 Germany, 11-5 Czech Republic.

Jürgen Klinsmann, who missed the semi-final because of a torn calf muscle, tested himself on the pitch an hour before kick-off and was passed fit to lead Germany.

In a goalless first half the balance of possession was with Germany, but the Czechs broke dangerously. They went ahead on the hour with a controversial penalty by Patrik Berger – TV replays showed that Matthias Sammer brought down Karel Poborsky inches outside the area.

Barely 20 minutes remained when the anxious Vogts introduced Oliver Bierhoff from the bench. Within 3 minutes the newcomer was at the far post to head the equaliser from Christian Ziege's free-kick.

Germany were transformed, and although all was still level at the end of the normal period, it needed only 5 minutes of Golden Goal time to decide. Bierhoff, close-marked on the edge of the box and with his back to goal, spun right for a fierce left-foot shot that was deflected and rolled over the line off Petr Kouba's finger-tips. It was a goal "out of nothing," and an inspired substitution had swung the game.

The Queen presented the trophy to Klinsmann to confirm Germany's sixth major title in 11 Finals (this their third out of 5 in the European Championship after 3 out of 6 in the World Cup).

And on his country's honours list Berti Vogts joined illustrious prize-winning predecessors in Sepp Herberger (pre-war to 1964), Helmut Schon (1964-78), Jupp Derwall (1978-84) and Franz Beckenbauer (1984-90).

Euro 96 Fair Play Award: England (trophy presented to Terry Venables on the field at half-time in Final).
UEFA Crowd Assessment Award: Holland. **Euro 96 Mascot:** Goaliath the Lion.
Total goals (excluding penalty shoot-outs): 64.
Tournament top scorer: Alan Shearer (England) 5.
Attendance aggregate (31 matches); 1,276,117.
Discipline: The referees showed 167 cards (7 red, 160 yellow).

Seven sendings-off at Euro 96 equalled the total of players dismissed in the entire history of European Championship finals (1 in 1968, 3 in 1976, 3 in 1984).

Davor Suker's 3 goals for Croatia gave him a record-equalling career total of 16 in European Championship football. They comprised 1 for Yugoslavia (1992 qual. Round) and 15 for Croatia (12 in qual. round for Euro 96, 3 in finals). Suker shares the record with West Germany's Gerd Muller (12 in qual. matches, 4 in finals) and Holland's Marco van Basten (11 and 5).

History: After the World Cup, the European Championship is football's most prestigious tournament. It was launched in 1958 and the trophy is the Henri Delaunay Cup, named after its French founder.

Later known as the Nations Cup and, since 1966, as the European Championship, the tournament spans two years, and the Final exactly midway between one World Cup and the next. Eight different countries have won the ten Finals, with Germany successful on three occasions.

Year	Venue	Winners		Runners-up	
1960	Paris	*U.S.S.R.	2	Yugoslavia	1
1964	Madrid	Spain	2	U.S.S.R.	1
1968	Rome	Italy	2	Yugoslavia	0
		(replay, after 1-1 draw)			
1972	Brussels	West Germany	3	U.S.S.R.	0
1976	Belgrade	*Czechoslovakia	2	West Germany	2
		(Czechoslovakia won 5-3 on penalties)			
1980	Rome	West Germany	2	Belgium	1
1984	Paris	France	2	Spain	0
1988	Munich	Holland	2	U.S.S.R.	0
1992	Gothenburg	Denmark	2	Germany	0
1996	London	†Germany	2	Czech Republic	1

(*After extra time; †decided in overtime)

• **Record scorer** in European Championship final series: **Michel Platini** with 9 goals when he captained France to victory in 1984. He scored in every match.
• The Finals in 2000 will be hosted jointly for the first time. Holland and Belgium were the only applicants by the deadline in September 1994.

EUROPEAN CHAMPIONSHIP 1994-96

HOW THEY QUALIFIED

(England as hosts)

GROUP 1

	P	W	D	L	F	A	Pts
ROMANIA	10	6	3	1	18	8	21
FRANCE	10	5	5	0	22	2	20
Slovakia	10	4	2	4	14	18	14
Poland	10	3	4	3	14	12	13
Israel	10	3	3	4	13	11	12
Azerbaijan	10	0	1	9	2	29	1

Results: Israel 2, Poland 1; Slovakia 0, France 0; Romania 3, Azerbaijan 0; France 0, Romania 0; Israel 2, Slovakia 2; Poland 1, Azerbaijan 0; Romania 3, Slovakia 2; Poland 0, France 0; Azerbaijan 0, Israel 2; Azerbaijan 0, France 2; Israel 1, Romania 1; Romania 2, Poland 1; Israel 0, France 0; Slovakia 4, Azerbaijan 1; Poland 4, Israel 3; France 4, Slovakia 0; Azerbaijan 1, Romania 4; Poland 5, Slovakia 0; Romania 2, Israel 1; France 1, Poland 1; Azerbaijan 0, Slovakia 1; France 10, Azerbaijan 0; Slovakia 1, Israel 0; Poland 0, Romania 0; Romania 1, France 3; Israel 2, Azerbaijan 0; Slovakia 4, Poland 1; Slovakia 0, Romania 2; Azerbaijan 0, Poland 0; France 2, Israel 0.

GROUP 2

	P	W	D	L	F	A	Pts
SPAIN	10	8	2	0	25	4	26
DENMARK	10	6	3	1	19	9	21
Belgium	10	4	3	3	16	12	15
Macedonia	10	1	4	5	9	18	7
Cyprus	10	1	4	5	5	19	7
Armenia	10	1	2	7	5	17	5

Results: Cyprus 1, Spain 2; Macedonia 1, Denmark 1; Belgium 2, Armenia 0; Armenia 0, Cyprus 0; Denmark 3, Belgium 1; Macedonia 0, Spain 2; Belgium 1, Macedonia 1; Spain 3, Denmark 0; Cyprus 2, Armenia 0; Belgium 1, Spain 4; Macedonia 3, Cyprus 0; Spain 1, Belgium 1; Cyprus 1, Denmark 1; Armenia 0, Spain 2; Belgium 2, Cyprus 0, Denmark 1, Macedonia 0; Armenia 2, Macedonia 2; Denmark 4, Cyprus 0; Macedonia 0, Belgium 5; Spain 1, Armenia 0; Armenia 0, Denmark 2; Belgium 1, Denmark 3; Spain 6, Cyprus 0; Macedonia 1, Armenia 2; Armenia 0, Belgium 2; Denmark 1, Spain 1; Cyprus 1, Macedonia 1; Spain 3, Macedonia 0; Cyprus 1, Belgium 1; Denmark 3, Armenia 1.

GROUP 3

	P	W	D	L	F	A	Pts
SWITZ'LAND	8	5	2	1	15	7	17
TURKEY	8	4	3	1	16	8	15
Sweden	8	2	3	3	9	10	9
Hungary	8	2	2	4	7	13	8
Iceland	8	1	2	5	3	12	5

Results: Iceland 0, Sweden 1; Hungary 2, Turkey 2; Turkey 5, Iceland 0; Switzerland 4, Sweden 2; Switzerland 1, Iceland 0; Sweden 2, Hungary 0; Turkey 1, Switzerland 2; Turkey 2, Sweden 1; Hungary 2, Switzerland 2; Hungary 1, Sweden 0; Switzerland 1, Turkey 2; Sweden 1, Iceland 1; Iceland 2, Hungary 1; Iceland 0, Switzerland 2; Sweden 0, Switzerland 0; Turkey 2, Hungary 0; Switzerland 3, Hungary 0; Iceland 0, Turkey 0; Hungary 1, Iceland 0; Sweden 2, Turkey 2.

GROUP 4

	P	W	D	L	F	A	Pts
CROATIA	10	7	2	1	22	5	23
ITALY	10	7	2	1	20	6	23
Lithuania	10	5	1	4	13	12	16
Ukraine	10	4	1	5	11	15	13
Slovenia	10	3	2	5	13	13	11
Estonia	10	0	0	10	3	31	0

Results: Estonia 0, Croatia 2; Slovenia 1, Italy 1; Ukraine 0, Lithuania 2; Estonia 0, Italy 2; Croatia 2, Lithuania 0; Ukraine 0, Slovenia 0; Ukraine 3, Estonia 0; Slovenia 1, Lithuania 2; Italy 1, Croatia 2; Italy 4, Estonia 1; Croatia 4, Ukraine 0; Slovenia 3, Estonia 0; Ukraine 0, Italy 2; Lithuania 0, Croatia 0; Lithuania 0, Italy 1; Croatia 2, Slovenia 0; Estonia 0, Ukraine 1; Lithuania 2, Slovenia 1; Estonia 1, Slovenia 3; Ukraine 1, Croatia 0; Estonia 0, Lithuania 1; Croatia 7, Estonia 1; Italy 1, Slovenia 0; Lithuania 1, Ukraine 3; Croatia 1, Italy 1; Slovenia 3, Ukraine 2; Lithuania 5, Estonia 0; Italy 3, Ukraine 1; Slovenia 1, Croatia 2; Italy 4, Lithuania 0.

GROUP 5

	P	W	D	L	F	A	Pts
CZECH REP	10	6	3	1	21	6	21
Holland	10	6	2	2	23	5	20
Norway	10	6	2	2	17	7	20
Belarus	10	3	2	5	8	13	11
Luxembourg	10	3	1	6	3	21	10
Malta	10	0	2	8	2	22	2

Results: Czech Rep 6, Malta 1; Luxembourg 0, Holland 4; Norway 1, Belarus 0; Malta 0, Czech Rep 0; Belarus 2, Luxembourg 0; Norway 1, Holland 1; Belarus 0, Norway 4; Holland 0, Czech Rep 0; Malta 0, Norway 1; Holland 5, Luxembourg 0; Malta 0, Luxembourg 1; Czech Rep 4, Belarus 2; Luxembourg 0, Norway 2; Holland 4, Malta 0; Belarus 1, Malta 1; Czech Rep 3, Holland 1; Norway 5, Luxembourg 0; Belarus 1, Holland 0; Luxembourg 1, Czech Rep 0; Norway 2, Malta 0; Norway 1, Czech Rep 1; Czech Rep 2, Norway 0; Luxembourg 1, Malta 0; Holland 1, Belarus 0; Belarus 0, Czech Rep 2; Malta 0, Holland 4; Luxembourg 0, Belarus 0; Malta 0, Belarus 2; Czech Rep 3, Luxembourg 0; Holland 3, Norway 0.

GROUP 6

	P	W	D	L	F	A	Pts
PORTUGAL	10	7	2	1	28	7	23
Rep Ireland	10	5	2	3	17	11	17
N. Ireland	10	5	2	3	21	15	17
Austria	10	5	1	4	29	14	16
Latvia	10	4	0	6	11	20	12
Liechtenstein	10	0	1	9	1	40	1

Results: N. Ireland 4, Liechtenstein 1; Liechtenstein 0, Austria 4; N. Ireland 1, Portugal 2; Latvia 0, Rep. Ireland 3; Latvia 1, Portugal 3; Austria 1, N. Ireland 2; Rep. Ireland 4, Liechtenstein 0; Portugal 1, Austria 0; Liechtenstein 0, Latvia 1; N. Ireland 0, Rep. Ireland 4; Portugal 8, Liechtenstein 0; Rep. Ireland 1, N. Ireland 1; Austria 5, Latvia 0; Rep. Ireland 1, Portugal 0; Latvia 0, N. Ireland 1; Austria 7, Liechtenstein 0; Portugal 3, Latvia 2; Liechtenstein 0, Rep. Ireland 0; N. Ireland 1, Latvia 2; Rep. Ireland 1, Austria 3, Liechtenstein 0, Portugal 7; Latvia 3, Austria 2; Portugal 1, N. Ireland 1; Austria 3, Rep. Ireland 1; Latvia 1, Liechtenstein 0; Rep. Ireland 2, Latvia 1; Austria 1, Portugal 1; Liechtenstein 0, N. Ireland 4; Portugal 3, Rep. Ireland 0; N. Ireland 5, Austria 3.

GROUP 7

	P	W	D	L	F	A	Pts
GERMANY	10	8	1	1	27	10	25
BULGARIA	10	7	1	2	24	10	22
Georgia	10	5	0	5	14	13	15
Moldova	10	3	0	7	11	27	9
Wales	10	2	2	6	9	19	8
Albania	10	2	2	6	10	16	8

Results: Wales 2, Albania 0; Georgia 0, Moldova 1; Moldova 3, Wales 2; Bulgaria 2, Georgia 0; Albania 1, Germany 2; Georgia 5, Wales 0; Bulgaria 4, Moldova 1; Wales 0, Bulgaria 3; Moldova 0, Germany 3; Albania 0, Georgia 1; Germany 2, Albania 1; Georgia 0, Germany 2; Bulgaria 3, Wales 1; Albania 3, Moldova 0; Germany 1, Wales 1; Moldova 0, Bulgaria 3; Georgia 2, Albania 0; Bulgaria 3, Germany 2; Wales 0, Georgia 1; Moldova 2, Albania 3; Germany 4, Georgia 1; Wales 1, Moldova 0; Albania 1, Bulgaria 1; Bulgaria 3, Albania 0; Germany 6, Moldova 1; Wales 1, Germany 2; Georgia 2, Bulgaria 1; Germany 3, Bulgaria 1; Albania 1, Wales 1; Moldova 3, Georgia 2.

GROUP 8

	P	W	D	L	F	A	Pts
RUSSIA	10	8	2	0	34	5	26
SCOTLAND	10	7	2	1	19	3	23
Greece	10	6	0	4	23	9	18
Finland	10	5	0	5	18	18	15
Faroe Isl.	10	2	0	8	10	35	6
San Marino	10	0	0	10	2	36	0

Results: Finland 0, Scotland 2; Faroe Isl. 1, Greece 5; Scotland 5, Faroe Isl. 1; Greece 4, Finland 0; Russia 4, San Marino 0; Scotland 1, Russia 1; Greece 2, San Marino 0; Finland 5, Faroe Isl. 0; Finland 4, San Marino 1; Greece 1, Scotland 0; Russia 0, Scotland 0; San Marino 0, Finland 2; San Marino 0, Scotland 2; Greece 0, Russia 3; Faroe Isl. 0, Finland 4; Russia 3, Faroe Isl. 0; Faroes 3, San Marino 0; Faroe Isl. 0, Scotland 2; San Marino 0, Russia 7; Finland 2, Greece 1; Scotland 1, Greece 0; Finland 0, Russia 6; Scotland 1, Finland 0; Faroe Isl. 2, Russia 5; San Marino 0, Greece 4; Russia 2, Greece 1; San Marino 1, Faroe Isl. 3; Scotland 5, San Marino 0; Russia 3, Finland 1; Greece 5, Faroe Isl. 0.

Play-off (at Anfield): Holland 2, Rep. Ireland 0.

QUOTE (Euro 96) UNQUOTE

GERMAN F.A., in £20,000 full page ad. In *The Times*: "Many thanks for the great hospitality in England, for the fair play shown by the English public and for the smooth organisation of Euro 96."

TERRY VENABLES, at the end of his reign as England coach: "Playing Spain, Holland and now Germany, we have competed at the highest level and I don't think we've got anything to be downhearted about. I wouldn't have changed anything – except the result against Germany. I wish Glenn (Hoddle) all the luck in the world. It helps if you can leave a team in useful shape, and that's something I think I've done."

RUUD GULLIT on BBC TV after a poor kick-out by Stanislav Cherchisov cost Russia a goal against Italy: "You have to remember, a goalkeeper is a goalkeeper because he can't play football."

ARRIGO SACCHI, Italy's coach, at start of tournament: "When it is over, they will either kiss my bald pate or throw tomatoes at it."

SCOTTISH FAN to manager Craig Brown after the 0-0 draw with Holland: "I'm in disgrace. I've missed my son's wedding to come to the game."

RICHARD MOLLER NIELSEN, Denmark's coach, on allowing players' wives and girl friends into the team camp: "I've nothing against it. Love is good for footballers, as long as it is not at half-time."

WORLD CUP 1998

France will host the finals of the 16th. Word Cup in 1998 with a **record assembly** of 32 nations (previously 24). The tournament will be staged over 33 days, starting June 10, at nine venues, with a programme of 64 matches (12 more than at US 94).

The **official logo** chosen by the French organisers takes the form of a football rising sun-like over part of the globe, and the **tournament mascot** will be a cockerel.

Draw for the finals of France 98 will be held in the open air at the Stade Velodrome in Marseille in December 1997.

The **Final** will take place on July 12 at the £223m., 80,000 all-seat Stade de France now under construction at St. Denis, just north of Paris.

World Cup 98 betting: 5-1 Brazil; 7-1 France, Germany; 8-1 Italy; 14-1 Holland, Spain; 20-1 England.

World Cup 2002: FIFA decided (June 1, 1996) that the tournament will be **jointly hosted** for the first time – by Japan and South Korea.

World Cup 2006: Host candidates to date are Brazil, Germany, South Africa and England.

QUALIFYING ROUND

The draw took place in Paris on Tuesday, December 12, 1995, with a record 171 entries (excluding hosts France and holders Brazil) from FIFA's 193 members. Bermuda and the Bahamas later withdrew for financial reasons.

Europe's entry was split into 9 groups, in which the first seeds were Denmark, Italy, Norway, Sweden, Russia, Spain, Holland, Romania and Germany.

EUROPE: 49 entries – 14 to qualify, plus France as hosts: 9 group winners and the runner-up with the best record; the other 8 to meet in 4 play-offs, home and away – winners qualify).

Group 1: Denmark, Greece, Croatia, Slovenia, Bosnia.
Group 2: Italy, **England**, Poland, Georgia, Moldova.
Group 3: Norway, Switzerland, Finland, Hungary, Azerbaijan.
Group 4: Sweden, **Scotland**, Austria, Latvia, Belarus, Estonia.
Group 5: Russia, Bulgaria, Israel, Cyprus, Luxembourg.
Group 6: Spain, Czech Republic, Slovakia, Yugoslavia, Malta, Faroe Islands.
Group 7: Holland, Belgium, Turkey, **Wales**, San Marino.
Group 8: Romania, **Rep. of Ireland**, Lithuania, Iceland, Macedonia, Liechtenstein.
Group 9: Germany, Portugal, **N. Ireland**, Ukraine, Albania, Armenia.

SOUTH AMERICA: 10 entries – 5 to qualify, Brazil as holders, plus 4 of the other 9 playing in mini-championship of home and away matches (April 24, 1996 to November 16, 1997): Argentina, Bolivia, Chile, Colombia, Ecuador, Paraguay, Peru, Uruguay and Venezuela.

AFRICA: 36 entries – 5 to qualify. Cameroon, Egypt, Morocco and Nigeria exempt until second qual. round.

First round (home and away, winners advance): Sudan v Zambia; Namibia v Mozambique; Tanzania v Ghana; Swaziland v Gabon; Uganda v Angola; Mauritius v Zaire; Malawi v S. Africa; Madagascar v Zimbabwe; Guinea-Bissau v Guinea; Rwanda v Tunisia; Congo v Ivory Coast; Kenya v Algeria; Burundi v Sierra Leone, Togo v Senegal; Gambia v Liberia; Mauritania v Burkino Faso.

Second round (drawn after 1st. Round): 5 leagues of 4 teams, group winners qualify.

ASIA: 36 entries – 3 or 4 qualify.

First round: 6 groups of 4 teams, 4 groups of 3. Ten winners advance to second round.

Group 1: Saudi Arabia, Malaysia, Bangladesh, Taiwan.
Group 2: Iran, Syria, Maldives, Kyrgyzstan.
Group 3: United Arab Emirates, Bahrain, Jordan.
Group 4: Japan, Oman, Nepal, Macao.
Group 5: Uzbekistan, Indonesia, Yemen, Cambodia.
Group 6: South Korea, Thailand, Hong Kong.
Group 7: Kuwait, Lebanon, Singapore.
Group 8: China, Turkmenistan, Vietnam, Tadikistan.
Group 9: Iraq, Kazakhstan, Pakistan.
Group 10: Qatar, India, Sri Lanka, Philippines.

Second round: 2 leagues of 5. Countries meet in one-off matches. Group winners qualify for France 98, runners-up to play off – winner qualifies, loser to play-off v Oceania group winner.

CONCACAF (North, Central America, Caribbean) – 30 entries, 3 qualify. Qualifying matches over 3 rounds, semi-final and final; 6 countries advance into home-and-away league series, top 3 qualify for France 98.
North America: USA, Canada, Mexico.
Central America: Nicaragua, Guatemala, Belize, Panama, Costa Rica, El Salvador, Honduras.
Caribbean Zone: Dominica, Antigua, Aruba, Dominican Republic, St. Kitts & Nevis, Guyana, Grenada, Trinidad & Tobago, Puerto Rico, St. Vincent, Cayman Islands, Cuba, St. Kitts, St. Lucia, Haiti, Surinam, Jamaica, Barbados, Dutch Antilles.

OCEANIA: 10 entries – 1 or 0 qualify. Winners of third round home-and-away play-off to meet Asia's fourth-placed team home and away, winners qualify for France 98. **Entries**: Australia, New Zealand, Fiji, Papua New Guinea, Tahiti, Solomon Islands, Vanuatu, Cook Islands, Tonga, Western Samoa.

First of the 639 matches scheduled in the World Cup 98 qualifying round took place in the Caribbean Zone on March 10, 1996: Dominica v Antigua (3-3).

The European qualifying groups started with 3 matches on April 24: Greece 2, Slovenia 0; Yogoslavia 3, Faroe Islands 1; Macedonia 3, Liechtenstein 0.

Wales played the first qualifying match among the **British countries** on June 2, winning 5-0 away to San Marino.

HOME COUNTRIES' WORLD CUP DATES

England (Group 2): **1996** – Sept. 1 Moldova (a); Oct. 9 Poland (h); Nov. 9 Georgia (a); **1997** – Feb. 12 Italy (h); Apr. 30 Georgia (h); May 31 Poland (a); Sept. 10 Moldova (h); Oct. 11 Italy (a).

N. Ireland (Group 9): **1996** – Aug. 31 Ukraine (h); Oct. 5 Armenia (h); Nov. 9 Germany (a); Dec. 14 Albania (h); **1997** Mar. 29 Portugal (h); Apr. 2 Ukraine (a); Apr. 30 Armenia (a); Aug. 20 Germany (h); Sept. 10 Albania (a); Oct. 11 Portugal (a).

Scotland (Group 4): **1996** – Aug. 31 Austria (a); Oct. 5 Latvia (a); Oct. 9 Estonia (a); Nov. 10 Sweden (h); **1997** – Mar. 29 Estonia (h); Apr. 2 Austria (h); Apr. 30 Sweden (a); June 8 Belarus (a); Sept. 6 Belarus (h); Oct. 11 Latvia (h).

Wales (Group 7): **1996** – June 2 San Marino 0, Wales 5; Aug. 31 San Marino (h); Oct. 5 Holland (h); Nov. 9 Holland (a); Dec. 14 Turkey (h); **1997** – Mar. 29 Belgium (h); Aug. 20 Turkey (a); Nov. 11 Belgium (a).

Rep. of Ireland (Group 8): **1996** – Aug. 31 Liechtenstein (a); Oct. 9 Macedonia (h); Nov. 10 Iceland (h); **1997** – Apr. 2 Macedonia (a); Apr. 30 Romania (a); June 7 Liechtenstein (h); Aug. 20 Lithuania (h); Sept. 6 Iceland (a); Sept. 9 Lithuania (a); Oct. 11 Romania (h).

WORLD CUP FINALS 1-2-3

Year	Venue	Winners	Runners-up	Score	Third
1930	Montevideo	Uruguay	Argentina	4-2	–
1934	Rome	*Italy	Czech'kia	2-1	Germany
1938	Paris	Italy	Hungary	4-2	Brazil
•1950	Rio de Janeiro	Uruguay	Brazil	2-1	–
1954	Berne	Germany	Hungary	3-2	Austria
1958	Stockholm	Brazil	Sweden	5-2	France
1962	Santiago	Brazil	Czech'kia	3-1	Chile
1966	Wembley	*England	W. Germany	4-2	Portugal
1970	Mexico City	Brazil	Italy	4-1	W. Germany
1974	Munich	W. Germany	Holland	2-1	Poland
1978	Buenos Aires	*Argentina	Holland	3-1	Brazil
1982	Madrid	Italy	W. Germany	3-1	Poland
1986	Mexico City	Argentina	W. Germany	3-2	France
1990	Rome	W. Germany	Argentina	1-0	Italy
1994	Los Angeles	†Brazil	Italy	0-0	Sweden

(•Finals on pool basis; *After extra time; †3-2 on penalties, after extra time)

World Champions: 4 – Brazil; 3 – Italy, West Germany; 2 – Argentina, Uruguay; 1 – England.
Next Finals: 1998 in France, 2002 Japan and South Korea joint hosts.

WORLD CUP-WINNING MANAGERS/COACHES

1930 Uruguay, Alberto Supicci; **1934** Italy, Vittorio Pozzo; **1938** Italy, Vittorio Pozzo; **1950** Uruguay, Juan Lopez; **1954** West Germany, Sepp Herberger; **1958** Brazil, Vicente Feola; **1962** Brazil, Aimore Moreira; **1966** England, Alf Ramsey; **1970** Brazil, Mario Zagalo; **1974** West Germany, Helmut Schoen; **1978** Argentina, Cesar Luis Menotti; **1982** Italy, Enzo Bearzot; **1986** Argentina, Carlos Bilardo; **1990** West Germany, Franz Beckenbauer; **1994** Brazil, Carlos Alberto Parreira.

QUOTE-UNQUOTE

GRAHAM KELLY, F.A. chief executive: "Our decision to apply to stage the 2006 World Cup in England has been crystallised during the European Championship. The behaviour of the fans has been a major plus and a big talking point within UEFA circles. The England supporters and the England team have done the game in this country a great service."

DON HOWE: "There is nothing you can know about football that cannot be learned from watching Germany. Physically, tactically, technically, mentally, they get it right almost every time."

BILL SHANKLY: "I'm only surprised that people are surprised by surprise results in football."

ALAN BUCKLEY, WBA manager, in season's briefest after-match Press conference: "First half OK, second half rubbish."

BRITISH AND IRISH INTERNATIONALS 1995-96

Note: In the senior Internationals that follow, * = new cap.

EUROPEAN CHAMPIONSHIP – QUALIFYING ROUND

SCOTLAND 1, GREECE 0

Hampden Park (34,910), Wednesday, August 16, 1995

Scotland: Leighton (Hibernian); McKimmie (Aberdeen), Calderwood (Tottenham), Boyd (Celtic), *T. McKinlay (Celtic), McAllister (Leeds, Capt.), McCall (Rangers), Collins (Celtic), Burley (Chelsea), Shearer (Aberdeen) (McCoist, Rangers, 72), Jackson (Hibernian) (Robertson, Hearts, 72). **Scorer**: McCoist (72). **Booked**: Burley.

Greece: Atmatzidis; Apostolakis, Karataidis, Kalitzakis, Dabizas, Tsalouchidis, Zagorakis (Georgiadis 79), Batista (Alexandris 51), Vryzas (Machlas 30), Tsartas, Kassapis. **Booked**: Kalitzakis.

Referee: P. Mikkelsen (Denmark). **Half-time:** 0-0.

PORTUGAL 1, NORTHERN IRELAND 1

Oporto (50,000), Sunday, September 3, 1995

Portugal: Vitor Baia; Secretario, Jorge Costa (Rui Barros 72), Oceano, Couto, Paulo Sousa, Figo, Paulinho Santos, Domingos, Rui Costa (Alves 82), Folha. **Scorer**: Domingos (47).

N. Ireland: Fettis (Hull); Morrow (Arsenal), Hill (Leicester), Hunter (Wrexham), Lomas (Man. City), Worthington (Leeds, Capt.), Gillespie (Newcastle), Magilton (Southampton), Lennon (Crewe), Hughes (Strasbourg), Dowie (Crystal Palace) (P. Gray, Sunderland, 77). **Scorer**: Hughes (66).

Referee: R. Harrel (France). **Half-time:** 0-0.

AUSTRIA 3, REPUBLIC OF IRELAND 1

Vienna (24,000), Wednesday, September 6, 1995

Austria: Konsel; Furstaller, Schottel, Pfeffer, Schopp, Kuhbauer, Pfeifenberger, Marasek, Stoger, Herzog, Polster (Cerny 79). **Scorer**: Stoger (3, 64, 77). **Booked**: Schottel.

Rep. of Ireland: A. Kelly (Sheff. Utd.); G. Kelly (Leeds), Kernaghan (Man. City), McGrath (Aston Villa), Irwin (Man. Utd.), Houghton (Crystal Palace) (Cascarino, Marseille, 67), Sheridan (Sheff. Wed.), Townsend (Aston Villa, Capt.), Keane (Man. Utd.), *Kennedy (Liverpool), Quinn (Man. City). **Scorer**: McGrath (74). **Booked**: Townsend, Kennedy, Keane.

Referee: A. Caker (Turkey). **Half-time:** 1-0.

SCOTLAND 1, FINLAND 0

Hampden Park (35,505), Wednesday, September 6, 1995

Scotland: Leighton (Hibernian); Boyd (Celtic), Calderwood (Tottenham), McKimmie (Aberdeen) (B. McKinlay, Dundee Utd., 89), Hendry (Blackburn), McLaren (Rangers), McAllister (Leeds, Capt.), Collins (Celtic), T. McKinlay (Celtic), Booth (Aberdeen) (Jackson, Hibernian, 80), Spencer (Chelsea) (McCoist, Rangers, 74). **Scorer**: Booth (10).

Finland: Laukkanen; Rissanen, Kanerva, Holmgren, Nieminen (Gronlund 63), Suominen, Myyry, Litmanen, Lindberg, Hjelm, Jarvinen.

Referee: V. Melnichuk (Ukraine). **Half-time:** 1-0.

WALES 1 MOLDOVA 0

Cardiff Arms Park (5,000), Wednesday, September 6, 1995

Wales: Southall (Everton); A. Williams (Reading), Symons (Man. City), Coleman (Crystal Palace), Bowen (Norwich), Horne (Everton, Capt.), Pembridge (Sheff. Wed.), Speed (Leeds), Rush (Liverpool) (Hartson, Arsenal, 68), Nogan (Reading) (Phillips, Nott'm. Forest, 45), Hughes (Chelsea). **Scorer**: Speed (55). **Booked**: Coleman.

Moldova: Ivanov; Fistican, Testimitanu, Culibaba, Rebeja (Gavriliuc 83), Stroenko, Oprea, Belous, Nani (Suharev 76), Cibotari, Clescento. **Sent-off**: Fistican (90).

Referee: G. Orrason (Iceland). **Half-time:** 0-0.

LIECHTENSTEIN 0, NORTHERN IRELAND 4

Vaduz (1,100), Wednesday, October 11, 1995

Liechtenstein: Oehry; Hefti, Frick (Hanselmann 78), Hilti (Ospelt 66), Hasler, Klaunzer, Telser, Stocker (Sele 45), Schadler, Zech, Oehri.

N. Ireland: Fettis (Hull) (*Wood, Walsall, 75); Lomas (Man. City), Hill (Leicester), Hunter (Wrexham), Worthington (Leeds, Capt.), McMahon (Tottenham) (McGibbon, Man. Utd., 80), Lennon (Crewe), O'Neill (Hibernian), Hughes (Strasbourg) (Rowland, West Ham, 89), Quinn (Reading), P. Gray (Sunderland). **Scorers**: O'Neill (36), McMahon (49), Quinn (55), Gray (72).

Referee: L. Michel (Slovakia). **Half-time:** 0-1.

REPUBLIC OF IRELAND 2, LATVIA 1

Lansdowne Road, Dublin (33,000), Wednesday, October 11, 1995

Rep. of Ireland: A. Kelly (Sheff. Utd.); G. Kelly (Leeds), McGrath (Aston Villa), Babb (Liverpool), Phelan (Man. City), McAteer (Liverpool), Kenna (Blackburn), Townsend (Aston Villa, Capt.), Staunton (Aston Villa), Quinn (Man. City), Aldridge (Tranmere) (D. Kelly, Sunderland, 79; Kennedy, Liverpool, 84). **Scorer**: Aldridge (61 pen, 64).

Latvia: Karavajevs; Shevljakovs, Stepanov, Zakresevskis, Troickis, Astafievs, Babicevs (Jelisejevs 71), Zemlinskis, Zeiberlins, Ivanovs, Rimkus. **Scorer**: Rimkus (78).

Referee: J-A. Marin (Spain). **Half-time:** 0-0.

WALES 1, GERMANY 2

Cardiff Arms Park (25,000), Wednesday, October 11, 1995

Wales: Southall (Everton); Symons (Man. City), Bowen (Norwich), Melville (Sunderland), *Jenkins (Swansea) (*Mardon, West Brom, 71), Blake (Sheff. Utd.) (G. Williams, Ipswich, 81), Horne (Everton, Capt.), Pembridge (Sheff. Wed.) (Hodges, Sheff. Utd., 81), Speed (Leeds), Giggs (Man. Utd.), Saunders (Galatasaray). **Scorer**: Symons (78). **Booked**: Southall, Saunders, Pembridge, Blake.

Germany: Kopke; Babbel (Worns 45), Sammer, Helmer, Freund, Hassler, Eilts, Moller, Ziege, Herrlich (Kuntz 73), Klinsmann. **Scorers**: Melville (75 og), Klinsmann (80). **Booked**: Ziege, Sammer.

Referee: I. Craciunescu (Romania). **Half-time:** 0-0.

ALBANIA 1, WALES 1

Tirana (5,000), Wednesday, November 15, 1995

Albania: Strakosha; Zmitani, Dema, Malko, Vata, Shulku, Pano, Lecbello, Bozgo (Zalla 78; Milori 83), Kushta (Bushey 57), Rakkli. **Scorer**: Kushta (5 pen). **Booked**: Lecbello.

Wales: Southall (Everton, Capt.); Young (Wolves), Bowen (Norwich), Melville (Sunderland), Jenkins (Huddersfield), Hughes (Luton) (*Savage, Crewe, 63), Phillips (Nott'm. Forest), Pembridge (Sheff. Wed.), *Taylor (Crystal Palace) (*Robinson, Charlton, 84), Saunders (Galatasaray), Giggs (Man. Utd.). **Scorer**: Pembridge (41). **Booked**: Bowen, Taylor, Pembridge.

Referee: D. Suheil (Israel). **Half-time:** 1-1.

NORTHERN IRELAND 5, AUSTRIA 3

Windsor Park, Belfast (8,400), Wednesday, November 15, 1995

N. Ireland: Fettis (Hull); Lomas (Man. City), Hunter (Wrexham), Hill (Leicester), Worthington (Leeds, Capt.), Gillespie (Newcastle), Lennon (Crewe), O'Neill (Hibernian), Hughes (Strasbourg), Dowie (West Ham) (Quinn, Reading, 82), P. Gray (Sunderland) (McDonald, Q.P.R., 79). **Scorers**: O'Neill (27, 78), Dowie (32 pen), Hunter (53), Gray (63).

Austria: Konsel; Feirsinger, Kogler, Pfeffer, Schopp, Kuhbauer (Wetl 45), Marasek, Herzog (Stumpf 45), Stoger, Pfeifenberger, Polster. **Scorers**: Schopp (56), Stumpf (70), Wetl (81).

Referee: L. Sundell (Sweden). **Half-time:** 2-0.

• N. Ireland's biggest home score since 5-0 v Cyprus, April 21, 1971.

PORTUGAL 3, REPUBLIC OF IRELAND 0

Lisbon (80,000), Wednesday, October 15, 1995

Portugal: Vitor Baia (Neno 86); Secretario, Helder, Couto, Paulinho Santos, Oceano, Paulo Sousa, Rui Costa, Figo, Joao Pinto (Folha 67), Domingos (Cadete 67). **Scorers**: Rui Costa (59), Helder (74), Cadete (89).

Rep. of Ireland: A. Kelly (Sheff. Utd.); G. Kelly (Leeds), McGrath (Aston Villa, Capt.), Babb (Liverpool), Irwin (Man. Utd.), McAteer (Liverpool), Kenna

(Blackburn), Staunton (Aston Villa) (Kernaghan, Man. City, 79), Kennedy (Liverpool), Quinn (Man. City), Aldridge (Tranmere). **Booked**: Babb, Quinn.

Referee: P. Ceccarini (Italy). **Half-time:** 0-0.

• Heaviest defeat for Rep. under manager Jack Charlton.

SCOTLAND 5, SAN MARINO 0

Hampden Park (30,306), Wednesday, November 15, 1995

Scotland: Leighton (Hibernian); McLaren (Rangers), Hendry (Blackburn), Calderwood (Tottenham), Boyd (Celtic), Gemmill (Nott'm. Forest), McAllister (Leeds, Capt.) (McCoist, Rangers, 47), Collins (Celtic) (B. McKinlay, Blackburn, 58), Nevin (Tranmere), Booth (Aberdeen) (Jackson, Hibernian, 65), Jess (Aberdeen). **Scorers**: Jess (30), Booth (45), McCoist (49), Nevin (71), Francini (90 og).

San Marino: S. Muccioli; Moroni, Guerra, M. Valentini, Manzaroli, Francini, Mazza (Della Valle 81), Matteoni, Gennari, Bacciocchi, Mularoni (Canti 51). **Booked**: Mularoni, Moroni, Guerra.

Referee: K. Bohunek (Czech Republic). **Half-time:** 2-0.

PLAY-OFF

REPUBLIC OF IRELAND 0, HOLLAND 2

Anfield (40,000), Thursday, December 13, 1995

Rep. of Ireland: A. Kelly (Sheff. Utd.); G. Kelly (Leeds), McGrath (Aston Villa), Babb (Liverpool), Irwin (Man. Utd.), Kenna (Blackburn), Sheridan (Sheff. Wed.), Townsend (Aston Villa, Capt.) (McAteer, Liverpool, 50), Phelan (Chelsea), Aldridge (Tranmere) (Kernaghan, Man. City, 72), Cascarino (Marseille). **Booked**: Kernaghan.

Holland: Van der Sar; Reiziger, Blind, Bogarde, R. de Boer, Seedorf, Davids, Bergkamp (de Kock 58), Overmars, Kluivert, Helder (Winter 78). **Scorers**: Kluivert (29, 89). **Booked**: Blind.

Referee: V. Zhuk (Belarus). **Half-time:** 0-1.

WORLD CUP – QUALIFYING ROUND

SAN MARINO 0, WALES 5

Stadio di Serravalle (1,613), Sunday, June 2, 1996

San Marino: S. Muccioli; Gasperoni, M. Valentini, Guerra, Gobbi, Casadei (Peverani 74), Manzaroli, Pasolini (A. Muccioli 70), Mazza, Mularoni (V. Valentini 50), Montagna. **Booked**: V. Valentini, Manzaroli.

Wales: Southall (Everton); Bowen (Norwich), Melville (Sunderland), Coleman (Blackburn), Pembridge (Sheff. Wed.), Horne (Everton, Capt.) (Savage, Crewe, 81), Browning (Bristol Rovers) (Goss, Norwich, 74), Robinson (Charlton) (Legg, Birmingham, 79), Hughes (Chelsea), Saunders (Galatasaray), Giggs (Man. Utd.). **Scorers**: Melville (20), Hughes (32, 43), Giggs (50), Pembridge (85). **Booked**: Hughes, Legg.

Referee: M. Lubos (Slovakia). **Half-time:** 0-3.

OTHER INTERNATIONALS

ENGLAND 0, COLOMBIA 0

Wembley (20,038), Wednesday, September 6, 1995

England: Seaman (Arsenal); G. Neville (Man. Utd.), Howey (Newcastle), Adams (Arsenal, Capt.), Le Saux (Blackburn), Wise (Chelsea), *Redknapp (Liverpool) (Barnes, Liverpool, 75), Gascoigne (Rangers) (Lee, Newcastle, 75), McManaman (Liverpool), Barmby (Middlesbrough), Shearer (Blackburn) (Sheringham, Tottenham, 75).

Colombia: Higuita; Santa, Bermudez, Mendoza, Perez, Lozano, Alvarez, Asprilla, Valderrama, Rincon, Valenciano. **Booked**: Asprilla, Rincon, Alvarez.

Referee: M. Batta (France).

NORWAY 0, ENGLAND 0

Oslo (21,006), Wednesday, October 11, 1995

Norway: Thorstvedt; Loken, Berg, R. Johnsen, Bjornebye, Rekdal, T. Flo, Bohinen, Leonhardsen (Solbakken 62), Jakobsen, Fjortoft (Brattbakk 78).

England: Seaman (Arsenal); G. Neville (Man. Utd.), Adams (Arsenal, Capt.), Pallister (Man. Utd.), Pearce (Nott'm. Forest), Wise (Chelsea) (*Stone, Nott'm. Forest, 66), Redknapp (Liverpool), Lee (Newcastle), McManaman (Liverpool), Barmby (Middlesbrough) (Sheringham, Tottenham, 66), Shearer (Blackburn).

Referee: K. Nilsson (Sweden).

SWEDEN 2, SCOTLAND 0

Stockholm (19,121), Wednesday, October 11, 1995

Sweden: B. Andersson; Lucic (Kamark 89), P. Andersson, Bjorklund, Nilsson, Schwarz, Alexandersson, Gudmundsson (Pringle 70), Petterson, K. Andersson (Erlingmark 80), Brolin. **Scorers**: Petterson (31), Schwarz (35).

Scotland: Leighton (Hibernian) (Goram, Rangers, 73); McKimmie (Aberdeen), Boyd (Celtic), Calderwood (Tottenham), Hendry (Blackburn), McLaren (Rangers), Burley (Chelsea) (B. McKinlay, Dundee Utd., 45), Robertson (Hearts) (Nevin, Tranmere, 73), McGinlay (Bolton) (Jess, Aberdeen, 45), McAllister (Leeds, Capt.) (Jackson, Hibernian, 60), Collins (Celtic).

Referee: D. Vega (Spain). **Half-time:** 2-0.

ENGLAND 3, SWITZERLAND 1

Wembley (29,874), Wednesday, November 15, 1995

England: Seaman (Arsenal); G. Neville (Man. Utd.), Adams (Arsenal, Capt.), Pallister (Man. Utd.), Pearce (Nott'm. Forest), Lee (Newcastle), Gascoigne (Rangers), Redknapp (Liverpool) (Stone, Nott'm. Forest, 5), McManaman (Liverpool), Sheringham (Tottenham), Shearer (Blackburn). **Scorers**: Pearce (45), Sheringham (56), Stone (78).

Switzerland: Pascolo; Hottiger, Geiger, Henchoz, Quentin (Vega 82), Ohrel, Fournier (Wolf 70), Sforza, Sutter (Grassi 80), Turkyilmaz, Knup. **Scorer**: Knup (41).

Referee: S. Puhl (Hungary). **Half-time:** 1-1.

ENGLAND 1, PORTUGAL 1

Wembley (28,592), Tuesday, December 12, 1995

England: Seaman (Arsenal); G. Neville (Man. Utd.), Adams (Arsenal, Capt.), Howey (Newcastle), Pearce (Nott'm. Forest) (Le Saux, Blackburn, 79), Stone (Nott'm. Forest), Gascoigne (Rangers), Wise (Chelsea) (McManaman, Liverpool, 79), Barmby (Middlesbrough) (*Southgate, Aston Villa, 79), Shearer (Blackburn), Ferdinand (Newcastle) (Beardsley, Newcastle, 65). **Scorer**: Stone (44). **Booked**: Howey.

Portugal: Neno; Secretario, Couto, Cadete, Dimas, Helder, Paulo Sousa (Paulo Alves 45), Joao Pinto (Dani 60), Figo (Domingos 45), Folha (Pedro 67), Sa Pinto. **Scorer**: Paulo Alves (58). **Booked**: Cadete.

Referee: R. Pedersen (Norway). **Half-time**: 1-0.

ITALY 3, WALES 0

Terni (20,000), Wednesday, January 24, 1996

Italy: Peruzzi (Toldo 45); Ferrara (Torricelli 45), Carboni, Di Matteo (Conte 23), Costacurta, Apolloni, Di Livio (Crippa 33), Albertini, Del Piero (Casiraghi 73), Zola, Ravanelli. **Scorers**: Del Piero (2), Ravanelli (50), Casiraghi (77).

Wales: Southall (Everton); Jenkins (Huddersfield), Coleman (Blackburn), Phillips (Nott'm. Forest), Williams (Reading), Symons (Man. City), Horne (Everton, Capt.), Hodges (Sheff. Utd.) (*Browning, Bristol Rovers, 57), Rush (Liverpool) (Taylor, Crystal Palace, 64), Hughes (Chelsea), Speed (Leeds) (Blake, Bolton, 77).

Referee: G. Goethals (Belgium). **Half-time**: 1-0.

ENGLAND 1, BULGARIA 0

Wembley (29,708), Wednesday, March 27, 1996

England: Seaman (Arsenal); G. Neville (Man. Utd.), Southgate (Aston Villa), Howey (Newcastle), Pearce (Nott'm. Forest, Capt.), Stone (Nott'm. Forest), Ince (Inter Milan), Gascoigne (Rangers) (Platt, Arsenal, 76), McManaman (Liverpool), Sheringham (Tottenham) (Lee, Newcastle, 76), Ferdinand (Newcastle) (*Fowler, Liverpool, 76). **Scorer**: Ferdinand (7). **Booked**: Pearce.

Bulgaria: Mihaylov (Popov 45); Ivanov, Kremenliev (Sirakov 85), Houbtchev, Iankov, Guintchev (Borimirov 45), Letchkov, Kiriakov, Iordanov (Guentchev 46), Kostadinov, Penev (Kischischev 85). **Booked**: Ivanov, Kremenliev.

Referee: G. Benkoe (Austria). **Half-time**: 1-0.

NORTHERN IRELAND 0, NORWAY 2

Windsor Park, Belfast (5,343), Wednesday, March 27, 1996

Northern Ireland: Fettis (Nott'm. Forest); Lomas (Man. City), Hill (Leicester), McDonald (Q.P.R.), Worthington (Leeds, Capt.) (Rowland, West Ham, 56), Gillespie (Newcastle), Magilton (Southampton) (Patterson, Luton, 45), Lennon (Leicester), Hughes (West Ham), O'Neill (Hibernian) (McMahon, Tottenham, 62), Dowie (West Ham).

Norway: Grodas (Thorstvedt 45); Haaland, Johnsen, Berg, Bjornebye, Rudi, Rekdal, Solbakken (Lundekvam 86), Leonhardsen (Jakobsen 24), Fjortoft (Ostenstad 74), Solskjaer. **Scorers**: Solskjaer (51), Ostenstad (78).

Referee: J. Ashman (Wales). **Half-time**: 0-0.

REPUBLIC OF IRELAND 0, RUSSIA 2

Lansdowne Road, Dublin (41,600), Wednesday, March 27, 1996

Rep. of Ireland: *Given (Blackburn); McGrath (Aston Villa), Kernaghan (Man. City), Staunton (Aston Villa), McAteer (Liverpool), Keane (Man. Utd.), Townsend (Aston Villa, Capt.) (Kenna, Blackburn, 45), Kennedy (Liverpool), Phelan (Chelsea), Quinn (Man. City) (Coyne, Motherwell, 83), Aldridge (Tranmere) (Cascarino, Marseille, 64). **Booked**: Staunton. **Sent-off**: Keane (88).

Russia: Cherchesov; Onopko, Nikiforov, Kovtun, Kanchelskis, Karpin, Radimov (Radchenko 45), Tsymbalar (Tetradze 45), Mostovoi, Kiriyakov (Simutenkov 67), Kolyvanov (Shalimov 70). **Scorers**: Mostovoi (34), Kolyvanov (54).

Referee: H. Luyten (Holland). **Half-time**: 0-1.

• Mick McCarthy's first match as Rep. of Ireland manager.

SCOTLAND 1, AUSTRALIA 0

Hampden Park (20,608), Wednesday, March 27, 1996

Scotland: Leighton (Hibernian); Burley (Chelsea), *O'Neil (Celtic) (Booth, Aberdeen, 45), Hendry (Blackburn), Boyd (Celtic), B. McKinlay (Blackburn) (Jackson, Hibernian, 75), McStay (Celtic) (Gallacher, Blackburn, 45), McAllister (Leeds), Collins (Celtic), McCoist (Rangers, Capt.) (Nevin, Tranmere, 80), Spencer (Chelsea). **Scorer**: McCoist (53).

Australia: Bosnich; T. Vidmar, Tobin, Horvat, Popovic, Van Blerk, Slater, A. Vidmar, Corica, Arnold, Veart (Teatto 68).

Referee: J. Van Dijk (Holland). **Half-time**: 0-0.

• Ally McCoist captain's Scotland in his 50th International.

CZECH REPUBLIC 2, REPUBLIC OF IRELAND 0

Prague (6,118), Wednesday, April 24, 1996

Czech Republic: Kouba; Hornak (Rada 73), Kadlec (Kubik 45), Repka, Latal (Nedved 59), Frydek, Nemecek (Bejbl 45), Berger, Hapal, Drulak, Kuka (Kerbr 78). **Scorers**: Frydek (61), Kuka (69).

Rep. of Ireland: Given (Blackburn); *Cunningham (Wimbledon), McGrath (Aston Villa), Babb (Liverpool) (Daish, Coventry, 66), Kenna (Blackburn), Houghton (Crystal Palace), Townsend (Aston Villa, Capt.), Kennedy (Liverpool), Irwin (Man. Utd.) (*Fleming, Middlesbrough, 45), Quinn (Man. City), *Moore (Middlesbrough).

Referee: H. Strampe (Germany). **Half-time**: 0-0.

DENMARK 2, SCOTLAND 0

Copenhagen (23,021), Wednesday, April 24, 1996

Denmark: Schmeichel (Krogh 45); Helveg, Rieper, Olsen, Risager (Laursen 81), Schjonberg, S. Nielsen, Thomsen, Beck, B. Laudrup, M. Laudrup (A. Nielsen 85). **Scorers**: M. Laudrup (7), B. Laudrup (27).

Scotland: Leighton (Hibernian) (Goram, Rangers, 45); McKimmie (Aberdeen), T. McKinlay (Celtic), Boyd (Celtic), Hendry (Blackburn) (B. McKinlay, Blackburn, 74), McCall (Rangers) (Gemmill, Nott'm. Forest, 45), Burley (Chelsea), Gallacher

(Blackburn) (McCoist, Rangers, 72), Spencer (Chelsea) (Jackson, Hibernian, 72), McAllister (Leeds, Capt.), Collins (Celtic).

Referee: J. Wegerees (Holland). **Half-time**: 0-2.

ENGLAND 0, CROATIA 0

Wembley (33,650), Wednesday, April 24, 1996

England: Seaman (Arsenal); G. Neville (Man. Utd.), Wright (Liverpool), Pearce (Nott'm. Forest), Ince (Inter Milan), Stone (Nott'm. Forest), Gascoigne (Rangers), Platt (Arsenal, Capt.), McManaman (Liverpool), Fowler (Liverpool), Sheringham (Tottenham). **Booked**: Pearce.

Croatia: Mrmic; Jerkan, Bilic, Stimac (Soldo 57), Pavlicic (Mladenovic 75), Asanovic, Boban (Stanic 45), Prosinecki, Jarni, Boksic (Pamic 70), Suker. **Booked**: Pavlicic, Asanovic.

Referee: Z. Przesmycki (Poland).

NORTHERN IRELAND 1, SWEDEN 2

Windsor Park, Belfast (5,666), Wednesday, April 24, 1996

N. Ireland: *Davison (Bolton); Patterson (Luton), Worthington (Leeds, Capt.) (*Quinn, Blackpool, 77), Hill (Leicester), Hunter (Wrexham), Morrow (Arsenal), *McCarthy (Port Vale), Lomas (Man. City), McMahon (Tottenham), O'Neill (Hibernian) (O'Boyle, St. Johnstone, 65), Rowland (West Ham). **Scorer**: McMahon (84).

Sweden: B. Andersson; R. Nilsson, P. Andersson, Bjorklund, Sundgren, Schwarz, Wilbran (Zetterberg 45), Ingesson, Thern, Dahlin (Larsson 88), K. Andersson (Pettersson 58). **Scorers**: Dahlin (21), Ingesson (58).

Referee: H. Dallas (Scotland). **Half-time**: 0-1.

SWITZERLAND 2, WALES 0

Lugano (8,000), Wednesday, April 24, 1996

Switzerland: Pascolo (Lehmann 84); Vogel (Hottiger 46), Vega, Henchoz, Quentin, Turkyilmaz (Comisetti 84), Ohrel (Lombardo 64), Sforza, Wicky (Koller 84), Grassi (Knup 76), Chapuisat (Sutter 64). **Scorers**: Coleman (32 og), Turkyilmaz (42 pen).

Wales: *Coyne (Tranmere) (*Marriott, Wrexham, 45); Symons (Man. City), Bowen (Norwich), Coleman (Blackburn) (*C. Edwards, Swansea, 88), Robinson (Charlton), Horne (Everton, Capt.) (Goss, Norwich, 65), Jones (Wimbledon) (Savage, Crewe, 65), Pembridge (Sheff. Wed.), *Legg (Birmingham) (Speed, Leeds, 29), Taylor (Sheff. Utd.) (*Davies, Man. Utd., 45), Hartson (Arsenal).

Referee: L. Stafoggia (Italy). **Half-time**: 2-0.

ENGLAND 3, HUNGARY 0

Wembley (34,184), Saturday, May 18, 1996

England: Seaman (Arsenal) (*Walker, Tottenham, 65); G. Neville (Man. Utd.), Wright (Liverpool) (Southgate, Aston Villa, 11), Pearce (Nott'm. Forest), Ince (Inter Milan) (*Campbell, Tottenham, 65), Anderton (Tottenham), Lee (Newcastle),

Platt (Arsenal, Capt.) (Wise, Chelsea, 65), *Wilcox (Blackburn), Sheringham (Tottenham), Ferdinand (Newcastle) (Shearer, Blackburn, 76). **Scorers**: Anderton (36, 62), Platt (52).

Hungary: Petry; Hahn, Banfi, Plokai, Balog (Illes 61), Mracsko (Aranyos 81), Urban, Sebok, Nagy (Telek 81), Horvath (Lisztes 81), Vincze (Egressy 79).

Referee: M. Merk (Germany). **Half-time**: 1-0.

CHINA 0, ENGLAND 3

Workers' Stadium, Beijing (65,000), Thursday, May 23, 1996

China: Ou Quliang; Wei Qun, Xu Hone, Fan Ziyi, Li Hong Ju, Xie Yuxing (Mi Ling 45), Jiang Feng (Gao Zhangxun 33), Ma Mingyu, Li Bing (Peng 45), Gao Fen, Hao Haidong.

England: Flowers (Blackburn) (Walker, Tottenham, 63); G. Neville (Man. Utd.), Adams (Arsenal, Capt.) (*Ehiogu, Aston Villa, 76), Southgate (Aston Villa), *P. Neville (Man. Utd.), Anderton (Tottenham), Redknapp (Liverpool), Gascoigne (Rangers), McManaman (Liverpool) (Stone, Nott'm. Forest, 80), Barmby (Middlesbrough) (Beardsley, Newcastle, 71), Shearer (Blackburn) (Fowler, Liverpool, 71). **Scorers**: Barmby (30, 53), Gascoigne (64).

Referee: P. Collina (Italy). **Half-time**: 0-1.

• Gary and Philip Neville first brothers in an England side since Bobby and Jack Charlton at the 1970 World Cup in Mexico. Philip Neville England's first 19-year-old since Lee Sharpe v Rep. of Ireland, March 1991.

HONG KONG GOLDEN XI 0, ENGLAND 1

Hong Kong Stadium (26,000), Sunday, May 26, 1996
(Caps not awarded)

Hong Kong XI: Hesford; Van der Sander (Shing Kit 80), Duxbury (ex-Man. Utd.), Watson (Everton), Fook Wing, Fairweather (ex-Wimbledon), Grainger, Roberts, Bullen, Grabo, Bajkusa (Cam Chuen 75).

England: Seaman (Arsenal); P. Neville (Man. Utd.), Adams (Arsenal), Howey (Newcastle) (Campbell, Tottenham, 59), Pearce (Nott'm. Forest), Stone (Nott'm. Forest) (Anderton, Tottenham, 62), Ince (Inter Milan), Platt (Arsenal, Capt.), McManaman (Liverpool) (Wilcox, Blackburn, 78), Ferdinand (Newcastle) (Shearer, Blackburn, 45), Sheringham (Tottenham) (Fowler, Liverpool, 71). **Scorer**: Ferdinand (33).

Referee: S. Setlarajan (Malaysia). **Half-time**: 0-1.

USA 2, SCOTLAND 1

Connecticut (8,526), Sunday, May 26, 1996

USA: Sommer; Burns, Lalas, Balboa, Agoos, Jones, Dooley (Kirovski 54), Harkes, Reyna (McBride 82), Ramos, Wynalda. **Scorers**: Wynalda (13 pen), Jones (72). **Booked**: Lalas.

Scotland: Leighton (Hibernian) (Walker, Partick, 81); Calderwood (Tottenham), Hendry (Blackburn, Capt.), Whyte (Middlesbrough), Burley (Chelsea) (McCall, Rangers, 60), Jackson (Hibernian) (Collins, Monaco, 45), Jess (Coventry), Gemmill (Nott'm. Forest) (McAllister, Leeds, 45), Boyd (Celtic), Booth (Aberdeen), Durie (Rangers) (Spencer, Chelsea, 45). **Scorer**: Durie (9). **Booked**: Booth.

Referee: E. Brizio-Carter (Brazil). **Half-time**: 1-1.

COLOMBIA 1, SCOTLAND 0

Miami (12,000), Wednesday, May 29, 1996

Colombia: Mondragon; Bermudez, Moreno, Ortiz (Herrera 45), Cassiani (Valderrama 45), Rincon, Estrada (Mendoza 45), Serna, Mafla (Asprilla 45), Valencia (Aristizabal 45), Valencieno (Alverez 45). **Scorer**: Asprilla (82). **Booked**: Moreno.

Scotland: Goram (Rangers); McKimmie (Aberdeen), McKinlay (Rangers), Boyd (Celtic), Hendry (Blackburn) (Burley, Chelsea, 45), Calderwood (Tottenham), Collins (Monaco), McAllister (Leeds, Capt.), McCall (Rangers), McCoist (Rangers) (Gallacher, Blackburn, 61), Spencer (Chelsea) (Jess, Coventry, 61). **Booked**: Boyd.

Referee: R. Dominguez (USA). **Half-time**: 0-0.

NORTHERN IRELAND 1, GERMANY 1

Windsor Park, Belfast (11,770), Wednesday, May 29, 1996

N. Ireland: Fettis (Nott'm. Forest); *Griffin (St. Johnstone), Hill (Leicester), Hunter (Wrexham), Worthington (Leeds, Capt.) (Rowland, West Ham, 45), Gillespie (Newcastle) (O'Boyle, St. Johnstone, 63), Lomas (Man. City), Magilton (Southampton), Hughes (West Ham), Dowie (West Ham), McMahon (Tottenham). **Scorer**: O'Boyle (79).

Germany: Khan; Helmer, Basler, Kohler, Ziege (Bode 45), Eilts, Moller, Scholl, Strunz, Klinsmann (Kuntz 45), Bierhoff (Bobic 45). **Scorer**: Scholl (80). **Booked**: Ziege, Scholl, Basler.

Referee: W. Young (Scotland). **Half-time**: 0-0.

REPUBLIC OF IRELAND 0, PORTUGAL 1

Lansdowne Road, Dublin (26,576), Wednesday, May 29, 1996

Rep. of Ireland: Given (Blackburn); Cunningham (Wimbledon), Kernaghan (Man. City) (*Breen, Birmingham, 88), Kenna (Blackburn), Fleming (Middlesbrough), McLoughlin (Portsmouth), *Farrelly (Aston Villa) (*Savage, Millwall, 59), Townsend (Aston Villa, Capt.), Phelan (Chelsea), Cascarino (Marseille) (Quinn, Man. City, 74), *Connolly (Watford) (*O'Neill, Norwich, 62).

Portugal: Vitor Baia; Paulinho Santos, Couto, Helder, Dimas, Paneira (Sa Pinto 45), Tavares, Oceano (Porfirio 67), Joao Pinto, Folha, Cadete (Secretario 72). **Scorer**: Folha (90). **Booked**: Oceano, Paulinho Santos.

Referee: C. Detruche (Switzerland). **Half-time**: 0-0.

REPUBLIC OF IRELAND 2, CROATIA 2

Lansdowne Road, Dublin (29,100), Sunday, June 2, 1996

Rep. of Ireland: Given (Blackburn); Breen (Birmingham) (Cascarino, Marseille, 76), Daish (Coventry), Kenna (Blackburn) (Kernaghan, Man. City, 66), Cunningham (Wimbledon) (Fleming, Middlesbrough, 60), McLoughlin (Portsmouth) (Savage, Millwall, 74), O'Brien (Tranmere), Kennedy (Liverpool), Phelan (Chelsea) (*Harte, Leeds, 45), O'Neill (Norwich) (Moore, Middlesbrough, 45), Quinn (Man. City, Capt.). **Scorers**: O'Neill (24), Quinn (89).

Croatia: Mrmic (Ladic 45); Stimac, Bilic, Jerkan, Stanic (Soldo 80), Boban,

Vlaovic (Jurcevic 74), Asanovic, Jarni, Suker, Boksic. **Scorers**: Suker (15), Boban (45).

Referee: P. Leduc (France). **Half-time**: 1-2.

HOLLAND 3, REPUBLIC OF IRELAND 1

Rotterdam (15,002), Tuesday, June 4, 1996

Holland: Van der Sar; Reiziger, Blind (de Kock 45), Bogarde, Witschge, R. de Boer (Winter 45), Seedorf, Davids, Hoekstra (Taument 28), Bergkamp, Cruyff (Cocu 75). **Scorers**: Bergkamp (27), Seedorf (77), Cocu (88). **Booked**: Cruyff.

Rep. of Ireland: Given (Blackburn); Breen (Birmingham), Kernaghan (Man. City, Capt.), Harte (Leeds), Kenna (Blackburn) (Fleming, Middlesbrough, 77), McLoughlin (Portsmouth), O'Brien (Tranmere) (Cunningham, Wimbledon, 71), Moore (Middlesbrough) (Kennedy, Liverpool, 45), Phelan (Chelsea), Connolly (Watford) (Quinn, Man. City, 65), Cascarino (Marseille) (O'Neill, Norwich, 45). **Scorer**: Breen (13).

Referee: F. Lambek (Denmark). **Half-time**: 1-1.

'B' INTERNATIONALS

SWEDEN 'B' 1, SCOTLAND 'B' 2

Gavle (2,500), Tuesday, October 10, 1995

Scotland 'B': Walker (Partick) (Gunn, Norwich, 65); Martin (Motherwell), Tweed (Hibernian), Whyte (Middlesbrough), Telfer (Coventry), Rae (Millwall) (Cameron, Raith, 65), Bernard (Aberdeen) (Lambert, Motherwell, 45), Gemmill (Nott'm. Forest), McKinnon (Motherwell), Creaney (Man. City), Shearer (Aberdeen, Capt.) (Brown, Kilmarnock, 70).

Scorers – Sweden: Andersson (77). **Scotland**: Shearer (36), Brown (85). **Half-time**: 0-1.

NORTHERN IRELAND 'B' 3, NORWAY 'B' 0

Coleraine (1,000), Tuesday, March 26, 1996

N. Ireland 'B': Davison (Bolton) (Wood, Walsall, 45); Wright (Norwich), Horlock (Swindon), Patterson (Luton) (Murdock, Man. Utd., 45), McGibbon (Man. Utd.), Lennon (Raith), McCarthy (Port Vale) (Graham, Q.P.R., 70), O'Boyle (St. Johnstone) (Robinson, Bournemouth, 45), Quinn (Blackpool) (Mulryne, Man. Utd., 61), Griffin (St. Johnstone), Black (Nott'm. Forest).

Scorers – N. Ireland 'B': Patterson (21), Quinn (66), Mulryne (87). **Half-time**: 1-0.

DENMARK 'B' 3, SCOTLAND 'B' 0

Nykobing (3,796), Tuesday, April 23, 1996

Scotland 'B': Walker (Partick) (Watt, Aberdeen, 45); McNamara (Celtic), O'Neil (Celtic), Martin (Motherwell), Whyte (Middlesbrough), Nevin (Tranmere), Jess (Coventry), Lambert (Motherwell), Glass (Aberdeen) (Cameron, Hearts, 45), McGinlay (Bolton) (Booth, Aberdeen, 45), Durie (Rangers) (Shearer, Aberdeen, 56).

Scorers – Denmark 'B': Larsen (43, 67), Bo Andersen (67). **Half-time**: 1-0.

US CUP

USA 2, REPUBLIC OF IRELAND 1

Boston (25,332), Sunday, June 9, 1996

USA: Friedel; Burns, Lalas, Balboa, Dooley, Agoos, Harkes, Reyna (Kirovski 77), Ramos (Lassiter 77), Jones, Wynalda (Caligiuri 88). **Scorers**: Ramos (58), Reyna (75).

Rep. of Ireland: Given (Blackburn); Kenna (Blackburn) (Fleming, Middlesbrough, 40), Phelan (Chelsea), Cunningham (Wimbledon), Kernaghan (Man. City, Capt.), Breen (Birmingham), McLoughlin (Portsmouth), Farrelly (Aston Villa), O'Brien (Tranmere) (O'Neill, Norwich, 87), Quinn (Man. City) (Savage, Millwall, 87), Connolly (Watford). **Scorer**: Connolly (56). **Half-time**: 0-0.

MEXICO 2, REPUBLIC OF IRELAND 2

New Jersey (21,322), Thursday, June 13, 1996

Mexico: O. Sanchez; Suarez, Davino, Lara, R. Garcia (Blanco 54), L. Garcia, Villa, Del Olmo, Sol, Alfaro, Palencia (Abundis 45). **Scorer**: L. Garcia (40, 70 pen).

Rep. of Ireland: Bonner (Celtic); Fleming (Middlesbrough), Breen (Birmingham), Daish (Coventry), Harte (Leeds), Kennedy (Liverpool) (Phelan, Chelsea, 72), Savage (Millwall), McLoughlin (Portsmouth), Moore (Middlesbrough), O'Neill (Norwich), Connolly (Watford). **Scorers**: Connolly (44), Davino (49 og). **Sent-off**: Daish (57), Quinn (57), McCarthy (manager, 60). **Half-time**: 1-1.

BOLIVIA 0, REPUBLIC OF IRELAND 3

New Jersey (14,624), Saturday, June 15, 1996

Bolivia: Sorio; Pena, Sanchez, Rimba, Castillo, Baldivieso, Etcheverry, Ramos (Cristalda 41), Cossio, Sandy, Moreno (Coimbra 45).

Rep. of Ireland: Given (Blackburn) (Bonner, Celtic, 86); Cunningham (Wimbledon) (Breen, Birmingham, 85), Kernaghan (Man. City, Capt.), Harte (Leeds), Fleming (Middlesbrough), Savage (Millwall), O'Brien (Tranmere) (McLoughlin, Portsmouth, 45), Phelan (Chelsea), Farrelly (Aston Villa) (Kennedy, Liverpool, 65), O'Neill (Norwich), Moore (Middlesbrough). **Scorers**: Harte (44), O'Neill (12, 32). **Half-time**: 0-3.

US Cup – final placings: 1 Mexico 5 points; **2** Rep. of Ireland 4 points; **3** USA 4 points; **4** Bolivia 3 points.

EUROPEAN UNDER-21 CHAMPIONSHIP

SCOTLAND 3, GREECE 0

Kilmarnock (2,517), Tuesday, August 15, 1995

Scotland: Stillie (Aberdeen); McNamara (Dunfermline) (McLaughlin, Celtic, 70), Gray (Celtic), Fullarton (St. Mirren) (Murray, Rangers, 58), Pressley (Dundee Utd., Capt.), Hannah (Dundee Utd.), Miller (Rangers), Glass (Aberdeen), Crawford (Raith) (Donnelly, Celtic, 62), Liddell (Barnsley), McCann (Dundee).

Scorers – Scotland: McNamara (16), Liddell (58 pen), Donnelly (68). **Half-time**: 1-0.

PORTUGAL 2, ENGLAND 0

Oporto (1,500), Saturday, September 2, 1995

England: Gerrard (Oldham, Capt.); P. Neville (Man. Utd.), Scimeca (Aston Villa), Elliott (Newcastle), Gordon (Crystal Palace), Sinclair (Q.P.R.), Beckham (Man. Utd.), Butt (Man. Utd.) (Bart-Williams, Nott'm. Forest, 45), Thompson (Bolton), Fowler (Liverpool), Shipperley (Southampton). **Sent-off**: Thompson (86).

Scorers – Portugal: Dani (23, 37). **Half-time**: 2-0.

AUSTRIA 1, REPUBLIC OF IRELAND 0

Amstetten (1,750), Tuesday, September 5, 1995

Rep. of Ireland: Given (Blackburn); Carr (Tottenham), Woods (Tranmere), Greene (Luton), Breen (Peterborough), Boland (Coventry), Kavanagh (Middlesbrough) (Scully, Crystal Palace, 42), Savage (Millwall), Launders (Crystal Palace), Perkins (Southend), Turner (Tottenham).

Scorer – Austria: Kouz (9). **Half-time**: 1-0.

WALES 1, MOLDOVA 0

Cardiff (500), Tuesday, September 5, 1995

Wales: Ward (Mansfield); Barnhouse (Swansea), R. Edwards (Bristol City, Capt.), Savage (Crewe) (Hughes, Swindon, 75), Page (Watford), Davies (Crystal Palace) (Baddeley, Cardiff, 45), Morgan (Tranmere), Evans (Shrewsbury), Taylor (Bristol Rovers), Jones (Liverpool), Coates (Swansea).

Scorer – Wales: Coates (16). **Half-time**: 1-0.

SCOTLAND 5, FINLAND 0

Cumbernauld (2,571), Wednesday, September 6, 1995

Scotland: Stillie (Aberdeen); McNamara (Dunfermline), Fullarton (St. Mirren), Glass (Aberdeen), Liddell (Barnsley) (Hamilton, Dundee, 65), McCann (Dundee), Murray (Rangers), Handyside (Grimsby), Dailly (Dundee Utd., Capt.), Locke (Hearts), Harper (Hibernian) (Crawford, Raith, 65).

Scorers – Scotland: Harper (21, 57, 69), Hamilton (79), Locke (87). **Half-time**: 1-0.

REPUBLIC OF IRELAND 1, LATVIA 0

Galway (6,000), Tuesday, October 10, 1995

Rep. of Ireland: Colgan (Chelsea); Carr (Tottenham), Greene (Luton), Breen (Peterborough), Savage (Millwall), Launders (Crystal Palace), Scully (Crystal Palace) (O'Byrne, UCD, 45), Hardy (Wrexham), Crawford (Newcastle) (O'Halloran, Middlesbrough, 45), Durkan (Wrexham), Moore (Middlesbrough) (O'Sullivan, Swindon, 45).

Scorer – Rep. of Ireland: Moore (1). **Half-time**: 1-0.

WALES 1, GERMANY 5

Cardiff (2,000), Tuesday, October 10, 1995

Wales: Ward (Mansfield); R. Edwards (Bristol City, Capt.), Savage (Crewe), Morgan (Tranmere) (Baddeley, Cardiff, 67), Evans (Shrewsbury), Jones (Liverpool) (Bird, Cardiff, 45), Coates (Swansea), Evans (Cardiff), C. Edwards (Swansea) (Twiddy, Plymouth, 67), Hughes (Bury), Hartson (Arsenal).

Scorers – Wales: Hartson (46). **Germany**: Jernies (37), Ricken (40, 52), Zickler (56), Rydlewitz (68). **Half-time**: 0-2.

ENGLAND 2, AUSTRIA 1

Middlesbrough (13,496), Tuesday, November 14, 1995

England: Oakes (Aston Villa); Watson (Newcastle), Elliott (Newcastle), Campbell (Tottenham), Unsworth (Everton), Butt (Man. Utd.), Bart-Williams (Nott'm. Forest) (Holland, Newcastle, 85), Roberts (Crystal Palace), Pollock (Middlesbrough) (Beckham, Man. Utd., 85), Fowler (Liverpool), Shipperley (Southampton).

Scorers – England: Fowler (18), Shipperley (34). **Austria**: Cemy (20). **Half-time**: 2-1.

PORTUGAL 3, REPUBLIC OF IRELAND 1

Leiria (25,000), Tuesday, November 14, 1995

Rep. of Ireland: Given (Swindon); Woods (Tranmere), Breen (Peterborough), Savage (Millwall) (Crawford, Newcastle, 62), Launders (Crystal Palace) (Turner, Tottenham, 28), Scully (Crystal Palace), Hardy (Wrexham), O'Sullivan (Swindon), Farrelly (Aston Villa), Coll (Tottenham) (Greene, Luton, 67), Carsley (Derby).

Scorers – Portugal: Porfirio (10), Conceicao (66), Litos (77). **Rep. of Ireland**: Savage (22). **Half-time**: 1-1.

SCOTLAND 1, SAN MARINO 0

Firhill Park, Glasgow (3,000), Tuesday, November 14, 1995

Scotland: Stillie (Aberdeen); McNamara (Dunfermline) (McNivern, Oldham, 45), Pressley (Dundee Utd., Capt.), Liddell (Barnsley), McCann (Dundee) (McLaughlin, Celtic, 45), Murray (Rangers), Donnelly (Celtic), Handyside (Grimsby), Dailly (Dundee Utd.), Hamilton (Dundee) (Freedman, Crystal Palace, 45), Sheerin (Southampton).

Scorer – Scotland: Valentino (52 og). **Half-time**: 0-0.

HUNGARY 2, SCOTLAND 1

(Quarter-final – 1st leg)
Budapest (15,000), Tuesday, March 12, 1996

Scotland: Stillie (Aberdeen); McNamara (Dunfermline), Pressley (Dundee Utd., Capt.), Glass (Aberdeen), Crawford (Raith) (Fullarton, St. Mirren, 72), Liddell (Barnsley), Murray (Rangers), Donnelly (Celtic), Dailly (Dundee Utd.), Locke (Hearts), Ritchie (Hearts).

Scorers – Hungary: Szanyo (13 pen), Zavadszky (80). **Scotland**: Glass (35). **Half-time**: 1-1.

SCOTLAND 3, HUNGARY 1

(Quarter-final – 2nd leg; Scotland won 4-3 on aggregate)
Easter Road, Edinburgh (9,173), Tuesday, March 26, 1996

Scotland: Stillie (Aberdeen); McNamara (Dunfermline) (Hamilton, Dundee, 45), Gray (Celtic), Fullarton (St. Mirren), Marshall (Arsenal), Pressley (Dundee Utd., Capt.), Liddell (Barnsley), McLaughlin (Celtic), Murray (Rangers) (Baker, St. Mirren, 45), Donnelly (Celtic), Dailly (Dundee Utd.) (Crawford, Raith, 72).

Scorers – Scotland: Dailly (42), Hamilton (84), Donnelly (86). **Hungary**: Egressy (30). **Half-time**: 1-1.

SPAIN 2, SCOTLAND 1

(Semi-final)
Barcelona (15,000), Tuesday, May 28, 1996

Scotland: Stillie (Aberdeen); Dailly (Dundee Utd.), Pressley (Dundee Utd., Capt.), Marshall (Arsenal), McNamara (Dunfermline), Miller (Rangers), Gray (Celtic) (Fullarton, St. Mirren, 72), Glass (Aberdeen), Donnelly (Celtic), Liddell (Barnsley) (Crawford, Raith, 72), Johnston (Hearts) (Hamilton, Dundee, 72).

Scorers – Spain: Oscar (25), De la Pena (35). **Scotland**: Marshall (29). **Half-time**: 2-1.

SCOTLAND 0, FRANCE 1

(3rd/4th place play-off)
Barcelona (6,000), Friday, May 31, 1996

Scotland: Stillie (Aberdeen) (Meldrum, Kilmarnock, 45); McNamara (Dunfermline), Pressley (Dundee Utd., Capt.), Marshall (Arsenal), Gray (Celtic), Donnelly (Celtic), Murray (Rangers), Miller (Rangers), Fullarton (St. Mirren), Dailly (Dundee Utd.) (Crawford, Raith, 66), Hamilton (Dundee) (Liddell, Barnsley, 45).

Scorer – France: Moreau (50). **Half-time**: 0-0.

1998 EUROPEAN UNDER-21 CHAMP. – QUAL. ROUND

SAN MARINO 0, WALES 3

Stadio di Serravalle (1,700), Saturday, June 1, 1996

Wales: Williams (Blackburn); Barnhouse (Swansea), Jarman (Cardiff), Hughes (Aston Villa), Huggins (Bristol City), Knott (Tottenham) (Bellamy, Norwich, 46), Robinson (Wolves), Young (Cardiff), Rowlands (Man. City), Hartson (Arsenal, Capt.), Thomas (Blackburn).

Scorers – Wales: Hartson (55, 74), Hughes (89). **Half-time**: 0-0.

OTHER UNDER-21 INTERNATIONALS

NORWAY 2, ENGLAND 2

Stavanger (2,640), Tuesday, October 10, 1995

England: D. Watson (Barnsley); S. Watson (Newcastle) (P. Neville, Man. Utd., 65), Gordon (Crystal Palace), Pearce (Blackburn), Campbell (Tottenham)

(Bowyer, Charlton, 65), Unsworth (Everton), Roberts (Crystal Palace), Pollock (Middlesbrough) (Holland, Newcastle, 65), Booth (Huddersfield) (Dichio, Q.P.R., 88), Joachim (Leicester), Shipperley (Southampton).

Scorers – Norway: Solskjaer (41), Lund (87). **England**: Campbell (62), Booth (77). **Half-time**: 1-0.

REPUBLIC OF IRELAND 0, RUSSIA 1

Drogheda (2,300), Tuesday, March 26, 1996

Rep. of Ireland: Murphy (Wimbledon); Carr (Tottenham) (Scully, Crystal Palace, 57), Kilbane (Preston), Harte (Leeds), Baker (Middlesbrough) (Coll, Tottenham, 45), Maher (Tottenham), Carey (Norwich), Turner (Tottenham) (O'Byrne, UCD, 57), O'Neill (Norwich), Launders (Crystal Palace) (Foley, Wolves, 73), Farrelly (Aston Villa).

Scorer – Russia: Semak (2). **Half-time**: 0-1.

ENGLAND 0, CROATIA 1

Middlesbrough (4,376), Tuesday, April 23, 1996

England: Day (Tottenham) (Davis, Luton, 71); O'Connor (Everton) (Carbon, Derby, 62), Rufus (Charlton, Capt.), Thatcher (Millwall) (Plummer, Q.P.R., 62), Brown (Man. City), Cooke (Man. Utd.), Holland (Newcastle), Ford (Leeds) (Hendrie, Aston Villa, 86), Briscoe (Sheff. Wed.), Gallen (Q.P.R.) (Moore, Tranmere, 71), Dyer (Crystal Palace).

Scorer – Croatia: Vucko (34). **Half-time**: 0-1.

UNDER-21 FESTIVAL, JUNE 1996

(Toulon, France – matches 40 mins. each way. Caps awarded)

ENGLAND 1, BELGIUM 0

(Friday, May 24)

England: Day (Tottenham); Brown (Man. City), Rufus (Charlton), Plummer (Q.P.R.), Holland (Newcastle), Stuart (Charlton), Cooke (Man. Utd.), Thornley (Man. Utd.) (Briscoe, Sheff. Wed., 70), Bowyer (Charlton), Beckham (Man. Utd.), Slade (Tottenham) (Moore, Tranmere, 70).

Scorer – England: Slade (36). **Half-time**: 1-0.

ENGLAND 0, ANGOLA 2

(Wednesday, May 28)

England: Marshall (Norwich); O'Connor (Everton) (Holland, Newcastle 45), Rufus (Charlton), Plummer (Q.P.R.) (Cooke, Man. Utd., 57), Stuart (Charlton), Beckham (Man. Utd.), Brown (Man. City), Challis (Q.P.R.), Briscoe (Sheff. Wed.), Moore (Tranmere) (Grant, Everton, 66), Slade (Tottenham).

Scorers – Angola: Muhongo (4 pen), Costa (63). **Half-time**: 0-1.

ENGLAND 1, PORTUGAL 3
(Thursday, May 30)

England: Davis (Luton); Brown (Man. City), Rufus (Charlton), Challis (Q.P.R.) (Plummer, Q.P.R., 45), Stuart (Charlton), Cooke (Man. Utd.), Beckham (Man. Utd.), Bowyer (Charlton), Thornley (Man. Utd.), Moore (Tranmere), Slade (Tottenham).

Scorers – England: Slade (46). **Portugal**: Nuno (18), Beto (57 pen), Dani (74). **Half-time**: 0-1.

ENGLAND 1, BRAZIL 2
(Saturday, June 1)

England: Day (Tottenham); Plummer (Q.P.R.), Rufus (Charlton), Stuart (Charlton), Briscoe (Sheff. Wed.), O'Connor (Everton), Bowyer (Charlton), Holland (Newcastle), Thornley (Man. Utd.), Slade (Tottenham), Moore (Tranmere).

Scorers – England: Moore (45). **Brazil**: Alex (55), Abailcon (61). **Half-time**: 1-0.

Final: Brazil 1, France 1 (aet; Brazil won 7-6 on pens.)

ENGLAND'S RECORD

England's first international was a 0-0 draw against Scotland in Glasgow, on the West of Scotland cricket ground, Partick, on November 30, 1872. Now, 124 years on, their complete International record, at the start of 1996-97, is:

P	W	D	L	F	A
725	411	174	140	1683	764

FIRST 'NO' TO ENGLAND

Burnley wing-half **Jimmy Adamson** was the first man to turn down an invitation to manage England – in 1963. He was the F.A.'s first choice when Walter Winterbottom retired, but felt he did not have enough experience. The job went to Alf Ramsey instead.

MICK IN THE MONEY

A crowd of 40,000 attended the Testimonial which the Republic of Ireland awarded new manager **Mick McCarthy** in recognition of his 57 caps. They saw a Republic XI beat Celtic 3-1 at Lansdowne Road, Dublin, on Sunday, May 26, and he benefited by an estimated £300,000.

HOOLIGAN HOTLINE

If you have any information, any time, about any person involved in football hooliganism, the **National Criminal Intelligence Service** await your call on free-phone number 0800-515495.

BRITISH AND IRISH INTERNATIONAL RESULTS

Note: In the results that follow, W.C. = World Cup, E.C. = European Championship. For Ireland, read Northern Ireland from 1921.

ENGLAND v. SCOTLAND

Played 108; England 44; Scotland 40; drawn 24. Goals: England 190, Scotland 168.

		E	S			E	S
1872	Glasgow	0	0	1931	Glasgow	0	2
1873	The Oval	4	2	1932	Wembley	3	0
1874	Glasgow	1	2	1933	Glasgow	1	2
1875	The Oval	2	2	1934	Wembley	3	0
1876	Glasgow	0	3	1935	Glasgow	0	2
1877	The Oval	1	3	1936	Wembley	1	1
1878	Glasgow	2	7	1937	Glasgow	1	3
1879	The Oval	5	4	1938	Wembley	0	1
1880	Glasgow	4	5	1939	Glasgow	2	1
1881	The Oval	1	6	1947	Wembley	1	1
1882	Glasgow	1	5	1948	Glasgow	2	0
1883	Sheffield	2	3	1949	Wembley	1	3
1884	Glasgow	0	1	1950	Glasgow (W.C.)	1	0
1885	The Oval	1	1	1951	Wembley	2	3
1886	Glasgow	1	1	1952	Glasgow	2	1
1887	Blackburn	2	3	1953	Wembley	2	2
1888	Glasgow	5	0	1954	Glasgow (W.C.)	4	2
1889	The Oval	2	3	1955	Wembley	7	2
1890	Glasgow	1	1	1956	Glasgow	1	1
1891	Blackburn	2	1	1957	Wembley	2	1
1892	Glasgow	4	1	1958	Glasgow	4	0
1893	Richmond	5	2	1959	Wembley	1	0
1894	Glasgow	2	2	1960	Glasgow	1	1
1895	Goodison Park	3	0	1961	Wembley	9	3
1896	Glasgow	1	2	1962	Glasgow	0	2
1897	Crystal Palace	1	2	1963	Wembley	1	2
1898	Glasgow	3	1	1964	Glasgow	0	1
1899	Birmingham	2	1	1965	Wembley	2	2
1900	Glasgow	1	4	1966	Glasgow	4	3
1901	Crystal Palace	2	2	1967	Wembley (E.C.)	2	3
1902	Birmingham	2	2	1968	Glasgow (E.C.)	1	1
1903	Sheffield	1	2	1969	Wembley	4	1
1904	Glasgow	1	0	1970	Glasgow	0	0
1905	Crystal Palace	1	0	1971	Wembley	3	1
1906	Glasgow	1	2	1972	Glasgow	1	0
1907	Newcastle	1	1	1973	Glasgow	5	0
1908	Glasgow	1	1	1973	Wembley	1	0
1909	Crystal Palace	2	0	1974	Glasgow	0	2
1910	Glasgow	0	2	1975	Wembley	5	1
1911	Goodison Park	1	1	1976	Glasgow	1	2
1912	Glasgow	1	1	1977	Wembley	1	2
1913	Stamford Bridge	1	0	1978	Glasgow	1	0
1914	Glasgow	1	3	1979	Wembley	3	1
1920	Sheffield	5	4	1980	Glasgow	2	0
1921	Glasgow	0	3	1981	Wembley	0	1
1922	Birmingham	0	1	1982	Glasgow	1	0
1923	Glasgow	2	2	1983	Wembley	2	0
1924	Wembley	1	1	1984	Glasgow	1	1
1925	Glasgow	0	2	1985	Glasgow	0	1
1926	Manchester	0	1	1986	Wembley	2	1
1927	Glasgow	2	1	1987	Glasgow	0	0
1928	Wembley	1	5	1988	Wembley	1	0
1929	Glasgow	0	1	1989	Glasgow	2	0
1930	Wembley	5	2	1996	Wembley (E.C.)	2	0

ENGLAND v. WALES

Played 97; England won 62; Wales 14; drawn 21. Goals: England 239, Wales 90.

		E	W
1879	The Oval	2	1
1880	Wrexham	3	2
1881	Blackburn	0	1
1882	Wrexham	3	5
1883	The Oval	5	0
1884	Wrexham	4	0
1885	Blackburn	1	1
1886	Wrexham	3	1
1887	The Oval	4	0
1888	Crewe	5	1
1889	Stoke	4	1
1890	Wrexham	3	1
1891	Sunderland	4	1
1892	Wrexham	2	0
1893	Stoke	6	0
1894	Wrexham	5	1
1895	London	1	1
1896	Cardiff	9	1
1897	Sheffield	4	0
1898	Wrexham	3	0
1899	Bristol	4	0
1900	Cardiff	1	1
1901	Newcastle	6	0
1902	Wrexham	0	0
1903	Portsmouth	2	1
1904	Wrexham	2	2
1905	Anfield	3	1
1906	Cardiff	1	0
1907	Fulham	1	1
1908	Wrexham	7	1
1909	Nottingham	2	0
1910	Cardiff	1	0
1911	Millwall	3	0
1912	Wrexham	2	0
1913	Bristol	4	3
1914	Cardiff	2	0
1920	Highbury	1	2
1921	Cardiff	0	0
1922	Anfield	1	0
1923	Cardiff	2	2
1924	Blackburn	1	2
1925	Swansea	2	1
1926	Selhurst Park	1	3
1927	Wrexham	3	3
1927	Burnley	1	2
1928	Swansea	3	2
1929	Stamford Bridge	6	0
1930	Wrexham	4	0
1931	Anfield	3	1
1932	Wrexham	0	0
1933	Newcastle	1	2
1934	Cardiff	4	0
1935	Wolverhampton	1	2
1936	Cardiff	1	2
1937	Middlesbrough	2	1
1938	Cardiff	2	4
1946	Manchester	3	0
1947	Cardiff	3	0
1948	Villa Park	1	0
1949	Cardiff (W.C.)	4	1
1950	Sunderland	4	2
1951	Cardiff	1	1
1952	Wembley	5	2
1953	Cardiff (W.C.)	4	1
1954	Wembley	3	2
1955	Cardiff	1	2
1956	Wembley	3	1
1957	Cardiff	4	0
1958	Birmingham	2	2
1959	Cardiff	1	1
1960	Wembley	5	1
1961	Cardiff	1	1
1962	Wembley	4	0
1963	Cardiff	4	0
1964	Wembley	2	1
1965	Cardiff	0	0
1966	Wembley (E.C.)	5	1
1967	Cardiff (E.C.)	3	0
1969	Wembley	2	1
1970	Cardiff	1	1
1971	Wembley	0	0
1972	Cardiff	3	0
1972	Cardiff (W.C.)	1	0
1973	Wembley (W.C.)	1	1
1973	Wembley	3	0
1974	Cardiff	2	0
1975	Wembley	2	2
1976	Wrexham	2	1
1976	Cardiff	1	0
1977	Wembley	0	1
1978	Cardiff	3	1
1979	Wembley	0	0
1980	Wrexham	1	4
1981	Wembley	0	0
1982	Cardiff	1	0
1983	Wembley	2	1
1984	Wrexham	0	1

ENGLAND v. IRELAND

Played 96; England won 74; Ireland 6; drawn 16. Goals: England 319, Ireland 80.

		E	I
1882	Belfast	13	0
1883	Aigburth, Liverpool	7	0
1884	Belfast	8	1
1885	Manchester	4	0
1886	Belfast	6	1
1887	Sheffield	7	0
1888	Belfast	5	1
1889	Goodison Park	6	1
1890	Belfast	9	1
1891	Wolverhampton	6	1
1892	Belfast	2	0
1893	Birmingham	6	1
1894	Belfast	2	2
1895	Derby	9	0
1896	Belfast	2	0
1897	Nottingham	6	0
1898	Belfast	3	2
1899	Sunderland	13	2
1900	Dublin	2	0
1901	Southampton	3	0
1902	Belfast	1	0
1903	Wolverhampton	4	0
1904	Belfast	3	1
1905	Middlesbrough	1	1
1906	Belfast	5	0
1907	Goodison Park	1	0
1908	Belfast	3	1
1909	Bradford (Park Ave)	4	0
1910	Belfast	1	1
1911	Derby	2	1
1912	Dublin	6	1
1913	Belfast	1	2
1914	Middlesbrough	0	3
1919	Belfast	1	1
1920	Sunderland	2	0
1921	Belfast	1	1
1922	West Bromwich	2	0
1923	Belfast	1	2
1924	Goodison Park	3	1
1925	Belfast	0	0
1926	Anfield	3	3
1927	Belfast	0	2
1928	Goodison Park	2	1
1929	Belfast	3	0
1930	Sheffield	5	1
1931	Belfast	6	2
1932	Blackpool	1	0
1933	Belfast	3	0
1935	Goodison Park	2	1
1935	Belfast	3	1
1936	Stoke	3	1
1937	Belfast	5	1
1938	Manchester	7	0
1946	Belfast	7	2
1947	Goodison Park	2	2
1948	Belfast	6	2
1949	Manchester (W.C.)	9	2
1950	Belfast	4	1
1951	Birmingham	2	0
1952	Belfast	2	2
1953	Goodison Park (W.C.)	3	1
1954	Belfast	2	0
1955	Wembley	3	0
1956	Belfast	1	1
1957	Wembley	2	3
1958	Belfast	3	3
1959	Wembley	2	1
1960	Belfast	5	2
1961	Wembley	1	1
1962	Belfast	3	1
1963	Wembley	8	3
1964	Belfast	4	3
1965	Wembley	2	1
1966	Belfast (E.C.)	2	0
1967	Wembley (E.C.)	2	0
1969	Belfast	3	1
1970	Wembley	3	1
1971	Belfast	1	0
1972	Wembley	0	1
1973	*Goodison Park	2	1
1974	Wembley	1	0
1975	Belfast	0	0
1976	Wembley	4	0
1977	Belfast	2	1
1978	Wembley	1	0
1979	Wembley (E.C.)	4	0
1979	Belfast	2	0
1979	Belfast (E.C.)	5	1
1980	Wembley	1	1
1982	Wembley	4	0
1983	Belfast	0	0
1984	Wembley	1	0
1985	Belfast (W.C.)	1	0
1985	Wembley (W.C.)	0	0
1986	Wembley (E.C.)	3	0
1987	Belfast (E.C.)	2	0

(* Switched from Belfast because of political situation in N. Ireland)

SCOTLAND v. WALES

Played 101; Scotland won 60; Wales 18; drawn 23. Goals: Scotland 238, Wales 112.

		S	W
1876	Glasgow	4	0
1877	Wrexham	2	0
1878	Glasgow	9	0
1879	Wrexham	3	0
1880	Glasgow	5	1
1881	Wrexham	5	1
1882	Glasgow	5	0
1883	Wrexham	4	1
1884	Glasgow	4	1
1885	Wrexham	8	1
1886	Glasgow	4	1
1887	Wrexham	2	0
1888	Edinburgh	5	1
1889	Wrexham	0	0
1890	Paisley	5	0
1891	Wrexham	4	3
1892	Edinburgh	6	1
1893	Wrexham	8	0
1894	Kilmarnock	5	2
1895	Wrexham	2	2
1896	Dundee	4	0
1897	Wrexham	2	2
1898	Motherwell	5	2
1899	Wrexham	6	0
1900	Aberdeen	5	2
1901	Wrexham	1	1
1902	Greenock	5	1
1903	Cardiff	1	0
1904	Dundee	1	1
1905	Wrexham	1	3
1906	Edinburgh	0	2
1907	Wrexham	0	1
1908	Dundee	2	1
1909	Wrexham	2	3
1910	Kilmarnock	1	0
1911	Cardiff	2	2
1912	Tynecastle	1	0
1913	Wrexham	0	0
1914	Glasgow	0	0
1920	Cardiff	1	1
1921	Aberdeen	2	1
1922	Wrexham	1	2
1923	Paisley	2	0
1924	Cardiff	0	2
1925	Tynecastle	3	1
1926	Cardiff	3	0
1927	Glasgow	3	0
1928	Wrexham	2	2
1929	Glasgow	4	2
1930	Cardiff	4	2
1931	Glasgow	1	1
1932	Wrexham	3	2
1933	Edinburgh	2	5
1934	Cardiff	2	3
1935	Aberdeen	3	2
1936	Cardiff	1	1
1937	Dundee	1	2
1938	Cardiff	1	2
1939	Edinburgh	3	2
1946	Wrexham	1	3
1947	Glasgow	1	2
1948	Cardiff (W.C.)	3	1
1949	Glasgow	2	0
1950	Cardiff	3	1
1951	Glasgow	0	1
1952	Cardiff (W.C.)	2	1
1953	Glasgow	3	3
1954	Cardiff	1	0
1955	Glasgow	2	0
1956	Cardiff	2	2
1957	Glasgow	1	1
1958	Cardiff	3	0
1959	Glasgow	1	1
1960	Cardiff	0	2
1961	Glasgow	2	0
1962	Cardiff	3	2
1963	Glasgow	2	1
1964	Cardiff	2	3
1965	Glasgow (E.C.)	4	1
1966	Cardiff (E.C.)	1	1
1967	Glasgow	3	2
1969	Wrexham	5	3
1970	Glasgow	0	0
1971	Cardiff	0	0
1972	Glasgow	1	0
1973	Wrexham	2	0
1974	Glasgow	2	0
1975	Cardiff	2	2
1976	Glasgow	3	1
1977	Glasgow (W.C.)	1	0
1977	Wrexham	0	0
1977	Anfield (W.C.)	2	0
1978	Glasgow	1	1
1979	Cardiff	0	3
1980	Glasgow	1	0
1981	Swansea	0	2
1982	Glasgow	1	0
1983	Cardiff	2	0
1984	Glasgow	2	1
1985	Glasgow (W.C.)	0	1
1985	Cardiff (W.C.)	1	1

SCOTLAND v. IRELAND

Played 92; Scotland won 61; Ireland 15; drawn 16. Goals: Scotland 254, Ireland 81.

		S	I			S	I
1884	Belfast	5	0	1935	Belfast	1	2
1885	Glasgow	8	2	1936	Edinburgh	2	1
1886	Belfast	7	2	1937	Belfast	3	1
1887	Belfast	4	1	1938	Aberdeen	1	1
1888	Belfast	10	2	1939	Belfast	2	0
1889	Glasgow	7	0	1946	Glasgow	0	0
1890	Belfast	4	1	1947	Belfast	0	2
1891	Glasgow	2	1	1948	Glasgow	3	2
1892	Belfast	3	2	1949	Belfast	8	2
1893	Glasgow	6	1	1950	Glasgow	6	1
1894	Belfast	2	1	1951	Belfast	3	0
1895	Glasgow	3	1	1952	Glasgow	1	1
1896	Belfast	3	3	1953	Belfast	3	1
1897	Glasgow	5	1	1954	Glasgow	2	2
1898	Belfast	3	0	1955	Belfast	1	2
1899	Glasgow	9	1	1956	Glasgow	1	0
1900	Belfast	3	0	1957	Belfast	1	1
1901	Glasgow	11	0	1958	Glasgow	2	2
1902	Belfast	5	1	1959	Belfast	4	0
1903	Glasgow	0	2	1960	Glasgow	5	1
1904	Dublin	1	1	1961	Belfast	6	1
1905	Glasgow	4	0	1962	Glasgow	5	1
1906	Dublin	1	0	1963	Belfast	1	2
1907	Glasgow	3	0	1964	Glasgow	3	2
1908	Dublin	5	0	1965	Belfast	2	3
1909	Glasgow	5	0	1966	Glasgow	2	1
1910	Belfast	0	1	1967	Belfast	0	1
1911	Glasgow	2	0	1969	Glasgow	1	1
1912	Belfast	4	1	1970	Belfast	1	0
1913	Dublin	2	1	1971	Glasgow	0	1
1914	Belfast	1	1	1972	Glasgow	2	0
1920	Glasgow	3	0	1973	Glasgow	1	2
1921	Belfast	2	0	1974	Glasgow	0	1
1922	Glasgow	2	1	1975	Glasgow	3	0
1923	Belfast	1	0	1976	Glasgow	3	0
1924	Glasgow	2	0	1977	Glasgow	3	0
1925	Belfast	3	0	1978	Glasgow	1	1
1926	Glasgow	4	0	1979	Glasgow	1	0
1927	Belfast	2	0	1980	Belfast	0	1
1928	Glasgow	0	1	1981	Glasgow (W.C.)	1	1
1929	Belfast	7	3	1981	Glasgow	2	0
1930	Glasgow	3	1	1981	Belfast (W.C.)	0	0
1931	Belfast	0	0	1982	Belfast	1	1
1932	Glasgow	3	1	1983	Glasgow	0	0
1933	Belfast	4	0	1984	Belfast	0	2
1934	Glasgow	1	2	1992	Glasgow	1	0

WALES v. IRELAND

Played 90; Wales won 42; Ireland 27; drawn 21. Goals: Wales 182, Ireland 127.

		W	I
1882	Wrexham	7	1
1883	Belfast	1	1
1884	Wrexham	6	0
1885	Belfast	8	2
1886	Wrexham	5	0
1887	Belfast	1	4
1888	Wrexham	11	0
1889	Belfast	3	1
1890	Shrewsbury	5	2
1891	Belfast	2	7
1892	Bangor	1	1
1893	Belfast	3	4
1894	Swansea	4	1
1895	Belfast	2	2
1896	Wrexham	6	1
1897	Belfast	3	4
1898	Llandudno	0	1
1899	Belfast	0	1
1900	Llandudno	2	0
1901	Belfast	1	0
1902	Cardiff	0	3
1903	Belfast	0	2
1904	Bangor	0	1
1905	Belfast	2	2
1906	Wrexham	4	4
1907	Belfast	3	2
1908	Aberdare	0	1
1909	Belfast	3	2
1910	Wrexham	4	1
1911	Belfast	2	1
1912	Cardiff	2	3
1913	Belfast	1	0
1914	Wrexham	1	2
1920	Belfast	2	2
1921	Swansea	2	1
1922	Belfast	1	1
1923	Wrexham	0	3
1924	Belfast	1	0
1925	Wrexham	0	0
1926	Belfast	0	3
1927	Cardiff	2	2
1928	Belfast	2	1
1929	Wrexham	2	2
1930	Belfast	0	7
1931	Wrexham	3	2
1932	Belfast	0	4
1933	Wrexham	4	1
1934	Belfast	1	1
1935	Wrexham	3	1
1936	Belfast	2	3
1937	Wrexham	4	1
1938	Belfast	0	1
1939	Wrexham	3	1
1947	Belfast	1	2
1948	Wrexham	2	0
1949	Belfast	2	0
1950	Wrexham (W.C.)	0	0
1951	Belfast	2	1
1952	Swansea	3	0
1953	Belfast	3	2
1954	Wrexham (W.C.)	1	2
1955	Belfast	3	2
1956	Cardiff	1	1
1957	Belfast	0	0
1958	Cardiff	1	1
1959	Belfast	1	4
1960	Wrexham	3	2
1961	Belfast	5	1
1962	Cardiff	4	0
1963	Belfast	4	1
1964	Swansea	2	3
1965	Belfast	5	0
1966	Cardiff	1	4
1967	Belfast (E.C.)	0	0
1968	Wrexham (E.C.)	2	0
1969	Belfast	0	0
1970	Swansea	1	0
1971	Belfast	0	1
1972	Wrexham	0	0
1973	*Goodison Park	0	1
1974	Wrexham	1	0
1975	Belfast	0	1
1976	Swansea	1	0
1977	Belfast	1	1
1978	Wrexham	1	0
1979	Belfast	1	1
1980	Cardiff	0	1
1982	Wrexham	3	0
1983	Belfast	1	0
1984	Swansea	1	1

(* Switched from Belfast because of political situation in N. Ireland)

OTHER BRITISH INTERNATIONAL RESULTS

ENGLAND

v. ALBANIA

		E	A			E	A
1989	Tirana (W.C.)	2	0	1989	Wembley (W.C.)	5	0

v. ARGENTINA

		E	A			E	A
1951	Wembley	2	1	1977	Buenos Aires	1	1
1953	* Buenos Aires	0	0	1980	Wembley	3	1
1962	Rancagua (W.C.)	3	1	1986	Mexico City (W.C.)	1	2
1964	Rio de Janeiro	0	1	1991	Wembley	2	2
1966	Wembley (W.C.)	1	0	(* Abandoned after 21 mins. – rain)			
1974	Wembley	2	2				

v. AUSTRALIA

		E	A			E	A
1980	Sydney	2	1	1983	Melbourne	1	1
1983	Sydney	0	0	1991	Sydney	1	0
1983	Brisbane	1	0				

v. AUSTRIA

		E	A			E	A
1908	Vienna	6	1	1958	Boras (W.C.)	2	2
1908	Vienna	11	1	1961	Vienna	1	3
1909	Vienna	8	1	1962	Wembley	3	1
1930	Vienna	0	0	1965	Wembley	2	3
1932	Stamford Bridge	4	3	1967	Vienna	1	0
1936	Vienna	1	2	1973	Wembley	7	0
1951	Wembley	2	2	1979	Vienna	3	4
1952	Vienna	3	2				

v. BELGIUM

		E	B			E	B
1921	Brussels	2	0	1936	Brussels	2	3
1923	Highbury	6	1	1947	Brussels	5	2
1923	Antwerp	2	2	1950	Brussels	4	1
1924	West Bromwich	4	0	1952	Wembley	5	0
1926	Antwerp	5	3	1954	Basle (W.C.)	4	4
1927	Brussels	9	1	1964	Wembley	2	2
1928	Antwerp	3	1	1970	Brussels	3	1
1929	Brussels	5	1	1980	Turin (E.C.)	1	1
1931	Brussels	4	1	1990	Bologna (W.C.)	1	0

v. BOHEMIA

		E	B
1908	Prague	4	0

v. BRAZIL

		E	B			E	B
1956	Wembley	4	2	1977	Rio de Janeiro	0	0
1958	Gothenburg (W.C.)	0	0	1978	Wembley	1	1
1959	Rio de Janeiro	0	2	1981	Wembley	0	1
1962	Vina del Mar (W.C.)	1	3	1984	Rio de Janeiro	2	0
1963	Wembley	1	1	1987	Wembley	1	1
1964	Rio de Janeiro	1	5	1990	Wembley	1	0
1969	Rio de Janeiro	1	2	1992	Wembley	1	1
1970	Guadalajara (W.C.)	0	1	1993	Washington	1	1
1976	Los Angeles	0	1	1995	Wembley	1	3

v. BULGARIA

		E	B			E	B
1962	Rancagua (W.C.)	0	0	1979	Sofia (E.C.)	3	0
1968	Wembley	1	1	1979	Wembley (E.C.)	2	0
1974	Sofia	1	0	1996	Wembley	1	0

v. CAMEROON

		E	C			E	C
1990	Naples (W.C.)	3	2	1991	Wembley	2	0

v. CANADA

		E	C
1986	Vancouver	1	0

v. CHILE

		E	C			E	C
1950	Rio de Janeiro (W.C.)	2	0	1984	Santiago	0	0
				1989	Wembley	0	0
1953	Santiago	2	1				

v. CHINA

		E	C
1996	Beijing	3	0

v. C.I.S. (formerly Soviet Union)

		E	C
1992	Moscow	2	2

v. COLOMBIA

		E	C			E	C
1970	Bogota	4	0	1995	Wembley	0	0
1988	Wembley	1	1				

v. CROATIA

		E	C
1995	Wembley	0	0

v. CYPRUS

		E	C			E	C
1975	Wembley (E.C.)	5	0	1975	Limassol (E.C.)	1	0

v. CZECHOSLOVAKIA

		E	C			E	C
1934	Prague	1	2	1975	* Bratislava (E.C.)	1	2
1937	Tottenham	5	4	1978	Wembley (E.C.)	1	0
1963	Bratislava	4	2	1982	Bilbao (W.C.)	2	0
1966	Wembley	0	0	1990	Wembley	4	2
1970	Guadalajara (W.C.)	1	0	1992	Prague	2	2
1973	Prague	1	1		(* Aband. 0-0, 17 mins. prev. day – fog)		
1974	Wembley (E.C.)	3	0				

v. DENMARK

		E	D			E	D
1948	Copenhagen	0	0	1982	Copenhagen (E.C.)	2	2
1955	Copenhagen	5	1	1983	Wembley (E.C.)	0	1
1956	W'hampton (W.C.)	5	2	1988	Wembley	1	0
1957	Copenhagen (W.C.)	4	1	1989	Copenhagen	1	1
1966	Copenhagen	2	0	1990	Wembley	1	0
1978	Copenhagen (E.C.)	4	3	1992	Malmo (E.C.)	0	0
1979	Wembley (E.C.)	1	0	1994	Wembley	1	0

v. EAST GERMANY

		E	EG			E	EG
1963	Leipzig	2	1	1974	Leipzig	1	1
1970	Wembley	3	1	1984	Wembley	1	0

v. ECUADOR

		E	Ec
1970	Quito	2	0

v. EGYPT

		E	Eg			E	Eg
1986	Cairo	4	0	1990	Cagliari (W.C.)	1	0

v. F.I.F.A.

		E	F			E	F
1938	Highbury	3	0	1963	Wembley	2	1
1953	Wembley	4	4				

v. FINLAND

		E	F			E	F
1937	Helsinki	8	0	1982	Helsinki	4	1
1956	Helsinki	5	1	1984	Wembley (W.C.)	5	0
1966	Helsinki	3	0	1985	Helsinki (W.C.)	1	1
1976	Helsinki (W.C.)	4	1	1992	Helsinki	2	1
1976	Wembley (W.C.)	2	1				

v. FRANCE

		E	F			E	F
1923	Paris	4	1	1929	Paris	4	1
1924	Paris	3	1	1931	Paris	2	5
1925	Paris	3	2	1933	Tottenham	4	1
1927	Paris	6	0	1938	Paris	4	2
1928	Paris	5	1	1947	Highbury	3	0

		E	F			E	F
1949	Paris	3	1	1966	Wembley (W.C.)	2	0
1951	Highbury	2	2	1969	Wembley	5	0
1955	Paris	0	1	1982	Bilbao (W.C.)	3	1
1957	Wembley	4	0	1984	Paris	0	2
1962	Sheffield (E.C.)	1	1	1992	Wembley	2	0
1963	Paris (E.C.)	2	5	1992	Malmo (E.C.)	0	0

v. GERMANY/WEST GERMANY

		E	G			E	G
1930	Berlin	3	3	1975	Wembley	2	0
1935	Tottenham	3	0	1978	Munich	1	2
1938	Berlin	6	3	1982	Madrid (W.C.)	0	0
1954	Wembley	3	1	1982	Wembley	1	2
1956	Berlin	3	1	1985	Mexico City	3	0
1965	Nuremberg	1	0	1987	Dusseldorf	1	3
1966	Wembley	1	0	1990	* Turin (W.C.)	1	1
1966	Wembley (W.C.F.)	4	2	1991	Wembley	0	1
1968	Hanover	0	1	1993	Detroit	1	2
1970	Leon (W.C.)	2	3	1996	† Wembley (E.C.)	1	1
1972	Wembley (E.C.)	1	3	(* England lost 3-4 on pens.)			
1972	Berlin (E.C.)	0	0	(†England lost 5-6 on pens.)			

v. GREECE

		E	G			E	G
1971	Wembley (E.C.)	3	0	1983	Wembley (E.C.)	0	0
1971	Athens (E.C.)	2	0	1989	Athens	2	1
1982	Salonika (E.C.)	3	0	1994	Wembley	5	0

v. HOLLAND

		E	H			E	H
1935	Amsterdam	1	0	1988	Wembley	2	2
1946	Huddersfield	8	2	1988	Dusseldorf (E.C.)	1	3
1964	Amsterdam	1	1	1990	Cagliari (W.C.)	0	0
1969	Amsterdam	1	0	1993	Wembley (W.C.)	2	2
1970	Wembley	0	0	1993	Rotterdam (W.C.)	0	2
1977	Wembley	0	2	1996	Wembley (E.C.)	4	1
1982	Wembley	2	0				

v. HUNGARY

		E	H			E	H
1908	Budapest	7	0	1978	Wembley	4	1
1909	Budapest	4	2	1981	Budapest (W.C.)	3	1
1909	Budapest	8	2	1981	Wembley (W.C.)	1	0
1934	Budapest	1	2	1983	Wembley (E.C.)	2	0
1936	Highbury	6	2	1983	Budapest (E.C.)	3	0
1953	Wembley	3	6	1988	Budapest	0	0
1954	Budapest	1	7	1990	Wembley	1	0
1960	Budapest	0	2	1992	Budapest	1	0
1962	Rancagua (W.C.)	1	2	1996	Wembley	3	0
1965	Wembley	1	0				

v. ICELAND

		E	I
1982	Reykjavik	1	1

v. REPUBLIC OF IRELAND

		E	RofI			E	RofI
1946	Dublin	1	0	1985	Wembley	2	1
1950	Goodison Park	0	2	1988	Stuttgart (E.C.)	0	1
1957	Wembley (W.C.)	5	1	1990	Cagliari (W.C.)	1	1
1957	Dublin (W.C.)	1	1	1990	Dublin (E.C.)	1	1
1964	Dublin	3	1	1991	Wembley (E.C.)	1	1
1977	Wembley	1	1	1995	* Dublin	0	1
1978	Dublin (E.C.)	1	1				
1980	Wembley (E.C.)	2	0				

(* Abandoned 27 mins. – crowd riot)

v. ISRAEL

		E	I			E	I
1986	Tel Aviv	2	1	1988	Tel Aviv	0	0

v. ITALY

		E	I			E	I
1933	Rome	1	1	1973	Wembley	0	1
1934	Highbury	3	2	1976	New York	3	2
1939	Milan	2	2	1976	Rome (W.C.)	0	2
1948	Turin	4	0	1977	Wembley (W.C.)	2	0
1949	Tottenham	2	0	1980	Turin (E.C.)	0	1
1952	Florence	1	1	1985	Mexico City	1	2
1959	Wembley	2	2	1989	Wembley	0	0
1961	Rome	3	2	1990	Bari (W.C.)	1	2
1973	Turin	0	2				

v. JAPAN

		E	J
1995	Wembley	2	1

v. KUWAIT

		E	K
1982	Bilbao (W.C.)	1	0

v. LUXEMBOURG

		E	L			E	L
1927	Luxembourg	5	2	1977	Luxembourg (W.C.)	2	0
1960	Luxembourg (W.C.)	9	0	1982	Wembley (E.C.)	9	0
1961	Highbury (W.C.)	4	1	1983	Luxembourg (E.C.)	4	0
1977	Wembley (W.C.)	5	0				

v. MALAYSIA

		E	M
1991	Kuala Lumpur	4	2

v. MALTA

		E	M			E	M
1971	Valletta (E.C.)	1	0	1971	Wembley (E.C.)	5	0

v. MEXICO

		E	M			E	M
1959	Mexico City	1	2	1969	Mexico City	0	0
1961	Wembley	8	0	1985	Mexico City	0	1
1966	Wembley (W.C.)	2	0	1986	Los Angeles	3	0

v. MOROCCO

		E	M
1986	Monterrey (W.C.)	0	0

v. NEW ZEALAND

		E	NZ			E	NZ
1991	Auckland	1	0	1991	Wellington	2	0

v. NIGERIA

		E	N
1994	Wembley	1	0

v. NORWAY

		E	N			E	N
1937	Oslo	6	0	1981	Oslo (W.C.)	1	2
1938	Newcastle	4	0	1992	Wembley (W.C.)	1	1
1949	Oslo	4	1	1993	Oslo (W.C.)	0	2
1966	Oslo	6	1	1994	Wembley	0	0
1980	Wembley (W.C.)	4	0	1995	Oslo	0	0

v. PARAGUAY

		E	P
1986	Mexico City (W.C.)	3	0

v. PERU

		E	P			E	P
1959	Lima	1	4	1961	Lima	4	0

v. POLAND

		E	P			E	P
1966	Goodison Park	1	1	1989	Katowice (W.C.)	0	0
1966	Chorzow	1	0	1990	Wembley (E.C.)	2	0
1973	Chorzow (W.C.)	0	2	1991	Poznan (E.C.)	1	1
1973	Wembley (W.C.)	1	1	1993	Chorzow (W.C.)	1	1
1986	Monterrey (W.C.)	3	0	1993	Wembley (W.C.)	3	0
1989	Wembley (W.C.)	3	0				

v. PORTUGAL

		E	P			E	P
1947	Lisbon	10	0	1964	Sao Paulo	1	1
1950	Lisbon	5	3	1966	Wembley (W.C.)	2	1
1951	Goodison Park	5	2	1969	Wembley	1	0
1955	Oporto	1	3	1974	Lisbon	0	0
1958	Wembley	2	1	1974	Wembley (E.C.)	0	0
1961	Lisbon (W.C.)	1	1	1975	Lisbon (E.C.)	1	1
1961	Wembley (W.C.)	2	0	1986	Monterrey (W.C.)	0	1
1964	Lisbon	4	3	1995	Wembley	1	1

v. ROMANIA

		E	R			E	R
1939	Bucharest	2	0	1981	Wembley (W.C.)	0	0
1968	Bucharest	0	0	1985	Bucharest (W.C.)	0	0
1969	Wembley	1	1	1985	Wembley (W.C.)	1	1
1970	Guadalajara (W.C.)	1	0	1994	Wembley	1	1
1980	Bucharest (W.C.)	1	2				

v. SAN MARINO

		E	SM			E	SM
1993	Wembley (W.C.)	6	0	1994	Bologna (W.C.)	7	1

v. SAUDI ARABIA

		E	SA
1988	Riyadh	1	1

v. SOVIET UNION (see also C.I.S.)

		E	SU			E	SU
1958	Moscow	1	1	1973	Moscow	2	1
1958	Gothenburg (W.C.)	2	2	1984	Wembley	0	2
1958	Gothenburg (W.C.)	0	1	1986	Tbilisi	1	0
1958	Wembley	5	0	1988	Frankfurt (E.C.)	1	3
1967	Wembley	2	2	1991	Wembley	3	1
1968	Rome (W.C.)	2	0				

v. SPAIN

		E	S			E	S
1929	Madrid	3	4	1968	Madrid (E.C.)	2	1
1931	Highbury	7	1	1980	Barcelona	2	0
1950	Rio de Janeiro (W.C.)	0	1	1980	Naples (E.C.)	2	1
1955	Madrid	1	1	1981	Wembley	1	2
1955	Wembley	4	1	1982	Madrid (W.C.)	0	0
1960	Madrid	0	3	1987	Madrid	4	2
1960	Wembley	4	2	1992	Santander	0	1
1965	Madrid	2	0	1996	* Wembley (E.C.)	0	0
1967	Wembley	2	0	(*England won 4-2 on pens.)			
1968	Wembley (E.C.)	1	0				

v. SWEDEN

		E	S			E	S
1923	Stockholm	4	2	1968	Wembley	3	1
1923	Stockholm	3	1	1979	Stockholm	0	0
1937	Stockholm	4	0	1986	Stockholm	0	1
1948	Highbury	4	2	1988	Wembley (W.C.)	0	0
1949	Stockholm	1	3	1989	Stockholm (W.C.)	0	0
1956	Stockholm	0	0	1992	Stockholm (E.C.)	1	2
1959	Wembley	2	3	1995	Elland Road	3	3
1965	Gothenburg	2	1				

v. SWITZERLAND

		E	S			E	S
1933	Berne	4	0	1952	Zurich	3	0
1938	Zurich	1	2	1954	Berne (W.C.)	2	0
1947	Zurich	0	1	1962	Wembley	3	1
1949	Highbury	6	0	1963	Basle	8	1

		E	S			E	S
1971	Basle (E.C.)	3	2	1981	Basle (W.C.)	1	2
1971	Wembley (E.C.)	1	1	1988	Lausanne	1	0
1975	Basle	2	1	1995	Wembley	3	1
1977	Wembley	0	0	1996	Wembley (E.C.)	1	1
1980	Wembley (W.C.)	2	1				

v. TUNISIA

		E	T
1990	Tunis	1	1

v. TURKEY

		E	T			E	T
1984	Istanbul (W.C.)	8	0	1991	Izmir (E.C.)	1	0
1985	Wembley (W.C.)	5	0	1992	Wembley (E.C.)	1	0
1987	Izmir (E.C.)	0	0	1992	Wembley (W.C.)	4	0
1987	Wembley (E.C.)	8	0	1993	Izmir (W.C.)	2	0

v. URUGUAY

		E	U			E	U
1953	Montevideo	1	2	1977	Montevideo	0	0
1954	Basle (W.C.)	2	4	1984	Montevideo	0	2
1964	Wembley	2	1	1990	Wembley	1	2
1966	Wembley (W.C.)	0	0	1995	Wembley	0	0
1969	Montevideo	2	1				

v. U.S.A.

		E	USA			E	USA
1950	Belo H. (W.C.)	0	1	1985	Los Angeles	5	0
1953	New York	6	3	1993	Boston	0	2
1959	Los Angeles	8	1	1994	Wembley	2	0
1964	New York	10	0				

v. YUGOSLAVIA

		E	Y			E	Y
1939	Belgrade	1	2	1966	Wembley	2	0
1950	Highbury	2	2	1968	Florence (E.C.)	0	1
1954	Belgrade	0	1	1972	Wembley	1	1
1956	Wembley	3	0	1974	Belgrade	2	2
1958	Belgrade	0	5	1986	Wembley (E.C.)	2	0
1960	Wembley	3	3	1987	Belgrade (E.C.)	4	1
1965	Belgrade	1	1	1989	Wembley	2	1

ENGLAND "B" TEAM RESULTS

(England score shown first)

1949	Finland (A)	4	0	1950	Switzerland (H)	5	0
1949	Holland (A)	4	0	1952	Holland (A)	1	0
1950	Italy (A)	0	5	1952	France (A)	1	7
1950	Holland (H)	1	0	1953	Scotland (A)	2	2
1950	Holland (A)	0	3	1954	Scotland (H)	1	1
1950	Luxembourg (A)	2	1	1954	Germany (A)	4	0

1954	Yugoslavia (A)	1	2
1954	Switzerland (A)	0	2
1955	Germany (H)	1	1
1955	Yugoslavia (H)	5	1
1956	Switzerland (H)	4	1
1956	Scotland (A)	2	2
1957	Scotland (H)	4	1
1978	W. Germany (A)	2	1
1978	Czechoslovakia (A)	1	0
1978	Singapore (A)	8	0
1978	Malaysia (A)	1	1
1978	N. Zealand (A)	4	0
1978	N. Zealand (A)	3	1
1978	N. Zealand (A)	4	0
1979	Austria (A)	1	0
1979	N. Zealand (H)	4	1
1980	U.S.A. (H)	1	0
1980	Spain (H)	1	0
1980	Australia (H)	1	0
1981	Spain (A)	2	3
1984	N. Zealand (H)	2	0
1987	Malta (A)	2	0
1989	Switzerland (A)	2	0
1989	Iceland (A)	2	0
1989	Norway (A)	1	0
1989	Italy (H)	1	1
1989	Yugoslavia (H)	2	1
1990	Rep. of Ireland (A)	1	4
1990	Czechoslovakia (H)	2	0
1990	Algeria (A)	0	0
1991	Wales (A)	1	0
1991	Iceland (H)	1	0
1991	Switzerland (H)	2	1
1991	Spanish XI (A)	1	0
1992	France (H)	3	0
1992	Czechoslovakia (A)	1	0
1992	C.I.S. (A)	1	1
1994	N. Ireland (H)	4	2
1995	Rep. of Ireland (H)	2	0

GREAT BRITAIN v. REST OF EUROPE (F.I.F.A.)

		GB	RofE
1947	Glasgow	6	1
1955	Belfast	1	4

SCOTLAND

v. ARGENTINA

		S	A
1977	Buenos Aires	1	1
1979	Glasgow	1	3
1990	Glasgow	1	0

v. AUSTRALIA

		S	A
1985	* Glasgow (W.C.)	2	0
1985	* Melbourne (W.C.)	0	0
1996	Glasgow	1	0

(* World Cup play-off)

v. AUSTRIA

		S	A
1931	Vienna	0	5
1933	Glasgow	2	2
1937	Vienna	1	1
1950	Glasgow	0	1
1951	Vienna	0	4
1954	Zurich (W.C.)	0	1
1955	Vienna	4	1
1956	Glasgow	1	1
1960	Vienna	1	4
1963	* Glasgow	4	1
1968	Glasgow (W.C.)	2	1
1969	Vienna (W.C.)	0	2
1978	Vienna (E.C.)	2	3
1979	Glasgow (E.C.)	1	1
1994	Vienna	2	1

(* Abandoned after 79 minutes)

v. BELGIUM

		S	B			S	B
1947	Brussels	1	2	1979	Brussels (E.C.)	0	2
1948	Glasgow	2	0	1979	Glasgow (E.C.)	1	3
1951	Brussels	5	0	1982	Brussels (E.C.)	2	3
1971	Liege (E.C.)	0	3	1983	Glasgow (E.C.)	1	1
1971	Aberdeen (E.C.)	1	0	1987	Brussels (E.C.)	1	4
1974	Brugge	1	2	1987	Glasgow (E.C.)	2	0

v. BRAZIL

		S	B			S	B
1966	Glasgow	1	1	1977	Rio de Janeiro	0	2
1972	Rio de Janeiro	0	1	1982	Seville (W.C.)	1	4
1973	Glasgow	0	1	1987	Glasgow	0	2
1974	Frankfurt (W.C.)	0	0	1990	Turin (W.C.)	0	1

v. BULGARIA

		S	B			S	B
1978	Glasgow	2	1	1990	Sofia (E.C.)	1	1
1986	Glasgow (E.C.)	0	0	1991	Glasgow (E.C.)	1	1
1987	Sofia (E.C.)	1	0				

v. CANADA

		S	C			S	C
1983	Vancouver	2	0	1983	Toronto	2	0
1983	Edmonton	3	0	1992	Toronto	3	1

v. CHILE

		S	C			S	C
1977	Santiago	4	2	1989	Glasgow	2	0

v. C.I.S. (formerly Soviet Union)

		S	C
1992	Norrkoping (E.C.)	3	0

v. COLOMBIA

		S	C			S	C
1988	Glasgow	0	0	1996	Miami	0	1

v. COSTA RICA

		S	C
1990	Genoa (W.C.)	0	1

v. CYPRUS

		S	C			S	C
1968	Nicosia (W.C.)	5	0	1989	Limassol (W.C.)	3	2
1969	Glasgow (W.C.)	8	0	1989	Glasgow (W.C.)	2	1

v. CZECHOSLOVAKIA

		S	C			S	C
1937	Prague	3	1	1972	Porto Alegre	0	0
1937	Glasgow	5	0	1973	Glasgow (W.C.)	2	1
1961	Bratislava (W.C.)	0	4	1973	Bratislava (W.C.)	0	1
1961	Glasgow (W.C.)	3	2	1976	Prague (W.C.)	0	2
1961	* Brussels (W.C.)	2	4	1977	Glasgow (W.C.)	3	1

(* World Cup play-off)

v. DENMARK

		S	D			S	D
1951	Glasgow	3	1	1972	Glasgow (W.C.)	2	0
1952	Copenhagen	2	1	1975	Copenhagen (E.C.)	1	0
1968	Copenhagen	1	0	1975	Glasgow (E.C.)	3	1
1970	Glasgow (E.C.)	1	0	1986	Neza (W.C.)	0	1
1971	Copenhagen (E.C.)	0	1	1996	Copenhagen	0	2
1972	Copenhagen (W.C.)	4	1				

v. EAST GERMANY

		S	EG			S	EG
1974	Glasgow	3	0	1983	Halle (E.C.)	1	2
1977	East Berlin	0	1	1986	Glasgow	0	0
1982	Glasgow (E.C.)	2	0	1990	Glasgow	0	1

v. ECUADOR

		S	E
1995	Toyama, Japan	2	1

v. EGYPT

		S	E
1990	Aberdeen	1	3

v. ESTONIA

		S	E			S	E
1993	Tallinn (W.C.)	3	0	1993	Aberdeen	3	1

v. FAROE ISLANDS

		S	F			S	F
1994	Glasgow (E.C.)	5	1	1995	Toftir (E.C.)	2	0

v. FINLAND

		S	F			S	F
1954	Helsinki	2	1	1992	Glasgow	1	1
1964	Glasgow (W.C.)	3	1	1994	Helsinki (E.C.)	2	0
1965	Helsinki (W.C.)	2	1	1995	Glasgow (E.C.)	1	0
1976	Glasgow	6	0				

v. FRANCE

		S	F			S	F
1930	Paris	2	0	1951	Glasgow	1	0
1932	Paris	3	1	1958	Orebro (W.C.)	1	2
1948	Paris	0	3	1984	Marseilles	0	2
1949	Glasgow	2	0	1989	Glasgow (W.C.)	2	0
1950	Paris	1	0	1990	Paris (W.C.)	0	3

v. GERMANY/WEST GERMANY

		S	G			S	G
1929	Berlin	1	1	1969	Hamburg (W.C.)	2	3
1936	Glasgow	2	0	1973	Glasgow	1	1
1957	Stuttgart	3	1	1974	Frankfurt	1	2
1959	Glasgow	3	2	1986	Queretaro (W.C.)	1	2
1964	Hanover	2	2	1992	Norrkoping (E.C.)	0	2
1969	Glasgow (W.C.)	1	1	1993	Glasgow	0	1

v. GREECE

		S	G			S	G
1994	Athens (E.C.)	0	1	1995	Glasgow	1	0

v. HOLLAND

		S	H			S	H
1929	Amsterdam	2	0	1982	Glasgow	2	1
1938	Amsterdam	3	1	1986	Eindhoven	0	0
1959	Amsterdam	2	1	1992	Gothenburg (E.C.)	0	1
1966	Glasgow	0	3	1994	Glasgow	0	1
1968	Amsterdam	0	0	1994	Utrecht	1	3
1971	Amsterdam	1	2	1996	Birmingham (E.C.)	0	0
1978	Mendoza (W.C.)	3	2				

v. HUNGARY

		S	H			S	H
1938	Glasgow	3	1	1960	Budapest	3	3
1955	Glasgow	2	4	1980	Budapest	1	3
1955	Budapest	1	3	1987	Glasgow	2	0
1958	Glasgow	1	1				

v. ICELAND

		S	I			S	I
1984	Glasgow (W.C.)	3	0	1985	Reykjavik (W.C)	1	0

v. IRAN

		S	I
1978	Cordoba (W.C.)	1	1

v. REPUBLIC OF IRELAND

		S	R of I			S	R of I
1961	Glasgow (W.C.)	4	1	1969	Dublin	1	1
1961	Dublin (W.C.)	3	0	1986	Dublin (E.C.)	0	0
1963	Dublin	0	1	1987	Glasgow (E.C.)	0	1

v. ISRAEL

		S	I			S	I
1981	Tel Aviv (W.C.)	1	0	1986	Tel Aviv	1	0
1981	Glasgow (W.C.)	3	1				

v. ITALY

		S	I			S	I
1931	Rome	0	3	1988	Perugia	0	2
1965	Glasgow (W.C.)	1	0	1992	Glasgow (W.C.)	0	0
1965	Naples (W.C.)	0	3	1993	Rome (W.C.)	1	3

v. JAPAN

		S	J
1995	Hiroshima	0	0

v. LUXEMBOURG

		S	L			S	L
1947	Luxembourg	6	0	1987	Esch (E.C.)	0	0
1986	Glasgow (E.C.)	3	0				

v. MALTA

		S	M			S	M
1988	Valletta	1	1	1993	Glasgow (W.C.)	3	0
1990	Valletta	2	1	1993	Valletta (W.C.)	2	0

v. NEW ZEALAND

		S	NZ
1982	Malaga (W.C.)	5	2

v. NORWAY

		S	N			S	N
1929	Bergen	7	3	1978	Glasgow (E.C.)	3	2
1954	Glasgow	1	0	1979	Oslo (E.C.)	4	0
1954	Oslo	1	1	1988	Oslo (W.C.)	2	1
1963	Bergen	3	4	1989	Glasgow (W.C.)	1	1
1963	Glasgow	6	1	1992	Oslo	0	0
1974	Oslo	2	1				

v. PARAGUAY

		S	P
1958	Norrkoping (W.C.)	2	3

v. PERU

		S	P			S	P
1972	Glasgow	2	0	1979	Glasgow	1	1
1978	Cordoba (W.C.)	1	3				

v. POLAND

		S	P			S	P
1958	Warsaw	2	1	1965	Glasgow (W.C.)	1	2
1960	Glasgow	2	3	1980	Poznan	0	1
1965	Chorzow (W.C.)	1	1	1990	Glasgow	1	1

v. PORTUGAL

		S	P			S	P
1950	Lisbon	2	2	1978	Lisbon (E.C.)	0	1
1955	Glasgow	3	0	1980	Glasgow (E.C.)	4	1
1959	Lisbon	0	1	1980	Glasgow (W.C.)	0	0
1966	Glasgow	0	1	1981	Lisbon (W.C.)	1	2
1971	Lisbon (E.C.)	0	2	1992	Glasgow (W.C.)	0	0
1971	Glasgow (E.C.)	2	1	1993	Lisbon (W.C.)	0	5
1975	Glasgow	1	0				

v. ROMANIA

		S	R			S	R
1975	Bucharest (E.C.)	1	1	1990	Glasgow (E.C.)	2	1
1975	Glasgow (E.C.)	1	1	1991	Bucharest (E.C.)	0	1
1986	Glasgow	3	0				

v. RUSSIA

		S	R			S	R
1994	Glasgow (E.C.)	1	1	1995	Moscow (E.C.)	0	0

v. SAN MARINO

		S	SM			S	SM
1991	Serravalle (E.C.)	2	0	1995	Serravalle (E.C.)	2	0
1991	Glasgow (E.C.)	4	0	1995	Glasgow (E.C.)	5	0

v. SAUDI ARABIA

		S	SA
1988	Riyadh	2	2

v. SOVIET UNION (see also C.I.S. and RUSSIA)

		S	SU			S	SU
1967	Glasgow	0	2	1982	Malaga (W.C.)	2	2
1971	Moscow	0	1	1991	Glasgow	0	1

v. SPAIN

		S	Sp			S	Sp
1957	Glasgow (W.C.)	4	2	1975	Valencia (E.C.)	1	1
1957	Madrid (W.C.)	1	4	1982	Valencia	0	3
1963	Madrid	6	2	1985	Glasgow (W.C.)	3	1
1965	Glasgow	0	0	1985	Seville (W.C.)	0	1
1975	Glasgow (E.C.)	1	2	1988	Madrid	0	0

v. SWEDEN

		S	Swe			S	Swe
1952	Stockholm	1	3	1980	Stockholm (W.C.)	1	0
1953	Glasgow	1	2	1981	Glasgow (W.C.)	2	0
1975	Gothenburg	1	1	1990	Genoa (W.C.)	2	1
1977	Glasgow	3	1	1995	Solna	0	2

v. SWITZERLAND

		S	Sw			S	Sw
1931	Geneva	3	2	1982	Berne (E.C.)	0	2
1948	Berne	1	2	1983	Glasgow (E.C.)	2	2
1950	Glasgow	3	1	1990	Glasgow (E.C.)	2	1
1957	Basle (W.C.)	2	1	1991	Berne (E.C.)	2	2
1957	Glasgow (W.C.)	3	2	1992	Berne (W.C.)	1	3
1973	Berne	0	1	1993	Aberdeen (W.C.)	1	1
1976	Glasgow	1	0	1996	Birmingham (E.C.)	1	0

v. TURKEY

		S	T
1960	Ankara	2	4

v. U.S.A.

		S	USA			S	USA
1952	Glasgow	6	0	1996	Connecticut	1	2
1992	Denver	1	0				

v. URUGUAY

		S	U			S	U
1954	Basle (W.C.)	0	7	1983	Glasgow	2	0
1962	Glasgow	2	3	1986	Neza (W.C.)	0	0

v. YUGOSLAVIA

		S	Y			S	Y
1955	Belgrade	2	2	1974	Frankfurt (W.C.)	1	1
1956	Glasgow	2	0	1984	Glasgow	6	1
1958	Vaasteras (W.C.)	1	1	1988	Glasgow (W.C.)	1	1
1972	Belo Horizonte	2	2	1989	Zagreb (W.C.)	1	3

v. ZAIRE

		S	Z
1974	Dortmund (W.C.)	2	0

WALES

v. ALBANIA

		W	A			W	A
1994	Cardiff (E.C.)	2	0	1995	Tirana (E.C.)	1	1

v. ARGENTINA

		W	A
1992	Gifu (Japan)	0	1

v. AUSTRIA

		W	A			W	A
1954	Vienna	0	2	1975	Wrexham (E.C.)	1	0
1955	Wrexham	1	2	1992	Vienna	1	1
1975	Vienna (E.C.)	1	2				

v. BELGIUM

		W	B			W	B
1949	Liege	1	3	1991	Brussels (E.C.)	1	1
1949	Cardiff	5	1	1992	Brussels (W.C.)	0	2
1990	Cardiff (E.C.)	3	1	1993	Cardiff (W.C.)	2	0

v. BRAZIL

		W	B			W	B
1958	Gothenburg (W.C.)	0	1	1966	Belo Horizonte	0	1
1962	Rio de Janeiro	1	3	1983	Cardiff	1	1
1962	Sao Paulo	1	3	1991	Cardiff	1	0
1966	Rio de Janeiro	1	3				

v. BULGARIA

		W	B			W	B
1983	Wrexham (E.C.)	1	0	1994	Cardiff (E.C.)	0	3
1983	Sofia (E.C.)	0	1	1995	Sofia (E.C.)	1	3

v. CANADA

		W	C			W	C
1986	Toronto	0	2	1986	Vancouver	3	0

v. CHILE

		W	C
1966	Santiago	0	2

v. COSTA RICA

		W	C
1990	Cardiff	1	0

v. CYPRUS

		W	C			W	C
1992	Limassol (W.C.)	1	0	1993	Cardiff (W.C.)	2	0

v. CZECHOSLOVAKIA (see also R.C.S.)

		W	C			W	C
1957	Cardiff (W.C.)	1	0	1977	Prague (W.C.)	0	1
1957	Prague (W.C.)	0	2	1980	Cardiff (W.C.)	1	0
1971	Swansea (E.C.)	1	3	1981	Prague (W.C.)	0	2
1971	Prague (E.C.)	0	1	1987	Wrexham (E.C.)	1	1
1977	Wrexham (W.C.)	3	0	1987	Prague (E.C.)	0	2

v. DENMARK

		W	D			W	D
1964	Copenhagen (W.C.)	0	1	1987	Copenhagen (E.C.)	0	1
1965	Wrexham (W.C.)	4	2	1990	Copenhagen	0	1
1987	Cardiff (E.C.)	1	0				

v. EAST GERMANY

		W	EG			W	EG
1957	Leipzig (W.C.)	1	2	1969	Dresden (W.C.)	1	2
1957	Cardiff (W.C.)	4	1	1969	Cardiff (W.C.)	1	3

v. ESTONIA

		W	E
1994	Tallinn	2	1

v. FAROE ISLANDS

		W	FI			W	FI
1992	Cardiff (W.C.)	6	0	1993	Toftir (W.C.)	3	0

v. FINLAND

		W	F			W	F
1971	Helsinki (E.C.)	1	0	1987	Wrexham (E.C.)	4	0
1971	Swansea (E.C.)	3	0	1988	Swansea (W.C.)	2	2
1986	Helsinki (E.C.)	1	1	1989	Helsinki (W.C.)	0	1

v. FRANCE

		W	F			W	F
1933	Paris	1	1	1953	Paris	1	6
1939	Paris	1	2	1982	Toulouse	1	0

v. GEORGIA

		W	G			W	G
1994	Tbilisi (E.C.)	0	5	1995	Cardiff (E.C.)	0	1

v. GERMANY/WEST GERMANY

		W	G			W	G
1991	Cardiff (E.C.)	1	0	1989	Cardiff (W.C.)	0	0
1968	Cardiff	1	1	1989	Cologne (W.C.)	1	2
1969	Frankfurt	1	1	1991	Cardiff (E.C.)	1	0
1977	Cardiff	0	2	1991	Nuremberg (E.C.)	1	4
1977	Dortmund	1	1	1995	Dusseldorf (E.C.)	1	1
1979	Wrexham (E.C.)	0	2	1995	Cardiff (E.C.)	1	2
1979	Cologne (E.C.)	1	5				

v. GREECE

		W	G			W	G
1964	Athens (W.C.)	0	2	1965	Cardiff (W.C.)	4	1

v. HOLLAND

		W	H			W	H
1988	Amsterdam (W.C.)	0	1	1992	Utrecht	0	4
1989	Wrexham (W.C.)	1	2				

v. HUNGARY

		W	H			W	H
1958	Sanviken (W.C.)	1	1	1963	Cardiff (E.C.)	1	1
1958	Stockholm (W.C.)	2	1	1974	Cardiff (E.C.)	2	0
1961	Budapest	2	3	1975	Budapest (E.C.)	2	1
1963	Budapest (E.C.)	1	3	1986	Cardiff	0	3

v. ICELAND

		W	I			W	I
1980	Reykjavik (W.C.)	4	0	1984	Cardiff (W.C.)	2	1
1981	Swansea (W.C.)	2	2	1991	Cardiff	1	0
1984	Reykjavik (W.C.)	0	1				

v. IRAN

		W	I
1978	Teheran	1	0

v. REPUBLIC OF IRELAND

		W	R of I			W	R of I
1960	Dublin	3	2	1990	Dublin	0	1
1979	Swansea	2	1	1991	Wrexham	0	3
1981	Dublin	3	1	1992	Dublin	1	0
1986	Dublin	1	0	1993	Dublin	1	2

v. ISRAEL

		W	I			W	I
1958	Tel Aviv (W.C.)	2	0	1984	Tel Aviv	0	0
1958	Cardiff (W.C.)	2	0	1989	Tel Aviv	3	3

v. ITALY

		W	I			W	I
1965	Florence	1	4	1988	Brescia	1	0
1968	Cardiff (W.C.)	0	1	1996	Terni	0	3
1969	Rome (W.C.)	1	4				

v. JAPAN

		W	J
1992	Matsuyama	1	0

v. KUWAIT

		W	K			W	K
1977	Wrexham	0	0	1977	Kuwait	0	0

v. LUXEMBOURG

		W	L			W	L
1974	Swansea (E.C.)	5	0	1990	Luxembourg (E.C.)	1	0
1975	Luxembourg (E.C.)	3	1	1991	Luxembourg (E.C.)	1	0

v. MALTA

		W	M			W	M
1978	Wrexham (E.C.)	7	0	1988	Valletta	3	2
1979	Valletta (E.C.)	2	0				

v. MEXICO

		W	M			W	M
1958	Stockholm (W.C.)	1	1	1962	Mexico City	1	2

v. MOLDOVA

		W	M			W	M
1994	Kishinev (E.C.)	2	3	1995	Cardiff (E.C.)	1	0

v. NORWAY

		W	N			W	N
1982	Swansea (E.C.)	1	0	1985	Wrexham	1	1
1983	Oslo (E.C.)	0	0	1985	Bergen	2	4
1984	Trondheim	0	1	1994	Cardiff	1	3

v. POLAND

		W	P			W	P
1973	Cardiff (W.C.)	2	0	1991	Radom	0	0
1973	Katowice (W.C.)	0	3				

v. PORTUGAL

		W	P			W	P
1949	Lisbon	2	3	1951	Cardiff	2	1

v. R.C.S. (formerly Czechoslovakia)

		W	RCS			W	RCS
1993	Ostrava (W.C.)	1	1	1993	Cardiff (W.C.)	2	2

v. REST OF UNITED KINGDOM

		W	R of UK			W	R of UK
1951	Cardiff	3	2	1969	Cardiff	0	1

v. ROMANIA

		W	R			W	R
1970	Cardiff (E.C.)	0	0	1992	Bucharest (W.C.)	1	5
1971	Bucharest (E.C.)	0	2	1993	Cardiff (W.C.)	1	2
1983	Wrexham	5	0				

v. SAN MARINO

		W	SM
1996	Serravalle (W.C.)	5	0

v. SAUDI ARABIA

		W	SA
1986	Dahran	2	1

v. SOVIET UNION

		W	SU			W	SU
1965	Moscow (W.C.)	1	2	1981	Tbilisi (W.C.)	0	3
1965	Cardiff (W.C.)	2	1	1987	Swansea	0	0
1981	Wrexham (W.C.)	0	0				

v. SPAIN

		W	S			W	S
1961	Cardiff (W.C.)	1	2	1984	Seville (W.C.)	0	3
1961	Madrid (W.C.)	1	1	1985	Wrexham (W.C.)	3	0
1982	Valencia	1	1				

v. SWEDEN

		W	S			W	S
1958	Stockholm (W.C.)	0	0	1990	Stockholm	2	4
1988	Stockholm	1	4	1994	Wrexham	0	2
1989	Wrexham	0	2				

v. SWITZERLAND

		W	S			W	S
1949	Berne	0	4	1996	Lugano	0	2
1951	Wrexham	3	2				

v. TURKEY

		W	T			W	T
1978	Wrexham (E.C.)	1	0	1980	Cardiff (W.C.)	4	0
1979	Izmir (E.C.)	0	1	1981	Ankara (W.C.)	1	0

v. URUGUAY

		W	U
1986	Wrexham	0	0

v. YUGOSLAVIA

		W	Y			W	Y
1953	Belgrade	2	5	1982	Titograd (E.C.)	4	4
1954	Cardiff	1	3	1983	Cardiff (E.C.)	1	1
1976	Zagreb (E.C.)	0	2	1988	Swansea	1	2
1976	Cardiff (E.C.)	1	1				

NORTHERN IRELAND

v. ALBANIA

		NI	A			NI	A
1965	Belfast (W.C.)	4	1	1983	Belfast (E.C.)	1	0
1965	Tirana (W.C.)	1	1	1992	Belfast (W.C.)	3	0
1983	Tirana (E.C.)	0	0	1993	Tirana (W.C.)	2	1

v. ALGERIA

		NI	A
1986	Guadalajara (W.C.)	1	1

v. ARGENTINA

		NI	A
1958	Halmstad (W.C.)	1	3

v. AUSTRALIA

		NI	A			NI	A
1980	Sydney	2	1	1980	Adelaide	2	1
1980	Melbourne	1	1				

v. AUSTRIA

		NI	A			NI	A
1982	Madrid (W.C.)	2	2	1991	Belfast (E.C.)	2	1
1982	Vienna (E.C.)	0	2	1994	Vienna (E.C.)	2	1
1983	Belfast (E.C.)	3	1	1995	Belfast (E.C.)	5	3
1990	Vienna (E.C.)	0	0				

v. BELGIUM

		NI	B			NI	B
1976	Liege (W.C.)	0	2	1977	Belfast (W.C.)	3	0

v. BRAZIL

		NI	B
1986	Guadalajara (W.C.)	0	3

v. BULGARIA

		NI	B			NI	B
1972	Sofia (W.C.)	0	3	1978	Sofia (E.C.)	2	0
1973	Sheffield (W.C.)	0	0	1979	Belfast (E.C.)	2	0

v. CANADA

		NI	C
1995	Edmonton	0	2

v. CHILE

		NI	C			NI	C
1989	Belfast	0	1	1995	Edmonton, Canada	0	2

v. COLOMBIA

		NI	C
1994	Boston (USA)	0	2

v. CYPRUS

		NI	C			NI	C
1971	Nicosia (E.C.)	3	0	1973	Nicosia (W.C.)	0	1
1971	Belfast (E.C.)	5	0	1973	Fulham (W.C.)	3	0

v. CZECHOSLOVAKIA

		NI	C			NI	C
1958	Halmstad (W.C.)	1	0	1958	Malmo (W.C.)	2	1

v. DENMARK

		NI	D			NI	D
1978	Belfast (E.C.)	2	1	1991	Odense (E.C.)	1	2
1979	Copenhagen (E.C.)	0	4	1992	Belfast (W.C.)	0	1
1986	Belfast	1	1	1993	Copenhagen (W.C.)	0	1
1990	Belfast (E.C.)	1	1				

v. FAROE ISLANDS

		NI	FI			NI	FI
1991	Belfast (E.C.)	1	1	1991	Landskrona, Sw. (E.C.)	5	0

v. FINLAND

		NI	F			NI	F
1984	Pori (W.C.)	0	1	1984	Belfast (W.C.)	2	1

v. FRANCE

		NI	F			NI	F
1951	Belfast	2	2	1982	Madrid (W.C.)	1	4
1952	Paris	1	3	1986	Paris	0	0
1958	Norrkoping (W.C.)	0	4	1988	Belfast	0	0
1982	Paris	0	4				

v. GERMANY/WEST GERMANY

		NI	G			NI	G
1958	Malmo (W.C.)	2	2	1982	Belfast (E.C.)	1	0
1960	Belfast (W.C.)	3	4	1983	Hamburg (E.C.)	1	0
1961	Berlin (W.C.)	1	2	1992	Bremen	1	1
1966	Belfast	0	2	1996	Belfast	1	1
1977	Cologne	0	5				

v. GREECE

		NI	G			NI	G
1961	Athens (W.C.)	1	2	1988	Athens	2	3
1961	Belfast (W.C.)	2	0				

v. HOLLAND

		NI	H			NI	H
1962	Rotterdam	0	4	1976	Rotterdam (W.C.)	2	2
1965	Belfast (W.C.)	2	1	1977	Belfast (W.C.)	0	1
1965	Rotterdam (W.C.)	0	0				

v. HONDURAS

		NI	H
1982	Zaragoza (W.C.)	1	1

v. HUNGARY

		NI	H			NI	H
1988	Budapest (W.C.)	0	1	1989	Belfast (W.C.)	1	2

v. ICELAND

		NI	I			NI	I
1977	Reykjavik (W.C.)	0	1	1977	Belfast (W.C.)	2	0

v. REPUBLIC OF IRELAND

		NI	R of I			NI	R of I
1978	Dublin (E.C.)	0	0	1993	Dublin (W.C.)	0	3
1979	Belfast (E.C.)	1	0	1993	Belfast (W.C.)	1	1
1988	Belfast (W.C.)	0	0	1994	Belfast (E.C.)	0	4
1989	Dublin (W.C.)	0	3	1995	Dublin (E.C.)	1	1

v. ISRAEL

		NI	I			NI	I
1968	Jaffa	3	2	1981	Belfast (W.C.)	1	0
1976	Tel Aviv	1	1	1984	Belfast	3	0
1980	Tel Aviv (W.C.)	0	0	1987	Tel Aviv	1	1

v. ITALY

		NI	I			NI	I
1957	Rome (W.C.)	0	1	1958	Belfast (W.C.)	2	1
1957	Belfast	2	2	1961	Bologna	2	3

v. LATVIA

		NI	L			NI	L
1993	Riga (W.C.)	2	1	1995	Riga (E.C.)	1	0
1993	Belfast (W.C.)	2	0	1995	Belfast (E.C.)	1	2

v. LIECHTENSTEIN

		NI	L			NI	L
1994	Belfast (E.C.)	4	1	1995	Eschen (E.C.)	4	0

v. LITHUANIA

		NI	L			NI	L
1992	Belfast (W.C.)	2	2	1993	Vilnius (W.C.)	1	0

v. MALTA

		NI	M			NI	M
1988	Belfast (W.C.)	3	0	1989	Valletta (W.C.)	2	0

v. MEXICO

		NI	M			NI	M
1966	Belfast	4	1	1994	Miami	0	3

v. MOROCCO

		NI	M
1986	Belfast	2	1

v. NORWAY

		NI	N			NI	N
1974	Oslo (E.C.)	1	2	1990	Belfast	2	3
1975	Belfast (E.C.)	3	0	1996	Belfast	0	2

v. POLAND

		NI	P			NI	P
1962	Katowice (E.C.)	2	0	1988	Belfast	1	1
1962	Belfast (E.C.)	2	0	1991	Belfast	3	1

v. PORTUGAL

		NI	P			NI	P
1957	Lisbon (W.C.)	1	1	1980	Lisbon (W.C.)	0	1
1957	Belfast (W.C.)	3	0	1981	Belfast (W.C.)	1	0
1973	Coventry (W.C.)	1	1	1994	Belfast (E.C.)	1	2
1973	Lisbon (W.C.)	1	1	1995	Oporto (E.C.)	1	1

v. ROMANIA

		NI	R			NI	R
1984	Belfast (W.C.)	3	2	1994	Belfast	2	0
1985	Bucharest (W.C.)	1	0				

v. SOVIET UNION

		NI	SU			NI	SU
1969	Belfast (W.C.)	0	0	1971	Moscow (E.C.)	0	1
1969	Moscow (W.C.)	0	2	1971	Belfast (E.C.)	1	1

v. SPAIN

		NI	S			NI	S
1958	Madrid	2	6	1985	Palma, Majorca	0	0
1963	Bilbao	1	1	1986	Guadalajara (W.C.)	1	2
1963	Belfast	0	1	1988	Seville (W.C.)	0	4
1970	Seville (E.C.)	0	3	1989	Belfast (W.C.)	0	2
1972	Hull (E.C.)	1	1	1992	Belfast (W.C.)	0	0
1982	Valencia (W.C.)	1	0	1993	Seville (W.C.)	1	3

v. SWEDEN

		NI	S			NI	S
1974	Solna (E.C.)	2	0	1981	Stockholm (W.C.)	0	1
1975	Belfast (E.C.)	1	2	1996	Belfast	1	2
1980	Belfast (W.C.)	3	0				

v. SWITZERLAND

		NI	S			NI	S
1964	Belfast (W.C.)	1	0	1964	Lausanne (W.C.)	1	2

v. TURKEY

		NI	T			NI	T
1968	Belfast (W.C.)	4	1	1985	Belfast (W.C.)	2	0
1968	Istanbul (W.C.)	3	0	1985	Izmir (W.C.)	0	0
1983	Belfast (E.C.)	2	1	1986	Izmir (E.C.)	0	0
1983	Ankara (E.C.)	0	1	1987	Belfast (E.C.)	1	0

v. URUGUAY

		NI	U			NI	U
1964	Belfast	3	0	1990	Belfast	1	0

v.YUGOSLAVIA

		NI	Y			NI	Y
1975	Belfast (E.C.)	1	0	1987	Sarajevo (E.C.)	0	3
1975	Belgrade (E.C.)	0	1	1990	Belfast (E.C.)	0	2
1982	Zaragoza (W.C.)	0	0	1991	Belgrade (E.C.)	1	4
1987	Belfast (E.C.)	1	2				

REPUBLIC OF IRELAND

v. ALBANIA

		R of I	A			R of I	A
1992	Dublin (W.C.)	2	0	1993	Tirana (W.C.)	2	1

v. ARGENTINA

		R of I	A			R of I	A
1951	Dublin	0	1	1980	Dublin	0	1
1979	* Dublin	0	0	(* Not regarded as full Int.)			

v. AUSTRIA

		R of I	A			R of I	A
1952	Vienna	0	6	1966	Vienna	0	1
1953	Dublin	4	0	1968	Dublin	2	2
1958	Vienna	1	3	1971	Dublin (E.C.)	1	4
1962	Dublin	2	3	1971	Linz (E.C.)	0	6
1963	Vienna (E.C.)	0	0	1995	Dublin (E.C.)	1	3
1963	Dublin (E.C.)	3	2	1995	Vienna (E.C.)	1	3

v. BELGIUM

		R of I	B			R of I	B
1928	Liege	4	2	1965	Dublin	0	2
1929	Dublin	4	0	1966	Liege	3	2
1930	Brussels	3	1	1980	Dublin (W.C.)	1	1
1934	Dublin (W.C.)	4	4	1981	Brussels (W.C.)	0	1
1949	Dublin	0	2	1986	Brussels (E.C.)	2	2
1950	Brussels	1	5	1987	Dublin (E.C.)	0	0

v. BOLIVIA

		R of I	B			R of I	B
1994	Dublin	1	0	1996	New Jersey	3	0

v. BRAZIL

		R of I	B			R of I	B
1974	Rio de Janeiro	1	2	1987	Dublin	1	0
1982	Uberlandia	0	7				

v. BULGARIA

		R of I	B			R of I	B
1977	Sofia (W.C.)	1	2	1979	Dublin (E.C.)	3	0
1977	Dublin (W.C.)	0	0	1987	Sofia (E.C.)	1	2
1979	Sofia (E.C.)	0	1	1987	Dublin (E.C.)	2	0

v. CHILE

		R of I	C			R of I	C
1960	Dublin	2	0	1982	Santiago	0	1
1972	Recife	1	2	1991	Dublin	1	1
1974	Santiago	2	1				

v. CYPRUS

		R of I	C			R of I	C
1980	Nicosia (W.C.)	3	2	1980	Dublin (W.C.)	6	0

v. CZECHOSLOVAKIA/CZECH REPUBLIC

		R of I	C			R of I	C
1938	Prague	2	2	1969	Dublin (W.C.)	1	2
1959	Dublin (E.C.)	2	0	1969	Prague (W.C.)	0	3
1959	Bratislava (E.C.)	0	4	1979	Prague	1	4
1961	Dublin (W.C.)	1	3	1981	Dublin	3	1
1961	Prague (W.C.)	1	7	1986	Reykjavik	1	0
1967	Dublin (E.C.)	0	2	1994	Dublin	1	3
1967	Prague (E.C.)	2	1	1996	Prague	0	2

v. DENMARK

		R of I	D			R of I	D
1956	Dublin (W.C.)	2	1	1979	Dublin (E.C.)	2	0
1957	Copenhagen (W.C.)	2	0	1984	Copenhagen (W.C.)	0	3
1968	*Dublin (W.C.)	1	1	1985	Dublin (W.C.)	1	4
1969	Copenhagen (W.C.)	0	2	1992	Copenhagen (W.C.)	0	0
1969	Dublin (W.C.)	1	1	1993	Dublin (W.C.)	1	1
1978	Copenhagen (E.C.)	3	3	(* Abandoned after 51 mins. – fog)			

v. ECUADOR

		R of I	E
1972	Natal	3	2

v. EGYPT

		R of I	E
1990	Palermo (W.C.)	0	0

v. ENGLAND (See England results)

v. FINLAND

		R of I	F			R of I	F
1949	Dublin (W.C.)	3	0	1990	Dublin	1	1
1949	Helsinki (W.C.)	1	1				

v. FRANCE

		R of I	F			R of I	F
1937	Paris	2	0	1976	Paris (W.C.)	0	2
1952	Dublin	1	1	1977	Dublin (W.C.)	1	0
1953	Dublin (W.C.)	3	5	1980	Paris (W.C.)	0	2
1953	Paris (W.C.)	0	1	1981	Dublin (W.C.)	3	2
1972	Dublin (W.C.)	2	1	1989	Dublin	0	0
1973	Paris (W.C.)	1	1				

v. GERMANY/WEST GERMANY

		R of I	G			R of I	G
1935	Dortmund	1	3	1960	Dusseldorf	1	0
1936	Dublin	5	2	1966	Dublin	0	4
1939	Bremen	1	1	1970	Berlin	1	2
1951	Dublin	3	2	1979	Dublin	1	3
1952	Cologne	0	3	1981	Bremen	0	3
1955	Hamburg	1	2	1989	Dublin	1	1
1956	Dublin	3	0	1994	Hanover	2	0

v. HOLLAND

		R of I	H			R of I	H
1932	Amsterdam	2	0	1983	Dublin (E.C.)	2	3
1934	Amsterdam	2	5	1988	G'kirchen (E.C.)	0	1
1935	Dublin	3	5	1990	Palermo (W.C.)	1	1
1955	Dublin	1	0	1994	Tilburg	1	0
1956	Rotterdam	4	1	1994	Orlando (W.C.)	0	2
1980	Dublin (W.C.)	2	1	1995	*Liverpool (E.C.)	0	2
1981	Rotterdam (W.C.)	2	2	1996	Rotterdam	1	3
1982	Rotterdam (E.C.)	1	2	(*Qual.	Round play-off)		

v. HUNGARY

		R of I	H			R of I	H
1934	Dublin	2	4	1969	Dublin (W.C.)	1	2
1936	Budapest	3	3	1969	Budapest (W.C.)	0	4
1936	Dublin	2	3	1989	Budapest (W.C.)	0	0
1939	Cork	2	2	1989	Dublin (W.C.)	2	0
1939	Budapest	2	2	1992	Gyor	2	1

v. ICELAND

		R of I	I			R of I	I
1962	Dublin (E.C.)	4	2	1983	Reykjavik (E.C.)	3	0
1962	Reykjavik (E.C.)	1	1	1986	Reykjavik	2	1
1982	Dublin (E.C.)	2	0				

v. IRAN

		R of I	I
1972	Recife	2	1

v. ISRAEL

		R of I	I			R of I	I
1984	Tel Aviv	0	3	1987	Dublin	5	0
1985	Tel Aviv	0	0				

v. ITALY

		R of I	I			R of I	I
1926	Turin	0	3	1985	Dublin	1	2
1927	Dublin	1	2	1990	Rome (W.C.)	0	1
1970	Florence (E.C.)	0	3	1992	Boston (U.S.A.)	0	2
1971	Dublin (E.C.)	1	2	1994	New York (W.C.)	1	0

v. LATVIA

		R of I	L			R of I	L
1992	Dublin (W.C.)	4	0	1994	Riga (E.C.)	3	0
1993	Riga (W.C.)	2	0	1995	Dublin (E.C.)	2	0

v. LITHUANIA

		R of I	L			R of I	L
1993	Vilnius (W.C.)	1	0	1993	Dublin (W.C.)	2	0

v. LUXEMBOURG

		R of I	L			R of I	L
1936	Luxembourg	5	1	1987	Luxembourg (E.C.)	2	0
1953	Dublin (W.C.)	4	0	1987	Luxembourg (E.C.)	2	1
1954	Luxembourg (W.C.)	1	0				

v. LIECHTENSTEIN

		R of I	L			R of I	L
1994	Dublin (E.C.)	4	0	1995	Eschen (E.C.)	0	0

v. MALTA

		R of I	M			R of I	M
1983	Valletta (E.C.)	1	0	1989	Valletta (W.C.)	2	0
1983	Dublin (E.C.)	8	0	1990	Valletta	3	0
1989	Dublin (W.C.)	2	0				

v. MEXICO

		R of I	M			R of I	M
1984	Dublin	0	0	1996	New Jersey	2	2
1994	Orlando (W.C.)	1	2				

v. MOROCCO

		R of I	M
1990	Dublin	1	0

v. NORTHERN IRELAND (See N. Ireland results)

v. NORWAY

		R of I	N			R of I	N
1937	Oslo (W.C.)	2	3	1973	Oslo	1	1
1937	Dublin (W.C.)	3	3	1976	Dublin	3	0
1950	Dublin	2	2	1978	Oslo	0	0
1951	Oslo	3	2	1984	Oslo (W.C.)	0	1
1954	Dublin	2	1	1985	Dublin (W.C.)	0	0
1955	Oslo	3	1	1988	Oslo	0	0
1960	Dublin	3	1	1994	New York (W.C.)	0	0
1964	Oslo	4	1				

v. POLAND

		R of I	P			R of I	P
1938	Warsaw	0	6	1964	Cracow	1	3
1938	Dublin	3	2	1964	Dublin	3	2
1958	Katowice	2	2	1968	Dublin	2	2
1958	Dublin	2	2	1968	Katowice	0	1

		R of I	P			R of I	P
1970	Dublin	1	2	1981	Bydgoscz	0	3
1970	Poznan	0	2	1984	Dublin	0	0
1973	Wroclaw	0	2	1986	Warsaw	0	1
1973	Dublin	1	0	1988	Dublin	3	1
1976	Poznan	2	0	1991	Dublin (E.C.)	0	0
1977	Dublin	0	0	1991	Poznan (E.C.)	3	3
1978	Lodz	0	3				

v. PORTUGAL

		R of I	P			R of I	P
1946	Lisbon	1	3	1992	Boston(U.S.A.)	2	0
1947	Dublin	0	2	1995	Dublin (E.C.)	1	0
1948	Lisbon	0	2	1995	Lisbon (E.C.)	0	3
1949	Dublin	1	0	1996	Dublin	0	1
1972	Recife	1	2				

v. ROMANIA

		R of I	R			R of I	R
1988	Dublin	2	0	1990	* Genoa	0	0

(* Rep. won 5-4 on pens.)

v. RUSSIA (See also Soviet Union)

		R of I	R			R of I	R
1994	Dublin	0	0	1996	Dublin	0	2

v. SCOTLAND

		R of I	S			R of I	S
1961	Glasgow (W.C.)	1	4	1969	Dublin	1	1
1961	Dublin (W.C.)	0	3	1986	Dublin (E.C.)	0	0
1963	Dublin	1	0	1987	Glasgow (E.C.)	1	0

v. SOVIET UNION (See also Russia)

		R of I	SU			R of I	SU
1972	Dublin (W.C.)	1	2	1984	Dublin (W.C.)	1	0
1973	Moscow (W.C.)	0	1	1985	Moscow (W.C.)	0	2
1974	Dublin (E.C.)	3	0	1988	Hanover (E.C.)	1	1
1975	Kiev (E.C.)	1	2	1990	Dublin	1	0

v. SPAIN

		R of I	S			R of I	S
1931	Barcelona	1	1	1965	Paris (W.C.)	0	1
1931	Dublin	0	5	1966	Dublin (E.C.)	0	0
1946	Madrid	1	0	1966	Valencia (E.C.)	0	2
1947	Dublin	3	2	1977	Dublin	0	1
1948	Barcelona	1	2	1982	Dublin (E.C.)	3	3
1949	Dublin	1	4	1983	Zaragoza (E.C.)	0	2
1952	Madrid	0	6	1985	Cork	0	0
1955	Dublin	2	2	1988	Seville (W.C.)	0	2
1964	Seville (E.C.)	1	5	1989	Dublin (W.C.)	1	0
1964	Dublin (E.C.)	0	2	1992	Seville (W.C.)	0	0
1965	Dublin (W.C.)	1	0	1993	Dublin (W.C.)	1	3
1965	Seville (W.C.)	1	4				

v. SWEDEN

		R of I	S			R of I	S
1949	Stockholm (W.C.)	1	3	1960	Malmo	1	4
1949	Dublin (W.C.)	1	3	1970	Dublin (E.C.)	1	1
1959	Dublin	3	2	1970	Malmo (E.C.)	0	1

v. SWITZERLAND

		R of I	S			R of I	S
1935	Basle	0	1	1975	Berne (E.C.)	0	1
1936	Dublin	1	0	1980	Dublin	2	0
1937	Berne	1	0	1985	Dublin (W.C.)	3	0
1938	Dublin	4	0	1985	Berne (W.C.)	0	0
1948	Dublin	0	1	1992	Dublin	2	1
1975	Dublin (E.C.)	2	1				

v. TRINIDAD & TOBAGO

		R of I	T&T
1982	Port of Spain	1	2

v. TUNISIA

		R of I	T
1988	Dublin	4	0

v. TURKEY

		R of I	T			R of I	T
1966	Dublin (E.C.)	2	1	1978	Dublin	4	2
1967	Ankara (E.C.)	1	2	1990	Izmir	0	0
1974	Izmir (E.C.)	1	1	1990	Dublin (E.C.)	5	0
1975	Dublin (E.C.)	4	0	1991	Istanbul (E.C.)	3	1
1976	Ankara	3	3				

v. URUGUAY

		R of I	U			R of I	U
1974	Montevideo	0	2	1986	Dublin	1	1

v. U.S.A.

		R of I	USA			R of I	USA
1979	Dublin	3	2	1992	Washington	1	3
1991	Boston	1	1	1996	Boston	1	2
1992	Dublin	4	1				

v. WALES

		R of I	W			R of I	W
1960	Dublin	2	3	1990	Dublin	1	0
1979	Swansea	1	2	1991	Wrexham	3	0
1981	Dublin	1	3	1992	Dublin	0	1
1986	Dublin	0	1	1993	Dublin	2	1

v. YUGOSLAVIA

		R of I	Y			R of I	Y
1955	Dublin	1	4	1988	Dublin	2	0

BRITISH CHAMPIONSHIP

WINNERS OF THE TITLE – COMPLETE RECORD

Season	Winner	Pts.
1883-84	Scotland	6
1884-85	Scotland	5
1885-86	England	5
	Scotland	5
1886-87	Scotland	6
1887-88	England	6
1888-89	Scotland	5
1889-90	Scotland	5
	England	5
1890-91	England	6
1891-92	England	6
1892-93	England	6
1893-94	Scotland	5
1894-95	England	5
1895-96	Scotland	5
1896-97	Scotland	5
1897-98	England	6
1898-99	England	6
1899-1900	Scotland	6
1900-01	England	5
1901-02	Scotland	5
1902-03	England	4
	Ireland	4
	Scotland	4
1903-04	England	5
1904-05	England	5
1905-06	England	4
	Scotland	4
1906-07	Wales	5
1907-08	Scotland	5
	England	5
1908-09	England	6
1909-10	Scotland	4
1910-11	England	5
1911-12	England	5
	Scotland	5
1912-13	England	4
1913-14	Ireland	5
1915-19	No contest	
1919-20	Wales	4
1920-21	Scotland	6
1921-22	Scotland	4
1922-23	Scotland	5
1923-24	Wales	6
1924-25	Scotland	6
1925-26	Scotland	6
1926-27	Scotland	4
	England	4
1927-28	Wales	5
1928-29	Scotland	6
1929-30	England	6
1930-31	Scotland	4
	England	4
1931-32	England	6
1932-33	Wales	5
1933-34	Wales	5
1934-35	England	4
	Scotland	4
1935-36	Scotland	4
1936-37	Wales	6
1937-38	England	4
1938-39	England	4
	Scotland	4
	Wales	4
1939-46	No contest	
1946-47	England	5
1947-48	England	5
1948-49	Scotland	6
1949-50	England	6
1950-51	Scotland	6
1951-52	Wales	5
	England	5
1952-53	England	4
	Scotland	4
1953-54	England	6
1954-55	England	6
1955-56	England	3
	Scotland	3
	Wales	3
	Ireland	3
1956-57	England	5
1957-58	England	4
	Ireland	4
1958-59	Ireland	4
	England	4
1959-60	England	4
	Scotland	4
	Wales	4
1960-61	England	6
1961-62	Scotland	6
1962-63	Scotland	6
1963-64	England	4
	Scotland	4
	Ireland	4
1964-65	England	5
1965-66	England	5
1966-67	Scotland	5
1967-68	England	5
1968-69	England	6
1969-70	England	4
	Scotland	4
	Wales	4
1970-71	England	5
1971-72	England	4
	Scotland	4
1972-73	England	6
1973-74	Scotland	4
	England	4
1974-75	England	4
1975-76	Scotland	6
1976-77	Scotland	5
1977-78	England	6
1978-79	England	5
1979-80	Ireland	5
1980-81	Declared Void †	
1981-82	England	6
1982-83	England	5
1983-84	Ireland	*3

* Title shared when countries finished level on points until 1983-84, when goal difference was used for the first and only time. The competition was discontinued after that season.

† Because of political unrest in Ireland.

INTERNATIONAL APPEARANCES SINCE THE WAR (1946-96)

(As at start of season 1996-7. Year shown = season, ie. 1996 = season 1995-6. *Also a pre-war International player. Totals include appearances as substitute).

ENGLAND

A'Court, A. (Liverpool, 1958-9) 5
Adams, T. (Arsenal, 1987-96) 45
Allen, A. (Stoke, 1960) 3
Allen, C. (Q.P.R., Tottenham, 1984-8) 5
Allen, R. (W.B.A., 1952-5) 5
Anderson, S. (Sunderland, 1962) 2
Anderson, V. (Nott'm F., Arsenal, Man. Utd., 1979-88) 30
Anderton, D. (Tottenham, 1994-6) . 16
Angus, J. (Burnley, 1961) 1
Armfield, J. (Blackpool, 1959-66) .. 43
Armstrong, D. (Middlesbrough, Southampton, 1980-4) 3
Armstrong, K. (Chelsea, 1955) 1
Astall, G. (Birmingham, 1956) 2
Astle, J. (W.B.A., 1969-70) 5
Aston, J. (Man. Utd., 1949-51) 17
Atyeo, J. (Bristol City, 1956-7) 6

Bailey, G. (Man. Utd., 1985) 2
Bailey, M. (Charlton, 1964-5) 2
Baily, E. (Tottenham, 1950-3) 9
Baker, J. (Hibernian, Arsenal, 1960-6) 8
Ball, A. (Blackpool, Everton, Arsenal, 1965-75) 72
Banks, G. (Leicester, Stoke, 1963-72) 73
Banks, T. (Bolton, 1958-9) 6
Bardsley, D. (Q.P.R., 1993) 2
Barham, M. (Norwich, 1983) 2
Barlow, R. (W.B.A., 1955) 1
Barmby, N. (Tottenham, Middlesbrough, 1995-6) 9
Barnes, J. (Watford, Liverpool, 1983-96) 79
Barnes, P. (Man. City, W.B.A., Leeds, 1978-82) 22
Barrass, M. (Bolton, 1952-3) 3
Barrett, E. (Oldham, Aston Villa, 1991-3) 3
Barton, W. (Wimbledon, Newcastle, 1995) 3
Batty, D. (Leeds, Blackburn, 1991-5) 17
Baynham, R. (Luton, 1956) 3
Beardsley, P. (Newcastle, Liverpool, Newcastle, 1986-96) 59
Beasant, D. (Chelsea, 1990) 2
Beattie, K. (Ipswich, 1975-8) 9
Bell, C. (Man. City, 1968-76) 48
Bentley, R. (Chelsea, 1949-55) 12
Berry, J. (Man. Utd., 1953-6) 4
Birtles, G. (Nott'm F., 1980-1) 3
Blissett, L. (Watford, AC Milan, 1983-4) 14
Blockley, J. (Arsenal, 1973) 1
Blunstone, F. (Chelsea, 1955-7) 5
Bonetti, P. (Chelsea, 1966-70) 7
Bould, S. (Arsenal, 1994) 2
Bowles, S. (Q.P.R., 1974-7) 5
Boyer, P. (Norwich, 1976) 1
Brabrook, P. (Chelsea, 1958-60) 3
Bracewell, P. (Everton, 1985-6) 3
Bradford, G. (Bristol Rovers, 1956) 1
Bradley, W. (Man. Utd., 1959) 3
Bridges, B. (Chelsea, 1965-6) 4
Broadbent, P. (Wolves, 1958-60) 7
Broadis, I. (Man. City, Newcastle, 1952-4) 14
Brooking, T. (West Ham, 1974-82) 47
Brooks, J. (Tottenham, 1957) 3
Brown, A. (W.B.A., 1971) 1
Brown, K. (West Ham, 1960) 1
Bull, S. (Wolves, 1989-91) 13
Butcher, T. (Ipswich, Rangers, 1980-90) 77
Byrne, G. (Liverpool, 1963-6) 2

Froggatt, R. (Sheff. Wed., 1953) 4

Garrett, T. (Blackpool, 1952-4) 3
Gascoigne, P. (Tottenham, Lazio, Rangers, 1989-96) 42
Gates, E. (Ipswich, 1981) 2
George, C. (Derby, 1977) 1
Gidman, J. (Aston Villa, 1977) 1
Gillard, I. (Q.P.R., 1975-6) 3
Goddard, P. (West Ham, 1982) 1
Grainger, C. (Sheff. Utd., Sunderland, 1956-7) 7
Gray, A. (Crystal P., 1992) 1
Greaves, J. (Chelsea, Tottenham, 1959-67) 57
Greenhoff, B. (Man. Utd., Leeds, 1976-80) 18
Gregory, J. (Q.P.R., 1983-4) 6

Hagan, J. (Sheff. Utd., 1949) 1
Haines, J. (W.B.A., 1949) 1
Hall, J. (Birmingham, 1956-7) 17
Hancocks, J. (Wolves, 1949-50) 3
Hardwick, G. (Middlesbrough, 1947-8) 13
Harford, M. (Luton, 1988-9) 2
Harris, G. (Burnley, 1966) 1
Harris, P. (Portsmouth, 1950-4) 2
Harvey, C. (Everton, 1971) 1
Hassall, H. (Huddersfield, Bolton, 1951-4) 5
Hateley, M. (Portsmouth, AC Milan, Monaco, Rangers, 1984-92) 32
Haynes, J. (Fulham, 1955-62) 56
Hector, K. (Derby, 1974) 2
Hellawell, M. (Birmingham, 1963) ... 2
Henry, R. (Tottenham, 1963) 1
Hill, F. (Bolton, 1963) 2
Hill, G. (Man. Utd., 1976-8) 6
Hill, R. (Luton, 1983-6) 3
Hinton, A. (Wolves, Nott'm F., 1963-5) 3
Hirst, D. (Sheff. Wed., 1991-2) 3
Hitchens, G. (Aston Villa, Inter Milan, 1961-2) 7
Hoddle, G. (Tottenham, Monaco, 1980-8) 53
Hodge, S. (Aston Villa, Tottenham, Nott'm F., 1986-91) 24
Hodgkinson, A. (Sheff. Utd., 1957-61) 5
Holden, D. (Bolton, 1959) 5
Holliday, E. (Middlesbrough, 1960) . 3
Hollins, J. (Chelsea, 1967) 1
Hopkinson, E. (Bolton, 1958-60) ... 14
Howe, D. (W.B.A., 1958-60) 23
Howe, J. (Derby, 1948-9) 3
Howey, S. (Newcastle, 1995-6) 4
Hudson, A. (Stoke, 1975) 2
Hughes, E. (Liverpool, Wolves, 1970-80) 62
Hughes, L. (Liverpool, 1950) 3
Hunt, R. (Liverpool, 1962-9) 34
Hunt, S. (W.B.A., 1984) 2
Hunter, N. (Leeds, 1966-75) 28
Hurst, G. (West Ham, 1966-72) 49

Ince, P. (Man. Utd., Inter Milan, 1993-6) 23

Jezzard, B. (Fulham, 1954-6) 2
Johnson, D. (Ipswich, Liverpool, 1975-80) 8
Johnston, H. (Blackpool, 1947-54) 10
Jones, M. (Leeds, Sheff. Utd., 1965-70) 3
Jones, R. (Liverpool, 1992-5) 8
Jones, W.H. (Liverpool, 1950) 2

Kay, A. (Everton, 1963) 1
Keegan, K. (Liverpool, Hamburg, Southampton, 1973-82) 63
Kennedy, A. (Liverpool, 1984) 2
Kennedy, R. (Liverpool, 1976-80) .. 17
Keown, M. (Everton, Arsenal, 1992-3) 11
Kevan, D. (W.B.A., 1957-61) 14
Kidd, B. (Man. Utd., 1970) 2
Knowles, C. (Tottenham, 1968) 4

Labone, B. (Everton, 1963-70) 26
Lampard, F. (West Ham, 1973-80) .. 2
Langley, J. (Fulham, 1958) 3
Langton, R. (Blackburn, Preston, Bolton, 1947-51) 11
Latchford, R. (Everton, 1978-9) 12
Lawler, C. (Liverpool, 1971-2) 4
*Lawton, T. (Chelsea, Notts County, 1947-9) 15
Lee, F. (Man. City, 1969-72) 27
Lee, J. (Derby, 1951) 1

Lee, R. (Newcastle, 1995-6) 7
Lee, S. (Liverpool, 1983-4) 14
Le Saux, G. (Blackburn, 1994-6) .. 12
Le Tissier, M. (Southampton, 1994-5) 6
Lindsay, A. (Liverpool, 1974) 4
Lineker, G. (Leicester, Everton, Barcelona, Tottenham, 1985-92) 80
Little, B. (Aston Villa, 1975) 1
Lloyd, L. (Liverpool, Nott'm F., 1971-80) 4
Lofthouse, N. (Bolton, 1951-9) 33
Lowe, E. (Aston Villa, 1947) 3

Mabbutt, G. (Tottenham, 1983-92) 16
Macdonald, M. (Newcastle, 1972-6) 14
Madeley, P. (Leeds, 1971-7) 24
Mannion, W. (Middlesbrough, 1947-52) 26
Mariner, P. (Ipswich, Arsenal, 1977-85) 35
Marsh, R. (Q.P.R., Man. City, 1972-3) 9
Martin, A. (West Ham, 1981-7) 17
Martyn, N. (Crystal P., 1992-3) 3
Marwood, B. (Arsenal, 1989) 1
Matthews, R. (Coventry, 1956-7) 5
*Matthews, S. (Stoke, Blackpool, 1947-57) 37
McDermott, T. (Liverpool, 1978-82) 25
McDonald, C. (Burnley, 1958-9) 8
McFarland, R. (Derby, 1971-7) 28
McGarry, W. (Huddersfield, 1954-6) 4
McGuinness, W. (Man. Utd., 1959) . 2
McMahon, S. (Liverpool, 1988-91) 17
McManaman, S. (Liverpool, 1995-6) 15
McNab, R. (Arsenal, 1969) 4
McNeil, M. (Middlesbrough, 1961-2) 9
Meadows, J. (Man. City, 1955) 1
Medley, L. (Tottenham, 1951-2) 6
Melia, J. (Liverpool, 1963) 2
Merrick, G. (Birmingham, 1952-4) . 23
Merson, P. (Arsenal, 1992-4) 14

Metcalfe, V. (Huddersfield, 1951) 2
Milburn, J. (Newcastle, 1949-56) ... 13
Miller, B. (Burnley, 1961) 1
Mills, M. (Ipswich, 1973-82) 42
Milne, G. (Liverpool, 1963-5) 14
Milton, C. (Arsenal, 1952) 1
Moore, R. (West Ham, 1962-74) . 108
Morley, A. (Aston Villa, 1982-3) 6
Morris, J. (Derby, 1949-50) 3
Mortensen, S. (Blackpool, 1947-54) 25
Mozley, B. (Derby, 1950) 3
Mullen, J. (Wolves, 1947-54) 12
Mullery, A. (Tottenham, 1965-72) .. 35

Neal, P. (Liverpool, 1976-84) 50
Neville, G. (Man. Utd., 1995-6) 14
Neville, P. (Man. Utd., 1996) 1
Newton, K. (Blackburn, Everton, 1966-70) 27
Nicholls, J. (W.B.A., 1954) 2
Nicholson, W. (Tottenham, 1951) 1
Nish, D. (Derby, 1973-4) 5
Norman, M. (Tottenham, 1962-5) .. 23

O'Grady, M. (Huddersfield, Leeds, 1963-9) 2
Osgood, P. (Chelsea, 1970-4) 4
Osman, R. (Ipswich, 1980-4) 11
Owen, S. (Luton, 1954) 3
Paine, T. (Southampton, 1963-6) .. 19
Pallister, G. (Middlesbrough, Man. Utd., 1988-96) 20
Palmer, C. (Sheff. Wed., 1992-4) .. 18
Parker, P. (Q.P.R., Man. Utd., 1989-94) 19
Parkes, P. (Q.P.R., 1974) 1
Parry, R. (Bolton, 1960) 2
Peacock, A. (Middlesbrough, Leeds, 1962-6) 6
Pearce, S. (Nott'm F., 1987-96) 70
Pearson, Stan (Man. Utd., 1948-52) 8
Pearson, Stuart (Man. Utd., 1976-8) 15
Pegg, D. (Man. Utd., 1957) 1
Pejic, M. (Stoke, 1974) 4
Perry, W. (Blackpool, 1956) 3
Perryman, S. (Tottenham, 1982) 1
Peters, M. (West Ham, Tottenham, 1966-74) 67

Phelan, M. (Man. Utd., 1990) 1
Phillips, L. (Portsmouth, 1952-5) 3
Pickering, F. (Everton, 1964-5) 3
Pickering, N. (Sunderland, 1983) 1
Pilkington, B. (Burnley, 1955) 1
Platt, D. (Aston Villa, Bari, Juventus, Sampdoria, Arsenal, 1990-96) ... 62
Pointer, R. (Burnley, 1962) 3
Pye, J. (Wolves, 1950) 1

Quixall, A. (Sheff. Wed., 1954-5) 5

Radford, J. (Arsenal, 1969-72) 2
Ramsey, A. (Southampton, Tottenham, 1949-54) 32
Reaney, P. (Leeds, 1969-71) 3
Redknapp, J. (Liverpool, 1996) 5
Reeves, K. (Norwich, Man. City, 1980) 2
Regis, C. (W.B.A., Coventry, 1982-8) 5
Reid, P. (Everton, 1985-8) 13
Revie, D. (Man. City, 1955-7) 6
Richards, J. (Wolves, 1973) 1
Richardson, K. (Aston Villa, 1994) .. 1
Rickaby, S. (W.B.A., 1954) 1
Rimmer, J. (Arsenal, 1976) 1
Ripley, S. (Blackburn, 1994) 1
Rix, G. (Arsenal, 1981-4) 17
Robb, G. (Tottenham, 1954) 1
Roberts, G. (Tottenham, 1983-4) 6
Robson, B. (W.B.A., Man. Utd., 1980-92) 90
Robson, R. (W.B.A., 1958-62) 20
Rocastle, D. (Arsenal, 1989-92) 14
Rowley, J. (Man. Utd., 1949-52) 6
Royle, J. (Everton, Man. City, 1971-7) 6
Ruddock, N. (Liverpool, 1995) 1

Sadler, D. (Man. Utd., 1968-71) 4
Salako, J. (Crystal P., 1991-2) 5
Sansom, K. (Crystal P., Arsenal, 1979-88) 86
Scales, J. (Liverpool, 1995) 3
Scott, L. (Arsenal, 1947-9) 17
Seaman, D. (Q.P.R., Arsenal, 1989-96) 29
Sewell, J. (Sheff. Wed., 1952-4) 6
Shackleton, L. (Sunderland, 1949-55) 5
Sharpe, L. (Man. Utd., 1991-4) 8
Shaw, G. (Sheff. Utd., 1959-63) 5
Shearer, A. (Southampton, Blackburn, 1992-6) 28
Shellito, K. (Chelsea, 1963) 1
Sheringham, E. (Tottenham, 1993-6) 20
Shilton, P (Leicester, Stoke, Nott'm. F., Southampton, Derby, 1971-90) 125
Shimwell, E. (Blackpool, 1949) 1
Sillett, P. (Chelsea, 1955) 3
Sinton, A. (Q.P.R., Sheff. Wed, 1992-4) 12
Slater, W. (Wolves, 1955-60) 12
Smith, A. (Arsenal, 1989-92) 13
Smith, L. (Arsenal, 1951-3) 6
Smith, R. (Tottenham, 1961-4) 15
Smith, T. (Birmingham, 1960) 2
Smith, T. (Liverpool, 1971) 1
Southgate, G. (Aston Villa, 1996) 9
Spink, N. (Aston Villa, 1983) 1
Springett, R. (Sheff. Wed., 1960-66) 33
Staniforth, R. (Huddersfield, 1954-5) 8
Statham, D. (W.B.A., 1983) 3
Stein, B. (Luton, 1984) 1
Stepney, A. (Man. Utd., 1968) 1
Sterland, M. (Sheff. Wed., 1989) 1
Steven, T. (Everton, Rangers, Marseille, 1985-92) 36
Stevens, G. (Everton, Rangers, 1985-92) 46
Stevens, G. (Tottenham, 1985-6) 7
Stewart, P. (Tottenham, 1992) 3
Stiles, N. (Man. Utd., 1965-70) 28
Stone, S. (Nott'm. F., 1996) 8
Storey, P. (Arsenal, 1971-3) 19
Storey-Moore, I. (Nott'm F., 1970) ... 1
Streten, B. (Luton, 1950) 1
Summerbee, M. (Man. City, 1968-73) 8
Sunderland, A. (Arsenal, 1980) 1
Swan, P. (Sheff. Wed., 1960-2) 19
Swift, W. (Man. City, 1947-9) 19

Talbot, B. (Ipswich, Arsenal, 1977-80) 6
Tambling, R. (Chelsea, 1963-6) 3
Taylor, E. (Blackpool, 1954) 1

Taylor, J. (Fulham, 1951) 2
Taylor, P. (Liverpool, 1948) 3
Taylor, P. (Crystal P., 1976) 4
Taylor, T. (Man. Utd., 1953-8) 19
Temple, D. (Everton, 1965) 1
Thomas, D. (Coventry, 1983) 2
Thomas, G. (Crystal P., 1991-2) 9
Thomas, D. (Q.P.R., 1975-6) 8
Thomas, M. (Arsenal, 1989-90) 2
Thompson, Peter (Liverpool, 1964-70) 16
Thompson, Phil (Liverpool, 1976-83) 42
Thompson, T. (Aston Villa, Preston, 1952-7) 2
Thomson, R. (Wolves, 1964-5) 8
Todd, C. (Derby, 1972-7) 27
Towers, A. (Sunderland, 1978) 3
Tueart, D. (Man. City, 1975-7) 6

Ufton, D. (Charlton, 1954) 1
Unsworth, D. (Everton, 1995) 1

Venables, T. (Chelsea, 1965) 2
Venison, B. (Newcastle, 1995) 2
Viljoen, C. (Ipswich, 1975) 2
Viollet, D. (Man. Utd., 1960) 2

Waddle, C. (Newcastle, Tottenham, Marseille, 1985-92) 62
Waiters, A. (Blackpool, 1964-5) 5
Walker, D. (Nott'm F., Sampdoria, 1989-94) 59
Walker, I. (Tottenham, 1996) 2
Wallace, D. (Southampton, 1986) ... 1
Walsh, P. (Luton, 1983-4) 5
Walters, M. (Rangers, 1991) 1
Ward, P. (Brighton, 1980) 1
Ward, T. (Derby, 1948) 2
Watson, D. (Sunderland, Man. City, Werder Bremen, Southampton, Stoke, 1974-82) 65
Watson, D. (Norwich, Everton, 1984-8) 12
Watson, W. (Sunderland, 1950-1) ... 4
Webb, N. (Nott'm F., Man. Utd., 1988-92) 26
Weller, K. (Leicester, 1974) 4
West, G. (Everton, 1969) 3
Wheeler, J. (Bolton, 1955) 1
White, D. (Man. City, 1993) 1
Whitworth, S. (Leicester, 1975-6) 7
Whymark, T. (Ipswich, 1978) 1
Wignall, F. (Nott'm F., 1965) 2
Wilcox, J. (Blackburn, 1996) 1
Wilkins, R. (Chelsea, Man. Utd., AC Milan, 1976-87) 84
Williams, B. (Wolves, 1949-56) 24
Williams, S. (Southampton, Arsenal, 1983-5) 6
Willis, A. (Tottenham, 1952) 1
Wilshaw, D. (Wolves, 1954-7) 12
Wilson, R. (Huddersfield, Everton, 1960-8) 63
Winterburn, N. (Arsenal, 1990-3) 2
Wise, D. (Chelsea, 1991-6) 12
Withe, P. (Aston Villa, 1981-5) 11
Wood, R. (Man. Utd., 1955-6) 3
Woodcock, A. (Nott'm F., Cologne, Arsenal, 1977-86) 42
Woods, C. (Norwich, Rangers, Sheff. Wed., 1984-93) 43
Worthington, F. (Leicester, 1974-5) . 8
Wright, I. (Crystal P., Arsenal, 1991-5) 20
Wright, M. (Southampton, Derby, Liverpool, 1984-96) 45
Wright, T. (Everton, 1968-70) 11
Wright, W. (Wolves, 1947-59) 105

Young, G. (Sheff. Wed., 1965) 1

NORTHERN IRELAND

Aherne, T. (Belfast Celtic, Luton, 1947-50) 4
Anderson, T. (Man. Utd., Swindon, Peterborough, 1973-9) 22
Armstrong, G. (Tottenham, Watford, Real Mallorca, W.B.A., 1977-86) 63

Barr, H. (Linfield, Coventry, 1962-3) 3
Best, G. (Man. Utd., Fulham, 1964-77) 37
Bingham, W. (Sunderland, Luton, Everton, Port Vale, 1951-64) 56
Black, K. (Luton, Nott'm Forest, 1988-94) 30

Blair, R. (Oldham, 1975-6) 5
Blanchflower, R.D. (Barnsley, Aston Villa, Tottenham, 1950-63) 56
Blanchflower, J. (Man. Utd., 1954-8) 12
Bowler, G. (Hull, 1950) 3
Braithwaite, R. (Linfield, Middlesbrough, 1962-5) 10
Brennan, R. (Luton, Birmingham, Fulham, 1949-51) 5
Briggs, W. (Man. Utd., Swansea, 1962-5) 2
Brotherston, N. (Blackburn, 1980-5) 27
Bruce, W. (Glentoran, 1961-7) 2

Campbell, D. (Nott'm F., Charlton, 1987-8) 10
Campbell, J. (Fulham, 1951) 2
Campbell, R. (Crusaders, 1963-5) 2
Campbell, R. (Bradford City, 1982) 2
Campbell, W. (Dundee, 1968-70) 6
Carey, J. (Man. Utd., 1947-9) 7
Casey, T. (Newcastle, Portsmouth, 1955-9) 12
Caskey, W. (Derby, Tulsa Roughnecks, 1979-82) 7
Cassidy, T. (Newcastle, Burnley, 1971-82) 24
Caughey, M. (Linfield, 1986) 2
Clarke, C. (Bournemouth, Southampton, Q.P.R., Portsmouth, 1986-93) 38
Cleary, J. (Glentoran, 1982-5) 5
Clements, D. (Coventry, Sheff. Wed., Everton, New York Cosmos, 1965-76) 48
Cochrane, A. (Coleraine, Burnley, Middlesbrough, Gillingham, 1976-84) 26
Cochrane, D. (Leeds, 1947-50) 10
Connell, T. (Coleraine, 1978) 1
Cowan, J. (Newcastle, 1970) 1
Coyle, F. (Coleraine, Nott'm F., 1956-8) 4
Coyle, L. (Derry C., 1989) 1
Coyle, R. (Sheff. Wed., 1973-4) 5
Craig, D. (Newcastle, 1967-75) 25
Crossan, E. (Blackburn, 1950-5) 3
Crossan, J. (Sparta Rotterdam, Sunderland, Man. City, Middlesbrough, 1960-68) 24
Cunningham, W. (St. Mirren, Leicester, Dunfermline, 1951-62) 30
Cush, W. (Glenavon, Leeds, Portadown, 1951-62) 26

D'Arcy, S. (Chelsea, Brentford, 1952-3) 5
Davison, A. (Bolton, 1996) 1
Dennison, R. (Wolves, 1988-94) 17
Devine, J. (Glentoran, 1990) 1
Dickson, D. (Coleraine, 1970-3) 4
Dickson, T. (Linfield, 1957) 1
Dickson, W. (Chelsea, Arsenal, 1951-5) 12
Doherty, L. (Linfield, 1985-8) 2
Doherty, P. (Derby, Huddersfield, Doncaster, 1946-50) 6
Donaghy, M. (Luton, Man. Utd., Chelsea, 1980-94) 91
Dougan, D. (Portsmouth, Blackburn, Aston Villa, Leicester, Wolves, 1958-73) 43
Douglas, J. (Belfast Celtic, 1947) 1
Dowd, H. (Glenavon, 1974) 3
Dowie, I. (Luton, West Ham, Southampton, Crystal P., 1990-6) 36
Dunlop, G. (Linfield, 1985-90) 4

Eglington, T. (Everton, 1947-9) 6
Elder, A. (Burnley, Stoke, 1960-70) 40

Farrell, P. (Everton, 1947-9) 7
Feeney, J. (Linfield, Swansea, 1947-50) 2
Feeney, W. (Glentoran, 1976) 1
Ferguson, W. (Linfield, 1966-7) 2
Ferris, R. (Birmingham, 1950-2) 3
Fettis, A. (Hull, Nott'm. F., 1992-6) 15
Finney, T. (Sunderland, Cambridge, 1975-80) 14
Fleming, G. (Nott'm F., Man. City, Barnsley, 1987-95) 31
Forde, J. (Ards, 1959-61) 4

Gallogly, C. (Huddersfield, 1951) 2
Gaston, R. (Coleraine, 1969) 1
Gillespie, K. (Man. Utd., 1995-6) ... 12
Gorman, W. (Brentford, 1947-8) 4
Graham, W. (Doncaster, 1951-9) .. 14
Gray, P. (Luton, Sunderland, 1993-6) 17
Gregg, H. (Doncaster, Man. Utd., 1954-64) 25
Griffin, D. (St. Johnstone, 1996) 1

Hamilton, B. (Linfield, Ipswich, Everton, Millwall, Swindon, 1969-80) 50
Hamilton, W. (Q.P.R., Burnley, Oxford, 1978-86) 41
Harkin, J. (Southport, Shrewsbury, 1968-70) 5
Harvey, M. (Sunderland, 1961-71) 34
Hatton, S. (Linfield, 1963) 2
Healy, F. (Coleraine, Glentoran, 1982-3) 4
Hegan, D. (W.B.A., Wolves, 1970-3) 7
Hill, C. (Sheff. Utd., Leicester, 1990-6) 14
Hill, J. (Norwich, Everton, 1959-64) .. 7
Hinton, E. (Fulham, Millwall, 1947-51) 7
Horlock, K. (Swindon, 1995) 2
Hughes, M. (Man. City, Strasbourg, 1992-6) 31
Hughes, P. (Bury, 1987) 3
Hughes, W. (Bolton, 1951) 1
Humphries, W. (Ards, Coventry, Swansea, 1962-5) 14
Hunter, A. (Blackburn, Ipswich, 1970-80) 53
Hunter, B. (Wrexham, 1995-6) 6
Hunter, V. (Coleraine, 1962) 2

Irvine, R. (Linfield, Stoke, 1962-5) .. 8
Irvine, W. (Burnley, Preston, Brighton, 1963-72) 23

Jackson, T. (Everton, Nott'm F., Man. Utd., 1969-77) 35
Jamison, J. (Glentoran, 1976) 1
Jennings, P. (Watford, Tottenham, Arsenal, Tottenham, 1964-86) .. 119
Johnston, W. (Glenavon, Oldham, 1962-6) 2
Jones, J. (Glenavon, 1956-7) 3

Keane, T. (Swansea, 1949) 1
Kee, P. (Oxford, Ards, 1990-5) 9
Keith, R. (Newcastle, 1958-62) 23
Kelly, H. (Fulham, Southampton, 1950-1) 4
Kelly, P. (Barnsley, 1950) 1

Lawther, W. (Sunderland, Blackburn, 1960-2) 4
Lennon, N. (Crewe, Leicester, 1994-6) 6
Lockhart, N. (Linfield, Coventry, Aston Villa, 1947-56) 8
Lomas, S. (Man. City, 1994-6) 12
Lutton, B. (Wolves, West Ham, 1970-4) 6

Magill, E. (Arsenal, Brighton, 1962-6) 26
Magilton, J. (Oxford, Southampton, 1991-6) 32
Martin, C. (Glentoran, Leeds, Aston Villa, 1947-50) 6
McAdams, W. (Man. City, Bolton, Leeds, 1954-62) 15
*McAlinden, J. (Portsmouth, Southend, 1947-9) 2
McBride, S. (Glenavon, 1991-2) 4
McCabe, J. (Leeds, 1949-54) 6
McCarthy, J. (Port Vale, 1996) 1
McCavana, T. (Coleraine, 1954-5) .. 3
McCleary, J. (Cliftonville, 1955) 1
McClelland, J. (Arsenal, Fulham, 1961-7) 6
McClelland, J. (Mansfield, Rangers, Watford, Leeds, 1980-90) 53
McCourt, F. (Man. City, 1952-3) 6
McCoy, R. (Coleraine, 1987) 1
McCreery, D. (Man. Utd., Q.P.R., Tulsa Roughnecks, Newcastle, 1976-90) 67
McCrory, S. (Southend, 1958) 1
McCullough, W. (Arsenal, Millwall, 1961-7) 10
McCurdy, C. (Linfield, 1980) 1
McDonald, A. (Q.P.R., 1986-96) 52
McElhinney, G. (Bolton, 1984-5) 6

McFaul, W. (Linfield, Newcastle, 1967-74) 6
McGarry, J. (Cliftonville, 1951) 3
McGaughey, M. (Linfield, 1985) 1
McGibbon, P. (Man. Utd., 1995-6) ... 4
McGrath, C. (Tottenham, Man. Utd., 1974-9) 21
McIlroy, J. (Burnley, Stoke, 1952-66) 55
McIlroy, S. (Man. Utd., Stoke, Man. City, 1972-87) 88
McKeag, W. (Glentoran, 1968) 2
McKenna, J. (Huddersfield, 1950-2) 7
McKenzie, R. (Airdrie, 1967) 1
McKinney, W. (Falkirk, 1966) 1
McKnight, A. (Celtic, West Ham, 1988-9) 10
McLaughlin, J. (Shrewsbury, Swansea, 1962-6) 12
McMahon, G. (Tottenham, 1995-6) . 7
McMichael, A. (Newcastle, 1950-60) 40
McMillan, S. (Man. Utd., 1963) 2
McMordie, A. (Middlesbrough, 1969-73) 21
McMorran, E. (Belfast Celtic, Barnsley, Doncaster, 1947-57) ... 15
McNally, B. (Shrewsbury, 1987-8) ... 5
McParland, P. (Aston Villa, Wolves, 1954-62) 34
Montgomery, F. (Coleraine, 1955) ... 1
Moore, C. (Glentoran, 1949) 1
Moreland, V. (Derby, 1979-80) 6
Morgan, S. (Port Vale, Aston Villa, Brighton, Sparta Rotterdam, 1972-9) 18
Morrow, S. (Arsenal, 1990-6) 19
Mullan, G. (Glentoran, 1983) 4

Napier, R. (Bolton, 1966) 1
Neill, T. (Arsenal, Hull, 1961-73) ... 59
Nelson, S. (Arsenal, Brighton, 1970-82) 51
Nicholl, C. (Aston Villa, Southampton, Grimsby, 1975-83) 51
Nicholl, J. (Man. Utd., Toronto Blizzard, Sunderland, Rangers, W.B.A., 1976-86) 73
Nicholson, J. (Man. Utd., Huddersfield, 1961-72) 41

O'Boyle, G. (Dunfermline, St. Johnstone, 1994-6) 8
O'Doherty, A. (Coleraine, 1970) 2
O'Driscoll, J. (Swansea, 1949) 3
O'Kane, W. (Nott'm F., 1970-5) 20
O'Neill, C. (Motherwell, 1989-91) 3
O'Neill, J. (Sunderland, 1962) 1
O'Neill, J. (Leicester, 1980-6) 39
O'Neill, M. (Distillery, Nott'm F., Norwich, Man. City, Notts Co., 1972-85) 64
O'Neill, M. (Newcastle, Dundee Utd., Hibernian, 1989-96) 29

Parke, J. (Linfield, Hibernian, Sunderland, 1964-8) 14
Patterson, D. (Crystal P., Luton, 1994-6) 10
Peacock, R. (Glasgow Celtic, Coleraine, 1952-62) 31
Penney, S. (Brighton, 1985-9) 17
Platt, J. (Middlesbrough, Ballymena, Coleraine, 1976-86) 23

Quinn, J. (Blackburn, Swindon, Leicester, Bradford City, West Ham, Bournemouth, Reading, 1985-96) 46
Quinn, J. (Blackpool, 1996) 1

Rafferty, W. (Wolves, 1980) 1
Ramsey, P. (Leicester, 1984-9) 14
Rice, P. (Arsenal, 1969-80) 49
Rogan, A. (Celtic, Sunderland, 1988-92) 16
Ross, W. (Newcastle, 1969) 1
Rowland, K. (West Ham, 1994-6) 8
Russell, A. (Linfield, 1947) 1
Ryan, R. (W.B.A., 1950) 1

Sanchez, L. (Wimbledon, 1987-9) ... 3
Scott, J. (Grimsby, 1958) 2
Scott, P. (Everton, York, Aldershot, 1976-9) 10
Sharkey, P. (Ipswich, 1976) 1
Shields, J. (Southampton, 1957) 1
Simpson, W. (Rangers, 1951-9) 12
Sloan, D. (Oxford, 1969-71) 2
Sloan, J. (Arsenal, 1947) 1
Sloan, T. (Man. Utd., 1979) 3

Smyth, S. (Wolves, Stoke, 1948-52) 9
Smyth, W. (Distillery, 1949-54) 4
Spence, D. (Bury, Blackpool, Southend, 1975-82) 27
*Stevenson, A. (Everton, 1947-8) 3
Stewart, A. (Glentoran, Derby, 1967-9) 7
Stewart, D. (Hull, 1978) 1
Stewart, I. (Q.P.R., Newcastle, 1982-7) 31
Stewart, T. (Linfield, 1961) 1

Taggart, G. (Barnsley, 1990-5) 35
Todd, S. (Burnley, Sheff. Wed., 1966-71) 11
Trainor, D. (Crusaders, 1967) 1
Tully, C. (Glasgow Celtic, 1949-59) 10

Uprichard, W. (Swindon, Portsmouth, 1952-59) 18

Vernon, J. (Belfast Celtic, W.B.A., 1947-52) 17

Walker, J. (Doncaster, 1955) 1
Walsh, D. (W.B.A., 1947-50) 9
Walsh, W. (Man. City, 1948-9) 5
Watson, P. (Distillery, 1971) 1
Welsh, E. (Carlisle, 1966-7) 4
Whiteside, N. (Man. Utd., Everton, 1982-90) 38
Williams, P. (W.B.A., 1991) 1
Wilson, D. (Brighton, Luton, Sheff. Wed., 1987-92) 24
Wilson, K. (Ipswich, Chelsea, Notts Co., Walsall, 1987-95) 42
Wilson, S. (Glenavon, Falkirk, Dundee, 1962-8) 12
Wood, T. (Walsall, 1996) 1
Worthington, N. (Sheff. Wed., Leeds, 1984-96) 64
Wright, T. (Newcastle, Nott'm F., 1989-94) 22

SCOTLAND

Aird, J. (Burnley, 1954) 4
Aitken, G. (East Fife, 1949-54) 8
Aitken, R. (Celtic, Newcastle, St. Mirren, 1980-92) 57
Albiston, A. (Man. Utd., 1982-6) 14
Allan, T. (Dundee, 1974) 2
Anderson, J. (Leicester, 1954) 1
Archibald, S. (Aberdeen, Tottenham, Barcelona, 1980-6) 27
Auld, B. (Celtic, 1959-60) 3

Baird, H. (Airdrie, 1956) 1
Baird, S. (Rangers, 1957-8) 7
Bannon, E. (Dundee Utd., 1980-6) 11
Bauld, W. (Hearts, 1950) 3
Baxter, J. (Rangers, Sunderland, 1961-8) 34
Bell, W. (Leeds, 1966) 2
Bernard, P. (Oldham, 1995) 2
Bett, J. (Rangers, Lokeren, Aberdeen, 1982-90) 26
Black, E. (Metz, 1988) 2
Black, I. (Southampton, 1948) 1
Blacklaw, A. (Burnley, 1963-6) 3
Blackley, J. (Hibernian, 1974-7) 7
Blair, J. (Blackpool, 1947) 1
Blyth, J. (Coventry, 1978) 2
Bone, J. (Norwich, 1972-3) 2
Booth, S. (Aberdeen, 1993-6) 13
Bowman, D. (Dundee Utd., 1992-4) 6
Boyd, T. (Motherwell, Chelsea, Celtic, 1991-6) 38
Brand, R. (Rangers, 1961-2) 8
Brazil, A. (Ipswich, Tottenham, 1980-3) 13
Bremner, D. (Hibernian, 1976) 1
Bremner, W. (Leeds, 1965-76) 54
Brennan, F. (Newcastle, 1947-54) ... 7
Brogan, J. (Celtic, 1971) 4
Brown, A. (East Fife, Blackpool, 1950-4) 14
Brown, H. (Partick, 1947) 3
Brown, J. (Sheff. Utd., 1975) 1
Brown, R. (Rangers, 1947-52) 3
Brown, W. (Dundee, Tottenham, 1958-66) 28

Brownlie, J. (Hibernian, 1971-6) 7
Buchan, M. (Aberdeen, Man. Utd., 1972-8) 34
Buckley, P. (Aberdeen, 1954-5) 3
Burley, C. (Chelsea, 1995-6) 12
Burley, G. (Ipswich, 1979-82) 11
Burns, F. (Man. Utd.. 1970) 1
Burns, K. (Birmingham, Nott'm F., 1974-81) 20
Burns, T. (Celtic, 1981-8) 8

Calderwood, C. (Tottenham, 1995-6) 14
Caldow, E. (Rangers, 1957-63) 40
Callaghan, T. (Dunfermline, 1970) ... 2
Campbell, R. (Falkirk, Chelsea, 1947-50) 5
Campbell, W. (Morton, 1947-8) 5
Carr, W. (Coventry, 1970-3) 6
Chalmers, S. (Celtic, 1965-7) 5
Clark, J. (Celtic, 1966-7) 4
Clark, R. (Aberdeen, 1968-73) 17
Clarke, S. (Chelsea, 1988-94) 6
Collins, J. (Hibernian, Celtic, 1988-96) 36
Collins, R. (Celtic, Everton, Leeds, 1951-65) 31
Colquhoun, E. (Sheff. Utd, 1972-3) . 9
Colquhoun, J. (Hearts, 1988) 1
Combe, J. (Hibernian, 1948) 3
Conn, A. (Hearts, 1956) 1
Conn, A. (Tottenham, 1975) 2
Connachan, E. (Dunfermline, 1962) 2
Connelly, G. (Celtic, 1974) 2
Connolly, J. (Everton, 1973) 1
Connor, R. (Dundee, Aberdeen, 1986-91) 4
Cooke, C. (Dundee, Chelsea, 1966-75) 16
Cooper, D. (Rangers, Motherwell, 1980-90) 22
Cormack, P. (Hibernian, 1966-72) ... 9
Cowan, J. (Morton, 1948-52) 25
Cowie, D. (Dundee, 1953-8) 20
Cox, C. (Hearts, 1948) 1
Cox, S. (Rangers, 1948-54) 25
Craig, J.P. (Celtic, 1968) 1
Craig, J. (Celtic, 1977) 1
Craig, T. (Newcastle, 1976) 1
Crawford, S. (Raith, 1995) 1
Crerand, P. (Celtic, Man. Utd., 1961-6) 16
Cropley, A. (Hibernian, 1972) 2
Cruickshank, J. (Hearts, 1964-76) .. 6
Cullen, M. (Luton, 1956) 1
Cumming, J. (Hearts, 1955-60) 9
Cunningham, W. (Preston, 1954-5) . 8
Curran, H. (Wolves, 1970-1) 5

Dalglish, K. (Celtic, Liverpool, 1972-87) 102
Davidson, J. (Partick, 1954-5) 8
Dawson, A. (Rangers, 1980-3) 5
Deans, D. (Celtic, 1975) 2
*Delaney, J. (Man. Utd., 1947-8) 4
Dick, J. (West Ham, 1959) 1
Dickson, W. (Kilmarnock, 1970-1) ... 5
Docherty, T. (Preston, Arsenal, 1952-9) 25
Dodds, D. (Dundee Utd., 1984) 2
Donachie, W. (Man. City, 1972-9) . 35
Dougall, C. (Birmingham, 1947) 1
Dougan, R. (Hearts, 1950) 1
Doyle, J. (Ayr, 1976) 1
Duncan, A. (Hibernian, 1975-6) 6
Duncan, D. (East Fife, 1948) 3
Duncanson, J. (Rangers, 1947) 1
Durie, G. (Chelsea, Tottenham, Rangers, 1988-96) 31
Durrant, I. (Rangers, 1988-94) 11

Evans, A. (Aston Villa, 1982) 4
Evans, R. (Celtic, Chelsea, 1949-60) 48
Ewing, T. (Partick, 1958) 2

Farm, G. (Blackpool, 1953-9) 10
Ferguson, D. (Dundee Utd., Everton, 1992-5) 5
Ferguson, D. (Rangers, 1988) 2
Ferguson, I. (Rangers, 1989-94) 8
Ferguson, R. (Kilmarnock, 1966-7) 7
Fernie, W. (Celtic, 1954-8) 12
Flavell, R. (Airdrie, 1947) 2
Fleck, R. (Norwich, 1990-1) 4
Fleming, C. (East Fife, 1954) 1
Forbes, A. (Sheff. Utd., Arsenal, 1947-52) 14
Ford, D. (Hearts, 1974) 3
Forrest, J. (Motherwell, 1958) 1

Forrest, J. (Rangers, Aberdeen, 1966-71) ... 5
Forsyth, A. (Partick, Man. Utd., 1972-6) ... 10
Forsyth, C. (Kilmarnock, 1964) ... 4
Forsyth, T. (Motherwell, Rangers, 1971-8) ... 22
Fraser, D. (W.B.A., 1968-9) ... 2
Fraser, W. (Sunderland, 1955) ... 2

Gabriel, J. (Everton, 1961-4) ... 2
Gallacher, K. (Dundee Utd., Coventry, Blackburn, 1988-96) ... 23
Galloway, M. (Celtic, 1992) ... 1
Gardiner, I. (Motherwell, 1958) ... 1
Gemmell, T. (St. Mirren, 1955) ... 2
Gemmell, T. (Celtic, 1966-71) ... 18
Gemmill, A. (Derby, Nott'm F., Birmingham, 1971-81) ... 43
Gemmill, S. (Nott'm F., 1995-6) ... 6
Gibson, D. (Leicester, 1963-5) ... 7
Gillespie, G. (Liverpool, 1988-91) ... 13
Gilzean, A. (Dundee, Tottenham, 1964-71) ... 22
Glavin, R. (Celtic, 1977) ... 1
Glen, A. (Aberdeen, 1956) ... 2
Goram, A. (Oldham, Hibernian, Rangers, 1986-96) ... 39
Gough, R. (Dundee Utd., Tottenham, Rangers, 1983-93) ... 61
Govan, J. (Hibernian, 1948-9) ... 6
Graham, A. (Leeds, 1978-81) ... 10
Graham, G. (Arsenal, Man. Utd., 1972-3) ... 12
Gray, A. (Aston Villa, Wolves, Everton, 1976-85) ... 20
Gray, E. (Leeds, 1969-77) ... 12
Gray, F. (Leeds, Nott'm F., 1976-83) ... 32
Grant, J. (Hibernian, 1958) ... 2
Grant, P. (Celtic, 1989) ... 2
Green, A. (Blackpool, Newcastle, 1971-2) ... 6
Greig, J. (Rangers, 1964-76) ... 44
Gunn, B. (Norwich, 1990-4) ... 6

Haddock, H. (Clyde, 1955-8) ... 6
Haffey, F. (Celtic, 1960-1) ... 2
Hamilton, A. (Dundee, 1962-6) ... 24
Hamilton, G. (Aberdeen, 1947-54) ... 5
Hamilton, W. (Hibernian, 1965) ... 1
Hansen, A. (Liverpool, 1979-87) ... 26
Hansen, J. (Partick, 1972) ... 2
Harper, J. (Aberdeen, Hibernian, 1973-8) ... 4
Hartford, A. (W.B.A., Man. City, Everton, 1972-82) ... 50
Harvey, D. (Leeds, 1973-7) ... 16
Haughney, M. (Celtic, 1954) ... 1
Hay, D. (Celtic, 1970-4) ... 27
Hegarty, P. (Dundee Utd., 1979-83) ... 8
Henderson, J. (Portsmouth, Arsenal, 1953-9) ... 7
Henderson, W. (Rangers, 1963-71) ... 29
Hendry, C. (Blackburn, 1994-6) ... 21
Herd, D. (Arsenal, 1959-61) ... 5
Herd, G. (Clyde, 1958-61) ... 5
Herriot, J. (Birmingham, 1969-70) ... 8
Hewie, J. (Charlton, 1956-60) ... 19
Holt, D. (Hearts, 1963-4) ... 5
Holton, J. (Man. Utd., 1973-5) ... 15
Hope, R. (W.B.A., 1968-9) ... 2
Houliston, W. (Queen of the South, 1949) ... 3
Houston, S. (Man. Utd., 1976) ... 1
Howie, H. (Hibernian, 1949) ... 1
Hughes, J. (Celtic, 1965-70) ... 8
Hughes, W. (Sunderland, 1975) ... 1
Humphries, W. (Motherwell, 1952) ... 1
Hunter, A. (Kilmarnock, Celtic, 1972-4) ... 4
Hunter, W. (Motherwell, 1960-1) ... 3
Husband, J. (Partick, 1947) ... 1
Hutchison, T. (Coventry, 1974-6) ... 17

Imlach, S. (Nott'm F., 1958) ... 4
Irvine, B. (Aberdeen, 1991-4) ... 9

Jackson, C. (Rangers, 1975-6) ... 8
Jackson, D. (Hibernian, 1995-6) ... 11
Jardine, A. (Rangers, 1971-80) ... 38
Jarvie, A. (Airdrie, 1971) ... 3
Jess, E. (Aberdeen, Coventry, 1993-6) ... 13
Johnston, M. (Watford, Celtic, Nantes, Rangers, 1984-92) ... 38
Johnston, W. (Rangers, WBA, 1966-78) ... 22

Johnstone, D. (Rangers, 1973-80) 14
Johnstone, J. (Celtic, 1965-75) 23
Johnstone, L. (Clyde, 1948) 2
Johnstone, R. (Hibernian, Man. City, 1951-6) 17
Jordan, J. (Leeds, Man. Utd., AC Milan, 1973-82) 52

Kelly, H. (Blackpool, 1952) 1
Kelly, J. (Barnsley, 1949) 2
Kennedy, J. (Celtic, 1964-5) 6
Kennedy, S. (Rangers, 1975) 5
Kennedy, S. (Aberdeen, 1978-82) ... 8
Kerr, A. (Partick, 1955) 2

Lambert P. (Motherwell, 1995) 2
Law, D. (Huddersfield, Man. City, Torino, Man. Utd., 1959-74) 55
Lawrence T. (Liverpool, 1963-9) 3
Leggat, G. (Aberdeen, Fulham, 1956-60) 18
Leighton, J. (Aberdeen, Man. Utd., Hibernian, 1983-96) 74
Lennox, R. (Celtic, 1967-70) 10
Leslie, L. (Airdrie, 1961) 5
Levein, C. (Hearts, 1990-5) 16
Liddell, W. (Liverpool, 1947-55) 28
Linwood, A. (Clyde, 1950) 1
Little, R. (Rangers, 1953) 1
Logie, J. (Arsenal, 1953) 1
Long, H. (Clyde, 1947) 1
Lorimer, P. (Leeds, 1970-6) 21

Macari, L. (Celtic, Man. Utd., 1972-8) 24
Macaulay, A. (Brentford, Arsenal, 1947-8) 7
MacDougall, E. (Norwich, 1975-6) .. 7
Mackay, D. (Hearts, Tottenham, 1957-66) 22
Mackay, G. (Hearts, 1988) 4
MacLeod, M. (Celtic, Borussia Dort., Hibernian, 1985-91) 20
Malpas, M. (Dundee Utd., 1984-93) 55
Marshall, G. (Celtic, 1992) 1
Martin, B. (Motherwell, 1995) 2
Martin, F. (Aberdeen, 1954-5) 6
Martin, N. (Hibernian, Sunderland, 1965-6) 3
Martis, J. (Motherwell, 1961) 1
Mason, J. (Third Lanark, 1949-51) .. 7
Masson, D. (Q.P.R., Derby, 1976-8) 17
Mathers, D. (Partick, 1954) 1
McAllister, G. (Leicester, Leeds, 1990-6) 44
McAvennie, F. (West Ham, Celtic, 1986-8) 5
McBride, J. (Celtic, 1967) 2
McCall, S. (Everton, Rangers, 1990-6) 36
McCalliog, J. (Sheff. Wed., Wolves, 1967-71) 5
McCann, R. (Motherwell, 1959-61) . 5
McClair, B. (Celtic, Man. Utd., 1987-93) 30
McCloy, P. (Rangers, 1973) 4
McCoist, A. (Rangers, 1986-96) 54
McColl, I. (Rangers, 1950-8) 14
McCreadie, E. (Chelsea, 1965-9) .. 23
MacDonald, A. (Rangers, 1976) 1
McDonald, J. (Sunderland, 1956) ... 2
McFarlane, W. (Hearts, 1947) 1
McGarr, E. (Aberdeen, 1970) 2
McGarvey, F. (Liverpool, Celtic, 1979-84) 7
McGhee, M. (Aberdeen, 1983-4) 4
McGinlay, J. (Bolton, 1995-6) 9
McGrain, D. (Celtic, 1973-82) 62
McGrory, J. (Kilmarnock, 1965-6) 3
McInally, A. (Aston Villa, Bayern Munich, 1989-90) 8
McInally, J. (Dundee Utd., 1987-93) 10
McKay, D. (Celtic, 1959-62) 14
McKean, R. (Rangers, 1976) 1
McKenzie, J. (Partick, 1954-6) 9
McKimmie, S. (Aberdeen, 1989-96) 40
McKinlay, T. (Celtic, 1996) 6
McKinlay, W. (Dundee Utd., Blackburn, 1994-6) 18
McKinnon, R. (Rangers, 1966-71) 28
McKinnon, R. (Motherwell, 1994-5) . 3
McLaren, A. (Preston, 1947-8) 4
McLaren, A. (Hearts, Rangers, 1992-6) 24
McLean, G. (Dundee, 1968) 1

McLean, T. (Kilmarnock, Rangers, 1969-71) 6
McLeish, A. (Aberdeen, 1980-93) . 77
McLeod, J. (Hibernian, 1961) 4
McLintock, F. (Leicester, Arsenal, 1963-71) 9
McMillan, I. (Airdrie, 1952-61) 6
McNaught, W. (Raith, 1951-5) 5
McNeill, W. (Celtic. 1961-72) 29
McPhail, J. (Celtic, 1950-4) 5
McPherson, D. (Hearts, Rangers, 1989-93) 27
McQueen, G. (Leeds, Man. Utd., 1974-81) 30
McStay, P. (Celtic, 1984-96) 73
Millar, J. (Rangers, 1963) 2
Miller, W. (Celtic, 1946-7) 6
Miller, W. (Aberdeen, 1975-90) 65
Mitchell, R. (Newcastle, 1951) 2
Mochan, N. (Celtic, 1954) 3
Moir, W. (Bolton, 1950) 1
Moncur, R. (Newcastle, 1968-72) .. 16
Morgan, W. (Burnley, Man. Utd., 1968-74) 21
Morris, H. (East Fife, 1950) 1
Mudie, J. (Blackpool, 1957-8) 17
Mulhall, G. (Aberdeen, Sunderland, 1960-4) 3
Munro, F. (Wolves, 1971-5) 9
Munro, I. (St. Mirren, 1979-80) 7
Murdoch, R. (Celtic, 1966-70) 12
Murray, J. (Hearts, 1958) 5
Murray, S. (Aberdeen, 1972) 1

Narey, D. (Dundee Utd., 1977-89) .. 35
Nevin, P. (Chelsea, Everton, Tranmere, 1987-96) 26
Nicholas, C. (Celtic, Arsenal, Aberdeen, 1983-9) 20
Nicol, S. (Liverpool, 1985-92) 27

O'Donnell, P. (Motherwell, 1994) 1
O'Hare, J. (Derby, 1970-2) 13
O'Neil, B. (Celtic, 1996) 1
Ormond, W. (Hibernian, 1954-9) 6
Orr, T. (Morton, 1952) 2

Parker, A. (Falkirk, Everton, 1955-6) 15
Parlane, D. (Rangers, 1973-7) 12
Paton, A. (Motherwell, 1952) 2
Pearson, T. (Newcastle, 1947) 2
Penman, A. (Dundee, 1966) 1
Pettigrew, W. (Motherwell, 1976-7) . 5
Plenderleith, J. (Man. City, 1961) 1
Provan, D. (Rangers, 1964-6) 5
Provan, D. (Celtic, 1980-2) 10

Quinn, P. (Motherwell, 1961-2) 9

Redpath, W. (Motherwell, 1949-52) 9
Reilly, L. (Hibernian, 1949-57) 38
Ring, T. (Clyde, 1953-8) 12
Rioch, B. (Derby, Everton, 1975-8) 24
Ritchie, W. (Rangers, 1962) 1
Robb, D. (Aberdeen, 1971) 5
Robertson, A. (Clyde, 1955) 5
Robertson, D. (Rangers, 1992-4) 3
Robertson, H. (Dundee, 1962) 1
Robertson, J. (Tottenham, 1964) 1
Robertson, J. (Nott'm F., Derby, 1978-84) 28
Robertson, J. (Hearts, 1991-6) 14
Robinson, R. (Dundee, 1974-5) 4
Rough, A. (Partick, Hibernian, 1976-86) 53
Rougvie, D. (Aberdeen, 1984) 1
Rutherford, E. (Rangers, 1948) 1

Schaedler, E. (Hibernian, 1974) 1
Scott, A. (Rangers, Everton, 1957-66) 16
Scott, J. (Hibernian, 1966) 1
Scott, J. (Dundee, 1971) 2
Scoular, J. (Portsmouth, 1951-3) 9
Sharp, G. (Everton, 1985-8) 12
Shaw, D. (Hibernian, 1947-9) 8
Shaw, J. (Rangers, 1947) 4
Shearer, D. (Aberdeen, 1994-6) 7
Shearer, R. (Rangers, 1961) 4
Simpson, N. (Aberdeen, 1983-8) 4
Simpson, R. (Celtic, 1967-9) 5
Sinclair, J. (Leicester, 1966) 1
Smith, D. (Aberdeen, Rangers, 1966-8) 2
Smith, G. (Hibernian, 1947-57) 18
Smith, H. (Hearts, 1988-92) 3
Smith, J.E. (Celtic, 1959) 2
Smith, J. (Aberdeen, Newcastle, 1968-74) 4

Souness, G. (Middlesbrough, Liverpool, Sampdoria, Rangers, 1975-86) 54
Speedie, D. (Chelsea, Coventry, 1985-9) 10
Spencer, J. (Chelsea, 1995-6) 12
Stanton, P. (Hibernian, 1966-74) ... 16
Steel, W. (Morton, Derby, Dundee, 1947-53) 30
Stein, C. (Rangers, Coventry, 1969-73) 21
Stephen, J. (Bradford, 1947-8) 2
Stewart, D. (Leeds, 1978) 1
Stewart, J. (Kilmarnock, Middlesbrough, 1977-9) 2
Stewart, R. (West Ham, 1981-7) ... 10
St. John, I. (Motherwell, Liverpool, 1959-65) 21
Strachan, G. (Aberdeen, Man. Utd., Leeds, 1980-92) 50
Sturrock, P. (Dundee Utd., 1981-7) 20

Telfer, W. (St. Mirren, 1954) 1
Thomson, W. (St. Mirren, 1980-4) ... 7
Thornton, W. (Rangers, 1947-52) ... 7
Toner, W. (Kilmarnock, 1959) 2
Turnbull, E. (Hibernian, 1948-58) 8

Ure, I. (Dundee, Arsenal, 1962-8) . 11

Waddell, W. (Rangers, 1947-55) ... 17
Walker, A. (Celtic, 1988-95) 3
Walker, N. (Hearts, 1993) 1
Wallace, I. (Coventry, 1978-9) 3
Wallace, W. (Hearts, Celtic, 1965-9) 7
Wardhaugh, J. (Hearts, 1955-7) 2
Wark, J. (Ipswich, Liverpool, 1979-85) 29
Watson, J. (Motherwell, Huddersfield, 1948-54) 2
Watson, R. (Motherwell, 1971) 1
Weir, A. (Motherwell, 1959-60) 6
Weir, P. (St. Mirren, Aberdeen, 1980-4) 6
White, J. (Falkirk, Tottenham, 1959-64) 22
Whyte, D. (Celtic, Middlesbrough, 1988-96) 9
Wilson, A. (Portsmouth, 1954) 1
Wilson, D. (Rangers, 1961-5) 22
Wilson, I. (Leicester, Everton, 1987-8) 5
Wilson, P. (Celtic, 1975) 1
Wilson, R. (Arsenal, 1972) 2
Wood, G. (Everton, Arsenal, 1978-82) 4
Woodburn, W. (Rangers, 1947-52) 24
Wright, K. (Hibernian, 1992) 1
Wright, S. (Aberdeen, 1993) 2
Wright, T. (Sunderland, 1953) 3

Yeats, R. (Liverpool, 1965-6) 2
Yorston, H. (Aberdeen, 1955) 1
Young, A. (Hearts, Everton, 1960-6) 8
Young, G. (Rangers, 1947-57) 53
Younger, T. (Hibernian, Liverpool, 1955-8) 24

WALES

Aizlewood, M. (Charlton, Leeds, Bradford City, Bristol C., Cardiff, 1986-95) 39
Allchurch, I. (Swansea, Newcastle, Cardiff, 1951-66) 68
Allchurch, L. (Swansea, Sheff. Utd., 1955-64) 11
Allen, B. (Coventry, 1951) 2
Allen, M. (Watford, Norwich, Millwall, Newcastle, 1986-94) 14

Baker, C. (Cardiff, 1958-62) 7
Baker, W. (Cardiff, 1948) 1
Barnes, W. (Arsenal, 1948-55) 22
Berry, G. (Wolves, Stoke, 1979-83) 5
Blackmore, C. (Man. Utd., 1985-94) 38
Blake, N. (Sheff. Utd., 1994-6) 6
Bodin, P. (Swindon, Crystal P., Swindon, 1990-5) 23
Bowen, D. (Arsenal, 1955-9) 19
Bowen, J. (Swansea, 1994) 1
Bowen, M. (Tottenham, Norwich, 1986-96) 37
Boyle, T. (Crystal P., 1981) 2

Browning, M. (Bristol R., 1996) 2
Burgess, R. (Tottenham, 1947-54) 32
Burton, A. (Norwich, Newcastle, 1963-72) 9

Cartwright, L. (Coventry, Wrexham, 1974-9) 7
Charles, Jeremy (Swansea, Q.P.R., Oxford, 1981-7) 19
Charles, John (Leeds, Juventus, Cardiff, 1950-65) 38
Charles, M. (Swansea, Arsenal, Cardiff, 1955-63) 31
Clarke, R. (Man. City, 1949-56) 22
Coleman, C. (Crystal P., Blackburn, 1992-6) 14
Cornforth, J. (Swansea, 1995) 2
Coyne, D. (Tranmere, 1996) 1
Crowe, V. (Aston Villa, 1959-63) ... 16
Curtis, A. (Swansea, Leeds, Southampton, Cardiff, 1976-87) 35

Daniel, R. (Arsenal, Sunderland, 1951-7) 21
Davies, A. (Man. Utd., Newcastle, Swansea, Bradford City, 1983-90) 13
Davies, C. (Charlton, 1972) 1
Davies, D. (Everton, Wrexham, Swansea, 1975-83) 52
Davies, E.R. (Newcastle, 1953-8) ... 6
Davies, G. (Fulham, Chelsea, Man. City, 1980-6) 16
Davies, R.T. (Norwich, Southampton, Portsmouth, 1964-74) 29
Davies, R.W. (Bolton, Newcastle, Man. Utd., Man. City, Blackpool, 1964-74) 34
Davies, S. (Man. Utd., 1996) 1
Davis, G. (Wrexham, 1978) 3
Deacy, N. (PSV Eindhoven, Beringen, 1977-9) 12
Derrett, S. (Cardiff, 1969-71) 4
Dibble, A. (Luton, Man. City, 1986-9) 3
Durban, A. (Derby, 1966-72) 27
Dwyer, P. (Cardiff, 1978-80) 10

Edwards, C. (Swansea, 1996) 1
Edwards, G. (Birmingham, Cardiff, 1947-50) 12
Edwards, I. (Chester, Wrexham, 1978-80) 4
Edwards, L. (Charlton, 1957) 2
Emanuel, W. (Bristol City, 1973) 2
England, M. (Blackburn, Tottenham, 1962-75) 44
Evans, B. (Swansea, Hereford, 1972-4) 7
Evans, I. (Crystal P., 1976-8) 13
Evans, R. (Swansea, 1964) 1

Felgate, D. (Lincoln, 1984) 1
Flynn, B. (Burnley, Leeds, 1975-84) 66
Ford, T. (Swansea, 1947-57) 38
Foulkes, W. (Newcastle, 1952-4) ... 11

Giggs, R. (Man. Utd., 1992-6) 16
Giles, D. (Swansea, Crystal P., 1980-3) 12
Godfrey, B. (Preston, 1964-5) 3
Goss, J. (Norwich, 1991-6) 9
Green, C. (Birmingham, 1965-9) ... 15
Griffiths, A. (Wrexham, 1971-7) 17
Griffiths, H. (Swansea, 1953) 1
Griffiths, M. (Leicester, 1947-54) ... 11

Hall, G. (Chelsea, 1988-92) 9
Harrington, A. (Cardiff, 1956-62) ... 11
Harris, C. (Leeds, 1976-82) 23
Harris, W. (Middlesbrough, 1954-8) 6
Hartson, J. (Arsenal, 1995-6) 5
Hennessey, T. (Birmingham, Nott'm F., Derby, 1962-73) 39
Hewitt, R. (Cardiff, 1958) 5
Hill, M. (Ipswich, 1972) 2
Hockey, T. (Sheff. Utd., Norwich, Aston Villa, 1972-4) 9
Hodges, G. (Wimbledon, Newcastle, Watford, Sheff. Utd., 1984-96) ... 18
Holden, A. (Chester, 1984) 1
Hole, B. (Cardiff, Blackburn, Aston Villa, Swansea, 1963-71) 30
Hollins, D. (Newcastle, 1962-6) 11
Hopkins, J. (Fulham, Crystal P., 1983-90) 16
Hopkins, M. (Tottenham, 1956-63) 34

Horne, B. (Portsmouth, Southampton, Everton, 1988-96) 54
Howells, R. (Cardiff, 1954) 2
Hughes, C. (Luton, 1992-6) 5
Hughes, I. (Luton, 1951) 4
Hughes, M. (Man. Utd., Barcelona, Bayern M., Man. Utd., Chelsea, 1984-96) 60
Hughes, W. (Birmingham, 1947) 3
Hughes, W.A. (Blackburn, 1949) 5
Humphreys, J. (Everton, 1947) 1

Jackett, K. (Watford, 1983-8) 31
James, E.G. (Blackpool, 1966-71) .. 9
James, L. (Burnley, Derby, Q.P.R., Swansea, Sunderland, 1972-83) 54
James, R. (Swansea, Stoke, Q.P.R., Leicester, Swansea, 1979-88) ... 47
Jarvis, A. (Hull, 1967) 3
Jenkins, S. (Swansea, Huddersfield, 1996) 3
Johnson, M. (Swansea, 1964) 1
Jones, A. (Port Vale, Charlton, 1987-90) 6
Jones, Barrie (Swansea, Plymouth, Cardiff, 1963-9) 15
*Jones, Bryn (Arsenal, 1947-9) 4
Jones, C. (Swansea, Tottenham, Fulham, 1954-69) 59
Jones, D. (Norwich, 1976-80) 8
Jones, E. (Swansea, Tottenham, 1947-9) 4
Jones, J. (Liverpool, Wrexham, Chelsea, Huddersfield, 1976-86) 72
Jones, K. (Aston Villa, 1950) 1
Jones, R. (Sheff. Wed., 1994) 1
*Jones, T.G. (Everton, 1946-9) 13
Jones, V. (Wimbledon, 1995-6) 5
Jones, W. (Bristol Rovers, 1971) 1

Kelsey, J. (Arsenal, 1954-62) 41
King, J. (Swansea, 1955) 1
Kinsey, N. (Norwich, Birmingham, 1951-6) 7
Knill, A. (Swansea, 1989) 1
Krzywicki, R. (W.B.A., Huddersfield, 1970-2) 8

Lambert, R. (Liverpool, 1947-9) 5
Law, B. (Q.P.R., 1990) 1
Lee, C. (Ipswich, 1965) 2
Leek, K. (Leicester, Newcastle, Birmingham, Northampton, 1961-5) 13
Legg, A. (Birmingham, 1996) 2
Lever, A. (Leicester, 1953) 1
Lewis, D. (Swansea, 1983) 1
Lloyd, B. (Wrexham, 1976) 3
Lovell, S. (Crystal P., Millwall, 1982-6) 6
Lowndes, S. (Newport, Millwall, Brighton, Barnsley, 1983-8) 10
Lowrie, G. (Coventry, Newcastle, 1948-9) 4
Lucas, M. (Leyton Orient, 1962-3) .. 4
Lucas, W. (Swansea, 1949-51) 7

Maguire, G. (Portsmouth, 1990-2) .. 7
Mahoney, J. (Stoke, Middlesbrough, Swansea, 1968-83) 50
Mardon, P. (W.B.A., 1996) 1
Marriott, A. (Wrexham, 1996) 1
Marustik, C. (Swansea, 1982-3) 6
Medwin, T. (Swansea, Tottenham, 1953-63) 29
Melville, A. (Swansea, Oxford, Sunderland, 1990-6) 27
Mielczarek, R. (Rotherham, 1971) .. 1
Millington, A. (W.B.A., Peterborough, Swansea, 1963-72) 21
Moore, G. (Cardiff, Chelsea, Man. Utd., Northampton, Charlton, 1960-71) 21
Morris, W. (Burnley, 1947-52) 5

Nardiello, D. (Coventry, 1978) 2
Neilson, A. (Newcastle, 1992-5) 4
Nicholas, P. (Crystal P., Arsenal, Crystal P., Luton, Aberdeen, Chelsea, Watford, 1979-92) 73
Niedzwiecki, E. (Chelsea, 1985-8) .. 2
Nogan, L. (Watford, Reading, 1991-6) 2
Norman, T. (Hull, 1986-8) 5
Nurse, M. (Swansea, Middlesbrough, 1960-3) 12

O'Sullivan, P. (Brighton, 1973-8) 3

Page, M. (Birmingham, 1971-9) 28

Palmer, D. (Swansea, 1957) 3
Parry, J. (Swansea, 1951) 1
Pascoe, C. (Swansea, Sunderland, 1984-92) 10
Paul, R. (Swansea, Man. City, 1949-56) 33
Pembridge, M. (Luton, Derby, Sheff. Wed., 1992-6) 16
Perry, J. (Cardiff, 1994) 1
Phillips, D. (Plymouth, Man. City, Coventry, Norwich, Nott'm. F., 1984-96) 62
Phillips, J. (Chelsea, 1973-8) 4
Phillips, L. (Cardiff, Aston Villa, Swansea, Charlton, 1971-82) 58
Pontin, K. (Cardiff, 1980) 2
Powell, A. (Leeds, Everton, Birmingham, 1947-51) 8
Powell, D. (Wrexham, Sheff. Utd. 1968-71) 11
Powell, I. (Q.P.R., Aston Villa, 1947-51) 8
Price, P. (Luton, Tottenham, 1980-4) 25
Pring, K. (Rotherham, 1966-7) 3
Pritchard, H. (Bristol City, 1985) 1

Rankmore, F. (Peterborough, 1966) 1
Ratcliffe, K. (Everton, Cardiff, 1981-93) 59
Reece, G. (Sheff. Utd., Cardiff, 1966-75) 29
Reed, W. (Ipswich, 1955) 2
Rees, A. (Birmingham, 1984) 1
Rees, J. (Luton, 1992) 1
Rees, R. (Coventry, W.B.A., Nott'm F., 1965-72) 39
Rees, W. (Cardiff, Tottenham, 1949-50) 4
Richards, S. (Cardiff, 1947) 1
Roberts, A. (Q.P.R., 1993) 1
Roberts, D. (Oxford, Hull, 1973-8) 17
Roberts, I. (Watford, Huddersfield, Leicester 1990-5) 7
Roberts, J. (Arsenal, Birmingham, 1971-6) 21
Roberts, J. (Bolton, 1949) 1
Roberts, P. (Portsmouth, 1974) 4
Robinson, J. (Charlton, 1996) 3
Rodrigues, P. (Cardiff, Leicester, Sheff. Wed. 1965-74) 40
Rouse, V. (Crystal P., 1959) 1
Rowley, T. (Tranmere, 1959) 1
Rush, I. (Liverpool, Juventus, Liverpool, 1980-96) 73

Saunders, D. (Brighton, Oxford, Derby, Liverpool, Aston Villa, Galatasaray, 1986-96) 52
Savage, R. (Crewe, 1996) 3
Sayer, P. (Cardiff, 1977-8) 7
Scrine, F. (Swansea, 1950) 2
Sear, C. (Man. City, 1963) 1
Sherwood, A. (Cardiff, Newport, 1947-57) 41
Shortt, W. (Plymouth, 1947-53) 12
Showers, D. (Cardiff, 1975) 2
Sidlow, C. (Liverpool, 1947-50) 7
Slatter, N. (Bristol Rovers, Oxford, 1983-9) 22
Smallman, D. (Wrexham, Everton, 1974-6) 7
Southall, N. (Everton, 1982-96) 86
Speed, G. (Leeds, 1990-6) 35
Sprake, G. (Leeds, Birmingham, 1964-75) 37
Stansfield, F. (Cardiff, 1949) 1
Stevenson, B. (Leeds, Birmingham, 1978-82) 15
Stevenson, N. (Swansea, 1982-3) .. 4
Stitfall, R. (Cardiff, 1953-7) 2
Sullivan, D. (Cardiff, 1953-60) 17
Symons, C. (Portsmouth, Man. City, 1992-6) 22

Tapscott, D. (Arsenal, Cardiff, 1954-9) 14
Taylor, G. (Crystal P., Sheff. Utd., 1996) 3
Thomas, D. (Swansea, 1957-8) 2
Thomas, M. (Wrexham, Man. Utd., Everton, Brighton, Stoke, Chelsea, W.B.A., 1977-86) 51
Thomas, M. (Newcastle, 1987) 1
Thomas, R. (Swindon, Derby, Cardiff, 1967-78) 50
Thomas, S. (Fulham, 1948-9) 4
Toshack, J. (Cardiff, Liverpool, Swansea, 1969-80) 40

Van den Hauwe, P. (Everton, 1985-9) 13
Vaughan, N. (Newport, Cardiff, 1983-5) 10
Vearncombe, G. (Cardiff, 1958-61) . 2
Vernon, R. (Blackburn, Everton, Stoke, 1957-68) 32
Villars, A. (Cardiff, 1974) 3

Walley, T. (Watford, 1971) 1
Walsh, I. (Crystal P., 1980-2) 18
Ward, D. (Bristol Rovers, Cardiff, 1959-62) 2
Webster, C. (Man. Utd., 1957-8) 4
Williams, A. (Reading, 1994-6) 7
Williams, D. (Norwich, 1986-7) 5
Williams, G. (Cardiff, 1951) 1
Williams, G. (Derby, Ipswich, 1988-96) 13
Williams, G.E. (W.B.A., 1960-9) 26
Williams, G.G. (Swansea, 1961-2) .. 5
Williams, H.J. (Swansea, 1965-72) . 3
Williams, H.T. (Newport, Leeds, 1949-50) 4
Williams, S. (W.B.A., Southampton, 1954-66) 43
Witcombe, D. (W.B.A., Sheff. Wed., 1947) 3
Woosnam, P. (Leyton Orient, West Ham, Aston Villa, 1959-63) 17

Yorath, T. (Leeds, Coventry, Tottenham, Vancouver Whitecaps, 1970-81) 59
Young, E. (Wimbledon, Crystal P., Wolves, 1990-6) 21

REPUBLIC OF IRELAND

Aherne, T. (Belfast Celtic, Luton, 1946-54) 16
Aldridge, J. (Oxford, Liverpool, Real Sociedad, Tranmere, 1986-96) .. 68
Ambrose, P. (Shamrock R., 1955-64) 5
Anderson, J. (Preston, Newcastle, 1980-9) 16

Babb, P. (Coventry, Liverpool, 1994-6) 20
Bailham, E. (Shamrock R., 1964) ... 1
Barber, E. (Bohemians, Birmingham, 1966) 2
Beglin, J. (Liverpool, 1984-7) 15
Braddish, S. (Dundalk, 1978) 1
Bonner, P. (Celtic, 1981-96) 80
Brady, L. (Arsenal, Juventus, Sampdoria, Inter-Milan, Ascoli, West Ham, 1975-90) 72
Brady, R. (Q.P.R., 1964) 6
Breen, G. (Birmingham, 1996) 6
*Breen, T. (Shamrock R., 1947) 3
Brennan, F. (Drumcondra, 1965) 1
Brennan, S. (Man. Utd., Waterford, 1965-71) 19
Browne, W. (Bohemians, 1964) 3
Buckley, L. (Shamrock R., Waregem, 1984-5) 2
Burke, F. (Cork Ath., 1952) 1
Byrne, A. (Southampton, 1970-4) .. 14
Byrne, J. (Q.P.R., Le Havre, Brighton, Sunderland, Millwall, 1985-93) ... 23
Byrne, P. (Shamrock R., 1984-6) 8

Campbell, A. (Santander, 1985) 3
Campbell, N. (St. Patrick's Ath., Fortuna Cologne, 1971-7) 11
Cantwell, N. (West Ham, Man. Utd., 1954-67) 36
Carey, B. (Man. Utd., Leicester, 1992-4) 3
*Carey, J. (Man. Utd., 1946-53) 21
Carolan, J. (Man. Utd., 1960) 2
Carroll, B. (Shelbourne, 1949-50) ... 2
Carroll, T. (Ipswich, 1968-73) 17
Cascarino, A. (Gillingham, Millwall, Aston Villa, Chelsea, Marseille, 1986-96) 61
Chandler, J. (Leeds, 1980) 2
Clarke, J. (Drogheda, 1978) 1
Clarke, K. (Drumcondra, 1948) 2
Clarke, M. (Shamrock R., 1950) 1
Clinton, T. (Everton, 1951-4) 3
Coad, P. (Shamrock R., 1947-52) 11
Coffey, T. (Drumcondra, 1950) 1
Colfer, M. (Shelbourne, 1950-1) 2
Conmy, O. (Peterborough, 1965-70) 5
Connolly, D. (Watford, 1996) 4
Conroy, G. (Stoke, 1970-7) 27

Conway, J. (Fulham, Man. City, 1967-77) 20
Corr, P. (Everton, 1949-50) 4
Courtney, E. (Cork Utd., 1946) 1
Coyle, O. (Bolton, 1994) 1
Coyne, T. (Celtic, Tranmere, Motherwell, 1992-6) 21
Cummins, G. (Luton, 1954-61) 19
Cuneen, T. (Limerick, 1951) 1
Cunningham, K. (Wimbledon, 1996) 6
Curtis, D. (Shelbourne, Bristol City, Ipswich, Exeter) 17
Cusack, S. (Limerick, 1953) 1

Daish, L. (Cambridge, Coventry, 1992-6) 5
Daly, G. (Man. Utd., Derby, Coventry, Birmingham, Shrewsbury, 1973-87) 45
Daly, M. (Wolves, 1978) 2
Daly, P. (Shamrock R., 1950) 1
Deacy, E. (Aston Villa, 1982) 4
De Mange, K. (Liverpool, Hull, 1987-9) 2
Dempsey, J. (Fulham, Chelsea, 1967-72) 19
Dennehy, J. (Cork Hibs., Nott'm F., Walsall, 1972-7) 11
Desmond, P. (Middlesbrough, 1950) 4
Devine, J. (Arsenal, 1980-5) 12
Donovan, D. (Everton, 1955-7) 5
Donovan, T. (Aston Villa, 1980) 1
Doyle, C. (Shelbourne, 1959) 1
Duffy, B. (Shamrock R., 1950) 1
Dunne, A. (Man. Utd., Bolton, 1962-76) 32
Dunne, J. (Fulham, 1971) 1
Dunne, P. (Man. Utd., 1965-7) 5
Dunne, S. (Luton, 1953-60) 15
Dunne, T. (St. Patrick's Ath., 1956-7) 3
Dunne, T. (Bolton, 1975) 1
Dunning, P. (Shelbourne, 1971) 2
Dunphy, E. (York, Millwall, 1966-71) 23
Dwyer, N. (West Ham, Swansea, 1960-5) 14

Eccles, P. (Shamrock R., 1986) 1
Eglington, T. (Shamrock R., Everton, 1946-56) 24

Fagan, E. (Shamrock R., 1973) 1
Fagan, F. (Man. City, Derby, 1955-61) 8
Fairclough, M. (Dundalk, 1982) 2
Fallon, S. (Celtic, 1951-5) 8
Farrell, P. (Shamrock R., Everton, 1946-57) 28
Farrelly, G. (Aston Villa, 1996) 3
Finucane, A. (Limerick, 1967-72) ... 11
Fitzgerald, F. (Waterford, 1955-6) ... 2
Fitzgerald, P. (Leeds, 1961-2) 5
Fitzpatrick, K. (Limerick, 1970) 1
Fitzsimons, A. (Middlesbrough, Lincoln, 1950-9) 26
Fleming, C. (Middlesbrough, 1996) 7
Fogarty, A. (Sunderland, Hartlepools, 1960-4) 11
Foley, T. (Northampton, 1964-7) 9
Fullam, J. (Preston, Shamrock R., 1961-70) 11

Gallagher, C. (Celtic, 1967) 2
Gallagher, M. (Hibernian, 1954) 1
Galvin, A. (Tottenham, Sheff. Wed., Swindon, 1983-90) 29
Gannon, E. (Notts. Co., Sheff. Wed., Shelbourne, 1949-55) 14
Gannon, M. (Shelbourne, 1972) 1
Gavin, J. (Norwich, Tottenham, Norwich, 1950-7) 7
Gibbons, A. (St. Patrick's Ath., 1952-6) 4
Gilbert, R. (Shamrock R., 1966) 1
Giles, C. (Doncaster, 1951) 1
Giles, J. (Man. Utd., Leeds, W.B.A., Shamrock R., 1960-79) 59
Given, S. (Blackburn, 1996) 7
Givens, D. (Man. Utd., Luton, Q.P.R., Birmingham, Neuchatel, Switz., 1969-82) 56
Glynn, D. (Drumcondra, 1952-5) 2
Godwin, T. (Shamrock R., Leicester, Bournemouth, 1949-58) 13
*Gorman, W. (Brentford, 1947) 2
Grealish, A. (Orient, Luton, Brighton, W.B.A., 1976-86) 45
Gregg, E. (Bohemians, 1978-80) 8

McGrath, P. (Man. Utd., Aston Villa, 1985-96) 82
Mackey, G. (Shamrock R., 1957) 3
McLoughlin, A. (Swindon, Southampton, Portsmouth, 1990-6) 24
McMillan, W. (Belfast Celtic, 1946) . 2
McNally, B. (Luton, 1959-63) 3
Macken, A. (Derby, 1977) 1
Malone, G. (Shelbourne, 1949) 1
Mancini, T. (Q.P.R., Arsenal, 1974-5) 5
Martin, C. (Glentoran, Leeds, Aston Villa, 1946-56) 30
Martin, M. (Bohemians, Man. Utd., 1972-83) 51
Meagan, M. (Everton, Huddersfield, Drogheda, 1961-70) 17
Milligan, M. (Oldham, 1992) 1
Mooney, J. (Shamrock R., 1965) 2
Moore, A. (Middlesbrough, 1996) 5
Moran, K. (Man. Utd., Sporting Gijon, Blackburn, 1980-94) 69
Moroney, T. (West Ham, 1948-54) 12
Morris, C. (Celtic, Middlesbrough, 1988-93) 35
Moulson, G. (Lincoln, 1948-9) 3
Mucklan, C. (Drogheda, 1978) 1
Mulligan, P. (Shamrock R., Chelsea, Crystal P., W.B.A., Shamrock R., 1969-80) 50
Munroe, L. (Shamrock R., 1954) 1
Murphy, A. (Clyde, 1956) 1
Murphy, B. (Bohemians, 1986) 1
Murphy, J. (Crystal P., 1980) 3
Murray, T. (Dundalk, 1950) 1

Newman, W. (Shelbourne, 1969) 1
Nolan, R. (Shamrock R., 1957-63) 10

O'Brien, F. (Philadelphia F., 1980) .. 4
O'Brien, L. (Shamrock R., Man. Utd., Newcastle, Tranmere, 1986-96) 15
O'Brien, R. (Notts Co., 1976-7) 4
O'Byrne, L. (Shamrock R., 1949) 1
O'Callaghan, B. (Stoke, 1979-82) ... 6
O'Callaghan, K. (Ipswich, Portsmouth, 1981-7) 21
O'Connell, A. (Dundalk, Bohemians, 1967-71) 2
O'Connor, T. (Shamrock R., 1950) .. 4
O'Connor, T. (Fulham, Dundalk, Bohemians, 1968-73) 7
O'Driscoll, J. (Swansea, 1949) 3
O'Driscoll, S. (Fulham, 1982) 3
O'Farrell, F. (West Ham, Preston, 1952-9) 9
*O'Flanagan, Dr. K. (Arsenal, 1947) 3
O'Flanagan, M. (Bohemians, 1947) 1
O'Hanlon, K (Rotherham, 1988) 1
O'Keefe, E. (Everton, Port Vale, 1981-5) 5
O'Leary, D. (Arsenal, 1977-93) 68
O'Leary, P. (Shamrock R., 1980-1) . 7
O'Neill, F. (Shamrock R., 1962-72) 20
O'Neill, J. (Everton, 1952-9) 17
O'Neill, J. (Preston, 1961) 1
O'Neill, K. (Norwich, 1996) 6
O'Regan, K. (Brighton, 1984-5) 4
O'Reilly, J. (Cork Utd., 1946) 3

Peyton, G. (Fulham, Bournemouth, Everton, 1977-92) 33
Peyton, N. (Shamrock R., Leeds, 1957-61) 6
Phelan, T. (Wimbledon, Man. City, Chelsea, 1992-6) 35

Quinn, N. (Arsenal, Man. City, 1986-96) 60

Richardson, D. (Shamrock R., Gillingham, 1972-80) 3
Ringstead, A. (Sheff. Utd., 1951-9) 20
Robinson, M. (Brighton, Liverpool, Q.P.R., 1981-6) 23
Roche, P. (Shelbourne, Man. Utd., 1972-6) 8
Rogers, E. (Blackburn, Charlton, 1968-73) 19
Ryan, G. (Derby, Brighton, 1978-85) 16
Ryan, R. (W.B.A., Derby, 1950-56) 16

Savage, D. (Millwall, 1996) 5
Saward, P. (Millwall, Aston Villa, Huddersfield, 1954-63) 18
Scannell, T. (Southend, 1954) 1
Scully, P. (Arsenal, 1989) 1
Sheedy, K. (Everton, Newcastle, 1984-93) 46
Sheridan, J. (Leeds, Sheff. Wed., 1988-96) 34
Slaven, B. (Middlesbrough, 1990-3) 7
Sloan, P. (Arsenal, 1946) 2
Smyth, M. (Shamrock R., 1969) 1
Staunton, S. (Liverpool, Aston Villa, 1989-96) 62
Stapleton, F. (Arsenal, Man. Utd., Ajax, Derby, Le Havre, Blackburn, 1977-90) 71
*Stevenson, A. (Everton, 1947-9) 6
Strahan, F. (Shelbourne, 1964-5) 5
Swan, M. (Drumcondra, 1960) 1
Synnott, N. (Shamrock R., 1978-9) . 3

Thomas, P. (Waterford, 1974) 2
Townsend, A. (Norwich, Chelsea, Aston Villa, 1989-96) 60
Traynor, T. (Southampton, 1954-64) 8
Treacy, R. (W.B.A., Charlton, Swindon, Preston, Shamrock R., 1966-80) 43
Tuohy, L. (Shamrock R., Newcastle, Shamrock R., 1956-65) 8
Turner, A. (Celtic, 1963) 2

Vernon, J. (Belfast Celtic, 1946) 2

Waddock, G. (Q.P.R., Millwall, 1980-90) 21
Walsh, D. (W.B.A., Aston Villa, 1946-54) 20
Walsh, J. (Limerick, 1982) 1
Walsh, M. (Blackpool, Everton, Q.P.R., Porto, 1976-85) 21
Walsh, M. (Everton, Norwich, 1982-3) 5
Walsh, W. (Man. City, 1947-50) 9
Waters, J. (Grimsby, 1977-80) 2
Whelan, R. (St. Patrick's Ath., 1964) 2
Whelan, R. (Liverpool, Southend, 1981-95) 53
Whelan, W. (Man. Utd., 1956-7) 4
Whittaker, R. (Chelsea, 1959) 1

INTERNATIONAL GOALSCORERS (1946-96)

(As at start of season 1996-7)

ENGLAND

Charlton, R 49
Lineker 48
Greaves 44
Finney 30
Lofthouse 30
Platt 28
Robson, B 26
Hurst 24
Mortensen 23
Channon 21
Keegan 21
Peters 20
Haynes 18
Hunt, R 18
Lawton 16
Taylor, T 16
Woodcock 16
Chivers 13
Mariner 13
Smith, R 13
Francis, T 12
Barnes, J 11
Douglas 11
Mannion 11
Clarke, A 10
Flowers, R 10
Lee, F 10
Milburn 10
Shearer 10
Wilshaw 10
Beardsley 9
Bell 9
Bentley 9
Hateley 9
Ball 8
Broadis 8
Byrne, J 8
Gascoigne 8
Hoddle 8
Kevan 8
Connelly 7
Coppell 7
Paine 7
Charlton, J 6
Johnson 6
Macdonald 6
Mullen 6
Rowley 6
Waddle 6
Anderton 5
Atyeo 5
Baily 5
Brooking 5
Carter 5
Edwards 5
Hitchens 5
Latchford 5
Neal 5

Pearce 5
Pearson, Stan 5
Pearson, Stuart 5
Pickering, F 5
Wright, I 5
Adams 4
Barnes, P 4
Bull 4
Dixon, K 4
Ferdinand 4
Hassall 4
Revie 4
Robson, R 4
Steven 4
Watson, Dave
(Sunderland) 4
Webb 4
Baker 3
Blissett 3
Butcher 3
Currie 3
Elliott 3
Francis, G 3
Grainger 3
Kennedy, R 3
McDermott 3
Matthews, S 3
Morris 3
O'Grady 3
Peacock 3
Ramsey 3
Sewell 3
Sheringham 3
Wilkins 3
Wright, W 3
Allen, R 2
Anderson 2
Barmby 2
Bradley 2
Broadbent 2
Brooks 2
Cowans 2
Eastham 2
Froggatt, J 2
Froggatt, R 2
Haines 2
Hancocks 2
Hunter 2
Ince 2
Lee, S 2
Moore 2
Perry 2
Pointer 2
Royle 2
Smith, A 2
Stone 2
Taylor, P 2
Tueart 2
Wignall 2
Worthington 2
A'Court 1
Astall 1
Beattie 1
Bowles 1
Bradford 1
Bridges 1
Chamberlain 1
Crawford 1
Dixon, L 1
Goddard 1
Hirst 1
Hughes, E 1
Kay 1
Keown 1
Kidd 1
Langton 1
Lawler 1
Lee, J 1
Lee, R 1
Le Saux 1
Mabbutt 1
Marsh 1
Medley 1
Melia1
Merson 1
Mullery 1
Nicholls 1
Nicholson 1
Palmer 1
Parry 1
Sansom 1
Shackleton 1
Stiles 1
Summerbee 1
Tambling 1
Thompson, Phil 1
Viollet 1
Wallace 1
Walsh 1
Weller 1
Wise 1
Withe 1
Wright, M 1

N. IRELAND

Clarke 13
Armstrong 12
Quinn, J 12
Bingham 10
Crossan, J 10
McIlroy, J 10
McParland 10
Best 9
Whiteside 9
Dougan 8
Dowie 8
Irvine, W 8
O'Neill, M (1972-85) ... 8
McAdams 7
Wilson, S 7
McLaughlin 6
Nicholson, J 6
Wilson, K 6
Cush 5
Gray 5
Hamilton, W 5
McIlroy, S 5
Simpson 5
Smyth, S 5
Taggart 5
Walsh, D 5
Anderson, T 4
Hamilton, B 4
Magilton 4
McGrath 4
McMorran 4
O'Neill, M. (1989-96) .. 4
Brotherston 3
Harvey, M 3
Lockhart 3
McDonald 3
McMordie 3
Morgan, S 3
Nicholl, C 3
Spence, D 3
Tully 3
Blanchflower, D 2
Casey 2
Clements 2
Doherty, P 2
Harkin 2
Hughes, M 2
Finney 2
McMahon 2
Neill, W 2

O'Neill, J 2
Peacock 2
Penney 2
Stewart, I 2
Barr 1
Black 1
Blanchflower, J 1
Brennan 1
Campbell, W 1
Caskey 1
Cassidy 1
Cochrane, T 1
Crossan, E 1
D'Arcy 1
Doherty, L 1
Elder 1
Ferguson 1
Ferris 1
Gillespie 1
Hill, C 1
Humphries 1
Hunter, A 1
Hunter, B 1
Johnston 1
Jones, J 1
Lomas 1
McClelland (1961) 1
McCrory 1
McCurdy 1
McGarry 1
Moreland 1
Morrow 1
Nelson 1
Nicholl, J 1
O'Boyle 1
O'Kane 1
Stevenson 1
Walker 1
Welsh 1
Wilson, D 1

SCOTLAND

Dalglish 30
Law 30
Reilly 22
McCoist 19
Johnston, M 14
Gilzean 12
Steel 12
Jordan 11
Collins, R 10
Johnstone, R 10
Stein 10
McStay 9
Mudie 9
St. John 9
Brand 8
Collins, J 8
Gemmill, A 8
Leggat 8
Robertson, J (1978-84) 8
Wilson, D 8
Gray, A 7
Wark 7
Brown, A 6
Cooper 6
Gough 6
Liddell 6
Rioch 6
Waddell 6
Booth 5
Durie 5
Henderson, W 5
Macari 5
Masson 5
McQueen 5
Murdoch 5
Nevin 5
Nicholas 5
O'Hare 5
Scott, A 5
Strachan 5
Young, A 5
Archibald 4
Caldow 4
Hamilton 4
Hartford 4
Herd, D. 4
Johnstone, J 4
Lorimer 4
Mackay, D 4
Mason 4
McAllister 4
McKinlay 4
McLaren 4
Smith, G 4
Souness 4
Baxter 3
Bremner, W 3
Chalmers 3
Gibson 3
Graham, G 3
Gray, E 3
Greig 3
Lennox 3
MacDougall 3
McGinlay 3
McInally, A 3
McNeill 3
McPhail 3
Morris 3
Robertson, J (1991-5) . 3
Sturrock 3
White 3
Baird, S 2
Bauld 2
Flavell 2
Fleming 2
Gallacher 2
Graham, A 2
Harper 2
Hewie 2
Holton 2
Houliston 2
Johnstone, D. 2
McClair 2
McGhee 2
McMillan 2
Pettigrew 2
Ring 2
Robertson, A 2
Shearer, D 2
Aitken, R 1
Bannon 1
Bett 1
Bone 1
Brazil 1
Buckley 1
Burns 1
Calderwood 1
Campbell, R 1
Combe 1
Conn 1
Craig 1
Crawford 1
Curran 1
Davidson 1
Docherty 1
Dodds 1
Duncan, M 1
Fernie 1
Gray, F 1
Gemmell, T 1
Henderson, J 1

Hendry	1
Howie	1
Hughes, J	1
Hunter, W	1
Hutchison	1
Jackson, C	1
Jardine	1
Jess	1
Johnstone, L	1
Linwood	1
Mackay, G	1
MacLeod	1
McAvennie	1
McCall	1
McCalliog	1
McKenzie	1
McKimmie	1
McKinnon	1
McLean	1
McLintock	1
Miller, W	1
Mitchell	1
Morgan	1
Mulhall	1
Murray, J	1
Narey	1
Ormond	1
Orr	1
Parlane	1
Provan, D	1
Quinn	1
Sharp	1
Stewart, R	1
Thornton	1
Wallace, I	1
Weir, A	1

WALES

Rush	28
Allchurch, I	23
Ford	23
Saunders	16
Charles, John	15
Jones, C	15
Hughes, M	14
Toshack	13
James, L	10
Davies, Ron	9
Vernon	8
Flynn	7
Walsh, I	7
Charles, Mel	6
Curtis, A	6
Griffiths, A	6
James, R	6
Medwin	6
Clarke, R	5
Leek	5
Deacy	4
Edwards, I	4
Giggs	4
Tapscott	4
Thomas, M	4
Woosnam	4
Allen, M	3
Bodin	3
Bowen, M	3
Coleman	3
England	3
Palmer, D	3
Pembridge	3
Rees, R	3
Davies, G	2
Durban, A	2
Dwyer	2
Edwards, G	2
Giles, D	2
Godfrey	2
Griffiths, M	2
Hodges	2
Horne	2
Jones, Barrie	2
Jones, Bryn	2
Lowrie	2
Nicholas	2
Phillips, D	2
Reece, G	2
Slatter	2
Speed	2
Williams, G.E	2
Yorath	2
Barnes	1
Blackmore	1
Blake	1
Bowen, D	1
Boyle, T	1
Burgess, R	1
Charles, Jeremy	1
Evans, I	1
Foulkes	1
Harris, C	1
Hewitt, R	1
Hockey	1
Jones, A	1
Jones, D	1
Jones, J	1
Krzywicki	1
Lovell	1
Mahoney	1
Melville	1
Moore, G.	1
O'Sullivan	1
Paul	1
Powell, A	1
Powell, D	1
Price, P	1
Roberts, P	1
Smallman	1
Symons	1
Young	1

REP. OF IRELAND

Stapleton	20
Aldridge	19
Givens	19
Cantwell	14
Quinn	14
Daly	13
Cascarino	12
Brady	9
Sheedy	9
Curtis	8
Grealish	8
Kelly, D	8
McGrath, P	8
Fitzsimons	7
Ringstead	7
Coyne	6
McEvoy	6
Martin, C	6
Moran	6
Townsend	6
Cummins	5
Fagan, F	5
Giles	5
Houghton	5
Lawrenson	5
Rogers	5
Sheridan	5
Staunton	5
Treacy	5
Walsh, D	5

Byrne, J	4	Gavin	2	Holmes	1
McGee	4	Hale	2	Hughton	1
Martin, M	4	Hand	2	Irwin	1
Robinson	4	Hurley	2	Keane	1
Tuohy	4	Leech	2	Kelly, G	1
Carey, J	3	McCarthy	2	Kernaghan	1
Coad	3	O'Connor	2	Mancini	1
Conway	3	O'Farrell	2	McCann	1
Farrell	3	O'Reilly, J	2	McLoughlin	1
Fogarty	3	Ambrose	1	Mooney	1
Haverty	3	Anderson	1	Moroney	1
O'Flanagan, K	3	Breen	1	Mulligan	1
O'Neill, K	3	Brown	1	O'Callaghan, K	1
Ryan, R	3	Byrne, A	1	O'Keefe	1
Waddock	3	Carroll	1	O'Leary	1
Walsh, M	3	Dempsey	1	O'Neill, F	1
Whelan	3	Duffy	1	O'Reilly, J.	1
Connelly	2	Fitzgerald, J	1	Ryan, G	1
Conroy	2	Fullam, J	1	Slaven	1
Dennehy	2	Galvin	1	Sloan	1
Eglington	2	Glynn	1	Strahan	1
Fallon	2	Grimes	1	Waters	1
Fitzgerald, P	2	Harte	1		

INTERNATIONAL FOOTBALL'S TV TOP TEN

(Source: Individuals Audience)

Date	Match	Est. Audience	Channel
26/6/96	England v Germany (Eur. Champ. s-final)	26,000,000	*BBC/ITV
4/7/90	England v W. Germany (World cup s-final)	25,200,000	BBC/ITV
8/7/90	W. Germany v Argentina (World Cup Final)	19,500,000	BBC/ITV
3/7/90	Italy v Argentina (World Cup s-final)	18,000,000	BBC/ITV
17/7/90	Brazil v Italy (World Cup Final)	17,500,000	BBC/ITV
22/6/86	England v Argentina (World Cup q-final)	15,350,000	BBC
13/10/93	Holland v England (World Cup)	14,075,000	ITV
5/7/82	England v Spain (World Cup)	13,650,000	ITV
6/6/81	England v Hungary (World Cup)	13,500,000	ITV
20/5/93	Arsenal v Sheffield. Wed. (FA Cup Final Rep)	13,440,000	BBC

(*BBC claimed 19.8m)

RECORDS SECTION

INDEX

GOALSCORING

(† Football League pre 1992-3. * Home team)

Highest: *Arbroath 36, Bon Accord (Aberdeen) 0, in **Scottish Cup** 1st Round, Sept. 12, 1885. On same day, also in Scottish Cup 1st Round, Dundee Harp beat Aberdeen Rovers 35-0.

Internationals: England 15, *France 0, in Paris, 1906 (Amateur); England 13 *Ireland 0, in Belfast, Feb. 18, 1882 (record in U.K.); *England 9, Scotland 3, at Wembley, Apr. 15, 1961; Biggest England win at Wembley: 9-0 v Luxembourg (E.Champ), Dec. 15, 1982.

Other record wins: Scotland: 11-0 v Ireland (Glasgow, Feb. 23, 1901); **Northern Ireland:** 7-0 v Wales (Belfast, Feb. 1, 1930); **Wales:** 11-0 v Ireland (Wrexham, Mar. 3, 1888); **Rep. of Ireland:** 8-0 v Malta (E. Champ., Dublin, Nov. 16, 1983).

Record International defeats: England: 1-7 v Hungary (Budapest, May 23, 1954); **Scotland:** 3-9 v England (Wembley, April 15, 1961); **Ireland:** 0-13 v England (Belfast, Feb. 18, 1882); **Wales:** 0-9 v Scotland (Glasgow, March 23, 1878); **Rep. of Ireland:** 0-7 v Brazil (Uberlandia, May 27, 1982).

World Cup: Qualifying round – New Zealand 13, Fiji 0, Aug. 16, 1981. **Finals – highest scorers:** Hungary 10, El Salvador 1 (Spain, June 15, 1982); Hungary 9, S. Korea 0 (Switzerland, June 17, 1954); Yugoslavia 9, Zaire 0 (W. Germany, June 18, 1974).

F.A. Cup: *Preston North End 26, Hyde 0, 1st Round, Oct. 15, 1887.

League Cup: *West Ham United 10, Bury 0 (2nd Round, 2nd Leg, Oct 25, 1983); *Liverpool 10, Fulham 0 (2nd Round, 1st Leg, Sept. 23, 1986). **Record Aggregates:** Liverpool 13, Fulham 2 (10-0h, 3-2a), Sept. 23-Oct. 7, 1986; West Ham 12, Bury 1 (2-1a, 10-0h), Oct. 4-25, 1983; Liverpool 11, Exeter 0 (5-0h, 6-0a), Oct 7-28, 1981.

F.A. Premier League (beginning 1992-3): *Manchester United 9; Ipswich 0, Mar. 4, 1995. **Record away win:** Nottingham Forest 7, *Sheff. Wednesday 1, Apr. 1, 1995.

† Football League (First Division): *Aston Villa 12, Accrington 2, Mar. 12, 1892; *Tottenham 10, Everton 4, Oct. 11, 1958 (highest 1st. Div. aggregate this century); *West Bromwich 12, Darwen 0, Apr. 4, 1892; *Nottingham Forest 12, Leicester Fosse 0, Apr. 21, 1909. **Record away wins:** Sunderland 9, *Newcastle United 1, Dec. 5, 1908; Wolves 9, *Cardiff City 1, Sept. 3, 1955.

New First Division (beginning 1992-3): *Newcastle 7, Leicester 1, May 9, 1993.

† **Second Division:** *Manchester City 11, Lincoln City 3, Mar. 23, 1895; *Newcastle United 13, Newport County 0, Oct. 5, 1946; *Small Heath 12, Walsall Town Swifts 0, Dec. 17, 1892; *Darwen 12, Walsall 0, Dec. 26, 1896; *Small Heath 12, Doncaster Rovers 0, Apr. 11, 1903. **Record away win:** Sheffield United 10, *Burslem Port Vale 0, Dec. 10, 1892.

New Second Division (beginning 1992-3): *Hartlepool 1, Plymouth 8, May 7, 1994.

† **Third Division:** *Gillingham 10, Chesterfield 0, Sept. 5, 1987; *Tranmere R. 9, Accrington Stanley 0, Apr. 18, 1959; *Brighton 9, Southend 1, Nov. 22, 1965; *Brentford 9, Wrexham 0, Oct. 15, 1963. **Record away win:** Fulham 8, *Halifax Town 0, Sept. 16, 1969.

New Third Division (beginning 1992-3): *Torquay 1, Scunthorpe 8, Oct. 28, 1995.

† **Third Division (North):** *Stockport County 13, Halifax Town 0 (still joint biggest win in F. League – see Div. 2) Jan. 6, 1934; *Tranmere Rovers 13, Oldham Athletic 4, Dec. 26, 1935. *(17 is highest Football League aggregate score).* **Record away win:** Barnsley 9, *Accrington Stanley 0, Feb. 3, 1934.

† **Third Division (South):** *Luton Town 12, Bristol Rovers 0, Apr. 13, 1936; *Gillingham 9, Exeter City 4, Jan. 7, 1951. **Record away win:** Walsall 8, *Northampton Town 0, Apr. 8, 1947.

† **Fourth Division:** *Oldham Ath. 11, Southport 0, Dec. 26, 1962; *Hartlepool 10, Barrow 1, Apr. 4, 1959; *Wrexham 10, Hartlepool U. 1, Mar. 3, 1962. **Record away win:** Rotherham Utd. 8, *Crewe Alex. 1, Sept. 8, 1973.

Scottish Premier Division – Highest aggregate: 11 goals – Celtic 8, Hamilton 3, Jan. 3, 1987. **Other highest team scores:** Aberdeen 8, Motherwell 0 (Mar. 26, 1979); Kilmarnock 1, Rangers 8 (Sept. 6, 1980); Hamilton 0, Celtic 8 (Nov. 5, 1988).

Scottish League Div. 1: *Celtic 11, Dundee 0, Oct. 26, 1895. **Record away win:** Hibs 11, *Airdrie 1, Oct. 24, 1959.

Scottish League Div. 2: *Airdrieonians 15, Dundee Wanderers 1, Dec. 1, 1894.

Record British score this century: Stirling Albion 20, Selkirk 0 (Scottish Cup 1st. Round, Dec. 8, 1984). Winger Davie Thompson (7 goals) was one of 9 Stirling players to score.

FOOTBALL LEAGUE – BEST IN SEASON
(Before restructure in 1992)

Div.		*Goals*	*Games*
1	W.R. (Dixie) Dean, Everton, 1927-8	60	39
2	George Camsell, Middlesbrough, 1926-7	59	37
3(S)	Joe Payne, Luton Town, 1936-7	55	39
3(N)	Ted Harston, Mansfield Town, 1936-7	55	41
3	Derek Reeves, Southampton, 1959-60	39	46
4	Terry Bly, Peterborough U., 1960-1	52	46

(Since restructure in 1992)

Div.		*Goals*	*Games*
1	Guy Whittingham, Portsmouth, 1992-3	42	46
2	Jimmy Quinn, Reading, 1993-4	35	46
3	Steve White, Hereford, 1995-6	29	40
	Andy Saville, Preston, 1995-6	29	44

F.A. PREMIER LEAGUE – BEST IN SEASON

Andy Cole **34 goals** (Newcastle – 40 games, 1993-4); Alan Shearer **34 goals** (Blackburn – 42 games, 1994-5).

FOOTBALL LEAGUE – BEST MATCH HAULS
(Before restructure in 1992)

Div.		*Goals*
1	Ted Drake (Arsenal), away to Aston V., Dec. 14, 1935	**7**
	James Ross (Preston N.E.) v Stoke, Oct 6, 1888	**7**
2	*Neville (Tim) Coleman (Stoke City) v. Lincoln, Feb. 23, 1957	**7**
	Tommy Briggs (Blackburn Rovers) v. Bristol Rovers, Feb. 5, 1955	**7**
3(S)	Joe Payne (Luton Town) v. Bristol Rovers, April 13, 1936	**10**
3(N)	Robert ('Bunny') Bell (Tranmere Rovers) v. Oldham Athletic, Dec. 26, 1935 – he also missed a penalty	**9**
3	Barrie Thomas (Scunthorpe Utd) v. Luton, April 24, 1965	**5**
	Keith East (Swindon Town) v. Mansfield, Nov. 20, 1965	**5**
	Steve Earle (Fulham) v. Halifax, Sept. 16, 1969	**5**
	Alf Wood (Shrewsbury Town) v. Blackburn Rov., Oct. 2, 1971	**5**
	Tony Caldwell (Bolton W.) v. Walsall, Sept 10, 1983	**5**
	Andy Jones (Port Vale) v. Newport Co., May 4, 1987	**5**
4	Bert Lister (Oldham Ath.) v. Southport, Dec. 26, 1962	**6**

* Scored from the wing

(Since restructure in 1992)

Div.	*Goals*
1	**4** in match – John Durnin (Oxford v Luton, 1992-3); Guy Whittingham (Portsmouth v Bristol R. 1992-3); Craig Russell (Sunderland v Millwall, 1995-6).
2	**4** in match – Ronnie Jepson (Exeter v Wrexham, 1993-4).
3	**5** in match – Tony Naylor (Crewe v Colchester, 1992-3); Steve Butler (Cambridge v Exeter, 1993-4).

F.A. PREMIER LEAGUE – BEST MATCH HAUL

5 goals in match: Andy Cole (Man. United v Ipswich, 1994-5).

SCOTTISH LEAGUE

Div.		*Goals*
1	Jimmy McGrory (Celtic) v. Dunfermline Athletic, Jan. 14, 1928	**8**
1	Owen McNally (Arthurlie) v. Armadale, Oct. 1, 1927	**8**
2	Jim Dyet (King's Park) v. Forfar Athletic, Jan. 2, 1930, on his debut for the club	**8**
2	John Calder (Morton) v. Raith Rovers, April 18, 1936	**8**
2	Norman Haywood (Raith Rovers) v. Brechin, Aug. 20, 1937	**8**
Prem.	Paul Sturrock (Dundee United) v. Morton, Nov. 20, 1984	**5**

SCOTTISH LEAGUE – BEST IN SEASON

Prem.	Brian McClair (Celtic, 1986-7)	**35**
1	William McFadyen (Motherwell, 1931-2)	**53**
2	*Jimmy Smith (Ayr, 1927-8 – 38 appearances)	**66**

(*British record)

CUP FOOTBALL

Scottish Cup: John Petrie (Arbroath) v. Bon Accord, at Arbroath, 1st Round, Sept. 12, 1885 .... **13**

F.A. Cup: Ted MacDougall (Bournemouth) v. Margate, 1st Round, Nov. 20, 1971 .... **9**

F.A. Cup Final: Billy Townley (Blackburn Rovers) v. Sheffield Wednesday, at Kennington Oval, 1890; Jimmy Logan (Notts County) v. Bolton Wanderers, at Everton, 1894; Stan Mortensen (Blackpool) v. Bolton Wanderers, at Wembley, 1953 .... **3**

League Cup: Frank Bunn (Oldham Athletic) v. Scarborough (3rd Round), Oct. 25, 1989 .... **6**

Scottish League Cup: Jim Fraser (Ayr) v. Dumbarton, Aug. 13, 1952 . **5**
Jim Forrest (Rangers) v. Stirling Albion, Aug. 17, 1966 .... **5**

Scottish Cup: Most goals in match since war: **10** by **Gerry Baker** (St. Mirren) in 15-0 win (1st. Round) v Glasgow Univ., Jan 30, 1960; **9** by his brother **Joe Baker** (Hibernian) in 15-1 win (2nd. Round) v Peebles Rov., Feb. 11, 1961.

AGGREGATE LEAGUE SCORING RECORDS

	Goals
* Arthur Rowley (1946-65, WBA, Fulham, Leicester, Shrewsbury)	**434**
† Jimmy McGrory (1922-38, Celtic, Clydebank)	**410**
Hughie Gallacher (1921-39, Airdrieonians, Newcastle,Chelsea, Derby, Notts County, Grimsby, Gateshead)	**387**
William ('Dixie') Dean (1923-37, Tranmere, Everton, Notts County)	**379**
Hugh Ferguson (1916-30, Motherwell, Cardiff City, Dundee)	**362**
▪Jimmy Greaves (1957-71, Chelsea, Tottenham, West Ham)	**357**
Steve Bloomer (1892-1914, Derby County, Middlesbrough, Derby County)	**352**
George Camsell (1923-39, Durham City, Middlesbrough)	**348**
Dave Halliday (1920-35, St. Mirren, Dundee, Sunderland, Arsenal, Man. City, Clapton Orient)	**338**
John Atyeo (1951-66, Bristol City)	**315**
Joe Smith (1908-29, Bolton, Stockport County)	**315**
Victor Watson (1920-36, West Ham, Southampton)	**312**
Bob McPhail (1920s–1930s, Airdrie, Rangers)	**306**

(* **Rowley** scored 4 for WBA, 27 for Fulham, 251 for Leicester, 152 for Shrewsbury. ▪ **Greaves's** 357 is record First Div. total. † **McGrory** scored 397 for Celtic, 13 for Clydebank.)

Most League goals for one club: 349 – Dixie Dean (Everton 1925-37); **326 – George Camsell** (Middlesbrough 1925-39); **315 – John Atyeo** (Bristol City 1951-66); **306 – Vic Watson** (West Ham 1920-35); **291 – Steve Bloomer** (Derby 1892-1906, 1910-14); **259 – Arthur Chandler** (Leicester 1923-35); **255 – Nat Lofthouse** (Bolton 1946-61); **251 – Arthur Rowley** (Leicester 1950-58).

Over 500 Goals: Jimmy McGrory (Celtic, Clydebank and Scotland) scored a total of 550 goals in his first-class career (1922-38).

Over 1,000 goals: Brazil's **Pele** is reputedly the game's all-time highest scorer with 1,282 goals in 1,365 matches (1956-77), but many of them were scored in friendlies for his club, Santos. He scored his 1,000th goal, a penalty, against Vasco da Gama in the Maracana Stadium, Rio, on November 19, 1969. Pele (born Oct. 23, 1940) played regularly for Santos from the age of 16. During his career, he was sent off once. He played 95 'A' Internationals for Brazil and in their World Cup-winning teams in 1958 and 1970. ● Pele (Edson Arantes do Nascimento) is now Brazil's Minister for Sport.

MOST LEAGUE GOALS IN SEASON: DEAN'S 60

W.R. ('Dixie') Dean, Everton centre-forward, created a League scoring record in 1927-8 with an aggregate of 60 in 39 First Division matches. He also scored three goals in F.A. Cup-ties, and 19 in representative games (total for the season 82).

George Camsell, of Middlesbrough, previously held the record with 59 goals in 37 Second Division matches in 1926-7, his total for the season being 75.

SHEARER'S RECORD 'FIRST'

Alan Shearer (Blackburn) is the first player to score more than 30 top-division goals in 3 successive seasons: 31 in 1993-4, 34 in 1994-5, 31 in 1995-6.

MOST GOALS IN A MATCH

TOP SCORE by a player in a first-class match is **13** in the Scottish Cup and **10** in the Football League.

October 6, 1888: James Ross for Preston N.E. (7-0 v. Stoke City) set a League record in its first season by scoring all **7**

December 14, 1935: Ted Drake for Arsenal in 7-1 win away to Aston Villa (Div. 1). Scored six goals with his first six shots and in all equalled Ross's Football League record by scoring **7**

February 5, 1955: Tommy Briggs for Blackburn Rovers v. Bristol Rovers set Second Division record during 8-3 win by scoring **7**

February 23, 1957: Neville ('Tim') Coleman for Stoke City v. Lincoln City (8-0) in Second Division set a record as a winger by scoring **7**

December 26, 1935: Robert ('Bunny') Bell for Tranmere Rovers v. Oldham Athletic (Div. III North) beat Drake's 12-day-old record in a 13-4 win by scoring . **9**

April 13, 1936: Joe Payne set the still-existing individual record on his debut as a centre-forward, for Luton Town v. Bristol Rovers (Div. III South). In a 12-0 win he scored **10**

September 12, 1885: John Petrie set the all-time British individual record for a first-class match when, in Arbroath's 36-0 win against Bon Accord (Scottish Cup first round), he scored **13**

OTHER BIG HAULS

Gerry Baker 10 for St. Mirren v. Glasgow University in Scottish Cup, January 30, 1960 (15-0).

Eric Gemmell for Oldham Athletic v. Chester in Third Division North (11-2), January 19, 1952, and **Albert Whitehurst** for Bradford City v. Tranmere Rovers (Third Division North) (8-0), March 6, 1929; both scored **seven**.

W.H. (Billy) Minter scored **seven** goals for St. Albans City in replayed F.A. Cup 4th Qualifying Round against Dulwich Hamlet, November 22, 1922. Dulwich won 8-7, and Minter's seven is still the most goals scored in one match by a player in a losing side.

Denis Law scored **seven** but finished a loser in Man. City's F.A. Cup 4th Round tie at Luton in 1961. The original match on January 28 was washed out (69 mins.) when City led 6-2 (Law 6). He scored a seventh when the game was played again, but Luton won 3-1.

Louis Page, England outside-left, when tried for the first time as centre-forward, accomplished the **double hat-trick** for Burnley in a First Division match against Birmingham, at St. Andrews, April 10, 1926. Burnley won 7-1.

Davie Wilson, Rangers outside-left, scored **six** goals from centre-forward at Falkirk in Scottish league, March 17, 1962. Result: 7-1.

MOST GOALS IN INTERNATIONAL FOOTBALL

SEVEN by

Vivian Woodward for England v France in Amateur International in Paris, November 1, 1906. Result 15-0.

SIX by

Nat Lofthouse for Football League v. Irish League, at Wolverhampton, September 24, 1952. Result: 7-1.

Joe Bambrick for Ireland against Wales, in Belfast, February 1, 1930. Result: 7-0.

W.C. Jordan in Amateur International for England v. France, at Park Royal, March 23, 1908. Result 12-0.

Vivian Woodward for England v. Holland in Amateur International, at Chelsea, December 11, 1909. Result: 9-1.

FIVE by

Oliver Vaughton for England v Ireland (Belfast), February 18, 1882. Result: 13-0.

Steve Bloomer for England v. Wales (Cardiff) March 16, 1896. Result: 9-1.

Hughie Gallacher for Scotland against Ireland (Belfast), February 23, 1929. Result: 7-3.

Willie Hall for England v. Ireland, at Old Trafford, Manchester, November 16, 1938. Five in succession (first three in 3 mins. – fastest International hat-trick). Result: 7-0.

Malcolm Macdonald for England v. Cyprus (Wembley) April 16, 1975. Result: 5-0.

Hughie Gallacher for Scottish League against Irish League (Belfast) November 11, 1925. Result: 7-3.

Barney Battles for Scottish League against Irish League (Firhill Park, Glasgow) October 31, 1928. Result: 8-2.

Bobby Flavell for Scottish League against Irish League (Belfast) April 30, 1947. Result: 7-4.

Joe Bradford for Football League v. Irish League (Everton) September 25, 1929. Result: 7-2.

Albert Stubbins for Football League v. Irish League (Blackpool) October 18, 1950. Result: 6-3.

Brian Clough for Football League v. Irish League (Belfast) September 23, 1959. Result: 5-0.

INTERNATIONAL TOP SHOTS

		Goals	*Games*
England	– Bobby Charlton (1958-70)	49	106
N. Ireland	– Colin Clarke (1986-92)	13	38
Scotland	– Denis Law (1958-74)	30	55
	– Kenny Dalglish (1971-86)	30	102
Wales	– Ian Rush (1980-96)	28	73
Rep. of I.	– Frank Stapleton (1977-90)	20	71

ENGLAND'S TOP MARKSMEN

(As at start of season 1996-97)

	Goals	*Games*
Bobby Charlton (1958-70)	49	106
Gary Lineker (1984-92)	48	80
Jimmy Greaves (1959-67)	44	57

Tom Finney (1946-58)	30	76
Nat Lofthouse (1950-58)	30	33
Vivian Woodward (1903-11)	29	23
Steve Bloomer (1895-1907)	28	23
David Platt (1989-96)	27	62
Bryan Robson (1979-91)	26	90
Geoff Hurst (1966-72)	24	49
Stan Mortensen (1947-53)	23	25
Tommy Lawton (1938-48)	22	23
Mike Channon (1972-77)	21	46
Kevin Keegan (1972-82)	21	63
Martin Peters (1966-74)	20	67
George Camsell (1929-36)	18	9
"Dixie" Dean (1927-32)	18	16
Johnny Haynes (1954-62)	18	56
Roger Hunt (1962-69)	18	34
Tommy Taylor (1953-57)	16	19
Tony Woodcock (1978-86)	16	42

'GOLDEN GOAL' DECIDERS

The Football League, in an experiment to avoid penalty shoot-outs, introduced a new "golden goal" system in the 1994-95 **Auto Windscreens Shield** to decide matches in the knock-out stages of the competition in which scores were level after 90 minutes. The first goal scored in overtime ended play.

Iain Dunn (Huddersfield) became the first player in British football to settle a match by this sudden-death method. His 107th-minute goal beat Lincoln 3-2 on Nov. 30, 1994, and to mark his "moment in history" he was presented with a golden football trophy.

The AWS Final of 1995 was decided when **Paul Tait** headed the only goal for Birmingham against Carlisle 13 minutes into overtime – the first time a match at Wembley had been decided by the "golden goal" formula.

First major International tournament match to be decided by sudden death was the final of the 1996 European Championship in which Germany beat Czech Rep. 2-1 by Oliver Bierhoff's goal in the 95th minute.

CONSECUTIVE GOALS FOR ENGLAND

Tinsley Lindley (Cambridge Univ.) scored in **NINE** consecutive Internationals for **England** in three seasons (March 1886-March 1888) – three games against each of Ireland, Wales and Scotland.

In modern times, **Paul Mariner** scored in six consecutive **England** appearances (7 goals) between November 1981 and June 1982.

LEAGUE GOAL RECORDS

The highest goal-scoring aggregates in the Football League, Premier and Scottish League are as follows:

FOR

	Goals	*Games*	*Club*	*Season*
Prem.	82	42	Newcastle	1993-4
Div. 1	128	42	Aston Villa	1930-1
New Div. 1	92	46	Newcastle	1992-3
Div. 2	122	42	Middlesbrough	1926-7
New Div. 2	88	46	W.B.A.	1992-3
	88	46	Plymouth	1993-4
Div. 3(S)	127	42	Millwall	1927-8
Div. 3(N)	128	42	Bradford City	1928-9

Div. 3	111	46	Q.P.R.	1961-2
New Div. 3	80	42	Mansfield Town	1994-5
Div. 4	134	46	Peterborough Utd.	1960-1
Scot. Prem.	101	44	Rangers	1991-2
Scot. L. 1	132	34	Hearts	1957-8
Scot. L. 2	142	34	Raith Rovers	1937-8
Scot. L. 3 (Modern)	69	36	Montrose	1994-5

AGAINST

	Goals	*Games*	*Club*	*Season*
Prem.	100	42	Swindon	1993-4
Div. 1	125	42	Blackpool	1930-1
New Div. 1	87	46	Bristol R.	1992-3
Div. 2	141	34	Darwen	1898-9
New Div. 2	102	46	Chester	1992- 3
Div. 3(S)	135	42	Merthyr T.	1929-30
Div. 3(N)	136	42	Nelson	1927-8
Div. 3	123	46	Accrington S.	1959-60
New Div. 3	84	46	Torquay	1995-6
Div. 4	109	46	Hartlepool	1959-60
Scot. Prem.	100	36	Morton	1984-5
Scot. Prem.	100	44	Morton	1987-8
Scot. L. 1	137	38	Leith A.	1931-2
Scot. L. 2	146	38	Edinburgh C.	1931-2
Scot. L. 3 (Modern)	82	36	Albion Rovers	1994-5

BEST DEFENSIVE RECORDS

*** Denotes under old offside law**

Div.	*Goals Agst.*	*Games*	*Club*	*Season*
Prem.	28	42	Arsenal	1993-4
1	16	42	Liverpool	1978-9
1	*15	22	Preston N.E.	1888-9
New Div. 1	33	46	Sunderland	1995-6
2	18	28	Liverpool	1893-4
2	*22	34	Sheffield W.	1899-1900
2	24	42	Birmingham C.	1947-8
2	24	42	Crystal Palace	1978-9
New Div. 2	34	46	Stoke	1992-3
New Div. 2	34	46	Swindon	1995-6
3(S)	*21	42	Southampton	1921-2
3(S)	30	42	Cardiff City	1946-7
3(N)	*21	38	Stockport C.	1921-2
3(N)	21	46	Port Vale	1953-4
3	30	46	Middlesbrough	1986-7
New Div. 3	20	46	Gillingham	1995-6
4	25	46	Lincoln City	1980-1

SCOTTISH LEAGUE

Div.	*Goals Agst.*	*Games*	*Club*	*Season*
Prem.	19	36	Rangers	1989-90
1	*12	22	Dundee	1902-3
1	*14	38	Celtic	1913-14
2	20	38	Morton	1966-7
2	*29	38	Clydebank	1922-3
2	29	36	East Fife	1995-6
New Div. 3	21	36	Brechin	1995-6

TOP SCORERS (LEAGUE ONLY)

		Goals	Div.
1995-6	Alan Shearer (Blackburn)	31	Prem.
1994-5	Alan Shearer (Blackburn)	34	Prem.
1993-4	Jimmy Quinn (Reading)	35	2
1992-3	Guy Whittingham (Portsmouth)	42	1
1991-2	Ian Wright (C. Palace 5, Arsenal 24)	29	1
1990-1	Teddy Sheringham (Millwall)	33	2
1989-90	Mick Quinn (Newcastle)	32	2
1988-9	Steve Bull (Wolves)	37	3
1987-8	Steve Bull (Wolves)	34	4
1986-7	Clive Allen (Tottenham Hotspur)	33	1
1985-6	Gary Lineker (Everton)	30	1
1984-5	Tommy Tynan (Plymouth)	31	3
	John Clayton (Tranmere)	31	4
1983-4	Trevor Senior (Reading)	36	4
1982-3	Luther Blissett (Watford)	27	1
1981-2	Keith Edwards (Hull 1 and Sheff U 35)	36	4
1980-1	Tony Kellow (Exeter City)	25	3
1979-80	Clive Allen (Queens Park Rangers)	28	2
1978-9	Ross Jenkins (Watford)	29	3
1977-8	Steve Phillips (Brentford)	32	4
	Alan Curtis (Swansea)	32	4
1976-7	Peter Ward (Brighton)	32	3
1975-6	Dixie McNeil (Hereford)	35	3
1974-5	Dixie McNeil (Hereford)	31	3
1973-4	Brian Yeo (Gillingham)	31	4
1972-3	Bryan (Pop) Robson (West Ham United)	28	1
1971-2	Ted MacDougall (Bournemouth)	35	3
1970-1	Ted MacDougall (Bournemouth)	42	4
1969-70	Albert Kinsey (Wrexham)	27	4
1968-9	Jimmy Greaves (Tottenham Hotspur)	27	1
1967-8	George Best (Manchester United)	28	1
	Ron Davies (Southampton)	28	1
1966-7	Ron Davies (Southampton)	37	1
1965-6	Kevin Hector (Bradford P.A.)	44	4
1964-5	Alick Jeffrey (Doncaster Rovers)	36	4
1963-4	Hugh McIlmoyle (Carlisle United)	39	4
1962-3	Jimmy Greaves (Tottenham Hotspur)	37	1
1961-2	Roger Hunt (Liverpool)	41	2
1960-1	Terry Bly (Peterborough United)	52	4

100 LEAGUE GOALS

Northampton Town, with **103** goals as Fourth Division Champions in 1987, were the first club to score a century of League goals for seven years – since 101 in season 1979-80 by Huddersfield Town (Div. 4 Champions). They are the last to do so.

Last League Champions to reach **100** League goals: **Tottenham** (115 in 1960-1). Last century of goals in the top division: **111** by runners-up **Tottenham** in 1962-3.

In **1930-1**, the Championship top three all scored a century of League goals: 1 Arsenal (127), 2 Aston Villa (128), 3 Sheffield Wednesday (102).

100 GOALS AGAINST

Swindon Town, relegated with 100 goals against in 1993-4, were the first top-division club to concede a century of League goals since **Ipswich** (121) went down in 1964. Most goals conceded in the top division: 125 by **Blackpool** in 1930-31, but they avoided relegation.

MOST GOALS IN TOP DIV. ON ONE DAY

This record has stood since December 26, 1963, when **66 goals** were scored in the ten First Division matches played.

MOST F.A. PREMIER LEAGUE GOALS ON ONE DAY

47, in nine matches on May 8, 1993 (last day of season).

FEWEST FIRST DIV. GOALS ON ONE DAY

For full/near full programme: **Ten goals** all by home clubs, in ten matches on April 28, 1923 (day of Wembley's first F.A. Cup Final).

ONE-DAY GOAL FEAST

Most goals scored in the Football League on one day: **209 (44 matches)** on February 1, 1936.

SIX-OUT-OF-SIX HEADERS

When **Oxford United** beat Shrewsbury Town 6-0 (Div. 2) on April 23, 1996, all six goals were headers.

FIVE IN A MATCH

Latest players to score 5 goals in a top-division match: **Tony Woodcock** (for Arsenal in 6-2 win away to Aston Villa) and **Ian Rush** (Liverpool 6, Luton 0), both on October 29, 1983; **Andy Cole** (Man. United 9, Ipswich 0) on March 4, 1995.

ALL–ROUND MARKSMAN

Alan Cork scored in four divisions of the Football League, in the F.A. Premier League and F.A. Premiership in his 18-season career with Wimbledon, Sheff. United, and Fulham (1977-95).

MOST CUP GOALS

F.A. Cup – most goals in one season: 15 by Albert (Sandy) Brown (Tottenham, 1900-1).

Most F.A. Cup goals in individual careers: 48 by Henry Cursham (Notts Co. 1880-87); this century: 42 by Ian Rush (39 for Liverpool, 3 for Chester, 1979-96). Denis Law was the previous highest F.A. Cup scorer this century with 41 goals for Huddersfield, Man. City and Man. United (1957-74).

Most F.A. Cup Final goals by individual: 5 by Ian Rush for Liverpool (2 in 1986, 2 in 1989, 1 in 1992).

HOTTEST CUP HOT-SHOT

Geoff Hurst scored 21 cup goals in season 1965-66: 11 League Cup, 4 F.A. Cup and 2 Cup-Winners' Cup for West Ham, and 4 in the World Cup for England.

SCORERS IN EVERY ROUND

Twelve players have scored in **every round** of the F.A. Cup in one season, from opening to Final inclusive: **Archie Hunter** (Aston Villa, winners 1887); **Albert (Sandy) Brown** (Tottenham, winners 1901); **Harry Hampton** (Aston Villa, winners 1905); **Harold Blackmore** (Bolton, winners 1929); **Ellis Rimmer** (Sheff. Wed., winners 1935); **Frank O'Donnell** (Preston, beaten 1937); **Stan Mortensen**

(Blackpool, beaten 1948); **Jack Milburn** (Newcastle, winners 1951); **Nat Lofthouse** (Bolton, beaten 1953); **Charlie Wayman** (Preston, beaten 1954); **Jeff Astle** (W.B.A., winners 1968); **Peter Osgood** (Chelsea, winners 1970).

Blackmore and the next seven completed their "set" in the Final at Wembley; Osgood did so in the Final replay at Old Trafford.

Only player to score in every **Football League Cup** round possible in one season: **Tony Brown** for W.B.A., winners 1965-6, with 9 goals in 10 games (after bye in Round 1).

TEN IN A ROW

Dixie McNeill scored for Wrexham in **ten successive** F.A. Cup rounds (18 goals): 11 in Rounds 1-6, 1977-8; 3 in Rounds 3-4, 1978-9; 4 in Rounds 3-4, 1979-80.

Stan Mortensen (Blackpool) scored 25 goals in 16 F.A. Cup rounds out of 17 (1946-51).

SIX GOALS IN FA CUP PROPER

George Best remains the last player to score **six goals** in the F.A. Cup proper – when Man. United won 8-2 away to Northampton in the fifth round, on February 7, 1970. Others to achieve this feat: **George Hilsdon** (for Chelsea v. Worksop, 1907-8); **Ronnie Rooke** (for Fulham v. Bury, 1938-9); and **Harold Atkinson** (for Tranmere v. Ashington, 1952-3).

Denis Law scored all **six** for Manchester City at Luton (6-2) in an F.A. Cup 4th Round tie on January 28, 1961, but none of them counted – the match was abandoned because of a waterlogged pitch.

Tony Philliskirk scored **five** when Peterborough Utd. beat Kingstonian 9-1 in an F.A. Cup 1st Round replay on November 25, 1992, but had them wiped from the records. With the score at 3-0, the Kingstonian goalkeeper was concussed by a coin thrown from the crowd and unable to play on. The F.A. ordered the match to be replayed at Peterborough behind closed doors, and Kingstonian lost 1-0.

QUICKEST GOALS AND RAPID SCORING

Six seconds after kick-off by **Albert Mundy** for Aldershot v. Hartlepool, October 25, 1958; **Barrie Jones** for Newport County v. Torquay United, March 31, 1962; **Keith Smith** for Crystal Palace v. Derby County, December 12, 1964.

9.6 seconds by **John Hewitt** for Aberdeen at Motherwell, 3rd Round, January 23, 1982 (fastest goal in Scottish Cup history).

A goal in **4 seconds** was claimed by **Jim Fryatt,** for Bradford P.A. v. Tranmere (Div. 4, April 25, 1965), and by **Gerry Allen** for Whitstable Town v. Danson (Kent League, March 3,1989). Backed by filmed evidence, **Damian Mori** scored in 4 seconds for Adelaide City v Sydney United (Australian National League, December 6, 1995).

Colin Cowperthwaite reputedly scored in **3½ seconds** for Barrow v. Kettering (Alliance Premier League) on December 8, 1979, but the timing was unofficial.

Phil Starbuck scored for Huddersfield only **3 seconds** after entering the field as 54th min. substitute at home to Wigan (Div. 2) on Easter Monday, April 12, 1993. A corner-kick was delayed, awaiting his arrival, and he scored with a header.

Malcolm Macdonald scored after **5 seconds** (officially timed) in Newcastle United's 7-3 win in a pre-season friendly at St. Johnstone on July 29, 1972. From the kick-off, the ball was passed to him, and Macdonald, spotting the goalkeeper off his line, promptly smashed a shot over him and into the net.

Scored first kick: Billy Foulkes (Newcastle United) for Wales v. England at Cardiff, October 20, 1951, in his first International match.

Six goals in seven minutes in Preston's record 26-0 F.A. Cup 1st Round win v. Hyde, October 15, 1887.

Five in 20 minutes: Frank Keetley in Lincoln's 9-1 win over Halifax in Div. III (North), January 16, 1932; **Brian Dear** for West Ham United v. West Bromwich Albion (6-1, Div.1) April 16, 1965.

Four in five minutes: by **John McIntyre** for Blackburn Rovers v. Everton (Div. 1), September 16, 1922; **W.G. Richardson** for West Bromwich Albion v. West Ham United (Div. 1), November 7, 1931.

Three in three minutes: Billy Lane for Watford v. Clapton Orient (Div.3S), December 20, 1933; **Johnny Hartburn** for Leyton Orient v Shrewsbury (Div. 3S), January 22, 1955; **Gary Roberts** for Brentford v. Newport, (Freight Rover Trophy, South Final), May 17, 1985; **Gary Shaw** for Shrewsbury v Bradford City (Div. 3), December 22, 1990.

Three in two minutes: Jimmy Scarth for Gillingham v. Leyton Orient (Div. 3S), November 1, 1952.

Arsenal scored six goals in 18 minutes (71-89 mins.) in 7-1 home win v. Sheffield Wednesday, February 15, 1992.

Sunderland scored eight goals in 28 minutes at Newcastle (9-1 Div 1), December 5, 1908.

Southend United scored all seven goals in 29 minutes in 7-0 win at home to Torquay (Leyland Daf Cup, Southern quarter-final), February 26, 1991. Score was 0-0 until 55th. minute.

Six goals in first 19 minutes by Tranmere when they beat Oldham 13-4 (Div. 3 North) on December 26, 1935.

Notts County scored six second-half goals in 12 minutes (Tommy Lawton 3, Jackie Sewell 3) when they beat Exeter 9-0 (Div. 3 South) at Meadow Lane on October 16, 1948.

Fastest International goal: 8.3 secs. by **Davide Gualtieri** for San Marino v England (World Cup qual., Bologna, November 17, 1993).

Fastest International hat-trick: 3½ minutes by **Willie Hall** for England v. N. Ireland at Old Trafford, Manchester, November 16, 1938. (Hall scored 5 in England's 7-0 win).

Fastest International goal by substitute: 5 seconds by Arsenal's **John Jensen** for Denmark v Belgium (Eur. Champ.), October 12, 1994.

Fastest England goals: 27 seconds by **Bryan Robson** v. France in World Cup at Bilbao, Spain on June 16, 1982; at Wembley: 38 seconds by **Bryan Robson** v Yugoslavia, December 13, 1989; 42 seconds by **Gary Lineker** v Malaysia in Kuala Lumpur, June 12, 1991.

Fastest F.A. Cup Final goals: 30 seconds by **John Devey**, for Aston Villa v W.B.A., 1895; at Wembley: 45 seconds by **Jack Milburn**, for Newcastle v. Manchester City, 1955.

Fastest F.A. Cup hat-tricks: In 3 minutes by **Billy Best** for Southend v Brentford (2nd. Round, December 7, 1968); 2 minutes 20 seconds by **Andy Locke** for Nantwich v Droylesden (1st. Qual. Round, September 9, 1995).

F.A. Premier League – fastest scoring: Four goals in 4 minutes, 44 seconds by Tottenham at home to Southampton on Sunday, February 7, 1993.

Fastest First Division hat-tricks since war: Graham Leggat, 3 goals in 3 minutes (first half) when Fulham beat Ipswich 10-1 on Boxing Day, 1963; **Nigel Clough,** 3 goals in 4 minutes (81, 82, 85 pen) when Nott'm Forest beat Q.P.R. 4-0 on Sunday, December 13, 1987.

F.A. Premier League – fastest hat-trick: 4½ minutes (26, 29, 31) by **Robbie Fowler** in Liverpool 3, Arsenal 0 on Sunday, August 28, 1994.

Fastest Premier League goals: 13 seconds by **Chris Sutton** for Blackburn at Everton, April 1, 1995; 13 seconds by **Dwight Yorke** for Aston Villa at Coventry, September 30, 1995.

Fastest Premier League goal by substitute: 13 seconds by Jamie Cureton for Norwich v Chelsea, December 10, 1994.

Fastest Scottish hat-trick: 2½ mins. by **Ian St. John** for Motherwell away to Hibernian (Scottish League Cup), August 15, 1959.

Fastest all-time hat-trick: Reported at 1 min. 50 secs. by **Maglioni** for Independiente against Gimnasia de la Plata in Argentina, March 18, 1973.

Fastest own goals: 8 seconds by Pat Kruse of Torquay, for Cambridge United (Div. 4), January 3, 1977; in **First Division**, 16 seconds by Steve Bould (Arsenal) away to Sheff. Wed., February 17, 1990.

FASTEST GOALS IN WORLD CUP FINAL SERIES

15 secs. by **Vaclav Masek** for Czechoslovakia v Mexico (in Chile, 1962).

27 secs. by **Bryan Robson** for England v France (in Bilbao, Spain, 1982).

TOP MATCH SCORES SINCE WAR

By English clubs: **13-0** by Newcastle v Newport (Div. 2, Oct. 1946); **13-2** by Tottenham v Crewe (F.A. Cup 4th. Rd. replay, Feb. 1960); **13-0** by Chelsea v Jeunesse Hautcharage, Lux. (Cup-Winners' Cup 1st. Rd., 2nd. Leg, Sept. 1971).

By Scottish club: **20-0** by Stirling Albion v Selkirk (E. of Scotland League) in Scottish Cup 1st. Rd. (Dec. 1984). That is the highest score in British first-class football this century, since Preston beat Hyde 26-0 in F.A. Cup, Oct. 1887.

GOALS BY WINGERS

	Season	Matches	Goals
Football League	(Div. I)		
Cliff Bastin (Arsenal)	1932-3	42	33
Scottish League	(Div. I)		
Bob Ferrier (Motherwell)	1929-30	27	32
Scottish League	(Div. II)		
Ken Dawson (Falkirk)	1935-6	34	39

GOALS BY GOALKEEPERS

Goalkeepers who have scored with long clearances include:

Pat Jennings for Tottenham away to Man. United (goalkeeper Alex Stepney) in the F.A. Charity Shield on August 12, 1967.

Peter Shilton for Leicester at Southampton (goalkeeper Campbell Forsyth) on October 14, 1967 (Div. 1).

Ray Cashley for Bristol City at home to Hull (goalkeeper Jeff Wealands) on September 18, 1973 (Div. 2).

Steve Sherwood for Watford away to Coventry (goalkeeper Raddy Avramovic) on January 14, 1984 (Div. 1).

Steve Ogrizovic for Coventry away to Sheff. Wednesday (goalkeeper Martin Hodge) on October 25, 1986 (Div. 1).

Andy Goram for Hibernian at home to Morton (goalkeeper David Wylie) on May 7, 1988 (Scottish Premier Div.).

Andy McLean, on Irish League debut, for Cliftonville v. Linfield (goalkeeper George Dunlop) on August 20, 1988.

Alan Paterson for Glentoran against Linfield (goalkeeper George Dunlop) on November 30, 1989 (Roadferry Cup Final at The Oval, Belfast).

Ray Charles for East Fife at Stranraer (goalkeeper Bernard Duffy) on February 28, 1990 (Scottish Div. 2).

Iain Hesford scored Maidstone's winner (3-2 v Hereford, Div. 4, November 2, 1991) with long kick-out that went first bounce past Tony Elliott in opposite goal.

Chris Mackenzie for Hereford at home to Barnet (goalkeeper Mark Taylor) in Div. 3, August 12, 1995.

Most goals by a goalkeeper in a League season: 5 (all penalties) by **Arthur**

Birch for Chesterfield (Div. 3 North), 1923-4.

Arthur Wilkie, Reading's goalkeeper at home to Halifax (Div. 3) on August 31, 1962, injured a hand, then played as a forward and scored twice in a 4-2 win.

Alan Fettis, N. Ireland goalkeeper, scored twice for Hull in Div. 2 in season 1994-5: as a substitute in 3-1 home win v Oxford (Dec. 17) and, when selected outfield, with last-minute winner (2-1) at Blackpool on May 6.

Peter Schmeichel, Man. United's goalkeeper, headed an 89th minute equaliser (2-2) from Ryan Giggs' corner in the UEFA Cup 1st. Round, 2nd leg against Rotor Volgograd (Russia) on September 26, 1995, but United lost the tie on away goals.

In League matches for Swansea City, **Roger Freestone** scored with a penalty at Oxford (Div. 2, April 30, 1995) and, in 1995-6 (Div. 2) with penalties at home to Shrewsbury (August 12) and Chesterfield (August 26).

MOST SCORERS IN MATCH

Liverpool set a Football League record with **EIGHT** scorers when they beat Crystal Palace 9-0 (Div.1) on September 12, 1989. Their marksmen were: Steve Nicol (7 and 88 mins), Steve McMahon (16), Ian Rush (45), Gary Gillespie (56), Peter Beardsley (61), John Aldridge pen. (67), John Barnes (79) and Glenn Hysen (82).

Fifteen years earlier, **Liverpool** went one better with **NINE** different scorers when they achieved their record win, 11-0 at home to Stromsgodset (Norway) in the Cup-Winners' Cup 1st. round, 1st leg on September 17, 1974.

Eight players scored for **Swansea City** when they beat Sliema, Malta, 12-0 in the Cup-Winners' Cup 1st round, 1st leg on September 15, 1982.

Nine **Stirling Albion** players scored in the 20-0 win against Selkirk in the Scottish Cup 1st. Round on December 8, 1984.

LONG SCORING RUNS

The record in England is held by **Bill Prendergast**, who scored on 13 consecutive appearances for Chester (Div. 3, Sept-Dec., 1938).

Dixie Dean scored in 12 consecutive games (23 goals) for Everton in Div. 2 in 1930-1.

Danish striker **Finn Dossing** scored in 15 consecutive matches (Scottish record) for Dundee United (Div. 1) in 1964-5.

In modern times, **John Aldridge** (Liverpool) scored in 10 successive First Division matches – the last game of season 1986-7 and the first nine in 1987-8.

Kevin Russell (Wrexham) scored in nine consecutive matches in Div. 4, March-May, 1988.

In the F.A. Premier League, **Mark Stein** scored in seven successive matches for Chelsea (Dec. 28, 1993-Feb. 5, 1994).

Ian Wright scored on 12 successive first-team appearances, including 7 Premiership, for Arsenal (Sept. 15-Nov. 23, 1994).

50-GOAL PLAYERS

With **52** goals for **Wolves** in 1987-8 (34 League, 12 Sherpa Van Trophy, 3 Littlewoods Cup, 3 F.A. Cup), **Steve Bull** became the first player to score 50 in a season for a League club since Terry Bly for 4th Division newcomers Peterborough United in 1960-1. Bly's 54 comprised 52 League goals and 2 in the F.A. Cup, and included 7 hat-tricks, still a post-war League record.

Bull was again the country's top scorer with 50 goals in season 1988-9: 37 League, 2 Littlewoods Cup and 11 Sherpa Van Trophy.

Between Bly and Bull, the highest individual scoring total for a season was 49 by two players: Ted MacDougall (Bournemouth 1970-1, 42 League, 7 F.A. Cup) and Clive Allen (Tottenham 1986-7, 33 League, 12 Littlewoods Cup, 4 F.A. Cup).

HOT SHOTS

Jimmy Greaves was First Division top scorer (League goals) six times in 11 seasons: 32 for Chelsea (1958-9), 41 for Chelsea (1960-1) and, for Tottenham, 37 in 1962-3, 35 in 1963-4, 29 in 1964-5 (joint top) and 27 in 1968-9.

Brian Clough (Middlesbrough) was the Second Division's leading scorer in three successive seasons: 40 goals in 1957-8, 42 in 1958-9 and 39 in 1959-60.

John Hickton (Middlesbrough) was top Div. 2 scorer three times in four seasons: 24 goals in 1967-8, 24 in 1969-70 and 25 in 1970-1.

MOST HAT-TRICKS

Nine by **George Camsell** (Middlesbrough) in Div. 2, 1926-7, is the record for one season. Most League hat-tricks in career: 37 by **Dixie Dean** for Tranmere and Everton (1924-38).

Most **top division** hat-tricks in a season since last war: 6 by **Jimmy Greaves** for Chelsea (1960-1). **Alan Shearer** scored 5 for Blackburn in the Premier League, season 1995-96.

Frank Osborne (Tottenham) scored three consecutive hat-tricks in Div. 1 in October-November 1925, against Liverpool (home), Leicester (away) and West Ham (home).

Tom Jennings (Leeds) scored hat-tricks in three successive First Div. matches (Sept-Oct, 1926): 3 goals v Arsenal, 4 at Liverpool, 4 v Blackburn.

Jack Balmer (Liverpool) scored hat-tricks in three successive First Div. matches (Nov. 1946): 3 goals v Portsmouth, 4 at Derby, 3 v Arsenal.

Gilbert Alsop scored hat-tricks in three successive matches for Walsall in Div. 3 South in April 1939: 3 goals at Swindon, 3 v Bristol City (home) and 4 v Swindon (home).

TRIPLE HAT-TRICKS

There have been three instances of **3 hat-tricks being scored** for **one team** in a Football League match:-

April 21, 1909: Enoch West, Billy Hooper and Arthur Spouncer scored 3 apiece for Nott'm. Forest (12-0 v Leicester Fosse, Div. 1).

March 3, 1962: Ron Barnes, Wyn Davies and Roy Ambler registered hat-tricks in Wrexham's 10-1 win against Hartlepool (Div. 4).

November 7, 1987: Tony Adcock, Paul Stewart and David White each scored 3 goals for Man. City in 10-1 win at home to Huddersfield (Div. 2).

For the first time in the Premiership, **three hat-tricks** were completed **on one day** (September 23, 1995): Tony Yeboah for Leeds at Wimbledon; Alan Shearer for Blackburn v Coventry; and Robbie Fowler with 4 goals for Liverpool v Bolton.

HAT-TRICKS v THREE 'KEEPERS

When West Ham beat Newcastle 8-1 (Div.1) at home on April 21, 1986 **Alvin Martin** scored 3 goals against different 'keepers: Martin Thomas injured a shoulder and was replaced, in turn, by outfield players Chris Hedworth and Peter Beardsley.

In 1948 **Jock Dodds** of Lincoln had done the same **against** West Ham, scoring past **Gregory**, **Moroney** and **Dick**. The Hammers lost 3-4.

On Oct. 16, 1993 (Div.3) **Chris Pike** (Hereford) scored a hat-trick against different goalkeepers. Opponents Colchester, beaten 5-0, had two 'keepers sent off for professional fouls.

TON UP – BOTH ENDS

Manchester City are the only club to **score and concede** a century of League goals in the same season. When fifth in the 1957-8 Championship, they scored 104 goals and gave away 100.

HALF AN OWN GOAL EACH

Chelsea's second goal in a 3-1 home win against Leicester City on December 18, 1954 was uniquely recorded as "shared own goal". Leicester defenders **Stan Milburn** and **Jack Froggatt**, both lunging at the ball in an attempt to clear, connected simultaneously and sent it rocketing into the net.

THE DAY IT RAINED GOALS

Saturday, February 1, 1936 has a permanent place in the Football League records, because on that afternoon the **44** matches played in the four divisions produced **209** goals – the most that have ever been scored on one day.
They piled up like this: 46 in Div.1; 46 in Div.2; 68 in Div.3 North; 49 in Div.3 South. Two matches in the Northern Section provided no fewer than 23 goals – Chester 12, York City 0, and Crewe Alexandra 5, Chesterfield 6.
There was only one 0-0 result (Aldershot v Bristol City, Div. 3 South).
• The previous record was set four years earlier on January 2, 1932, when 205 goals were scored in 43 League matches: 56 in Div.1, 49 in Div.2, 57 in Div.3 South and 43 in Div.3 North.

TOURNAMENT TOP SHOTS

Most individual goals in a World Cup Final series: 13 by **Just Fontaine** for France, in Sweden, 1958.

Most in European Championship Finals: 9 by **Michel Platini** for France, in France 1984.

MOST GOALS ON CLUB DEBUT

Jim Dyet scored **eight** goals for King's Park against Forfar Athletic (Jan. 2, 1930).

Len Shackleton scored **six** times in Newcastle United's 13-0 win v. Newport County (Div. 2, Oct. 5, 1946) in the week he joined them from Bradford Park Avenue.

MOST GOALS ON LEAGUE DEBUT

Five by **George Hilsdon**, for Chelsea (9-2) v Glossop, Div. 2 Sept. 1, 1906.

Alan Shearer, with three goals for Southampton (4-2) v Arsenal, April 9, 1988, became, at 17, the youngest player to score a First Division hat-trick on his full debut.

CLEAN-SHEET RECORDS

On the way to promotion from Div. 3 last season, **Gillingham's** ever-present goalkeeper **Jim Stannard** set a new clean-sheet record. In 46 matches, he achieved 29 shut-outs (17 at home, 12 away), beating the 28 by Ray Clemence for Liverpool (42 matches in Div. 1, 1978-9) and the previous best in a 46-match programme of 28 by Port Vale (Div. 3 North, 1953-4). In conceding only 20 League goals in 1995-6, Gillingham created a defensive record for the lower divisions.

Chris Woods, Rangers' England goalkeeper, set a British record in season

1986-7 by going 1,196 minutes without conceding a goal. The sequence began in the UEFA Cup match against Borussia Moenchengladbach on Nov. 26, 1986 and ended when Rangers were sensationally beaten 1-0 at home by Hamilton in the Scottish Cup 3rd. Round on Jan. 31, 1987 with a 70th.-minute goal by Adrian Sprott.

The previous British record of 1,156 minutes without a goal conceded was held by Aberdeen goalkeeper **Bobby Clark** (season 1970-1).

There have been three instances of clubs keeping 11 consecutive clean sheets in the Football League: Coventry City (Div. 2, 1919-20), Millwall (Div. 3 South, 1925-6) and Reading (Div. 4, 1978-9). In that sequence, Reading goalkeeper Steve Death set the existing Football League shut-out record of 1,103 minutes.

Mark Leonard (Chesterfield) kept a clean sheet in 8 consecutive Div.3 away games (Jan-April 1994). Believed an away-match record in British football.

Sebastiano Rossi kept a clean sheet in 8 successive away matches for AC Milan (Nov. 1993-Apr. 1994).

A world record of 1,275 minutes without conceding a goal was set in 1990-1 by **Abel Resino**, the Atletico Madrid goalkeeper. He was finally beaten by Sporting Gijon's Enrique in Atletico's 3-1 win on March 19, 1991.

In International football, the record is held by **Dino Zoff** with a shut-out for Italy (Sept. 1972 to June 1974) lasting 1,142 minutes.

LOW SCORING

Fewest goals by any club in season in Football League: **24** by **Stoke City** (Div. 1, 42 matches, 1984-5); **24** by **Watford** (Div. 2, 42 matches, 1971-2). In 46-match programme, **27** by **Stockport County** (Div. 3, 1969-70).

Arsenal were the lowest Premier League scorers in its opening season (1992-3) with 40 goals in 42 matches, but won both domestic cup competitions. **Ipswich** were the lowest Premiership scorers (35) in 1993-4, **Crystal Palace** lowered that figure to 34 in 1994-5, and **Man. City** set the Premiership's fewest-goals record with only 33 when relegated last season.

LONG TIME NO SCORE

Longest non-scoring sequences in Football League: 11 matches by **Coventry City** in 1919-20 (Div. 2); 11 matches by **Hartlepool United** in 1992-3 (Div. 2). After beating Crystal Palace 1-0 in the F.A. Cup 3rd round on Jan. 2, they went 13 games and 2 months without scoring (11 League, 1 F.A. Cup, 1 Autoglass Trophy). The sequence ended after 1,227 blank minutes with a 1-1 draw at Blackpool (League) on March 6.

In the **Premier League** (Oct.-Jan. season 1994-5) Crystal Palace failed to score in nine consecutive matches.

The British non-scoring record is held by Scottish club **Stirling Albion**: 14 consecutive matches (13 League, 1 Scottish Cup) and 1,292 minutes play, from Jan. 31, 1981 until Aug. 8, 1981 (when they lost 4-1 to Falkirk in the League Cup).

In season 1971-2, **Mansfield Town** did not score in any of their first nine home games in Div. 3.

F.A. CUP CLEAN SHEETS

Most consecutive F.A. Cup matches without conceding a goal: 12 by **Bradford City**. The sequence spanned 8 rounds, from 3rd. in 1910-11 to 4th. Round 3rd. replay in 1911-12, and included winning the Cup in 1911.

ATTENDANCES

GREATEST WORLD CROWDS

World Cup, Maracana Stadium, Rio de Janeiro, July 16, 1950. Final match (Brazil v. Uruguay) attendance 199,850; receipts £125,000.

Total attendance in three matches (including play-off) between Santos (Brazil) and AC Milan for the Inter-Continental Cup (World Club Championship) 1963, exceeded 375,000.

BRITISH RECORD CROWDS

Most to pay: 149,547, Scotland v. England, at Hampden Park, Glasgow, April 17, 1937. This was the first all-ticket match in Scotland (receipts £24,000).

At Scottish F.A. Cup Final: 146,433, Celtic v. Aberdeen, at Hampden Park, April 24, 1937. Estimated another 20,000 shut out.

For British club match (apart from a Cup Final): 143,470, Rangers v. Hibernian, at Hampden Park, March 27, 1948.

F.A. Cup Final: 126,047, Bolton Wanderers v. West Ham United, at Wembley, April 28, 1923. Estimated 150,000 in stadium.

World Cup Qualifying Ties: 120,000, Cameroon v. Morocco, Yaounde, November 29, 1981; 107,580, Scotland v. Poland, Hampden Park, October 13, 1965.

European Cup: 135,826, Celtic v. Leeds United (semi-final) at Hampden Park, Glasgow, April 15, 1970.

European Cup Final: 127,621, Real Madrid v. Eintracht Frankfurt, at Hampden Park, Glasgow, May 18, 1960.

European Cup-Winners' Cup Final: 100,000, West Ham v. TSV Munich, at Wembley, May 19, 1965.

Scottish League: 118,567, Rangers v. Celtic, January 2, 1939.

Scottish League Cup Final: 107,609, Celtic v. Rangers, at Hampden Park, October 23, 1965.

English League – Premier League: 53,926, Man. United v Nott'm. F, Sunday, April 28, 1996; **First Div.:** 83,260, Manchester United v. Arsenal, January 17, 1948 (at Maine Road); **Second Div.:** 68,029, Aston Villa v. Coventry City, October 30, 1937; **Third Div. South:** 51,621, Cardiff City v. Bristol City, April 7, 1947; **Third Div. North:** 49,655, Hull City v. Rotherham United, December 25, 1948; **Third Div.:** 49,309, Sheff. Wed. v. Sheff. United, December 26, 1979; **Fourth Div.:** 37,774, Crystal Palace v. Millwall, March 31, 1961.

In English Provinces: 84,569, Manchester City v. Stoke City (F.A. Cup 6th Round), March 3, 1934.

Record for Under-21 International: 25,863, England v. Rep. of Ireland at Newcastle, November 15, 1994.

Record for friendly match: 104,679, Rangers v. Eintract Frankfurt, at Hampden Park, Glasgow, October 17, 1961.

Record Football League aggregate (season): 41,271,414 (1948-9) – 88 clubs.

Record Football League aggregate (single day): 1,269,934, December 27, 1949.

Record average home League attendance for season: 57,758 by Man. United in 1967-8.

Long-ago League attendance aggregates: 10,929,000 in 1906-07 (40 clubs); 28,132,933 in 1937-8 (88 clubs).

Last 1m. crowd aggregate, League: 1,007,200, December 27, 1971.

Record Amateur match attendance: 100,000 for F.A. Amateur Cup Final, Pegasus v. Harwich & Parkeston at Wembley, April 11, 1953.

Record Cup-tie aggregate: 265,199, at two matches between Rangers and Morton, in the Scottish Cup Final, 1947-8.

Abandoned match attendance records: In **England** – 63,480 at Newcastle v. Swansea F.A. Cup 3rd round, Jan. 10, 1953, abandoned 8 mins (0-0), fog.

In Scotland: 94,596 at Scotland v. Austria (4-1), Hampden Pak, May 8, 1963.

Referee Jim Finney ended play (79 minutes) after Austria had two players sent off and one carried off.

What is still **Colchester United's** record crowd (19,072) was for the F.A. Cup 1st round tie v. Reading on Nov. 27, 1948, abandoned 35 minutes (0-0), fog.

SMALLEST CROWDS

Lowest post-war League attendance: 450 Rochdale v. Cambridge United (Div. 3, February 2, 1974).

Lowest First Division crowds since the war: 3,121 for Wimbledon v. Sheff. W., Oct. 2, 1991; 3,231 for Wimbledon v. Luton, Sept. 7, 1991; 3,270 for Wimbledon v. Coventry, Dec. 28, 1991; 3,496 for Wimbledon v. Luton, Feb. 14, 1990.

Lowest top-division crowd at a major ground since the war: 4,554 for Arsenal v Leeds United (May 5, 1966) – fixture clashed with live TV coverage of Cup-Winners' Cup Final (Liverpool v Borussia Dortmund).

Lowest Saturday post-war top-division crowd: 3,231 for Wimbledon v. Luton, Sept. 7, 1991 (Div. 1).

Lowest F.A. Premier League crowds: 3,039 for Wimbledon v Everton, Jan. 26, 1993 (smallest top-division attendance since war); 3,386 Wimbledon v Oldham, Dec. 12, 1992.

Smallest League Cup attendance at top-division ground: 1,987 for Wimbledon v Bolton (2nd Round, 2nd Leg) Oct. 6, 1992.

Smallest Wembley crowds for England matches: 15,628 v Chile (Rous Cup, May 23, 1989 – affected by Tube strike); 20,038 v Colombia (Friendly, Sept. 6, 1995); 21,432 v Czech. (Friendly, Apr. 25, 1990); 21,142 v. Japan (Umbro Cup, June 3, 1995); 23,600 v. Wales (British Championship, Feb. 23, 1983); 23,659 v Greece (Friendly, May 17, 1994); 23,951 v. East Germany (Friendly, Sept. 12, 1984); 24,000 v. N. Ireland (British Championship, Apr. 4, 1984); 25,756 v. Colombia (Rous Cup, May 24, 1988); 25,837 v Denmark (Friendly, Sept. 14, 1988).

Other smallest Int. crowds – N.Ireland: 2,500 v Chile (Belfast, May 26, 1989 – clashed with ITV live screening of Liverpool v Arsenal Championship decider); **Scotland:** 7,843 v N.Ireland (Hampden Park, May 6, 1969); **Wales:** 2,315 v N.Ireland (Wrexham, May 27, 1982).

Smallest attendance for any England match: 2,378 v San Marino (World Cup) at Bologna (Nov. 17, 1993). Tie clashed with Italy v Portugal (World Cup) shown live on Italian TV.

F.A. CUP CROWD RECORD (OUTSIDE FINAL)

The first F.A. Cup-tie shown on closed-circuit TV (5th. Round, Saturday, March 11, 1967, kick-off 7pm) drew a total of 105,000 spectators to Goodison Park and Anfield.

This is the biggest attendance for a single F.A. Cup match other than the Final. At Goodison, 64,851 watched the match "for real", while 40,149 saw the TV version on eight giant screens at Anfield. Everton beat Liverpool 1-0.

LOWEST SEMI-FINAL CROWD

The smallest F.A. Cup semi-final attendance since the war was 17,987 for Man. United v. Crystal Palace replay, at Villa Park on April 12, 1995. Palace supporters largely boycotted tie after a fan died in car-park clash outside pub in Walsall before first match. Previous lowest: 25,963 for Wimbledon v Luton, at Tottenham on April 9, 1988.

Lowest quarter-final crowd since the war: 10,084 for Cambridge United v Crystal Palace on March 10, 1990.

Smallest F.A. Cup 3rd. Round attendances, for matches between League clubs: 1,833 for Chester v Bournemouth (at Macclesfield) Jan. 5, 1991; 1,966 for Aldershot v Oxford Utd., Jan. 10, 1987.

PRE-WEMBLEY CUP FINAL CROWDS

At Crystal Palace

1895	42,560	1902	48,036	1908	74,967
1896	48,036	Replay	33,050	1909	67,651
1897	65,891	1903	64,000	1910	76,980
1898	62,017	1904	61,734	1911	69,098
1899	73,833	1905	101,117	1912	54,434
1900	68,945	1906	75,609	1913	120,028
1901	110,802	1907	84,584	1914	72,778

At Old Trafford

1915 50,000

At Stamford Bridge

1920	50,018	1921	72,805	1922	53,000

RECEIPTS RECORDS

Wembley Stadium underwent its first considerable alteration during 1962-3 in preparation for the World Cup in 1966. Higher admission fees at the 1963 F.A. Cup Final resulted in 100,000 spectators paying a record £89,000.

This is how Wembley's receipts record have risen since then:–

1968	F.A. Cup Final (Everton v W.B.A.)	£110,000
1968	Europan Cup Final (Man. United v Benfica)	£120,000
1976	F.A. Cup Final (Southampton v Man. United)	£420,000
1978	F.A. Cup Final (Ipswich v Arsenal)	£500,000
1981	England v Hungary (World Cup)	£671,000
1982	F.A. Cup Final (Tottenham v Q.P.R.) (plus £605,000 for replay)	£886,000
1984	F.A. Cup Final (Everton v Watford)	£919,000
*1985	F.A. Cup Final (Man. United v Everton)	£1,100,000
1986	F.A. Cup Final (Liverpool v Everton)	£1,100,000
†1987	League Cup Final (Arsenal v Liverpool)	£1,000,000
1987	F.A. Cup Final (Coventry v Tottenham)	£1,286,737
1988	F.A. Cup Final (Wimbledon v Liverpool)	£1,422,814
1989	F.A. Cup Final (Liverpool v Everton)	£1,600,000
1990	League Cup Final (Nott'm Forest v Oldham)	£1,650,000
1990	F.A. Cup Final (Man. United v Crystal P. – first match)	£2,000,000
1991	League Cup Final (Man. United v Sheff. Wed.)	£2,000,000
1991	F.A. Cup Final (Nott'm F. v Tottenham)	£2,016,000
1992	F.A. Cup Final (Liverpool v Sunderland)	£2,548,174
1993	F.A. Cup Final (Arsenal v Sheff. W. – first match) (Replay took receipts for both matches to £4,695,200)	£2,818,000
1994	F.A. Cup Final record (Man. United v Chelsea)	£2,962,167
1995	League Cup Final record (Liverpool v Bolton)	£2,600,000

(* Britain's first £1m. gate; †First £1m. gate for League Cup Final)

Record England match receipts: £1,500,000 (v. Brazil, Wembley, Sunday, May 17, 1992 – att: 53,428)

Record Friendly International receipts: £1,392,515 for England v Denmark at Wembley, March 9, 1994 (att: 71,970).

Euro 96 Wembley match receipts not available before going to press.

EARLY CUP FINAL RECEIPTS

1885	(Blackburn Rovers v Queens Park)	£442
1913	(Aston Villa v Sunderland)	£9,406
1923	(Bolton v West Ham, first Wembley Final)	£27,776
1939	(Portsmouth v Wolves)	£29,000
1946	(Derby v Charlton)	£45,000

WORLD RECORD MATCH RECEIPTS

£4,300,000 for **World Cup Final**, Argentina v West Germany (Rome, July 8, 1990).

BRITISH RECORD RECEIPTS

£2,962,167 at the **1994 F.A. Cup Final**, Man. United v Chelsea.

INTERNATIONAL RECORDS

MOST APPEARANCES

Peter Shilton, England goalkeeper, then aged 40, retired from International football after the 1990 World Cup Finals with the then world record number of caps – 125. Previous record (119) was set by **Pat Jennings**, Northern Ireland's goalkeeper from 1964-86, who retired at 41 at the end of the 1986 World Cup in Mexico. Shilton's England career spanned 20 seasons from his debut against East Germany at Wembley on Nov. 25, 1970.

Four players have completed a century of appearances in full International matches for England. **Billy Wright** of Wolves, was the first, retiring in 1959 with a total of 105 caps.

Bobby Charlton, of Manchester United, beat Wright's record in the World Cup match against West Germany in Leon, Mexico, in June 1970 and **Bobby Moore,** of West Ham, overtook Charlton's 106 caps against Italy in Turin, in June 1973. Moore played 108 times for England, a record that stood until **Peter Shilton** reached 109 against Denmark in Copenhagen (June 7, 1989).

Kenny Dalglish became Scotland's first 100-cap International v. Romania (Hampden Park, March 26, 1986).

BRITAIN'S MOST-CAPPED PLAYERS

(As at start of season 1996-97)

England	
Peter Shilton	125
Bobby Moore	108
Bobby Charlton	106
Billy Wright	105
Scotland	
Kenny Dalglish	102
Alex McLeish	77
Jim Leighton	74
Paul McStay	73
Wales	
Neville Southall	86
Peter Nicholas	73
Ian Rush	73
Joey Jones	72

N. Ireland

Pat Jennings	119
Mal Donaghy	91
Sammy McIlroy	88

Republic of Ireland

Paul McGrath	82
Pat Bonner	80
Liam Brady	72
Frank Stapleton	71

MOST CAPS IN ROW

Most consecutive International appearances: 70 by **Billy Wright**, for England from October 1951 to May 1959. He played 105 of England's first 108 post-war matches. **England captains most times: Billy Wright** and **Bobby Moore**, 90 each.

WORLD'S MOST-CAPPED PLAYERS

147 – Majid Abdullah (Saudi Arabia); 127 Thomas Ravelli (Sweden); 125 – Peter Shilton (England); 122 – Lothar Matthaus (Germany); 119 – Pat Jennings (N. Ireland); 117 – Heinz Hermann (Switzerland); 115 – Bjorn Nordqvist (Sweden); 112 – Dino Zoff (Italy); 111 — Hector Chumpitaz (Peru); 111 – Alain Geiger (Switzerland); 110 – Pele (Brazil); 110 – Andoni Zubizaretta (Spain); 109 – Oleg Blokhin (USSR); 108 – Bobby Moore (England); 108 – Ladislau Boloni (Romania); 108 – Park Kyung Hoon (S. Korea); 106 – Bobby Charlton (England); 105 – Billy Wright (England); 105 – Gregorz Lato (Poland); 104 – Thorbjorn Svenssen (Norway); 103 – Franz Beckenbauer (W. Germany); 102 – Kenny Dalglish (Scotland); 102 – Kazimierz Deyna (Poland); 102 – Joachim Streich (E. Germany); 102 Morten Olsen (Denmark); 102 – Soon-Ho Choi (S. Korea); 100 – Jozsef Bozsik (Hungary); 100 – Djalma Santos (Brazil); 100 – Hans-Juergen Doerner (E. Germany); 100 – Gheorghe Hagi (Romania).

ENGLAND'S WORLD CUP-WINNERS

At Wembley, July 30, 1966, 4-2 v West Germany (2-2 after 90 mins), scorers Hurst 3, Peters. Team: Banks; Cohen, Wilson, Stiles, Charlton (J.), Moore (Captain), Ball, Hurst, Charlton (R.), Hunt, Peters. Manager **Alf Ramsey** fielded that same eleven in six successive matches (an England record): the World Cup quarter-final, semi-final and Final, and the first three games of the following season. England wore red shirts in the Final and Her Majesty the Queen presented the Cup to Bobby Moore. The players each received a £1,000 bonus, less tax. The match was shown live on TV (in black and white).

BIGGEST WORLD CUP WINS

(Source: *World Soccer*)

Score	Opponents	Date	Venue	Stage
13-0	New Zealand v Fiji	16.08.81	Auckland	qual
12-0	West Germany v Cyprus	21.05.70	Essen	qual
11-0	Mexico v St. Vincent	6.12.92	Mexico City	qual
11-1	Hungary v Greece	25.03.38	Budapest	qual
11-1	Trinidad v Antigua	10.11.74	Port of Spain	qual
10-0	Soviet Union* v Finland	15.08.58	Helsinki	qual
10-0	Australia v Fiji	14.08.82	Melbourne	qual

10-0	Norway v San Marino	9.09.92	Oslo	qual
10-1	Hungary v El Salvador	15.06.82	Elche	finals
10-1	Kuwait v Macao	3.05.93	Kuala Lumpur	qual
9-0	Spain v Portugal	11.03.34	Madrid	qual
9-0	Hungary v South Korea	17.06.54	Zurich	finals
9-0	England* v Luxembourg	19.10.62	Luxembourg	qual
9-0	Holland v Norway	1.11.74	Rotterdam	qual
9-0	Rumania v Finland	14.10.74	Bucharest	qual
9-0	Yugoslavia v Zaire	18.06.74	Gelsenkirchen	finals
9-0	Austria v Malta	30.04.78	Salzburg	qual
9-0	East Germany v Malta	29.10.78	Potsdam	qual
9-0	South Korea v Nepal	25.05.90	Seoul	qual

(* = away team)

WORLD CUP TWICE STOLEN

Four months before the 1966 World Cup Finals in England the World Cup itself, the gold Jules Rimet Trophy, insured for £30,000, was stolen while on exhibition in London. One week later, March 27, the Cup, undamaged and wrapped in a copy of the *News of the World*, was found in the front garden of his home at Norwood, London, by a man and his dog. The finder obtained rewards exceeding £5,000; the dog, Pickles, became famous overnight.

To commemorate their third triumph in 1970, Brazil were given the Jules Rimet Trophy to keep permanently, and it was replaced for competition by the F.I.F.A. World Cup. But, on December 19, 1983, the original cup vanished from the Brazilian Confederation offices. Two men were arrested, but the Jules Rimet Cup was never seen again; it had been melted down. A replica, valued at £25,000 and made in West Germany, was presented to Brazil at a ceremony in Frankfurt in March 1984.

WORLD CUP 'FIRSTS'

First World Cup match on artificial turf: Canada v U.S.A. (Vancouver, September 24, 1976); **first World Cup match staged indoors**: U.S.A. v Canada (Seattle, October 20, 1976). First **World Cup Finals match** indoors: U.S.A. v Switzerland (Detroit, June 18, 1994).

BRAZIL'S RECORD RUN

Brazil hold the record for the longest unbeaten sequence in International football: 37 matches (30W, 7D, goals 85-18) from December 1993 until they lost 2-0 to Mexico in the CONCACAF Gold Cup Final on January 21, 1996. The previous record of 32 matches undefeated was held by Hungary.

ALL-SEATED INTERNATIONALS

The first **all-seated crowd** (30,000) for a full International in Britain saw **Wales** and **West Germany** draw 0-0 at Cardiff Arms Park on May 31, 1989. The terraces were closed.

England's first all-seated International at Wembley was against Yugoslavia (2-1) on December 13, 1989 (attendance 34,796). The terracing behind the goals was closed for conversion to seating.

England's first **full-house all-seated** International at Wembley was for England v Brazil (1-0) on March 28, 1990, when a capacity 80,000 crowd paid record British receipts of £1,200,000.

FIRST BLACK CAPS

England's first black player was Nottingham Forest full-back **Viv Anderson** against Czechoslovakia at Wembley on November 29, 1978.

Aston Villa's **Ugo Ehiogu** was **England's** first black captain (U-21 v Holland at Portsmouth, April 27, 1993).

Paul Ince (Man. United) became the first black player to captain **England** in a **full International** (v U.S.A., Boston, June 9, 1993).

First black British International was **Eddie Parris** (Bradford Park Avenue) for Wales against N. Ireland in Belfast on December 5, 1931.

PLAYED FOR MORE THAN ONE COUNTRY

Multi-nationals in senior International football include: **Johnny Carey** (1938-53) – caps Rep. of Ireland 29, N. Ireland 7; **Ferenc Puskas** (1945-62) – caps Hungary 84, Spain 4; **Alfredo di Stefano** (1950-6) – caps Argentina 7, Spain 31; **Ladislav Kubala** (1948-58) – caps Hungary 3, Czechoslovakia 11, Spain 19, only player to win full Int. honours with 3 countries.

Everton's **Peter Farrell** and **Tommy Eglington** played for N. Ireland and the Republic of Ireland in seasons directly after the last war.

John Reynolds (West Bromwich Albion) played for both England and Ireland in the 1890s.

Robert Evans (Sheffield United) had played 10 times for Wales when capped for England, in 1910-11. He was born in Chester of Welsh parents.

FATHER & SON SAME-DAY CAPS

Iceland made father-and-son Int. history when they beat Estonia 3-0 in Tallin. Arnor Gudjohnsen (35) started the match and was replaced (62 mins.) by his 17-year-old son Eidur.

LATEST HAT-TRICKS v ENGLAND

May 17, 1959, scorer **Juan Seminario** (Peru 4, England 1, Lima); June 15, 1988, scorer **Marco Van Basten** (Holland 3, England 1, European Championship, Dusseldorf).

NO-SAVE GOALKEEPERS

Chris Woods did not have one save to make when England beat San Marino 6-0 (World Cup) at Wembley on February 17, 1993. He touched the ball only six times throughout the match.

Gordon Banks had a similar no-save experience when England beat Malta 5-0 (European Championship) at Wembley on May 12, 1971. Malta did not force a goal-kick or corner, and the four times Banks touched the ball were all from back passes.

FIFA PIONEERS

FIFA, now with a membership of 198 countries, began in 1904 with seven founder nations: Belgium, Denmark, France, Holland, Spain, Sweden and Switzerland.

FAMOUS CLUB FEATS

Home Runs: Sunderland were undefeated at home in Football League (Div. 1) in seasons 1891-2, 2-3, 4-5 and 5-6, losing only one home match in 1893-4. **Brentford** won all 21 home games in 1929-30 in the Third Division (South). Others have won all home games in a smaller programme.

Record Home Run: Liverpool went 85 competitive first-team games unbeaten at home between losing 2-3 to Birmingham on January 21, 1978 and 1-2 to Leicester on January 31, 1981. They comprised 63 in the League, 9 League Cup, 7 in European competition and 6 F.A. Cup.

Millwall were unbeaten at home in the League for 59 consecutive matches from 1964-67.

Third to First: Charlton Athletic, in 1936, became the first club to advance from the Third to First Division in successive seasons. **Queen's Park Rangers** were the second club to achieve the feat in 1968, and **Oxford United** did it in 1984 and 1985 as Champions of each division. **Derby County** (1987), **Middlesbrough** (1988), **Sheffield United** (1990) and **Notts County** (1991) were the latest to climb from Third Division to First in successive seasons.

Fourth to First: Northampton Town, in 1965 became the first club to rise from the Fourth to the First Division. **Swansea City** climbed from the Fourth Division to the First (three promotions in four seasons), 1977-8 to 1980-1. **Watford** did so in five seasons, 1977-8 to 1981-2. **Carlisle United** climbed from Fourth Division to First, 1964-74.

Non-League to First: When **Wimbledon** finished third in the Second Division in 1986, they completed the phenomenal rise from non-League football (Southern League) to the First Division in nine years. Two years later they won the F.A. Cup.

Tottenham Hotspur, in 1960-1, not only carried off the First Division Championship and the F.A. Cup for the first time this century but set up other records by opening with 11 successive wins, registering most First Division wins (31), most away wins in the League's history (16), and equalling Arsenal's First Division record of 66 points. They already held the Second Division record of 70 points (1919-20).

Arsenal repeated Tottenham's Double feat by winning the F.A. Cup and the League in 1970-1. **Liverpool** did the Double in 1985-6, **Manchester United** in 1993-4.

Manchester United's dual success again in 1995-6 made them the first English club to complete the Double **twice**.

Arsenal, in 1993, became the first club to win both English domestic cup competitions (F.A. Cup and League Cup) in the same season.

Preston North End, in season 1888-9, won the first League Championship without losing a match and the F.A. Cup without having a goal scored against them throughout the competition.

Bury, in 1903, also won the F.A. Cup without conceding a goal.

Liverpool won the League Championship in 1964, the F.A. Cup in 1965 and the Championship again in 1966. In 1978 they became the first British club to win the European Cup in successive seasons. **Nott'm. Forest** repeated the feat in 1979 and 1980.

Liverpool won the League Championship six times in eight seasons (1976-83) under **Bob Paisley's** management. During his nine years in charge at Anfield – he succeeded Bill Shankly July 1974 – they won a total of 20 major prizes: 6 League titles, 3 European Cups, 3 League (Milk) Cups, 1 UEFA Cup, 1 European Super Cup and 6 F.A. Charity Shields (1 shared).

Triple Triumph: Liverpool are the only Football League club to win three major competitions in one season. In 1983-4 (their first under manager **Joe Fagan**) they were League Champions, League Cup winners and European Cup winners.

Arsenal supplied seven men (still a record) to the England team v. Italy at Highbury on November 14, 1935. They were: Frank Moss, George Male, Eddie Hapgood, Wilf Copping, Ray Bowden, Ted Drake and Cliff Bastin. In addition, Arsenal's Tom Whittaker was England's trainer.

Since then, the most players from one club in an England team was six from **Liverpool** against Switzerland at Wembley in September 1977. The side also included a Liverpool old boy, Kevin Keegan (Hamburg).

COVENTRY UNIQUE

Coventry City are the only club to have played in the Premier League, all four previous divisions of the Football League and in both sections (North and South) of the old Third Division.

Grimsby Town were the other club to play in the four divisions of the Football League and its two Third Division sections.

FAMOUS UPS & DOWNS

Sunderland: Relegated in 1958 after maintaining First Division status since their election to the Football League in 1890. They dropped into Division 3 for the first time in 1987.

Aston Villa: Relegated with **Preston North End**, to the Third Division in 1970.

Arsenal up: When the League was extended in 1919, Woolwich Arsenal (sixth in Division Two in 1914-15, last season before the war) were elected to Division One. Arsenal have been in Div. 1 ever since.

Spurs down: At the same meeting Chelsea (due for relegation) retained their place in Division One but the bottom club (Tottenham Hotspur) had to go down to Division Two.

Preston and Burnley down: Preston North End, the first League Champions in season 1888-9, dropped into the Fourth Division in 1985. So did Burnley, also among the League's original members in 1888. In 1986, Preston were required to apply for re-election.

Wolves' fall: Wolverhampton Wanderers, another of the Football League's original members, completed the fall from First Division to Fourth in successive seasons (1984-5-6).

Lincoln out: Lincoln City became the first club to suffer automatic demotion from the Football League when they finished bottom of Div. 4 in season 1986-7. They were replaced by Scarborough, champions of the GM Vauxhall Conference. Lincoln regained their place a year later.

Swindon up and down: In the 1990 play-offs, Swindon Town won promotion to the First Division for the first time, but remained in the Second Division because of financial irregularities.

MOST CHAMPIONSHIP WINS

Liverpool, by winning the First Division in 1976-7, established a record of 10 Championship victories. They have since increased the total to 18.

CHAMPIONS: FEWEST PLAYERS

Liverpool used only 14 players (five ever-present) when they won the League Championship in season 1965-6. **Aston Villa** also called on no more than 14 players to win the title in 1980-81, with seven ever-present.

MOST PLAYERS USED IN LEAGUE SEASON

46: By **Birmingham City** in 1995-6.

42: By **Coventry** and **Sheff. Wed.** (both 1919-20) and by **Hull City** (1946-7), in each case in a season following a break in League football because of war.

BEST OF CENTURY

Arsenal (1990-91) were the first League Champions this century to lose only once. **Preston** were undefeated first Champions in 1888-9, but played only 22 matches.

LEAGUE HAT-TRICKS

Huddersfield Town created a record in 1925-6 by winning the League Championship for the third year in succession.

Arsenal equalled this League hat-trick in 1933-4-5, and **Liverpool** in 1982-3-4.

'SUPER DOUBLE' WINNERS

Since the war, there have been three instances of players appearing in and then managing F.A. Cup and Championship-winning teams:

Joe Mercer: Player in Arsenal Championship teams 1948, 1953 and in their 1950 F.A. Cup side; manager of Man. City when they won Championship 1968, F.A. Cup 1969.

Kenny Dalglish: Player in Liverpool Championship-winning teams 1979, 1980, 1982, 1983, 1984, player-manager 1986, 1988, 1990: player-manager when Liverpool won F.A. Cup (to complete Double) 1986; manager of Blackburn Rovers, Champions 1995.

George Graham: Played in Arsenal's Double-winning team in 1971, and as manager took them to Championship success in 1989 and 1991 and the F.A. Cup – League Cup double in 1993.

CHAMPIONS IN SUCCESSIVE SEASONS

Preston North End (1888-9, 1889-90).
Sunderland (1891-2, 1892-3).
Aston Villa (1895-6, 1896-7, 1898-9, 1899-1900).
Sheffield Wednesday (1902-3, 1903-4, 1928-9, 1929-30).
Liverpool (1921-2, 1922-3, 1975-6, 1976-7, 1978-9, 1979-80, 1981-2, 1982-3, 1983-4).
Portsmouth (1948-9, 1949-50).
Manchester United (1955-6, 1956-7, 1993-4).
Wolverhampton Wanderers (1957-8, 1958-9).

The Second Division Championship and League Championship have been won in successive seasons by **Liverpool** (1905-6), **Everton** (1931-2), **Tottenham** (1950-1) and **Ipswich Town** (1961-2).

Oxford United became the first club to win the Third and Second Division Championships in successive years (1984, 1985).

Wolves are the only club to win the Fourth and Third Division Championships in successive years (1988, 1989).

BACK FIRST TIME

The following clubs won promotion the season after losing their position in the First Division of the League (*as Champions):

Sheffield Wednesday *1899-1900, *1951-2, *1955-6, *1958-9, 1990-1; **Bolton Wanderers** 1899-1900, *1908-9, 1910-11; **West Bromwich Albion** *1901-2;

Manchester City *1902-3, *1909-10, 1950-1; **Burnley** *1897-8.

Small Heath 1902-3; **Liverpool** *1904-5; **Nottingham Forest** *1906-7; **Preston North End** *1912-13, 1914-15; **Notts County** *1913-14; **Derby County** *1914-15.

Tottenham Hotspur *1919-20, 1977-8; **Leeds United** 1927-8, 1931-2; **Middlesbrough** *1928-9; **Everton** *1930-1; **Manchester United** 1937-8, *1974-5; **Huddersfield Town** 1952-3.

Aston Villa *1959-60, 1987-8; **Chelsea** 1962-3; *1988-9; **Norwich City** 1974-5, 1981-2, *1985-6; **Wolverhampton Wanderers** 1976-7, 1982-3; **Birmingham City** 1979-80, 1984-5.

West Ham, relegated in 1992, won promotion to the **Premier League** in 1993; **Crystal Palace** and **Nott'm. Forest** both returned to the Premiership in 1994, a year after relegation; so did **Leicester City** in 1996.

ORIGINAL TWELVE

The original 12 members of the Football League (formed in 1888) were: **Accrington, Aston Villa, Blackburn Rovers, Bolton Wanderers, Burnley, Derby County, Everton, Notts County, Preston North End, Stoke, West Bromwich Albion** and **Wolverhampton Wanderers**.

Results on the opening day (September 8, 1888): Bolton 3, Derby 6; Everton 2, Accrington 1; Preston 5, Burnley 2; Stoke 0, W.B.A. 2; Wolves 1, Aston Villa 1. Preston had the biggest first-day crowd: 6,000. Blackburn Rovers and Notts County did not play that day. They kicked off a week later (September 15) – Blackburn 5, Accrington 5; Everton 2, Notts County 1.

FASTEST CLIMB – FOURTH DIV. TO FIRST

Three promotions in four seasons by two clubs – **Swansea City:** 1978 third in Div.4; 1979 third in Div.3; 1981 third in Div.2; **Wimbledon:** 1983 Champions of Div.4; 1984 second in Div.3; 1986 third in Div.2.

MERSEYSIDE RECORD

Liverpool is the only city to have staged top-division football – through Everton or Liverpool – in **every season** since the Football League began in 1888.

LEAGUE RECORDS

MOST POINTS IN A SEASON

The following records applied before the introduction of three points for a win in the Football League in 1981-2.

Lincoln City set a **Football League** record in season 1975-6 with 74 points from 46 games, (including 32 victories) in **Division 4**.

First Division: Liverpool (1978-9), 68 points from 42 matches.

Second Division: Tottenham Hotspur (1919-20), 70 points from 42 matches.

Third Division: Aston Villa (1971-2) 70 points from 46 matches.

Since 3 points for win (pre-Premier League):

First Division: Everton (1984-5) and Liverpool (1987-8) 90 points: **Second Division:** Chelsea (1988-9) 99 points; **Third Division:** Bournemouth (1986-7) 97 points; **Fourth Division:** Swindon Town (1985-6) 102 points – record for any division, beating York City's 101 points in 1983-4.

Since change of League format:
Premier League: Man. United (1993-4) 92 points; **First Division**: Newcastle (1992-3) 96 points; **Second Division**: Stoke City (1992-3) 93 points; **Third Division**: Carlisle United (1994-5) 91 points.

Fewest Points: Doncaster Rovers, 8 points (of possible 68) in Second Division, 1904-5. Stirling Albion 6 points (of possible 60) in Scottish League Division A, 1954-5.

DOUBLE CHAMPIONS

Nine men have played in and later managed League Championship-winning teams:

Ted Drake	Player – Arsenal 1934, 1935, 1938. Manager – Chelsea 1955.
Bill Nicholson	Player – Tottenham 1951. Manager – Tottenham 1961.
Alf Ramsey	Player – Tottenham 1951. Manager – Ipswich 1962.
Joe Mercer	Player – Everton 1939, Arsenal 1948, 1953. Manager – Manchester City 1968.
Dave Mackay	Player – Tottenham 1961. Manager – Derby County 1975.
Bob Paisley	Player – Liverpool 1947. Manager – Liverpool 1976, 1977, 1979, 1980, 1982, 1983.
Howard Kendall	Player – Everton 1970. Manager – Everton 1985, 1987.
Kenny Dalglish	Player – Liverpool 1979, 1980, 1982, 1983, 1984. Player-Manager – Liverpool 1986, 1988, 1990. Manager – Blackburn 1995.
George Graham	Player – Arsenal 1971. Manager – Arsenal 1989, 1991.

MOST LEAGUE CHAMPIONSHIP MEDALS

Kenny Dalglish: 9 – 8 for Liverpool (5 as player, 1979-80-82-83-84; 3 as manager, 1986-88-90); 1 for Blackburn (as manager, 1995). As a player he also won 4 Scottish Championship medals with Celtic (1972-73-74-77). **Phil Neal**: 8 for Liverpool (1976-77-79-80-82-83-84-86); **Alan Hansen**: 8 for Liverpool (1979-80-82-83-84-86-88-90).

ARRIVALS AND DEPARTURES

The following are the Football League arrivals and departures since 1923:

Year	In	Out
1923	Doncaster Rovers	Stalybridge Celtic
	New Brighton	
1927	Torquay Athletic	Aberdare Athletic
1928	Carlisle United	Durham City
1929	York City	Ashington
1930	Thames	Merthyr Tydfil
1931	Mansfield Town	Newport County
	Chester	Nelson
1932	Aldershot	Thames
	Newport County	Wigan Borough
1938	Ipswich Town	Gillingham
1950	Colchester United	
	Gillingham	
	Scunthorpe United	
	Shrewsbury Town	
1951	Workington	New Brighton
1960	Peterborough United	Gateshead
1962	Oxford United	Accrington Stanley (resigned)

1970	Cambridge United	Bradford P.A.
1972	Hereford United	Barrow
1977	Wimbledon	Workington
1978	Wigan Athletic	Southport
1987	Scarborough	Lincoln City
1988	Lincoln City	Newport County
1989	Maidstone United	Darlington
1990	Darlington	Colchester United
1991	Barnet	
1992	Colchester United	Aldershot, Maidstone (resigned)
1993	Wycombe W.	Halifax Town

Leeds City were expelled from Div. 2 in October, 1919; Port Vale took over their fixtures.

EXTENSIONS TO FOOTBALL LEAGUE

Clubs	*Season*	*Clubs*	*Season*
12 to 14	1891-2	40 to 44	1919-20
*14 to 28	1892-3	+44 to 66	1920-1
28 to 31	1893-4	† 66 to 86	1921-2
31 to 32	1894-5	86 to 88	1923-4
32 to 36	1898-9	88 to 92	1950-1
36 to 40	1905-6	92 to 93	1991-2

* Second Division formed. + Third Division (South) formed from Southern League clubs. † Third Division (North) formed.

League reduced to 70 clubs and three divisions on the formation of the F.A. Premier League in 1992; increased to 72 season 1994-5, when Premier League reduced to 20 clubs.

RECORD RUNS

Nottingham Forest hold the record unbeaten sequence in the English League – 42 matches spanning the last 26 of season 1977-8 and the first 16 of 1978-9. The run began in November 1977 and ended on December 9, 1978 when Forest lost 0-2 at Liverpool. Their sequence comprised 21 wins and 21 draws.

Best debuts: Ipswich Town won the First Division at their first attempt in 1961-2. **Peterborough United** in their first season in the Football League (1960-1) not only won the Fourth Division but set a scoring record for the League of 134 goals. **Hereford United** were promoted from the Fourth Division in their first League season, 1972-3. **Wycombe Wanderers** were promoted from the Third Division (via the play-offs) in their first League season, 1993-4.

Record winning sequence: 14 consecutive League victories by three clubs (all in Second Division): **Manchester United** 1904-5, **Bristol City** 1905-6 and **Preston** 1950-1. Since then, **Reading** have gone closest to equalling this record with 13 successive League wins in Div. 3 from the start of season 1985-6.

Best starts in "old" First Division: 11 consecutive victories by **Tottenham** in 1960-1; 10 by **Manchester United** in 1985-6. **Newcastle** won their first 11 matches in the **"new" First Division** in 1992-3.

Longest unbeaten sequence (all competitions): 40 by **Nott'm. Forest**, March-December 1978. It comprised 21 wins, 19 draws in 29 League matches, 6 League Cup, 4 European Cup, 1 Charity Shield.

Longest unbeaten start to League season: 29 matches – **Leeds United,** Div. 1 1973-4 (19 wins, 10 draws, goals 51-16); **Liverpool,** Div. 1 1987-8 (22 wins, 7 draws, goals 67-13).

Most consecutive League matches unbeaten in a season: 30 **Burnley** (21 wins, 9 draws, goals 68-17), September 6, 1920 – March 25, 1921, Div. 1.

Longest winning sequence in Div. 1: 13 matches by **Tottenham** – last two of season 1959-60, first 11 of 1960-1.

Longest winning one-season sequences in Championship: 13 matches by **Preston N.E.** in 1891-2 (September 12–January 2); 13 by **Sunderland**, also in 1891-2 (November 14–April 2).

Premier League's record unbeaten run: 25 matches (15W, 10D) by Nott'm. Forest (Feb.-Nov. 1995). It ended with a 7-0 defeat at Blackburn.

WORST SEQUENCES

Cambridge United experienced the longest run without a win in Football League history in season 1983-4: 31 matches (21 lost, 10 drawn) between October 8 and April 23. They finished bottom of the Second Division.

Previous worst no-win League sequence was 30 by **Crewe Alexandra** (Div. 3 North) in season 1956-7.

Worst losing start to a League season: 12 consecutive defeats by **Manchester United** (Div. 1) in 1930-1.

Worst Premier League start: **Swindon Town 15** matches without win (6 draws, 9 defeats), 1993-4.

Longest non-winning start to League season: 25 matches (4 draws, 21 defeats) by **Newport County**, Div. 4 (Aug. 15, 1970 – Jan. 9, 1971). Worst no-win League starts since then: 16 matches by **Burnley** (9 draws, 7 defeats in Div. 2, 1979-80); 16 by **Hull City** (10 draws, 6 defeats in Div. 2, 1989-90); 16 by **Sheffield United** (4 draws, 12 defeats in Div. 1, 1990-91).

Most consecutive League defeats: 18 by **Darwen** (Div. 1) 1898-9. **In modern times:** 15 by Walsall (Div. 2, 1988-9), longest such sequence since last War.

Most League defeats in season: 33 by **Rochdale** (Div. 3 North) 1931-2; by **Cambridge United** (Div. 3) 1984-5; by **Newport County** (Div. 4) 1987-8; by **Chester City** (Div. 2) 1992-3.

Most home League defeats in season: 18 by **Cambridge United** (Div. 3, 1984-5).

Away League defeats record: 24 in row by **Nelson** (Div. 3 North) – 3 in April 1930 followed by all 21 in season 1930-31. They then dropped out of League.

UNBEATEN LEAGUE SEASON

Only two clubs have completed a Football League season unbeaten: **Preston N.E.** (22 matches in 1888-9, the League's first season) and **Liverpool** (28 matches in Div. 2, 1893-4).

100 PER CENT HOME RECORD

Brentford provided the last instance of a club winning every home Football League fixture in a season: 21 Third Division South matches at Griffin Park in 1929-30. **Liverpool** won all 14 home matches in Div. 2 in 1893-4.

Rotherham United just failed to equal that record in 1946-7 (Div. 3 North). They won the first 20 home games, then drew the last, 3-3 v Rochdale.

WORST HOME RUN

Most consecutive home League defeats: 8 by **Rochdale** in Div. 3 North in season 1931-2.

Between November 1958 and October 1959 **Portsmouth** drew 2 and lost 14 out of 16 consecutive home games.

MOST AWAY WINS IN SEASON

Doncaster Rovers won 18 of their 21 away League fixtures as Div. 3 North Champions in 1946-7.

AWAY WINS RECORD

Most **consecutive away wins** in the Football League: **8 by Tottenham** (Div. 1) at start of 1960-1, after ending previous season with 2 away League wins.

100 PER CENT HOME WINS ON ONE DAY

Div. 1 – All 11 home teams won on Feb. 13, 1926 and on Dec. 10, 1955. **Div. 2** – All 12 home teams won on Nov. 26, 1988.

In **Div. 3**, all 12 home teams won in the week-end programme of Oct. 18-19, 1968.

NO HOME WINS IN DIV. ON ONE DAY

Div. 1 – 8 away wins, 3 draws in 11 matches on Sept. 6, 1986. **Div. 2** – 7 away wins, 4 draws in 11 matches on Dec. 26, 1987. **Premier League** – 6 away wins, 5 draws in 11 matches on Dec. 26, 1994.

MOST DRAWS IN A SEASON (FOOTBALL LEAGUE)

23 by **Norwich City** (Div. 1, 1978-79) and **Exeter City** (Div. 4, 1986-87). Norwich played 42 matches, Exeter 46.

MOST DRAWS IN ONE DIV. ON ONE DAY

On September 18, 1948 **nine** out of 11 First Division matches were drawn.

MOST DRAWS IN PREMIER DIV. PROGRAMME

In the week-end of December 2, 3, 4, 1995, seven out of the ten matches finished level.

HIGHEST-SCORING DRAWS IN LEAGUE

Leicester City 6, Arsenal 6 (Div. 1 April 21, 1930) **Charlton Athletic 6, Middlesbrough 6** (Div 2 October 22, 1960)

Latest 6-6 draw in first-class football was between Tranmere Rovers and Newcastle United in the Zenith Data Systems Cup 1st. Round on October 1, 1991. The score went from 3-3 at 90 minutes to 6-6 after extra time, and Tranmere won the tie 3-2 on penalties.

Most recent 5-5 draws in top division: Southampton v Coventry (Div. 1, May 4, 1982); Q.P.R. v Newcastle (Div. 1, Sept. 22, 1984).

DRAWS RECORDS

Most consecutive drawn matches in Football League: 8 by **Torquay United** (Div. 3), Oct. 25 – Dec. 13, 1969.

Longest sequence of draws by the same score: six 1-1 results by **Q.P.R.** in season 1957-8.

IDENTICAL RECORDS

There is only **one instance** of two clubs in one division finishing a season with identical records. In 1907-8, **Blackburn Rovers** and **Woolwich Arsenal** were bracketed equal 14th. in the First Division with these figures: P38, W12, D12, L14, Goals 51-63, Pts. 36.

The total of **1195 goals** scored in the Premier League in season 1993-4 was **repeated** in 1994-5.

CHAMPIONS OF ALL DIVISIONS

Wolves and **Burnley** are the only clubs to have won the Championships of the old **Divisions 1, 2, 3 and 4**. Wolves were also **Champions** of the **Third Division North**.

UPS & DOWNS RECORD

Northampton Town went from **Fourth Division** to **First** and back again in nine seasons (1961-9). **Carlisle United** did the same from 1974-87.

NIGHTMARE STARTS

Most goals conceded by a goalkeeper on League debut: 13 by **Steve Milton** when Halifax Town lost 13-0 at Stockport (Div. 3 North) on January 6, 1934.

Post-war: 11 by Lincoln City (11-1) against Crewe's new goalkeeper **Dennis Murray** (Div. 3 North) on September 29, 1951.

RELEGATION ODD SPOTS

In season 1937-8, **Manchester City** were the highest-scoring team in the First Division with 80 goals (3 more than Champions Arsenal), but they finished in 21st place and were relegated – a year after winning the Championship. They scored more goals than they conceded (77).

Twelve years earlier, in 1925-6, City went down to Division 2 despite totalling 89 goals – still the most scored in any division by a relegated team. Man. City also scored 31 F.A. Cup goals that season, but lost the Final 1-0 to Bolton.

Cardiff City were relegated from Div. 1 in season 1928-9, despite conceding fewest goals in the division (59). They also scored fewest (43).

RELEGATION TREBLES

Two Football League clubs have been relegated three seasons in succession. **Bristol City** fell from First Division to Fourth in 1980-1-2, and **Wolves** did the same in 1984-5-6.

OLDEST CLUBS

Oldest Association Football Club is **Sheffield F.C.** (formed in 1855). The minute book for 1857 is still in existence.

The oldest Football League clubs are: **Notts County**, 1862; **Nottingham Forest**, 1865; and **Sheffield Wednesday**, 1866.

FOUR DIVISIONS

In **May, 1957**, the Football League decided to re-group the two sections of the Third Division into Third and Fourth Divisions in **season 1958-9**.

The Football League was reduced to three divisions on the formation of the F.A. Premier League in **1992**.

THREE UP – THREE DOWN

The Football League Annual General Meeting of June 1973 agreed to adopt the promotion and relegation system of three up and three down.

The **new system** came into effect in **season 1973-4** and applied only to the first three divisions; four were still relegated from the Third and four promoted from the Fourth.

It was the first change in the promotion and relegation system for the top two divisions in 81 years.

MOST LEAGUE APPEARANCES

Players with more than 700 Football League appearances (as at end of season 1995-6):-

996 **Peter Shilton** 1966-93 (286 Leicester, 110 Stoke, 202 Nott'm. Forest, 188 Southampton, 175 Derby, 34 Plymouth, 1 Bolton).

824 **Terry Paine** 1956-77 (713 Southampton, 111 Hereford).

797 **Tommy Hutchison** 1968-91 (165 Blackpool, 314 Coventry, 46 Man. City, 92 Burnley, 180 Swansea). In addition, 68 Scottish League apps. for Alloa 1965-68, giving career League app. total of 865.

782 **Robbie James** 1973-94 (484 Swansea, 48 Stoke, 87 Q.P.R., 23 Leicester, 89 Bradford C., 51 Cardiff).

777 **Alan Oakes** 1959-84 (565 Man. City, 211 Chester, 1 Port Vale).

770 **John Trollope** 1960-80 (all for Swindon, record total for one club).

764 **Jimmy Dickinson** 1946-65 (all for Portsmouth).

762 **Roy Sproson** 1950-72 (all for Port Vale).

758 **Billy Bonds** 1964-88 (95 Charlton, 663 West Ham).

758 **Ray Clemence** 1966-88 (48 Scunthorpe, 470 Liverpool, 240 Tottenham).

757 **Pat Jennings** 1963-86 (48 Watford, 472 Tottenham, 237 Arsenal).

757 **Frank Worthington** 1966-88 (171 Huddersfield, 210 Leicester, 84 Bolton, 75 Birmingham, 32 Leeds, 19 Sunderland, 34 Southampton, 31 Brighton, 59 Tranmere, 23 Preston, 19 Stockport).

749 **Ernie Moss** 1968-88 (469 Chesterfield, 35 Peterborough, 57 Mansfield, 74 Port Vale, 11 Lincoln, 44 Doncaster, 26 Stockport, 23 Scarborough, 10 Rochdale).

746 **Les Chapman** 1966-88 (263 Oldham, 133 Huddersfield, 70 Stockport, 139 Bradford C., 88 Rochdale, 53 Preston).

743 **Alan Ball** 1963-84 (146 Blackpool, 208 Everton, 177 Arsenal, 195 Southampton, 17 Bristol Rovers).

743 **John Hollins** 1963-84 (465 Chelsea, 151 QPR, 127 Arsenal).

743 **Phil Parkes** 1968-91 (52 Walsall, 344 Q.P.R., 344 West Ham, 3 Ipswich).

732 **Mick Mills** 1966-88 (591 Ipswich, 103 Southampton, 38 Stoke).

731 **Asa Hartford** 1967-90 (213 W.B.A., 260 Man. City, 3 Nott'm. F., 81 Everton, 28 Norwich, 81 Bolton, 45 Stockport, 4 Oldham, 16 Shrewsbury).

731 **Ian Callaghan** 1959-81 (640 Liverpool, 76 Swansea, 15 Crewe).

725 **Steve Perryman** 1969-90 (655 Tottenham, 17 Oxford Utd., 53 Brentford).

722 **Martin Peters** 1961-81 (302 West Ham, 189 Tottenham, 207 Norwich, 24 Sheffield United).

718 **Mike Channon** 1966-86 (511 Southampton, 72 Man. City, 4 Newcastle, 9 Bristol Rov., 88 Norwich, 34 Portsmouth).

718 **Phil Neal** 1968-89 (186 Northampton, 455 Liverpool, 77 Bolton).

716 **Ron Harris** 1961-83 (655 Chelsea, 61 Brentford).

716 **Mike Summerbee** 1959-79 (218 Swindon, 357 Man. City, 51 Burnley, 3 Blackpool, 87 Stockport).

705 **John Wile** 1968-86 (205 Peterborough, 500 W.B.A.).

• **Stanley Matthews** made 701 League apps. 1932-65 (322 Stoke, 379 Blackpool), incl. 3 for Stoke at start of 1939-40 before season abandoned (war).

LONGEST LEAGUE SEQUENCE

Harold Bell, centre-half of Tranmere Rovers, was ever-present for the first nine post-war seasons (1946-55), achieving a League record of 401 consecutive matches. Counting F.A. Cup games, his run of successive appearances totalled 459.

The longest League sequence since Bell's was 394 appearances by goalkeeper **Dave Beasant** for Wimbledon, Newcastle and Chelsea. His nine-year run began on August 29, 1981 and was ended by a broken finger sustained in Chelsea's League Cup-tie against Portsmouth on October 31, 1990. Beasant's 394 consecutive League games comprised 304 for Wimbledon (1981-8), 20 for Newcastle (1988-9) and 70 for Chelsea (1989-90).

Phil Neal made 366 consecutive First Division appearances for Liverpool between December 1974 and September 1983, a remarkable sequence for an outfield player in top-division football.

EVER-PRESENT DEFENCE

The **entire defence** of Huddersfield Town played in all 42 Second Division matches in season 1952-3, namely, Bill Wheeler (goal), Ron Staniforth and Laurie Kelly (full-backs), Bill McGarry, Don McEvoy and Len Quested (half-backs). In addition, Vic Metcalfe played in all 42 League matches at outside-left.

FIRST SUBSTITUTE USED IN LEAGUE

Keith Peacock (Charlton), away to Bolton (Div. 2) on August 21, 1965.

FROM PROMOTION TO CHAMPIONS

Clubs who have become Champions of England a year after winning promotion: **Tottenham** (manager Arthur Rowe) 1950, 1951; **Ipswich** (Alf Ramsey) 1961, 1962; **Nott'm. Forest** (Brian Clough) 1977, 1978.

CHAMPIONSHIP FOUR-TIMER

Eric Cantona played in Championship-winning teams for four consecutive seasons: 1990-91 Marseille (France); 1991-2 Leeds; 1992-3 and 1993-4 Man. U..

THREE-NATION CHAMPION

Trevor Steven earned eight Championship medals, in three countries: two with Everton (1985, 1987); five with Rangers (1990, 1991, 1993, 1994, 1995) and one with Marseille in 1992.

LEEDS NO-WAY AWAY

Leeds United, in 1992-3, provided the first instance of a club failing to win an away League match in the season following Championship success.

PIONEERS IN 1888 and 1992

Three clubs among the twelve who formed the Football League in 1888 were also founder members of the F.A. Premier League: **Aston Villa**, **Blackburn Rovers** and **Everton**.

CHAMPIONS (MODERN) WITH TWO CLUBS – PLAYERS

Francis Lee (Man. C. 1968, Derby 1975); **Ray Kennedy** (Arsenal 1971, Liverpool 1979, 1980, 1982); **Archie Gemmill** (Derby 1972, 1975, Nott'm. F. 1978); **John McGovern** (Derby 1972, Nott'm. F. 1978) **Larry Lloyd** (Liverpool 1973, Nott'm. F. 1978); **Peter Withe** (Nott'm. F. 1978, Aston Villa 1981); **John Lukic** (Arsenal 1989, Leeds 1992); **Kevin Richardson** (Everton 1985, Arsenal 1989); **Eric Cantona** (Leeds 1992, Man. United 1993, 1994, 1996); **David Batty** (Leeds 1992, Blackburn 1995), **Bobby Mimms** (Everton 1987, Blackburn 1995).

CLUB CLOSURES

Four clubs have left the Football League in mid-season: **Leeds City** (expelled Oct. 1919); **Wigan Borough** (Oct. 1931, debts of £20,000); **Accrington Stanley** (March 1962, debts £62,000); **Aldershot** (March 1992, debts £1.2m.). **Maidstone United**, with debts of £650,000, closed August 1992, on the eve of the season.

FOUR-DIVISION 'KEEPER

In season 1986-7, **Eric Nixon**, Manchester City goalkeeper, became the first player to appear in **all four divisions** of the Football League **in one season**. He served two clubs in Div. 1: Man. City (5 League games) and Southampton (4); in Div. 2 Bradford City (3); in Div. 3 Carlisle (16); and in Div. 4 for Wolves (16). Total appearances: 44.

FATHERS & SONS

When player-manager **Ian Bowyer** (39) and **Gary Bowyer** (18) appeared together in the **Hereford United** side at Scunthorpe (Div.4, April 21, 1990), they provided the first instance of father and son playing in the same team in a Football League match for 39 years. Ian Bowyer played as substitute, and Gary scored Hereford's injury-time equaliser in a 3-3 draw.

Alec and **David Herd** were the previous father-and-son duo in League football – for **Stockport County**, 2-0 winners at Hartlepool (Div.3 North) on May 5, 1951.

When **Preston N.E.** won 2-1 at Bury in Div. 3 on January 13, 1990, the opposing goalkeepers were brothers: **Alan Kelly** (21) for Preston and **Gary** (23) for Bury. Their father, **Alan Kelly Senior**, (who kept goal for Preston in the 1964 F.A. Cup Final and won 47 Rep. of Ireland caps) flew from America to watch the sons he taught to keep goal line up on opposite sides.

THREE BROTHERS IN DIV. 1 SIDE

Southampton provided the first instance for 68 years of three brothers appearing together in a First Division side on October 22, 1988, when **Danny Wallace** (24) and his 19-year-old twin brothers **Rodney** and **Ray**, played against Sheffield Wednesday.

A previous instance in Div. 1 was provided by the Middlesbrough trio, William, John and George Carr, in 1920.

SHORTEST MATCH

The 0-0 score in the **Bradford City v. Lincoln City Third Division fixture** on May 11, 1985, abandoned through fire after 40 minutes, was subsequently confirmed as a result. It is the shortest officially completed League match on record, and only the third instance in Football League history of the score of an unfinished match being allowed to stand.

The other occasions: **Middlesbrough 4, Oldham 1** (Div. 1, April 3, 1915), abandoned after 55 minutes when Oldham defender Billy Cook refused to leave the field after being sent off; **Barrow 7, Gillingham 0** (Div. 4, Oct. 9, 1961), abandoned after 75 minutes because of bad light, the match having started late because of Gillingham's delayed arrival.

The last 60 seconds of **Birmingham v Stoke** (Div. 3, 1-1, on Feb. 29, 1992) were played behind locked doors. The ground had been cleared after a pitch invasion.

The First Division fixture, **Sheff. Wednesday v. Aston Villa** (Nov. 26, 1898), was abandoned through bad light after 79½ mins. with Wednesday leading 3-1. The Football League ruled that the match should be completed, and the remaining 10½ minutes were played **four months later** (Mar. 13, 1899), when Wednesday added another goal to make the result 4-1.

A crucial **Manchester derby** (Div.1) was abandoned after 85 minutes, and the result stood, on April 27, 1974, when a pitch invation at Old Trafford followed the only goal, scored for City by Denis Law, which relegated Manchester United – Law's former club.

F.A. CUP RECORDS

CHIEF F.A. CUP WINNERS

Nine Times: Manchester United.
Eight Times: Tottenham Hotspur.
Seven Times: Aston Villa.
Three Times in Succession: The Wanderers (1876-7-8) and Blackburn Rovers (1884-5-6).
Trophy Handed Back: The F.A. Cup became the Wanderers' absolute property in 1878, but they handed it back to the Association on condition that it was not to be won outright by any club.
In Successive Years by Professional Clubs: Blackburn Rovers (in 1890 and 1891); Newcastle United (in 1951 and 1952); Tottenham Hotspur (in 1961 and 1962) and Tottenham again (in 1981 and 1982).
Record Final-tie score: Bury 6, Derby County 0 (1903).
Most F.A. Cup wins at Wembley: Manchester United 8, Arsenal 6, Tottenham Hotspur 6, Newcastle United 5, Liverpool 5.

F.A. CUP: SECOND DIVISION WINNERS

Notts County (1894), Wolves (1908), Barnsley (1912), West Bromwich Albion (1931), Sunderland (1973), Southampton (1976), West Ham United (1980). When Tottenham won the Cup in 1901 they were a Southern League club.

THIRD DIVISION SEMI-FINALISTS

Millwall (1937), Port Vale (1954), York City (1955), Norwich City (1959), Crystal Palace (1976), Plymouth Argyle (1984).

FOURTH DIVISION QUARTER-FINALISTS

Oxford United (1964), Colchester United (1971), Bradford City (1976), Cambridge United (1990).

F.A. CUP – FOUR TROPHIES

The new F.A. Cup, presented at Wembley in 1992, is a replica of the one it replaced and which had been in existence since 1911. The old F.A. Cup is now a museum piece at Lancaster Gate, the F.A. explaining: "It was falling apart and was not going to last much longer."

The new trophy is the fourth F.A. Cup. This is what happened to its predecessors:

1895 First F.A. Cup stolen from shop in Birmingham while held by Aston Villa. Never seen again.

1910 Second F.A. Cup presented to Lord Kinnaird on completing 21 years as F.A. president.

1992 Third F.A. Cup "gracefully retired" after 80 years' service (1911-91).

FINALISTS RELEGATED

F.A. Cup Final clubs relegated in same season: Man. City 1926, Leicester 1969, Brighton 1983. All lost at Wembley and went down to Div. 2.

GIANT-KILLING IN F.A. CUP

(* Home team; R = Replay; Season 1996 = 1995-6)

Season	Home team		Opponent	
1996	*Hitchin	2	Bristol R.	1
1996	*Woking	2	Barnet	1R
1996	*Bury	0	Blyth S.	2
1996	*Gravesend & N.	2	Colchester	0
1995	*Kingstonian	2	Brighton	1
1995	*Enfield	1	Cardiff	0
1995	*Marlow	2	Oxford	0
1995	*Woking	1	Barnet	0R
1995	*Hitchin	4	Hereford	2R
1995	*Torquay	0	Enfield	1R
1995	*Altrincham	1	Wigan	0
1995	*Wrexham	2	Ipswich	1
1995	*Scarboro'	1	Port Vale	0
1994	*Colchester	3	Sutton	4
1994	*Yeovil	1	Fulham	0
1994	*Torquay	0	Sutton	1
1994	*Halifax	2	W.B.A.	1
1994	*Birmingham	1	Kid'minster	2
1994	*Stockport	2	Q.P.R.	1
1994	*Liverpool	0	Bristol C.	1R
1994	*Arsenal	1	Bolton	3R
1994	*Leeds	2	Oxford	3R
1994	*Luton	2	Newcastle	0R
1994	*Kid'minster	1	Preston	0
1994	*Cardiff	1	Man. C.	0
1993	*Hereford	1	Yeovil	2R
1993	*Torquay	2	Yeovil	5
1993	*Altrincham	2	Chester	0R
1993	*Cardiff	2	Bath	3
1993	*Ch'field	2	Macc'field	2R
	(Macclesfield won on pens).			
1993	*Marine	4	Halifax	1
1993	*Stafford	2	Lincoln	1R
1993	*Hartlepool	1	Crystal P.	0
1993	*Liverpool	0	Bolton	2R
1992	*Fulham	0	Hayes	2
1992	*Crawley	4	N'thampton	2
1992	*Telford	2	Stoke	1R
1992	*Aldershot	0	Enfield	1
1992	*Halifax	1	Witton A.	2R
1992	*Maidstone	1	Kettering	2
1992	*Walsall	0	Yeovil	1R
1992	*Farnboro'	4	Torquay	3
1992	*Wrexham	2	Arsenal	1
1991	*Scarboro'	0	Leek	2
1991	*N 'hampton	0	Barnet	1R
1991	*Hayes	1	Cardiff	0R
1991	*Chorley	2	Bury	1
1991	*Shrewsbury	1	Wimbledon	0
1991	*W.B.A.	2	Woking	4
1990	*Aylesbury	1	Southend	0
1990	*Scarboro'	0	Whitley Bay	1
1990	*Welling	1	Gillingham	0R
1990	*Whitley Bay	2	Preston	0
1990	*N'hampton	1	Coventry	0
1990	*Cambridge	1	Millwall	0R
1989	*Sutton	2	Coventry	1
1989	*Halifax	2	Kettering	3R
1989	*Kettering	2	Bristol R.	1
1989	*Bognor	2	Exeter	1
1989	*Leyton O	0	Enfield	1R
1989	*Altrincham	3	Lincoln	2
1989	*Wrexham	2	Runcorn	3R
1988	*Sutton	3	Aldershot	0
1988	*Peterboro'	1	Sutton	3
1988	*Carlisle	2	Macc'field	4
1988	*Macc'field	4	Rotherham	0
1988	*Chester	0	Runcorn	1
1988	*Cambridge	0	Yeovil	1

1987 *Caernarfon . 1	Stockport 0
1987 Chorley .... 3 (at Bolton)	Wolves ..... 0 R
1987 *Telford 3	Burnley 0
1987 *York C. 1	Caernarfon 2 R
1987 *Aldershot 3	Oxford U 0
1987 *Wigan 1	Norwich C 0
1987 *Charlton 1	Walsall 2
1986 *Stockport 0	Telford 1
1986 *Wycombe ... 2	Colchester 0
1986 *Dagenham . 2	Cambridge U 1
1986 *Blackpool 1	Altrincham 2
1986 *B'ham 1	Altrincham 2
1986 *Peterboro' ... 1	Leeds 0
1985 *Telford 2	Lincoln 1
1985 *Preston 1	Telford 4
1985 *Telford 2	Bradford C. .. 1
1985 *Telford 3	Darlington . 0 R
1985 *Blackpool 0	Altrincham 1
1985 *Wimbledon . 1	Nott'm. F .. 0 R
1985 *Orient 2	W.B.A. 1
1985 *Dagenham .. 1	Peterboro' 0
1985 *Swindon 1	Dagenham 2 R
1985 *York 1	Arsenal 0
1984 *Halifax 2	Whitby 3
1984 *B'mouth 2	Man. Utd 0
1984 *Telford 3	Stockport 0
1984 *Telford 3	N'hampton 2 R
1984 Telford 4	*Rochdale 1
1983 *Cardiff 2	Weymouth 3
1981 *Exeter 3	Leicester .. 1 R
1981 *Exeter 4	Newcastle . 0 R
1980 *Halifax 1	Man. C 0
1980 *Harlow 1	Leicester .. 0 R
1980 *Chelsea 0	Wigan 1
1979 *Newport 2	West Ham 1
1978 *Wrexham 4	Newcastle . 1 R
1978 *Stoke 2	Blyth S 3
1976 *Leeds U 0	Crystal P. 1
1975 *Brighton 0	Leatherhead . 1
1975 *Burnley 0	Wimbledon ... 1
1972 *Hereford 2	Newcastle . 1 R
1971 *Colchester .. 3	Leeds U 2
1969 *Mansfield 3	West Ham 0
1967 *Swindon 3	West Ham . 0 R
1967 *Man. U 1	Norwich C 2
1966 *Ipswich T 2	Southport . 3 R
1965 *Peterboro' ... 2	Arsenal 1
1964 *Newcastle ... 1	Bedford T 2
1964 *Aldershot 2	Aston V .... 1 R
1961 *Grimsby 1	Kings Lynn ... 2
1961 *Chelsea 1	Crewe A 2
1960 *Man. C 1	South'ton 5
1959 *Norwich C ... 3	Man. U 0
1959 *Worcester ... 2	Liverpool 1
1959 *Tooting 3	Bournem'th .. 1
1959 *Tooting 2	N'mpton 1
1958 *Newcastle ... 1	Scunthorpe .. 3
1957 *Wolves 0	Bournem'th .. 1
1957 *B'mouth 3	Tottenham 1
1957 *Derby 1	N. Brighton ... 3
1956 *Derby C 1	Boston U 6
1955 *York C 2	Tottenham 1
1955 *Blackpool 0	York C 2
1954 *Arsenal 1	Norwich C 2
1954 *Port Vale 2	Blackpool 0
1952 *Everton 1	Leyton O 3
1949 *Yeovil T 2	Sunderland .. 1
1948 *Colchester .. 1	Hud'field 0
1948 *Arsenal 0	Bradford 1
1938 *Ch'lmsf'd C . 4	South'ton 1
1933 *Walsall 2	Arsenal 0
1922 *Everton 0	Crystal P. 6

YEOVIL TOP GIANT-KILLERS

Yeovil's first round victory against Fulham in season 1993-4 gave them a total of 17 F.A. Cup wins against League opponents. They hold another non-League record by reaching Round 3 eleven times.

This is Yeovil's triumphant Cup record against League clubs: 1924-5 Bournemouth 3-2; 1934-5 Crystal P. 3-0, Exeter 4-1; 1938-9 Brighton 2-1; 1948-9 Bury 3-1, Sunderland 2-1; 1958-9 Southend 1-0; 1960-1 Walsall 1-0; 1963-4 Southend 1-0, Crystal P. 3-1; 1970-1 Bournemouth 1-0; 1972-3 Brentford 2-1; 1987-8 Cambridge 1-0; 1991-2 Walsall 1-0; 1992-3 Torquay 5-2, Hereford 2-1; 1993-4 Fulham 1-0.

NON-LEAGUE BEST IN F.A. CUP

Apart from Tottenham winning the Cup as a Southern League team in 1901, the **furthest progress** by non-League clubs has been to the **5th. Round**, on 5 occasions: Colchester 1948, Yeovil 1949, Blyth Spartans 1978, Telford 1985 and Kidderminster 1994.

Greatest number of non-League sides to reach the **3rd. Round** is 6 in 1978:

Blyth, Enfield, Scarborough, Tilbury, Wealdstone and Wigan.

Most to reach **Round 4**: 3 in 1957 (Rhyl, New Brighton, Peterborough) and 1975 (Leatherhead, Stafford and Wimbledon).

TOP-DIVISION SCALPS

Victories in F.A. Cup by non-League clubs over top-division teams this century:- Season 1900-1 (Final, replay); **Tottenham** 3, Sheffield Utd. 1 (Spurs then in Southern League); 1919-20 **Cardiff City** 2, Oldham Athletic 0, and Sheffield Wed. 0, **Darlington** 2; 1923-4 **Corinthians** 1, Blackburn Rovers 0; 1947-8 **Colchester Utd.** 1, Huddersfield Town 0; 1948-9 **Yeovil Town** 2, Sunderland 1; 1971-2 **Hereford Utd.** 2, Newcastle 1; 1974-5 Burnley 0, **Wimbledon** 1; 1985-6 Birmingham City 1, **Altrincham** 2; 1988-9 **Sutton United** 2, Coventry City 1.

MOST WEMBLEY FINALS

Five players have appeared in five F.A. Cup Finals at Wembley:-

- Joe Hulme (Arsenal: 1927, lost; 1930 won; 1932 lost; 1936 won; Huddersfield Town: 1938 lost).
- Johnny Giles (Man. United: 1963 won; Leeds Utd: 1965 lost; 1970 drew at Wembley, lost replay at Old Trafford; 1972 won; 1973 lost).
- Pat Rice (all for Arsenal: 1971 won; 1972 lost; 1978 lost; 1979 won; 1980 lost).
- Frank Stapleton (Arsenal: 1978 lost; 1979 won; 1980 lost; Man. United: 1983 won; 1985 won).
- Ray Clemence (Liverpool: 1971 lost; 1974 won; 1977 lost; Tottenham: 1982 won; 1987 lost).

Stapleton and Clemence also played in a replay, making six actual F.A. Cup Final appearances for each of them.

Glenn Hoddle made six F.A. Cup Final appearances at Wembley: 5 for Tottenham (incl. 2 replays), in 1981, 1982 and 1987, and 1 for Chelsea in 1994.

F.A. CUP SEMI-FINALS AT WEMBLEY

1991 Tottenham 3, Arsenal 1; **1993** Sheff. Wed. 2, Sheff. Utd. 1; Arsenal 1, Tottenham 0; **1994** Chelsea 2, Luton 0; Man. Utd. 1, Oldham 1.

FIRST F.A. CUP ENTRANTS (1871-2)

Barnes, Civil Service, Crystal Palace, Clapham Rovers, Donnington School (Spalding), Hampstead Heathens, Harrow Chequers, Hitchin, Maidenhead, Marlow, Queen's Park (Glasgow), Reigate Priory, Royal Engineers, Upton Park and Wanderers. Total 15. Three scratched.

Record F.A. Cup entry .... **674 in 1921**

CUP 'FIRSTS'

Out of Country: Cardiff City, by defeating Arsenal 1-0 in the 1927 Final at Wembley, became the first and only club to take the F.A. Cup out of England. **All-English Winning XI:** First club to win the F.A. Cup with all-English XI was West Bromwich Albion, in 1888. Others since: Bolton (1958), Man. City (1969), West Ham (1964 and 1975). **Non-English Winning XI:** Liverpool in 1986 (Mark Lawrenson, born Preston, a Rep. of Ireland player). **Won both Cups: Old Carthusians** won the F.A. Cup in 1881 and the F.A. Amateur Cup in 1894 and 1897. **Wimbledon** won Amateur Cup in 1963, F.A. Cup in 1988.

MOST GAMES NEEDED TO WIN F.A. CUP

Barnsley played a record 12 matches (20 hours' football) to win the F.A. Cup in season 1911-12. All six replays (one in Rd. 1, three in Rd. 4 and one in each of semi-final and Final) were brought about by goalless draws.

Arsenal played 11 F.A. Cup games when winning the trophy in 1979. Five of them were in the 3rd. Rd. against Sheffield Wedneday.

LONGEST F.A. CUP TIES

6 matches (11 hours): **Alvechurch v. Oxford City** (4th. qual. round, 1971-2). Alvechurch won 1-0.

5 matches (9 hours, 22 mins – record for competition proper): **Stoke City v. Bury** (3rd. round, 1954-5). Stoke won 3-2.

5 matches: Chelsea v Burnley (4th. round, 1955-6). Chelsea won 2-0.

5 matches: Hull v. Darlington (2nd. round, 1960-1). Hull won 3-0.

5 matches: Arsenal v. Sheff. Wed. (3rd. round, 1978-9). Arsenal won 2-0.

Other marathons (qualifying comp., all 5 matches, 9 hours): **Barrow v. Gillingham** (last qual. round, 1924-5) – winners Barrow; **Leyton v Ilford** (3rd. qual. round, 1924-5) – winners Leyton; **Falmouth Town v. Bideford** (3rd. qual. round, 1973-4) – winners Bideford.

F.A. Cup marathons ended in season 1991-2, when the penalty shoot-out was introduced to decide ties still level after one replay and extra time.

LONGEST ROUND

The longest round in F.A. Cup history was the **third round** in **season 1962-3**. It took 66 days to complete, lasting from January 5 to March 11, and included 261 postponements because of bad weather.

RE-STAGED F.A. CUP TIES

Sixth round, March 9, 1974: Newcastle 4, Nott'm. Forest 3. Match declared void by F.A. and ordered to be replayed following a pitch invasion after Newcastle had a player sent off. Forest claimed the hold-up caused the game to change its pattern. The tie went to two further matches at Goodison Park (0-0, then 1-0 to Newcastle).

Third round, January 5, 1985: Burton Albion 1, Leicester 6 (at Derby). Burton goalkeeper Paul Evans was hit on the head by a missile thrown from the crowd, and continued in a daze. The F.A. ordered the tie to be played again, behind closed doors at Coventry (Leicester won 1- 0).

First round replay, November 25, 1992: Peterborough 9 (Tony Philliskirk 5), Kingstonian 1. Match expunged from records because, at 3-0 after 57 mins, Kingstonian were reduced to ten men when goalkeeper Adrian Blake was concussed by a 50 pence coin thrown from the crowd. The tie was re-staged on the same ground behind closed doors (Peterborough won 1-0).

WAR-TIME MARATHON

Match of 203 minutes: Stockport County's second-leg tie with Doncaster Rovers in the Third Division North Cup, March 30, 1946, lasted 203 minutes and a replay was still necessary.

F.A. CUP FINAL HAT-TRICKS

There have been only three in the history of the competition: **Billy Townley** (Blackburn Rovers, 1890), **Jimmy Logan** (Notts Co., 1894) and **Stan Mortensen** (Blackpool, 1953).

FIVE WINNING MEDALS

The Hon. A.F. Kinnaird (The Wanderers and Old Etonians), **C.H.R. Wollaston** (The Wanderers) and **James Forrest** (Blackburn Rovers) each earned five F.A. Cup winners' medals. Kinnaird, later president of the F.A., played in nine of the first 12 F.A. Cup Finals, and was on the winning side three times for The Wanderers, in 1873 (captain), 1877, 1878 (captain) and twice as captain of Old Etonians (1879, 1882).

MOST WINNERS' MEDALS THIS CENTURY

3 – the list includes modern players **Bruce Grobbelaar**, **Ian Rush** and **Steve Nicol** (all Liverpool); **Bryan Robson** (3 times winning captain) and **Mark Hughes** (Man. United).

MOST F.A. CUP APPEARANCES

88 by **Ian Callaghan** (79 for Liverpool, 7 for Swansea, 2 for Crewe); 86 by **Stanley Matthews** (37 for Stoke, 49 for Blackpool); 86 by **Peter Shilton** for six clubs (Leicester, Stoke, Nott'm. Forest, Southampton, Derby and Plymouth); 84 by **Bobby Charlton** (80 for Man. United, 4 for Preston N.E.).

THREE-CLUB FINALISTS

Two players have appeared in the F.A. Final for three clubs: **Harold Halse** for Man. United (1909), Aston Villa (1913) and Chelsea (1915); **Ernie Taylor** for Newcastle (1951), Blackpool (1953) and Man. United (1958).

CAPTAIN'S CUP DOUBLE

Martin Buchan is the only player to have captained Scottish and English F.A. Cup-winning teams – Aberdeen in 1970 and Manchester United in 1977.

MEDALS BEFORE AND AFTER

Two players appeared in F.A. Cup Final teams before and after the war: **Raich Carter** was twice a winner (Sunderland 1937, Derby 1946) and **Willie Fagan** twice on the losing side (Preston 1937, Liverpool 1950).

STARS WHO MISSED OUT

Great players who never won an F.A. Cup winner's medal include: **Tommy Lawton, Tom Finney, Johnny Haynes, Gordon Banks, George Best, Terry Butcher** and **Peter Shilton**.

CUP WINNERS AT NO COST

Not one member of **Bolton Wanderers'** 1958 F.A. Cup-winning team cost the club a transfer fee. Five were Internationals.

ALL-INTERNATIONAL CUP WINNERS

In **Man. United's** 1985 Cup-winning team v. Everton, all 11 players were full Internationals, as was the substitute who played.

NO-CAP CUP WINNERS

Sunderland, in 1973, were the last F.A. Cup-winning team not to include an International player, although some were capped later.

HIGH SCORING SEMI-FINALS

The **record team score** in F.A. Cup semi-finals is 6: 1891-2 WBA 6, Nott'm. Forest 2; 1907-8 Newcastle 6, Fulham 0; 1933-4 Man. City 6, Aston Villa 1.

Most goals in semi-finals (aggregate): 17 in 1892 (4 matches) and 1899 (5 matches). In modern times: 15 in 1958 (3 matches, including Man. United 5, Fulham 3 – highest-scoring semi-final since last war); 16 in 1989-90 (Crystal Palace 4, Liverpool 3; Man. United v Oldham 3-3, 2-1. **All 16 goals** in those three matches were scored by **different players**.

Last hat-trick in an F.A. Cup semi-final was scored by **Alex Dawson** for Man. United in 5-3 replay win against Fulham at Highbury in 1958.

FOUR SPECIAL AWAYS

For the only time in F.A. Cup history, **all four quarter-finals** in season 1986-7 were won by the away team.

F.A. CUP – DRAWS RECORD

In season 1985-6, **seven** of the eight F.A. Cup 5th. Round ties went to replays – a record for that stage of the competition.

LUCK OF THE DRAW

In the F.A. Cup on Jan. 11, 1947, eight of **London**'s ten Football League clubs involved in the 3rd. Round were drawn at home (including Chelsea v Arsenal). Only Crystal Palace played outside the capital (at Newcastle).

Contrast: In the 3rd. Round in Jan. 1992, Charlton were the only London club drawn at home (against Barnet), but the venue of the Farnborough v West Ham tie was reversed on police instruction. So Upton Park staged Cup-ties on successive days, with West Ham at home on the Saturday and Charlton (who shared the ground) on Sunday.

Arsenal were drawn away in every round on the way to reaching the F.A. Cup Finals of 1971 and 1972. **Man. United** won the Cup in 1990 without playing once at home.

F.A. CUP: ALL FIRST DIVISION VICTIMS

Only instance of an F.A. Cup-winning club meeting **First Division** opponents in every round was provided by Man. United in 1947-8. They beat Aston Villa, Liverpool, Charlton, Preston, then Derby County in the semi-final and Blackpool in the Final.

HOME ADVANTAGE

For the first time in F.A. Cup history, all eight ties in the 1992-3 5th. Round were won (no replays) by the **clubs drawn at home**. Only other instance of eight home wins at the "last 16" stage of the F.A. Cup was in 1889-90, in what was then the 2nd. Round.

SIXTH ROUND ELITE

For the first time in F.A. Cup 6th. Round history, dating from 1926, when the format of the competition changed, **all eight quarter-finalists** in 1995-6 were from the top division.

CUP FINAL HYMN

"**Abide With Me**" was introduced into the F.A. Cup Final community singing in 1927, and has been sung ever since with the exception of 1959. So many complaints followed its omission that it was restored the following year.

LONGEST UNBEATEN RUN IN F.A. CUP

Blackburn Rovers: 24 matches (21 wins, 2 draws, 1 walkover, from Dec. 1883-Nov. 1886), including F.A. Cup hat-trick.

TOP CLUB DISTINCTION

Since the Football League began in 1888, there has never been an F.A. Cup Final in which **neither club** represented the top division.

SPURS OUT – AND IN

Tottenham Hotspur were banned, pre-season, from the 1994-5 F.A. Cup competition because of financial irregularities, but were readmitted on appeal and reached the semi-finals.

F.A. CUP FINAL GUESTS OF HONOUR

1923	King George V, The Duke of Devonshire
1924	Duke of York
1925	Duke of York
1926	King George V
1927	King George V
1928	King George V and Queen Mary, Duke and Duchess of York
1929	Prince of Wales
1930	King George V
1931	Duke of Gloucester
1932	King George V and Queen Mary
1933	Duke of York
1934	King George V
1935	Prince of Wales
1936	Sir Charles Clegg, President of the FA
1937	King George VI and Queen Elizabeth
1938	King George VI
1939	King George VI
1946	King George VI, Queen Elizabeth, Princess Elizabeth
1947	Duke and Duchess of Gloucester
1948	King George VI
1949	Princess Elizabeth, Duke of Gloucester
1950	King George VI
1951	King George VI, Queen Elizabeth, Duke of Gloucester, Prince William, Princess Mary
1952	Sir Winston Churchill
1953	Queen Elizabeth II
1954	Queen Mother, Princess Margaret
1955	Princess Mary, Duke of Edinburgh
1956	Queen Elizabeth II
1957	Queen Elizabeth II and Duke of Edinburgh
1958	Queen Elizabeth II and Duke of Edinburgh
1959	Queen Elizabeth II and Duke of Edinburgh
1960	Duke of Gloucester
1961	Duchess of Kent
1962	Queen Elizabeth II and Duke of Edinburgh
1963	Queen Elizabeth II and Duke of Edinburgh
1964	Earl of Harewood

1965	Queen Elizabeth II and Duke of Edinburgh
1966	Princess Margaret
1967	Duke and Duchess of Kent
1968	Princess Alexandra
1969	Princess Anne
1970	Princess Margaret
1970rep	Sir Dr Andrew Stephen
1971	Duke and Duchess of Kent
1972	Queen Elizabeth II and Duke of Edinburgh, Duke and Duchess of Kent
1973	Duke of Kent
1974	Princess Anne, Duke of Kent
1975	Duke and Duchess of Kent
1976	Queen Elizabeth II and Duke of Edinburgh
1977	Duke and Duchess of Kent
1978	Princess Alexandra
1979	Prince of Wales
1980	Duke and Duchess of Kent
1981	Queen Mother
1981rep	Prince Michael of Kent
1982	Princess Anne
1982rep	Duke of Kent
1983	Duke of Kent
1983rep	Princess Michael of Kent
1984	Duke and Duchess of Kent
1985	Duke of Kent
1986	Duchess of Kent
1987	Duchess of Kent
1988	Princess of Wales
1989	Duke and Duchess of Kent
1990	Duke and Duchess of Kent
1990rep	Duke and Duchess of Kent
1991	Prince and Princess of Wales, Duke and Duchess of Kent
1992	Duke and Duchess of Kent
1993	Duke and Duchess of Kent
1993rep	Duchess of Kent
1994	Duchess of Kent
1995	Prince of Wales and Duke of Kent
1996	Duke and Duchess of Kent

LEAGUE CUP RECORDS

(See also League Cup and Goalscoring Sections)

Highest scores: West Ham 10-0 v Bury (2nd. Rd., 2nd. Leg 1983-4; agg. 12-1); Liverpool 10-0 v Fulham (2nd. Rd., 1st. Leg 1986-7; agg. 13-2).
Most League Cup goals (career): 49 Geoff Hurst (43 West Ham, 6 Stoke, 1960-75); 48 Ian Rush (Liverpool); 42 John Aldridge (Newport, Oxford, Liverpool, Tranmere 1979 to date).
Highest scorer (season): 12 Clive Allen (Tottenham 1986-7 in 9 apps).
Most goals in match: 6 Frank Bunn (Oldham v Scarborough, 3rd. Rd., 1989-90).
Fewest goals conceded by winners: 3 by Leeds (1967-8), Tottenham (1970-1), Aston Villa (1995-6).
Most winner's medals: 5 Ian Rush (Liverpool).
Most appearances in Final: 6 Kenny Dalglish (Liverpool 1978-87), Ian Rush (Liverpool 1971-95).
Alan Hardaker Man of the Match Award was introduced in the 1990 Final, in recognition of the League's late secretary who proposed the competition in 1960.
League Cup sponsors: Milk Cup 1981-6, Littlewoods Cup 1987-90, Rumbelows Cup 1991-2, Coca-Cola Cup since 1993.

DISCIPLINE

SENDINGS-OFF

The total of 320 players with Premier League and Football League clubs sent off in first-team competitions last season was 56 fewer than the record 376 in 1994-5.

It comprised 279 in League matches (57 Premiership, 221 Endsleigh Football League, 1 in play-offs); 13 in F.A. Cup; 17 Coca-Cola League Cup; 2 European

Champions' League; 1 Cup-Winners' Cup; 6 Auto Windscreens Shield; 2 Anglo-Italian Cup.

Clubs with the worst red-card records in 1995-6 were Hartlepool (10), Wycombe (8), Gillingham (8). Among Premiership clubs, Wimbledon had most dismissals with 8 (all League).

Three clubs did not have a player sent off last season in first-team football: Tottenham, Watford and Swindon.

Season-by-season dismissals from the Eighties: **1981-2**, 157 (132 League); **1982-3**, 242 (211 League); **1983-4**, 173 (150 League); **1984-5**, 183 (163 League); **1985-6**, 207 (185 League); **1986-7**, 219 (193 League); **1987-8**, 217 (197 League, incl. 2 in play-offs); **1988-9**, 192 (173 League, incl. 1 in play-offs); **1989-90**, 183 (162 in League, incl. 1 in play-offs); **1990-1**, 238 (204 League, incl. 2 in play-offs); **1991-2**, 278 (245 League, incl. 1 in play-offs); **1992-3**, 277 (229 in League, incl. 3 in play-offs); **1993-4,** 288 (239 in League, incl. 6 in play-offs); **1994-5**, 376 (309 in League, incl. 5 in play-offs); 1995-6, 320 (279 in League, incl. 1 in play-offs).

November 20, 1982 was the **worst day** for dismissals **in football history** with 15 players sent off (3 League, 12 in the F.A. Cup first round). That was also the blackest day for disciplinary action in the F.A. Cup (previous worst – eight on January 9, 1915).

Most players ordered off in **League football on one day**: 13 on Dec. 14, 1985 (also 4 in Scottish League); 13 on Aug. 19, 1995; 13 on Sept. 9, 1995.

Most players sent off in one **Football League programme**: 15 in week-end of Sat., Dec. 22 (11) and Sun., Dec. 23 (4), 1990.

● In the entire first season of post-war League football (1946-7) only 12 players were sent off, followed by 14 in 1949-50, and the total League dismissals for the first nine seasons after the war was 104.

Worst pre-war total was 28 in each of seasons 1921-2 and 1922-3.

ENGLAND SENDINGS-OFF

Ray Wilkins became only the fourth player England have had sent off in their International history (1872 to date) when he was dismissed for a second bookable offence – throwing ball at referee – in the World Cup Finals match against Morocco in Monterrey on June 6, 1986:-

June 5, 1968 **Alan Mullery**	v. Yugoslavia (Florence, Eur. Champ.)
June 6, 1973 **Alan Ball**	v. Poland (Chorzow, World Cup qual.)
June 15, 1977 **Trevor Cherry**	v. Argentina (Buenos Aires, friendly)
June 6, 1986 **Ray Wilkins**	v. Morocco (Monterrey, World Cup Finals)

Other countries: Most recent sendings-off of players representing the other Home Countries: **N. Ireland – Iain Dowie** v. Norway (Friendly, Belfast, March 1996); **Scotland – John Spencer** v. Japan (Kirin Cup, Hiroshima, May 1995); **Wales – Vinnie Jones** v. Georgia (European Champ., Cardiff, June 1995); **Rep. of Ireland – Liam Daish** v Mexico (US Cup, New Jersey, June 1996).

England dismissals at other levels:-

U-23 (4): **Stan Anderson** (v Bulgaria, Sofia, May 19, 1957); **Alan Ball** (v Austria, Vienna, June 2, 1965); **Kevin Keegan** (v E. Germany, Magdeburg, June 1, 1972); **Steve Perryman** (v Portugal, Lisbon, Nov. 19, 1974).

U-21 (10): **Sammy Lee** (v Hungary, Keszthely, June 5, 1981); **Mark Hateley** (v Scotland, Hampden Park, April 19, 1982); **Paul Elliott** (v Denmark, Maine Road, Manchester, March 26, 1986); **Tony Cottee** (v W. Germany, Ludenscheid, September 8, 1987); **Julian Dicks** (v Mexico, Toulon, France, June 12, 1988); **Jason Dodd** (v Mexico, Toulon, France, May 29, 1991; 3 Mexico players also sent off in that match); **Matthew Jackson** (v France, Toulon, France, May 28, 1992); **Robbie Fowler** (v Austria, Kafkenberg, October 11, 1994); **Alan Thompson** (v Portugal, Oporto, September 2, 1995; **Terry Cooke** (v Portugal, Toulon, May 30, 1996.

England 'B' (1): **Neil Webb** (v Algeria, Algiers, December 11, 1990).

FOUR OFF IN ONE MATCH

There have been five instances of four Football League club players being sent off in one match:

Jan. 8, 1955 Crewe v. Bradford (Div. 3 North), two players from each side.

Dec. 13, 1986 Sheff. United (1 player) v. Portsmouth (3) in Div. 2.

Aug. 18, 1987 Port Vale v. Northampton (Littlewoods Cup 1st. Round, 1st. Leg), two players from each side.

Dec. 12, 1987 Brentford v. Mansfield (Div. 3), two players from each side.

Sept. 6, 1992 First instance in British first-class football of **four players from one side** being sent off in one match. Hereford United's seven survivors, away to Northampton (Div. 3), held out for a 1-1 draw.

Four Stranraer players were sent off away to Airdrie (Scottish Div. 1) on Dec. 3, 1994, the most dismissals for one club in the Scottich records.

Modern instances of **three players from one side** being sent off:

Dec. 13, 1986 Portsmouth (away to Sheff. United, Div. 2); **Aug. 23, 1989** Falkirk (home to Hearts, Scottish Skol Cup 3rd. Round); **Apr. 20, 1992** Newcastle (away to Derby, Div. 2); **May 2, 1992** Bristol City (away to Watford, Div. 2).

Aug. 24, 1994: Three Sheff. United players, and one from Udinese, were sent off in the Anglo-Italian Cup at Bramall Lane on Aug. 24, 1994. In addition, United manager Dave Bassett was ordered from the bench.

Most dismissals one team, one match: Five players of America Tres Rios in first ten minutes after disputed goal by opponents Itaperuna in Brazilian cup match in Rio de Janeiro on Nov. 23, 1991. Tie then abandoned and awarded to Itaperuna.

Eight dismissals in one match: Four on each side in S. American Super Cup quarter-final (Gremio, Brazil v Penarol, Uruguay) in Oct. 1993.

Five dismissals in one season – Dave Caldwell (twice with Chesterfield, 3 times with Torquay) in 1987-88.

First instance of **four dismissals in Scottish match**: three **Rangers** players (all English – Terry Hurlock, Mark Walters, Mark Hateley) and **Celtic's** Peter Grant in Scottish Cup quarter-final at Parkhead on Mar. 17, 1991 (Celtic won 2-0).

Four players (3 Hamilton, 1 Airdrie) were sent off in Scottish Div. 1 match on Oct. 30, 1993.

Four players (3 Ayr, 1 Stranraer) were sent off in Scottish Div. 1 match on Aug. 27, 1994.

FASTEST SENDINGS-OFF

World record – 10 secs: Giuseppe Lorenzo (Bologna) for striking opponent in Italian League match v Parma, December 9, 1990.

Domestic – 19 secs: Mark Smith (Crewe goalkeeper at Darlington, Div. 3, Mar. 12, 1994). **In Div. 1 – 85 secs: Liam O'Brien** (Man. Utd. at Southampton, Jan. 3, 1987). **Premier League – 72 secs: Tim Flowers** (Blackburn goalkeeper v Leeds, Feb. 1, 1995).

In World Cup – 55 secs: Jose Batista (Uruguay v. Scotland at Neza, Mexico, June 13, 1986).

In European competition – 90 secs: Sergei Dirkach (Dynamo Moscow v Ghent UEFA Cup 3rd round, 2nd leg, December 11, 1991).

MOST SENDINGS-OFF IN CAREER

21 – Willie Johnston (Rangers 7, WBA 6, Vancouver Whitecaps 4, Hearts 3, Scotland 1).

WEMBLEY SENDINGS-OFF

Manchester United's **Kevin Moran** is the only player to be sent off in the F.A. Cup Final (v. Everton, 1985).

Arsenal's **Lee Dixon** became the seventh player ordered off in major soccer at Wembley when dismissed in the F.A. Cup semi-final against Tottenham (April 1993), and **Andrei Kanchelskis** (Man. U.) was sent off in the 1994 League Cup Final v Aston Villa. The others, besides Moran, Dixon and Kanchelskis:

Aug. 1948 Boris Stankovic (Yugoslavia) v. Sweden, Olympic Games.
July 1966 Antonio Rattin (Argentina captain) v. England, World Cup.
Aug. 1974 Billy Bremner (Leeds) and **Kevin Keegan** (Liverpool) in F.A. Charity Shield.
Mar. 1977 Gilbert Dresch (Luxembourg) v. England, World Cup.
June 1995 Tetsuji Hashiratani (Japan) v. England (Umbro Cup).

In addition, three players have been sent off in **Play-off Finals** at Wembley: **Peter Swan** (Port Vale v W.B.A., 1993) and two Stockport players, **Mike Wallace** and **Chris Beaumont**, against Burnley, 1994.

WEMBLEY'S SUSPENDED CAPTAINS

Suspension has prevented four **club captains** playing at Wembley in modern finals, in successive years.

Three were in F.A. Cup Finals – **Glenn Roeder** (Q.P.R., 1982), **Steve Foster** (Brighton, 1983) and **Wilf Rostron** (Watford, 1984) – and Sunderland's **Shaun Elliott** was barred from the 1985 Milk Cup Final.

Roeder was banned from Q.P.R.'s 1982 Cup Final replay against Tottenham, and Foster was ruled out of the first match in Brighton's 1983 Final against Manchester United.

DECISIONS REVOKED

Sendings-off cancelled by F.A. on "second evidence": **Season 1994-5** Kevin Scott (Tottenham v QPR); Alvin Martin (West Ham v Sheff. Wed.); **season 1995-6** Vinnie Jones (Wimbledon v Liverpool); Henning Berg (Blackburn v Liverpool).

BOOKINGS RECORDS

Most players of one Football League club booked in one match is **TEN** – members of the Mansfield Town team away to Crystal Palace in F.A. Cup third round, January 1963.

Fastest bookings – 3 seconds after kick-off, **Vinnie Jones** (Chelsea, home to Sheff. Utd., F.A. Cup fifth round, February 15, 1992); 5 seconds after kick-off: **Vinnie Jones** (Sheff. Utd., away to Man. City, Div. 1, January 19, 1991). He was sent-off (54 mins) for second bookable offence.

FIGHTING TEAM-MATES

Charlton's **Mick Flanagan** and **Derek Hales** were sent off for fighting each other five minutes from end of F.A. Cup 3rd Round tie at home to Southern League Maidstone on Jan. 9, 1979.

On Sept. 28, 1994 the Scottish F.A. suspended Hearts players **Graeme Hogg** and **Craig Levein** for ten matches for fighting each other in a pre-season "friendly" v Raith.

PLAYERS JAILED

Ten professional footballers found guilty of conspiracy to fraud by "fixing" matches for betting purposes were given prison sentences at Nottingham Assizes on Jan. 26, 1965.

Jimmy Gauld (Mansfield Town), described as the central figure, was given four years. Among the others sentenced, Tony Kay (Sheff. Wed., Everton & England), Peter Swan (Sheff. Wed. & England) and David "Bronco" Layne (Sheff. Wed.) were suspended from football for life by the F.A.

LONG SUSPENSIONS

The longest suspension in modern times for a player in British football was imposed on Man. United's French international captain **Eric Cantona**, following his attack on a spectator as he left the pitch after being sent off at Crystal Palace (Prem. League) on Jan. 25, 1995. He was banned from football for 8 months.

The club immediately suspended him to the end of the season and fined him 2 weeks' wages (est. £20,000). Then, on a disrepute charge, the F.A. fined him £10,000 and extended the ban to September 30 (which FIFA confirmed as world wide).

A subsequent 2-weeks' jail sentence on Cantona for assault was altered, on appeal, to 120 hours' community service, which took the form of coaching schoolboys in the Manchester area.

Mark Dennis, the Q.P.R. defender, was sent off for the 11th time in his career away to Tottenham (Div. 1) on November 14, 1987. (Two of those dismissals were for after-match tunnel offences; in addition, Dennis had then been cautioned 64 times in ten seasons and answered two disrepute charges concerning newspaper articles).

On December 10, the F.A. imposed on him a 53-day suspension, which was amended on appeal (January 25) to an 8-match ban. This was the longest suspension of a Football League player since **Kevin Keegan** (Liverpool) and **Billy Bremner** (Leeds) were each banned for 5 weeks (10 matches) after being sent off in the F.A. Charity Shield at Wembley in August 1974.

On December 6, 1988 Dennis was sent off for **12th. time** in career (Q.P.R. v. Fulham reserves) and fined £1,000.

Up to the end of season 1993-4, **Steve Walsh** (Leicester) had been sent off 11 times in his 12-season career (4 times with Wigan, 7 with Leicester; ten times in League, once in F.A. Cup; ten times away, once at home).

Before the disciplinary points system was introduced in season 1972-73, offenders were suspended for a specific number of weeks. Other lengthy suspensions imposed by the F.A. for on-field offences:

November 1969: Derek Dougan (Wolves) 8 weeks; **John Fitzpatrick** (Man. Utd.) 8 weeks.

January 1970: Ronnie Rees (Nott'm Forest) 6 weeks; **George Best** (Man. Utd.) 6 weeks.

December 1971: Kevin Lewis (Man. United) 5 months; **Denis Hollywood** and **Brian O'Neil** (both Southampton) 9 weeks.

October 1987: Steve Walsh (Leicester) 9 matches – original ban of 6 games (following the sixth sending-off of his career) increased to 9 when he reached 21 disciplinary points.

April 1988: Chris Kamara (Swindon) suspended to end of season (6 matches).

October 1988: Paul Davis (Arsenal) suspended for 9 matches, and fined a record £3,000, for breaking jaw of Glen Cockerill (Southampton).

January 1992: Frank Sinclair (Chelsea) suspended for 9 matches (fined £600) after clash of heads with referee while playing for W.B.A. on loan.

January 1993: Alan Gough, Fulham goalkeeper, suspended for 42 days by

F.A. for assaulting referee in Autoglass Trophy match at Gillingham on December 8.

November 1994: Andy Townsend (Aston Villa) suspended for 6 matches (3 for 21 discip. points, 3 for sending-off).

Seven-month ban: Frank Barson, 37-year-old Watford centre-half, sent off at home to Fulham (Div. 3 South) on September 29, 1928, was suspended by the F.A. for the remainder of the season.

Twelve-month ban: Oldham Athletic full-back **Billy Cook** was given a 12-month suspension for refusing to leave the field when sent off at Middlesbrough (Div. 1), on April 3, 1915. The referee abandoned the match with 35 minutes still to play, and the score (4-1 to Middlesbrough) was ordered to stand.

Long Scottish ban: Billy McLafferty, Stenhousemuir striker, was banned (April 14) for 8½ months, to Jan. 1, 1993, and fined £250 for failing to appear at a disciplinary hearing after being sent off against Arbroath on Feb. 1.

Twelve-match ban: On May 12, 1994 Scottish F.A. suspended then Rangers forward **Duncan Ferguson** for 12 matches for violent conduct v Raith on Apr. 16. On Oct. 11, 1995, Ferguson (then with Everton) sent to jail for 3 months for the assault (served 44 days); Feb. 1, 1996 Scottish judge quashed 7 months that remained of SFA ban on Ferguson.

FINES – MODERN

For space reasons, this section has been condensed. Fuller details appeared seasonally in previous Annuals.

1988 (July) **Chelsea** fined record £75,000 by F.A. following serious crowd trouble at play-off v Middlesbrough in May.

1988 (November) League fine **Tottenham** £15,000 for failing to fulfil opening-day fixture v Coventry (ground not ready after close-season improvements).

1989 (February) **Brian Clough**, Nott'm. F. manager, fined £5,000 by F.A. (and banned from touchline for rest of season) for striking spectators at League Cup quarter-final v Q.P.R.

1989 (March) **Wimbledon** fined £10,000 by F.A. for making unauthorised loans to players.

1989 (June) League fine **Bradford City** £10,000 for poaching manager Terry Yorath from Swansea. **1989** (November) **Paul McGrath** (Aston Villa) fined £8,500 by F.A. (record for disrepute charge against player) following newspaper criticism of former club, Man. United. F.A. fine **Norwich** £50,000, **Arsenal** £20,000 following player-brawl at Highbury.

1989 (December) **West Ham** and **Wimbledon** each fined £20,000 after player-brawl at League Cup-tie.

1990 (February) **Swindon Town** fined £7,500 by F.A., their former manager **Lou Macari** £1,000 and censured, their chairman **Brian Hillier** suspended from football for 3 years for breach of rules re betting on matches (Newcastle v Swindon, F.A. Cup 4th. Round, Jan. 1988).

1990 (June) **Swindon Town** (promoted to Div.1 via play-offs) demoted to Div. 3, then, on appeal, to Div. 2, by League after pleading guilty to 36 charges of irregular payments to players over four-year period.

1990 (September) **Chesterfield** fined £12,500 by League for failing to fulfil League Cup-tie when hit by injuries.

1990 (November) F.A. deduct 2 League points from **Arsenal**, 1 from **Man. United** and fine both clubs £50,000, following mass player-brawl at Old Trafford.

1991 (January) League fine **Chelsea** record £105,000 for making illegal payments to three players.

1991 (April) League fine **Tottenham** £20,000 (£15,000 of it suspended) for late arrival at Chelsea.

1991 (November) League fine **Tottenham** £17,500 for late payment of transfer instalment to Chelsea for Gordon Durie.

1992 (January) **Birmingham** fined £10,000 by League for fielding ineligible player.

1992 (February) F.A. fine **Michael Thomas** (Liverpool) £3,000 for press criticism of his former manager George Graham (Arsenal).

1992 (April) F. A. fine **Birmingham** £50,000 (suspended to end of season 1992-3) after pitch invasion v Stoke.

1992 (August) F.A. fine **Southampton** £20,000 (£15,000 suspended) for previous season's disciplinary record (5 sent off, 80 cautions, 11 suspensions). F.A. fine **Kevin Keegan** (Newcastle manager) £1,000 on disrepute charge (assistant **Terry McDermott** fined £250) for comments to referee at Derby, April 20. F.A. warn **Kenny Dalglish** (Blackburn manager) on disrepute charge for comments to referee v Wolves, April 14.

1992 (October) *F.A. ban **Gordon Durie** (Tottenham) 3 matches for "feigning injury" v Coventry, Aug. 18 (*ban quashed by F.A. Appeal Board, Dec. 16).

1992 (November) F.A give **Joe Kinnear** (Wimbledon manager) 5-match touchline ban and £750 fine (suspended) for comments to referee at Blackburn, Sept. 19. F.A. fine **Vinnie Jones** (Wimbledon) record individual sum of £20,000 on disrepute charge for narrating "Soccer's hard men" video; Jones also given 6-month playing ban (suspended for 3 years). **Barnet** fined £50,000 by F. League after investigation into club's financial affairs.

1993 (January) Sequel to League match at Tottenham, Dec. 12: F.A. fine Arsenal manager **George Graham** £500 for remarks to referee, suspend **Ian Wright** for 3 matches for throwing punch at opponent.

1993 (March) F.A. fine **Martin Allen** (West Ham) £1,000 (4-match ban) as season's first player to reach 41 discip. points (12 bookings). F.A. fine **Eric Cantona** (Man. U.) £1,000 for spitting at spectators at Leeds, Feb. 8.

1993 (April) F.A. fine **Vinnie Jones** (Wimbledon) £1,000 (4-match ban) for reaching 41 discip. points (his 4th suspension of season). F.A. fine **Man. City** £50,000 (suspended) following F.A. Cup 6th Round pitch invasion v Tottenham, March 7. **Graeme Souness** (Liverpool manager) fined £500 by F.A. and warned for "insulting behaviour" to referee at Crystal Palace, March 23.

1993 (May) League fine **Barnet** £25,000 for irregular payment to player, and warn that further indiscretion could cost them League status.

1993 (August) F.A. fine **Ian Wright** (Arsenal) £5,000 for 'improper gesture' to linesman at F.A. Cup Final replay v Sheff. Wed.. F.A. punish clubs for poor disap. records, season 1992-3: **Southampton** fined £25,000 (suspended), £10,000 of prev. year's fine activated; **Wimbledon** £25,000 (suspended); **Sheff. Utd.** £20,000 (suspended).

1993 (October) F.A. fine **Jim Smith** (Portsmouth manager) £750 for 'insulting comments to referee'; UEFA fine **Cardiff** £1,000 for coin-throwing incident v Standard Liege (CWC).

1993 (November) F.A. fine **Tottenham** £25,000 for 'poaching' manager Ossie Ardiles from WBA. F. League fine **Watford** £10,000 for illegal approach when signing manager Glenn Roeder from Gillingham. UEFA fine **Aberdeen** £4,500 and **Man. U.** £2,260 for offences at European matches. F.A. fine **Bristol C.** £40,000 (£30,000 suspended for 2 years) for improper claims to Football Trust over ground improvements. F.A. fine **Aston Villa** and **Notts Co.** £30,000 each for breach of rules when signing players from Australia.

1994 (January) FIFA fine **Welsh F.A.** £7,055 over incident at Wales-Romania World Cup match in which fan killed by rocket-flare.

1994 (February) F. League fine **Birmingham** £55,000 for 'poaching' manager Barry Fry from Southend.

1994 (March) F.A. fine **Sunderland** £5,000 for 'poaching' Mick Buxton (manager) from Huddersfield. Welsh F.A. fine **Cardiff** £25,000, **Swansea** £30,000 (suspended to season's end) for crowd trouble in match at Cardiff, Dec. 22. **Alex Ferguson** (Man. U. manager) fined £250 by F.A. for remarks to referee at 'A' team match.

1994 (April) F.A. Premier League fine **Everton** record £75,000 (plus £50,000 compensation) for 'poaching' manager Mike Walker from Norwich.

1994 (June) In **heaviest punishment** ever handed out by F.A., **Tottenham** fined £600,000, deducted 12 Premiership points at start of season 1994-5 and banned from F.A. Cup for same season for 'financial irregularities' involving loans to players during previous administration at club (see Dec. 1994 re appeal). F.A. give **Millwall** 3 sentences (first 2 suspended for 2 years) after crowd trouble at play-off v Derby: fined £100,000; ordered to play 2 matches behind closed doors; 3 League points deducted if further disturbances, home or away, before Dec. 31.

1994 (September) F.A. fine **Ian Wright** (Arsenal) £750 for making "gestures' to fans at Q.P.R., April 27.

1994 (October) Football League fine **Preston** £2,500 for late arrival at Darlington (Aug. 13). UEFA fine **Aston Villa** £12,500 for pitch invasion, home to Inter Milan (UEFA Cup, Sept. 29).

1994 (November) UEFA fine **Aston Villa** £9,367 for pitch invasion after UEFA home leg v Trabzonspor (Nov. 1). F.A. fine **Des Walker** (Sheff. W.) £1,200, plus 3-match ban, for head-butting opponent v Ipswich (Nov. 16). F.A. fine **John Fashanu** (Aston Vila) (£6,000) on misconduct charge (newspaper criticism of Eric Cantona (Man. U.).

1994 (December) F.A. suspend **Paul Merson** (Arsenal) 2 months from senior football while under treatment for drug abuse.

1995 (January) F.A. fines: **Ian Wright** (Arsenal) £1,000 (4-match ban) for reaching 41 discip. points; **Terry Hurlock** (Fulham) £350, with total 6-week ban for 51 discip. points; **Alan Ball** (Southampton manager) £500 for comments to linesman at Q.P.R. (Dec. 28); **Joe Jordan** (Bristol C. manager) £250 for remarks to match official; **Martin Edwards** (Man. U. Chairman) £100 for remarks to referee at Arsenal (Nov. 26).

1995 (March) League fine **Sunderland** £2,500 for fielding ineligible player (Dominic Matteo, loan transfer from Liverpool registered after transfer deadline). F.A. fines (for 41 discip. points): **Steve Bruce** (Man. U.) £750 and 2-match ban; **Mike Milligan** (Norwich) £500 and 2-match ban; **Francis Benali** (Southampton) £350 and 3-match ban.

1995 (April) F.A. fines: **Robbie Fowler** (Liverpool) £1,000 for hitching shorts to spectators at Leicester, Dec. 26; **Tim Sherwood** (Blackburn) £1,000 and 1-match ban (41 discip. points); **Ken Monkou** (Southampton) £350 and 1-match ban (41 discip. points); **Joe Kinnear** (Wimbledon manager) £1,500 and 6-month touchline ban to Oct. 31 on misconduct charges (verbal abuse of referees); **Vinnie Jones** (Wimbledon) £1,750 on misconduct charge (swearing at Newcastle manager Kevin Keegan after match); **Terry Hurlock** (Fulham) £400 and 4-match suspension (totalling 15-game ban in 1994-5) as first player to reach 61 discip. points in a season.

1995 (May) F.A. fines: **Gary Neville** (Man. U.) and **Carlton Palmer** (Sheff. W.) each £1,000 (41 discip. points); **Roy Keane** (Man. U.) £5,000 on disrepute charge after being sent off in F.A. Cup s-final v Crystal P.

1995 (August) F.A. give suspended fines to 5 clubs for previous season's poor disciplinary records: **QPR** (£25,000), **Wimbledon** (£25,000), **Burnley** (£10,000), **Chester** (£10,000), **Fulham** (£10,000).

1995 (September) UEFA suspend **Vinnie Jones** (Wales) for 5 matches (sent off v Georgia, June); UEFA fine **Rangers** £2,500 for supporters' misconduct in Cyprus (E. Cup, August).

1995 (October) F.A. suspend **Julian Dicks** (West Ham) 3 matches on disrepute charge (alleged stamping on Chelsea's John Spencer, Sept. 11).

1995 (November) UEFA fine **Chelsea** £17,000 for misconduct by "unofficial" supporters away to Real Zaragoza (CWC Sf, April 6); F.A. fine **Robert Fleck** (Norwich) £1,000 for abuse of official at Sheff. Utd., Sept. 9); Blackburn fine **Graeme Le Saux** and **David Batty** for brawling away to Spartak Moscow (E. Champions' League, Nov. 22); **UEFA suspend** Le Saux and Batty each for 2 European club matches.

1995 (December) F.A. fine **Bournemouth** £5,000 (suspended) following crowd trouble v Crewe (Sept. 16).

1996 (January) **Tottenham** and **Wimbledon** each given 1-year Euro ban (active for 5 years) by UEFA for fielding weak team in last summer's Inter Toto Cup; on appeal, UEFA quash ban, impose fines instead – **Tottenham** £90,000, **Wimbledon** £60,000 (Premier League's 20 clubs each to pay £9,000 to cover fines/costs. F.A. fine **Man. United** £20,000 for illegal approach to 17-year-old David Brown (Oldham). F.A. fine **Bryan Robson** (Mid'bro' player-manager) £750 and Boro' players **Neil Cox** and **Nigel Pearson** each £500 for abusive remarks to referee at Blackburn, Dec. 16.

1996 (February) **Leyton Orient** sack **Roger Stanislaus** after F.A. ban him for 12 months – first British-based player to test positive for taking performance-enhancing drug, cocaine-related). F.A. fine **Vinnie Jones** £2,000 (his 5th. large fine in 3 years) for newspaper attack on Chelsea's Ruud Gullit and foreign players generally; F.A. fine **Gary Megson** (Norwich manager) £1,000 on disrepute charge (incident at Derby, Jan. 1).

1996 (March) F.A. fine **Keith Curle** (Man. City) £500 for remarks made to referee (v Everton, Feb. 10).

1996 (April) F.A. fine **Mark Hughes** (Chelsea) £1,000, plus 2-match ban, for reaching 45 discip. points (his third suspension of season); F.A. fine **Mark Ford** (Leeds) £75, with 1-match ban (45 discip. points); **Faustino Asprilla** (Newcastle) fined £10,000 by F.A. and banned from first match 1996-7, on misconduct charges for elbowing/head-butting Keith Curle (Man. City) at Maine Road, Feb. 24 (Curle cleared).

MANAGERS

INTERNATIONAL RECORDS

(As at start of season 1996-97)

	P	W	D	L	F	A
Bryan Hamilton (N. Ireland – appointed Feb. 1994)	18	6	3	9	25	29
Craig Brown (Scotland – appointed Sept. 1993)	25	12	4	9	30	21
Bobby Gould (Wales – appointed Aug. 1995)	6	2	1	3	8	8
Mick McCarthy (Rep. of Ireland – appointed Feb. 1996)	8	1	2	5	9	14

FINAL RECORDS OF LAST NATIONAL MANAGERS

	P	W	D	L	F	A
Terry Venables (England 1994-6)	23	11	11	1	35	13
Billy Bingham (N. Ireland, *2 spells)	117	40	33	44	112	127
Andy Roxburgh (Scotland 1986-93)	61	23	19	19	67	60
Mike Smith (Wales, †2 spells)	48	17	11	20	55	57
Jack Charlton (Rep. of Ireland 1986-95)	93	46	30	17	127	62

(*Bingham managed N. Ireland 1967-71, 1980-93.
He also coached Greece 1971-3).
(†Smith managed Wales 1974-9, 1994-5;
second spell record: P9, W2, D1, L6, Goals 8-19).

ENGLAND'S MANAGERS

1946-62:	**Walter Winterbottom** (P139, W78, D33, L28).
1963-74:	**Sir Alf Ramsey** (P113, W69, D27, L17).
1974:	**Caretaker – Joe Mercer** (P7, W3, D3, L1).
1974-77:	**Don Revie** (P29, W14, D8, L7).
1977-82:	**Ron Greenwood** (P55, W33, D12, L10).
1982-90:	**Bobby Robson** (P95, W47, D30, L18).
1990-93:	**Graham Taylor** (P38, W18, D13, L7).
1994-96:	**Terry Venables**, coach (P23, W11, D11, L1).

INTERNATIONAL MANAGER CHANGES

England: Walter Winterbottom 1946-62 (initially coach); **Alf Ramsey** (Feb. 1963-May 1974); **Joe Mercer** (caretaker May 1974); **Don Revie** (July 1974-July 1977); **Ron Greenwood** (Aug. 1977-July 1982); **Bobby Robson** (July 1982-July 1990); **Graham Taylor** (July 1990-Nov. 1993); **Terry Venables**, coach (Jan. 1994-June 1996); **Glenn Hoddle**, coach (from June 1996).

N. Ireland (modern): **Billy Bingham** (1967-Aug. 1971); **Terry Neill** (Aug. 1971-Mar. 1975); **Dave Clements** (Player-Manager Mar. 1975-1976); **Danny Blanchflower** (June 1976-Nov. 1979); **Billy Bingham** (Feb. 1980-Nov. 1993); **Bryan Hamilton** (since Feb. 1994).

Scotland (modern): **Bobby Brown** (Feb. 1967-July 1971); **Tommy Docherty** (Sept. 1971- Dec. 1972); **Willie Ormond** (Jan. 1973-May 1977); **Ally MacLeod** (May 1977-Sept.1978); **Jock Stein** (Oct. 1978-Sept. 1985); **Alex Ferguson** (caretaker Oct. 1985-June 1986); **Andy Roxburgh**, coach (July 1986-Sept. 1993); **Craig Brown** (since Sept. 1993).

Wales (modern): **Mike Smith** (July 1974-Dec. 1979); **Mike England** (Mar. 1980-Feb. 1988); **David Williams** (caretaker Mar. 1988); **Terry Yorath** (Apr. 1988-Nov. 1993); **John Toshack** (Mar. 1994, one match); **Mike Smith** (Mar. 1994-June 1995); **Bobby Gould** (since Aug. 1995).

Rep. of Ireland (modern): **Liam Tuohy** (Sept. 1971-Nov. 1972); **Johnny Giles** (Oct. 1973-Apr. 1980, initially player-manager); **Eoin Hand** (June 1980-Nov. 1985); **Jack Charlton** (Feb. 1986-Dec. 1995); **Mick McCarthy** (since Feb. 1996).

LONGEST-SERVING LEAGUE MANAGERS – ONE CLUB

Fred Everiss, secretary-manager of W.B.A. for 46 years (1902-48); since last war, **Sir Matt Busby**, in charge of Man. United for 26 seasons (Oct 1945-June 1971).

SHORT-TERM MANAGERS

		Departed
3 Days	Bill Lambton (Scunthorpe United)	April 1959
7 Days	Tim Ward (Exeter City)	March 1953
7 Days	Kevin Cullis (Swansea City)	February 1996
13 Days	Johnny Cochrane (Reading)	April 1939
16 Days	Jimmy McIlroy (Bolton Wanderers)	November 1970
20 Days	Paul Went (Leyton Orient)	October 1981
28 Days	Tommy Docherty (Q.P.R.)	December 1968
41 Days	Steve Wicks (Lincoln City)	October 1995
44 Days	Brian Clough (Leeds United)	September 1974
44 Days	Jock Stein (Leeds United)	October 1978
48 Days	John Toshack (Wales)	March 1994
49 Days	Brian Little (Wolves)	October 1986
61 Days	Bill McGarry (Wolves)	November 1985
63 Days	Dave Booth (Peterborough United)	January 1991

• In May 1984, Crystal Palace named **Dave Bassett** as manager, but he changed his mind four days later, without signing the contract, and returned to Wimbledon.

EARLY-SEASON MANAGER SACKINGS

1994 Kenny Hibbitt (Walsall) and Kenny Swain (Wigan) 20 days; **1993** Peter Reid (Man. C.) 12 days; **1991** Don Mackay (Blackburn) 14 days; **1989** Mick Jones (Peterborough) 12 days; **1980** Bill McGarry (Newcastle) 13 days; **1979** Dennis Butler (Port Vale) 12 days; **1977** George Petchey (Leyton O.) 13 days; **1977** Willie Bell (Birmingham) 16 days; **1971** Len Richley (Darlington) 12 days.

FEWEST MANAGERS

West Ham United have had only eight managers in their history: Syd King, Charlie Paynter, Ted Fenton, Ron Greenwood, John Lyall, Lou Macari, Billy Bonds and Harry Redknapp.

RECORD START FOR MANAGER

Arsenal were unbeaten in 17 League matches from the start of season 1947-8 under new manager Tom Whittaker.

MANAGER DOUBLES

Only three managers have won the League Championship with different clubs: **Herbert Chapman** with Huddersfield Town (1923-4, 1924-5) and Arsenal (1930-1, 1932-3); **Brian Clough** with Derby County (1971-2) and Nottingham Forest (1977-8); **Kenny Dalglish** with Liverpool (1985-6, 1987-8, 1989-90) and Blackburn (1994-5).

Only manager to win the F.A. Cup with different clubs: **Billy Walker** (Sheff. Wed. 1935, Nott'm. Forest 1959).

Kenny Dalglish (Liverpool) is the only man to achieve the Championship/F.A. Cup double as both player and manager.

FIRST CHAIRMAN-MANAGER

On December 20, 1988, after two years on the board, Dundee United manager **Jim McLean** was elected chairman, too. Scotland's longest-serving manager (appointed by United on November 24, 1971) resigned at end of season 1992-3 (remained chairman).

FIRST DIV (Old)/PREM. LGE. PLAYER–MANAGERS

Les Allen (Q.P.R. 1968-9); **Johnny Giles** (W.B.A. 1976-7); **Howard Kendall** (Everton 1981-2); **Kenny Dalglish** (Liverpool, 1985-90); **Trevor Francis** (Q.P.R., 1988-9); **Terry Butcher** (Coventry, 1990-1), **Peter Reid** (Man. City, 1990-93), **Trevor Francis** (Sheff. Wed., 1991-4), **Glenn Hoddle**, (Chelsea, 1993-5), **Bryan Robson** (Middlesbrough, since May 1994), **Ray Wilkins** (Q.P.R., since November 1994), **Ruud Gullit** (Chelsea 1996).

MANAGERS OF POST-WAR CHAMPIONS

1947 George Kay (Liverpool); **1948** Tom Whittaker (Arsenal); **1949** Bob Jackson (Portsmouth); **1950** Bob Jackson (Portsmouth); **1951** Arthur Rowe (Tottenham); **1952** Matt Busby (Man. United); **1953** Tom Whittaker (Arsenal).

1954 Stan Cullis (Wolves); **1955** Ted Drake (Chelsea); **1956** Matt Busby (Man. United); **1957** Matt Busby (Man. United); **1958** Stan Cullis (Wolves); **1959** Stan Cullis (Wolves); **1960** Harry Potts (Burnley).

1961 *Bill Nicholson (Tottenham); **1962** Alf Ramsey (Ipswich); **1963** Harry Catterick (Everton); **1964** Bill Shankly (Liverpool); **1965** Matt Busby (Man. United); **1966** Bill Shankly (Liverpool); **1967** Matt Busby (Man United).

1968 Joe Mercer (Man. City); **1969** Don Revie (Leeds); **1970** Harry Catterick (Everton); **1971** *Bertie Mee (Arsenal); **1972** Brian Clough (Derby); **1973** Bill Shankly (Liverpool); **1974** Don Revie (Leeds).

1975 Dave Mackay (Derby); **1976** Bob Paisley (Liverpool); **1977** Bob Paisley (Liverpool); **1978** Brian Clough (Nott'm. Forest); **1979** Bob Paisley (Liverpool); **1980** Bob Paisley (Liverpool); **1981** Ron Saunders (Aston Villa).

1982 Bob Paisley (Liverpool); **1983** Bob Paisley (Liverpool); **1984** Joe Fagan (Liverpool); **1985** Howard Kendall (Everton); **1986** *Kenny Dalglish (Liverpool – player/manager); **1987** Howard Kendall (Everton).

1988 Kenny Dalglish (Liverpool – player/manager); **1989** George Graham (Arsenal); **1990** Kenny Dalglish (Liverpool); **1991** George Graham (Arsenal); **1992** Howard Wilkinson (Leeds); **1993** Alex Ferguson (Man. United); **1994** *Alex Ferguson (Man. United); **1995** Kenny Dalglish (Blackburn); **1996** Alex Ferguson (Man. United).

(* Double winners)

ALEX FERGUSON TOP ANGLO MANAGER

Alex Ferguson has the most successful managerial record with Scottish and English clubs combined. With **Aberdeen** (1978-86) he won ten top prizes: 3 Scottish Championships, 4 Scottish Cups, 1 Scottish League Cup, 1 Cup-Winners' Cup, 1 European Super Cup.

With **Manchester United** he has won 8 major trophies in the last 6 seasons: 1990 F.A. Cup, 1991 Cup-Winners' Cup, 1992 League Cup, 1993 League Championship, 1994 League Championship and F.A. Cup, 1996 Championship and F.A. Cup.

MOST SUCCESSFUL ENGLISH-CLUB MANAGER

Bob Paisley, with 20 trophies for Liverpool (1974-83): 6 League Championships, 3 European Cups, 3 League Cups, 1 UEFA Cup, 1 European Super Cup, 6 Charity Shields (1 shared).

RELEGATION 'DOUBLES'

Managers associated with two clubs relegated in same season: **Billy McNeill** in 1986-7 (Man. City and Aston Villa both relegated to Div. 2; **Dave Bassett** in 1987-8 (Watford down to Div. 2, Sheff. Utd. down to Div. 3).

WEMBLEY STADIUM

Wembley is favourite to defeat Manchester and be named England's new national stadium. The decision is due in October, and in June Wembley unveiled plans for a £160m. "stadium of dreams" redevelopment in which only the famous Twin Towers will survive. The super stadium will accommodate 80,000 seated in space-age comfort. It will have a retractable roof and rail station with direct link to the Channel Tunnel. One question: Why only 80,000?

Over the past ten years, more than £80m. has been spent, transforming the stadium that opened in 1923 into an arena to match its "Venue of Legends" slogan.

Improvements include the conversion to all-seating (capacity 80,000) in season 1989-90, construction of the spectacular Olympic Gallery that encircles the stadium (capacity 4,000), installation of modern box office and walkways directly linking station to ground.

Wembley remains the national home of English football and its new charisma was rewarded in May 1992 with the allocation of a fifth European Cup Final after an interval of 14 years.

ORIGINAL CONTRACT

The **Empire Stadium** was built at a cost of **£750,000**. Its construction included 25,000 tons of concrete, 2,000 tons of steel and 104 turnstiles. The original contract (May 1921) between the F.A. and the British Empire Exhibition was for the Cup Final to be played there for 21 years.

INVASION DAY

Memorable scenes were witnessed at the **first F.A. Cup Final at Wembley, April 28, 1923**, between **Bolton Wanderers** and **West Ham United**. An accurate return of the attendance could not be made owing to thousands breaking in, but there were probably more than 150,000 spectators present. The match was delayed for 40 minutes owing to the crowd invading the playing pitch. Official attendance was 126,047.

Gate receipts totalled £27,776. The two clubs and the Football Association each received £6,365 and the F.A. refunded £2,797 to ticket-holders who were unable to get to their seats. Admission has since been by ticket only.

ENGLAND THERE UNTIL 2002

Under an agreement signed in 1983, the Football Association are contracted to playing **England's home matches***, the F.A. Cup Final and Charity Shield at Wembley Stadium until 2002.

* Exception was v Sweden (Umbro Cup) at Elland Road, Leeds, on June 8, 1995 – first England home game played away from Wembley since Poland at Goodison Park on Jan. 5, 1966.

England previously played elsewhere on their own soil on May 12, 1973, when they met N. Ireland on Everton's ground. Officially, that was a home fixture for Ireland, but the venue was switched from Belfast for security reasons.

MODERN CAPACITY

Capacity of the now all-seated **Wembley Stadium** is 80,000. The last 100,000 attendance was for the 1985 F.A. Cup Final between Man. United and Everton.

WEMBLEY'S FIRST UNDER LIGHTS

November 30, 1955 (England 4, Spain 1), when the floodlights were switched on after 73 minutes (afternoon match played in damp, foggy conditions).

First Wembley International played throughout under lights: England 8, N. Ireland 3 on evening of November 20, 1963 (att: 55,000).

WEMBLEY HAT-TRICKS

Three players have scored hat-tricks in major finals at Wembley: **Stan Mortensen** for Blackpool v Bolton (F.A. Cup Final, 1953), **Geoff Hurst** for England v West Germany (World Cup Final, 1966) and **David Speedie** for Chelsea v Man. City (Full Members Cup, 1985).

ENGLAND'S WEMBLEY DEFEATS

England have lost 14 matches to foreign opponents at Wembley:

Nov.	1953	3-6 v Hungary	May	1981	0-1 v Brazil
Oct.	1959	2-3 v Sweden	Oct.	1982	1-2 v W. Germany
Oct.	1965	2-3 v Austria	Sept.	1983	0-1 v Denmark
Apr.	1972	1-3 v W. Germany	June	1984	0-2 v Russia
Nov.	1973	0-1 v Italy	May	1990	1-2 v Uruguay
Feb.	1977	0-2 v Holland	Sept.	1991	0-1 v Germany
Mar.	1981	1-2 v Spain	June	1995	1-3 v Brazil

But a 15th. defeat came in **Euro 96**. After drawing the semi-final with Germany 1-1, England went out 6-5 on penalties.

FASTEST GOALS AT WEMBLEY

In first-class matches: **38 seconds** by **Bryan Robson** in England's 2-1 win against Yugoslavia on December 13, 1989; **44 seconds** by **Bryan Robson** for England in 4-0 win v N. Ireland on February 23, 1982; **45 seconds** by **Jack Milburn** for Newcastle in the 1955 F.A. Cup Final against Man. City.

Fastest goal in **any** match at Wembley: **20 seconds** by **Maurice Cox** for Cambridge University against Oxford on December 5, 1979.

FOUR WEMBLEY HEADERS

When **Wimbledon** beat Sutton United 4-2 in the F.A. Amateur Cup Final at Wembley on May 4, 1963, Irish centre-forward **Eddie Reynolds** headed all four goals.

ENGLAND POSTPONEMENT

Fog at Wembley on November 21, 1979 caused England's European Championship match against Bulgaria to be postponed 24 hours.

WEMBLEY ONE-SEASON DOUBLES

In 1989, **Nottingham Forest** became the first club to win two Wembley Finals in the same season (Littlewoods Cup and Simod Cup).

In 1993, **Arsenal** made history there as the first club to win the League (Coca-Cola) Cup and the F.A. Cup in the same season. They beat Sheffield Wednesday 2-1 in both finals.

SUDDEN DEATH DECIDERS

First Wembley Final decided on sudden death (first goal scored in overtime): April 23, 1995 – **Birmingham** beat Carlisle (1-0, Paul Tait 103 mins.) to win Auto Windscreens Shield.

First instance of a "golden goal" deciding a major International tournament was at Wembley on June 30, 1996, when **Germany** beat the Czech Republic 2-1 in the European Championship Final with Oliver Bierhoff's goal in the 95th. minute.

SHADOWS OVER SOCCER

DAYS OF TRAGEDY – CLUBS

Season 1988-9 brought the worst disaster in the history of British sport, with the death of *95 Liverpool supporters (200 injured) at the **F.A. Cup semi-final** against Nott'm. Forest at **Hillsborough, Sheffield**, on Saturday, April 15. The tragedy built up in the minutes preceding kick-off, when thousands surged into the ground at the Leppings Lane end. Many were crushed in the tunnel between entrance and terracing, but most of the victims were trapped inside the perimeter fencing behind the goal. The match was abandoned without score after six minutes' play. The dead included seven women and girls, two teenage sisters and two teenage brothers. The youngest victim was a boy of ten, the oldest 67-year-old Gerard Baron, whose brother Kevin played for Liverpool in the 1950 Cup Final. (*Total became 96 in March 1993, when Tony Bland died after being in a coma for nearly four years).

The two worst disasters in one season in British soccer history occurred at the end of 1984-5. On May 11, the last Saturday of the League season, 56 people (two of them visiting supporters) were burned to death – and more than 200 taken to hospital – when fire destroyed the main stand at the **Bradford City-Lincoln City** match at Valley Parade.

The wooden, 77-year-old stand was full for City's last fixture before which, amid scenes of celebration, the club had been presented with the Third Division Championship trophy. The fire broke out just before half-time and, within five minutes, the entire stand was engulfed.

Eighteen days later, on May 29, at the European Cup Final between **Liverpool** and **Juventus** at the Heysel Stadium, Brussels, 39 spectators (31 of them Italian) were crushed or trampled to death and 437 injured. The disaster occurred an hour before the scheduled kick-off when Liverpool supporters charged a Juventus section of the crowd at one end of the stadium, and under pressure, a retaining wall collapsed.

The sequel was a 5-year ban by UEFA on English clubs generally in European competition, with a 6-year ban on Liverpool.

On May 26, 1985 ten people were trampled to death and 29 seriously injured in a crowd panic on the way into the **Olympic Stadium, Mexico City** for the Mexican Cup Final between local clubs National University and America.

More than 100 people died and 300 were injured in a football disaster at Nepal's national stadium in Katmandu in March 1988. There was a stampede when a violent hailstorm broke over the capital. Spectators rushed for cover, but the stadium exits were locked, and hundreds were trampled in the crush.

In South Africa, on January 13, 1991 40 black fans were trampled to death (50 injured) as they tried to escape from fighting that broke out at a match in the gold-mining town of Orkney, 80 miles from Johannesburg. The friendly, between top teams **Kaiser Chiefs** and **Orlando Pirates**, attracted a packed crowd of 20,000. Violence erupted after the referee allowed Kaiser Chiefs a disputed second-half goal to lead 1-0.

Disaster struck at the French Cup semi-final (May 5, 1992), with the death of 15 spectators and 1,300 injured when a temporary metal stand collapsed in the Corsican town of Bastia. The tie between Second Division **Bastia** and French Champions **Marseille** was cancelled.

A total of 318 died and 500 were seriously injured when the crowd rioted over a disallowed goal at the National Stadium in Lima, Peru, on May 24, 1964. **Peru** and **Argentina** were competing to play in the Olympic Games in Tokyo.

That remained sport's heaviest death toll until October 20, 1982, when (it was revealed only in July 1989) 340 Soviet fans were killed in Moscow's Lenin Stadium at the UEFA Cup second round first leg match between **Moscow Spartak** and **Haarlem (Holland)**. They were crushed on an open stairway when a last-minute Spartak goal sent departing spectators surging back into the ground.

Among other crowd disasters abroad: **June 1968** – 74 died in **Argentina**. Panic broke out at the end of a goalless match between River Plate and Boca Juniors at Nunez, Buenos Aires, when Boca supporters threw lighted newspaper torches onto fans in the tiers below.

February 1974 – 49 killed in **Egypt** in crush of fans clamouring to see Zamalek play Dukla Prague.

September 1971 – 44 died in **Turkey**, when fighting among spectators over a disallowed goal (Kayseri v Siwas) led to a platform collapsing.

The then worst disaster in the history of British football, in terms of loss of life, occurred at Glasgow Rangers' ground at **Ibrox Park**, January 2, 1971.

Sixty-six people were trampled to death (100 injured) as they tumbled down Stairway 13 just before the end of the **Rangers v. Celtic** New Year's match. That disaster led to the 1975 Safety of Sports Grounds legislation.

The Ibrox tragedy eclipsed even the Bolton disaster in which 33 were killed and about 500 injured when a wall and crowd barriers collapsed near a corner-flag at the **Bolton v. Stoke** F.A. Cup sixth round tie on March 9, 1946. The match was completed after half an hour's stoppage.

In a previous crowd disaster at **Ibrox** on April 5, 1902 part of the terracing collapsed during the Scotland v. England International and 25 people were killed. The match, held up for 20 minutes, ended 1-1, but was never counted as an official International.

Eight leading players and three officials of **Manchester United** and eight newspaper representatives were among the 23 who perished in the air crash at Munich on February 6, 1958, during take-off following a European Cup-tie in Belgrade. The players were Roger Byrne, Geoffrey Bent, Eddie Colman, Duncan Edwards, Mark Jones, David Pegg, Tommy Taylor and Liam Whelan, and the officials were Walter Crickmer (secretary), Tom Curry (trainer) and Herbert

Whalley (coach). The newspaper representatives were Alf Clarke, Don Davies, George Follows, Tom Jackson, Archie Ledbrooke, Henry Rose, Eric Thompson and Frank Swift (former England goalkeeper of Manchester City).

On May 14, 1949, the entire team of Italian Champions, **Torino,** 8 of them Internationals, were killed when the aircraft taking them home from a match against Benfica in Lisbon crashed at Superga, near Turin. The total death toll of 28 included all the club's reserve players, the manager, trainer and coach.

On December 9, 1987, the 18-strong team squad of **Alianza Lima,** one of Peru's top clubs, were wiped out, together with 8 officials and several youth players, when a military aircraft taking them home from Puccalpa, crashed into the sea off Ventillana, ten miles from Lima. The only survivor among 43 on board was a member of the crew.

On April 28, 1993, 18 members of **Zambia's International** squad and 5 ZFA officials died when the aircraft carrying them to a World Cup qualifying tie against Senegal crashed into the Atlantic soon after take-off from Libreville, Gabon.

DAYS OF TRAGEDY – PERSONAL

Sam Wynne, Bury right-back, collapsed five minutes before half-time in the First Division match away to Sheffield United on April 30, 1927, and died in the dressing-room.

In the Rangers v. Celtic Scottish match on September 5, 1931, **John Thomson**, the 23-year-old Celtic and Scottish International goalkeeper, sustained a fractured skull when diving at an opponent's feet just before half-time and died the same evening.

Sim Raleigh (Gillingham), injured in a clash of heads at home to Brighton (Div. 3 South) on December 1, 1934, continued to play but collapsed in second half and died in hospital the same night.

James Thorpe, 23-year-old Sunderland goalkeeper, was injured during the First Division match at home to Chelsea on February 1, 1936 and died in a diabetic coma three days later.

Derek Dooley, Sheffield Wednesday centre-forward and top scorer in 1951-52 in the Football League with 46 goals in 30 matches, broke a leg in the League match at Preston on February 14, 1953, and, after complications set in, had to lose the limb by amputation.

John White (27), Tottenham Hotspur's Scottish International forward, was killed by lightning on a golf course at Enfield, North London in July, 1964.

Two players were killed by lightning during the Army Cup Final replay at Aldershot in April, 1948.

Tommy Allden (23), Highgate United centre-half was struck by lightning during Highgate's Amateur Cup quarter-final with Enfield Town on February 25, 1967. He died the following day. Four other players were also struck but recovered.

Roy Harper died while refereeing the York City–Halifax Town (Div. 4) match on May 5, 1969.

Jim Finn collapsed and died from a heart attack while refereeing Exeter v Stockport (Div. 4) on September 16, 1972.

Scotland manager **Jock Stein**, 62, collapsed and died minutes after the Wales-Scotland World Cup qualifying match (1-1) at Cardiff on September 10, 1985.

David Longhurst, 25-year-old York City forward, died after being carried off two minutes before half-time in the Fourth Division fixture at home to Lincoln City on September 8, 1991. The match was abandoned (0-0) and the inquest revealed that Longhurst suffered from a rare heart condition.

GREAT SERVICE

"For services to Association Football", **Stanley Matthews** (Stoke City, Blackpool and England), already a C.B.E., became the first professional footballer to receive a knighthood. This was bestowed in 1965, his last season.

Before he retired and five days after his 50th birthday, he played for Stoke to set a record as the oldest First Division footballer (v. Fulham, February 6, 1965).

Over a brilliant span of 33 years, he played in 886 first-class matches, including 54 full Internationals (plus 31 in war time), 701 League games (including 3 at start of season 1939-40, which was abandoned on the outbreak of war) and 86 F.A. Cup-ties, and scored 95 goals. He was never booked in his career.

Sir Stanley celebrated his 81st birthday last season (February 1, 1996). After spending a number of years in Toronto, he made his home back in the Potteries in 1989, having previously returned to his hometown, Hanley, Stoke-on-Trent in October, 1987 to unveil a life-size bronze statue of himself.

The inscription reads: "Sir Stanley Matthews, CBE. Born Hanley, 1 February 1915. His name is symbolic of the beauty of the game, his fame timeless and international, his sportsmanship and modesty universally acclaimed. A magical player, of the people, for the people."

On his home-coming in 1989, Sir Stanley was made President of Stoke City, the club he joined as a boy of 15 and served as a player for 20 years between 1931 and 1965.

In July 1992 FIFA honoured him with their "Gold merit award" for outstanding services to the game.

Former England goalkeeper **Peter Shilton**, still playing in 1994-5 at 45, has made more first-class appearances (1,378) than any other footballer in British history. He took his record total of League games to 996 with one appearance as substitute for Bolton (away to Stoke, May 3, 1995) after leaving Plymouth (player-manager) in January. In addition, he made one play-off appearance for Bolton. He retired from International football after the 1990 World Cup in Italy with 125 caps, then a world record.

Shilton's career spanned 30 seasons, 20 of them on the International stage. He made his League debut for Leicester City in May 1966, two months before England won the World Cup.

His 1,379 first-class appearances comprised a record 996 in the Football League, 125 Internationals, 102 League Cup, 86 F.A. Cup, 13 for England U-23s, 4 for the Football League and 52 other matches (European Cup, UEFA Cup, World Club Championship, Charity Shield, European Super Cup, Full Members' Cup, Play-offs, Screen Sports Super Cup, Anglo-Italian Cup, Texaco Cup, Simod Cup, Zenith Data Systems Cup and Autoglass Trophy).

Shilton has appeared more times at Wembley (57) than any other player: 52 for England, 2 League Cup Finals, 1 F.A. Cup Final, 1 Charity Shield match, and 1 for the Football League. He passed a century of League appearances with each of his first five clubs: Leicester (286), Stoke (110), Nott'm. Forest (202), Southampton (188) and Derby (175).

His club honours, all gained with Nott'm. Forest: League Championship 1978, League Cup 1979, European Cup 1979 and 1980, PFA Player of Year 1978.

Two other British footballers, also goalkeepers, have made more than 1,000 first-class appearances:

Ray Clemence, formerly with Tottenham, Liverpool and England, retired through injury in season 1987-8 after a career total of 1,119 matches starting in 1965-6. Clemence played 50 times for his first club, Scunthorpe; 665 for Liverpool; 337 for Tottenham; his 67 representative games included 61 England caps.

A third great British goalkeeper, **Pat Jennings**, ended his career (1963-86) with a total of 1,098 first-class matches for Watford, Tottenham, Arsenal and

N. Ireland. They were made up of 757 in the Football League, 119 full Internationals, 84 F.A. Cup appearances, 72 League/Milk Cup, 55 European club matches, 2 Charity Shield, 3 Other Internationals, 1 Under-23 cap, 2 Texaco Cup, 2 Anglo-Italian Cup and 1 Super Cup. Jennings played his 119th. and final International on his 41st birthday, June 12, 1986, against Brazil in Guadalajara in the Mexico World Cup.

KNIGHTS OF SOCCER

In the Queen's Birthday Honours (June 11, 1994), **Bobby Charlton**, England's record goalscorer and a Manchester United legend, became the fourth former professional footballer to receive a knighthood for services to the game. The others were **Stanley Matthews** (1965), **Alf Ramsey** (1967) and **Matt Busby** (1968).

PENALTIES

It is now **105 years** since the **penalty-kick** was introduced to the game, following a proposal to the Irish F.A. in 1890 by William McCrum, son of the High Sheriff for Co. Omagh, and approved by the International Football Board on June 2, 1891.

First penalty scored in a first-class match was by John Heath, for Wolves v Accrington Stanley (5-0 in Div. 1, September 14, 1891).

The greatest influence of the penalty has come since the 1970s, with the introduction of the shoot-out to settle deadlocked ties in various competitions.

Man. United were the first club to win a competitive match in British Football via a shoot-out (4-3 v Hull, Watney Cup semi-final, August 1970).

In season 1991-2, penalty shoot-outs were introduced to decide **F.A. Cup ties** still level after one replay and extra time.

Wembley saw its first penalty contest 22 years ago in the Charity Shield. So, since 1974, many major matches across the world have been settled thus, including:-

1974 F.A. Charity Shield (Wembley): Liverpool beat Leeds 6-5 (after 1-1).
1976 Eur. Champ. Final (Belgrade): Czech. beat W. Germany 5-3 (after 2-2).
1980 Cup-Winners' Cup Final (Brussels): Valencia beat Arsenal 5-4 (0-0).
1982 World Cup s-final (Seville): West Germany beat France 5-4 (after 3-3).
1984 European Cup Final (Rome): Liverpool beat AS Roma 4-2 (after 1-1).
1984 UEFA Cup Final: Tottenham (home) beat Anderlecht 4-3 (2-2 agg.).
1984 Eur. Champ. s-final (Lyon, France): Spain beat Denmark 5-4 (after 1-1).
1986 European Cup Final (Seville): Steaua Bucharest beat Barcelona 2-0 (0-0). Barcelona missed all four penalties taken.
1986 World Cup q-finals (in Mexico): France beat Brazil 4-3 (after 1-1); West Germany beat Mexico 4-1 (after 0-0); Belgium beat Spain 5-4 (after 1-1).
1987 Freight Rover Trophy Final (Wembley): Mansfield Town beat Bristol City 5-4 (after 1-1).
1987 Scottish League (Skol) Cup Final (Hampden Park): Rangers beat Aberdeen 5-3 (after 3-3).
1988 European Cup Final (Stuttgart): PSV Eindhoven beat Benfica 6-5 (after 0-0).
1988 UEFA Cup Final: Bayer Leverkusen (home) beat Espanol 3-2 (3-3 agg.).
1990 Scottish F.A. Cup Final (Hampden Park): Aberdeen beat Celtic 9-8 (0-0).

1990 World Cup (in Italy): 2nd. Round: Rep. of Ireland beat Rumania 5-4 (after 0-0); q-final: Argentina beat Yugoslavia 3-2 (after 0-0); s-finals: Argentina beat Italy 4-3 (after 1-1); West Germany beat England 4-3 (1-1).

1991 European Cup Final (Bari): Red Star Belgrade beat Marseille 5-3 (after 0-0).

1991 Barclays League Play-off (4th. Div. Final – Wembley): Torquay beat Blackpool 5-4 (after 2-2).

1992 F.A. Cup s-final replay (Villa Park): Liverpool beat Portsmouth 3-1 (after 0-0).

1992 Barclays League Play-off (4th. Div. Final – Wembley): Blackpool beat Scunthorpe 4-3 (after 1-1).

1992 Eur. Champ. s-final (Gothenburg): Denmark beat Holland 5-4 (after 2-2).

1992 African Nations Cup Final (Dakar): Ivory Coast beat Ghana 11-10 (after 0-0)

1993 Barclays League Play-off: (3rd Div. Final – Wembley): York beat Crewe 5-3 (after 1-1).

1993 F.A. Charity Shield (Wembley): Man. Utd. beat Arsenal 5-4 (after 1-1).

1994 League (Coca-Cola) Cup s-final: Aston Villa beat Tranmere 5-4 (after 4-4, 1-3a, 3-1h).

1994 Autoglass Trophy Final (Wembley): Swansea beat Huddersfield 3-1 (after 1-1).

1994 World Cup (in U.S.A.): **2nd. Round**: Bulgaria beat Mexico 3-1 (after 1-1); q-final: Sweden beat Rumania 5-4 (after 2-2); **Final**: Brazil beat Italy 3-2 (after 0-0).

1994 Scottish League (Coca-Cola) Cup Final (Ibrox Park): Raith beat Celtic 6-5 (after 2-2).

1995 Cup-Winners' Cup s-final: Arsenal beat Sampdoria away 3-2 (5-5 agg.)

1995 Copa America Final (Montevideo): Uruguay beat Brazil 5-3 (after 1-1).

1996 European Cup Final (Rome): Juventus beat Ajax 4-2 (after 1-1).

1996 European U-21 Champ. Final (Barcelona): Italy beat Spain 4-2 (after 1-1).

1996 Eur. Champ. q-finals: England beat Spain (Wembley) 4-2 after 0-0; France beat Holland (Anfield) 5-4 after 0-0; **E. Champ. s-finals**: Germany beat England (Wembley) 6-5 after 1-1; Czech Republic beat France (Old Trafford) 6-5 after 0-0.

Footnote: Highest-recorded score in a penalty shoot-out in Britain was **Aldershot's 11-10** victory at home to **Fulham** after their 1-1 draw in the Freight Rover Trophy Southern quarter-final on February 10, 1987. Seven spot-kicks were missed or saved in a record 28-penalty shoot-out at senior level.

Longest-recorded penalty shoot-out was in South America in 1988 – **Argentinos Juniors** beat **Racing Club 20-19**.

F.A. CUP SHOOT-OUTS

In **five seasons** since the introduction of this method to settle F.A. Cup ties (from Round 1) that are level after two matches, a total of **23 ties** have been decided by such means (5 in 1991-2, 6 in 1992-3, 4 in 1993-4, 4 in 1994-5, 4 in 1995-6).

But the **first** penalty contest in the F.A. Cup took place **23** years ago. In days of the play-off for third place, the 1972 match was delayed until the eve of the following season when losing semi-finalists **Birmingham** and **Stoke** met at St. Andrew's on Aug. 5. The score was 0-0 and Birmingham won 4-3 on penalties.

MISSED CUP FINAL PENALTIES

John Aldridge (Liverpool) became the first player to miss a penalty in the F.A. Cup Final at Wembley – and the second in the competition's history (previously

Charlie Wallace, of Aston Villa, in the 1913 Final against Sunderland at Crystal Palace) – when Wimbledon's Dave Beasant saved his shot in May 1988. Seven previous penalties had been scored in this Final at Wembley.

Tottenham's **Gary Lineker** saw his penalty saved by Nott'm. Forest goalkeeper Mark Crossley in the 1991 F.A. Cup Final.

Another crucial penalty miss at Wembley was by Arsenal's **Nigel Winterburn,** Luton's Andy Dibble saving his spot-kick in the 1988 Littlewoods Cup Final, when a goal would have put Arsenal 3-1 ahead. Instead, they lost 3-2.

Winterburn was the third player to fail with a League Cup Final penalty at Wembley, following ***Ray Graydon** (Aston Villa) against Norwich in 1975 and **Clive Walker** (Sunderland), who shot wide in the 1985 Milk Cup Final, also against Norwich, who won 1-0. * Graydon had his penalty saved by Kevin Keelan, but scored from the rebound and won the cup for Villa (1-0).

Derby's Martin Taylor saved a penalty from **Eligio Nicolini** in the Anglo-Italian Cup Final at Wembley on March 27, 1993, but Cremonese won 3-1.

LEAGUE PENALTIES RECORD

Most penalties in Football League match: Five – 4 to Crystal Palace (3 missed), 1 to Brighton (scored) in Div. 2 match at Selhurst Park on March 27 (Easter Monday), 1989. Palace won 2-1. Three of the penalties were awarded in a 5-minute spell. The match also produced 5 bookings and a sending-off.

Man. City provided the previous instance of a team missing 3 penalties in a match – against Newcastle (Div. 1) in January, 1912.

SPOT-KICK HAT-TRICKS

Danish International **Jan Molby**'s first hat-trick in English football, for Liverpool in their 3-1 win at home to Coventry (Littlewoods Cup, 4th round replay, Nov. 26, 1986) comprised three goals from the penalty spot.

It was the first such hat-trick in a major match for two years – since **Andy Blair** scored three penalties for Sheff. Wed. against Luton (Milk Cup 4th. round, Nov. 20 1984).

Portsmouth's **Kevin Dillon** scored a penalty hat-trick in the Full Members Cup (2nd rd.) at home to Millwall (3-2) on Nov. 4, 1986.

Alan Slough scored an away-match hat-trick of penalties for Peterborough, beaten 4-3 at Chester (Div. 3, Apr. 29, 1978).

MOST PENALTY GOALS (LEAGUE) IN SEASON

Thirteen by **Francis Lee** for Man. City (Div. 1) in 1971-2. His goal total for the season was 33. In season 1988-9, **Graham Roberts** scored 12 League penalties for Second Division Champions Chelsea.

PENALTY-SAVE SEQUENCES

Ipswich goalkeeper **Paul Cooper** saved eight of the ten penalties he faced in 1979-80. **Roy Brown** (Notts Co.) saved six in a row in season 1972-3.

Andy Lomas, goalkeeper for Chesham United (Diadora League) claimed a record eight **consecutive** penalty saves – three at the end of season 1991-2 and five in 1992-3.

Mark Bosnich (Aston Villa) saved five in two consecutive matches in 1993-4: three in Coca-Cola Cup semi-final penalty shoot-out v Tranmere (Feb. 26), then two in Premiership at Tottenham (Mar. 2).

MISSED PENALTIES SEQUENCE

Against Wolves in Div. 2 on Sept. 28, 1991, **Southend United** missed their seventh successive penalty (five of them the previous season).

SCOTTISH RECORDS

(See also under 'Goals')

RANGERS' MANY RECORDS

Rangers' record-breaking feats include:-

League Champions: 46 times (once joint holders) – world record.

Winning every match in Scottish League (1898-9 season).

Major hat-tricks: Rangers have completed the domestic treble (League Championship, League Cup and Scottish F.A. Cup) a record five times (1948-9, 1963-4, 1975-6, 1977-8, 1992-3).

League & Cup double: 14 times.

CELTIC'S GRAND SLAM

Celtic's record in 1966-7 was the most successful by a British club in one season. They won the **Scottish League**, the **Scottish Cup**, the **Scottish League Cup**, the **Glasgow Cup** and became the first British club to win the **European Cup**.

Celtic have twice achieved the Scottish treble (League Championship, League Cup and F.A. Cup), in 1966-7 and 1968-9.

They have won the Scottish Cup most times (30), and have completed the League and Cup double 11 times.

SCOTTISH CUP HAT-TRICKS

Aberdeen's feat of winning the Scottish F.A. Cup in 1982-3-4 made them only the third club to achieve that particular hat-trick.

Queen's Park did it twice (1874-5-6 and 1880-1-2), and **Rangers** have won the Scottish Cup three years in succession on three occasions: 1934-5-6, 1948-9-50 and 1962-3-4.

SCOTTISH CUP FINAL DISMISSALS

Three players have been sent off in the Scottish F.A. Cup Final: **Jock Buchanan** (Rangers v. Kilmarnock, 1929), **Roy Aitken** (Celtic v. Aberdeen, 1984) and **Walter Kidd** (Hearts captain v. Aberdeen, 1986).

CELTIC'S RECORD 62

Celtic hold the Scottish League record run of success with 62 matches undefeated, from November 13, 1915 to April 21, 1917, when Kilmarnock won 2-0 at Parkhead.

Greenock Morton in 1963-4 were undefeated in home League matches, obtained a record 67 points out of 72 and scored 135 goals, clinching promotion as early as February 29.

Queen's Park did not have a goal scored against them during the first seven seasons of their existence (1867-74, before the Scottish League was formed).

WORST HOME SEQUENCE

After winning promotion to Div. 1 in 1992, **Cowdenbeath** went a record 40 consecutive home League matches without a win. They ended the sequence when beating Arbroath 1-0 on April 2, 1994.

ALLY'S RECORDS

Ally McCoist became the first player to complete 200 goals in the Premier Division when he scored Rangers' winner (2-1) at Falkirk on December 12, 1992. His first was against Celtic in September 1983, and he reached 100 against Dundee on Boxing Day 1987. He ended 1995-6 with a total of 235 League goals for Rangers.

When McCoist, as sub, scored Rangers' winning goal against Hibernian in the League Cup Final (Oct. 1993), he earned a record eighth winner's medal in the competition, all with the Ibrox club.

STURROCK'S RECORD

Paul Sturrock set an individual scoring record for the Scottish Premier Division with 5 goals in Dundee United's 7-0 win at home to Morton on November 17, 1984.

DOUBLE SCOTTISH FINAL

Rangers v. Celtic drew **129,643** and **120,073** people to the Scottish Cup Final and replay at Hampden Park, Glasgow, in 1963. Receipts for the two matches totalled £50,500.

CHAMPION NINE TIMES

Alan Morton won **nine** Scottish Championship medals with Rangers in 1921-23-24-25-27-28-29-30-31.

SCOTTISH CUP – NO DECISION

The **Scottish F.A.** withheld their Cup and medals in 1908-9 after Rangers and Celtic played two drawn games at Hampden Park. Spectators rioted.

GREAT SCOTS

In February 1988, the Scottish F.A. launched a national **Hall of Fame**, initially comprising the first 11 Scots to make 50 International appearances, to be joined by all future players to reach that number of caps. Each member receives a gold medal, invitation for life at all Scotland's home matches, and has his portrait hung at Scottish F.A. headquarters in Glasgow. Latest to qualify was Ally McCoist, who captained Scotland on his 50th. appearance against Australia at Hampden Park on March 27, 1996.

NOTABLE SCOTTISH 'FIRSTS'

• The father of League football was a Scot, **William McGregor**, a draper in Birmingham. The 12-club Football League kicked off in September 1888, and McGregor was its first president.

• **Hibernian** were the first British club to play in the European Cup. They reached the semi-final when it began in 1955-6.

• **Celtic** were Britain's first winners of the European Cup, in 1967.

• Scotland's First Division became the **Premier Division** in season 1975-6.

• Football's **first International** was staged at the West of Scotland cricket ground, Partick, on November 30, 1872: Scotland 0, England 0.

• Scotland introduced its **League Cup** in 1945-6, the first season after the war. It was another 15 years before the Football League Cup was launched.

• The Scottish F.A. Cup has been **sponsored** for the last seven seasons, and Tennents' contract continues in 1996-7 .

• Scotland pioneered the use in British football of **two substitutes** per team in League and Cup matches.

• The world's **record football score** belongs to Scotland and has stood for 111 years: Arbroath 36, Bon Accord 0 (Scottish Cup first round) on September 12, 1885.

• The Scottish F.A. introduced the **penalty shoot-out** to their Cup Final in 1990.

• On Jan. 22, 1994 all six matches in the **Scottish Premier Division** ended as draws.

SCOTTISH CUP SHOCK RESULTS

1885-86 (1) Arbroath 36, Bon Accord 0
1921-22 (F) Morton 1, Rangers 0
1937-38 (F) East Fife 4, Kilmarnock 2 (replay, after 1-1)
1960-61 (F) Dunfermline 2, Celtic 0 (replay, after 0-0)
1966-67 (1) Berwick Rangers1, Rangers 0
1979-80 (3) Hamilton 2, Keith 3
1984-85 (1) Stirling Albion 20, Selkirk 0
1984-85 (3) Inverness Thistle 3, Kilmarnock 0
1986-87 (3) Rangers 0, Hamilton 1
1994-95 (4) Stenhousemuir 2, Aberdeen 0
Scottish League (Coca-Cola) Cup Final shock
1994-95 Raith 2, Celtic 2 (Raith won 6-5 on pens.)

SCOTTISH FINES (Modern)

1989 (June) fine **Hearts** £93,000, following TV infringement at UEFA Cup q-final.
1990 (May) S.F.A. fine Rangers manager **Graeme Souness** record £5,000 for breaking touchline ban v Hearts on Feb. 17, and extend Souness trackside ban to May 1992. **1991** (February) S.F.A. fine **Rangers** £10,000 and order them to forfeit £13,000 sponsorship money for failing to carry out sponsors' agreement at Cup-tie v Dunfermline in January.
1991 (June) S.F.A. fine **Dundee Utd.** £12,000 for incidents involving referee at Scottish Cup Final defeat by Motherwell.
1992 (October) UEFA fine **Hibernian** £5,730 for crowd trouble at UEFA Cup match v Anderlecht.
1993 (March) UEFA fine **Rangers** £8,000 (later halved) for crowd misconduct away to Bruges in European Cup.
1993 (May) **Rangers** fined £5,000 by League under rule covering "tapping" of players with other clubs.

1993 (August) S.F.A. fine **Airdrie** £10,000, **Dundee** £5,000 for poor disciplinary records, season 1992-3.

1993 (November) UEFA fine **Aberdeen** £4,500 for fan misconduct v Torino (CWC).

1994 (January) S.F.A. fine **Rangers** coach **John McGregor** £3,000 and ban him from touchline until year 2000 for using foul and abusive language to referee at reserve match.

1994 (August) Scottish League fine **Celtic** record £100,000 for poaching manager Tommy Burns from Kilmarnock.

1994 (August) S.F.A. fines for prev. season's disciplinary records: **Dundee** £10,000; **Cowdenbeath, East Fife, Stranraer** each £1,000.

1994 (November) S.F.A fine **Celtic** manager **Tommy Burns** £2,000 and assistant **Billy Stark** each £2,000 for breach of contract when leaving Kilmarnock.

1995 (March) S.F.A. fine **Celtic** manager **Tommy Burns** £1,000 and ban him from touchline for rest of season (verbal abuse of referee).

1995 (August) S.F.A. fine five clubs for poor disciplinary records in 1994-5: **Dundee Utd.** (£5,000), **Falkirk** (£5,000), **Cowdenbeath, East Fife** and **Stranraer** (each £2,000).

MISCELLANEOUS

NATIONAL ASSOCIATIONS FORMED

F. A. on Oct. 26 .... **1863**
Scottish F.A. **1873**
F.A. of Wales **1876**
Irish F.A. **1904**
Federation of International Football Associations (FIFA) **1904**

NATIONAL COMPETITIONS LAUNCHED

F. A. Cup **1871**
Scottish Cup **1873**
Welsh Cup **1877**
Irish Cup **1880**
Football League **1888**
F.A. Premier League **1992**
Scottish League **1890**
Football League Cup **1960**
Scottish League Cup **1945**
World (Jules Rimet) Cup, at Montevideo **1930**
International Championship **1883-4**
Youth International (16-18 age-groups) **1946-7**
Olympic Games Tournament, at Shepherd's Bush **1908**

INNOVATIONS

Size of Ball: Fixed in **1872.**

Shinguards: Introduced and registered by Sam Weller Widdowson (Nottingham Forest & England) in **1874.**

Referee's Whistle: First used on Nottingham Forest's ground in **1878.**

Professionalism: Legalised in England in the summer of **1885** as a result of agitation by Lancashire clubs.

Goal-nets: Invented and patented in **1890** by Mr. Brodie of Liverpool. They were first used in the North v. South match in January, **1891.**

Referees and Linesmen: Replaced umpires and referees in January, **1891.**

Penalty-kick: Introduced at Irish F.A.'s request in the season **1891-2.** The penalty law ordering the goalkeeper to remain on the goal-line came into force in September, **1905,** and the order to stand on his goal-line until the ball is kicked arrived in **1929-30.**

White ball: First came into official use in **1951.**

Floodlighting: First F.A. Cup-tie (replay), Kidderminster Harriers v. Brierley Hill Alliance, **1955.**

Electrified pitch to beat frost tried by Everton at Goodison Park in **1958.**

First Soccer Closed-circuit TV: At Coventry City ground in October 1965 (10,000 fans saw their team win at Cardiff, 120 miles away).

Substitutes (one per team) were first allowed in Football League matches at the start of season **1965-6**. Three substitutes (one a goalkeeper) allowed, two of which could be used, in Premier League matches, **1992-93**. The Football League introduced three substitutes for **1993-94**.

Three points for a win: This was introduced by the Football League in **1981-2.**

Offside law amended, player 'level' no longer offside, and 'professional foul' made sending-off offence, **1990**.

Penalty shoot-outs introduced to decide F.A. Cup ties level after one replay and extra time, **1991-2**.

New back-pass rule – goalkeeper must not handle ball kicked to him by team-mate, **1992**.

1994: 3 points for win introduced in World Cup Finals group matches in USA. Also by Scottish League at start of season 1994-5.

CUP AND LEAGUE DOUBLES

League Championship and F.A. Cup: Preston North End, 1889; Aston Villa, 1897; Tottenham Hotspur, 1961; Arsenal, 1971; Liverpool 1986; Man. United 1994, 1996.

F.A. Cup and Promotion: West Bromwich Albion, 1931.

F.A. Cup and Football League Cup: Arsenal, 1993

League Championship and Football League Cup: Nottingham Forest, 1978; Liverpool, 1982; Liverpool, 1983; Liverpool, 1984.

Scottish League Championship and Cup Double: Rangers, (14): 1928-30-34-35-49-50-53-63-64-76-78-92-93-96. Celtic, (11): 1907-8-14-54-67-69-71-72-74-77-88. Aberdeen, (1): 1984.

Scottish Treble (Championship, Cup, League Cup): Rangers 5 times (1949-64-76-78-93); Celtic twice (1967-69).

DERBY DAYS: COMPLETE LEAGUE RESULTS

Arsenal v Tottenham: Played 118 (all in top div.); Arsenal 47 wins, Tottenham 44, Drawn 27.

Aston Villa v Birmingham: Played 96; Villa 39, Birmingham 32, Drawn 25.

Everton v Liverpool: Played 154 (all in top div.); Liverpool 56, Everton 52, Drawn 46.

Ipswich v Norwich: Played 60; Ipswich 31, Norwich 20, Drawn 9.

Man. City v Man. United: Played 124; United 48, City 32, Drawn 44.

Middlesbrough v Newcastle: Played 88; Newcastle 33, Middlesbrough 31, Drawn 24.

Newcastle v Sunderland: Played 116; Newcastle 42, Sunderland 39, Drawn 35 (incl. 1990 play-offs – Sunderland win and draw).

Nott'm. Forest v Notts Co.: Played 86; Forest 35, County 28, Drawn 23.

Sheff. United v Sheff. Wed.: Played 98; United 37, Wednesday 31, Drawn 30.
Port Vale v Stoke City: Played 36; Stoke 14, Port Vale 12, Drawn 10.
Bristol City v Bristol Rovers: Played 78; City 30, Rovers 23, Drawn 25.
Celtic v Rangers: Played 240; Rangers 93, Celtic 74, Drawn 73.
Dundee v Dundee United: Played 98; United 50, Dundee 29, Drawn 19.
Hearts v Hibernian: Played 206; Hearts 84, Hibernian 61, Drawn 61.

YOUNGEST AND OLDEST

Youngest Caps	**Age**
Norman Whiteside (N. Ireland v. Yugoslavia, June 17, 1982)	**17** years, **42** days
Ryan Giggs (Wales v. Germany, October 16, 1991)	**17** years, **332** days
James Prinsep (England v. Scotland, April 5, 1879)	**17** years **252** days
Denis Law (Scotland v. Wales, October 18, 1958)	**18** years, **235** days
Jimmy Holmes (Rep. of Ireland v. Austria, May 30, 1971)	**17** years **200** days

England's Youngest cap this century: Duncan Edwards (v. Scotland, April 2, 1955), 18 years, 183 days.
Youngest England scorer: Tommy Lawton (19 years, 6 days) – penalty against Wales, Ninian Park, Cardiff, October 22, 1938.
Youngest England captain: Bobby Moore (v Czech., away, May 29, 1963), 22 years, 1 month, 17 days.
Youngest player to appear in World Cup Finals: Norman Whiteside (N. Ireland v. Yugoslavia in Spain – June 17, 1982, age 17 years and 42 days (record previously held by Pele – 17 years and 237 days when playing for Brazil in 1958 World Cup in Sweden).
Youngest First Division player: Derek Forster (Sunderland goalkeeper v. Leicester, August 22, 1964) aged 15 years, 185 days.
Youngest First Division scorer: At 16 years and 57 days, schoolboy Jason Dozzell (substitute after 30 minutes for Ipswich Town at home to Coventry City on February 4, 1984). Ipswich won 3-1 and Dozzell scored their third goal.
Youngest F.A. Premier League player: Neil Finn (West Ham goalkeeper at Man. City, January 1, 1996) 17 years, 3 days.
Youngest F.A. Premier League scorer: Andy Turner (Tottenham v Everton, September 5, 1992), 17 years, 166 days.
Youngest First Division hat-trick scorer: Alan Shearer, aged 17 years, 240 days, in Southampton's 4-2 home win v. Arsenal (April 9, 1988) on his full debut.
Youngest to complete 100 Football League goals: Jimmy Greaves (20 years, 261 days) when he did so for Chelsea v. Man. City, November 19, 1960.
Youngest Football League scorer: Ronnie Dix (for Bristol Rovers v. Norwich, Div. 3 South, March 3, 1928) aged 15 years, 180 days.
Youngest players in Football League: Albert Geldard (Bradford v. Millwall, Div. 2, September 16, 1929) aged 15 years, 158 days; Ken Roberts (Wrexham v. Bradford, Div. 3 North, September 1, 1951) also 15 years, 158 days.
Youngest player in Scottish League: Goalkeeper Ronnie Simpson (Queens Park) aged 15 in 1946.
Youngest player in F.A. Cup: Andy Awford, Worcester City's England Schoolboy defender, aged 15 years, 88 days when he substituted in second half away to Borehamwood (3rd. qual-round) on October 10, 1987.
Youngest player in F.A. Cup proper: Scott Endersby (15 years, 279 days) when he kept goal for Kettering Town v. Tilbury in first round on November 26, 1977.
Youngest Wembley Cup Final captain: Barry Venison (Sunderland v. Norwich City, Milk Cup Final, March 24, 1985 – replacing suspended captain Shaun Elliott), aged 20 years, 7 months, 8 days.
Youngest F.A. Cup-winning captain: Bobby Moore (West Ham, 1964, v Preston), aged 23 years, 20 days.

Youngest F.A. Cup Final captain: David Nish was 21 years and 7 months old when he captained Leicester C. against Man. City at Wembley on April 26, 1969.

Youngest F.A. Cup Final player: James Prinsep (Clapham Rovers v Old Etonians, 1879) aged 17 years, 245 days.

Youngest F.A. Cup Final player this century: Paul Allen (West Ham v. Arsenal, 1980) aged 17 years, 256 days.

Youngest F.A. Cup Final scorer: Norman Whiteside (Man. United v. Brighton in 1983 replay at Wembley), aged 18 years, 19 days.

Youngest F.A. Cup Final managers: Stan Cullis, Wolves (33) v Leicester, 1949; Steve Coppell, Crystal Palace (34) v Man. United, 1990.

Youngest player in Football League Cup: Kevin Davies (Chesterfield sub at West Ham, 2nd Round, 2nd Leg on September 22, 1993) aged 16 years, 180 days.

Youngest Wembley scorer: Norman Whiteside (Man. United v. Liverpool, Milk Cup Final, March 26, 1983) aged 17 years, 324 days.

Youngest Wembley Cup Final goalkeeper: Chris Woods (18 years, 125 days) for Nott'm Forest v. Liverpool, League Cup Final on March 18, 1978.

Youngest Wembley F.A. Cup Final goalkeeper: Peter Shilton (19 years, 7 months) for Leicester City v. Man. City, April 26, 1969.

Youngest senior International at Wembley: Blendi Nollbani (Albania's World Cup goalkeeper v. England, April 26, 1989), aged 17 years, 19 days.

Youngest scorer in full International: Mohamed Kallon (Sierra Leone v Congo, African Nations Cup, April 22, 1995), aged 15 years, 6 months, 16 days.

Youngest F.A. Cup Final referee: Kevin Howley, of Middlesbrough, aged 35 when in charge of Wolves v. Blackburn, 1960.

Youngest player in England U-23 team: Duncan Edwards (v. Italy, Bologna, January 20, 1954), aged 17 years, 3 months.

Youngest player in England U-21 team: Lee Sharpe (v. Greece, away, February 7, 1989), aged 17 years, 8 months.

Youngest player in Scotland U-21 team: Christian Dailly (v Rumania, Hampden Park, Sept. 11, 1990), aged 16 years, 11 months.

Youngest player in senior football: Cameron Campbell Buchanan, Scottish-born outside right, aged 14 years, 57 days when he played for Wolves v. W.B.A. in War-time League match, September 26, 1942.

Youngest player in peace-time senior match: Eamon Collins (Blackpool v. Kilmarnock, Anglo-Scottish Cup quarter-final 1st. leg, September 9, 1980) aged 14 years, 323 days.

Oldest player to appear in Football League: New Brighton manager Neil McBain (51 years, 120 days) as emergency goalkeeper away to Hartlepool United (Div. 3 North, March 15, 1947).

Other oldest post-war League players: Sir Stanley Matthews (Stoke, 1965, 50 years, 5 days); Peter Shilton (Bolton 1995, 45 years, 239 days); Alf Wood (Coventry, 1958, 43 years, 199 days); Tommy Hutchison (Swansea, 1991, 43 years, 172 days).

Oldest Football League debut: Andrew Cunningham, for Newcastle United at Leicester (Div. 1) on February 2, 1929, aged 38 years, 2 days.

Oldest player to appear in First Division: Sir Stanley Matthews (Stoke City v. Fulham, February 6, 1965), aged 50 years, 5 days.

Oldest player in Premier League: Goalkeeper John Burridge (half-time substitute for Man. City v Newcastle, 0-0, April 29, 1995), aged 43 years, 4 months, 26 days.

Oldest F.A. Cup Final player: Walter (Billy) Hampson (Newcastle Utd. v. Aston Villa on April 26, 1924), aged 41 years, 8 months.

Oldest F.A. Cup-winning team: Arsenal 1950 (average age 31 years, 2 months). Eight of the players were over 30, with the three oldest centre-half Leslie Compton 37, and skipper Joe Mercer and goalkeeper George Swindin, both 35.

Oldest player capped by England: Stanley Matthews (v. Denmark, Copenhagen, May 15, 1957), aged 42 years and 104 days.

Oldest England scorer: Stanley Matthews (v N. Ireland, Belfast, October 6, 1956), aged 41 years, 248 days.

Oldest British International player: Billy Meredith (Wales v. England at Highbury, March 15, 1920), aged 45 years, 8 months.

Oldest "new cap": Arsenal centre-half Leslie Compton, at 38 years, 2 months when he made his England debut in 4-2 win against Wales at Sunderland on November 15, 1950. **For Scotland:** Goalkeeper Ronnie Simpson (Celtic) at 36 v England at Wembley, April 15, 1967.

Longest Football League career: This spanned 32 years and 10 months, by Stanley Matthews (Stoke, Blackpool, Stoke) from March 19, 1932 until February 6, 1965.

Smallest F.A. Cup-winning captain: 5ft. 4in. – Bobby Kerr (Sunderland v. Leeds, 1973).

SHIRT NUMBERING

Numbering players in Football League matches was made compulsory in 1939. Players wore numbered shirts (1-22) in the F.A. Cup Final as an experiment in 1933 (Everton v. Man. City).

Squad numbers for players were introduced by the F.A. Premier League at the start of the season 1993-4. They were optional in the Football League.

Names on shirts: For first time, players wore names as well as numbers on shirts in League Cup and F.A. Cup Finals, 1993.

SUBSTITUTES

In **1965**, the Football League, by 39 votes to 10, agreed that **one substitute** be allowed for an injured player at any time during a League match.

Two substitutes per team were approved for the League (Littlewoods) Cup and F.A. Cup in season 1986-7 and two were permitted in the Football League for the first time in 1987-8.

Three substitutes (one a goalkeeper), two of which could be used, introduced by the Premier League for 1992-3. The Football League followed suit for 1993-4.

Three substitutes (one a goalkeeper) were allowed at the World Cup Finals for the first time at US '94.

Three substitutes (any position) introduced by Premier League and Football League in 1995-6.

When Leigh Roose, the Welsh goalkeeper, was injured against England at Wrexham, March 16, 1908, David Davies (Bolton Wanderers) was allowed to take his place as substitute. Thus Wales used 12 players. England won 7-1.

The **first recorded use of a substitute was in 1889** (Wales v. Scotland at Wrexham on April 15) when Sam Gillam arrived late – although he was a Wrexham player – and Alf Pugh (Rhostellyn) was allowed to keep goal until he turned up. The match ended 0-0.

First substitute to score in F.A. Cup Final: Eddie Kelly (Arsenal v. Liverpool, 1971).

END OF WAGE LIMIT

Freedom from the maximum wage system – in force since the formation of the Football League in 1888 – was secured by the Professional Footballers' Association in 1961. About this time Italian clubs renewed overtures for the transfer of British stars and Fulham's **Johnny Haynes** became the first British player to earn a wage of £100 a week.

GREATEST SHOCKS

Excluding such tragedies as the Munich air crash (Feb. 1958), the Bradford fire disaster (May 1985), Heysel (May 1985) and Hillsborough (April 1989), here in date order are, arguably, the greatest shocks in football history:

(1)	Jan. 1933	F.A. Cup 3rd. Round: Walsall 2, Arsenal 0.
(2)	Jan. 1949	F.A. Cup 4th. Round: Yeovil 2, Sunderland 1.
(3)	June 1950	World Cup Finals: U.S.A. 1, England 0 (Belo Horizonte, Brazil).
(4)	Nov. 1953	England 3, Hungary 6 (Wembley).
(5)	Sept. 1962	Cup-Winners' Cup 1st. Round, 1st. Leg: Bangor 2, Napoli 0.
(6)	Mar. 1966	World Cup stolen in London (found a week later).
(7)	June 1966	World Cup Finals: N. Korea 1, Italy 0 (Middlesbrough).
(8)	Jan. 1967	Scottish Cup 1st. Round: Berwick Rangers 1, Glasgow Rangers 0.
(9)	Mar. 1969	League Cup Final: Swindon Town 3, Arsenal 1.
(10)	Feb. 1971	F.A. Cup 5th. Round: Colchester United 3, Leeds 2.
(11)	Jan. 1972	F.A. Cup 3rd. Round: Hereford United 2, Newcastle 1.
(12)	July 1974	Bill Shankly retires as Liverpool manager.
(13)	May 1973	F.A. Cup Final: Sunderland 1, Leeds 0.
(14)	May 1976	F.A. Cup Final: Southampton 1, Man. Utd. 0.
(15)	July 1977	England manager Don Revie defects to coach United Arab Emirates.
(16)	June 1982	World Cup Finals: Algeria 2, West Germany 1 (Gijon, Spain).
(17)	Jan. 1984	F.A. Cup 3rd. Round: Bournemouth 2, Manchester United (holders) 0.
(18)	May 1988	F.A. Cup Final: Wimbledon 1, Liverpool 0 .
(19)	June 1990	World Cup Finals: Cameroon 1, Argentina (World Champions) 0 (Milan).
(20)	Sept. 1990	European Championship (Qual. Round): Faroe Islands 1, Austria 0.
(21)	Feb. 1991	Kenny Dalglish resigns as Liverpool manager.
(22)	Jan. 1992	F.A. Cup 3rd. Round: Wrexham 2, Arsenal 1.
(23)	June 1992	European Championship Final: Denmark 2, Germany (World Champions) 0.
(24)	June 1993	U.S. Cup '93: U.S.A. 2, England 0 (Foxboro, Boston).
(25)	July 1994	World Cup Finals: Bulgaria 2, Germany 1 (New York).

OTHER INTERNATIONAL SHOCKS

(Read in conjunction with Greatest Shocks above)

1982	Spain 0, N. Ireland 1 (World Cup Finals in Spain).
1990	Scotland 0, Costa Rica 1 (World Cup Finals in Italy).
1990	Sweden 1, Costa Rica 2 (World Cup Finals in Italy).
1993	Argentina 0, Colombia 5 (World Cup qual. round).
1993	France 2, Israel 3 (World Cup qual. round).
1993	San Marino score fastest goal in Int. records: 8.3 secs. v England (World Cup qual. round).
1994	Moldova 3, Wales 0; Georgia 5, Wales 0 (both Euro. Champ. qual. round).
1995	Belarus 1, Holland 0 (European Champ. qual. round).

GREAT RECOVERIES

On December 21, 1957, Charlton Athletic were losing 5-1 against Huddersfield Town (Div. 2) at The Valley with only 28 minutes left. From the 15th minute, they were reduced to ten men by injury, but they won 7-6, with left-winger Johnny Summers scoring five goals. Huddersfield remain the only team to score six times in a League match and lose.

Among other notable comebacks: on November 12, 1904 (Div. 1), Sheffield Wednesday were losing 0-5 at home to Everton, but drew 5-5. At Anfield on December 4, 1909 (Div.1), Liverpool trailed 2-5 to Newcastle at half-time, then won 6-5. On Boxing Day, 1927, in Div. 3 South, Northampton Town won 6-5 at home to Luton Town after being 1-5 down at half-time. On September 22, 1984 (Div. 1), Q.P.R. drew 5-5 at home to Newcastle after trailing 0-4 at half-time. On April 12, 1993 (Div. 1) Swindon were 1-4 down at Birmingham with 30 minutes left, but won 6-4.

Other astonishing turnabouts in Div.1 include: Grimsby (3-5 down) won 6-5 at W.B.A. on Apr. 30, 1932; and Derby beat Man. Utd. 5-4 (from 1-4) on Sept. 5, 1936.

With 5 minutes to play, Ipswich were losing 3-0 at Barnsley (Div. 1, March 9, 1996), but drew 3-3.

MATCHES OFF

Worst day for postponements: Feb. 9, 1963, when 57 League fixtures in England and Scotland were frozen off. Only 7 Football League matches took place, and the entire Scottish programme was wiped out

Worst other weather-hit days:

Jan. 12, 1963 and Feb. 2, 1963 – on both those Saturdays, only 4 out of 44 Football League matches were played.

Jan. 1, 1979 – 43 out of 46 Football League fixtures postponed.

Jan. 17, 1987 – 37 of 45 scheduled Football League fixtures postponed; only 2 Scottish matches survived.

Feb. 8-9, 1991 – only 4 of the week-end's 44 Barclays League matches survived the freeze-up (4 of the postponements were on Friday night). In addition, 11 Scottish League matches were off.

Jan. 27, 1996 – 44 Cup and League matches in England and Scotland were frozen off. The ten fixtures played comprised 3 F.A. Cup (4th. Round), 1 in Div. 1, 5 in Scottish Cup (3rd. Round), 1 in Scottish Div. 2.

Fewest matches left on one day by postponements was during the Second World War – Feb. 3, 1940 when, because of snow, ice and fog only one out of 56 regional league fixtures took place. It resulted Plymouth Argyle 10, Bristol City 3.

The Scottish Cup second round tie between Inverness Thistle and Falkirk in season 1978-9 was **postponed 29 times** because of snow and ice. First put off on Jan. 6, it was eventually played on Feb. 22. Falkirk won 4-0.

Pools Panel's busiest days: Jan. 17, 1987 and Feb. 9, 1991 – on both dates they gave their verdict on 48 postponed coupon matches.

FEWEST 'GAMES OFF'

Season 1947-8 was the best since the war for Football League fixtures being played to schedule. Only **six** were postponed.

LONGEST SEASON

The latest that League football has been played in a season was **June 7, 1947**. The season was extended because of mass postponements caused by bad weather in mid-winter.

The latest the F.A. Cup competition has ever been completed was in season 1981-2, when Tottenham beat Q.P.R. 1-0 in a Final replay at Wembley on May 27.

Worst winter hold-up was in season 1962-3. The Big Freeze began on Boxing Day and lasted until March, with nearly 500 first-class matches postponed. The F.A. Cup 3rd. Round was the longest on record – it began with only three out of 32 ties playable on January 5 and ended 66 days and 261 postponements later on March 11. The Lincoln-Coventry tie was put off 15 times. The Pools Panel was launched that winter, on January 26, 1963.

Hottest day for a Football League programme is believed to have been Saturday, September 1, 1906, when temperatures across the country were over 90°.

LEAGUE SECRETARIES

In February 1989, the Football League confirmed the appointment of **David Dent**, 52, as secretary in succession to Graham Kelly, who became chief executive of the F.A.

Mr. Dent, previously assistant and formerly with Coventry City, is only the **sixth secretary** of the League in its 107-year history, following: **Harry Lockett** (1888-1902), **Tom Charnley** (1902-33), **Fred Howarth** (1933-57), **Alan Hardaker** (1957-79) and **Graham Kelly** (1979-88).

F.A. Premier League (1992 to date): Chief executive – Rick Parry; Secretary – Mike Foster.

FOOTBALL ASSOCIATION SECRETARIES

Ebenezer Morley (1863-66), **Robert Willis** (1866-68), **R.G. Graham** (1868-70), **Charles Adcock** (1870-95, paid from 1887), 1895-1934 **Sir Frederick Wall**, 1934-62 **Sir Stanley Rous**, 1962-73 **Denis Follows**, 1973-89 **Ted Croker** (latterly chief executive), 1989 to date **Graham Kelly** (chief executive).

FOOTBALL'S SPONSORS

Football League: Canon 1983-6; Today Newspaper 1986-7; Barclays 1987-93; Endsleigh Insurance 1993-6; Nationwide 1996-9.

League Cup: Milk Cup 1982-6; Littlewoods 1987-90; Rumbelows 1991-2; Coca-Cola Cup 1993 to date.

Premier League: Carling 1993-7.

F.A. Cup: Littlewoods 1994-8.

SOCCER HEADQUARTERS

Football Association: 16 Lancaster Gate, London W2 3LW. Chief Executive – Graham Kelly. **F.A. Premier League:** 16 Lancaster Gate, London W2 3LW. Chief Executive – Rick Parry.

Football League: Lytham St. Annes, Lancashire FY8 1JG. Secretary – David Dent. **Professional Footballers Association:** 2 Oxford Court, Bishopsgate, Manchester M2 3WQ. Chief Executive: Gordon Taylor.

Football Trust: Walkden House, 10 Melton Street, London NW1 2EB. Chief Executive: Peter Lee.

Scottish Football Association: 6 Park Gardens, Glasgow G3 7YF. Chief Executive – James Farry.**Scottish Football League:** 188 West Regent Street, Glasgow G2 4RY. Secretary – Peter Donald. **Irish Football Association:** 20 Windsor Avenue, Belfast BT9 6EG. Secretary – David Bowen. **Irish Football League:** 87 University Street, Belfast BT7 1HP. Secretary – Mervyn Brown. **League of Ireland:** 80 Merrion Square, Dublin 2. Secretary – Eamonn Morris. **Republic of Ireland F.A.:** 80 Merrion Square, Dublin 2.

Welsh Football Association: 3 Westgate Street, Cardiff, S. Glamorgan CF1 1JF. **FIFA:** FIFA House, Hitzigweg 11, CH-8032 Zurich, Switzerland. Secretary – Sepp Blatter. **UEFA:** Chemin de la Redoute 54, Case Postale 303, CH-1260, Nyon, Geneva, Switzerland. Secretary – Gerhard Aigner.

WORLD'S LARGEST STADIA

(Source: *FIFA NEWS*)

Capacity 165,000: Maracana, Rio de Janeiro, Brazil; **150,000** Rungnado Stadium, Pyongyang, Korea DPR; **125,000** Magalhaes Pinto Stadium, Belo Horizonte, Brazil; **120,000** Morumbi Stadium, Sao Paulo, Brazil; Stadium of Light, Lisbon, Portugal; Krirangan Stadium, Salt Lake, Calcutta; Senayan Stadium, Jakarta, Indonesia; **119,000** Castelao Stadium, Fortaleza, Brazil; **115,000** Arrudao Stadium, Recife, Brazil; Azteca Stadium, Mexico City; Nou Camp, Barcelona, Spain; **114,000** Bernabeu Stadium, Madrid; **100,000** Nasser Stadium, Cairo, Egypt; Azadi Stadium, Tehran, Iran; Red Star Stadium, Belgrade, Yugoslavia; Central Stadium, Kiev, USSR.

NEW HOMES OF SOCCER

Newly-constructed League grounds in Britain since the war: 1946 Hull City (Boothferry Park); 1950 Port Vale (Vale Park); 1955 Southend United (Roots Hall); 1988 Scunthorpe United (Glanford Park); 1988 St. Johnstone (McDiarmid Park); 1990 Walsall (Bescot Stadium); 1990 Wycombe (Adams Park); 1992 Chester City (Deva Stadium, Bumpers Lane); 1993 Millwall (New Den); 1994 Clyde (Broadwood Stadium); 1994 Huddersfield Town (Alfred McAlpine Stadium, Kirklees); 1994 Northampton Town (Sixfields Stadium); 1995 Middlesbrough (Riverside Stadium).

GROUND-SHARING

Crystal Palace and **Charlton Athletic** (Selhurst Park, 1985-91); **Bristol Rovers** and **Bath City** (Twerton Park, Bath, 1986-96); **Partick Thistle** and **Clyde** (Firhill Park, Glasgow, 1986-91; in seasons 1990-1, 1991-2 **Chester** shared **Macclesfield Town's** ground (Moss Rose). **Crystal Palace** and **Wimbledon** now share Selhurst Park, starting season 1991-2, when **Charlton** rented Upton Park from **West Ham**. **Clyde** moved to Douglas Park, **Hamilton Academical**'s home, in 1991-2. **Stirling Albion** shared **Stenhousemuir's** ground, Ochilview Park, in 1992-3. In 1993-4, **Clyde** shared **Partick's** home until moving to their new ground. In 1994-5, **Celtic** shared Hampden Park with **Queen's Park** (while Celtic Park redeveloped); **Hamilton** shared **Partick's** ground. **Airdrie** shared **Clyde's** Broadwood stadium. **Bristol Rovers** have left Bath City's ground for the start of season 1996-7, sharing Bristol Rugby Club's Memorial Ground.

ARTIFICIAL TURF

Q.P.R. were the first British club to install an artificial pitch, in 1981. They were followed by **Luton Town** in 1985, and **Oldham Athletic** and **Preston in 1986**. Q.P.R. reverted to grass in 1988, as did Luton and promoted Oldham in season 1991-2 (when artificial pitches were banned in Div. 1). **Preston** were the last Football League club playing "on plastic" in 1993-4, and their Deepdale ground was restored to grass for the start of 1994-5.

Stirling Albion were the **first Scottish club** to play on plastic, in season 1987-8.

ALL-SEATER DEADLINE

Following the **Taylor Report**, Premier League and First Division grounds in England were required to be all-seated by August 1994. But the deadline was extended (May 1994) for five clubs planning to move to new stadiums: Derby, Grimsby, Middlesbrough, Portsmouth and Sunderland.

F.A. SOCCER SCHOOL

The Football Association's **national soccer school**, at Lilleshall, aimed at providing the backbone of England's World Cup challenge in the 1990s, was opened by the Duke of Kent (President) on September 4, 1984. It was sponsored by GM Motors, and the first intake comprised 25 boys aged fourteen.

To date the School of Excellence has produced four England Internationals: Nick Barmby, Andy Cole, Sol Campbell and Ian Walker.

DOUBLE RUNNERS-UP

There have been eight instances of clubs finishing **runner-up in both the League Championship and F.A. Cup in the same season**: 1928 Huddersfield Town; 1932 Arsenal; 1939 Wolves; 1962 Burnley; 1965 and 1970 Leeds United; 1986 Everton; 1995 Manchester United.

CORNER-KICK RECORDS

Not a single corner-kick was recorded when **Newcastle United** drew 0-0 at home to **Portsmouth** (Div.1) on December 5, 1931.

The record for **most corners** in a match for one side is believed to be **Sheffield United's 28** to West Ham's 1 in Div.2 at Bramall Lane on October 14, 1989. For all their pressure, Sheff. United lost 2-0.

Nott'm. Forest led Southampton 22-2 on corners (Premier League, Nov. 28, 1992) but lost the match 1-2.

Tommy Higginson (Brentford) once passed back to his own goalkeeper from a corner kick.

'PROFESSIONAL FOUL' DIRECTIVE

After the 1990 World Cup Finals, F.I.F.A. dealt with the "**professional foul**", incorporating this directive into the Laws of the Game: "If, in the opinion of the referee, a player who is moving towards his opponents' goal, with an obvious opportunity to score, is intentionally impeded by an opponent through unlawful means – thus denying the attacking player's team the aforesaid goalscoring opportunity – the offender should be sent from the field of play."

SACKED AT HALF-TIME

Leyton orient sacked **Terry Howard** on his 397th. appearance for the club – at half-time in a Second Division home defeat against Blackpool (Feb. 7, 1995) for "an unacceptable performance". He was fined two weeks' wages, given a free transfer and moved to Wycombe Wanderers.

MOST GAMES BY 'KEEPER FOR ONE CLUB

At the end of 1995-6, **Alan Knight** had made 620 League appearances for Portsmouth, over 19 season, a record for a goalkeeper at one club. The previous holder was Peter Bonetti with 600 League games for Chelsea (20 seasons, 1960-79).

COLOURFUL REFS

With the launch of the F.A. Premier League in 1992-3, referees wore **green, purple** or **yellow shirts**. Traditional all-black kit was still used when there was a clash with team colours.

PLAYED TWO GAMES ON SAME DAY

Jack Kelsey played full-length matches for both club and country on Wednesday, November 26, 1958. In the afternoon he kept goal for Wales in a 2-2 draw against England at Villa Park, and he then drove to Highbury to help Arsenal win 3-1 in a prestigious floodlit friendly against Juventus.

On the same day, winger **Danny Clapton** played for England (against Wales and Kelsey) and then in part of Arsenal's match against Juventus.

On November 11, 1987, **Mark Hughes** played for Wales against Czechoslovakia (European Championship) in Prague, then flew to Munich and went on as substitute that night in a winning Bayern Munich team, to whom he was on loan from Barcelona.

On February 16, 1993 goalkeeper **Scott Howie** played in Scotland's 3-0 U-21 win v Malta at Tannadice Park, Dundee (k.o. 1.30pm) and the same evening played in Clyde's 2-1 home win v Queen of South (Div. 2).

GOING PUBLIC

Manchester United became the fourth British club (after Tottenham, Hibernian and Millwall) to "go public" with a Stock Exchange share issue in June 1991. Others to follow since: Chelsea, Preston, Celtic, Leeds, Newcastle.

FIRST 'MATCH OF THE DAY'

BBC TV (recorded highlights): Liverpool 3, Arsenal 2 on August 22, 1964.
First complete match to be televised: Arsenal 3, Everton 2 on August 29, 1936.
First League match televised in colour: Liverpool 2, West Ham 0 on November 15, 1969.

OLYMPIC SOCCER WINNERS

1908 Great Britain (in London); **1912** Great Britain (Stockholm); **1920** Belgium (Antwerp); **1924** Uruguay (Paris); **1928** Uruguay (Amsterdam); **1932** No soccer in Los Angeles Olympics.

1936 Italy (Berlin); **1948** Sweden (London); **1952** Hungary (Helsinki); **1956** USSR (Melbourne); **1960** Yugoslavia (Rome); **1964** Hungary (Tokyo).

1968 Hungary (Mexico); **1972** Poland (Munich); **1976** E. Germany (Montreal); **1980** Czechoslovakia (Moscow); **1984** France (Los Angeles); **1988** USSR (Seoul); **1992** Spain (Barcelona); **1996** Venue Atlanta.

Highest scorer in Final tournament: Ferenc Bene (Hungary) 12 goals, 1964.

Record crowd for Olympic Soccer Final: 108,800 (France v. Brazil, Los Angeles 1984).

MOST AMATEUR CUP WINS

Bishop Auckland set the F.A. Amateur Cup record with 10 wins, and in 1957 became the only club to carry off the trophy in three successive seasons. Five wins: Clapton and Crook Town. The competition was discontinued after the Final on April 20, 1974. (Bishop's Stortford 4, Ilford 1, at Wembley).

POOLS – RECORD WINS

Twenty-three winners have crashed the £2m. barrier since Littlewoods raised the Treble Chance top prize to that limit at the start of season 1991-2 but, due to the National Lottery, there were none in 1995-6.

The Pools began in 1923. Launched with a capital of £100, Littlewoods distributed 4,000 coupons outside Manchester United's ground. Only 35 were returned, stakes totalled £4-7s.-6d. and the first pay-out was £2-12s.

The Treble Chance was introduced in 1946. Prize-money "firsts": £100,000 — 1950; £200,000 — 1957; £500,000 – 1972; £1m. – 1986; £1.5m. – 1990; £2m. – 1991.

Top Winners (all Littlewoods; * = Summer Pools)

Date	Name & Area	£
19/11/94	Syndicate from Worsley, Manchester	2,924,622
22/10/94	Syndicate from Wigan	2,615,854
14/1/95	Andy Paliunovas, Gloucester	2,326,792
27/8/94	Dave Yeomans, Worcester	2,293,110
23/7/94	Maurice Remington, Leicester	*2,281,399
1/10/94	Syndicate from Leeds	2,275,052
7/1/95	Co. Durham Man	2,273,430
6/8/94	David Caldwell, Cheam, Surrey	*2,267,636
16/7/94	Rohan Mitchell, Royal Navy	*2,261,401
24/9/94	Somerset Man	2,257,953
12/2/94	Barry Mallett, Dovercourt, Essex	2,255,387
13/6/92	Justin Daniels, Bournemouth	*2,246,113
11/4/92	South London Man	2,137,917
2/5/92	Suffolk Man	2,110,436
11/12/93	Judith and Terry Smith, Portland	2,077,683
27/11/93	Mary Brown, Liverpool	2,075,151
26/10/91	Rodica Woodcock, South-east London	2,072,220
24/6/95	Audrey Grieve, Scotland	*2,069,767
6/3/93	Terry Saxon (syndicate), Newport, Gwent	2,055,559
8/5/93	Bill Forbes (syndicate), Birmingham	2,029,668
1/2/92	Joyce Beynon, Llantrisant, Mid-Glamorgan	2,027,493
31/10/92	Charlie Hill, Blackpool	2,008,137
15/2/92	Pat Unwin, Stoke-on-Trent	2,000,000

- Jim Wright, from Teignmouth, Devon, set a Fixed Odds record with a payment of £654,375 (Ladbrokes, May 1993). He placed a £1,000 each-way pre-season treble on the champions of the three Football League divisions – Newcastle (8-1), Stoke (6-1), Cardiff (9-1).

POOLS PANEL

The **Pools Panel** was introduced in January 1963 during the **Big Freeze winter**. Originally, 30 coupon matches had to be postponed for the panel to operate; in later seasons the figure was ten and, starting in 1988-9, they gave their verdict when only one coupon fixture was off. The panel assembles at a hotel (originally in London and since 1984 in Manchester) every weekend from the beginning of November to the end of April.

Last season (1995-6) it comprised Roger Hunt (Chairman), Ronnie Simpson, Gordon Banks and Tony Green.

Their busiest day was Jan. 27, 1996, when, because of postponements, they were required to adjudicate on 54 matches (incl. 11 in the Conference).

THE FOOTBALL TRUST

The Football Trust was founded in 1975, an initiative of the Pools companies, Littlewoods, Vernons and Zetters. The Trust helps football at all levels, from the top – grants for the redevelopment of our national stadia and League clubs, safety and improvement grants, support for the Pyramid, closed circuit television and transport projects – down to the grass roots, including providing strips and equipment for schoolboys and schoolgirl teams.

The Trust's priority is to help clubs implement the recommendations of the Taylor Report. Grants are awarded for new stadia, new stands, cover and safety work. Since 1990 the Trust has allocated more than £132m. to projects costing over £240m.

RECORD TESTIMONIALS

Two nights after Man. United completed the Double in May, 1994, 42,079 packed Old Trafford for **Mark Hughes'** testimonial (1-3 Celtic). The estimated proceeds of £500,000 equalled the British testimonial record of **Ally McCoist's** match (Rangers 1, Newcastle 2) on August 3, 1993.

The match for **Bryan Robson**, Man. United and England captain, against Celtic at Old Trafford on Tuesday, November 20, 1990 was watched by a crowd of 41,658, and receipts of £300,000 were a then record for a testimonial.

Kenny Dalglish's testimonial (Liverpool v Real Sociedad) at Anfield on August 14, 1990 attracted 30,461 spectators, with receipts estimated at £150,000.

On December 4, 1990, **Willie Miller**'s testimonial (Aberdeen v World XI) packed Pittodrie to its 22,500 capacity, and raised an estimated £150,000.

The match for 82-year-old **Sir Matt Busby**, between Man. United and a Rep. of Ireland XI at Old Trafford on Sunday, August 11, 1991 was watched by 35,410 (estimated benefit £250,000).

Ian Rush's testimonial brought an estimated £250,000 from a 25,856 crowd at Anfield on December 6, 1994 (Liverpool 6, Celtic 0).

Three lucrative testimonials were staged in May 1996. Arsenal's **Paul Merson** earned a reported £400,000 (a percentage to charity) from his match against an Int. XI at Highbury (May 9, att: 31,626); the Republic of Ireland's new manager **Mick McCarthy** received an estimated £300,000 from a 40,000 who saw Celtic beaten 3-0 at Lansdowne Road, Dublin on May 26; and **Stuart Pearce** benefited by some £200,000 from a turn-out of 23,815 when Nott'm. Forest beat Newcastle 6-5 at the City Ground on May 8.

WHAT IT USED TO COST . . .

Minimum admission to League football was one shilling in 1939. After the war, it was increased to 1s. 3d. in 1946; 1s. 6d. in 1951; 1s. 9d. in 1952; 2s. in 1955; 2s. 6d. in 1960; 4s. in 1965; 5s. in 1968; 6s. in 1970; and 8s. (40p) in 1972. After that, the fixed minimum charge was dropped.

ENGLAND TOP EURO-PRIZE WINNERS

There have been **115 European club competitions** since the Champions' Cup was launched in season 1955-6; 41 for the European Cup, 38 for the Fairs/UEFA Cup and 36 for the Cup-Winners' Cup.

Despite the five-year enforced absence that followed the Heysel disaster in 1985, **English clubs** still head the European prize list, Arsenal's success in the 1994 Cup-Winners' Cup taking the total to 24 triumphs: 8 in the Champions' Cup, 7 in the Cup-Winners' Cup and 9 in the Fairs/UEFA Cup.

Italy are second with 23 Euro prizes, followed by Spain (21) and West Germany/Germany (13). The 115 winners have come from 16 countries.

England's 24 prizes are shared among 13 clubs: Liverpool 6 (4 EC, 2 UEFA); Tottenham 3 (1 CWC, 2 UEFA); Leeds 2 (2 UEFA); Man. United 2 (1 EC, 1 CWC); Nott'm. Forest 2 (2 EC); Arsenal 2 (1 UEFA, 1 CWC); Aston Villa 1 (EC); Chelsea 1 (CWC); Everton 1 (CWC); Ipswich 1 (UEFA); Man. City 1 (CWC); Newcastle 1 (UEFA); West Ham 1 (CWC).

Scotland's three successes have been achieved by Celtic (EC); Rangers and Aberdeen (both CWC).

EUROPEAN TRIUMPHS, COUNTRY BY COUNTRY

	European Cup	Cup-Winners' Cup	UEFA Cup	Total
England	8	7	9	24
Italy	9	6	8	23
Spain	7	6	8	21
West Germany/Germany	4	4	5	13
Holland	6	1	3	10
Belgium	–	3	1	4
Portugal	3	1	–	4
Scotland	1	2	–	3
USSR	–	3	–	3
Sweden	–	–	2	2
Yugoslavia	1	–	1	2
Czechoslovakia	–	1	–	1
East Germany	–	1	–	1
France	1	1	–	2
Hungary	–	–	1	1
Romania	1	–	–	1
Total:	41	36	38	115

BRITAIN'S 27 TROPHIES IN EUROPE

Arsenal's success in the 1993-4 Cup-Winners' Cup took the number of British club triumphs in European to 27 (nine in each competition):

European Cup (9)	Cup-Winners' Cup (9)	Fairs/UEFA Cup (9)
1967 Celtic	1963 Tottenham	1968 Leeds Utd.
1968 Man. United	1965 West Ham Utd.	1969 Newcastle Utd.
1977 Liverpool	1970 Man. City	1970 Arsenal
1978 Liverpool	1971 Chelsea	1971 Leeds Utd.
1979 Nott'm Forest	1972 Rangers	1972 Tottenham
1980 Nott'm Forest	1983 Aberdeen	1973 Liverpool
1981 Liverpool	1985 Everton	1976 Liverpool
1982 Aston Villa	1991 Man. United	1981 Ipswich Town
1984 Liverpool	1994 Arsenal	1984 Tottenham

EUROPEAN CLUB COMPETITIONS – SCORING RECORDS

European Cup – Record aggregate: 18-0 by Benfica v Dudelange (Lux) (8-0a, 10-0h), prelim. round, 1965-6.

Record single-match score: 12-0 by Feyenoord v KR Reykjavik (Ice), 1st. round, 1st. leg, 1969-70 (aggregate was 16-0).

Cup-Winners' Cup – Record aggregate: 21-0 by Chelsea v Jeunesse Hautcharage (Lux) (8-0a, 13-0h), 1st. round, 1971-2.

Record single-match score: 16-1 by Sporting Lisbon v Apoel Nicosia, 2nd. round, 1st. leg, 1963-4 (aggregate was 18-1).

UEFA Cup (prev. Fairs Cup) – Record aggregate: 21-0 by Feyenoord v US Ramelange (Lux) (9-0h, 12-0a), 1st. round, 1972-3.

Record single-match score: 14-0 by Ajax Amsterdam v Red Boys (Lux) 1st. round, 2nd leg, 1984-5 (aggregate also 14-0).

Record British score in Europe: 13-0 by **Chelsea** at home to Jeunesse Hautcharage (Lux) in Cup-Winners'Cup 1st. round, 2nd. leg, 1971-2. Chelsea's overall 21-0 in that tie is highest aggregate by British club in Europe.

Individual scoring records for European tie (over two legs): **8 goals** by **Jose Altafini** for the AC Milan v US Luxembourg (European Cup, prelim. round, 1962-3, agg. 14-0) and by **Peter Osgood** for Chelsea v Jeunesse Hautcharage (Cup-Winners' Cup, 1st. round 1971-2, agg. 21-0). Altafini and Osgood each scored 5 goals at home, 3 away.

Individual single-match scoring record in European competition: **6 goals** by **Lothar Emmerich** when Borussia Dortmund beat Floriana (Malta) 8-0 in Cup-Winners' Cup 1st. round, 2nd. leg, 1965-6.

Most goals in single European campaign: **15** by **Jurgen Klinsmann** for Bayern Munich (UEFA Cup 1995-6).

Most goals (career total) **by British player in European competition**: **31** by **Peter Lorimer** (Leeds, in 9 campaigns).

EUROPEAN FOOTBALL – BIG RECOVERIES

In the 41-year history of European competition, only four clubs have survived a **4-goal** deficit:

1961-2 (Cup-Winners' Cup 1st. Rd.): Leixoes (Portugal) beat Chaux de Fonds 7-6 on agg. (lost 2-6a, won 5-0h).

1962-3 (Fairs Cup 2nd. Rd.): Valencia (Spain) beat **Dunfermline** 1-0 in play-off in Lisbon after 6-6 agg. (Valencia won 4-0h, lost 2-6a).

1984-5 (UEFA Cup 2nd. Rd.): Partizan Belgrade beat **Q.P.R.** on away goals (lost 2-6 away, at Highbury, won 4-0 home).

1985-6 (UEFA Cup 3rd. Rd.): Real Madrid beat Borussia Moenchengladbach on away goals (lost 1-5a, won 4-0h) and went on to win competition.

In the **European Cup**, there are eight instances of clubs reaching the next round after **arrears of three goals** in the first leg:

1958-9 (Prel. Rd.) Schalke beat KB Copenhagen (0-3, 5-2, 3-1).

1965-6 (Q-final) Partizan Belgrade beat Sparta Prague (1-4, 5-0).

1970-1 (S-final) Panathinaikos beat Red Star Belgrade on away goal (1-4, 3-0).

1975-6 (2nd. Rd.) Real Madrid beat **Derby County** (1-4, 5-1).

1985-6 (S-final) Barcelona beat IFK Gothenburg on pens. (0-3, 3-0).

1988-9 (1st. Rd.) Werder Bremen beat Dynamo Berlin (0-3, 5-0).

1988-9 (2nd. Rd.) Galatasaray (Turkey) beat Neuchatel Xamax (Switz.) (0-3, 5-0).

1992-3 (1st. Rd.) **Leeds** beat VfB Stuttgart 2-1 in play-off in Barcelona. Over two legs, VfB won on away goal (3-0h, 1-4 away) but UEFA ordered third match because they broke "foreigners" rule in team selection.

In the **Cup-Winners' Cup**, six clubs have survived a **3-goal** deficit:
1963-4 (Q-final) Sporting Lisbon beat **Man. United** (1-4, 5-0).
1963-4 (S-final) MTK Budapest beat **Celtic** (0-3, 4-0).
1978-9 (2nd. Rd.) Barcelona beat Anderlecht on pens. (0-3, 3-0).
1980-1 (1st. Rd.) Carl Zeiss Jena beat AS Roma (0-3, 4-0).
1984-5 (Q-final) Rapid Vienna beat Dynamo Dresden (0-3, 5-0).
1989-90 (1st. Rd.) Grasshoppers (Switz.) beat Slovan Bratislava (0-3, 4-0).

In the **Fairs Cup/UEFA Cup**, there have been 20 occasions when clubs have survived a deficit of **3 goals**, the most notable example being the 1988 UEFA Cup Final, which Bayer Leverkusen won 3-2 on pens., having lost the first leg 0-3 away to Espanol and won the return 3-0 to level the aggregate.

Apart from Leeds, **Kilmarnock** are the only British club to win a European tie from a 3-goal, first leg deficit: 0-3, 5-1 v Eintracht Frankfurt (UEFA Cup 1st. Round, 1964-5).

Three English clubs have gone out of the **UEFA Cup** after leading 3-0 from the first leg: 1975-6 (2nd. Rd.) **Ipswich** lost 3-4 on agg. to Bruges; 1976-7 (Q-final) **Q.P.R.** lost on pens. to AEK Athens after 3-3 agg; 1977-8 (3rd. Rd.) **Ipswich** lost on pens. to Barcelona after 3-3 agg.

HEAVIEST ENGLISH-CLUB DEFEATS IN EUROPE

(Single-leg scores)

European Cup: Ajax 5, Liverpool 1 (2nd. Rd.), Dec. 1966; Real Madrid 5, Derby 1 (2nd. Rd.), Nov. 1975.
Cup-Winners' Cup: Sporting Lisbon 5, Man. Utd. 0 (Q-final), Mar. 1964.
Fairs/UEFA Cup: Bayern Munich 6, Coventry 1 (2nd. Rd.), Oct. 1970.

SHOCK ENGLISH-CLUB DEFEATS

1968-69 (E. Cup, 1st. Rd.): Man. City beaten by Fenerbahce, 1-2 agg.
1971-72 (CWC, 2nd. Rd.): Chelsea beaten by Atvidaberg on away goals.
1993-94 (E. Cup, 2nd. Rd.): Man. United beaten by Galatasaray on away goals.
1994-95 (UEFA Cup, 1st. Rd.): Blackburn beaten by Trelleborgs, 2-3 agg.

P.F.A. FAIR PLAY TROPHY (Bobby Moore Fair Play Trophy from 1993)

1988 Liverpool
1989 Liverpool
1990 Liverpool
1991 Nott'm. Forest
1992 Portsmouth
1993 Norwich
1994 Crewe
1995 Crewe
1996 Crewe

WORLD YOUTH CHAMPIONSHIP – FINALS

1977 (Tunis) Soviet Union 2, Mexico 2 (Soviet won 9-8 on pens.); **1979** (Tokyo) Argentina 3, Soviet Union 1; **1981** (Sydney) W. Germany 4, Qatar 0; **1983** (Mexico City) Brazil 1, Argentina 0; **1985** (Moscow) Brazil 1, Spain 0; **1987** (Santiago) Yugoslavia 1, W. Germany 1 (Yugoslavia won 5-4 on pens.); **1989** (Riyadh) Portugal 2, Nigeria 0; **1991** (Lisbon) Portugal 0, Brazil 0 (Portugal won 4-2 on pens.); **1993** (Sydney) Brazil, 2 Ghana 1; **1995** (Qatar) Argentina 2, Brazil 0.

RECORD MEDALS SALE

At Christies' fifth annual Football Memorabilia sale in Glasgow on Oct. 20, 1993, trophies, caps and medals earned by **Ray Kennedy**, 42-year-old former England, Arsenal and Liverpool player, fetched a record total of £88,407. Kennedy, who suffers from Parkinson's Disease, received £73,000 after commission.

The P.F.A. paid £31,080 for a total of 60 lots – including a record £16,000 for his 1977 European Cup winner's medal – to be exhibited at their Manchester museum. An anonymous English collector paid £17,000 for the medal and plaque commemorating Kennedy's part in the Arsenal Double in 1971.

Previous record for one player's medals, shirts etc. collection: £30,000 (**Bill Foulkes**, Man. Utd. in 1992). The sale of **Dixie Dean**'s medals etc. in 1991 realised £28,000.

VARSITY MATCH

Oxford beat **Cambridge** 2-1 in the 112th Varsity soccer match at Fulham on April 6 last. Cambridge have won 45, Oxford 42, with 25 draws.

LONGEST UNBEATEN CUP RUN

Liverpool established the longest unbeaten Cup sequence by a Football League club: 25 successive rounds in the League/Milk Cup between semi-final defeat by Nottingham Forest (1-2 agg.) in 1980 and defeat at Tottenham (0-1) in the third round on October 31, 1984. During this period Liverpool won the tournament in four successive seasons, a feat no other Football League club has achieved in any competition.

HIGH HALF-TIME SCORES

Tottenham 10, Crewe 1 (F.A. Cup 4th. Rd. replay, Feb. 3, 1960; result 13-2); Tranmere 8, Oldham 1 (Div. 3N., Dec. 26, 1935; result 13-4); Chester 8, York 0 (Div. 3N., Feb. 1, 1936; result 12-0; believed to be record half-time scores in League football).

- Only instance of club failing to win League match after leading 5-0 at half-time: Sheff. Wed. 5, Everton 5 (Div. 1, Nov. 12, 1904; Wednesday scored 5 in first half, Everton 5 in second).

TOP SECOND-HALF TEAM

Most goals scored by a team in one half of a League match is eleven. Stockport led Halifax 2-0 at half-time in Div. 3 North on Jan. 6, 1934 and won 13-0.

FIVE NOT ENOUGH

Last team to score 5 in League match and lose: Reading, beaten 7-5 at Doncaster (Div. 3, Sept. 25, 1982).

LONG SERVICE WITH ONE CLUB

Bob Paisley was associated with Liverpool for 57 years from 1939, when he joined them from Bishop Auckland, until he died in February 1996. He served them as player, trainer, coach, assistant-manager, manager, director and vice-president.

Ronnie Moran, who joined Liverpool in 1952, is still with the club as coach.

Ernie Gregory served West Ham for 52 years as goalkeeper and coach. He joined them as boy of 14 from school in 1935, retired in May 1987.

Ted Sagar, Everton goalkeeper, 23 years at Goodison Park (1929-52, but only 16 League seasons because of War).

Roy Sproson, defender, played 21 League seasons for his only club, Port Vale (1950-71).

Pat Bonner, goalkeeper, 18 seasons with Celtic (1978-96).

Danny McGrain, defender, 17 years with Celtic (1970-87).

LONGEST CURRENT MEMBERSHIPS OF TOP DIVISION

Arsenal (since 1919), **Everton** (1954), **Liverpool** (1962), **Coventry** (1967).

TIGHT AT HOME

Fewest home goals conceded in League season (modern times): 4 by **Liverpool** (Div. 1, 1978-9); 4 by **Man. United** (Premier League, 1994-5).

LIVERPOOL'S LEAGUE CUP RECORDS

First club to win competition 5 times. **Ian Rush** first player to collect 5 winners' medals in League Cup: 1981-82-83-84-95.

Rush also first to play in 6 winning teams in Cup Finals **at Wembley**, all with Liverpool (F.A. Cup 1986-89-92; League Cup 1982-83-95).

TRIBUNAL-FEE RECORDS

Top tribunal fee: £2.5m for **Chris Bart-Williams** (Sheff. Wed. to Nott'm. Forest, June 1995).

Biggest discrepancy: **Andy Walker**, striker, Bolton to Celtic, June 1994: Bolton asked £2.2m, Celtic offered £250,000. Tribunal decided £550,000.

LONGEST THROW-IN?

That by Notts County's **Andy Legg** was measured (season 1994-5) at 41 metres (45 yards) and claimed as the longest throw by any footballer in the world.

BALL JUGGLING: WORLD RECORD CLAIM

Sam Ik (South Korea) juggled a ball non-stop for 18 hours, 11 minutes, 4 seconds in March 1995.

SUBS' SCORING RECORD

Barnet's 5-4 home win v Torquay (Div. 3, Dec. 28, 1993) provided the first instance of **all four substitutes** scoring in a major League match in England.

FOOTBALL'S OLDEST ANNUAL

Now in its 110th edition, this publication began as the 16-page ***Athletic News Football Supplement & Club Directory*** in 1887. From the long-established ***Athletic News***, it became the ***Sunday Chronicle Annual*** in 1946, the ***Empire News*** in 1956, the ***News of the World & Empire News*** in 1961 and, since 1965, the ***News of the World Annual***.

LEAGUE CHAMPIONS' RECORDS

Season	Champions	P	W	D	L	F	A	Pts
1888-89	Preston North End	22	18	4	0	74	15	40
1889-90	Preston North End	22	15	3	4	71	30	33
1890-91	Everton	22	14	1	7	63	29	29
1891-92	Sunderland	26	21	0	5	93	36	42
1892-93	Sunderland	30	22	4	4	100	36	48
1893-94	Aston Villa	30	19	6	5	84	42	44
1894-95	Sunderland	30	21	5	4	80	37	47
1895-96	Aston Villa	30	20	5	5	78	45	45
1896-97	Aston Villa	30	21	5	4	73	38	47
1897-98	Sheffield United	30	17	8	5	56	31	42
1898-99	Aston Villa	34	19	7	8	76	40	45
1899-1900	Aston Villa	34	22	6	6	77	35	50
1900-01	Liverpool	34	19	7	8	59	35	45
1901-02	Sunderland	34	19	6	9	50	35	44
1902-03	Sheffield Wednesday	34	19	4	11	54	36	42
1903-04	Sheffield Wednesday	34	20	7	7	48	28	47
1904-05	Newcastle United	34	23	2	9	72	33	48
1905-06	Liverpool	38	23	5	10	79	46	51
1906-07	Newcastle United	38	22	7	9	74	46	51
1907-08	Manchester United	38	23	6	9	81	48	52
1908-09	Newcastle United	38	24	5	9	65	41	53
1909-10	Aston Villa	38	23	7	8	84	42	53
1910-11	Manchester United	38	22	8	8	72	40	52
1911-12	Blackburn Rovers	38	20	9	9	60	43	49
1912-13	Sunderland	38	25	4	9	86	43	54
1913-14	Blackburn Rovers	38	20	11	7	78	42	51
1914-15	Everton	38	19	8	11	76	47	46
1915-19	No competition – First World War							
1919-20	West Bromwich Albion	42	28	4	10	104	47	60
1920-21	Burnley	42	23	13	6	79	36	59
1921-22	Liverpool	42	22	13	7	63	36	57
1922-23	Liverpool	42	26	8	8	70	31	60
1923-24	Huddersfield Town	42	23	11	8	60	33	57
1924-25	Huddersfield Town	42	21	16	5	69	28	58
1925-26	Huddersfield Town	42	23	11	8	92	60	57
1926-27	Newcastle United	42	25	6	11	96	58	56
1927-28	Everton	42	20	13	9	102	66	53
1928-29	Sheffield Wednesday	42	21	10	11	86	62	52
1929-30	Sheffield Wednesday	42	26	8	8	105	57	60
1930-31	Arsenal	42	28	10	4	127	59	66
1931-32	Everton	42	26	4	12	116	64	56
1932-33	Arsenal	42	25	8	9	118	61	58
1933-34	Arsenal	42	25	9	8	75	47	59
1934-35	Arsenal	42	23	12	7	115	46	58
1935-36	Sunderland	42	25	6	11	109	74	56
1936-37	Manchester City	42	22	13	7	107	61	57
1937-38	Arsenal	42	21	10	11	77	44	52
1938-39	Everton	42	27	5	10	88	52	59

Season	Champions	P	W	D	L	F	A	Pts
1939-46	No competition – Second World War							
1946-47	Liverpool	42	25	7	10	84	52	57
1947-48	Arsenal	42	23	13	6	81	32	59
1948-49	Portsmouth	42	25	8	9	84	42	58
1949-50	Portsmouth	42	22	9	11	74	38	53
1950-51	Tottenham Hotspur	42	25	10	7	82	44	60
1951-52	Manchester United	42	23	11	8	95	52	57
1952-53	Arsenal	42	21	12	9	97	64	54
1953-54	Wolverhampton Wanderers	42	25	7	10	96	56	57
1954-55	Chelsea	42	20	12	10	81	57	52
1955-56	Manchester United	42	25	10	7	83	51	60
1956-57	Manchester United	42	28	8	6	103	54	64
1957-58	Wolverhampton Wanderers	42	28	8	6	103	47	64
1958-59	Wolverhampton Wanderers	42	28	5	9	110	49	61
1959-60	Burnley	42	24	7	11	85	61	55
1960-61	Tottenham Hotspur	42	31	4	7	115	55	66
1961-62	Ipswich Town	42	24	8	10	93	67	56
1962-63	Everton	42	25	11	6	84	42	61
1963-64	Liverpool	42	26	5	11	92	45	57
1964-65	Manchester United	42	26	9	7	89	39	61
1965-66	Liverpool	42	26	9	7	79	34	61
1966-67	Manchester United	42	24	12	6	84	45	60
1967-68	Manchester City	42	26	6	10	86	43	58
1968-69	Leeds United	42	27	13	2	66	26	67
1969-70	Everton	42	29	8	5	72	34	66
1970-71	Arsenal	42	29	7	6	71	29	65
1971-72	Derby County	42	24	10	8	69	33	58
1972-73	Liverpool	42	25	10	7	72	42	60
1973-74	Leeds United	42	24	14	4	66	31	62
1974-75	Derby County	42	21	11	10	67	49	53
1975-76	Liverpool	42	23	14	5	66	31	60
1976-77	Liverpool	42	23	11	8	62	33	57
1977-78	Nottingham Forest	42	25	14	3	69	24	64
1978-79	Liverpool	42	30	8	4	85	16	68
1979-80	Liverpool	42	25	10	7	81	30	60
1980-81	Aston Villa	42	26	8	8	72	40	60
1981-82	Liverpool	42	26	9	7	80	32	87
1982-83	Liverpool	42	24	10	8	87	37	82
1983-84	Liverpool	42	22	14	6	73	32	80
1984-85	Everton	42	28	6	8	88	43	90
1985-86	Liverpool	42	26	10	6	89	37	88
1986-87	Everton	42	26	8	8	76	31	86
1987-88	Liverpool	40	26	12	2	87	24	90
1988-89	Arsenal	38	22	10	6	73	36	76
1989-90	Liverpool	38	23	10	5	78	37	79
1990-91	Arsenal	38	24	13	1	74	18	83
1991-92	Leeds United	42	22	16	4	74	37	82
1992-93	Manchester United	42	24	12	6	67	31	84
1993-94	Manchester United	42	27	11	4	80	38	92
1994-95	Blackburn Rovers	42	27	8	7	80	39	89
1995-96	Manchester United	38	25	7	6	73	35	82

OLYMPIC SOCCER FINALS

Year	Venue	Participants	Winners	Runners-up	Score	Attendance	Tournament Top Scorer
1908	London	6	Great Britain	Denmark	2-0	8,000	11 – Sophus Nielsen (Denmark)
1912	Stockholm	13	Great Britain	Denmark	4-2	14,000	10 – Gottfried Fuchs (Germany)
1920	Antwerp	14	Belgium	Czechoslovakia	2-0		7 – Herbert Karlsson (Sweden)
	(Final abandoned 39 mins – Czechs disqualified after walking off in protest when player sent off)						
1924	Paris	23	Uruguay	Switzerland	3-0	41,000	8 – Pedro Petrovic (Uruguay)
1928	Amsterdam	17	Uruguay	Argentina	2-1 (Replay after 1-1)		9 – Domingo Tarasconi (Argentina)
1932	Los Angeles – No soccer tournament						
1936	Berlin	16	Italy	Austria	2-1	100,000	7 – Annibale Frossi (Italy)
1948	London	18	Sweden	Yugoslavia	3-1		7 – Gunnar Nordahl (Sweden)
1952	Helsinki	25	Hungary	Yugoslavia	2-0	60,000	7 – Rajko Mitic & Branko Zebec (both Yugoslavia)
1956	Melbourne	11	USSR	Yugoslavia	1-0	100,000	4 – Dimitar Milanov (Bulgaria)
1960	Rome	16	Yugoslavia	Denmark	3-1		7 – Milan Galic & Borivoje Kostic (both Yugoslavia)
1964	Tokyo	14	Hungary	Czechoslovakia	2-1	80,000	12 – Ferenc Bene (Hungary)
1968	Mexico	16	Hungary	Bulgaria	4-1		7 – Kunishige Kamamoto (Japan)
1972	Munich	16	Poland	Hungary	2-1		9 – Kazimierz Deyna (Poland)
1976	Montreal	13	E. Germany	Poland	3-1	71,619	6 – Andrzej Szarmach (Poland)
1980	Moscow	16	Czechoslovakia	E. Germany	1-0	80,000	5 – Sergey Andreev (USSR)
*1984	Los Angeles	16	France	Brazil	2-0	108,800	5 – Damel Xuereb (France); Bovivoje Cvetkovic & Stjepan Deveric (both Yugoslavia)
1988	Seoul	16	USSR	Brazil	2-1	74,000	7 – Farias Romario (Brazil)
1992	Barcelona	16	Spain	Poland	3-2	95,000	7 – Andrzej Juskowiak (Poland)

(*Total of 1,421,627 spectators attended the 32 matches, including record crowd of 108,800 for Olympic Final).

TRANSFER TRAIL

By Albert Sewell

First British player to be transferred for £1m. was **Trevor Francis**, from Birmingham to Nott'm. Forest (£1,180,000) in Feb. 1979.

These are the "**Transfer Millionaire**" deals that have involved British players and/or British clubs, key as follows:

* = British record fee at that time
A = First £1m. British transfer
B = Record all-British deal
C = Record for goalkeeper
D = Record for defender
E = Record deal between English and Scottish clubs
F = Record fee paid by Scottish club
G = Record fee to Scottish club
H = Record all-Scottish deal
J = Record for winger
K = Record for teenager
L = Most expensive foreign import
M = Record English-club signing
N = Record British striker
(● Fees as at time of transfer, i.e. not including any subsequent increases)

	Player	From	To	Date	£
BMN*	Stan Collymore	Nottm. F.	Liverpool	6/95	8,500,000
L*	Dennis Bergkamp	Inter Milan	Arsenal	6/95	7,500,000
*	Andy Cole	Newcastle	Man. Utd.	1/95	7,000,000
	Fabrizio Ravanelli	Juventus	Mid'bro'	7/96	7,000,000
	Faustino Asprilla	Parma	Newcastle	2/96	6,700,000
*	David Platt	Bari	Juventus	6/92	6,500,000
*	Paul Ince	Man. Utd.	Inter Milan	6/95	6,000,000
	Les Ferdinand	Q.P.R.	Newcastle	6/95	6,000,000
*	David Platt	Aston Villa	Bari	7/91	5,500,000
*	Paul Gascoigne	Tottenham	Lazio	6/92	5,500,000
	Nick Barmby	Tottenham	Mid'bro'	8/95	5,250,000
	David Platt	Juventus	Sampdoria	7/93	5,200,000
G	Trevor Steven	Rangers	Marseille	8/91	5,000,000
	Chris Sutton	Norwich	Blackburn	7/94	5,000,000
J	Andrei Kanchelskis	Man. Utd.	Everton	8/95	5,000,000
	Roberto Di Matteo	Lazio	Chelsea	7/96	4,900,000
	David Platt	Sampdoria	Arsenal	7/95	4,750,000
	Juninho	Sao Paulo	Mid'bro'	10/95	4,750,000
	Chris Armstrong	Crystal P.	Tottenham	6/95	4,500,000
F	Paul Gascoigne	Lazio	Rangers	7/95	4,300,000
	Jason McAteer	Bolton	Liverpool	9/95	4,500,000
	Tomas Brolin	Parma	Leeds	11/95	4,300,000
	Ruel Fox	Newcastle	Tottenham	10/95	4,200,000
*	Chris Waddle	Tottenham	Marseille	7/89	4,250,000
H	Duncan Ferguson	Dundee U.	Rangers	7/93	4,000,000
E	Duncan Ferguson	Rangers	Everton	12/94	4,000,000
D	Warren Barton	Wimbledon	Newcastle	6/95	4,000,000
	David Batty	Blackburn	Newcastle	2/96	4,000,000
	Emerson	FC Porto	Mid'bro'	5/96	4,000,000
	Roy Keane	Nott'm. F.	Man. Utd.	7/93	3,750,000
	Phil Babb	Coventry	Liverpool	9/94	3,600,000
	John Scales	Wimbledon	Liverpool	9/94	3,500,000
	Savo Milosevic	P'zan. Belgrade	Aston Villa	6/95	3,500,000
	Alan Stubbs	Bolton	Celtic	5/96	3,500,000
	Gary Speed	Leeds	Everton	6/96	3,500,000
	Tony Yeboah	Eint. F'furt	Leeds	1/95	3,400,000
*	Alan Shearer	Southampton	Blackburn	7/92	3,300,000
	Mark Draper	Leicester	Aston Villa	7/95	3,250,000
*	Ian Rush	Liverpool	Juventus	6/87	3,200,000
	Gheorghe Popescu	Tottenham	Barcelona	5/95	3,200,000
	Garry Flitcroft	Man. City	Blackburn	3/96	3,200,000

	Daniel Amokachi	Bruges	Everton	8/94	3,000,000
	Dean Saunders	Derby	Liverpool	7/91	2,900,000
	Gheorghe Popescu	PSV Eindhov'n	Tottenham	9/94	2,900,000
	Ian Rush	Juventus	Liverpool	8/88	2,800,000
	Chris Coleman	Crystal P.	Blackburn	12/95	2,800,000
	Gary Lineker	Everton	Barcelona	6/86	2,750,000
	Andy Sinton	Q.P.R.	Sheff. W.	8/93	2,750,000
	David Batty	Leeds	Blackburn	10/93	2,750,000
	Brian Deane	Sheff. Utd.	Leeds	7/93	2,700,000
	Des Walker	Sampdoria	Sheff. W.	7/93	2,700,000
	Paul Warhust	Sheff. W.	Blackburn	9/93	2,700,000
	Darren Peacock	Q.P.R.	Newcastle	3/94	2,700,000
	Basile Boli	Marseille	Rangers	6/94	2,700,000
	Andy Booth	Huddersfield	Sheff. Wed.	7/96	2,700,000
	Philippe Albert	Anderlecht	Newcastle	8/94	2,650,000
	Carlton Palmer	Sheff. W.	Leeds	6/94	2,600,000
	Ilie Dumitrescu	Steaua Buch.	Tottenham	7/94	2,600,000
K	Lee Bowyer	Charlton	Leeds	7/96	2,600,000
	Jonas Bjorklund	Vicenza	Rangers	7/96	2,600,000
	Keith Curle	Wimbledon	Man. City	8/91	2,500,000
	Ian Wright	Crystal P.	Arsenal	9/91	2,500,000
	Terry Phelan	Wimbledon	Man. City	8/92	2,500,000
	Craig Short	Notts Co.	Derby	9/92	2,500,000
	Kevin Gallacher	Coventry	Blackburn	3/93	2,500,000
	Neil Ruddock	Tottenham	Liverpool	7/93	2,500,000
	Bryan Roy	Foggia	Nott'm. F.	6/94	2,500,000
	John Hartson	Luton	Arsenal	1/95	2,500,000
	Gareth Southgate	Crystal P.	Aston Villa	6/95	2,500,000
	David Ginola	Paris St. Germain	Newcastle	7/95	2,500,000
	Stefan Schwarz	Arsenal	Fiorentina	7/95	2,500,000
	Oleg Salenko	Valencia	Rangers	7/95	2,500,000
	Kevin Campbell	Arsenal	Nott'm. F.	6/95	2,500,000
	Chris Bart-Williams	Sheff. W.	Nott'm. F.	6/95	2,500,000
	Darko Kovacevic	Sheff. W.	R. Sociedad	6/96	2,500,000
	Franck Lebouef	Strasbourg	Chelsea	6/96	2,500,000
	Trevor Steven	Marseille	Rangers	7/92	2,400,000
	Craig Short	Derby	Everton	7/95	2,400,000
	Florin Raducioiu	Espanol	West Ham	7/96	2,400,000
*	Mark Hughes	Man. Utd.	Barcelona	5/86	2,300,000
	Gary Pallister	Mid'bro'	Man. Utd.	8/89	2,300,000
	Paul Stewart	Tottenham	Liverpool	7/92	2,300,000
	Dean Saunders	Liverpool	Aston Villa	9/91	2,300,000
	Paul Furlong	Watford	Chelsea	5/94	2,300,000
	Andreas Thom	B. Leverkusen	Celtic	7/95	2,300,000
	Dan Petrescu	Sheff. W.	Chelsea	10/95	2,300,000
	Michael Johansen	FC Copenhagen	Bolton	6/96	{2,280,000
	Per Frandsen	FC Copenhagen	Bolton	6/96	
	Nigel Clough	Nott'm. Forest	Liverpool	6/93	2,275,000
	Ruel Fox	Norwich	Newcastle	2/94	2,250,000
	Paul Kitson	Derby	Newcastle	9/94	2,250,000
	Tony Cottee	West Ham	Everton	7/88	2,200,000
	Mark Wright	Derby	Liverpool	7/91	2,200,000
	Gordon Durie	Chelsea	Tottenham	8/91	2,200,000
	Stan Collymore	Southend	Nott'm. F.	6/93	2,200,000
	Brian Laudrup	Fiorentina	Rangers	6/94	2,200,000
	Vinny Samways	Tottenham	Everton	8/94	2,200,000
	Teddy Sheringham	Nott'm. F.	Tottenham	8/92	2,100,000
	Robert Fleck	Norwich	Chelsea	8/92	2,100,000
	Andy Townsend	Chelsea	Aston Villa	7/93	2,100,000
	Paul Gascoigne	Newcastle	Tottenham	7/88	2,000,000
	Alexei Mikhailichenko	Sampdoria	Rangers	6/91	2,000,000

	Player	From	To	Date	Fee
	Teddy Sheringham	Millwall	Nott'm. F.	7/91	2,000,000
	Paul Parker	Q.P.R.	Man. Utd.	8/91	2,000,000
	David Rocastle	Arsenal	Leeds	7/92	2,000,000
	Martin Keown	Everton	Arsenal	2/93	2,000,000
C	Tim Flowers	Southampton	Blackburn	11/93	2,000,000
	Jurgen Klinsmann	Monaco	Tottenham	7/94	2,000,000
	Dion Dublin	Man. Utd.	Coventry	9/94	2,000,000
	Tommy Johnson	Derby	Aston Villa	1/95	2,000,000
	Glenn Helder	Vit. Arnhem	Arsenal	2/95	2,000,000
	Darko Kovacevic	R.S. Belgrade	Sheff. W.	10/95	2,000,000
	Dejan Stefanovic	R.S. Belgrade	Sheff. W.	10/95	2,000,000
	Noel Whelan	Leeds	Coventry	12/95	2,000,000
	Eoin Jess	Aberdeen	Coventry	2/96	2,000,000
	Ben Thatcher	Millwall	Wimbledon	7/96	2,000,000
	Peter Beardsley	Newcastle	Liverpool	7/87	1,900,000
	Georgi Kinkladze	Dynamo Tbilisi	Man. City	7/95	1,900,000
	Dean Richards	Bradford C.	Wolves	5/95	1,850,000
	Mark Hughes	Barcelona	Man. Utd.	6/88	1,800,000
	Marco Gabbiadini	Sunderland	Crystal P.	9/91	1,800,000
	Andy Roberts	Millwall	Crystal P.	7/95	1,800,000
	Andrea Silenzi	Torino	Nott'm. F.	7/95	1,800,000
	Kit Symons	Portsmouth	Man. City	8/95	1,800,000
	Andrew Cole	Bristol City	Newcastle	3/93	1,750,000
	Jason Dozzell	Ipswich	Tottenham	8/93	1,750,000
	Stefan Schwarz	Benfica	Arsenal	6/94	1,750,000
	Phil O'Donnell	Motherwell	Celtic	9/94	1,750,000
	Billy McKinlay	Dundee U.	Blackburn	10/95	1,750,000
	Liam Daish	Birmingham	Coventry	2/96	1,750,000
	Dalian Atkinson	Sheff. W.	Real S'dad	8/90	1,700,000
	Paul Stewart	Man. City	Tottenham	6/88	1,700,000
	Earl Barrett	Oldham	Aston Villa	2/92	1,700,000
	Slaven Bilic	Karlsruhe	West Ham	12/95	1,650,000
	Darren Anderton	Portsmouth	Tottenham	6/92	1,700,000
	Earl Barrett	Aston Villa	Everton	1/95	1,700,000
	Dennis Wise	Wimbledon	Chelsea	7/90	1,600,000
	Rod Wallace	Southampton	Leeds	5/91	1,600,000
	Dalian Atkinson	Real S'dad	Aston Villa	7/91	1,600,000
	Anders Limpar	Arsenal	Everton	3/94	1,600,000
	Shaka Hislop	Reading	Newcastle	8/95	1,575,000
	Igor Stimac	Hadjuk Split	Derby	10/95	1,570,000
	Trevor Steven	Everton	Rangers	6/89	1,525,000
*	Bryan Robson	W.B.A.	Man. Utd.	10/81	1,500,000
	Ray Wilkins	Man. Utd.	AC Milan	6/84	1,500,000
	Richard Gough	Tottenham	Rangers	10/87	1,500,000
	Neil Webb	Nott'm. F.	Man. Utd.	6/89	1,500,000
	Mo Johnston	Nantes	Rangers	7/89	1,500,000
	Paul Ince	West Ham	Man. Utd.	9/89	1,500,000
	Tony Cascarino	Millwall	Aston Villa	3/90	1,500,000
	Chris Whyte	W.B.A.	Leeds	6/90	1,500,000
	Kingsley Black	Luton	Nott'm. F.	8/91	1,500,000
	Mo Johnston	Rangers	Everton	11/91	1,500,000
	Michael Thomas	Arsenal	Liverpool	12/91	1,500,000
	Des Walker	Nott'm. F.	Sampdoria	5/92	1,500,000
	Stuart Slater	West Ham	Celtic	8/92	1,500,000
	Peter Beardsley	Everton	Newcastle	6/93	1,500,000
	Colin Cooper	Millwall	Nott'm. F.	6/93	1,500,000
	Julian Dicks	West Ham	Liverpool	9/93	1,500,000
	Alan Kernaghan	Mid'bro'	Man. City	9/93	1,500,000
	Mark Stein	Stoke	Chelsea	10/93	1,500,000
	David May	Blackburn	Man. Utd.	5/94	1,500,000
	Nicky Summerbee	Swindon	Man. City	6/94	1,500,000

Ian Nolan	Tranmere	Sheff. W.	8/94	1,500,000
Don Hutchison	Liverpool	West Ham	8/94	1,500,000
Jeff Kenna	Southampton	Blackburn	3/95	1,500,000
Mark Kennedy	Millwall	Liverpool	3/95	1,500,000
Mark Hughes	Man. Utd.	Chelsea	6/95	1,500,000
Dean Saunders	Aston Villa	Galatasaray	7/95	1,500,000
Gordan Petric	Dundee U.	Rangers	7/95	1,500,000
Steve Wright	Aberdeen	Rangers	7/95	1,500,000
Gerry Taggart	Barnsley	Bolton	8/95	1,500,000
John Salako	Crystal P.	Coventry	8/95	1,500,000
Mark Hateley	Rangers	Q.P.R.	9/95	1,500,000
Graham Fenton	Aston Villa	Blackburn	10/95	1,500,000
Richard Shaw	Crystal P.	Coventry	11/95	1,500,000
Marc Degryse	Anderlecht	Sheff. W.	7/95	1,500,000
Ilie Dumitrescu	Tottenham	West Ham	1/96	1,500,000
Andy Sinton	Sheff. W.	Tottenham	1/96	1,500,000
Julian Joachim	Leicester	Aston Villa	2/96	1,500,000
Erik Bo Andersen	Aalborg	Rangers	2/96	1,500,000
Jon Newsome	Norwich	Sheff. W.	3/96	1,500,000
Dean Saunders	Galatasaray	Nott'm. F.	6/96	1,500,000
Ole Gunnar Solskjar	Molde	Man. Utd.	7/96	1,500,000
Paul Furlong	Chelsea	Birmingham	7/96	1,500,000
* Andy Gray	Aston Villa	Wolves	9/79	1,469,000
* Steve Daley	Wolves	Man. City	9/79	1,437,500
Oleg Kuznetsov	Dynamo Kiev	Rangers	10/90	1,400,000
Carl Tiler	Barnsley	Nott'm. F.	5/91	1,400,000
Paul Elliott	Celtic	Chelsea	7/91	1,400,000
Jose Dominguez	Birmingham	Sp. Lisbon	6/95	1,400,000
Mikhail Kavelashvili	Sp. Vladikavkaz	Man. City	3/96	1,400,000
Kenny Sansom	Crystal P.	Arsenal	8/80	1,350,000
John Fashanu	Wimbledon	Aston Villa	8/94	1,350,000
Jurgen Klinsmann	Tottenham	B. Munich	7/95	1,350,000
David Seaman	Q.P.R.	Arsenal	5/90	1,300,000
Tony Dorigo	Chelsea	Leeds	5/91	1,300,000
Tommy Johnson	Notts Co.	Derby	3/92	1,300,000
Dave McPherson	Hearts	Rangers	6/92	1,300,000
Stuart Ripley	Mid'bro'	Blackburn	7/92	1,300,000
Dan Petrescu	Genoa	Sheff. W.	8/94	1,300,000
Jan Aage Fjortoft	Swindon	Mid'bro'	3/95	1,300,000
Mark Rieper	Brondby	West Ham	5/95	1,300,000
Kevin Reeves	Norwich	Man. City	3/80	1,250,000
Ian Wallace	Coventry	Nott'm. F.	7/80	1,250,000
Clive Allen	Arsenal	Crystal P.	8/80	1,250,000
Garry Birtles	Nott'm. F.	Man. Utd.	10/80	1,250,000
Frank McAvennie	Celtic	West Ham	3/89	1,250,000
Andy Linighan	Norwich	Arsenal	7/90	1,250,000
Mark Walters	Rangers	Liverpool	8/91	1,250,000
Mark Pembridge	Luton	Derby	5/92	1,250,000
Gavin Peacock	Newcastle	Chelsea	7/93	1,250,000
Colin Calderwood	Swindon	Tottenham	7/93	1,250,000
Tony Daley	Aston Villa	Wolves	5/94	1,250,000
Mark Draper	Notts. Co	Leicester	7/94	1,250,000
David Rocastle	Man. City	Chelsea	8/94	1,250,000
Alan McLaren	Hearts	Rangers	10/94	1,250,000
Chris Kiwomya	Ipswich	Arsenal	1/95	1,250,000
Ned Zelic	Bor. Dortmund	Q.P.R.	7/95	1,250,000
Clive Allen	Q.P.R.	Arsenal	6/80	1,200,000
Trevor Francis	Nott'm. F.	Man. City	9/81	1,200,000
Gary Lineker	Barcelona	Tottenham	6/89	1,200,000
Danny Wallace	Southampton	Man. Utd.	9/89	1,200,000
Andy Townsend	Norwich	Chelsea	7/90	1,200,000

	Stuart McCall	Everton	Rangers	8/91	1,200,000
	Chris Woods	Rangers	Sheff. W.	8/91	1,200,000
	Dale Gordon	Norwich	Rangers	11/91	1,200,000
	Marco Gabbiadini	Crystal P.	Derby	1/92	1,200,000
	Eric Cantona	Leeds	Man. Utd.	11/92	1,200,000
	Guy Whittingham	Portsmouth	Aston Villa	8/93	1,200,000
	Gordon Durie	Tottenham	Rangers	11/93	1,200,000
	Pierre van Hooijdonk	NAC Breda	Celtic	1/95	1,200,000
	Gordon Watson	Sheff. W.	Southampton	3/95	1,200,000
	Nigel Clough	Liverpool	Sheff. W.	1/96	1,200,000
	Steve Claridge	Birmingham	Leicester	3/96	1,200,000
	Marcus Stewart	Bristol Rovers	Huddersfield	7/96	1,200,000
	Ronnie Johnsen	Besiktas	Man. Utd.	7/96	1,200,000
A*	Trevor Francis	Birmingham	Nott'm. F.	2/79	1,180,000
	Paul Telfer	Luton	Coventry	6/95	1,150,000
	Gary Lineker	Leicester	Everton	6/85	1,100,000
	Mike Newell	Leicester	Everton	6/89	1,100,000
	Alan McInally	Aston Villa	Bayern M.	6/89	1,100,000
	John Aldridge	Liverpool	Real S'dad	9/89	1,100,000
	Tony Cascarino	Aston Villa	Celtic	7/91	1,100,000
	Steve Staunton	Liverpool	Aston Villa	8/91	1,100,000
	Mike Newell	Everton	Blackburn	11/91	1,100,000
	John Jensen	Brondby	Arsenal	7/92	1,100,000
	Bruce Dyer	Watford	Crystal P.	3/94	1,100,000
	Peter Beagrie	Everton	Man. City	3/94	1,100,000
	Don Goodman	Sunderland	Wolves	12/94	1,100,000
	David Burrows	Everton	Coventry	3/95	1,100,000
	Simon Osborn	Reading	Q.P.R.	7/95	1,100,000
	Justin Fashanu	Norwich	Nott'm. F.	8/81	1,000,000
	Luther Blissett	Watford	AC Milan	6/83	1,000,000
	Steve Archibald	Tottenham	Barcelona	7/84	1,000,000
	Mark Hateley	AC Milan	Monaco	6/87	1,000,000
	Clive Allen	Tottenham	Bordeaux	5/88	1,000,000
	Gary Stevens	Everton	Rangers	7/88	1,000,000
	Dean Saunders	Oxford U.	Derby	10/88	1,000,000
	Clive Allen	Bordeaux	Man. City	7/89	1,000,000
	Nigel Martyn	Bristol R.	Crystal P.	11/89	1,000,000
	Roy Wegerle	Luton	Q.P.R.	12/89	1,000,000
	Mark Ward	West Ham	Man. City	12/89	1,000,000
	John Lukic	Arsenal	Leeds	5/90	1,000,000
	Gary McAllister	Leicester	Leeds	6/90	1,000,000
	Tony Coton	Watford	Man. City	7/90	1,000,000
	Anders Limpar	Cremonese	Arsenal	7/90	1,000,000
	Alan McLoughlin	Swindon	Southampton	12/90	1,000,000
	Gary Penrice	Watford	Aston Villa	3/91	1,000,000
	Andy Goram	Hibernian	Rangers	6/91	1,000,000
	Peter Beardsley	Liverpool	Everton	8/91	1,000,000
	Tony Mowbray	Mid'bro'	Celtic	11/91	1,000,000
	Roy Wegerle	Q.P.R.	Blackburn	3/92	1,000,000
	David James	Watford	Liverpool	6/92	1,000,000
	Chris Waddle	Marseille	Sheff. W.	6/92	1,000,000
	Dion Dublin	Cambridge U.	Man. Utd.	8/92	1,000,000
	Chris Armstrong	Millwall	Crystal P.	9/92	1,000,000
	Roy Wegerle	Blackburn	Coventry	3/93	1,000,000
	Eddie McGoldrick	Crystal P.	Arsenal	6/93	1,000,000
	Jon Newsome	Leeds	Norwich	6/94	1,000,000
	Joey Beauchamp	Oxford U.	West Ham	6/94	1,000,000
	John Moncur	Swindon	West Ham	6/94	1,000,000
	Steve Sedgley	Tottenham	Ipswich	6/94	1,000,000
	Steve Froggatt	Aston Villa	Wolves	7/94	1,000,000
	Ian Taylor	Sheff. W.	Aston Villa	12/94	1,000,000

Keith Gillespie	Man. Utd.	Newcastle	1/95	1,000,000
Mark Robins	Norwich	Leicester	1/95	1,000,000
Gerry Creaney	Portsmouth	Man. City	9/95	1,000,000
Mark Atkins	Blackburn	Wolves	9/95	1,000,000
Sasa Curcic	Part. Belgrade	Bolton	10/95	1,000,000
Nathan Blake	Sheff. Utd.	Bolton	12/95	1,000,000
Simon Osborn	Q.P.R.	Wolves	12/95	1,000,000
Regi Blinker	Feyenoord	Sheff. W.	3/96	1,000,000
Niklas Gudmundsson	Halmstad	Blackburn	3/96	1,000,000
Ashley Ward	Norwich	Derby	3/96	1,000,000
Gary Croft	Grimsby	Blackburn	3/96	1,000,000
Nikola Jerkan	Real Oviedo	Nottm. F.	7/96	1,000,000
Iwan Roberts	Leicester	Wolves	7/96	1,000,000

Record stages: Prior to Trevor Francis becoming the subject of the first £1m. transfer, this is how the record was broken, stage by stage from the time of the first £1,000 deal in 1905:

Player	From	To	Date	£
Alf Common	Sunderland	Mid'bro'	2/1905	1,000
Syd Puddefoot	West Ham	Falkirk	2/22	5,000
Warney Cresswell	S. Shields	Sunderland	3/22	5,500
Bob Kelly	Burnley	Sunderland	12/25	6,500
David Jack	Bolton	Arsenal	10/28	10,890
Bryn Jones	Wolves	Arsenal	8/38	14,500
Billy Steel	Morton	Derby	9/47	15,000
Tommy Lawton	Chelsea	Notts Co.	11/47	20,000
Len Shackleton	Newcastle	Sunderland	2/48	20,500
Johnny Morris	Man. Utd.	Derby	2/49	24,000
Eddie Quigley	Sheff. W.	Preston	12/49	26,000
Trevor Ford	Aston Villa	Sunderland	10/50	30,000
Jackie Sewell	Notts Co.	Sheff. W.	3/51	34,500
Eddie Firmani	Charlton	Sampdoria	7/55	35,000
John Charles	Leeds	Juventus	4/57	65,000
Denis Law	Man. City	Torino	6/61	100,000
Denis Law	Torino	Man. Utd.	7/62	115,000
Allan Clarke	Fulham	Leicester	6/68	150,000
Allan Clarke	Leicester	Leeds	6/69	165,000
Martin Peters	West Ham	Tottenham	3/70	200,000
Alan Ball	Everton	Arsenal	12/71	220,000
David Nish	Leicester	Derby	8/72	250,000
Bob Latchford	Birmingham	Everton	2/74	350,000
Graeme Souness	Mid'bro'	Liverpool	1/78	352,000
Kevin Keegan	Liverpool	Hamburg	6/77	500,000
David Mills	Mid'bro'	W.B.A.	1/79	516,000

• **World's first £1m. transfer:** Guiseppe Savoldi, Bologna to Napoli, July 1975.

TOP FOREIGN SIGNINGS

Player	From	To	Date	£
Gianluigi Lentini	Torino	AC Milan	7/92	13,000,000
Gianluca Vialli	Sampdoria	Juventus	6/92	12,500,000
Jean-Pierre Papin	Marseille	AC Milan	6/92	10,000,000
Alen Boksic	Marseille	Lazio	10/93	8,400,000
Dennis Bergkamp	Ajax	Inter Milan	6/93	8,000,000
Roberto Baggio	Juventus	AC Milan	7/95	8,000,000
Roberto Baggio	Fiorentina	Juventus	5/90	7,700,000
Daniel Fonseca	Cagliari	Napoli	6/92	7,000,000
Igor Shalimov	Foggia	Inter Milan	5/92	6,500,000
David Platt	Bari	Juventus	6/92	6,500,000

Ruud Gullit	PSV Eindh'n	AC Milan	6/87	6,000,000
Luca Marchegiani	Torino	Lazio	7/93	6,000,000
Thomas Hassler	Juventus	Roma	7/91	5,800,000
K-H. Riedle	Wer. Bremen	Lazio	4/90	5,500,000
Claudio Caniggia	Atalanta	Roma	5/92	5,500,000
K-H. Riedle	Lazio	B. Dortmund	7/93	5,500,000
Thomas Hassler	Cologne	Juventus	4/90	5,400,000
Dragan Stojkovic	Red Star	Marseille	7/90	5,250,000
Diego Maradona	Barcelona	Napoli	6/84	5,000,000
Thomas Doll	Hamburg	Lazio	6/91	5,000,000
Christian Karembeu	Nantes	Sampdoria	7/95	5,000,000
Romario	Flamenco	Valencia	7/96	5,000,000
Diego Maradona	Boca Juniors	Barcelona	6/82	4,800,000
Lajos Detari	Eint. F'furt	Olympiakos	7/88	4,700,000
Hristo Stoichkov	Barcelona	Parma	7/95	4,600,000
Diego Maradona	Napoli	Seville	9/92	4,500,000
George Weah	Paris SG	AC Milan	5/95	4,500,000
Clarence Seedorf	Ajax	Sampdoria	7/95	4,500,000
Roberto Carlos	Palmeiras	Inter Milan	7/95	4,500,000
Paulo Futre	At. Madrid	Benfica	1/93	4,200,000
Rui Barros	Porto	Juventus	7/88	4,000,000
Ronald Koeman	PSV Eindh'n	Barcelona	7/89	4,000,000
Martin Vazquez	Real Madrid	Torino	6/90	4,000,000
Jurgen Kohler	Bayern M.	Juventus	6/91	4,000,000
Dejan Savicevic	Red Star	AC Milan	12/91	4,000,000
Sensia Mihajlovic	Red Star	Roma	6/92	4,000,000
Gheorghe Hagi	Real Madrid	Brescia	7/92	4,000,000
Matthias Sammer	Inter Milan	B. Dortmund	1/93	4,000,000
Ronaldo	Cruzeiro	PSV Eindh'n	8/94	4,000,000
Youri Djorkaeff	Paris St. Germain	Inter Milan	5/96	4,000,000

WORLD RECORD GOALKEEPER FEE

£7.5m for **Gianluca Pagliuca** (Sampdoria to Inter Milan, Aug. 1994).

RECORD FEE BETWEEN NON-LEAGUE CLUBS

£85,000 for **Carl Alford**, 24-year-old striker from Kettering (GMVC) to neighbours Rushden & Diamonds (Beazer Homes League), March 1996.

SOCCER DIARY 1995-96

July 1995

3 Man. City appoint **Alan Ball** manager, from Southampton. **Dean Saunders**, A. Villa to **Galatasaray**, Turkey (coach Graeme Souness) in £1.5m move. **5** Transfers: **Mark Hughes**, Man. Utd. to **Chelsea** (£1.5m), **Mark Draper**, Leicester to **A. Villa** (£3.25m). **6 Newcastle** sign **David Ginola** (£2.5m) from Paris SG. **Southend** appoint **Ronnie Whelan** player-manager. **10 Arsenal** sign **David Platt** from Sampdoria – £4.75m deal takes Platt's career fees to world record £22.15m. **Paul Gascoigne**, Lazio to **Rangers** (£4.3m). **13 George Graham**, sacked Arsenal manager, banned from football world-wide for year until June 30, 1996 after FA inquiry finds him guilty of misconduct in accepting £425,000 "bung" from Norwegian agent Rune Hauge when Arsenal signed John Jensen and Pal Lydersen. **14 Stefan Schwarz**, **Arsenal** to Fiorentina (£2.5m). **Alan Ball**, on first day in charge of **Man. C.**, signs Georgian Int. **Georgi Kinkladze** from Dynamo Tbilisi (£1.9m). **Southampton** appoint **Dave Merrington**, 50, manager after 11 years on coaching staff. **17** Transfers: **Everton** pay £2.4m for **Craig Short** (Derby); **Crystal P.** sign **Andy Roberts** from Millwall (valued £2.25m in part-exchange for Ricky Newman). **19** Third Div. **Wigan** sign 3 Spaniards: **Jesus Seba** from Real Zaragoza, **Roberto Martinez** and **Isidro Diaz** (Balaguer). **Mark Pembridge**, Derby to **Sheff. W.** (£900,000), **David Hopkin**, Chelsea to **Crystal P.** (£850,000). Arsenal striker **Alan Smith** forced to retire through knee injury. **Jamie Hughes** (Tranmere) given 2-year suspended ban by FA for drugs offence. **21 Andrei Kanchelskis** (Man. Utd.) agrees £5m transfer (completed Aug. 25) – **Everton's** record fee. **24** Premier League players **Bruce Grobbelaar** (So'ton), **John Fashanu** (A. Villa) and **Hans Segers** (Wimbledon) charged with taking bribes to rig results (1991-5), bailed until Oct. 11. **Nott'm. F.** pay Torino £1.8m for **Andrea Silenzi** (first Italian Int. in English football). **25 Diego Maradona** signs for Boca Juniors, Arg. **26 Dalian Atkinson** (A. Villa to Fenerbahce, Turk.) £600,000; **QPR** pay club record £1.25m for **Ned Zelic** (Bor. Dortmund). **28** Scottish deals: **Rangers** sign Russian Int. striker **Oleg Salenko** from Valencia (£2.5m) and Serbian defender **Gordan Petric** from Dundee U. (£1.5m); **Celtic** pay club record £2.3m for German Int. **Andreas Thom** (Bayer Leverkusen). **31** Falkirk manager **Jim Jefferies** moves to **Hearts**, replacing Tommy McLean.

August 1995

1 Bolton pay club record £1.5m for **Gerry Taggart** (Barnsley). **2 Graham Turner**, ex-Wolves manager, appointed director of football at **Hereford**. **5 Mid'bro'** pay club record £5.25m for **Nick Barmby** (Tottenham). **8 Nott'm. F.** ordered to pay Sheff. W. **record tribunal fee** (£2.5m) for **Chris Bart-Williams**. **9 Newcastle** sign goalkeeper **Shaka Hislop** for £1.575m (Reading record). **10 Alex Ferguson** flies to Paris to talk suspended **Eric Cantona** into staying with Man. Utd. **Charlie Nicholas** leaves Celtic for Clyde. **12 Football League** (Endsleigh) season kicks off. **13 Charity Shield** (Wembley, Sunday): **Everton** 1, Blackburn 0. **16 E. Champ**: **Scotland** 1, Greece 0. **17 Bobby Gould** surprise choice as **Wales'** new manager (2½-year contract). **Marco van Basten** (30), AC Milan and Holland striker, forced to retire by ankle injury. **Man. C.** sign **Kit Symons** from Portsmouth (valued £1.8m in part-exchange deal) and goalkeeper **Eike Immel** (£400,000) from Vfb Stuttgart. **18** Premier League introduces **Chairmen's Charter** (also covering directors and chief execs) in search of highest standards of professionalism and integrity in club boardrooms. **19** First day of **Premiership** season: **Man. Utd.** (11-4 title favs) lose 3-1 at Aston V. **England** call off home match v war-torn Croatia (Sept. 6), replace fixture with Colombia. **25 Everton** complete £5m signing of **Andrei Kanchelskis** from Man. Utd. month after player agreed move. Draws for 1st. Round of European club comps. **26 Mid'bro'** open Riverside Stadium with 2-0 win v Chelsea. FA double **minimum admission** to Cup matches (from prelim. round) to £4. **28 Roy Keane** (Man. Utd.) sent off in 2-1 win at Blackburn. **31** Cartilage op. for Arsenal's **David Platt**; second hernia op. for **Duncan Ferguson** (Everton).

September 1995

3 E. Champ: Portugal 1, **N. Ireland** 1. **4** Season's first **manager casualties**: Mike Walsh leaves **Bury** (Stan Ternent takes over), **Lincoln** sack Sam Ellis (replaced by Steve Wicks). **6** Ints: **England** 0, Colombia 0. **E. Champ**: **Scotland** 1, Finland 0; **Wales** 1, Moldova 0; Austria 3, **Rep. of Ireland** 1. **Jason McAteer**, Bolton to Liverpool (£4.5m, taking **Roy Evans' spending** to £22m). **9 Liverpool** lose 1-0 away to ten-man Wimbledon (Vinnie Jones' sending off later revoked). **12 Tony Yeboah hat-trick** in Leeds 3-0 win away to Monaco (UEFA Cup 1/1). **13** Champions' Lge: **Blackburn** 0, Spartak Moscow 1; Steaua Bucharest 1, **Rangers** 0. **16** Champions **Blackburn** lose 0-3 at Liverpool, fourth defeat in first 6 Prem. games. **Julian Dicks** (West Ham) sent off at Arsenal (ninth dismissal of career). **20 Coca-Cola Cup** (2/1): **Man. Utd.** 0, York 3. **Dynamo Kiev** thrown out of European comps. for 2 years for attempting to bribe referee in Champions' League match. **22 Crystal P.** sign Bristol R. striker **Gareth Taylor** (£1.75m). **23 Robbie Fowler** scores 4 in Liverpool 5, Bolton 2. **26 Man. Utd.** go out of UEFA Cup (1st. Rd.) on away goals; agg. 2-2 v Rotor Volgograd (**Peter Schmeichel scores**). **27 Champions' Lge**: Rosenborg, Nor. 2, **Blackburn** 1.

October 1995

1 Man. Utd. 2, Liverpool 2 (**Eric Cantona**, returning from 8-month ban, scored United's penalty equaliser). **2 Andrew Plumb**, former Nott'm. F. ticket-office manager, jailed for 2 years on theft/false accounting charges 1991-93. **Swansea** manager **Frank Burrows** resigns. **3 Coca-Cola Cup** (2/2): York 1, Man. Utd. 3 (**York win 4-3 agg**); Charlton 3, Wimbledon 3 (**Charlton win 8-7 agg**). **4 Tottenham** sign **Ruel Fox** from Newcastle (£4.2m). **5 Lars Bohinen**, Nott'm. F. to **Blackburn** (£700,000). **8 Mid'bro'** sign Brazilian Int. **Juninho** from Sao Paulo (£4.75m). **9 Wigan** sack manager **Graham Barrow. 11** Ints: Norway 0, **England** 0; Sweden 2, **Scotland** 0. E. Champ: **Wales** 1, Germany 2; Liechtenstein 0, **N. Ireland** 4; **Rep. of Ireland** 2, Latvia 1. **Russia** (2-1 v Greece) first group qualifiers for Euro 96. **Duncan Ferguson** (Everton) loses appeal against 3-month sentence (May 25) for head-butting offence when playing for Rangers, April 1994; first British Int. jailed for onfield offence (will be released Nov. 24 after 44 days). Bruce Grobbelaar, John Fashanu, Hans Segers remanded on bail to Dec. 1 on match-fixing charges. **13 Chelsea** sign Romanian Int. **Dan Petrescu** from Sheff. W. (£2.3m); **Bolton** pay Partizan Belgrade £1m for **Sasa Curcic. David O'Leary**, 37 (Arsenal, Leeds and Rep. of Ireland) retires because of Achilles injury. **15 Lincoln** (bottom Div. 3) sack Steve Wicks after 41 days, make **John Beck** their third manager of season. **17** Boro's new Brazilian **Juninho** arrives on Teeside to carnival reception. **24 John Still** (**Peterborough** manager) resigns. **27** In Man. Utd. 2, Mid'bro' 0, **Roy Keane** sent off for third time in 6 months. **29 Torquay** sack player-manager **Don O'Riordan** day after 8-1 home defeat v Scunthorpe. **31** UEFA Cup (2/2): **Liverpool** 0, Brondby 1 (0-1 agg.); PSV Eindhoven 3, **Leeds** 0 (8-3 agg.); **Nott'm. F.** 0 Auxerre 0 (1-0 agg.). **John Deehan** appointed **Wigan** manager.

November 1995

1 Champions' Lge: **Blackburn** 0, Legia Warsaw 0; **Rangers** 0, Juventus 4. **2** CWC (2/2) Feyenoord 1, **Everton** 0 (agg. 1-0); **Celtic** 0, Paris SG 3 (agg. 0-4). **6 Vinnie Jones** (Wimbledon) sent off at Nott'm. F. (tenth dismissal of career). **8 Scottish FA** reject **Duncan Ferguson's** appeal against suspension (for head-butting offence while Rangers player). **11 FA Cup (1)**: **Shrewsbury** set club record with 11-2 win v Marine; **Oxford** 9, Dorchester 1; **Fulham** 7, Swansea 0. **13 Graham Taylor** resigns as manager of **Wolves** (19th in Div. 1). **15 England** 3, Switzerland 1; E. Champ: **Scotland** 5, San Marino 0; Albania 1, **Wales** 1; **N. Ireland** 5, Austria 3; Portugal 3, **Rep. of Ireland** 0 (Rep. of I. to meet Holland in play-off, Dec. 13, for final qual. place). **17 Leeds** pay club record £4.5m for **Tomas Brolin** (Parma). **18 Prem**: Blackburn 7, Nott'm. F. 0. **20** Manager **Liam Brady** leaves **Brighton**, replaced by coach **Jimmy Case**. **22** Champions' Lge: **Rangers** 1, Steaua Bucharest 1; Spartak Moscow 3, **Blackburn** 0 (Greame Le Saux and David Batty exchange blow on field). Blackburn fine Batty £3,000, Le Saux a reported £10,000. **26 Scottish Coca-Cola Cup Final**: Aberdeen 2, Dundee 0. **27 Bradford C.** sack manager **Lennie Lawrence** (assistant **Chris Kamara** in charge to end of season). **28 Football League** announce £125m **5-year live TV contract** with BSkyB from season 1996-97 (Divs 1, 2, 3, Coca-Cola Cup and play-off finals). **World Club Cup** (Tokyo): Ajax 0, Gremio (Brazil) 0; Ajax win 4-3 pens. **30 FA** agree **£130m 4-year TV** package with Sky (£55m), ITV (£60m) and BBC (£15m) w/effect season 1997-8 to 2001.

December 1995

1 Aberdeen sign Hull striker **Dean Windass** (£700,000). **Match-fixing charges** against Bruce Grobbelaar, John Fashanu and Hans Segers adjourned to Jan. 3. **4** FA Cup **3rd. Rd. draw** made by Terry Venables/Denis Law at Lancaster Gate; Chelsea v Newcastle is only all-Prem. tie. **Jim Platt** replaces David Hodgson as **Darlington** manager. **5 Bolton** sign **Scott Sellars** from Newcastle (£750,000). **Peter Beardsley** receives MBE from the Queen at Buckingham Palace. UEFA Cup (3/2): Lyon 0, **Nott'm. F.** 0, (0-1 agg.). **6** Champions' Lge: **Blackburn** 4 (Paul Warhurst sent off), Rosenborg 1; Bor. Dortmund 2, **Rangers** 2 (Paul Gascoigne sent off). **7** Manager **Mark McGhee** leaves Leicester for **Wolves. Bryan Hamilton's** contract as **N. Ireland** manager extended by 2½ years. **Duncan Ferguson** (Everton) has 12-match ban (7 remain) suspended by Edinburgh court – to be reviewed in New Year. **9 Sunderland** go top of Div. 1 with 6-0 win over **leaders Millwall** (who will be relegated at season's end). **12 England** 1, Portugal 1. **Paris: Draw for 1998 World Cup. Dave Bassett** resigns after 8 years as **Sheff. Utd.** manager; replaced by **Howard Kendall**. FA Cup **2nd. Rd. replay**: Walsall 8, Torquay 4 aet (h-t 1-1; 90 mins 3-3). **Peterborough** confirm caretaker **Mick Halsall** as manager. **13 E. Champ. play-off** (Anfield): Rep. of Ireland lose 2-0 to Holland in **Jack Charlton's last match** as manager. **Blackburn** sign **Chris Coleman** from Crystal P. for £2.8m (of which previous club Swansea receive £1m). **14** In Central London County Court, Recorder finds against England coach **Terry Venables** in case brought by Jeremy Fugler, suing Scribes' West (Venables' London club) for unpaid £20,000 bill; claim almost halved; Fugler ordered to pay half his costs. **15 Luxembourg**: European Court of Justice upholds **Bosman** ruling (Sept. 20), barring transfer fees for out-of-contract players and removing limit on clubs fielding foreign players. **National Lottery** makes £23m gift towards £51m reconstruction of **Hampden Park. England** stripped of 4th. UEFA Cup place in 1996-7 because Tottenham/Wimbledon fielded weak teams in last summer's Intertoto Cup. **16 Graeme Le Saux** (England & Blackburn) suffers dislocated right ankle and broken tibia v Mid'bro', ruled out until next season. **17** Birmingham ICC: **Draw for Euro 96 Finals**. Manager **Martin O'Neill** leaves Norwich; Luton manager **Terry Westley** resigns. **19 Switzerland** sack English coach **Roy Hodgson** (Inter Milan), appoint Portugal's Artur Jorge. **21 Jack Charlton resigns** after nearly ten years as Rep. of Ireland manager. FA Prem. Lge. Board decide **Stan Collymore** not entitled to £425,000 share of his £8.5m transfer from Nott'm. F. to Liverpool. **Bolton** sign Sheff. Utd. striker **Noel Blake** (£1m). Three Div. 1 clubs name **new managers**: Leicester (Martin O'Neill), Luton (Lennie Lawrence), Norwich (Gary Megson). **26 Vinnie Jones** (Wimbledon) sent off (11th time in career) in 2-1 win at Chelsea. **27 Man. Utd.** 2, Newcastle 0. **28 West Ham** sign Croatian Int. defender **Slaven Bilic** from Karlsruhe (£1.65m).

January 1996

1 Ian Rush awarded **MBE** in New Year Honours. Tottenham 4, Man. Utd. 1. **2 Bolton**, Bottom of Prem. Lge. by 8 points, sack joint-manager **Roy McFarland**, put **Colin Todd** in sole charge. **3** Bruce Grobbelaar, John Fashanu and Hans Segers remanded on match-rigging charges, to appear before Southampton magistrates on Mar. 18. **5 Millwall** sign Spartak Moscow pair Sergei Yuran and Vaseli Kulkov. **6 FA Cup 3rd. Rd**: Man. Utd. 2, Sunderland 2; in Liverpool's 7-0 win v Rochdale, **Ian Rush** scores his **42nd. FA Cup goal**, beating Denis Law's record this century. **10 Terry Venables** announces he will **quit as England coach** after Euro 96 to concentrate on series of legal battles due in court in autumn. **12 Man. Utd.**, found guilty by FA of **illegal approach** to 16-year-old Matthew Wicks, are unpunished apart from paying costs of 2 hearings. **15 Ossie Ardiles** appointed coach of Japanese J-League club S-Pulse Shimuzu (**Steve Perryman** his assistant). **16** Premier Lge. clubs refuse entry to 1996 **Intertoto Cup. FA Cup 3rd. Rd. replay: Chelsea** win 4-2 on pens at Newcastle after 2-2 draw. **19 Nigel Clough**, Liverpool to **Man. C.** (£1.2m); **Andy Sinton**, Sheff. W. to **Tottenham** (£1.5m). **Man. Utd.** sign Man. C. goalkeeper **Tony Coton** (£400,000). **20 Newcastle** win 2-1 v Bolton, go **12 points clear** of Liverpool and Man. Utd. – biggest Champ. lead since Man. Utd. 13 points ahead of Blackburn in Jan. 1993. **23 Carlisle** appoint **Mervyn Day** manager from coach. **24 FA ban** Chelsea striker **Mark Hughes** for 5 matches for 33 points and sending-off at Everton. Italy 3, **Wales** 0. **26 Newcastle** agree club record £6.7m signing of Colombian Int. **Faustino Asprilla** from Parma (see Feb. 8). On appeal, UEFA fine Tottenham £90,000, Wimbledon £60,000 and quash 1-year Euro ban for fielding weak teams in Intertoto Cup last summer. **27** Snow and ice cause **postponement of 55 matches** in England/Scotland (incl. all 11 in Conference); only 3 FA Cup 4th. Round ties played. **29 Man. Utd.** fined £20,000 by FA for poaching schoolboy David Brown (17) from Oldham.

February 1996

1 Everton and **Liverpool** receive **Freedom of City of Liverpool**. Judgment in Edinburgh quashes remaining 7 games of 12-match ban imposed by Scottish FA on **Duncan Ferguson** (Everton, prev. Rangers) for head-butting opponent, April 1994. **FA suspend** Leyton Orient defender **Roger Stanislaus** for year – first British-based player barred for using banned substance to enhance playing performance (tested positive for cocaine). Orient sack Stanislaus. **2 FA inquiry** into Birmingham v Millwall (Nov. 4) orders Birmingham to play 1 home game behind closed doors if further crowd trouble before Dec. 31, 1996. **5 Rep. of Ireland** appoint Millwall's **Mick McCarthy** (37) their new manager. **8 Crystal P.** (16th. in Div. 1) appoint **Dave Bassett** manager. **Millwall** appoint **Jimmy Nicholl** from Raith. After 2-week delay, **Newcastle** (Champ. leaders by 9 points) complete £6.7m signing of **Faustino Asprilla** from Parma. **Mid'bro'** sign another Brazilian Int., defender **Branco** (free agent) from Internacional, Brazil. **12** Manager **Jimmy Mullen** leaves **Burnley** after 5 seasons. **13 FA fine Vinnie Jones** (Wimbledon) £2,000 for newspaper attack on Ruud Gullit (Chelsea) and other foreign players. **FA warn Arsenal manager Bruce Rioch** after touchline confrontation with Newcastle coach Terry McDermott (Coca-Cola Cup q-final, Jan. 10). **14** Death of **Liverpool legend Bob Paisley** (77), most successful manager in English football. Manager **Kevin Cullis** leaves **Swansea** after 7 days in job (2 defeats). **FA Cup 4th. Rd. replay shocks**: **Port Vale** 2, Everton 1; **Grimsby** 3, West Ham 0. **17 Sean Connolly**, chief exec. FA of Ireland, resigns. **18 FA Cup 5**: Man. Utd. 2, Man. C. 1. **19 FA Cup 5**: Nott'm. F. 0, Tottenham 0 (aband. 14 mins, snow). Two months after Bosman ruling, UEFA confirm **restrictions scrapped on foreign players** in club comps. **20 Coventry** sign **Eoin Jess** (Aberdeen, £2m) and **Liam Daish** (Birmingham, £1.75m). Neil Lennon, Crewe to Leicester (£750,000). **Watford** sack manager **Glenn Roeder**. **Fulham** make coach **Micky Adams** player-manager (Ian Branfoot to gen. manager). **22 Graham Taylor** returns to **Watford** as gen. manager (Luther Blissett coach). **Swansea** sign **Jan Molby** (free) from Liverpool as **player-manager**, their 5th. manager of season. **23 Julian Joachim**, Leicester to Aston V. (£1.5m). **25 Man. Utd.** win 6-0 at Bolton, cut Newcastle's lead to 4 points. **29 Newcastle** sign **David Batty** from Blackburn – £4m fee takes Kevin Keegan's spending to £45m.

March 1996

4 Man. Utd. complete season's double v Newcastle, ending their 100% home record (Cantona, 1-0), and close to within point of leaders. **5 UEFA Cup q-f/1**: Bayern Munich 2, **Nott'm. F.** 1. **7** Long-awaited work permits granted to **Ilie Dumitrescu** (Tottenham to West Ham, £1.5m, Jan. 18) and **Marc Hottiger** (Newcastle to Everton, £750,000, Jan. 19). **7** In High Court, **England coach Terry Venables** awarded nearly £50,000 damages against former business partner Paul Kirby, but allowed only half of estimated £100,000 costs. **Adrian Heath** is new **Burnley** manager. **10 FIFA Int. Board** decide **linesmen** to be known as "**referee's assistants**" w/effect July 1. **11 Swindon** sack **John Trollope** after 37 years' service as player, manager, youth coach. **Scunthorpe** replace Dave Moore with their former manager **Mick Buxton**. **14 Derby** sign **Ashley Ward** from Norwich (£1m). **17 Anglo-It. Cup Final** (Wembley): Port Vale 2, Genoa 5. **18 Newcastle** (3-0 v West Ham) regain Champ. lead day after Man. Utd. went top on goal diff. **19 UEFA Cup q-f/2**: **Nott'm. F.** 1, Bayern Munich 5 (agg. 2-7). **21 Garry Flitcroft**, Man. C. to **Blackburn** (£3.2m). **24 Coca-Cola Cup Final** (Wembley): Aston V. 3, Leeds 0. **Man. Utd.** (1-0 v Tottenham) go 4 points clear of Newcastle (beaten 2-0 at Arsenal prev. day). **Les Ferdinand** (Newcastle) voted **PFA Player of Year**. **27 England** 1, Bulgaria 0; **Scotland** 1, Australia 0; **N. Ireland** 0, Norway 2; **Rep. of Ireland** 0, Russia 2. **28** Main signings on **transfer deadline day**; Gary Croft, Grimsby to Blackburn (£1m), Mikhail Kavelashvili, Spartak Vladikavkaz (Russia) to Man. C. (£1.4m). **31 FA Cup s-finals**: Man. Utd. 2, Chelsea 1; Liverpool 3, Aston V. 0.

April 1996

3 Liverpool 4, Newcastle 3 in **Premiership epic**. **FA fine Mark Hughes** (Chelsea) £1,000, plus 2-match ban, for reaching 45 discip. points. **5 USA** launches ten-club **Major League Soccer**. **6 Scottish Cup s-final**: Hearts 2, Aberdeen 1. Steve Harkness (Liverpool) suffers double fracture of leg in 1-0 defeat at Coventry. **7 Scottish Cup s-final**: Rangers 2, Celtic 1. **8** (Easter Mon.) **Graham Fenton** scores twice in last 5 mins as Blackburn beat Newcastle 2-1; **Man. Utd.** (1-0 v Coventry) 6 points clear. Coventry defender **David Busst** suffers compound fracture of leg. **9 Leslie Silver** (71) retires after 14 years as **Leeds chairman**. **12 Tranmere** promote **John Aldridge** to player-manager, ending 9-year reign of John King. **Huddersfield** sack striker **Craig Whitington** after second positive drug test in less than year. **13 Man. Utd.**, beaten 3-1 at Southampton, **change colours** at half-time, from second-choice grey to blue. **14 Auto Windscreen Shield Final** (Wembley): Rotherham 2, Shrewsbury 1. **17** Groin op. for **Alan Shearer** after scoring 2 in Blackburn's 3-2 win v Wimbledon. A. Villa right-back **Gary Charles** fractures ankle v West Ham. **20 Sunderland** (not playing) **promoted** to Premier League. **Eric Cantona** voted Football Writers' **Footballer of Year**. **23 Swindon** (3-1 at Chesterfield) win Div. 2. **Brighton** relegated to Div. 3 after 2-1 defeat at Notts Co. **24 England** 0, Croatia 0; Denmark 2, **Scotland** 0; Switzerland 2, **Wales** 0; **N. Ireland** 1, Sweden 2; Czech Rep. 2, **Rep. of Ireland** 0. **25** Manager **Bryan Robson** signs 2-year extension of contract with **Mid'bro'** (to 1999); **West Ham** extend manager **Harry Redknapp's** contract to **May 2001**. **27 QPR relegated** to Div. 1 despite 3-0 win v West Ham; **Bolton** (0-1 v So'ton) relegated year after promotion; Brighton v York **abandoned** 16 mins (0-0), pitch invasion; **Sunderland** win Div. 1, **Luton** relegated; **Preston** (2-0 at Hartlepool) are Div. 3 Champions. **28 Man. Utd.** (5-0 v Nott'm. F.) are 6 points, 7 goals clear of Newcastle. **Derby** (2-1 v Crystal P.) promoted to Premier Lge. **Rangers** beat Aberdeen 3-1, clinch **8th. successive Scottish League title** with hat-trick by **Paul Gascoigne** on day he is voted **Scottish PFA Player of Year**. **29** After Newcastle win 1-0 at Leeds, **Kevin Keegan** attacks Man. Utd. manager Alex Ferguson on Sky TV (over Ferguson's previous comments on Leeds' commitment). **30** Newcastle striker **Faustino Asprilla** fined £10,000 by FA and banned 1 match (start of next season) on misconduct charge for elbowing Keith Curle (Man. C.) at Maine Road., Feb. 24. Manager **Eddie May** resigns at **Torquay** (bottom Div. 3).

May 1996

1 UEFA Cup Final (1): Bayern Munich 2, Bordeaux 0. **2** FA name Chelsea manager **Glenn Hoddle** (38) next **England coach**. He succeeds Terry Venables after Euro 96; 4-year contract from June 1. Galatasaray (Turkey) **sack coach Graeme Souness** after 1 year. **Robert Chase quits Norwich** after ten years as chairman. Crystal P. fan **Matthew Simmons** jailed for contempt for attacking prosecuting solicitor in court after Croydon Magistrates found him guilty of provoking Eric Cantona's attack on him (Jan. 1995), fined him £500 plus £200 costs and banned him from British grounds for year. **Peter Swales**, former Man. C. chairman, dies after heart attack. **4 Oxford** clinch promotion to Div. 1; **Bury** join Preston and Gillingham in Div. 2. Last-match **crowd trouble** at Hull v Bradford C. and Ipswich v Millwall. **5** (Sun) **Man. Utd.** (3-0 at Mid'bro') take third Premier League title in 4 seasons; **Man. C.** (2-2 v Liverpool) relegated. **Millwall**, Div. 1 leaders in Dec., relegated with Watford, Luton. **7 Birmingham** sack manager **Barry Fry**. **Trevor Phillips** quits as FA commercial director. **8 Cup-Winners' Cup Final** (Brussels): Paris SG 1, Rapid Vienna 0. **9 York** win 3-1 at Brighton in season's final League game (re-staged after abandonment, April 27); York stay in Div. 2, send **Carlisle** down. **10 Chelsea** appoint Glenn Hoddle's successor – promote **Ruud Gullit** to player-coach. **Birmingham** appoint **Trevor Francis** manager. **11 Man. Utd.** (1-0 v Liverpool) achieve **record ninth FA Cup triumph** and become **first English club to complete Double twice**. **13 Bristol R.** appoint **Ian Holloway** (ex-QPR) player-manager; John Ward out. **14 Mid'bro'** sign third Brazilian, **Emerson** from FC Porto (£4m). **15** Next England coach Glenn Hoddle appoints Scot **John Gorman** his assistant. Manager **Mick Docherty** leaves **Rochdale**. **UEFA Cup Final (2)**: Bordeaux 1, Bayern Munich 3 (1-5 agg.); **Jurgen Klinsmann** scores 15th. goal for Bayern in this UEFA Cup, a new individual record in European comps. **16 Scottish play-off** (2nd. leg): **Dundee Utd.** 2, Partick 1 aet (agg. 3-2); Dundee Utd. promoted to Premier Div., **Partick** relegated to Div. 1. **Alex Ferguson** signs new 4-year contract with Man.

Utd. **17 Bobby Robson** leaves FC Porto to replace Johan Cruyff as **Barcelona** coach. **Liverpool win FA Youth Cup** for first time (2-1 v Crystal P., 4-1 agg.). **18 England** 3, Hungary 0 (**Mark Wright** injures knee, out of Euro 96). **Rochdale** appoint **Graham Barrow** manager. **19 Scottish Cup Final: Rangers** beat Hearts 5-1 to complete Double for **14th. time. 20 Ian Rush** joins **Leeds** (2-year contract) on free transfer from Liverpool. **John Collins**, out of contract with Celtic, signs for **Monaco. 21 Watford** promote **Kenny Jackett** from youth coach to first-team manager (Graham Taylor gen. manager). **Graeme Souness** wins libel damages (est. £100,000) from *Mail on Sunday* over allegations about his transfer activities when manager of Liverpool. Relegated **Falkirk** appoint **Eamonn Bannon** manager. **22 European Cup Final** (Rome): **Juventus** beat Ajax 4-2 on pens after 1-1. Man. Utd. captain **Steve Bruce** (35) joins Birmingham on free transfer. Blackpool chairman **Owen Oyston** jailed for 6 years on rape and indecent assault charges. **23** China 0, **England** 3 (Beijing). **24** Two days after lifting European Cup for Juventus, **Gianluca Vialli** agrees to join Chelsea – first signing by new player-coach Ruud Gullit. **Everton** to sign **Gary Speed** from Leeds (£3.5m). **25 Div. 3 Play-off Final** (Wembley): **Plymouth** 1, Darlington 0; Plymouth fan dies after pre-match fight outside stadium. **26** Hong Kong Golden Select 0, **England** 1. **Div. 2 Play-off Final** (Wembley): **Bradford C.** 2, Notts Co. 0. USA 2, **Scotland** 1 (Connecticut). **27 Div. 1 Play-off Final** (Wembley): **Leicester** 2, Crystal P. 1 (aet). **28** Terry Venables names **England's Euro 96** squad. **29** Ints: **N. Ireland** 1, Germany 1; **Rep. of Ireland** 0, Portugal 1. **Blackpool sack** manager **Sam Allardyce. Cathay Pacific** airline complain to FA about damage done inside jet bringing England tour party home from Hong Kong; FA to hold inquiry. **30 Nationwide Building Society** agree 3-year, £5.25m sponsorship with **Football League**. Colombia 1, **Scotland** 0 (Miami). **31 FIFA** announce that **Japan** and **S. Korea** will **co-host World Cup** in 2002. **Barry Fry** (sacked by Birmingham) becomes owner-manager of Peterborough.

June 1996

2 World Cup: San Marino 0, **Wales** 5. **Int: Rep. of Ireland** 2, Croatia 2. **3 Fourteen police** share £1.2m. damages for stress suffered at **Hillsborough Disaster**, 1989. **Scotland** extend manager **Craig Brown**'s contract to World Cup 98. **4 Terry Venables** defends England players against "grossly exaggerated" claims of misconduct on flight home from Hong Kong. **Int**: Holland 3, **Rep. of Ireland** 1. Wales captain **Barry Horne** leaves Everton for **Birmingham** (£250,000). **5 Torquay** appoint Youth coach **Kevin Hodges** player-coach. **6 Premier League** agree new 4-year, **£670m. TV deal** with Sky (plus BBC £73m) from season 1997-98. **Sunderland** sign **Alex Rae** from Millwall (£750,000). **8 Euro 96 kicks off: England** 1, Switzerland 1. **US Cup** (Boston): USA 2, **Rep. of Ireland** 1. **10 Euro 96**: Holland 0, **Scotland** 0. **12 US Cup** (New Jersey): Mexico 2, **Rep. of Ireland** 2. **14 Southampton** sack manager **Dave Merrington. 15 Euro 96: England 2**, Scotland 0. **Neville Southall**, Everton & Wales goalkeeper, **awarded MBE** in Queen's Birthday Honours. **US Cup** (New Jersey): **Rep. of Ireland** 3, Bolivia 0 – Rep's **first win**, after 8 games, for new manager **Mick McCarthy. 18 Euro 96: England** 4, Holland 1; **Scotland** 1, Switzerland 0. **21 Mike Walker** returns to **Norwich** as manager after 2½ years, replacing Gary Megson. **Everton** complete £3.5m. signing of **Gary Speed** from Leeds. **Mick Wadsworth** appointed **Scarborough** manager. **22 Euro 96 Qf: England** 0, Spain 0 (England win 4-2 on pens.). **24** New **Chelsea manager Ruud Gullit** pays club record fee (£2.5m.) for French Int. defender **Franck Lebouef** from Strasbourg. **26 Euro 96 Sf: England** 1, Germany 1 (Germany win 6-5 on pens.). Gangs go on late-night rampage in Trafalgar Square; other outbursts of violence across country, including Birmingham, Bradford, Swindon, Mansfield, Nottingham, Luton, Bedford, Dunstable. **Nott'm. Forest** sign striker **Dean Saunders** from Galatasaray (£1.5m.). **27 Wembley** reveal plans for **£160m. rebuilding** of stadium. **29** England left-back **Stuart Pearce** retires from Int. football. **30 Euro 96 Final**: Germany beat Czech Rep. 2-1 in overtime.

(For full details of Euro 96, see European Championship section).

FINAL WHISTLE – OBITUARIES 1995-96

July

DENIS ALLEN, 56, from a strong footballing family, was father of Martin, uncle to Clive, Paul and Bradley, and brother of Les, who played in Tottenham's Double-winning team of 1961. Played more than 400 first-team matches for Reading, Charlton and Bournemouth (1961-70).

MIKE NAYLOR, 59, managing director of Endsleigh Insurance (Football League sponsors), killed when his Bentley crashed into a tree near Plaisance, South-West France.

August

JOHNNY CAREY, 76, was a Man. United legend in the Matt Busby era, captaining them to F.A. Cup success against Blackpool in 1948 and a member of their Championship-winning team of 1952. Outstanding at right-back, he played in ten out of 11 positions (including goal) and was capped for Rep. of Ireland (29 times) and N. Ireland (7), also captained Rest of World against Great Britain at Hampden Park, 1947. Dublin-born, he joined United from Irish club St. James's Gate for £200 in 1936. Made 306 League apps. for them (1937-52). Footballer of Year 1949. Went into management with Blackburn in 1953 and subsequently with Everton (1958-61), Leyton Orient (1961-63), Nott'm. Forest (1963-68) and back to Blackburn (1970-71).

DICK FOSS, 82, launched the careers of a galaxy of stars as Chelsea's youth-team manager 1952-66. They included Jimmy Greaves, Peter Bonetti, Bobby Smith, Terry Venables, John Hollins, Ken Shellito and Bobby Tambling. Joined Chelsea from amateurs Southall in 1936 and, at inside-forward and wing-half, played more than 200 times for the club, including war-time League South Cup Finals at Wembley in 1944 and 1945.

September

DAVE BOWEN, 67, who died after a short illness, captained Wales when they reached the 1958 World Cup quarter-finals in Sweden (losing to Pele's goal for Brazil). He also managed Wales part-time from 1964-74. As player, won 19 caps, all from 1955-59 while with Arsenal, having joined them from Northampton Town in 1950. Returned to Northampton as player-manager in 1959 and took them from Fourth to First Division in 1960s. A "miracle worker" for club and country, he also served Town as secretary, director and, until he died, president.

DIRCEU, 43, Brazilian Int. midfielder who played in World Cups of 1974 and 1978 and was in squad for 1982 Finals. Killed in car crash in Rio.

ALBERT JOHANNESON, 55, was the first black player to appear in the F.A. Cup Final, in Leeds side beaten by Liverpool in 1965. The left-winger joined Leeds from a S. African black township and scored 67 goals in 200 matches for them (1960-69) before playing out career with York. Died alone at his tower-block home in Leeds.

MICHAEL MILLETT, England U-18 and Wigan Athletic defender, died in car crash the day before his 18th birthday. Former England Schoolboy captain.

ERIK NILSSON, 79, played 57 times for Sweden (1938-52) and member of their team that won 1948 Olympic tournament in London.

GUNNAR NORDAHL, 73, who died in Sardinia, was one of Sweden's greatest players – scored 43 goals in 34 Ints. Moved from IFK Norrkoping to AC Milan in 1949 and scored 210 goals in 257 matches for the Italian club. Was one of 5 brothers, 4 of them capped by Sweden.

FRED SCOTT, 78, was a right-winger with York pre-war and war-time guest with Charlton. Fetched York's record fee of £4,500 when moving to Nott'm. Forest in Sept. 1946, and helped them win Div. 3 South in 1951 and clinch promotion to First Division in his last game in 1957. In 11 seasons with Forest made 322 League and Cup apps. and scored 46 goals.

HAROLD SHEPHERDSON, 76, Middlesbrough's trainer from 1950 and England's for 171 Ints. from 1957-74 (including 1966 World Cup triumph) under managers Walter Winterbottom and Alf Ramsey. Served Boro' for 50 years in various capacities, starting as player in 1934.

October

STAN ALDOUS, 72, was one of the best centre half-backs in Leyton Orient's history. Although not making his debut until he was 27 (signed from Gravesend & Northfleet in 1950), he played 327 League and Cup games over 8 seasons, and captained Orient to the Third Div. South championship in 1956.

November

ERIC BRYANT, 74, wrote a page in F.A. Cup history when his extra-time goal for Southern League Yeovil beat Sunderland 2-1 on the famous Huish slope in the 4th Round on Jan. 29, 1949. The centre-forward joined Yeovil from Mansfield and left them in Oct. 1949 to resume his League career briefly with Plymouth and later Leyton Orient.

LESTER FINCH, 86, one of the outstanding amateurs of his time, was a left-winger who played for Barnet for 20 years until 1948, earning an Amateur Cup-winner's medal in 1946. Won 16 amateur caps for England (1933-39) and played for Great Britain in 1936 Olympics. Among pro' clubs for whom he guested in wartime were Tottenham, Chelsea, Wolves and Nott'm. Forest, and he played for the full England side in a wartime Int. against Wales in 1941.

BILL MASON, 87, began career with Fulham in 1928 and was QPR's regular goalkeeper in 5 seasons up to the war with 160 League and Cup apps. (1934-39).

PAT McKENNA, 75, left-back in Aberdeen side that won the first Scottish League Cup in 1946 and the Scottish Cup for the first time in 1947. Later played for Plymouth, Arbroath, Derry City and finally captained Fraserburgh in the Highland League.

ALAN NICHOLLS, 22, former England U-21 goalkeeper, was killed (with driver) when the motor-cycle, on which he was a passenger, crashed on the A1 near Peterborough. Plymouth Argyle's regular 'keeper in seasons 1993-4-5. Was returning home after playing for Conference club Stalybridge Celtic when he died.

ALEC WHITE, 79, left-back whose Chelsea career (1937-48) was disrupted by the war, in which he played twice for Scotland in Army Ints. v England. Left Chelsea for Swindon, later Southport, before returning home to Scotland.

December

EDDIE CLAMP, 61, a sharp-tackling wing-half, served Wolves for the first nine of his 13 years in League football (1952-65). Helped Stan Cullis's team win League Championships in 1958 and 1959, winning 4 England caps in 1958 (3 of them in the World Cup in Sweden, in all-Wolves half-back line with Billy Wright and Bill Slater). Moved to Arsenal (£34,500) in Sept. 1961, then to Stoke, where he played in the veterans' team that won promotion as Div. 2 Champions in 1963. Ended League career at Peterborough. On retirement ran building and decorating business at Wednesfield, Staffs.

HARRY CRIPPS, 54, who as a fearsome full-back was the embodiment of Millwall over 13 seasons (447 apps., 1961-73), died of heart attack. A fierce shot brought him 40 goals. Was member of Millwall side unbeaten at The Den for 59 League games (1964-67). Began with West Ham and on leaving Millwall made Charlton his third London club. Later became assistant-manager there, also at Southend (under Bobby Moore) and subsequently coached at Winchester School.

BASIL EASTERBROOK, 75, was for 30 years football and cricket correspondent of the *Kemsley* group and then *Thomson Regional Newspapers*. Began with his native *Torquay Times*, then worked for the *Sheffield Star*. Spent his retirement from 1983 watching his beloved Torquay United.

WALTER GALBRAITH, 77, pre-war left-back with Clyde, served a long managerial career in lower regions of the Football League: New Brighton, Grimsby, Accrington Stanley, Bradford Park Avenue and Tranmere before 3 years with Hibernian (1961-64). Returned to Bradford and finally managed Stockport (1969-70).

GEORGE RUMBOLD, 84, pre-war full-back and free-kick specialist with Crystal Palace and Clapton Orient, post-war with Ipswich (1946-50).

REG STOCKILL, 82, who played in Arsenal's Championship team of 1932-33, died in hospital at York. Was the only non-Int. in that Arsenal side. Had scored York's first Football League goal in 1929, and Arsenal signed him from non-League Scarborough for £500 in 1931 (plus £300 after 3 first-team apps.).

January 1996

BOBBY COWELL, 73, a right-back who specialised in goal-line clearances, won 3 FA Cup-winner's medals with Newcastle in 1951-52-55. Joined them from Blackhall Colliery in 1943 (wartime) and played 289 League games, helping them win promotion to the First Division in 1948.

JOHNNY GARVIE, 68, scored 78 goals in 184 League apps. for Lincoln City (1950-56) and starred in side that won Div. 3 North in 1951-52. Began with Hibernian and spent 1 season with Preston before joining Lincoln. Completed League career with Carlisle (1956-57).

JACK HATHER, 70, left-winger known as the "Flying Englishman" with Aberdeen, for whom he scored 104 goals in 351 senior apps. over 12 seasons (1948-60). Helped Dons win Scottish Championship in 1955 and played in 3 Scottish Cup Finals (1953-54-59).

BOBBY LANGTON, 77, left-winger who spent career with 3 Lancashire First Div. clubs and capped 11 times by England (1947-51). Made debut pre-war with Blackburn in 1937, joined Preston in 1948 and Bolton the following year. Played in 1953 Cup Final v Blackpool, and returned to Blackburn for 3 seasons before retiring in 1956.

NORRIE McCATHIE, 34, Dunfermline captain and defensive rock, died accidentally, with hairdresser Amanda Burns, from carbon monoxide poisoning at his cottage near the Fife town. Joined Dunfermline from Cowdenbeath in 1981 and made 563 apps. for the club. Captained them when promoted to Premier Div. in 1987 and 1989 and to the 1992 League Cup Final. Was club Player of Year in 1995.

HARRY POTTS, 75, was Burnley's most successful manager, taking them to League Championship success in 1959-60, the F.A. Cup Final in 1962 and developing a prodigious youth scheme that, at the time, enabled the club to keep up with their powerful neighbours. As inside-forward played 13 years of war-interrupted career with Burnley (promotion to Div. 1 and Cup Final in 1947). Moved to Everton (£20,000) in 1950, then coached Wolves before starting in management with Shrewsbury. Managed Burnley 1958-70, then gen. manager to 1972, Blackpool manager (1972-76) and second spell in charge of Burnley from 1977-79.

GEORGE THOMSON, 86, Scottish president of Chelsea FC.

DAI WARD, 61, inside-forward, scored 150 goals in 316 League apps. in 4-club career from 1954-64: Bristol R., Cardiff, Watford and Brentford. Capped twice by Wales (v England in 1959, 1962).

February

CORNELIUS (NEIL) FRANKLIN, 74, won his 27 caps at centre-half in England's first 27 post-war Ints. Made headlines when, just before the 1950 World Cup Finals, he left Stoke City (maximum wage £12 a week) with clubmate George Mountfield to play for Bogota in Colombia. Was lured by offer of £5,000 a week, but the big money never materialised and within 2 months Franklin and his family flew home. The Bogota episode ended his Int. career. Stoke, whom he joined in 1939, sold him to Hull for £22,500 in Feb. 1951, and after 5 years there he played for Crewe and Stockport, then with non-League Macclesfield and Wellington. Coached Apoel, Cyprus for year, and managed Colchester (1963-68). Then gave up football to manage a pub at Oswaldtwistle, Lancs.

PETER HOWARD, 68, was, as a *Daily Mail* photographer, a hero of the Man. United air crash in Munich in Feb. 1958. Risked his life to rescue survivors in the snow.

ERNEST JACKSON, 81, served Sheffield United for 32 years as wing-half, trainer and, in 1955, temporary manager. Locally-born, he made 229 League apps. Either side of the war (1933-48), earned an FA Cup runners-up medal v Arsenal in 1936 and helped United win promotion to Div. 1 in 1939.

BOB PAISLEY, 77, who died in a Liverpool nursing home on Feb. 14, was the most successful manager in English football, taking 13 major prizes – 6 League Championships, 3 European Cups, 3 League Cups and 1 UEFA Cup, to Anfield in his 9 years in charge (1974-83). Only the F.A. Cup was missing.

He was reluctant to succeed Bill Shankly and tried to talk him into carrying on, but said he would do his best – and became another Liverpool legend. As the trophies piled up, he would remind the players at the start of every new season: "First is first, second is nowhere."

Among the stars he signed were Kenny Dalglish, Alan Hansen and Graeme Souness. What the players thought of him was reflected when they sent him up Wembley's 39 steps to receive the League Cup in 1983. Manager of the Year a record 6 times, he was awarded the OBE in 1977.

He was one of the last of the "old school" managers. On retirement, 44 years after joining Liverpool as a player, he became a director until ill health ended a 53-year association in 1992.

Born at Hetton-le-Hole, Co. Durham, he won an Amateur Cup winner's medal with Bishop Auckland in 1939 just before signing for Liverpool. He returned from Army service with the Royal Artillery to play 252 League matches as a sturdy wing-half, and earned a Championship medal in 1947.

He moved into the famous Boot Room in 1954, serving in turn as physio, second and first-team trainer, assistant-manager and as Shankly's successor in July 1974.

His own achievements were played down, and when he retired to cardigan and slippers in 1983 he said: "I've never wanted a lot of fuss, like to keep things low key and down to earth. I don't talk a lot of tactics. We don't have coaching – we just have damned good players. I've never made much money out of football, but no-one ever got more enjoyment from the game than I did."

HELMUT SCHOEN, 80, was the "man in the cap" under whom West Germany won the European Championship in 1972 and the World Cup in 1974 after being World Cup runners-up to England in 1966. His complete Int. record (1964-78) read: P139, W87, D31, L21. Among the great players produced by Schoen's Germany were Franz Beckenbauer, Gerd Muller and goalkeeper Sepp Maier. As player himself (inside-left) won 16 caps from 1937. Died in Wiesbaden, from Alzheimer's Disease.

ALAN SEALEY, 53, hero of West Ham's Cup-Winners' Cup Final triumph in 1965 with 2 goals in Final v TSV Munich at Wembley, died from a heart attack. Made 108 first-team apps. for the club and after leaving Upton Park in 1967 played briefly for Plymouth, then Romford in old Southern League. A cousin of goalkeeper Les Sealey, he returned to West Ham as a scout.

March

ALAN BROWN, 81, Burnley centre-half and captain of their 1947 promotion and Cup Final team. Began with Huddersfield in 1933. Left Burnley for Notts County in 1948, returning to Turf Moor as manager (1954-57) and launching highly successful youth policy. Subsequently managed Sunderland (1957-64), Sheff. Wed. (1964-68, including 1966 F.A. Cup Final) and Sunderland again (1968-72). After coaching in Norway, retired to live in North Devon and had heart by-pass operation at age of 70.

CISSIE CHARLTON, 84, mother of Sir Bobby and Jack. She came from a famous football family – 4 Milburn brothers played for Leeds, and Newcastle's Jackie Milburn was a cousin.

ERIC WHITE, 70, Brentford's long-serving Press officer and deputy president, died from a heart attack. For over 40 years he gave his services voluntarily as programme editor, and co-wrote the club history *100 Years of Brentford* in 1989. He was Brentford through and through, and his devoted contribution to the club and unfailing helpfulness to the media could not be overstated.

May

ERIC HOUGHTON, 85, pre-war Aston Villa and England left-winger (7 caps), was one of the hardest dead-ball kickers with many of his 200+ goals for Villa (1928-46) blasted from free-kicks or penalties. He helped the club win the Second Div. in 1938 (2 years after relegation). Moved to Notts County in 1946 as player, then manager (Div. 3 South champions, 1950). Returned to Villa as manager in Sept. 1953, leading them to F.A. Cup Final victory v Man. United in 1957, but was

sacked in Nov. 1958. One of Villa's most dedicated servants returned to join the board (1972-79) and became senior vice-president in 1983.
ADEMIR MENEZES, 74, played in Brazil team beaten by Uruguay in 1950 World Cup Final, died in Rio. Scored 35 goals in 41 Ints.
PETER SWALES, 62, chairman of Man. City for 21 years until ousted in take-over in Feb. 1994 and replaced by Francis Lee, died after heart attack. In his time was chairman of F.A. Int. Committee.

June
CLIFF HOLTON, 67, Arsenal centre-forward in the 1952 FA Cup Final against Newcastle, died while on holiday in Spain. One of the hardest shots in football, he scored 83 goals in 198 apps. for Arsenal, having joined them as a full-back from Oxford City. After leaving Highbury, he played for Watford, Northampton, Crystal Palace, Charlton and Leyton Orient. In 1959-60 he set the Watford record of 48 goals in a season, and in his 6-club senior career he scored a total of 293 goals in 570 League apps.
BOBBY KEETCH, 54, Fulham's cavalier centre-half in the era of Johnny Haynes, Jimmy Hill and Bobby Robson, died suddenly from a stroke. He played 102 League games for the club (1962-66), then spent two seasons with QPR. The working-class Londoner with man-about-town style – he once declined the team bus to travel to a Fulham away match in a chauffeur-driven Rolls Royce – became a successful businessman/entrepreneur. He was into art collecting, and the moving figure behind the opening of the "Football Football" theme restaurant in the West End. Terry Venables said: "He was the greatest friend any man could have. Through the times I've had when it was really bad, he would ring me every day."
ALAN WEEKS, 72, BBC TV sports commentator from 1951-96, died after being ill for only a short time. Although best known for his ice-skating commentaries, he reported football for 22 of his 45 years at the microphone, including 4 World Cups.

(Sources: National and provincial newspapers, Association of Football Statisticians and FIFA News)

MILESTONES OF SOCCER

1848 First code of rules compiled at Cambridge Univ.
1855 Sheffield F.C., world's oldest football club, formed
1862 Notts County (oldest League club) formed
1863 Football Association founded – their first rules of game agreed
1871 F.A. Cup introduced
1872 First official International: Scotland 0, England 0. Corner-kick introduced
1873 Scottish F.A. formed; Scottish Cup introduced
1874 Shinguards introduced. Oxford v Cambridge, first match
1875 Crossbar introduced (replacing tape)
1876 F.A. of Wales formed
1877 Welsh Cup introduced
1878 Referee's whistle first used
1880 Irish F.A. founded; Irish Cup introduced
1883 Two-handed throw-in introduced
1885 Record first-class score (Arbroath 36, Bon Accord 0 – Scottish Cup). Professionalism legalised
1886 International Board formed
1887 Record F.A. Cup score (Preston N.E. 26, Hyde 0)
1888 Football League founded by Wm. McGregor. First matches on Sept. 8
1889 Preston win Cup and League (first club to complete Double)
1890 Scottish League and Irish League formed
1891 Goal-nets introduced. Penalty-kick introduced
1892 Inter-League games began. Football League Second Division formed

1893 F.A. Amateur Cup launched
1894 Southern League formed
1895 F.A. Cup stolen from Birmingham shop window – never recovered
1897 First Players' Union formed. Aston Villa win Cup and League
1898 Promotion and relegation introduced
1901 Maximum wage rule in force. Tottenham Hotspur first professional club to take F.A. Cup South. First 100,000 attendance (110,802) at F.A. Cup Final
1902 Ibrox Park disaster (25 killed). Welsh League formed
1904 F.I.F.A. founded (7 member countries)
1905 First £1,000 transfer (Alf Common, Sunderland to Middlesbrough)
1907 Players' Union revived
1908 Transfer fee limit (£350) fixed in January and withdrawn in April.
1911 New F.A. Cup trophy – in use to 1991. Transfer deadline introduced
1914 King George V first reigning monarch to attend F.A. Cup Final
1916 Entertainment Tax introduced
1919 League extended to 44 clubs
1920 Third Division (South) formed
1921 Third Division (North) formed
1922 Scottish League (Div. II) introduced
1923 Beginning of football pools. First Wembley Cup Final
1924 First International at Wembley (England 1, Scotland 1). Rule change allows goals to be scored direct from corner-kicks
1925 New offside law
1926 Huddersfield Town complete first League Championship hat-trick
1927 First League match broadcast (radio): Arsenal v Sheff. Utd. (Jan 22). First radio broadcast of Cup Final (winners Cardiff C.). Charles Clegg, president of F.A., becomes first knight of football
1928 First £10,000 transfer – David Jack (Bolton to Arsenal). W.R. ('Dixie') Dean (Everton) creates League record – 60 goals in season. Britain withdraws from F.I.F.A.
1930 Uruguay first winners of World Cup
1931 West Bromwich Albion win Cup and promotion
1933 Players numbered for first time in Cup Final (1-22)
1934 Sir Frederick Wall retires as F.A. secretary; successor Stanley Rous. Death of Herbert Chapman (Arsenal manager)
1935 Arsenal equal Huddersfield Town's Championship hat-trick record. Official two-referee trials
1936 Joe Payne's 10-goal League record (Luton 12, Bristol Rovers 0)
1937 British record attendance: 149,547 at Scotland v England match
1938 First live TV transmission of F.A. Cup Final. F.A.'s 75th anniversary. Football League 50th Jubilee. New pitch marking – arc on edge of penalty-area. Laws of Game re-drafted by Stanley Rous. Arsenal pay record £14,500 fee for Bryn Jones (Wolverhampton Wanderers)
1939 Compulsory numbering of players in Football League. First six-figure attendance for League match (Rangers v Celtic, 118,567). All normal competitions suspended for duration of Second World War
1944 Death of Sir Frederick Wall (84), F.A. secretary 1896-1934
1945 Scottish League Cup introduced
1946 British associations rejoin F.I.F.A.. Bolton disaster (33 killed) during F.A. Cup tie with Stoke City. Walter Winterbottom appointed England's first director of coaching
1947 Great Britain beat Rest of Europe 6-1 at Hampden Park, Glasgow. First £20,000 transfer – Tommy Lawton, Chelsea to Notts Co.
1949 Stanley Rous, secretary F.A., knighted. England's first home defeat outside British Champ. (0-2 v Eire)
1950 Football League extended from 88 to 92 clubs. World record crowd (203,500) at World Cup Final, Brazil v Uruguay, in Rio. Scotland's first home defeat by foreign team (0-1 v Austria)
1951 White ball comes into official use
1952 Newcastle first club to win F.A. Cup at Wembley in successive seasons
1953 England's first Wembley defeat by foreign opponents (3-6 v Hungary)

1954 Hungary beat England 7-1 in Budapest

1955 First F.A. Cup match under floodlights (prelim. round replay, Sept. 14): Kidderminster Harriers v Brierley Hill Alliance

1956 First F.A. Cup ties under floodlights in competition proper (Jan. 7). First League match by floodlight (Feb. 22, Portsmouth v Newcastle). Real Madrid win the first European Cup

1957 Last full Football League programme on Christmas Day. Entertainment Tax withdrawn

1958 Manchester United air crash at Munich (Feb. 6). League re-structured into four divisions

1959 Football League establish fixtures copyright; pools must pay for use

1960 Record transfer fee: £55,000 for Denis Law (Huddersfield to Man. C.). Wolves win Cup, miss Double and Championship hat-trick by one goal. For fifth time in ten years F.A. Cup Final team reduced to ten men by injury. F.A. recognise Sunday football. Football League Cup launched

1961 Tottenham complete the first Championship-F.A. Cup double this century. Maximum wage (£20 a week) abolished in High Court challenge by George Eastham. First British £100-a-week wage paid (by Fulham to Johnny Haynes). First £100,000 British transfer – Denis Law, Man. C. to Torino. Sir Stanley Rous elected president of F.I.F.A.

1962 Man. United raise record British transfer fee to £115,000 for Denis Law

1963 F.A. Centenary. Football League's 75th anniversary. Season extended to end of May due to severe winter. First pools panel. English "retain and transfer" system ruled illegal in High Court test case

1964 Rangers' second great hat-trick – Scottish Cup, League Cup and League. Football League and Scottish League guaranteed £500,000 a year in new fixtures copyright agreement with Pools. First televised 'Match of the Day' (BBC2): Liverpool 3, Arsenal 2 (August 22)

1965 Bribes scandal – ten players jailed (and banned for life by F.A.) for match-fixing 1960-63. Stanley Matthews knighted in farewell season. Arthur Rowley (Shrewsbury Town) retires with record of 434 League goals. Substitutes allowed for injured players in Football League matches (one per team)

1966 England win World Cup (Wembley)

1967 Alf Ramsey, England manager, knighted; O.B.E. for captain Bobby Moore. Celtic become first British team to win European Cup. First substitutes allowed in F.A. Cup Final (Tottenham v Chelsea) but not used. Football League permit loan transfers (two per club)

1968 First F.A. Cup Final televised live in colour (BBC2 – W.B.A. v Everton). Manchester United first English club to win European Cup

1971 Arsenal win League Championship and F.A. Cup

1973 Football League introduce 3-up, 3-down promotion/relegation between Divisions 1, 2 and 3 and 4-up, 4-down between Divisions 3 and 4

1974 First F.A. Cup ties played on Sunday (Jan. 6). League football played on Sunday for first time (Jan. 20). Last F.A. Amateur Cup Final. Joao Havelange (Brazil) succeeds Sir Stanley Rous as F.I.F.A. president

1975 Scottish Premier Division introduced

1976 Football League introduce goal difference (replacing goal average)

1977 Liverpool achieve the double of League Championship and European Cup. Don Revie defects to Saudi Arabia when England manager – successor Ron Greenwood

1978 Freedom of contract for players accepted by Football League. P.F.A. lifts ban on foreign players in English football. Football League introduce Transfer Tribunal. Viv Anderson (Nottingham Forest) first black player to win a full England cap. Willie Johnston (Scotland) sent home from World Cup Finals in Argentina after failing dope test

1979 First all-British £500,000 transfer – David Mills, M'bro' to W.B.A. First British million pound transfer (Trevor Francis – B'ham to Nott'm. F.). Andy Gray moves from Aston Villa to Wolves for a record £1,469,000 fee

1981 Tottenham win 100th F.A. Cup Final. Liverpool first British side to win

European Cup three times. Three points for a win introduced by Football League. Q.P.R. install Football League's first artificial pitch. Sept. 29, death of Bill Shankly, manager-legend of Liverpool 1959-74. Record British transfer – Bryan Robson (W.B.A. to Man. Utd.), £1,500,000

1982 Aston Villa become sixth consecutive English winners of European Cup. Tottenham retain F.A. Cup – first club to do so since Spurs 1961 and 1962. Football League Cup becomes the (sponsored) Milk Cup

1983 Liverpool complete the League Championship-Milk Cup double for second year running. Manager Bob Paisley retires. Aberdeen first club to do Cup-Winners' Cup and domestic Cup double. Football League clubs vote to keep own match receipts. Football League sponsored by Canon, Japanese camera and business equipment manufacturers – 3-year agreement starting 1983-4. Football League agree 2-year contract for live TV coverage of ten matches per season (5 Friday night, BBC, 5 Sunday afternoon, ITV)

1984 One F.A. Cup tie in rounds 3, 4, 5 and 6 shown live on TV (Friday or Sunday). Aberdeen take Scottish Cup for third successive season, win Scottish Championship, too. Tottenham win UEFA Cup on penalty shoot-out. Liverpool win European Cup on penalty shoot-out to complete unique treble with Milk Cup and League title (as well as Championship hat-trick). N. Ireland win the final British Championship. France win European Championship – their first honour. F.A. National Soccer School opens at Lilleshall. Britain's biggest score this century: Stirling Alb. 20, Selkirk 0 (Scottish Cup)

1985 Bradford City fire disaster – 56 killed. First £1m. receipts from match in Britain (F.A. Cup Final). Kevin Moran (Man. United) first player to be sent off in F.A. Cup Final. Celtic win 100th Scottish F.A. Cup Final. European Cup Final horror (Liverpool v Juventus, riot in Brussels) 39 die. UEFA ban all English clubs indefinitely from European competitions. No TV coverage at start of League season – first time since 1963 (resumption delayed until January 1986). Sept: first ground-sharing in League history – Charlton move from The Valley to Selhurst Park (C. Palace)

1986 Liverpool complete League and Cup double in player-manager Kenny Dalglish's first season in charge. Swindon (4th Div. Champions) set League points record (102). League approve reduction of First Division to 20 clubs by 1988. Everton chairman Philip Carter elected president of Football League. July 18, death of Sir Stanley Rous (91). 100th edition of *News of the World* Football Annual. League Cup sponsored for next three years by Littlewoods (£2m.). Football League voting majority (for rule changes) reduced from ¾ to ⅔. Wales move HQ from Wrexham to Cardiff after 110 years. Two substitutes in F.A. Cup and League (Littlewoods) Cup. Two-season League/TV deal (£6.2m.):- BBC and ITV each show seven live League matches per season, League Cup semi-finals and Final. Football League sponsored by *Today* newspaper. Luton Town first club to ban all visiting supporters; as sequel are themselves banned from League Cup. Oldham and Preston install artificial pitches, making four in F. League (following Q.P.R. and Luton).

1987 May: F. League introduce play-off matches to decide final promotion/relegation places in all divisions. Re-election abolished – bottom club in Div. 4 replaced by winners of GM Vauxhall Conference. Two substitutes approved for Football League 1987-88. Red and yellow disciplinary cards (scrapped 1981) re-introduced by League and F.A.. Football League sponsored by Barclays. First Div. reduced to 21 clubs

1988 Football League Centenary. First Division reduced to 20 clubs

1989 Soccer gets £74m. TV deal: £44m. over 4 years, ITV; £30m. over 5 years, BBC/BSB. But it costs Philip Carter the League Presidency. Ted Croker retires as F.A. chief executive; successor Graham Kelly, from Football League. Hillsborough disaster: 95 die at F.A. Cup semi-final (Liverpool v Nott'm. F.). Arsenal win closest-ever Championship with last kick. Peter Shilton sets England record with 109 caps.

1990 Nott'm. Forest win last Littlewoods Cup Final. Both F.A. Cup semi-finals played on Sunday and televised live. Play-off finals move to Wembley; Swindon win place in Div. 1, then relegated back to Div. 2 (breach of financial regulations) – Sunderland promoted instead. Pools betting tax cut from 42½ to 40%. England reach World Cup semi-final in Italy and win F.I.F.A. Fair Play Award. Peter Shilton retires as England goalkeeper with 125 caps (world record). Graham Taylor (Aston Villa) succeeds Bobby Robson as England manager. Int. Board amend offside law (player 'level' no longer offside). F.I.F.A. make "pro foul" a sending-off offence. English clubs back in Europe (Man. U. and Aston V.) after 5-year exile

1991 First F.A. Cup semi-final at Wembley (Tottenham 3, Arsenal 1). Bert Millichip (F.A. chairman) and Philip Carter (Everton chairman) knighted. End of artificial pitches in Div. 1 (Luton, Oldham). Scottish League reverts to 12-12-14 format (as in 1987-8). Penalty shoot-out introduced to decide F.A. Cup ties level after one replay

1992 Introduction of fourth F.A. Cup (previous trophy withdrawn). F.A. launch Premier League (22 clubs). Football League reduced to three divisions (71 clubs). Record TV-sport deal: BSkyB/BBC to pay £304m. for 5-year coverage of Premier League. ITV do £40m., 4-year deal with F. League. Channel 4 show Italian football live (Sundays). F.I.F.A. approve new back-pass rule (goalkeeper must not handle ball kicked to him by team-mate). New League of Wales formed. Record all-British transfer, £3.3m.: Alan Shearer (So'ton to Blackburn). Charlton return to The Valley after 7-year absence.

1993 Barclays end 6-year sponsorship of F. League. For first time both F.A. Cup semi-finals at Wembley (Sat., Sun.). Arsenal first club to complete League Cup/F.A. Cup double. Rangers pull off Scotland's domestic treble for fifth time. F.A. in record British sports sponsorship deal (£12m. over 4 years) with brewers Bass for F.A. Carling Premiership, from Aug. Brian Clough retires after 18 years as Nott'm. F. manager; as does Jim McLean (21 years manager of Dundee U.). Football League agree 3-year, £3m. sponsorship with Endsleigh Insurance. Premier League introduce squad numbers with players' names on shirts. Record British transfer: Duncan Ferguson, Dundee U. to Rangers (£4m.). Record English-club signing: Roy Keane, Nott'm. F. to Man. U. (£3.75m.). Graham Taylor resigns as England manager after World Cup exit (Nov.). Death in Feb. of Bobby Moore (51), England World-Cup winning captain 1966.

1994 Death of Sir Matt Busby (Jan.). Terry Venables appointed England coach (Jan.). Man. United complete the Double. Last artificial pitch in English football goes – Preston revert to grass, summer 1994. Bobby Charlton knighted. Scottish League format changes to four divisions of ten clubs. Record British transfer: Chris Sutton, Norwich to Blackburn (£5m.). Sept: FA announce first sponsorship of F.A. Cup – Littlewoods Pools (4-year, £14m. deal, plus £6m. for Charity Shield). Death of Billy Wright, 70 (Sept).

1995 New record British transfer: Andy Cole, Newcastle to Man. U. (£7m.). First England match abandoned through crowd trouble (v Rep. of Ireland, Dublin). Blackburn Champions for first time since 1914. Premiership reduced to 20 clubs. British transfer record broken again (June): Stan Collymore, Nott'm. F. to Liverpool (£8½m.). Starting season 1995-96, teams allowed to use 3 substitutes per match, not necessarily including a goalkeeper. Dec: European Court of Justice upholds Bosman ruling, barring transfer fees for players out of contract and removing limit on number of foreign players clubs can field.

1996 Death in Feb. of Bob Paisley (77), ex-Liverpool, most successful manager in English Football. F.A. appoint Chelsea manager Glenn Hoddle to succeed Terry Venables as England coach after Euro 96. Man. United first English club to achieve Double twice (and in 3 seasons). Football League completes £125m., 5-year TV deal with BSkyB starting 1996-97. England stage European Championship, reach semi-finals, lose on pens to tournament winners Germany.

NATIONAL REFEREES 1996-97

From a list of 69 National List referees (ten of them newcomers), a panel of 19 will take charge of Premier League matches this season. Eight of them are on the FIFA list.

Match fees – Premier League and FA Cup (from 3rd. Round): referees £350 (previously £325); assistant-referees (formerly linesmen) £150 (£135). Nationwide Football League: referees £185 (£175); assistant-referees £90 (£87.50).

- ▲ ALCOCK, Paul (Redhill, Surrey)
- ALLISON, David (Lancaster)
- ▲ ASHBY, Gerald (Worcester)
- BAILEY, Mike (Impington, Cambs.)
- BAINES, Steve (Chesterfield)
- ▲ BARBER, Graham (Warwick)
- BARRY, Neale (Scunthorpe)
- • BATES, Tony (Stoke-on-Trent)
- BENNETT, Steve (Dartford)
- ▲ BODENHAM, Martin (Looe, Cornwall)
- BRANDWOOD, John (Lichfield)
- ▲ BURGE, Keith (Tonypandy)
- BURNS, Bill (Scarborough)
- BUTLER, Alan (Sutton-in-Ashfield)
- CAIN, George (Bootle)
- • CODDINGTON, Brian (Sheffield)
- CRUIKSHANKS, Ian (Hartlepool)
- ▲ DANSON, Paul (Leicester)
- ▲ DILKES, Roger (Mossley, Lancs.)
- ▲ DUNN, Steve (Bristol)
- †▲ DURKIN, Paul (Portland, Dorset)
- D'URSO, Andrew (Billericay, Essex)
- †▲ ELLERAY, David (Harrow-on-the-Hill)
- • FINCH, Carl (Bury St Edmunds)
- FLETCHER, Mike (Warley, W. Midlands)
- • FOY, Chris (St Helens)
- FRANKLAND, Graham (Middlesbrough)
- FURNANDIZ, Roger (Doncaster)
- †▲ GALLAGHER, Dermot (Banbury)
- • HALSEY, Mark (Welwyn Garden City, Herts.)
- HARRIS, Rob (Oxford)
- HEILBRON, Terry (Newton Aycliffe)
- †▲ JONES, Peter (Loughborough)
- • JONES, Trevor (Barrow-in-Furness)
- KIRKBY, John (Sheffield)
- KNIGHT, Barry (Orpington)
- LAWS, David (Whitley Bay)
- • LAWS, Graham (Whitley Bay)
- LEACH, Ken (Wolverhampton)
- LEAKE, Tony (Darwen, Lancs.)
- †▲ LODGE, Steve (Barnsley)
- LOMAS, Eddie (Manchester)
- LUNT, Terry (Ashton-in-Makerfield, Lancs.)
- LYNCH, Kevin (Knaresborough)
- MATHIESON, Scott (Stockport)
- ORR, David (Iver, Bucks.)
- PEARSON, Roy (Peterlee, Durham)
- PIERCE, Mike (Portsmouth)
- †▲ POLL, Graham (Tring, Herts.)
- POOLEY, Graham (Bishop's Stortford)
- POULAIN, Richard (Huddersfield)
- • PUGH, David (Wirral)
- †▲ REED, Mike (Birmingham)
- REJER, Paul (Tipton, W. Midlands)
- RENNIE, Uriah (Sheffield)
- RICHARDS, Phil (Preston)
- ▲ RILEY, Mike (Leeds)
- • ROBINSON, Paul (Hull)
- SINGH, Gurnam (Wolverhampton)
- STRETTON, Frazer (Nottingham)
- • STYLES, Rob (Waterlooville, Hants.)
- TAYLOR, Paul (Cheshunt, Herts.)
- WEST, Trevor (Hull)
- WILEY, Alan (Burntwood, Staffs.)
- WILKES, Clive (Gloucester)
- ▲ WILKIE, Alan (Chester-le-Street)
- †▲ WILLARD, Gary (Worthing)
- ▲ WINTER, Jeff (Stockton-on-Tees)
- WOLSTENHOLME, Eddie (Blackburn)

(† FIFA list; ▲ Premier League; • New appointment)

ENGLISH LEAGUE ROLL CALL

APPEARANCES & SCORERS 1995-96

(Figures in brackets = appearances as substitute)

F.A. CARLING PREMIERSHIP

ARSENAL

Ground: Arsenal Stadium, Highbury, London N5 1BU.
Telephone: 0171-704-4000. **Clubcall**: 0891 202020. **Club Nickname**: Gunners.
First-choice Colours: Red shirts; white shorts; white stockings.

Adams, T 21
Bergkamp, D 33
Bould, S 19
Clarke, A .... 4(2)
Dickov, P .... 1(6)
Dixon, L 38
Hartson, J .... 15(4)
Helder, G .... 15(9)
Hillier, D .... 3(2)
Hughes, S .... –(1)
Jensen, J .... 13(2)
Keown, M 34
Linighan, A .... 17(1)
McGoldrick, E .... –(1)
McGowan, G 1
Marshall, S .... 10(1)
Merson, P 38
Morrow, S .... 3(1)
Parlour, R .... 20(2)
Platt, D .... 27(2)
Rose, M .... 1(3)
Seaman, D 38
Shaw, P .... –(3)
Winterburn, N 36
Wright, I 31

League Goals (49): Wright 15, Bergkamp 11, Platt 6, Merson 5, Hartson 4, Dixon 2, Winterburn 2, Adams 1, Dickov 1, Helder 1, Marshall 1.
Coca-Cola Cup Goals (17): Wright 7, Bergkamp 5, Adams 2, Bould 1, Hartson 1, Keown 1. **FA Cup Goals (1)**: Wright 1.
'Player of Year' 1996: David Seaman.
Average Home League Attendance 1995-96: 37,568. **Capacity for 1996-97**: 38,500 (all-seated).
Record Attendance: 73,295 v Sunderland (Div. 1) 9 March 1935.

ASTON VILLA

Ground: Villa Park, Trinity Road, Birmingham B6 6HE.
Telephone: 0121-327-2299. **Clubcall**: 0891 121148. **Club Nickname**: Villans.
First-choice Colours: Claret and blue shirts; white shorts; claret stockings.

Bosnich, M 38
Browne, P 2
Carr, F 1
Charles, G 34
Davis, N .... –(2)
Draper, M 36
Ehiogu, U 36
Farrelly, G .... 1(4)
Fenton, G .... –(3)
Hendrie, L .... 2(1)
Joachim, J .... 4(7)
Johnson, T .... 17(6)
McGrath, P .... 29(1)
Milosevic, S .... 36(1)
Murray, S 3
Scimeca, R .... 7(10)
Southgate, G 31
Spink, N .... –(2)
Staunton, S .... 11(2)
Taylor, I .... 24(1)
Tiler, C 1
Townsend, A .... 32(1)
Wright, A 38
Yorke, D 35

League Goals (52): Yorke 19, Milosevic 10, Johnson 5, Taylor 3, Draper 2, Joachim 2, McGrath 2, Townsend 2, Wright 2, Charles 1, Ehiogu 1, Southgate 1, Opponents 2.
Coca-Cola Cup Goals (16): Yorke 6, Johnson 2, Draper 1, Ehiogu 1, Milosevic 1, Southgate 1, Staunton 1, Taylor 1, Townsend 1, Opponent 1. **F.A. Cup Goals (8)**: Draper 2, Yorke 2, Carr 1, Johnson 1, Milosevic 1, Taylor 1.
'Player of Year' 1996: Dwight Yorke.
Average Home League Attendance 1995-96: 32,614. **Capacity for 1996-97**: 39,339 (all-seated).
Record Attendance: 76,588 v Derby County (F.A. Cup 6) 2 March 1946.

BLACKBURN ROVERS

Ground: Ewood Park, Blackburn, Lancashire BB2 4JF.
Telephone: 01254-698888. **Clubcall**: 0891 121179. **Club Nickname**: Rovers

First-choice Colours: Blue and white shirts; white shorts; blue and white stockings.

Atkins, M .... –(4)
Batty, D 23
Berg, H 38
Bohinen, L .... 17(2)
Coleman, C .... 19(1)
Fenton, G .... 4(10)
Flitcroft, G 3
Flowers, T 37
Gallacher, K .... 14(2)
Gundmundsson, N . 1(3)
Hendry, C 33
Holmes, M .... 8(1)
Kenna, J 32
Le Saux, G .... 13(1)
McKinlay, B .... 13(5)
Makel, L .... –(3)
Marker, N .... 8(1)
Mimms, B .... 1(1)
Newell, M .... 26(4)
Pearce, I 12
Ripley, S 28
Shearer, A 35
Sherwood, T 33
Sutton, C .... 9(4)
Warhurst, P .... 1(9)
Wilcox, J 10

League Goals (61): Shearer 31, Fenton 6, Bohinen 4, Sherwood 4, Newell 3, Wilcox 3, Gallacher 2, McKinlay 2, Batty 1, Hendry 1, Holmes 1, Le Saux 1, Marker 1, Pearce 1.
Coca-Cola Cup Goals (8): Shearer 5, Newell 1, Sutton 1, Opponent 1. **F.A. Cup Goals**: None. **European Cup Goals (5)**: Newell 4, Shearer 1. **Charity Shield Goals**: None.
'Player of Year' 1996: Colin Hendry.
Average Home League Attendance 1995-96: 27,714. **Capacity for 1996-97**: 31,500 (all-seated).
Record Attendance: 61,783 v Bolton Wanderers (F.A. Cup 6) 2 March 1929.

BOLTON WANDERERS

Ground: Burnden Park, Manchester Road, Bolton, Lancashire BL3 2QR.
Telephone: 01204-389200. **Clubcall**: 0891 121164. **Club Nickname**: Trotters.
First-choice Colours: White shirts; blue shorts; blue stockings.

Bergsson, G 34
Blake, N .... 14(4)
Branagan, K 31
Burnett, W .... –(1)
Coleman, S 12
Coyle, O .... 2(3)
Curcic, S 28
Davison, A 2
De Freitas, F ...... 17(10)
Fairclough, C 33
Green, S .... 26(5)
Lee, D .... 9(9)
McAnespie, S .... 7(2)
McAteer, J 4
McGinlay, J .... 29(3)
Paatelainen, M-M 12(3)
Patterson, M .... 12(4)
Phillips, J 37
Sellars, S 22
Small, B 1
Sneekes, R .... 14(3)
Strong, G .... –(1)
Stubbs, A .... 24(1)
Taggart, G 11
Taylor, S .... –(1)
Thompson, A .... 23(3)
Todd, A .... 9(3)
Ward, G 5

League Goals (39): McGinlay 6, De Freitas 5, Bergsson 4, Curcic 4, Stubbs 4, Green 3, Sellars 3, Todd 2, Blake 1, Coleman 1, Lee 1, Paatelainen 1, Patterson 1, Sneekes 1, Taggart 1, Thompson 1.
Coca-Cola Cup Goals (7): McGinlay 2, Sneekes 2, Curcic 1, Patterson 1, Thompson 1. **F.A. Cup Goals (3)**: Curcic 2, McGinlay 1.
'Player of Year' 1996: Keith Branagan.
Average Home League Attendance 1995-96: 18,822. **Capacity for 1996-97**: 22,291 (seats 8,759, standing 13,542).
Record Attendance: 69,912 v Manchester City (F.A. Cup 5) 18 February 1933.

CHELSEA

Ground: Stamford Bridge, Fulham Road, London SW6 1HS.
Telephone: 0171-385-5545. **Clubcall**: 0891 121159. **Club Nickname**: Blues.
First-choice Colours: Blue shirts; blue shorts; white stockings.

Burley, C .... 16(6)
Clarke, S .... 21(1)
Dow, A 1
Duberry, M 22
Furlong, P .... 14(14)
Gullit, R 31
Hall, G 5
Hitchcock, K 12
Hughes, M 31
Johnsen, E .... 18(4)
Kharine, D 26
Lee, D .... 29(2)
Minto, S 10
Morris, J .... –(1)
Myers, A 20
Newton, E .... 21(3)
Peacock, G .... 17(11)
Petrescu, D .... 22(2)
Phelan, T 12
Rocastle, D 1
Sinclair, F .... 12(1)

Spackman, N .... 13(3)
Spencer, J .... 23(5)
Stein, M .... 7(1)
Wise, D .... 34(1)

League Goals (46): Spencer 13, Hughes 8, Wise 7, Peacock 5, Furlong 3, Gullit 3, Petrescu 2, Hall 1, Lee 1, Newton 1, Sinclair 1, Opponent 1.
Coca-Cola Cup Goals: None. **F.A. Cup Goals (15)**: Hughes 4, Gullit 3, Duberry 2, Peacock 2, Furlong 1, Petrescu 1, Spencer 1, Wise 1.
'Player of Year' 1996: To be announced.
Average Home League Attendance 1995-96: 25,466. **Capacity for 1996-97**: 28,000 (all-seated).
Record Attendance: 82,905 v Arsenal (Div. 1) 12 October 1935.

COVENTRY CITY

Ground: Highfield Road, King Richard Street, Coventry CV2 4FW.
Telephone: 01203-234000. **Clubcall**: 0891 121166. **Club Nickname**: Sky Blues.
First-choice Colours: Sky blue shirts; navy shorts; navy stockings.

Barnwell, J .... –(1)
Boland, W .... 2(1)
Borrows, B 21
Burrows, D 11
Busst, D .... 16(1)
Christie, I .... –(1)
Cook, P .... 2(1)
Daish, L 11
Dublin, D 34
Filan, J 13
Hall, M .... 24(1)
Isaias, M .... 9(2)
Jess, E .... 9(3)
Lamptey, N .... 3(3)
Ndlovu, P .... 27(5)
Ogrizovic, S 25
Pickering, A .... 26(4)
Rennie, D .... 9(2)
Richardson, K 33
Salako, J .... 34(3)
Shaw, R 21
Strachan, G .... 5(7)
Telfer, P 31
Whelan, N 21
Whyte, C 1
Williams, P .... 30(2)

League Goals (42): Dublin 14, Whelan 8, Ndlovu 5, Salako 3, Busst 2, Isaias 2, Rennie 2, Williams 2, Daish 1, Jess 1, Telfer 1, Opponent 1.
Coca-Cola Cup Goals (7): Lamptey 2, Busst 1, Ndlovu 1, Richardson 1, Salako 1, Williams 1. **F.A. Cup Goals (6)**: Dublin 2, Pickering 1, Salako 1, Telfer 1, Whelan 1.
'Player of Year' 1996: Paul Williams.
Average Home League Attendance 1995-96: 18,507. **Capacity for 1996-97**: 23,500 (all-seated).
Record Attendance: 51,455 v Wolves (Div. 2) 29 April 1967.

EVERTON

Ground: Goodison Park, Liverpool L4 4EL.
Telephone: 0151-330-2200. **Clubcall**: 0891 121199. **Club Nickname**: Toffees.
First-choice Colours: Blue shirts; white shorts; blue stockings.

Ablett, G 13
Amokachi, D .... 17(8)
Barlow, S .... –(3)
Barrett, E 8
Branch, M .... 1(2)
Ebbrell, J .... 24(1)
Ferguson, D .... 16(2)
Grant, A .... 12(6)
Hinchcliffe, A .... 23(5)
Holmes, P 1
Horne, B .... 25(1)
Hottiger, M 9
Jackson, M 14
Kanchelskis, A 32
Limpar, A .... 22(6)
O'Connor, J .... 3(1)
Parkinson, J 28
Rideout, P .... 19(6)
Samways, V .... 3(1)
Short, C .... 22(1)
Southall, N 38
Stuart, G .... 26(2)
Unsworth, D .... 28(3)
Watson, D 34

League Goals (64): Kanchelskis 16, Stuart 10, Amokachi 6, Rideout 6, Ferguson 5, Ebbrell 4, Hinchcliffe 3, Limpar 3, Parkinson 3, Unsworth 2, Grant 1, Horne 1, Hottiger 1, Samways 1, Short 1, Watson 1.
Coca-Cola Cup Goals (2): Hinchcliffe 1, Stuart 1. **F.A. Cup Goals (8)**: Stuart 3, Ferguson 2, Ablett 1, Amokachi 1, Ebbrell 1. **European Cup-Winners' Cup Goals (6)**: Amokachi 1, Ebbrell 1, Grant 1, Rideout 1, Stuart 1, Unsworth 1.
Charity Shield Goals (1): Samways 1.
'Player of Year' 1996: Andrei Kanchelskis.
Average Home League Attendance 1995-96: 35,435. **Capacity for 1996-97**: 40,200 (all-seated).
Record Attendance: 78,299 v Liverpool (Div. 1) 18 September 1948.

LEEDS UNITED

Ground: Elland Road, Leeds, West Yorkshire LS11 0ES.
Telephone: 0113-271-6037. **Clubcall**: 0891 121180. **Club Nickname**: United.
First-choice Colours: White shirts; white shorts; white stockings.

Beeney, M 10
Beesley, P .... 8(2)
Blunt, J .... 2(1)
Bowman, R .... 1(2)
Brolin, T .... 17(2)
Chapman, L 2
Couzens, A .... 8(6)
Deane, B .... 30(4)
Dorigo, T 17
Ford, M 12
Gray, A .... 12(3)
Harte, I .... 2(2)
Jackson, M .... –(1)
Jobson, R 12
Kelly, G 34
Kewell, H 2
Lukic, J 28
McAllister, G 36
Masinga, P .... 5(3)
Maybury, A 1
Palmer, C 35
Pemberton, J .... 16(1)
Radebe, L .... 10(3)
Speed, G 29
Tinkler, M .... 5(4)
Wallace, R .... 12(12)
Wetherall, D 34
Whelan, N .... 3(5)
White, D .... 1(3)
Worthington, N ..... 12(4)
Yeboah, T 22

League Goals (40): Yeboah 12, Deane 7, McAllister 5, Brolin 4, Wetherall 4, Palmer 2, Speed 2, Dorigo 1, Jobson 1, Wallace 1, White 1.
Coca-Cola Cup Goals (13): Speed 3, Yeboah 3, Deane 2, Masinga 2, Couzens 1, McAllister 1, Opponent 1. **F.A. Cup Goals (7)**: McAllister 3, Deane 1, Speed 1, Wallace 1, Yeboah 1. **UEFA Cup Goals (6)**: Yeboah 3, McAllister 1, Palmer 1, Speed 1.
'Player of Year' 1996: Tony Yeboah.
Average Home League Attendance 1995-96: 32,580. **Capacity for 1996-97**: 40,000 (all-seated).
Record Attendance: 57,892 v Sunderland (F.A. Cup 5) 15 March 1967.

LIVERPOOL

Ground: Anfield Road, Liverpool L4 0TH.
Telephone: 0151-263-2361. **Clubcall**: 0891 121184. **Club Nickname**: Reds.
First-choice Colours: Red shirts; red shorts; red stockings.

Babb, P 28
Barnes, J 36
Bjornebye, S 2
Clough, N .... 1(1)
Collymore, S .... 30(1)
Fowler, R .... 36(2)
Harkness, S .... 23(1)
James, D 38
Jones, R 33
Kennedy, M .... 1(3)
McAteer, J .... 27(1)
McManaman, S 38
Matteo, D 5
Redknapp, J .... 19(4)
Ruddock, N .... 18(2)
Rush, I .... 10(9)
Scales, J 27
Thomas, M .... 18(8)
Wright, M 28

League Goals (70): Fowler 28, Collymore 14, McManaman 6, Ruddock 5, Rush 5, Barnes 3, Redknapp 3, Wright 2, Harkness 1, Thomas 1, Opponents 2.
Coca-Cola Cup Goals (7): Fowler 2, Harkness 1, McManaman 1, Rush 1, Scales 1, Thomas 1. **F.A. Cup Goals (19)**: Fowler 6, Collymore 5, McAteer 3, McManaman 2, Rush 1, Opponents 2. **UEFA Cup Goals (2)**: McManaman 1, Redknapp 1.
'Player of Year' 1996: Robbie Fowler.
Average Home League Attendance 1995-96: 39,553. **Capacity for 1996-97**: 41,000 (all-seated).
Record Attendance: 61,905 v Wolves (F.A. Cup 4) 2 February 1952.

MANCHESTER CITY

Ground: Maine Road, Moss Side, Manchester M14 7WN.
Telephone: 0161-224-5000. **Clubcall**: 0891 121184. **Club Nickname**: Citizens.
First-choice Colours: Sky blue shirts; white shorts; white stockings.

Beagrie, P .... 4(1)
Brightwell, I .... 26(3)
Brown, M .... 16(5)
Clough, N 15
Creaney, G .... 6(9)
Curle, K 32
Edghill, R 13
Ekelund, R .... 2(2)
Flitcroft, G 25
Foster, J 4
Frontzeck, M .... 11(1)
Hiley, S .... 2(4)
Immel, E 38
Ingram, R 5
Kavelashvili, M .... 3(1)
Kernaghan, A .... 4(2)
Kerr, D .... –(1)
Kinkladze, G 37
Lomas, S .... 32(1)
Mazzarelli, G .... –(2)
Phelan, T 9

Phillips, M .... 2(9)	Rosler, U .... 34(2)	Symons, K 38
Quinn, N .... 24(8)	Summerbee, N .... 33(4)	Walsh, P 3

League Goals (33): Rosler 9, Quinn 8, Kinkladze 4, Creaney 3, Lomas 3, Clough 2, Symons 2, Kavelashvili 1, Summerbee 1.
Coca-Cola Cup Goals (4): Rosler 2, Curle 1, Quinn 1. **F.A. Cup Goals (10)**: Quinn 2, Rosler 2, Clough 1, Creaney 1, Flitcroft 1, Kinkladze 1, Lomas 1, Opponent 1.
'Player of Year' 1996: Georgi Kinkladze.
Average Home League Attendance 1995-96: 27,869. **Capacity for 1996-97**: 31,257 (all-seated).
Record Attendance: 84,569 v Stoke City (F.A. Cup 6) 3 March 1934.

MANCHESTER UNITED

Ground: Sir Matt Busby Way, Old Trafford, Manchester M16 0RA.
Telephone: 0161-872-1661/930-1968. **Clubcall**: 0891 121161. **Club Nickname**: Red Devils. **First-choice Colours**: Red shirts; white shorts; black stockings.

Beckham, D .... 26(7)	Irwin, D 31	Parker, P .... 5(1)
Bruce, S 30	Keane, R 29	Pilkington, K .... 2(1)
Butt, N .... 31(1)	McClair, B .... 12(10)	Prunier, W 2
Cantona, E 30	May, D .... 11(5)	Schmeichel, P 36
Cole, A .... 32(2)	Neville, G .... 30(1)	Scholes, P .... 16(10)
Cooke, T .... 1(3)	Neville, P .... 21(3)	Sharpe, L .... 21(10)
Davies, S .... 1(5)	O'Kane, J .... –(1)	Thornley, B .... –(1)
Giggs, R .... 30(3)	Pallister, G 21	

League Goals (73): Cantona 14, Cole 11, Giggs 11, Scholes 10, Beckham 7, Keane 6, Sharpe 4, McClair 3, Butt 2, Bruce 1, Irwin 1, May 1, Pallister 1, Opponent 1.
Coca-Cola Cup Goals (3): Scholes 2, Cooke 1. **F.A. Cup Goals (14)**: Cantona 5, Cole 2, Sharpe 2, Beckham 1, Butt 1, Giggs 1, Parker 1, Scholes 1. **UEFA Cup Goals (2)**: Schmeichel 1, Scholes 1.
'Player of Year' 1996: Eric Cantona.
Average Home League Attendance 1995-96: 41,700. **Capacity for 1996-97**: 54,000 (all-seated).
Record Attendance: 76,962 Wolves v Grimsby Town (F.A. Cup Semi-final) 25 March 1939. **Club record:** 70,504 v Aston Villa (Div. 1) 27 December 1920.
Note: 83,260 saw Man. United v Arsenal (Div. 1) 17 January 1948 (at Maine Road).

MIDDLESBROUGH

Ground: Cellnet Riverside Stadium, Middlesbrough, Cleveland TS3 6RS.
Telephone: 01642-227227. **Clubcall**: 0891 424200. **Club Nickname**: Boro.
First-choice Colours: Red shirts; white shorts; red stockings.

Barmby, N 32	Hignett, C .... 17(5)	Pearson, N 36
Barron, M 1	Juninho .... 20(1)	Pollock, J 31
Blackmore, C .... 4(1)	Kavanagh, G 6	Robson, B .... 1(1)
Branco .... 5(2)	Liddle, C .... 12(1)	Stamp, P .... 11(1)
Campbell, A .... 1(1)	Miller, A 6	Summerbell, M .... –(1)
Cox, G 35	Moore, A .... 5(7)	Vickers, S 32
Fjortoft, J .... 27(1)	Moreno, J .... 2(5)	Walsh, G 32
Fleming, C 13	Morris, C .... 22(1)	Whelan, P .... 9(4)
Freestone, C .... 2(1)	Mustoe, R 21	Whyte, D .... 24(1)
Hendrie, J .... 7(5)	O'Halloran, K .... 2(1)	Wilkinson, P .... 2(1)

League Goals (35): Barmby 7, Fjortoft 6, Hignett 5, Cox 2, Juninho 2, Morris 2, Stamp 2, Fleming 1, Freestone 1, Hendrie 1, Kavanagh 1, Mustoe 1, Pollock 1, Vickers 1, Whelan 1, Opponent 1.
Coca-Cola Cup Goals (7): Fjortoft 2, Hignett 2, Barmby 1, Mustoe 1, Vickers 1.
F.A. Cup Goals (2): Barmby 1, Pollock 1.
'Player of Year' 1996: Steve Vickers.

Average Home League Attendance 1995-96: 29,283. **Capacity for 1996-97**: 30,500 (all-seated).
Record Attendance: 53,596 v Newcastle United (Div. 1) 27 December 1949.

NEWCASTLE UNITED

Ground: St. James' Park, Newcastle-upon-Tyne, Tyne and Wear NE1 4ST.
Telephone: 0191-232-8361. **Clubcall**: 0891 121190. **Club Nickname**: Magpies.
First-choice Colours: Black and white shirts; black shorts; black stockings.

Albert, P .... 19(4)
Asprilla, F .... 11(3)
Barton, W .... 30(1)
Batty, D 11
Beardsley, P 35
Beresford, J .... 32(1)
Clark, L .... 22(6)
Elliott, R ....5(1)
Ferdinand, L 37
Fox, R .... 2(2)
Gillespie, K .... 26(2)
Ginola, D 34
Hislop, S 24
Hottiger, M .... –(1)
Howey, S 28
Huckerby, D .... –(1)
Kitson, P .... 2(5)
Lee, R 36
Peacock, D .... 33(1)
Sellars, S .... 2(3)
Srnicek, P .... 14(1)
Watson, S .... 15(8)

League Goals (66): Ferdinand 25, Beardsley 9, Lee 8, Ginola 5, Albert 4, Gillespie 4, Watson 3, Asprilla 2, Clark 2, Kitson 2, Batty 1, Howey 1.
Coca-Cola Cup Goals (13): Ferdinand 3, Beardsley 2, Peacock 2, Albert 1, Barton 1, Gillespie 1, Lee 1, Sellars 1, Watson 1. **F.A. Cup Goals (3)**: Albert 1, Beardsley 1, Ferdinand 1.
'Player of Year' 1996: Les Ferdinand.
Average Home League Attendance 1995-96: 36,507. **Capacity for 1996-97**: 36,610 (all-seated).
Record Attendance: 68,386 v Chelsea (Div. 1) 3 September 1930.

NOTTINGHAM FOREST

Ground: City Ground, Nottingham NG2 5FJ.
Telephone: 01159-526000. **Clubcall**: 0891 121174. **Club Nickname**: Reds.
First-choice Colours: Red shirts; white shorts; red stockings.

Allen, C .... 1(2)
Bart-Williams, C 33
Black, K .... 1(1)
Bohinen, L 7
Campbell, K 21
Chettle, S 37
Cooper, C 37
Crossley, M 38
Gemmill, S .... 26(5)
Guinan, S .... 1(1)
Haaland, A .... 12(4)
Howe, S .... 4(5)
Irving, R .... –(1)
Lee, J .... 21(7)
Lyttle, D .... 32(1)
McGregor, P .... 7(7)
Pearce, S 31
Phillips, D .... 14(4)
Roy, B .... 25(3)
Silenzi, A .... 3(6)
Stone, S 34
Woan, I 33

League Goals (50): Lee 8, Roy 8, Woan 8, Stone 7, Cooper 5, Campbell 3, Pearce 3, Howe 2, McGregor 2, Allen 1, Gemmill 1, Lyttle 1, Opponent 1.
Coca-Cola Cup Goals (4): Bohinen 2, Pearce 1, Silenzi 1. **F.A. Cup Goals (10)**: Campbell 3, Woan 3, Pearce 2, Roy 1, Silenzi 1. **UEFA Cup Goals (6)**: Stone 2, Chettle 1, McGregor 1, Roy 1, Woan 1.
'Player of Year' 1996: Stuart Pearce.
Average Home League Attendance 1995-96: 26,083. **Capacity for 1996-97**: 30,602 (all-seated).
Record Attendance: 49,945 v Manchester United (Div. 1) 28 October 1967.

QUEENS PARK RANGERS

Ground: Rangers Stadium, South Africa Road, Shepherds Bush, London W12 7PA.
Telephone: 0181-743-0262. **Clubcall**: 0891 121162. **Club Nickname**: Rangers.
First-choice Colours: Blue and white shirts; white shorts; white stockings.

Allen, B .... 5(3)
Bardsley, D .... 28(1)
Barker, S 33
Brazier, M .... 6(5)
Brevett, R 27
Challis, T .... 10(1)
Charles, L .... –(4)
Dichio, D .... 21(8)
Gallen, K .... 26(4)
Goodridge, G .... –(7)
Hateley, M .... 10(4)
Holloway, I .... 26(1)
Impey, A .... 28(1)
McDonald, A .... 25(1)
Maddix, D .... 20(2)

Murray, P 1	Quashie, N 11	Sommer, J 33
Osborn, S .... 6(3)	Ready, K .... 16(7)	Wilkins, R .... 11(4)
Penrice, G .... –(3)	Roberts, T 5	Yates, S 30
Plummer, C .... –(1)	Sinclair, T 37	Zelic, N .... 3(1)

League Goals (38): Dichio 11, Gallen 8, Barker 5, Impey 3, Hateley 2, Sinclair 2, Allen 1, Brevett 1, Goodridge 1, Holloway 1, McDonald 1, Osborn 1, Ready 1. **Coca-Cola Cup Goals (6)**: Dichio 2, Gallen 1, Impey 1, Ready 1, Sinclair 1. **F.A. Cup Goals (3)**: Quashie 2, Sinclair 1.
'Player of Year' 1996: Trevor Sinclair.
Average Home League Attendance 1995-96: 16,044. **Capacity for 1996-97**: 19,100 (all-seated).
Record Attendance: 35,353 v Leeds United (Div. 1) 27 April 1974.

SHEFFIELD WEDNESDAY

Ground: Hillsborough, Sheffield, South Yorkshire S6 1SW.
Telephone: 01142-343122. **Clubcall**: 0891 121186. **Club Nickname**: Owls.
First-choice Colours: Blue and white shirts; blue shorts; blue stockings.

Atherton, P 36	Kovacevic, D .... 8(8)	Sheridan, J .... 13(4)
Blinker, R 9	Newsome, J 8	Sinton, A .... 7(3)
Bright, M .... 15(10)	Nicol, S .... 18(1)	Stefanovic, D .... 5(1)
Briscoe, L .... 22(4)	Nolan, I 29	Waddle, C .... 23(9)
Degryse, M .... 30(4)	Pearce, A 3	Walker, D 36
Donaldson, O .... 1(2)	Pembridge, M ...... 24(1)	Watts, J .... 9(2)
Hirst, D .... 29(1)	Petrescu, D 8	Whittingham, G .... 27(2)
Humphreys, R .... 1(4)	Platts, M .... –(2)	Williams, M .... 2(3)
Hyde, G .... 14(11)	Pressman, K 30	Woods, C 8
Ingesson, K .... 3(2)		

League Goals (48): Hirst 13, Degryse 8, Bright 7, Whittingham 6, Kovacevic 4, Blinker 2, Pembridge 2, Waddle 2, Donaldson 1, Hyde 1, Newsome 1, Watts 1. **Coca-Cola Cup Goals (10)**: Degryse 4, Bright 3, Hirst 1, Pembridge 1, Whittingham 1. **F.A. Cup Goals**: None.
'Player of Year' 1996: Marc Degryse
Average Home League Attendance 1995-96: 24,877. **Capacity for 1996-97**: 40,000 (all-seated).
Record Attendance: 72,841 v Manchester City (F.A. Cup 5) 17 February 1934.

SOUTHAMPTON

Ground: The Dell, Milton Road, Southampton, Hampshire SO15 2XH.
Telephone: 01703-220505. **Clubcall**: 0891 121178. **Club Nickname**: Saints.
First-choice Colours: Red and white shirts; black shorts; red and white stockings.

Beasant, D 36	Le Tissier, M 34	Robinson, M .... –(5)
Benali, F .... 28(1)	McDonald, P .... –(1)	Shipperley, N 37
Bennett, F .... 5(6)	Maddison, N .... 13(2)	Tisdale, P .... 5(4)
Charlton, S .... 24(2)	Magilton, J 31	Venison, B .... 21(1)
Dodd, J 37	Maskell, C .... –(1)	Walters, M .... 4(1)
Grobbelaar, B 2	Monkou, K .... 31(1)	Warren, C .... 1(5)
Hall, R 30	Neilson, A .... 15(3)	Watson, G .... 18(7)
Heaney, N .... 15(3)	Oakley, M .... 5(5)	Widdrington, T ..... 20(1)
Hughes, D .... 6(5)		

League Goals (34): Le Tissier 7, Shipperley 7, Magilton 3, Watson 3, Dodd 2, Heaney 2, Monkou 2, Widdrington 2, Hall 1, Hughes 1, Maddison 1, Tisdale 1, Opponents 2.
Coca-Cola Cup Goals (8): Le Tissier 2, Shipperley 2, Watson 2, Hall 1, Monkou 1. **F.A. Cup Goals (10)**: Shipperley 3, Magilton 2, Dodd 1, Hall 1, Le Tissier 1, Oakley 1, Watson 1.
'Player of Year' 1996: Dave Beasant.

Average Home League Attendance 1995-96: 14,819. **Capacity for 1996-97**: 15,300 (all-seated).
Record Attendance: 31,044 v Manchester United (Div. 1) 8 October 1969.

TOTTENHAM HOTSPUR

Ground: White Hart Lane, 748 High Road, Tottenham, London N17 0AP.
Telephone: 0181-365-5000. **Spurs Line**: 0891 335555. **Club Nickname**: Spurs. **First-choice Colours**: White shirts; navy shorts; navy stockings.

Anderton, D .... 6(2)
Armstrong, C 36
Austin, D 28
Calderwood, C ..... 26(3)
Campbell, S 31
Caskey, D 3
Cundy, J .... –(1)
Dozzell, J .... 24(4)
Dumitrescu, I 5
Edinburgh, J .... 15(7)
Fox, R 26
Howells, D 29
Kerslake, D 2
McMahon, G .... 7(7)
Mabbutt, G 32
Nethercott, S .... 9(4)
Rosenthal, R .... 26(7)
Scott, K .... –(2)
Sheringham, T 38
Sinton, A .... 8(1)
Slade, S .... 1(4)
Walker, I 38
Wilson, C 28

League Goals (50): Sheringham 16, Armstrong 15, Fox 5, Dozzell 3, Howells 3, Anderton 2, Campbell 1, Rosenthal 1, Opponents 4.
Coca-Cola Cup Goals (9): Armstrong 3, Sheringham 3, Howells 1, Rosenthal 1, Opponent 1. **F.A. Cup Goals (12)**: Sheringham 5, Armstrong 4, Rosenthal 2, Wilson 1.
'Player of Year' 1996: Teddy Sheringham.
Average Home League Attendance 1995-96: 30,510. **Capacity for 1996-97**: 33,083 (all-seated).
Record Attendance: 75,038 v Sunderland (F.A. Cup 6) 5 March 1938.

WEST HAM UNITED

Ground: Boleyn Ground, Green Street, Upton Park, London E13 9AZ.
Telephone: 0181-548-2748. **Clubcall**: 0891 121165. **Club Nickname**: Hammers. **First-choice Colours**: Claret and blue shirts; white shorts; claret and blue stockings.

Allen, M 3
Bilic, S 13
Bishop, I 35
Boere, J .... –(1)
Boogers, M .... –(4)
Breacker, T .... 19(3)
Brown, K 3
Cottee, T .... 30(3)
Dani .... 3(7)
Dicks, J 34
Dowie, I 33
Dumitrescu, I .... 2(1)
Ferdinand, R .... –(1)
Finn, N 1
Gordon, D .... –(1)
Harkes, J .... 6(5)
Hughes, M 28
Hutchison, D .... 8(4)
Lampard, F .... –(2)
Lazaridis, S .... 2(2)
Martin, A .... 10(4)
Miklosko, L 36
Moncur, J .... 19(1)
Potts, S 34
Rieper, M .... 35(1)
Rowland, K .... 19(4)
Sealey, L .... 1(1)
Slater, R .... 16(6)
Watson, M .... –(1)
Whitbread, A .... –(2)
Williamson, D .... 28(1)

League Goals (43): Cottee 10, Dicks 10, Dowie 8, Williamson 4, Dani 2, Hutchison 2, Rieper 2, Slater 2, Allen 1, Bishop 1, Opponent 1.
Coca-Cola Cup Goals (5): Cottee 2, Bishop 1, Dicks 1, Moncur 1. **F.A. Cup Goals (3)**: Dowie 1, Hughes 1, Moncur.
'Player of Year' 1996: Julian Dicks.
Average Home League Attendance 1995-96: 22,340. **Capacity for 1996-97**: 25,985 (all-seated).
Record Attendance: 43,322 v Tottenham Hotspur (Div. 1) 17 October 1970.

WIMBLEDON

Ground: Selhurst Park, London SE25 6PY.
Telephone: 0181-771-2233. **Clubcall**: 0891 121175. **Club Nickname**: Crazy Gang. **First-choice Colours**: Blue shirts; blue shorts; blue stockings.

Ardley, N .... 4(2)
Blackwell, D 8
Blissett, G .... –(4)
Castledine, S .... 2(2)
Clarke, A .... 9(9)
Cunningham, K .... 32(1)
Earle, R 37
Ekoku, E .... 28(3)
Elkins, G .... 7(3)

Euell, J .... 4(5)	Holdsworth, D ...... 31(2)	Reeves, A .... 21(3)
Fear, P 4	Jones, V .... 27(4)	Segers, H .... 3(1)
Fitzgerald, S .... 2(2)	Kimble, A 31	Skinner, J 1
Gayle, M .... 21(13)	Leonhardsen, O 28	Sullivan, N 16
Goodman, J .... 9(18)	McAllister, B 2	Talboys, S .... 3(2)
Harford, M .... 17(4)	Pearce, A .... 6(1)	Thorn, A .... 11(3)
Heald, P 18	Perry, C .... 35(2)	Tracey, S 1

League Goals (55): Earle 11, Holdsworth 10, Ekoku 7, Goodman 6, Gayle 5, Leonhardsen 4, Jones 3, Clarke 2, Euell 2, Castledine 1, Harford 1, Reeves 1, Opponents 2.
Coca-Cola Cup Goals (7): Holdsworth 4, Earle 2, Clarke 1. **F.A. Cup Goals (11)**: Ekoku 3, Goodman 3, Holdsworth 2, Clarke 1, Earle 1, Leonhardsen 1.
'Player of Year' 1996: Oyvind Leonhardsen.
Average Home League Attendance 1995-96: 13,246. **Capacity for 1996-97**: 26,309 (all-seated).
Record Attendance: 30,115 v Manchester United (Premier Division), Selhurst Park, 9 May 1993; 45,701 v Leeds United (F.A. Cup 4R), switched from Plough Lane to Selhurst Park, 10 Feb. 1975.

ENDSLEIGH INSURANCE LEAGUE – FIRST DIVISION

BARNSLEY

Ground: Oakwell, Barnsley, South Yorkshire S71 1ET.
Telephone: 01226-211211. **Clubcall**: 0891 121152. **Club Nickname**: Tykes.
First-choice Colours: Red shirts; white shorts; red stockings.

Archdeacon, O ... 36(12)	Jackson, C .... 6(2)	Redfearn, N 45
Bishop, C .... 12(1)	Jones, S 4	Regis, D .... 4(8)
Bochenski, S .... –(2)	Kane, P 4	Sheridan, D .... 39(3)
Bullock, M .... 25(15)	Liddell, A 43	Shirtliff, P 31
Butler, L .... 1(2)	Molby, J 5	Shotton, M 2
Davis, S 27	Moses, A .... 21(4)	Ten Heuvel, L .... 1(2)
De Zeeuw, A 31	O'Connell, B .... 20(5)	Van der Velden, C . 6(1)
Eaden, N 46	Payton, A .... 37(3)	Viveash, A 2
Fleming, G .... 2(1)	Rammell, A .... 11(9)	Watson, D 45
Hurst, G .... –(5)		

League Goals (60): Payton 17, Redfearn 14, Liddell 9, Davis 5, Rammell 4, Archdeacon 3, Eaden 2, Bullock 1, De Zeeuw 1, Moses 1, O'Connell 1, Regis 1, Viveash 1.
Coca-Cola Cup Goals (4): Payton 3, Rammell 1. **F.A. Cup Goals (1)**: Redfearn 1.
'Player of Year' 1996: Arjan de Zeeuw.
Average Home League Attendance 1995-96: 8,086. **Capacity for 1996-97**: 19,007 (all-seated).
Record Attendance: 40,255 v Stoke City (F.A. Cup 5) 15 February 1936.

BIRMINGHAM CITY

Ground: St. Andrew's, Birmingham B9 4NH.
Telephone: 0121-772-0101. **Clubcall**: 0891 121188. **Club Nickname**: Blues.
First-choice Colours: Blue shirts; white shorts; blue stockings.

Barber, F 1	Castle, S .... 12(3)	Donowa, L .... 5(8)
Barnes, P .... 15(1)	Charlery, K .... 8(8)	Edwards, A .... 36(1)
Barnes, S .... –(2)	Claridge, S 28	Finnan, S .... 6(6)
Bass, J 5	Cooper, G .... 16(3)	Forsyth, R .... 12(14)
Bennett, I 24	Cornforth, J 8	Frain, J .... 22(1)
Bowen, J .... 16(7)	Daish, L .... 16(1)	Francis, K .... 11(8)
Breen, G .... 17(1)	Devlin, P 16	Grainger, M 8
Bull, G .... 3(3)	Doherty, N .... –(2)	Greimink, B 20

Hiley, S 5
Hill, D 5
Hunt, J .... 43(2)
Johnson, M .... 31(2)
Legg, A .... 9(3)
Lowe, K .... –(2)
Martin, J .... 1(5)
Muir, I 1

Otto, R .... 6(12)
Peschisolido, P ...... 7(2)
Poole, G .... 27(1)
Preece, D 6
Rea, S .... –(1)
Richardson, I .... 3(2)
Rushfeldt, S .... 3(4)

Sahlin, D .... –(1)
Samways, V 12
Sansome, P 1
Sheridan, J .... 1(1)
Tait, P .... 23(4)
Ward, M 13
Whyte, C 4

League Goals (61): Hunt 11, Claridge 8, Barnes (P.) 7, Devlin 7, Bowen 4, Charlery 4, Francis 3, Tait 3, Ward 3, Forsyth 2, Otto 2, Breen 1, Castle 1, Doherty 1, Edwards 1, Finnan 1, Legg 1, Peschisolido 1.
Coca-Cola Cup Goals (17): Francis 4, Bowen 2, Charlery 2, Daish 2, Hunt 2, Claridge 1, Cooper 1, Edwards 1, Rushfeldt 1, Opponent 1. **F.A. Cup Goals (2)**: Hunt 1, Poole 1. **Anglo-Italian Cup Goals (10)**: Bowen 2, Bull 1, Castle 1, Claridge 1, Edwards 1, Hunt 1, Poole 1, Opponents 2.
'Player of Year' 1996: Jon Hunt.
Average Home League Attendance 1995-96: 18,090. **Capacity for 1996-97**: 25,899 (all-seated).
Record Attendance: 66,844 v Everton (F.A. Cup 5) 11 February 1939.

CHARLTON ATHLETIC

Ground: The Valley, Floyd Road, Charlton, London SE7 8BL.
Telephone: 0181-293-4567. **Clubcall**: 0891 121146. **Club Nickname**: Robins.
First-choice Colours: Red shirts; white shorts; red stockings.

Allen, B 10
Ammann, M .... 10(1)
Balmer, S .... 30(3)
Bowyer, L 41
Brown, S .... 17(2)
Chandler, D .... –(1)
Chapple, P .... 13(3)
Garland, P 3
Grant, K .... 20(10)
Humphrey, J 28

Jackson, M 8
Jones, K .... 24(1)
Leaburn, C .... 38(2)
Linger, P .... 2(6)
Mortimer, P .... 13(5)
Nelson, G .... 12(18)
Newton, S .... 39(2)
Petterson, A 9
Robinson, J .... 42(1)

Robson, M .... 12(16)
Rufus, R .... 40(1)
Salmon, M 27
Stuart, J 27
Sturgess, P 13
Walsh, C .... 5(1)
Whyte, C .... 10(1)
Whyte, D .... 11(14)
Williams, P .... 2(7)

League Goals (57): Leaburn 9, Bowyer 8, Grant 7, Robinson 6, Mortimer 5, Newton 5, Allen 3, Nelson 3, Chapple 2, Stuart 2, Whyte (D.) 2, Balmer 1, Linger 1, Robson 1, Opponents 2.
Play-offs – Appearances: Allen 1(1), Balmer 2, Bowyer 2, Brown 2, Jackson 2, Leaburn 2, Nelson 1(1), Newton 2, Petterson 2, Robinson 2, Robson 1, Rufus 1, Stuart –(1), Whyte (C.) 2, Whyte (D.) –(2). **Goals (1)**: Newton 1. **Coca-Cola Cup Goals (11)**: Bowyer 5, Robinson 2, Garland 1, Grant 1, Leaburn 1, Newton 1. **F.A. Cup Goals (6)**: Grant 2, Bowyer 1, Mortimer 1, Robinson 1, Whyte (D.) 1.
'Player of Year' 1996: John Robinson.
Average Home League Attendance 1995-96: 11,185. **Capacity for 1996-97**: 14,986 (all-seated).
Record Attendance: 75,031 v Aston Villa (F.A. Cup 5) 12 February 1938.

CRYSTAL PALACE

Ground: Selhurst Park, London SE25 6PU.
Telephone: 0181-768-6000. **Clubcall**: 0891 400333. **Club Nickname**: Eagles.
First-choice Colours: Red and blue shirts; white shorts; white stockings.

Andersen, L .... 12(4)
Boere, J .... –(7)
Boxall, D 1
Brown, K .... 5(1)
Coleman, C 17
Cox, I .... 1(3)
Cundy, J 4
Davies, G .... 17(3)

Dowie, I 4
Dyer, B .... 21(14)
Edworthy, M 44
Freedman, D .... 37(2)
Gale, T 2
Gordon, D 34
Hopkin, D .... 41(1)
Houghton, R 41

Launders, B .... –(2)
McKenzie, L .... 4(8)
Martyn, N 46
Matthew, D .... 4(4)
Ndah, G .... 17(6)
Pitcher, D 36
Quinn, R 1
Roberts, A .... 36(2)

Rodger, S .... 14(10)	Sparrow, P 1	Vincent, J .... 19(4)
Scully, A .... –(2)	Taylor, G .... 18(2)	Veart, C .... 5(7)
Shaw, R 15	Tuttle, D .... 9(1)	

League Goals (67): Freedman 20, Dyer 13, Gordon 8, Hopkin 8, Houghton 4, Ndah 4, Brown 2, Davies 2, Dowie 2, Boere 1, Taylor 1, Tuttle 1, Opponent 1.
Play-offs – Appearances: Andersen 1, Brown 3, Dyer –(2), Edworthy 3, Freedman 3, Hopkin 1, Houghton 3, Martyn 3, Ndah 3, Pitcher 3, Quinn 2(1), Roberts 3, Rodger –(1), Tuttle 3, Veart 2(1). **Goals (4)**: Brown 1, Houghton 1, Roberts 1, Veart 1. **Coca-Cola Cup Goals (6)**: Hopkin 4, McKenzie 1, Vincent 1. **F.A. Cup Goals (3)**: Cox 1, Dyer 1, Taylor 1.
'Player of Year' 1996: Andy Roberts.
Average Home League Attendance 1995-96: 15,248. **Capacity for 1996-97**: 26,000 (all-seated).
Record Attendance: 51,482 v Burnley (Div. 2) 11 May 1979.

DERBY COUNTY

Ground: The Baseball Ground, Shaftesbury Crescent, Derby DE23 8NB.
Telephone: 01332-340105. **Clubcall**: 0891 121187. **Club Nickname**: Rams.
First-choice Colours: White shirts; black shorts; white stockings.

Boden, C 4	Nicholson, S .... 19(1)	Sutton, S 7
Carbon, M .... 2(4)	Powell, C 19	Trollope, P .... 7(10)
Carsley, L .... 31(4)	Powell, D 37	Van der Laan, R 39
Cooper, K .... –(1)	Preece, D .... 10(3)	Ward, A .... 5(2)
Flynn, S .... 29(13)	Rowett, G .... 34(1)	Wassall, D .... 16(1)
Gabbiadini, M ...... 33(6)	Simpson, P .... 21(18)	Webster, S 3
Harkes, J .... 7(1)	Stallard, M 3	Willems, R .... 31(2)
Hodges, G .... 1(8)	Stimac, I 27	Wrack, D .... 2(7)
Hoult, R .... 40(1)	Sturridge, D .... 33(6)	Yates, D 38
Kavanagh, J .... 8(1)		

League Goals (71): Sturridge 20, Gabbiadini 11, Willems 11, Simpson 10, Van der Laan 6, Powell (D.) 5, Flynn 2, Yates 2, Carsley 1, Preece 1, Stimac 1, Ward 1.
Coca-Cola Cup Goals (4): Gabbiadini 1, Simpson 1, Stallard 1, Willems 1. **F.A. Cup Goals (2)**: Gabbiadini 1, Simpson 1.
'Player of Year' 1996: Dean Yates.
Average Home League Attendance 1995-96: 14,327. **Capacity for 1996-97**: 18,000 (all-seated).
Record Attendance: 41,826 v Tottenham Hotspur (Div. 1) 20 September 1969.

GRIMSBY TOWN

Ground: Blundell Park, Cleethorpes, South Humberside DN35 7PY.
Telephone: 01472-697111. **Clubcall**: 0891 555855. **Club Nickname**: Mariners.
First-choice Colours: Black and white shirts; black shorts; white stockings.

Bonetti, I 19	Gambaro, E .... –(1)	Neil, J 1
Butler, P 3	Groves, P 46	Pearcey, J 2
Childs, G .... 33(2)	Handyside, P 30	Rodger, G .... 14(2)
Clare, D .... –(1)	Jewell, P .... 2(3)	Shakespeare, C ... 24(4)
Crichton, P 44	Jobling, K 3	Smith, R 18
Croft, G 36	Laws, B .... 21(6)	Southall, N .... 28(5)
Dobbin, J .... 21(5)	Lester, J .... –(5)	Walker, J .... 1(1)
Fickling, A .... 5(6)	Lever, M .... 23(1)	Warner, V 3
Flatts, M .... 4(1)	Livingstone, S ...... 33(5)	Watson, T .... –(2)
Forrester, J .... 23(5)	McDermott, J .... 27(1)	Woods, N .... 24(8)
Gallimore, A 10	Mendonca, C 8	

League Goals (55): Livingstone 11, Groves 10, Forrester 5, Mendonca 4, Bonetti 3, Childs 3, Dobbin 3, Woods 3, Shakespeare 2, Southall 2, Croft 1, Gallimore 1, Jewell 1, Laws 1, Lever 1, McDermott 1, Walker 1, Opponents 2.
Coca-Cola Cup Goals (2): Southall 1, Woods 1. **F.A. Cup Goals (12)**: Forrester 3, Livingstone 2, Woods 2, Bonetti 1, Childs 1, Groves 1, Laws 1, Southall 1.

'Player of Year' 1996: Paul Groves.
Average Home League Attendance 1995-96: 5,992. **Capacity for 1996-97**: 8,700 (all-seated).
Record Attendance: 31,651 v Wolves (F.A. Cup 5) 20 February 1937.

HUDDERSFIELD TOWN

Ground: Alfred McAlpine Stadium, Leeds Road, Huddersfield, West Yorkshire HD1 6PX.
Telephone: 01484-420335. **Clubcall**: 0891 121635. **Club Nickname**: Terriers.
First-choice Colours: Blue and white shirts; white shorts; white stockings.

Baldry, S .... 3(11)
Booth, A 43
Brown, K 5
Bullock, D 42
Collins, S .... 18(12)
Cowan, T 43
Crosby, G .... –(1)
Dalton, P 29
Dunn, I .... 3(11)
Duxbury, L 3
Dyson, J .... 15(2)
Edwards, R 13
Francis, S 43
Gray, K 38
Jenkins, S 31
Jepson, R .... 40(3)
Logan, R 2
Makel, L 33
Norman, T 3
Reid, P .... 8(5)
Rowe, R .... 6(8)
Scully, P 25
Sinnott, L 32
Thornley, B 12
Trevitt, S 4
Turner, A .... 2(3)
Ward, M .... 7(1)
Whitney, J .... 3(1)

League Goals (61): Booth 16, Jepson 12, Edwards 7, Bullock 6, Dalton 5, Collins 3, Cowan 2, Makel 2, Thornley 2, Jenkins 1, Rowe 1, Scully 1, Turner 1, Opponents 2.
Coca-Cola Cup Goals (6): Booth 3, Bullock 1, Collins 1, Dalton 1. **F.A. Cup Goals (7)**: Booth 2, Jepson 2, Bullock 1, Cowan 1, Rowe 1.
'Player of Year' 1996: Tom Cowan.
Average Home League Attendance 1995-96: 13,151. **Capacity for 1996-97**: 14,996 (seats 5,495, standing 9,501).
Record Attendance: 67,037 v Arsenal (F.A. Cup 6) 27 February 1932.

IPSWICH TOWN

Ground: Portman Road, Ipswich, Suffolk IP1 2DA.
Telephone: 01473-219211. **Clubcall**: 0839 664488. **Club Nickname**: Blues.
First-choice Colours: Blue shirts; white shorts; white stockings.

Appleby, R, ... –(3)
Barber, F 1
Chapman, L .... 2(4)
Forrest, C 21
Gregory, N .... 5(12)
Linighan, D 2
Marshall, I 35
Mason, P .... 24(2)
Mathie, A 39
Milton, S .... 34(3)
Mowbray, T 19
Palmer, S 5
Petterson, A 1
Scowcroft, J .... 13(10)
Sedgley, S 40
Slater, S .... 11(6)
Stockwell, M .... 33(4)
Swailes, C .... 4(1)
Tanner, A .... 3(7)
Taricco, M .... 36(3)
Thompson, N 6
Thomsen, C .... 35(1)
Uhlenbeek, G .... 37(3)
Vaughan, T .... 19(6)
Wark, J .... 13(1)
Williams, G 42
Wright, R 23
Yallop, F .... 3(4)

League Goals (79): Marshall 19, Mathie 18, Milton 9, Mason 7, Sedgley 4, Uhlenbeek 4, Gregory 2, Mowbray 2, Scowcroft 2, Slater 2, Thomsen 2, Wark 2, Stockwell 1, Thompson 1, Vaughan 1, Williams 1, Opponents 2.
Coca-Cola Cup Goals(2): Sedgley 1, Thomsen 1. **F.A. Cup Goals (3):** Mason 3.
Anglo-Italian Cup Goals (9): Mason 3, Gregory 2, Mathie 1, Mowbray 1, Sedgley 1, Tanner 1.
'Player of Year' 1996: Simon Milton.
Average Home League Attendance 1995-96: 12,604. **Capacity for 1996-97**: 22,600 (all-seated).
Record Attendance: 38,010 v Leeds United (F.A. Cup 6) 8 March 1975.

LEICESTER CITY

Ground: City Stadium, Filbert Street, Leicester LE2 7FL.
Telephone: 01162-555000. **Clubcall**: 0891 121185. **Club Nickname**: Foxes.
First-choice Colours: Blue shirts; white shorts; blue stockings.

Blake, M .... 6(2)
Carey, B .... 16(3)
Claridge, S 14
Corica, S 16
Gee, P .... 1(1)
Grayson, S .... 39(2)
Heskey, E .... 20(10)
Hill, C .... 24(3)
Izzet, M .... 8(1)
Joachim, J .... 14(8)

Kaamark, P 1
Kalac, Z 1
Lawrence, J .... 10(5)
Lennon, N .... 14(1)
Lewis, N .... 10(4)
Lowe, D .... 21(7)
McMahon, S .... 1(2)
Parker, G .... 36(4)
Philpott, L .... 1(5)
Poole, K 45

Roberts, I .... 34(3)
Robins, M .... 19(12)
Rolling, F 17
Smith, R 1
Taylor, S 39
Walsh, S 37
Watts, J 9
Whitlow, M .... 41(1)
Willis, J .... 11(1)

League Goals (66): Roberts 19, Heskey 7, Robins 6, Taylor 6, Claridge 5, Walsh 4, Lowe 3, Parker 3, Whitlow 3, Corica 2, Grayson 2, Carey 1, Izzet 1, Joachim 1, Lennon 1, Lewis 1, McMahon 1.
Play-offs – Appearances: Claridge 3, Grayson 3, Heskey 3, Hill –(1), Izzet 3, Kalac –(1), Lennon 3, Parker 2(1), Poole 3, Robins 1(1), Taylor 3, Walsh 3, Watts 3, Whitlow 3. **Goals (3)**: Parker 2, Claridge 1. **Coca-Cola Cup Goals (6)**: Robins 4, Joachim 1, Roberts 1.**F.A. Cup Goals:** None.
'Player of Year' 1996: Garry Parker.
Average Home League Attendance 1995-96: 16,530. **Capacity for 1996-97**: 22,526 (all-seated).
Record Attendance: 47,298 v Tottenham Hotspur (F.A. Cup 5) 18 February 1928.

LUTON TOWN

Ground: Kenilworth Stadium, 1 Maple Road, Luton, Bedfordshire LU4 8AW.
Telephone: 01582-411622. **Clubcall**: 0891 121123. **Club Nickname**: Hatters.
First-choice Colours: White shirts; blue shorts; blue and white stockings.

Alexander, G .... 35(2)
Chenery, B 2
Davis, K 6
Davis, S 36
Douglas, S .... 3(5)
Evers, S 1
Feuer, I 38
Grant, K 10
Guentchev, B ..... 25(10)
Harvey, R .... 28(8)
Hughes, C .... 21(2)

James, J .... 23(4)
Johnson, G .... 5(1)
Johnson, M .... 33(2)
Linton, D .... 6(4)
McLaren, P .... 9(3)
Marshall, D .... 23(3)
Oakes, S .... 26(3)
Oldfield, D .... 23(11)
Patterson, D .... 21(2)
Peake, T .... 15(3)

Riseth, V .... 6(5)
Sommer, J 2
Taylor, J .... 18(10)
Thomas, M .... 25(2)
Thorpe, T .... 23(10)
Tomlinson, G .... 1(6)
Vilstrup, J .... 6(1)
Waddock, G .... 32(4)
Wilkinson, P 3
Woodsford, J .... 1(2)

League Goals (40): Guentchev 9, Marshall 9, Thorpe 7, Grant 3, Oakes 3, Davis (S.) 2, Oldfield 2, Alexander 1, Douglas 1, Harvey 1, Hughes 1, McLaren 1.
Coca-Cola Cup Goals (2): Marshall 1, Johnson (M.) 1. **F.A. Cup Goals (1)**: Marshall 1.
'Player of Year' 1996: Ian Feuer.
Average Home League Attendance 1995-96: 7,223. **Capacity for 1996-97**: 9,970 (all-seated).
Record Attendance: 30,069 v Blackpool (F.A. Cup 6) 4 March 1959.

MILLWALL

Ground: The New Den, Zampa Road, London SE16 3LN.
Telephone: 0171-232-1222. **Clubcall**: 0891 400300. **Club Nickname**: Lions.
First-choice Colours: Blue shirts; white shorts; blue stockings.

Bennett, M .... 1(1)
Berry, G 1
Black, K .... 1(2)
Bowry, B .... 33(5)
Cadette, R .... –(1)
Carter, T 4
Connor, J .... 7(1)
Dixon, K .... 15(7)

Dolby, T .... 6(4)
Doyle, M .... 15(3)
Forbes, S .... –(4)
Fuchs, U .... 21(11)
Gordon, D 6
Keller, K 42
Kulkov, V 6
Lavin, G .... 18(2)

McRobert, L .... 1(6)
Malkin, C .... 39(4)
Neill, L .... 5(8)
Newman, R .... 34(2)
Rae, A 37
Rogan, A .... 4(4)
Savage, D .... 17(10)
Stevens, K 39

Taylor, S .... 12(10)	Webber, D .... 8(8)	Witter, T .... 30(1)
Thatcher, B .... 41(1)	Weir, M 8	Yuran, S 13
Van Blerk, J 42		

League Goals (43): Rae 13, Malkin 11, Dixon 5, Fuchs 5, Bowry 2, Stevens 2, Black 1, Newman 1, Van Blerk 1, Witter 1, Yuran 1.
Coca-Cola Cup Goals (4): Taylor 2, Rae 1, Savage 1. **F.A. Cup Goals (3)**: Rae 2, Malkin 1.
'Player of Year' 1996: Ben Thatcher.
Average Home League Attendance 1995-96: 9,571. **Capacity for 1996-97**: 20,146 (all-seated).
Record Attendance (at previous ground, The Den): 48,672 v Derby County (F.A. Cup 5) 20 February 1937.

NORWICH CITY

Ground: Carrow Road, Norwich, Norfolk NR1 1JE.
Telephone: 01603-760760. **Clubcall**: 0891 101500. **Club Nickname**: Canaries.
First-choice Colours: Yellow shirts; green shorts; yellow stockings.

Adams, N .... 40(2)	Gunn, B 43	Prior, S .... 42(2)
Akinbiyi, A .... 13(9)	Johnson, A .... 23(3)	Rush, M .... –(1)
Bowen, M .... 30(1)	Marshall, A 3	Scott, K .... 5(7)
Bradshaw, C .... 18(3)	Milligan, M .... 21(7)	Sheron, M .... 2(5)
Carey, S .... 6(3)	Mills, D .... 8(6)	Simpson, K 1
Crook, I .... 27(1)	Molby, J 3	Sutch, D .... 7(6)
Cureton, J .... 4(8)	Newman, R .... 15(8)	Ullathorne, R .... 26(3)
Eadie, D .... 29(2)	Newsome, J .... 26(1)	Ward, A 28
Fleck, R .... 37(4)	O'Neill, K .... 12(7)	Wright, J 1
Goss, J .... 9(7)	Polston, J .... 27(3)	

League Goals (59): Fleck 10, Ward 10, Johnson 7, Eadie 6, Newsome 4, Akinbiyi 3, Adams 2, Bowen 2, Crook 2, Cureton 2, Milligan 2, Scott 2, Bradshaw 1, Goss 1, Newman 1, O'Neill 1, Prior 1, Sheron 1, Opponent 1.
Coca-Cola Cup Goals (16): Ward 3, Akinbiyi 2, Fleck 2, Sheron 2, Crook 1, Eadie 1, Johnson 1, Mills 1, Molby 1, Ullathorne 1, Opponent 1. **F.A. Cup Goals (1)**: Newsome 1.
'Player of Year' 1996: Spencer Prior.
Average Home League Attendance 1995-96: 14,581. **Capacity for 1996-97**: 21,994 (all-seated).
Record Attendance: 43,984 v Leicester City (F.A. Cup 6) 30 March 1963.

OLDHAM ATHLETIC

Ground: Boundary Park, Oldham, Lancashire OL1 2PA.
Telephone: 0161-624-4972. **Clubcall**: 0891 121142. **Club Nickname**: Latics.
First-choice Colours: Red and blue shirts; white shorts; red stockings.

Banger, N .... 8(5)	Halle, G 37	Orlygsson, T .... 15(1)
Barlow, S .... 21(5)	Hallworth, J .... 10(1)	Pemberton, M .... –(2)
Beckford, D .... 12(8)	Henry, N 14	Pointon, N .... 3(1)
Beresford, D .... 8(20)	Hughes, A .... 10(5)	Redmond, S .... 37(3)
Bernard, P 7	Jobson, R 12	Richardson, L 27
Brennan, M .... 23(2)	Lonergan, D .... 1(1)	Rickers, P 23
Creaney, G .... 8(1)	McCarthy, S .... 30(5)	Serrant, C 20
Fleming, C .... 21(1)	McNivern, S .... 14(1)	Snodin, I .... 24(2)
Gannon, J 5	Makin, C 39	Vonk, M 5
Gerrard, P 36	Olney, I 1	Wilkinson, P 4
Graham, R .... 31(1)		

League Goals (54): Richardson 11, McCarthy 10, Barlow 7, Brennan 3, Halle 3, Banger 2, Beckford 2, Beresford 2, Creaney 2, Makin 2, Bernard 1, Graham 1, Hughes 1, Redmond 1, Serrant 1, Vonk 1, Wilkinson 1, Opponents 3.
Coca-Cola Cup Goals (1): Halle 1. **F.A. Cup Goals (2)**: Beckford 2. **Anglo-Italian Cup Goals (2)**: McCarthy 1, Wilkinson 1.

'Player of Year' 1996: Lee Richardson.
Average Home League Attendance 1995-96: 6,634. **Capacity for 1996-97**: 13,700 (all-seated).
Record Attendance: 47,671 v Sheffield Wednesday (F.A. Cup 4) 25 January 1930.

PORTSMOUTH

Ground: Fratton Park, Frogmore Road, Portsmouth, Hampshire PO4 8RA.
Telephone: 01705-731204. **Clubcall**: 0891 121182. **Club Nickname**: Pompey.
First-choice Colours: Blue shirts; white shorts; red stockings.

Allen, M 27	Griffiths, C .... 2(12)	Rees, J .... 15(6)
Awford, A .... 17(1)	Hall, P .... 44(2)	Russell, L .... 17(2)
Bradbury, L .... 3(9)	Hinshelwood, D 5	Simpson, F .... 27(3)
Burton, D .... 24(8)	Igoe, S .... 4(18)	Stimson, M 14
Butters, G 37	Knight, A 42	Symons, K 1
Carter, J .... 31(4)	McLoughlin, A ...... 38(2)	Thomson, A .... 15(1)
Creaney, G 3	Perrett, R .... 8(1)	Walsh, P 21
Dobson, A .... 7(2)	Pethick, R .... 30(8)	Whitbread, A 13
Durnin, J .... 30(11)	Poom, M 4	Wood, P .... 13(2)
Gittens, J .... 14(1)		

League Goals (61): Hall 10, McLoughlin 10, Burton 7, Simpson 5, Walsh 5, Allen 4, Carter 4, Creaney 3, Durnin 3, Butters 2, Griffiths 2, Awford 1, Gittens 1, Rees 1, Stimson 1, Wood 1, Opponent 1.
Coca-Cola Cup Goals: None. **F.A. Cup Goals**: None.
'Player of Year' 1996: Alan Knight.
Average Home League Attendance 1995-96: 9,406. **Capacity for 1996-97**: 11,000 (all-seated).
Record Attendance: 51,385 v Derby County (F.A. Cup 6) 26 February 1949.

PORT VALE

Ground: Vale Park, Burslem, Stoke-on-Trent, Staffordshire ST6 1AW.
Telephone: 01782-814134. **Clubcall**: 0891 121636. **Club Nickname**: Valiants.
First-choice Colours: White shirts; black shorts; black stockings.

Aspin, N 22	Hill, A 35	Samuel, R 9
Bogie, I .... 27(5)	Kent, K .... –(1)	Sandeman, B 1
Corden, W 2	Lawton, C 2	Stokes, D .... 16(2)
Foyle, M .... 24(1)	McCarthy, J .... 44(1)	Talbot, S .... 8(12)
Glover, D .... 27(2)	Mills, L .... 20(12)	Tankard, A .... 28(1)
Glover, L .... 17(7)	Musselwhite, P 39	Van Heusden, A 7
Griffiths, G .... 40(1)	Naylor, T .... 30(9)	Walker, R .... 21(14)
Guppy, S .... 43(1)	Porter, A .... 44(1)	

League Goals (59): Naylor 11, Porter 10, McCarthy 8, Mills 8, Foyle 7, Guppy 4, Bogie 3, Glover (L.) 3, Griffiths 2, Aspin 1, Samuel 1, Opponent 1.
Coca-Cola Cup Goals (3): Glover (D.) 1, Glover (L.) 1, Mills 1. **F.A. Cup Goals (9)**: Bogie 2, Foyle 2, Walker 2, McCarthy 1, Naylor 1, Porter 1. **Anglo-Italian Cup Goals (18)**: Foyle 4, Mills 4, Naylor 3, Glover (L.) 2, McCarthy 2, Guppy 1, Porter 1, Talbot 1.
'Player of Year' 1996: Jon McCarthy.
Average Home League Attendance 1995-96: 8,227. **Capacity for 1996-97**: 22,356 (seats 17,616, standing 4,740).
Record Attendance: 50,000 v Aston Villa (F.A. Cup 5) 20 February 1960.

READING

Ground: Elm Park, Norfolk Road, Reading, Berkshire RG3 2EF.
Telephone: 01189-507878. **Clubcall**: 0891 121000. **Club Nickname**: Royals.
First-choice Colours: Blue and white shirts; white shorts; white stockings.

Bernal, A 34	Brown, K 12	Codner, R .... 3(1)
Booty, M 17	Caskey, D 15	Freeman, A .... –(1)

Gilkes, M .... 36(8)
Gooding, M .... 37(3)
Gordon, N .... –(1)
Hammond, N 5
Hoslgrove, P .... 27(3)
Hopkins, J 14
Jones, T .... 13(8)
Kerr, D .... 4(4)
Lambert, J .... 10(5)
Lovell, S .... 28(7)
McPherson, K 16
Meaker, M .... 15(6)
Mihaylov, B 16
Morley, T .... 14(3)
Nogan, L .... 32(7)
Parkinson, P .... 36(6)
Quinn, J .... 20(15)
Sheppard, S 18
Sutton, S 2
Swales, S .... 4(5)
Thorp, M 2
Wdowczyk, D .... 29(1)
Williams, A 31
Williams, M .... 11(3)
Wood, C 5

League Goals (54): Quinn 11, Nogan 10, Lovell 7, Lambert 4, Morley 4, Gooding 3, Williams (A.) 3, Bernal 2, Caskey 2, Kerr 2, Booty 1, Brown 1, Holsgrove 1, Williams (M.) 1, Opponents 2.
Coca-Cola Cup Goals (10): Quinn 4, Lovell 2, Lambert 1, Morley 1, Nogan 1, Opponent 1. **F.A. Cup Goals (3)**: Quinn 2, Morley 1.
'Player of Year' 1996: Mick Gooding.
Average Home League Attendance 1995-96: 8,918. **Capacity for 1996-97**: 15,000 (seats 2,242, standing 12,758).
Record Attendance: 33,042 v Brentford (F.A. Cup 5) 17 February 1927.

SHEFFIELD UNITED

Ground: Bramall Lane, Sheffield, South Yorkshire S2 4SU.
Telephone: 0114-273-8955. **Clubcall**: 0891 888650. **Club Nickname**: Blades.
First-choice Colours: Red and white shirts; black shorts; black stockings.

Ablett, G 12
Angell, B 6
Battersby, T .... 3(7)
Beard, M .... 13(7)
Blake, N .... 20(2)
Blount, M .... 7(1)
Cowans, G .... 18(2)
Davidson, R 1
Fitzgerald, S 6
Flo, J .... 17(2)
Foran, M .... 6(1)
Gage, K 2
Gannon, J 12
Gayle, B .... 3(2)
Hawes, S 1
Heath, A .... –(4)
Hodges, G .... 15(7)
Hodgson, D .... 12(4)
Holland, P .... 11(7)
Hutchison, D .... 18(1)
Kelly, A .... 34(1)
Mercer, W 1
Muggleton, C .... –(1)
Nilsen, R 39
Patterson, M 21
Reed, J .... –(2)
Rogers, P .... 13(3)
Scott, A .... 3(4)
Scott, R .... 2(3)
Short, C .... 13(2)
Starbuck, P .... 5(6)
Taylor, G 10
Tracey, S 11
Tuttle, D 26
Veart, C .... 17(10)
Vonk, M 17
Walker, A .... 12(2)
Ward, M .... 39(3)
White, D .... 24(4)
Whitehouse, D ..... 36(2)

League Goals (57): Blake 11, Walker 8, White 7, Veart 5, Flo 4, Hodges 4, Whitehouse 4, Angell 2, Hutchison 2, Patterson 2, Taylor 2, Battersby 1, Holland 1, Scott (R.) 1, Starbuck 1, Tuttle 1, Ward 1.
Coca-Cola Cup Goals (4): Flo 1, Holland 1, Veart 1, Whitehouse 1. **F.A. Cup Goals (2)**: Veart 1, Whitehouse 1.
'Player of Year' 1996: Alan Kelly.
Average Home League Attendance 1995-96: 12,901. **Capacity for 1996-97**: 23,459 (all-seated).
Record Attendance: 68,287 v Leeds United (F.A. Cup 5) 15 February 1936.

SOUTHEND UNITED

Ground: Roots Hall, Victoria Avenue, Southend-on-Sea, Essex SS2 6NQ.
Telephone: 01702-304050. **Clubcall**: 0839 664444. **Club Nickname**: Shrimpers. **First-choice Colours**: Blue shirts; blue shorts; blue stockings.

Ansah, A .... –(4)
Barness, A 5
Belsvik, P 3
Bodley, M .... 38(1)
Boere, J 6
Brown, K 6
Byrne, P .... 38(3)
Charlery, K .... 2(1)
Dublin, K .... 42(1)
Gridelet, P .... 37(3)
Hails, J .... 39(3)
Hone, M .... 11(5)
Iorfa, D .... 1(1)
Jones, G .... 14(9)
Lapper, M .... 23(1)
McNally, M 20
Marsh, M 40
Powell, C 27
Rammell, A .... 6(1)
Read, P .... 3(1)
Regis, D .... 25(4)
Roget, L .... 4(4)
Royce, S 46
Stimson, M 10

Sussex, A .... 1(1)	Tilson, S .... 23(5)	Whelan, R 1
Thomson, A .... 22(11)	Turner, A .... 4(2)	Willis, R .... 9(1)

League Goals (52): Regis 8, Thomson 6, Byrne 5, Marsh 5, Hails 4, Dublin 3, Tilson 3, Willis 3, Boere 2, Gridelet 2, Jones 2, McNally 2, Rammell 2, Belsvik 1, Bodley 1, Read 1, Roget 1, Opponent 1.
Coca-Cola Cup Goals (2): Byrne 1, Jones 1. **F.A. Cup Goals**: None. **Anglo-Italian Cup Goals (3)**: Marsh 1, Regis 1, Tilson 1.
'Player of Year' 1996: Simon Royce.
Average Home League Attendance 1995-96: 5,898. **Capacity for 1996-97**: 12,485 (all-seated).
Record Attendance: 31,033 v Liverpool (F.A. Cup 3) 10 January 1979.

STOKE CITY

Ground: Victoria Ground, Stoke-on-Trent ST4 4EG.
Telephone: 01782-413511. **Clubcall**: 0891 121040. **Club Nickname**: Potters.
First-choice Colours: Red and white shirts; white shorts; white stockings.

Beeston, C .... 13(3)	Gleghorn, N 46	Sandford, L 46
Brightwell, D .... –(1)	Keen, K .... 27(6)	Scott, K .... 6(1)
Carruthers, M ..... 10(14)	Muggleton, C 6	Sheron, M .... 23(5)
Clarkson, I 43	Orlygsson, T .... 6(1)	Sigurdsson, L 46
Cranson, I .... 23(1)	Overson, V 18	Sinclair, R 1
Devlin, M .... 5(5)	Peschisolido, P .... 20(6)	Sturridge, S .... 30(10)
Dreyer, J .... 4(15)	Potter, G .... 38(3)	Wallace, R 44
Gayle, J .... 5(5)	Prudhoe, M 39	Whittle, J .... 7(1)

League Goals (60): Sheron 15, Sturridge 13, Gleghorn 9, Peschisolido 6, Wallace 6, Carruthers 3, Gayle 3, Keen 3, Cranson 1, Potter 1.
Play-offs – Appearances: Carruthers –(1), Clarkson 2, Devlin 2, Gleghorn 2, Potter 2, Prudhoe 2, Sandford 2, Sheron 2, Sigurdsson 2, Sturridge 2, Wallace 2, Whittle 2. **Goals**: None. **Coca-Cola Cup Goals (1)**: Peschisolido 1. **F.A. Cup Goals (1)**: Sturridge 1. **Anglo-Italian Cup Goals (4)**: Peschisolido 2, Dreyer 1, Wallace 1.
'Player of Year' 1996: Ray Wallace.
Average Home League Attendance 1995-96: 12,275. **Capacity for 1996-97**: 24,054 (seats 8,979, standing 15,075).
Record Attendance: 51,380 v Arsenal (Div. 1) 29 March 1937.

SUNDERLAND

Ground: Roker Park, Grantham Road, Sunderland, Tyne & Wear SR6 9SW.
Telephone: 0191-514-0332. **Clubcall**: 0891 121140. **Club Nickname**: Roker-ites. **First-choice Colours**: Red and white shirts; black shorts; red stockings.

Agnew, S .... 26(3)	Cooke, T 6	Kubicki, D 46
Aiston, S .... 4(10)	Given, S 17	Melville, A 40
Angell, B 2	Gray, Martin .... 4(3)	Mullin, J .... 5(5)
Armstrong, G .... –(1)	Gray, Michael 45	Ord, R .... 41(1)
Atkinson, B .... 5(2)	Gray, P .... 29(4)	Russell, C .... 35(6)
Ball, K .... 35(1)	Hall, G .... 8(6)	Scott, M 43
Bracewell, P 38	Howey, L .... 17(9)	Smith, M .... 9(11)
Bridges, M .... 2(13)	Kelly, D .... 9(1)	Stewart, P .... 11(1)
Chamberlain, A 29		

League Goals (59): Russell 13, Gray (P.) 9, Scott 6, Agnew 5, Ball 4, Bridges 4, Melville 4, Gray (Michael) 3, Howey 3, Kelly 2, Smith 2, Mullin 1, Ord 1, Stewart 1, Opponent 1.
Coca-Cola Cup Goals (4): Howey 2, Angell 1, Opponent 1. **F.A. Cup Goals (3)**: Agnew 1, Gray (P.) 1, Russell 1
'Player of Year' 1996: Richard Ord.
Average Home League Attendance 1995-96: 17,482. **Capacity for 1996-97**: 22,657 (seats 7,000, standing 15,657).
Record Attendance: 75,118 v Derby County (F.A. Cup 6) 8 March 1933.

TRANMERE ROVERS

Ground: Prenton Park, Prenton Road West, Birkenhead, Merseyside L42 9PN.
Telephone: 0151-608-4194. **Clubcall**: 0891 121646. **Club Nickname**: Rovers.
First-choice Colours: White shirts; white shorts; white stockings.

Aldridge, J 45	Irons, K .... 25(7)	Mungall, S .... 2(4)
Bennett, G .... 26(3)	Jones, G .... 17(6)	Nevin, P .... 39(1)
Branch, G .... 11(10)	Kenworthy, J .... –(4)	O'Brien, L .... 18(4)
Brannan, G 44	McGreal, J 32	Rogers, D .... 25(1)
Cook, P 15	Mahon, A .... –(2)	Stevens, G .... 33(1)
Coyne, D 46	Moore, I .... 27(9)	Teale, S 29
Garnett, S .... 17(1)	Morgan, A .... –(4)	Thomas, T 31
Higgins, D .... 16(1)	Morrissey, J .... 8(8)	

League Goals (64): Aldridge 27, Bennett 9, Moore 9, O'Brien 4, Irons 3, Nevin 3, Branch 2, Rogers 2, Cook 1, Jones 1, Morgan 1, Opponents 2.
Coca-Cola Cup Goals (6): Aldridge 2, Jones 2, Brannan 1, Moore 1. **F.A. Cup Goals**: None.
'Player of Year' 1996: Danny Coyne.
Average Home League Attendance 1995-96: 7,861. **Capacity for 1996-97**: 16,789 (all-seated).
Record Attendance: 24,424 v Stoke City (F.A. Cup 4) 5 February 1972.

WATFORD

Ground: Vicarage Road, Watford, Hertfordshire WD1 8ER.
Telephone: 01923-496000. **Clubcall**: 0891 104104. **Club Nickname**: Hornets.
First-choice Colours: Yellow shirts; black shorts; black stockings.

Andrews, W .... –(1)	Hodge, S 2	Palmer, S 35
Barnes, D 10	Holdsworth, D ...... 26(1)	Payne, D .... 9(3)
Bazeley, D .... 35(6)	Johnson, R .... 17(3)	Penrice, G .... 4(3)
Beadle, P 3	Lavin, G 16	Phillips, K .... 26(1)
Caskey, D 6	Ludden, D .... 9(3)	Pitcher, G .... 2(6)
Cherry, S 4	Millen, K .... 32(1)	Porter, G .... 28(1)
Connolly, D .... 7(4)	Miller, K 42	Ramage, C .... 34(2)
Dixon, K .... 8(3)	Mooney, T .... 38(4)	Simpson, C .... –(1)
Foster, C 26	Moralee, J .... 17(8)	Ward, D 1
Gibbs, N .... 8(1)	Neill, W 1	White, D .... 9(7)
Hessenthaler, A 30	Page, R .... 16(3)	Wilkinson, P 4
Hill, D 1		

League Goals (62): Ramage 15, Phillips 11, Connolly 8, Mooney 6, Foster 4, White 4, Moralee 3, Bazeley 1, Caskey 1, Holdsworth 1, Johnson 1, Millen 1, Palmer 1, Payne 1, Penrice 1, Pitcher 1, Porter 1, Opponent 1.
Coca-Cola Cup Goals (3): Bazeley 1, Johnson 1, Phillips 1. **F.A. Cup Goals (1)**: Mooney 1.
'Player of Year' 1996: Tommy Mooney.
Average Home League Attendance 1995-96: 9,457. **Capacity for 1996-97**: 22,000 (all-seated).
Record Attendance: 34,099 v Manchester United (F.A. Cup 4) 3 February 1969.

WEST BROMWICH ALBION

Ground: The Hawthorns, Halfords Lane, West Bromwich, West Midlands B71 4LF.
Telephone: 0121-525-8888. **Clubcall**: 0891 121193. **Club Nickname**: Baggies.
First-choice Colours: Blue and white shirts; white shorts; white stockings.

Agnew, P 3	Coldicott, S .... 21(12)	Fettis, A 3
Angell, B .... –(3)	Comyn, A 3	Gilbert, D .... 35(5)
Ashcroft, L .... 11(15)	Cunnington, S .... 8(1)	Hamilton, I .... 39(2)
Brien, A 2	Darby, J .... 19(2)	Hargreaves, C .... –(1)
Burgess, D 45	Donovan, K .... 28(6)	Holmes, P 18
Butler, P 9	Edwards, P .... 14(3)	Hunt, A .... 44(1)

King, P 4	Phelan, M 1	Smith, D .... 8(7)
Mardon, P .... 35(4)	Raven, P 40	Sneekes, R 13
Naylor, S 27	Reece, P 1	Spink, N 15
Nicholson, S 18	Rees, A .... 3(6)	Taylor, R .... 39(3)

League Goals (60): Taylor 17, Hunt 14, Sneekes 10, Gilbert 5, Ashcroft 4, Raven 4, Hamilton 3, Burgess 2, Darby 1.
Coca-Cola Cup Goals (8): Taylor 3, Burgess 2, Donovan 2, Hunt 1. **F.A. Cup Goals (3)**: Coldicott 1, Hunt 1, Raven 1. **Anglo-Italian Cup Goals (7)**: Taylor 3, Herbert 1, Hunt 1, Raven 1, Rees 1.
'Player of Year' 1996: Andy Hunt.
Average Home League Attendance 1995-96: 15,061. **Capacity for 1996-97**: 25,386 (all-seated).
Record Attendance: 64,815 v Arsenal (F.A. Cup 6) 6 March 1937.

WOLVERHAMPTON WANDERERS

Ground: Molineux, Waterloo Road, Wolverhampton, West Midlands WV1 4QR.
Telephone: 01902-655000. **Clubcall**: 0891 121103. **Club Nickname**: Wolves.
First-choice Colours: Gold shirts; black shorts; gold stockings.

Atkins, M .... 26(6)	Froggatt, S .... 13(5)	Samways, V 3
Birch, P .... 5(2)	Goodman, D .... 43(1)	Shirtliff, P 2
Bull, S .... 42(2)	Jones, P 8	Smith, J .... 10(3)
Corica, S 17	Kelly, D .... 3(2)	Stowell, M 38
Cowans, G .... 10(6)	Law, B .... 5(2)	Thomas, G .... –(2)
Crowe, G .... 1(1)	Masters, N 3	Thompson, A 45
Daley, T .... 16(2)	Osborn, S 21	Venus, M .... 19(3)
De Wolf, J .... 14(1)	Pearce, D .... 3(2)	Williams, M .... 5(7)
Emblen, N .... 30(3)	Rankine, M .... 27(5)	Wright, J .... 4(3)
Ferguson, D .... 26(7)	Richards, D .... 36(1)	Young, E 30
Foley, D .... 1(4)		

League Goals (56): Goodman 16, Bull 15, Thompson 6, Daley 3, Atkins 2, Emblen 2, Osborn 2, Young 2, Crowe 1, De Wolf 1, Ferguson 1, Froggatt 1, Law 1, Richards 1, Williams 1, Opponent 1.
Coca-Cola Cup Goals (11): Goodman 3, Atkins 2, Daley 1, Emblen 1, Ferguson 1, Venus 1, Williams 1, Wright 1. **F.A. Cup Goals (4)**: Bull 2, Ferguson 1, Goodman 1.
'Player of Year' 1996: Steve Bull.
Average Home League Attendance 1995-96: 24,786. **Capacity for 1996-97**: 28,500 (all-seated).
Record Attendance: 61,315 v Liverpool (F.A. Cup 5) 11 February 1939.

SECOND DIVISION

BLACKPOOL

Ground: Bloomfield Road, Blackpool, Lancashire FY1 1BA.
Telephone: 01253-404331. **Clubcall**: 0891 121648. **Club Nickname**: Seasiders. **First-choice Colours**: Tangerine shirts; tangerine shorts; tangerine stockings.

Allardyce, C .... –(1)	Brown, R .... 2(1)	Linighan, D 29
Banks, S 24	Bryan, M .... 44(2)	Lydiate, J .... 30(2)
Barber, F 1	Capleton, M 1	Mellon, M 45
Barlow, A 34	Charnock, P .... –(4)	Morrison, A 29
Beech, C .... 3(15)	Darton, S .... 5(4)	Nixon, F 20
Bonner, M .... 41(1)	Ellis, T .... 41(2)	Pascoe, C .... –(1)
Bradshaw, D 25	Gouck, A .... 8(8)	Philpott, L .... 4(6)
Brown, P .... 5(8)	Holden, R .... 19(3)	Preece, A .... 37(4)

Quinn, J .... 42(2) Watson, A .... 14(13) Yallop, F 3
Thorpe, L .... –(1)

League Goals (67): Ellis 14, Preece 14, Quinn 9, Mellon 6, Watson 6, Linighan 4, Bonner 3, Morrison 3, Holden 2, Barlow 1, Bryan 1, Gouck 1, Lydiate 1, Opponents 2.
Play-offs – Appearances: Bonner 2, Bradshaw 2, Brown –(1), Bryan 2, Ellis 2, Gouck 2, Linighan 2, Mellon 2, Morrison 2, Nixon 2, Philpott –(1), Preece 2, Quinn –(2), Watson 2. **Goals (2)**: Bonner 1, Ellis 1. **Coca-Cola Cup Goals (3)**: Ellis 2, Mellon 1. **F.A. Cup Goals (5)**: Quinn 3, Lydiate 1, Preece 1. **Auto Windscreens Shield Goals (5)**: Beech 2, Quinn 2, Mellon 1.
'Player of Year' 1996: Micky Mellon.
Average Home League Attendance 1995-96: 5,818. **Capacity for 1996-97**: 9,701 (seats 2,987, standing 6,714).
Record Attendance: 38,098 v Wolves (Div. 1) 17 September 1955.

A.F.C. BOURNEMOUTH

Ground: Dean Court, Bournemouth, Dorset BH7 7AF.
Telephone: 01202-395381. **Clubcall**: 0891 121163. **Club Nickname**: Cherries.
First-choice Colours: Red and black shirts; white shorts; white stockings.

Andrews, I 26
Bailey, J .... 36(7)
Beardsmore, R 44
Brissett, J 43
Casper, C 16
Coll, O 8
Cox, I 8
Cureton, J .... –(5)
Dean, M .... 4(1)
Duberry, M 7
Fletcher, S .... 4(4)
Glass, J 13
Holland, M 43
Howe, E .... 4(1)
Jones, S 44
McElhatton, M .... 2(2)
Mean, S .... 13(1)
Mitchell, P .... 2(2)
Morris, M .... 28(3)
Moss, N 7
Murray, R .... 30(5)
Ndah, G 12
Oldbury, M .... 2(10)
O'Neill, J .... 2(4)
Pennock, A .... 16(1)
Rawlinson, M .... 3(16)
Robinson, S .... 35(5)
Santos, A .... –(3)
Scott, K 8
Strong, S .... –(1)
Town, D .... 1(6)
Victory, J .... 5(11)
Young, N .... 40(1)

League Goals (51): Jones 18, Holland 10, Robinson 7, Bailey 4, Brissett 3, Ndah 2, Casper 1, Fletcher 1, Mean 1, Morris 1, Murray 1, Scott 1, Victory 1.
Coca-Cola Cup Goals (5): Jones 3, Morris 1, Oldbury 1. **F.A. Cup Goals (1)**: Robinson 1. **Auto Windscreens Shield Goals (3)**: Brissett 2, Robinson 1.
'Player of Year' 1996: Matthew Holland.
Average Home League Attendance 1995-96: 4,213. **Capacity for 1996-97**: 11,000 (seats 3,080, standing 7,920).
Record Attendance: 28,779 v Manchester United (F.A. Cup 6) 2 March 1957.

BRADFORD CITY

Ground: The Pulse Stadium, Valley Parade, Bradford, West Yorkshire BD8 7DY.
Telephone: 01274-773355. **Clubcall**: 0891 888640. **Club Nickname**: Bantams.
First-choice Colours: Claret and amber shirts; black shorts; claret stockings.

Brightwell, D .... 21(1)
Bullimore, W .... 1(1)
Duxbury, L 30
Foley, S .... –(1)
Ford, J .... 18(1)
Gould, J 9
Grayston, N 2
Hamilton, D .... 18(6)
Harper, S 1
Huxford, R .... 21(5)
Jacobs, W 28
Jewell, P .... 7(10)
Kernaghan, A 5
Kiwomya, A .... 7(9)
Liburd, R 33
Midgley, C .... –(5)
Mitchell, G .... 32(1)
Mohan, N 39
Murray, S .... 25(9)
Ormondroyd, I ...... 28(9)
Robson, G .... 4(2)
Showler, P .... 29(4)
Shutt, C .... 22(12)
Stallard, M .... 20(1)
Tolson, N .... 12(19)
Ward, G 36
Wright, T .... 28(6)
Youds, E 30

League Goals (71): Stallard 9, Showler 8, Shutt 8, Tolson 8, Ormondroyd 6, Duxbury 4, Mohan 4, Wright 4, Youds 4, Hamilton 3, Jewell 3, Kiwomya 2, Murray 2, Huxford 1, Liburd 1, Midgley 1, Mitchell 1, Opponents 2.
Play-offs – Appearances: Brightwell 2, Duxbury 3, Gould 3, Hamilton 3, Huxford

2(1), Jacobs 3, Kiwomya 2(1), Liburd 1, Mitchell 2, Mohan 3, Ormondroyd 1(1), Shutt 3, Stallard 3, Tolson –(1), Wright –(1), Youds 2. **Goals (5)**: Hamilton 2, Stallard 2, Shutt 1. **Coca-Cola Cup Goals (13)**: Showler 4, Ormondroyd 3, Wright 2, Youds 2, Hamilton 1, Tolson 1. **F.A. Cup Goals (6)**: Jacobs 2, Showler 2, Ormondroyd 1, Robson 1. **Auto Windscreens Shield Goals (2)**: Murray 1, Tolson 1.
'Player of Year' 1996: Carl Shutt.
Average Home League Attendance 1995-96: 5,708 **Capacity for 1996-97**: 18,000 (seats 10,521, standing 7,479).
Record Attendance: 39,146 v Burnley (F.A. Cup 4) 11 March 1911.

BRENTFORD

Ground: Griffin Park, Braemar Road, Brentford, Middlesex TW8 0NT.
Telephone: 0181-847-2511. **Clubcall**: 0891 121108. **Club Nickname**: Bees.
First-choice Colours: Red and white shirts; black shorts; black stockings.

Abrahams, P	14(3)	Dearden, K	41	McGhee, D	31(5)
Anderson, I	25	Fernandes, T	5	Martin, D	14(5)
Annon, D	–(1)	Forster, N	37(1)	Mundee, D	5(1)
Ansah, A	6	Grainger, M	33	Omigie, J	3(8)
Asaba, C	5(5)	Greene, D	11	Ravenscroft, C	1
Ashby, B	31(2)	Harvey, L	38(2)	Smith, P	46
Bates, J	36	Hooker, J	4	Statham, B	17
Bent, M	8(4)	Hurdle, G	11(3)	Sussex, A	3
Canham, S	14	Hutchings, C	20(3)	Taylor, R	42
Davis, P	5				

League Goals (43): Taylor 11, Forster 5, McGhee 5, Bates 4, Smith 4, Abrahams 3, Grainger 3, Anderson 2, Asaba 2, Ansah 1, Ashby 1, Bent 1, Martin 1.
Coca-Cola Cup Goals (7): Forster 2, Anderson 1, Grainger 1, Harvey 1, McGhee 1, Taylor 1. **F.A. Cup Goals (10)**: Bent 3, Taylor 3, Smith 2, Ashby 1, Opponent 1.
Auto Windscreens Shield Goals (2): Forster 1, Taylor 1.
'Player of Year' 1996: Robert Taylor.
Average Home League Attendance 1995-96: 4,768. **Capacity for 1996-97**: 13,870 (seats 3,905, standing 9,965).
Record Attendance: 39,626 v Preston N.E. (F.A. Cup 6) 5 March 1938.

BRIGHTON & HOVE ALBION

Ground: Goldstone Ground, Newtown Road, Hove, East Sussex BN3 7DE.
Telephone: 01273-778855. **Club Line**: 0891 440066. **Club Nickname**: Seagulls. **First-choice Colours**: Blue and white shirts; blue shorts; white stockings.

Allan, D	8	Fox, S	–(6)	Mundee, D	31(1)
Andrews, P	–(8)	Hobson, G	9	Myall, S	27(6)
Berry, G	6	Johnson, R	19(1)	Osman, R	11(1)
Bull, G	10	McCarthy, P	33	Parris, G	38
Byrne, J	15(10)	McDonald, P	5	Rowe, E	9
Case, J	–(2)	McDougald, D	34(3)	Rust, N	46
Chapman, I	36	McGarrigle, K	8(6)	Smith, P	28(3)
Coughlan, D	1	Maskell, C	15	Storer, S	28(10)
Foster, S	8	Minton, J	37(2)	Tuck, S	7(1)
Fox, M	–(2)	Munday, S	6(3)	Wilkins, D	31(4)

League Goals (46): Minton 8, McDougald 4, Maskell 4, Chapman 3, Mundee 3, Rowe 3, Wilkins 3, Berry 2, Bull 2, Byrne 2, Myall 2, Parris 2, Storer 2, Foster 1, McCarthy 1, McGarrigle 1, Smith 1, Opponents 2.
Coca-Cola Cup Goals: None. **F.A. Cup Goals (6)**: McDougald 3, Byrne 2, Smith 1. **Auto Windscreens Shield Goals (8)**: Bull 2, McDougald 2, McCarthy 1, Mundee 1, Storer 1, Opponent 1.
'Player of Year' 1996: Ian Chapman.
Average Home League Attendance 1995-96: 5,448. **Capacity for 1996-97**: 13,600 (seats 5,110, standing 8,490).
Record Attendance: 36,747 v Fulham (Div. 2) 27 December 1958.

BRISTOL CITY

Ground: Ashton Gate, Bristol BS3 2EJ.
Telephone: 0117-963-2812. **Clubcall**: 0891 121176. **Club Nickname**: Robins.
First-choice Colours: Red shirts; white shorts; red stockings.

Agostino, P .... 29(11)	Dykstra, S 8	Nugent, K .... 29(5)
Armstrong, G 6	Edwards, R .... 18(1)	Owers, G .... 34(3)
Baird, I 1	Fowler, J .... 6(4)	Partridge, S .... 3(6)
Barber, P 3	Hansen, V .... 7(1)	Paterson, S .... 16(2)
Barclay, D .... –(2)	Hewlett, M 27	Plummer, D .... 1(10)
Barnard, D .... 33(1)	Kite, P .... 3(1)	Seal, D .... 19(11)
Bent, J .... 33(7)	Kuhl, M 46	Shail, M .... 9(3)
Bryant, M .... 31(2)	McLeary, A .... 30(1)	Starbuck, P 5
Carey, L .... 22(1)	Maskell, C 5	Tinnion, B .... 27(3)
Dryden, R .... 17(1)	Munro, S 3	Welch, K 35

League Goals (55): Agostino 10, Seal 10, Nugent 8, Kuhl 6, Barnard 4, Tinnion 3, Bent 2, Hewlett 2, Owers 2, Dryden 1, Maskell 1, Partridge 1, Paterson 1, Starbuck 1, Opponents 3.
Coca-Cola Cup Goals (4): Seal 3, Agostino 1. **F.A. Cup Goals**: None. **Auto Windscreens Shield Goals (2)**: Edwards 1, Seal 1.
'Player of Year' 1996: Martin Kuhl.
Average Home League Attendance 1995-96: 7,017. **Capacity for 1996-97**: 21,900 (all-seated).
Record Attendance: 43,335 v Preston N.E. (F.A. Cup 5) 16 February 1935.

BRISTOL ROVERS

Ground: Avonfields House, Somerdale, Keynsham, Bristol BS18 2DJ.
Telephone: 0117-986-9999. **Clubcall**: 0891 664422. **Club Nickname**: Pirates.
First-choice Colours: Blue and white shirts; white shorts; blue stockings.

Archer, L .... 13(6)	Hayfield, M .... 3(3)	Skinner, J .... 23(5)
Armstrong, C .... 13(1)	Low, J .... –(1)	Sterling, W .... 28(2)
Beadle, P .... 26(1)	McLean, I .... 4(3)	Stewart, M 44
Browning, M 45	Matthew, D 8	Taylor, G 7
Channing, J .... 35(1)	Miller, P .... 37(1)	Tillson, A 38
Clark, B .... 38(1)	Morgan, S 5	Tovey, P 8
Collett, A 26	Parkin, B 20	White, T .... –(2)
Davis, M .... 1(3)	Paul, M .... 9(4)	Wright, I .... 15(3)
French, J .... 3(7)	Pritchard, D 12	Wyatt, M .... 3(1)
Gurney, A .... 42(1)		

League Goals (57): Stewart 21, Beadle 12, Gurney 6, Browning 4, Miller 4, Taylor 4, Clark 2, Archer 1, French 1, Paul 1, Tillson 1.
Coca-Cola Cup Goals (5): Stewart 4, Miller 1. **F.A. Cup Goals (1)**: Archer 1.
Auto Windscreens Shield Goals (11): Stewart 5, Archer 1, Browning 1, Davis 1, French 1, Matthew 1, Tillson 1.
'Player of Year' 1996: Andy Tillson.
Average Home League Attendance 1995-96: 5,279. **Capacity for 1996-97**: To be confirmed.
Record Attendance (at previous ground, Eastville): 38,472 v Preston N.E. (F.A. Cup 4) 30 January 1960.

BURNLEY

Ground: Turf Moor, Brunshaw Road, Burnley, Lancashire BB10 4BX.
Telephone: 01282-700000. **Clubcall**: 0891 121153. **Club Nickname**: Clarets.
First-choice Colours: Claret and blue shirts; white shorts; white stockings.

Adams, D .... –(2)	Cooke, A .... 10(13)	Harrison, G 35
Beresford, M 36	Dowell, W 1	Heath, A .... 5(2)
Bishop, C 9	Eyres, D .... 39(3)	Helliwell, I .... 3(1)
Borland, J 1	Francis, J .... 4(18)	Hoyland, J .... 21(2)
Brass, C .... 7(2)	Harper, A .... 3(1)	Joyce, W .... 42(1)

McDonald, P .... 8(1)
McMinn, T .... 7(3)
Mahorn, P .... 3(5)
Nogan, K 46
Parkinson, G 29
Pender, J 1
Philliskirk, T .... 7(1)
Randall, A .... 12(3)
Robinson, L .... 11(5)
Russell, W 10
Smith, P .... 3(7)
Swan, P .... 31(1)
Thompson, S 18
Vinnicombe, C 35
Weller, P .... 24(1)
Winstanley, M 45

League Goals (56): Nogan 20, Eyres 6, Cooke 5, Joyce 5, Swan 5, Winstanley 3, Francis 2, Robinson 2, Vinnicombe 2, Harrison 1, McDonald 1, Mahorn 1, Philliskirk 1, Weller 1, Opponent 1.
Coca-Cola Cup Goals (4): Nogan 3, Randall 1. **F.A. Cup Goals (1)**: Eyres 1.
Auto Windscreens Shield Goals (3): Nogan 3.
'Player of Year' 1996: Kurt Nogan.
Average Home League Attendance 1995-96: 9,064. **Capacity for 1996-97**: 22,100 (all-seated).
Record Attendance: 54,775 v Huddersfield Town (F.A. Cup 4) 23 February 1924.

CARLISLE UNITED

Ground: Brunton Park, Warwick Road, Carlisle, Cumbria CA1 1LL.
Telephone: 01228-26237. **Clubcall**: 0891 230011. **Club Nickname**: Cumbrians.
First-choice Colours: Blue shirts; white shorts; white stockings.

Allen, C 3
Aspinall, W .... 36(6)
Atkinson, B 2
Bennett, G 26
Caig, A 33
Conway, P .... 13(9)
Currie, D .... 41(1)
Delap, R .... 5(14)
Donachie, D .... –(1)
Dowell, W .... 2(5)
Edmondson, D ..... 40(2)
Elliott, A 13
Fuller, C 1
Gallimore, T 36
Hayward, S .... 36(2)
Hopper, T .... 1(4)
McAllindon, G .... –(3)
Moore, N 12
Murray, P .... 23(5)
Peacock, L .... 12(10)
Philliskirk, T 3
Prokas, R .... 17(3)
Reeves, D 43
Robinson, J .... 18(2)
Smart, A .... 3(1)
Thomas, R .... 28(8)
Thorpe, J .... 16(18)
Walling, D 43

League Goals (57): Reeves 13, Currie 9, Aspinall 6, Bennett 5, Hayward 4, Conway 3, Delap 3, Gallimore 2, Peacock 2, Robinson 2, Walling 2, Edmondson 1, Murray 1, Philliskirk 1, Thomas 1, Thorpe 1, Opponent 1.
Coca-Cola Cup Goals (4): Reeves 2, Aspinall 1, Walling 1. **F.A. Cup Goals (1)**: Reeves 1. **Auto Windscreens Shield Goals (10)**: Reeves 3, Edmondson 2, Aspinall 1, Bennett 1, Currie 1, Hayward 1, Thomas 1.
'Player of Year' 1996: David Currie.
Average Home League Attendance 1995-96: 5,704. **Capacity for 1996-97**: 16,651 (seats 7,987, standing 8,664).
Record Attendance: 27,500 v Birmingham (F.A. Cup 3) 5 January 1957; 27,500 v Middlesbrough (F.A. Cup 5) 7 January 1970.

CHESTERFIELD

Ground: Recreation Ground, Saltergate, Chesterfield, Derbyshire S40 4SX.
Telephone: 01246-209765. **Clubcall**: 0891 555818. **Club Nickname**: Spireites.
First-choice Colours: Blue shirts; white shorts; blue stockings.

Beasley, A 11
Carr, D 1
Curtis, T 46
Davies, K .... 28(1)
Dyche, S .... 39(2)
Fairclough, W .... –(2)
Hazel, D .... 16(5)
Hewitt, J .... 23(4)
Holland, P .... 16(1)
Howard, J .... 16(13)
Jules, M .... 28(4)
Law, N 38
Lormor, T .... 38(3)
Lund, G .... 6(2)
McDougald, J 9
Madden, L 1
Mercer, B 34
Morris, A .... 14(2)
Moss, D .... 6(7)
Narbett, J .... 11(6)
Perkins, C .... 18(4)
Pierce, D 1
Roberts, D .... 6(8)
Robinson, P .... 38(1)
Rogers, L 20
Williams, M 42

League Goals (56): Lormor 13, Robinson 9, Law 7, Morris 5, Davies 4, McDougald 3, Williams 3, Hewitt 2, Holland 2, Howard 2, Jules 2, Lund 1, Narbett 1, Opponents 2.

Coca-Cola Cup Goals (1): Roberts 1. **F.A. Cup Goals (4)**: Davies 2, Lormor 2.
Auto Windscreens Shield Goals (6): Roberts 2, Robinson 2, Law 1, Lormor 1.
'Player of Year' 1996: Mark Williams.
Average Home League Attendance 1995-96: 4,884. **Capacity for 1996-97**: 6,000 (seats 3,408, standing 2,592).
Record Attendance: 30,698 v Newcastle United (Div. 2) 7 April 1939.

CREWE ALEXANDRA

Ground: Gresty Road, Crewe, Cheshire CW2 6EB.
Telephone: 01270-213014. **Clubcall**: 0891 664564. **Club Nickname**: Alex.
First-choice Colours: Red shirts; white shorts; red stockings.

Adebola, D .... 20(9)
Barr, B .... 15(2)
Blissett, G 10
Booty, M 21
Clarkson, P .... 1(4)
Collier, D .... 2(4)
Collins, W .... 38(5)
Edwards, R .... 29(3)
Ellison, L .... –(1)
Garvey, S .... 18(10)
Gayle, M 46
Lennon, N 25
Lightfoot, C .... 5(1)
Little, C .... 7(5)
McAllister, B 13
Macauley, S .... 27(2)
Murphy, D .... 41(1)
Ridings, D 1
Rivers, M .... 24(9)
Savage, R .... 28(2)
Smith, S .... 24(5)
Tierney, F .... 21(1)
Unsworth, L .... 15(13)
Westwood, A .... 31(2)
Whalley, G 44

League Goals (77): Edwards 15, Murphy 10, Rivers 10, Adebola 8, Macauley 7, Savage 7, Westwood 4, Booty 2, Garvey 2, Lennon 2, Tierney 2, Whalley 2, Blissett 1, Collins 1, Little 1, McAllister 1, Smith 1, Opponent 1.
Play-offs – Appearances: Adebola 1, Barr –(1), Blissett 1, Collins 1(1), Gayle 2, Lightfoot 2, Little 1, McAllister 2, Macauley 2, Murphy 1, Ridings 1, Rivers 1(1), Savage 2, Tierney –(2), Unsworth 2, Westwood 2, Whalley 1. **Goals (2)**: Little 1, Rivers 1. **Coca-Cola Cup Goals (9)**: Edwards 4, Adebola 1, Collins 1, Lennon 1, Unsworth 1, Whalley 1. **F.A. Cup Goals (11)**: Adebola 2, Edwards 2, Rivers 2, Booty 1, Murphy 1, Unsworth 1, Westwood 1, Whalley 1. **Auto Windscreens Shield Goals (8)**: Collins 1, Garvey 1, Macauley 1, Murphy 1, Rivers 1, Savage 1, Whalley 1, Opponent 1.
'Player of Year' 1996: Mark Gayle.
Average Home League Attendance 1995-96: 3,974. **Capacity for 1996-97**: 6,000 (seats 5,000, standing 1,000).
Record Attendance: 20,000 v Tottenham Hotspur (F.A. Cup 4) 30 January 1960

HULL CITY

Ground: Boothferry Park, Boothferry Road, Hull, North Humberside HU4 6EU.
Telephone: 01482-351119. **Clubcall**: 0891 664550. **Club Nickname**: Tigers.
First-choice Colours: Amber shirts; black shorts; amber stockings.

Abbott, G 31
Allison, N .... 33(2)
Brown, L .... 21(2)
Carroll, R 23
Dakin, S .... 2(4)
Darby, D 8
Davison, B 11
Dewhurst, R 16
Fettis, A .... 4(3)
Fewings, P .... 16(9)
Fidler, R .... –(1)
Gilbert, K .... 6(7)
Gordon, G .... 3(10)
Graham, J 24
Hobson, G .... 28(1)
Humphries, G .... 9(3)
Lawford, C .... 20(11)
Lee, C .... 25(3)
Lowthorpe, A .... 15(4)
Mann, N .... 34(4)
Marks, J 4
Mason, A .... 10(10)
Maxfield, S .... 3(1)
Peacock, R .... 39(6)
Quigley, M .... 9(4)
Trevitt, S 25
Watson, T 4
Wharton, P .... 7(2)
Wilkinson, I 8
Williams, A .... 33(1)
Wilson, S 19
Windass, D 16

League Goals (36): Peacock 7, Abbott 6, Davison 4, Windass 4, Gordon 3, Allison 2, Fewings 2, Brown 1, Darby 1, Graham 1, Lee 1, Mann 1, Mason 1, Quigley 1, Wilkinson 1.
Coca-Cola Cup Goals (5): Windass 3, Allison 1, Fewings 1. **F.A. Cup Goals**: None.
Auto Windscreens Shield Goals (4): Fewings 1, Lawford 1, Mann 1, Windass 1.
'Player of Year' 1996: Roy Carroll.
Average Home League Attendance 1995-96: 3,803. **Capacity for 1996-97**: 12,996 (seats 5,495, standing 7,501).

Record Attendance: 55,019 v Manchester United (F.A. Cup 6) 26 February 1949.

NOTTS COUNTY

Ground: Meadow Lane, Nottingham NG2 3HJ.
Telephone: 0115-952-9000. **Clubcall**: 0891 888684. **Club Nickname**: Magpies.
First-choice Colours: Black and white shirts; black shorts; black stockings.

Agana, T .... 20(9)	Hoyle, C 2	Richardson, I 15
Arkins, V .... 17(6)	Hunt, J 10	Rogers, P 21
Ashcroft, L .... 4(2)	Jemson, N .... 2(1)	Short, C .... –(2)
Baraclough, I 35	Jones, G .... 16(2)	Simpson, M .... 18(5)
Battersby, A .... 14(7)	Legg, A .... 24(1)	Strodder, G 43
Derry, S 12	McSwegan, G .... –(3)	Turner, P 12
Devlin, P 26	Marsden, C 3	Walker, R 11
Finnan, S .... 14(3)	Martindale, G ...... 13(3)	Ward, D 46
Gallagher, T .... 21(1)	Mills, G .... 11(2)	White, D .... 18(2)
Galloway, M .... 7(2)	Murphy, S 39	Wilder, C 9
Hogg, G 10	Nicol, S 13	

League Goals (63): White 8, Arkins 7, Battersby 7, Devlin 6, Martindale 6, Jones 5, Legg 4, Murphy 3, Strodder 3, Agana 2, Baraclough 2, Finnan 2, Gallagher 2, Nicol 2, Rogers 2, Hunt 1, Turner 1.
Play-offs – Appearances: Agana 3, Baraclough 3, Battersby 3, Derry 3, Finnan 3, Jones 1(1), Martindale 2(1), Murphy 3, Richardson 3, Rogers 3, Strodder 3, Ward 3. **Goals (3)**: Martindale 2, Finnan 1. **Coca-Cola Cup Goals (6)**: White 6. **F.A. Cup Goals (4)**: Legg 2, Gallagher 1, Rogers 1. **Auto Windscreens Shield Goals (5)**: Devlin 2, Agana 1, Murphy 1, White 1.
'Player of Year' 1996: Shaun Murphy.
Average Home League Attendance 1995-96: 5,130. **Capacity for 1996-97**: 20,300 (all-seated).
Record Attendance: 47,310 v York City (F.A. Cup 6) 12 March 1955.

OXFORD UNITED

Ground: Manor Ground, London Road, Headington, Oxford OX3 7RS.
Telephone: 01865-61503. **Clubline**: 0891 440055. **Club Nickname**: U's.
First-choice Colours: Yellow shirts; navy shorts; navy stockings.

Aldridge, M .... 15(3)	Ford, M .... 43(1)	Murphy, M .... 13(21)
Allen, C .... 13(11)	Ford, R .... 26(2)	Powell, P .... 1(2)
Angel, M .... 16(11)	Gilchrist, P 42	Robinson, L .... 40(1)
Beauchamp, J ...... 25(7)	Gray, M .... 6(1)	Rush, D .... 41(2)
Biggins, W .... 8(2)	Lewis, M .... 5(14)	Smith, D 45
Carter, T 12	Marsh, S .... 2(3)	Whitehead, P 34
Druce, M .... 1(7)	Massey, S .... 33(2)	Wood, S .... 10(1)
Elliott, M 45	Moody, P .... 30(12)	

League Goals (76): Moody 17, Rush 11, Aldridge 9, Elliott 8, Beauchamp 7, Murphy 5, Massey 4, Allen 3, Ford (R.) 3, Gilchrist 3, Ford (M.) 2, Angel 1, Biggins 1, Smith 1, Opponent 1.
Coca-Cola Cup Goals (7): Allen 2, Biggins 1, Moody 1, Murphy 1, Robinson 1, Smith 1. **F.A. Cup Goals (16)**: Moody 5, Massey 4, Ford (R.) 2, Wood 2, Beauchamp 1, Ford (M.) 1, Rush 1. **Auto Windscreens Shield Goals (7)**: Murphy 2, Rush 2, Angel 1, Moody 1, Opponent 1.
'Player of Year' 1996: Matt Elliott.
Average Home League Attendance 1995-96: 5,876. **Capacity for 1996-97**: 9,572 (seats 2,803, standing 6,769).
Record Attendance: 22,730 v Preston N.E. (F.A. Cup 6) 29 February 1964.

PETERBOROUGH UNITED

Ground: London Road, Peterborough, Cambridge PE2 8AL.
Telephone: 01733-63947. **Clubcall**: 0891 424300. **Club Nickname**: Posh.
First-choice Colours: Blue shirts; white shorts; white stockings.

Ansah, A .... –(2)
Ashley, K 9
Basham, M .... 13(1)
Blount, M .... 4(1)
Breen, G 25
Carter, D .... 30(7)
Charlery, K 19
Clark, S .... 39(1)
Codner, R .... 1(1)
Dobson, T 4
Drury, A .... –(1)
Ebdon, M 39
Farrell, S .... 20(6)
Foran, M 17
Furnell, A .... –(1)
Grazioli, G .... 2(1)
Gregory, D .... –(3)
Griffiths, C 4
Heald, G 40
Hooper, D 4
Inman, N 1
Le Bihan, N .... 16(8)
McGleish, S .... 3(9)
Manuel, B 13
Martindale, G .... 26(5)
Meredith, T .... 1(1)
Morrison, D .... 21(3)
Power, L .... 25(12)
Rioch, G .... 13(5)
Robinson, S 5
Sedgemore, B ...... 13(4)
Shaw, P 12
Sheffield, J 46
Spearing, T 9
Williams, L .... 32(1)
Williams, S .... –(3)

League Goals (59): Martindale 15, Farrell 9, Charlery 7, Power 6, Shaw 5, Heald 4, Ebdon 2, Morrison 2, Ansah 1, Basham 1, Carter 1, Clark 1, Foran 1, Grazioli 1, Griffiths 1, Manuel 1, Spearing 1.
Coca-Cola Cup Goals (5): Manuel 3, Le Bihan 1, Martindale 1. **F.A. Cup Goals (6)**: Farrell 3, Le Bihan 2, Ebdon 1. **Auto Windscreens Shield Goals (7)**: McGleish 2, Martindale 2, Clark 1, Farrell 1, Power 1.
'Player of Year' 1996: Jon Sheffield.
Average Home League Attendance 1995-96: 4,655. **Capacity for 1996-97**: 15,500 (seats 11,000, standing 4,500).
Record Attendance: 30,096 v Swansea (F.A. Cup 5) 20 February 1965.

ROTHERHAM UNITED

Ground: Millmoor, Rotherham, South Yorkshire S60 1HR.
Telephone: 01709-512434. **Clubcall**: 0891 664442. **Club Nickname**: Merry Millers. **First-choice Colours**: Red shirts; white shorts; red and white stockings.

Berry, T .... 33(3)
Blades, P .... 34(3)
Bowyer, G .... 23(4)
Breckin, I .... 37(2)
Clarke, M 40
Davison, R 1
Garner, D 31
Goater, S 44
Goodwin, S .... 25(1)
Hayward, A .... 22(14)
Hurst, P .... 32(8)
James, M .... –(1)
Jeffrey, M 22
Jemson, N 16
McGlashan, J .... 13(3)
McLean, I 9
Monington, M .... 7(4)
Moore, I .... 10(1)
Muggleton, C 6
Pettinger, P .... –(1)
Pike, M .... –(2)
Richardson, N ...... 23(2)
Roscoe, A .... 44(1)
Smith, S .... 11(3)
Viljoen, N .... 5(3)
Wilder, C 18

League Goals (54): Goater 18, Berry 7, Jeffrey 5, Jemson 5, Goodwin 4, Hayward 2, McGlashan 2, Richardson 2, Roscoe 2, Viljoen 2, Blades 1, Breckin 1, Garner 1, Hurst 1, Opponent 1.
Coca-Cola Cup Goals (7): Goater 3, Hayward 2, Jeffrey 1, McGlashan 1. **F.A. Cup Goals (3)**: Goater 2, McGlashan 1. **Auto Windscreens Shield Goals (15)**: Jemson 4, Goodwin 3, Hayward 2, Roscoe 2, Berry 1, Garner 1, Goater 1, Richardson 1.
'Player of Year' 1996: Matthew Clarke.
Average Home League Attendance 1995-96: 3,413. **Capacity for 1996-97**: 11,514 (seats 4,467, standing 7,047).
Record Attendance: 25,000 v Sheff. Wed. (Div. 2) 26 January 1952; 25,000 v Sheff. Utd. (Div. 2) 13 December 1952.

SHREWSBURY TOWN

Ground: Gay Meadow, Shrewsbury, Shropshire SY2 2AB.
Telephone: 01743-360111. **Clubcall**: 0891 888611. **Club Nickname**: Town.
First-choice Colours: Blue shirts; blue shorts; blue stockings.

Anthrobus, S ...... 27(12)
Berkley, A .... 36(2)
Boden, C 5
Clarke, T 15
Cope, J .... –(1)
Currie, D .... 11(2)
Dempsey, M .... 17(11)
Edwards, P 31
Evans, P .... 25(9)
Hughes, M 2
Jackson, D .... –(1)
Kay, J 7
Lynch, T .... 22(3)
Megson, G 2
Reed, I .... 9(2)
Robinson, C .... 2(2)
Rowbotham, D ..... 20(6)
Scott, R 36
Seabury, K .... 26(8)
Spink, D .... 32(2)
Stevens, I .... 27(5)

Stewart, S 4
Summerfield, K ...... –(1)
Taylor, M 38
Walton, D 35
Watson, M 1
Whiston, P 28
Withe, C .... 30(2)
Woods, R .... 18(5)
Wray, S .... –(3)

League Goals (58): Stevens 12, Anthrobus 10, Rowbotham 8, Scott 6, Spink 6, Evans 3, Lynch 3, Currie 2, Dempsey 2, Reed 2, Whiston 2, Berkley 1, Taylor 1. **Coca-Cola Cup Goals (3)**: Lynch 1, Rowbotham 1, Seabury 1. **F.A. Cup Goals (17)**: Scott 3, Spink 2, Dempsey 2, Evans 2, Whiston 2, Anthrobus 1, Rowbotham 1, Stevens 1, Withe 1, Opponent 1. **Auto Windscreens Shield Goals (15)**: Stevens 7, Taylor 2, Dempsey 1, Evans 1, Scott 1, Walton 1, Woods 1, Opponent 1.
'Player of Year' 1996: Ian Stevens.
Average Home League Attendance 1995-96: 3,348. **Capacity for 1996-97**: 8,000 (seats 3,000, standing 5,000).
Record Attendance: 18,917 v Walsall (Div. 3) 26 April 1961.

STOCKPORT COUNTY

Ground: Edgeley Park, Hardcastle Road, Edgeley, Stockport SK3 9DD.
Telephone: 0161-286-8888. **Clubcall**: 0891 121638. **Club Nickname**: County.
First-choice Colours: Blue shirts; white shorts; blue stockings.

Armstrong, A .... 44(2)
Beaumont, C .... 38(5)
Bennett, T 24
Bound, M 26
Chalk, M .... 5(5)
Connelly, S .... 42(1)
Croft, B .... –(3)
Dickins, M 1
Dinning, T .... 1(9)
Durkan, K .... 11(5)
Eckhardt, J .... 30(5)
Edwards, N 45
Flynn, M 46
Gannon, J .... 22(1)
Helliwell, I .... 18(4)
Jeffers, J .... 21(2)
Landon, R .... 7(4)
Marsden, C .... 19(1)
Mike, A .... 4(4)
Mutch, A 11
Oliver, M .... 7(2)
Thornley, B .... 8(2)
Todd, L 42
Ware, P .... 22(5)
Williams, M .... 12(5)

League Goals (61): Armstrong 13, Helliwell 9, Eckhardt 6, Flynn 6, Bound 5, Landon 4, Mutch 4, Jeffers 3, Ware 3, Bennett 1, Dinning 1, Gannon 1, Marsden 1, Oliver 1, Thornley 1, Williams 1, Opponent 1.
Coca-Cola Cup Goals (6): Armstrong 2, Gannon 2, Chalk 1, Eckhardt 1. **F.A. Cup Goals (11)**: Eckhardt 4, Armstrong 3, Bound 1, Helliwell 1, Opponents 2. **Auto Windscreens Shield Goals (1)**: Ware 1.
'Player of Year' 1996: Neil Edwards.
Average Home League Attendance 1995-96: 5,903. **Capacity for 1996-97**: 12,100 (seats 9,350, standing 2,750).
Record Attendance: 27,833 v Liverpool (F.A. Cup 5) 11 February 1950.

SWANSEA CITY

Ground: Vetch Field, Swansea, West Glamorgan SA1 3SU.
Telephone: 01792-474114. **Clubcall**: 0891 121639. **Club Nickname**: Swans.
First-choice Colours: White shirts; white shorts; white stockings.

Ampadu, K .... 40(2)
Barnhouse, D .... 12(3)
Barnwell-Edinboro, J 2(2)
Basham, M .... 9(2)
Beresford, D .... 4(1)
Brown, L .... 3(1)
Chapman, L 7
Chapple, S .... 15(7)
Clode, M .... 25(6)
Coates, J .... 7(11)
Cook, A .... 30(3)
Cornforth, J 17
Dennison, R 9
Edwards, C .... 36(2)
Freestone, R 45
Garnett, S 9
Heggs, C .... 28(4)
Hodge, J .... 34(7)
Hurst, G 2
Jenkins, S 15
Jones, L 1
Jones, S .... 16(1)
Lampard, F .... 8(1)
McDonald, C .... 3(4)
Mardenborough, S 1
Molby, J 12
O'Leary, K 1
Pascoe, C .... 9(4)
Penney, D 28
Perrett, D .... 2(2)
Thomas, D .... 3(13)
Torpey, S .... 41(1)
Walker, K .... 32(1)

League Goals (43): Torpey 16, Heggs 5, Chapman 4, Ampadu 2, Chapple 2, Cornforth 2, Edwards 2, Freestone 2, Molby 2, Basham 1, Hodge 1, Lampard 1, Pascoe 1, Thomas 1, Opponent 1.
Coca-Cola Cup Goals (4): Hodge 2, Ampadu 1, Torpey 1. **F.A. Cup Goals**: None. **Auto Windscreens Shield Goals (1)**: Torpey 1.

'Player of Year' 1996: Roger Freestone.
Average Home League Attendance 1995-96: 2,996. **Capacity for 1996-97**: 15,385 (seats 3,400, standing 11,985).
Record Attendance: 32,796 v Arsenal (F.A. Cup 4) 17 February 1968.

SWINDON TOWN

Ground: County Ground, County Road, Swindon, Wiltshire SN1 2ED.
Telephone: 01793-430430. **Clubcall**: 0891 121640. **Club Nickname**: Robins.
First-choice Colours: Red shirts; red shorts; red stockings.

Allen, P .... 25(2)
Allison, W .... 43(1)
Beauchamp, J .... 1(2)
Bodin, P .... 32(1)
Collins, L .... 2(3)
Cowe, S .... 4(7)
Culverhouse, I 46
Digby, F 25
Drysdale, J .... 10(3)
Finney, S .... 22(8)
Given, S 5
Gooden, T .... 14(12)
Grant, T 3
Horlock, K .... 44(1)
Leitch, S 7
Ling, M .... 12(4)
McMahon, S .... 20(2)
Murray, E .... 3(1)
O'Sullivan, W .... 27(7)
Preece, D 7
Robinson, M 46
Seagraves, M ...... 25(3)
Smith, A .... 2(6)
Talia, F 16
Taylor, S 43
Thorne, P .... 22(4)

League Goals (71): Allison 17, Finney 12, Horlock 12, Thorne 10, Taylor 7, Gooden 3, O'Sullivan 3, Bodin 2, Cowe 1, Grant 1, Murray 1, Preece 1, Robinson 1.
Coca-Cola Cup Goals (5): Allison 1, Beauchamp 1, Finney 1, Gooden 1, Horlock 1. **F.A. Cup Goals (10)**: Horlock 3, Allison 2, Finney 2, Allen 1, Bodin 1, Ling 1.
Auto Windscreens Shield Goals (3): Finney 1, Ling 1, Thorne 1.
'Player of Year' 1996: Shaun Taylor.
Average Home League Attendance 1995-96: 10,602. **Capacity for 1996-97**: 15,746 (all-seated).
Record Attendance: 32,000 v Arsenal (F.A. Cup 3) 15 January 1972.

WALSALL

Ground: Bescot Stadium, Bescot Crescent, Walsall, West Midlands WS1 4SA.
Telephone: 01922-22791. **Clubcall**: 0891 555800. **Club Nickname**: Saddlers.
First-choice Colours: Red shirts; black shorts; white stockings.

Bradley, D 45
Butler, M .... 13(15)
Daniel, R .... 23(2)
Evans, W .... 20(3)
Houghton, S .... 38(2)
Keister, J .... 9(11)
Kerr, J .... –(1)
Lightbourne, K ..... 37(6)
Marsh, C .... 39(2)
Mountfield, D 28
Ntamark, C .... 34(8)
O'Connor, M 41
Palmer, C 15
Platt, C .... –(4)
Ricketts, M .... –(1)
Rogers, D .... 23(2)
Roper, I .... 3(2)
Ryder, S .... 1(2)
Smith, C .... –(1)
Viveash, A 31
Walker, J 26
Watkiss, S .... 14(1)
Wilson, K 46
Wood, T 20

League Goals (60): Lightbourne 15, Wilson 15, O'Connor 9, Houghton 6, Butler 4, Marsh 2, Platt 2, Bradley 1, Mountfield 1, Ricketts 1, Opponents 4.
Coca-Cola Cup Cup Goals (4): Evans 1, Houghton 1, O'Connor 1, Wilson 1.
F.A. Cup Goals (13): Lightbourne 3, Bradley 2, Houghton 2, Marsh 2, Wilson 2, O'Connor 1, Opponent 1. **Auto Windscreens Shield Goals (11)**: Lightbourne 6, Butler 2, O'Connor 1, Viveash 1, Wilson 1.
'Player of Year' 1996: Adrian Viveash.
Average Home League Attendance 1995-96: 3,982. **Capacity for 1996-97**: 9,000 (seats 6,700, standing 2,300).
Record Attendance (at previous ground, Fellows Park): 25,433 v Newcastle United (Div. 2) 29 August 1961.

WREXHAM

Ground: Racecourse Ground, Mold Road, Wrexham, Clwyd LL11 2AN.
Telephone: 01978-262129. **Clubcall**: 0891 121642. **Club Nickname**: Robins.
First-choice Colours: Red shirts; white shorts; red stockings.

Brace, D 16	Hughes, B .... 11(11)	Morris, S .... 4(9)
Brammer, D 11	Humes, A .... 26(1)	Owen, G .... 11(7)
Chalk, M 19	Hunter, B .... 30(1)	Phillips, W .... 43(1)
Connolly, K .... 45(1)	Jones, B .... 39(1)	Russell, K .... 37(3)
Cross, J .... 4(3)	Jones, L 20	Skinner, C .... 21(2)
Durkan, K .... 6(3)	McGregor, M .... 27(5)	Ward, P .... 33(1)
Hardy, P 41	Marriott, A 46	Watkin, S .... 16(13)

League Goals (76): Connolly 18, Jones (L.) 9, Russell 7, Watkin 7, Phillips 5, Ward 5, Chalk 4, Humes 3, Hunter 3, Morris 3, Skinner 3, Brammer 2, Owen 2, Brace 1, McGregor 1, Opponents 3.
Coca-Cola Cup Goals (2): Russell 1, Watkin 1. **F.A. Cup Goals (3)**: Connolly 1, Hunter 1, Watkin 1. **Auto Windscreens Shield Goals (4)**: Connolly 2, Hughes 1, Ward 1.
'Player of Year' 1996: Wayne Phillips.
Average Home League Attendance 1995-96: 3,705. **Capacity for 1996-97**: 9,500 (seats 5,000, standing 4,500).
Record Attendance: 34,445 v Manchester United (F.A. Cup 4) 26 January 1957.

WYCOMBE WANDERERS

Ground: Adams Park, Hillbottom Road, High Wycombe, Bucks. HP1 4HJ.
Telephone: 01494-472100. **Clubcall**: 0891 446855. **Club Nickname**: Blues.
First-choice Colours: Blue shirts; blue shorts; blue stockings.

Bell, M .... 40(1)	Farrell, D .... 27(6)	Markman, D .... –(2)
Blissett, G 4	Foran, M 5	Moussaddik, C 1
Brown, S 38	Garner, S .... 8(5)	Patterson, G .... 31(6)
Carroll, D 46	Hardyman, P .... 12(3)	Roberts, B 15
Castledine, S 7	Hemmings, T .... –(3)	Rowbotham, J 27
Clark, A .... 1(2)	Howard, T .... 36(3)	Ryan, K .... 18(5)
Cousins, J .... 28(2)	Hyde, P 17	Skiverton, T .... 3(1)
Crossley, M 12	Lawrence, M .... 1(2)	Soloman, J .... 6(1)
De Souza, M .... 38(5)	McGavin, S .... 22(9)	Stapleton, S 1
Dykstra, S 13	McGorry, B .... –(4)	Williams, J .... 23(6)
Evans, T .... 26(2)		

League Goals (63): De Souza 18, Carroll 8, Williams 8, Farrell 7, Ryan 4, Castledine 3, Evans 3, Blissett 2, Garner 2, Howard 2, McGavin 2, Bell 1, Crossley 1, Patterson 1, Skiverton 1.
Coca-Cola Cup Goals (3): De Souza 2, Crossley 1. **F.A. Cup Goals (1)**: Patterson 1. **Auto Windscreens Shield Goals (1)**: Howard 1.
'Player of Year' 1996: David Carroll.
Average Home League Attendance 1995-96: 4,573. **Capacity for 1996-97**: 9,447 (seats 7,249, standing 2,198).
Record Attendance (at previous ground Loakes Park): 15,850 v St. Albans City (FA Amateur Cup 4).

YORK CITY

Ground: Bootham Crescent, York, North Yorkshire YO3 7AQ.
Telephone: 01904-624447. **Clubcall**: 0891 664545. **Club Nickname**: Minstermen. **First-choice Colours**: Red shirts; blue shorts; navy stockings.

Atkin, P .... 25(5)	Himsworth, G .... 7(1)	Pepper, N .... 39(1)
Atkinson, P .... 20(2)	Jordan, S .... 18(8)	Peverell, N .... 11(9)
Baker, P .... 11(7)	Kiely, D 40	Randall, A .... 13(3)
Barnes, P 30	McMillan, A 46	Scaife, N .... –(1)
Barras, A 32	Matthews, R .... 14(3)	Sharples, J 10
Bull, G 15	Murty, G .... 31(3)	Stephenson, P ..... 24(3)
Bushell, S .... 17(6)	Naylor, G .... 20(5)	Tutill, S 25
Cresswell, R .... 9(7)	Osborne, W .... 5(1)	Warrington, A 6
Curtis, A .... –(1)	Oxley, S .... 1(1)	Williams, D .... 16(2)
Hall, W .... 21(2)		

League Goals (58): Barnes 15, Pepper 9, Bull 8, Naylor 7, Baker 5, Barras 3, Murty 2, Stephenson 2, Cresswell 1, Himsworth 1, Jordan 1, McMillan 1, Matthews 1, Peverell 1, Opponent 1.
Coca-Cola Cup Goals (11): Barnes 5, Baker 2, Barras 1, Jordan 1, Pepper 1, Peverell 1. **F.A. Cup Goals:** None. **Auto Windscreens Shield Goals (6)**: Barnes 2, Barras 1, Peverell 1, Stephenson 1, Williams 1.
'Player of Year' 1996: Andy McMillan.
Average Home League Attendance 1995-96: 3,538. **Capacity for 1996-97**: 9,500 (seats 3,500, standing 6,000).
Record Attendance: 28,123 v Huddersfield Town (F.A. Cup 6) 5 March 1938.

THIRD DIVISION

BARNET

Ground: Underhill Stadium, Westcombe Drive, Barnet, Herts. EN5 2BE.
Telephone: 0181-441-6932. **Clubcall**: 0891 121544. **Club Nickname**: Bees.
First-choice Colours: Black and amber shirts; black and amber shorts; black and amber stockings.

Adams, K	1	Gale, S	44	Scott, P	19(1)
Brady, M	1(1)	Hodges, L	34(6)	Simpson, P	24
Campbell, J	14(10)	Howarth, L	19	Smith, P	–(1)
Charles, L	2(3)	McDonald, D	30(2)	Stimson, M	5
Codner, R	8	Mills, D	5(14)	Taylor, M	45
Cooper, M	26(7)	Newell, P	1	Thomas, G	16
Devine, S	35	Pardew, A	41	Thompson, N	1(1)
Dunwell, R	3(10)	Primus, L	42	Tomlinson, M	17(8)
Dyer, A	30(5)	Robbins, T	9(6)	Wilson, P.	29(4)
Freedman, D	5				

League Goals (65): Devine 19, Hodges 17, Cooper 8, Primus 4, Wilson 4, Freedman 3, Dyer 2, Tomlinson 2, Campbell 1, Dunwell 1, Gale 1, Robbins 1, Simpson 1, Opponent 1.
Coca-Cola Cup Goals: None. **F.A. Cup Goals (3)**: Devine 1, Hodges 1, Primus 1. **Auto Windscreens Shield Goals (2)**: Cooper 1, Robbins 1.
'Player of Year' 1996: Mark Taylor.
Average Home League Attendance 1995-96: 2,282. **Capacity for 1996-97**: 3,887 (seats 1,774, standing 2,113).
Record Attendance: 11,026 v Wycombe W. (F.A. Amateur Cup 4) 1954.

BURY

Ground: Gigg Lane, Bury, Lancashire BL9 9HR.
Telephone: 0161-764-4881. **Clubcall**: 0891 121197. **Club Nickname**: Shakers.
First-choice Colours: White shirts; blue shorts; blue stockings.

Bimson, S	16	Jackson, M	31	Paskin, J	–(11)
Brabin, G	5	Johnrose, L	34	Pugh, D	42
Bracey, L	21	Johnson, D	21(14)	Reid, N	13(4)
Carter, M	28(4)	Kelly, G	25	Reid, S	20(2)
Cross, R	13	Lancaster, D	1(4)	Richardson, N	3(2)
Daws, N	33(4)	Lucketti, C	42	Rigby, T	33(8)
Edwards, P	4	Matthews, R	11(5)	Sertori, M	4(7)
Harle, M	–(1)	Matthewson, T	16	Stant, P	27(7)
Hughes, I	30(2)	Mulligan, J	–(2)	West, D	32(5)
Hulme, K	–(1)	Parker, S	–(1)	Woodward, A	1

League Goals (66): Carter 16, Pugh 10, Stant 10, Rigby 7, Johnrose 5, Johnson 5, Jackson 4, Matthews 4, Daws 1, Lucketti 1, Sertori 1, West 1, Opponent 1.
Coca-Cola Cup Goals (9): Stant 4, Carter 2, Daws 1, Johnson 1, Rigby 1. **F.A. Cup Goals**: None. **Auto Windscreens Shield Goals**: None.
'Player of Year' 1996: Chris Lucketti.

Average Home League Attendance 1995-96: 3,262 **Capacity for 1996-97**: 11,862 (seats 9,362, standing 2,500).
Record Attendance: 35,000 v Bolton Wanderers (F.A. Cup 3) 9 January 1960.

CAMBRIDGE UNITED

Ground: Abbey Stadium, Newmarket Road, Cambridge CB5 8LN.
Telephone: 01223-566500. **Clubcall**: 0891 555885. **Club Nickname**: U's.
First-choice Colours: Black and amber shirts; black shorts; black and amber stockings.

Adekola, D .... 1(4)
Barnwell-Edinboro, J .. 7
Barrett, S 31
Barrick, D .... 2(1)
Beall, M 15
Benjamin, T .... –(5)
Butler, S 16
Clark, P 2
Corazzin, C 31
Craddock, J .... 44(2)
Davies, M 15
Fowler, J .... –(2)
Granville, D .... 31(4)
Gutzmore, L .... –(2)
Hayes, A 1
Howes, S .... –(1)
Hyde, M .... 20(4)
Illman, N .... 1(4)
Jeffrey, A .... 20(7)
Joseph, Marc .... 10(2)
Joseph, Matthew 42
Kyd, M .... 3(6)
Middleton, C .... 38(2)
Middleton, L .... 1(2)
Pack, L .... 3(9)
Palmer, L 30
Perkins, D .... 1(1)
Pick, G .... 1(2)
Rattle, J .... 7(2)
Raynor, P 35
Richards, T .... 15(4)
Robinson, D .... 4(13)
Stock, R .... 15(2)
Thompson, D .... 14(1)
Turner, R 10
Vowden, C .... 22(1)
Wanless, P 14
Watson, M .... 1(3)
Westley, S 3
Wosahlo, B .... –(4)

League Goals (61): Butler 10, Corazzin 10, Middleton (C.) 8, Beall 4, Hyde 4, Craddock 3, Raynor 3, Turner 3, Barnwell-Edinboro 2, Joseph (Matthew) 2, Adekola 1, Barrick 1, Kyd 1, Palmer 1, Perkins 1, Richards 1, Robinson 1, Stock 1, Wanless 1, Watson 1, Opponents 2.
Coca-Cola Cup Goals (2): Corazzin 2. **F.A. Cup Goals (1)**: Butler 1. **Auto Windscreens Shield Goals (1)**: Adekola 1.
'Player of Year' 1996: Jody Craddock.
Average Home League Attendance 1995-96: 2,767. **Capacity for 1996-97**: 9,667 (seats 3,242, standing 6,425).
Record Attendance: 14,000 v Chelsea (Friendly) 1 May 1970.

CARDIFF CITY

Ground: Ninian Park, Sloper Road, Cardiff, South Glamorgan CF1 8SX.
Telephone: 01222-398636. **Clubcall**: 0891 121171. **Club Nickname**: Bluebirds.
First-choice Colours: Blue shirts; blue shorts; blue stockings.

Adams, D .... 8(5)
Baddeley, L .... 27(3)
Bird, A .... 9(3)
Bolesan, M .... –(1)
Brazil, D .... 19(1)
Dale, C 44
Dobbs, G 3
Downing, K .... 3(1)
Evans, A 1
Evans, T 1
Flack, S .... 5(5)
Fleming, H .... 20(2)
Gardner, J .... 32(3)
Harding, P 36
Harper, A 5
Haworth, S .... 7(6)
Ingram, C .... 4(4)
Jarman, L .... 31(1)
Johnson, G .... 1(4)
Jones, I 1
McGorry, B 7
Oatway, A 2
Osman, R .... 14(1)
Perry, J .... 13(1)
Philliskirk, T 28
Rodgerson, I .... 28(5)
Scott, A .... –(1)
Scully, A .... 13(1)
Searle, D 41
Shaw, P 6
Wigg, N .... 14(7)
Williams, D 42
Williams, S 4
Young, S .... 37(4)

League Goals (41): Dale 21, Gardner 4, Philliskirk 4, Adams 3, Bird 3, Flack 1, Ingram 1, Rodgerson 1, Searle 1, Opponents 2.
Coca-Cola Cup Goals (4): Dale 2, Bird 1, Rodgerson 1. **F.A. Cup Goals (3)**: Dale 2, Jarman 1. **Auto Windscreens Shield Goals (7)**: Dale 5, Adams 2.
'Player of Year' 1996: Carl Dale.
Average Home League Attendance 1995-96: 3,420. **Capacity for 1996-97**: 12,695 (seats 10,371, standing 2,324).
Record Attendance: 61,566 Wales v England 14 October 1961. **Club record**: 57,800 v Arsenal (Div. 1) 22 April 1953.

CHESTER CITY

Ground: Deva Stadium, Bumpers Lane, Chester CH1 4LT.
Telephone: 01244-371376. **Clubcall**: 0891 664554. **Club Nickname**: Blues.
First-choice Colours: Blue and white shirts; blue shorts; blue and white stockings.

Alsford, J .... 22(2)	Flitcroft, D .... 7(2)	Regis, C 29
Bishop, E .... 7(2)	Jackson, P 36	Richardson, N ...... 36(1)
Brien, T 8	Jenkins, I .... 12(1)	Rimmer, S .... 30(11)
Brown, G .... 1(2)	Kenworthy, J .... 5(2)	Rodgers, D .... 14(6)
Burnham, J 40	Milner, A .... 35(7)	Ryan, D .... 2(2)
Chambers, L .... 2(6)	Murphy, J .... 1(17)	Shelton, G .... 10(1)
Cutler, N 1	Noteman, K .... 27(6)	Stewart, B 45
Davidson, R 19	Preece, R 1	Whelan, S .... 35(4)
Fisher, N .... 43(1)	Priest, C .... 38(1)	

League Goals (72): Priest 13, Rimmer 13, Noteman 9, Regis 7, Bishop 5, Milner 4, Richardson 4, Murphy 3, Fisher 2, Whelan 2, Burnham 1, Chambers 1, Davidson 1, Flitcroft 1, Jackson 1, Kenworthy 1, Rogers 1, Ryan 1, Shelton 1, Opponent 1.
Coca-Cola Cup Goals (8): Milner 3, Bishop 2, Chambers 1, Murphy 1, Whelan 1.
F.A. Cup Goals (1): Milner 1. **Auto Windscreens Shield Goals (1)**: Richardson 1.
'Player of Year' 1996: Peter Jackson.
Average Home League Attendance 1995-96: 2,674. **Capacity for 1996-97**: 5,734 (seats 3,094, standing 2,640).
Record Attendance (at previous ground, Sealand Road): 20,500 v Chelsea (F.A. Cup 3) 16 January 1952.

COLCHESTER UNITED

Ground: Layer Road, Colchester, Essex CO2 7JJ.
Telephone: 01206-574042. **Clubcall**: 0891 664646. **Club Nickname**: U's.
First-choice Colours: Blue and white shirts; white shorts; white stockings.

Abrahams, P 8	Duguid, K .... 7(9)	Lewis, B .... 1(1)
Adcock, T 41	Dunne, J .... 2(3)	Locke, A .... 22(3)
Ball, S .... 6(2)	Emberson, C 41	McCarthy, T 44
Betts, S 45	English, T .... 20(1)	McGleish, S .... 10(5)
Boyce, R .... –(2)	Fry, C .... 35(3)	Mardenborough, S . 4(8)
Caesar, G 23	Gibbs, P .... 13(11)	Petterson, A 5
Cawley, P 42	Greene, D 14	Reinelt, R .... 12(9)
Cheetham, M .... 25(3)	Gregory, D .... 7(3)	Whitton, S .... 10(2)
Dennis, J .... 24(8)	Kinsella, M 45	

League Goals (61): Adcock 12, Reinelt 7, McGleish 6, Betts 5, Kinsella 5, Dennis 3, Gibbs 3, Locke 3, Abrahams 2, Caesar 2, Cheetham 2, Fry 2, Mardenborough 2, Whitton 2, Ball 1, Cawley 1, Duguid 1, Dunne 1, Greene 1.
Play-offs Appearances: Betts 2, Caesar 2, Cawley 2, Dennis 2, Emberson 2, Fry 2, Gibbs 2, Kinsella 2, Locke –(1), McCarthy 2, McGleish 2, Reinelt 2, Whitton –(1). **Goals (2)**: Kinsella 2. **Coca-Cola Cup Goals (3)**: Adcock 1, Cheetham 1, Kinsella 1. **F.A. Cup Goals**: None. **Auto Windscreens Shield Goals (9)**: Adcock 4, Betts 2, Cawley 1, Kinsella 1, Reinelt 1.
'Player of Year' 1996: Tony Adcock.
Average Home League Attendance 1995-96: 3,274. **Capacity for 1996-97**: 7,291 (seats 871, standing 6,420).
Record Attendance: 19,072 v Reading (F.A. Cup 1) 27 November 1948.

DARLINGTON

Ground: Feethams, Darlington, County Durham DL1 5JB.
Telephone: 01325-465097. **Clubcall**: 0891 101555. **Club Nickname**: Quakers.
First-choice Colours: Black and white shirts; black shorts; black stockings.

Appleby, M .... 42(1)	Blake, R .... 23(6)	Carmichael, M ...... 11(2)
Bannister, G .... 39(2)	Brumwell, P .... 16(11)	Carss, A .... 13(14)
Barnard, M 37	Burridge, J 3	Crosby, A 45

Gaughan, S .... 34(7)	Naylor, G .... 3(1)	Pollitt, M 15
Gregan, S 38	Neves, R .... 3(2)	Quetongo, D 1
Guinan, S 3	Newell, P 21	Robinson, P .... –(4)
Himsworth, G .... 26(2)	Olsson, P 34	Shaw, S .... 36(5)
Lucas, D 6	Painter, R .... 33(2)	Stephens, A 1
McMahon, S .... 6(5)	Paulo, P .... 4(2)	Twynham, G 2
Mattison, P .... 1(5)	Pepper, G .... –(1)	Worboys, G .... 6(8)
Muir, I 4		

League Goals (60): Blake 11, Bannister 10, Painter 8, Appleby 6, Olsson 4, Barnard 3, Gaughan 3, Himsworth 3, Carmichael 2, Carss 2, Worboys 2, Crosby 1, Guinan 1, McMahon 1, Muir 1, Naylor 1, Shaw 1.
Play-offs – Appearances: Appleby 3, Bannister 3, Barnard 3, Blake 3, Brumwell 2(1), Carmichael 2(1), Carss 2, Crosby 3, Gaughan 3, Gregan 3, Mattison –(1), Newell 3, Painter 3. **Goals (4)**: Appleby 1, Blake 1, Gregan 1, Painter 1.
Coca-Cola Cup Goals (1): Carss 1. **F.A. Cup Goals (6)**: Bannister 1, Brumwell 1, Gaughan 1, Olsson 1, Painter 1, Shaw 1. **Auto Windscreens Shield Goals (2)**: Appleby 1, Olsson 1.
'Player of Year' 1996: Gary Bannister.
Average Home League Attendance 1995-96: 2,408. **Capacity for 1996-97**: 7,048 (seats 1,100, standing 5,948).
Record Attendance: 21,023 v Bolton Wanderers (League Cup 3) 14 November 1960.

DONCASTER ROVERS

Ground: Belle Vue, Doncaster, South Yorkshire DN4 5HT.
Telephone: 01302-539441. **Clubcall**: 0891 664420. **Club Nickname**: Rovers.
First-choice Colours: Red and white shirts; white shorts; red stockings.

Ashley, K 3	Jones, G .... 31(1)	Peel, N 2
Barker, R .... 5(1)	Kirby, R .... 32(4)	Robertson, P .... 12(4)
Brabin, G 31	Knight, J .... 1(3)	Schofield, J .... 40(1)
Brodie, S 5	Marquis, P 15	Smith, M .... 12(1)
Carmichael, M ...... 19(8)	Maxfield, S .... 12(7)	Speight, M 1
Clark, I .... 14(9)	Meara, J .... –(1)	Suckling, P 21
Colcombe, S .... 21(9)	Measham, I .... 7(3)	Utley, D 1
Cramb, C .... 20(1)	Moore, D 35	Warren, L .... 40(2)
Darby, D .... 8(9)	Murphy, J .... 17(6)	Wilcox, R 4
Doling, S .... –(1)	Norbury, M .... 2(3)	Williams, D 17
Gore, I 5	Noteman, K 4	Williams, P .... 2(1)
Hackett, W 7	O'Connor, G 8	Wright, J 13
Harper, S .... –(1)	Parrish, S .... 39(2)	

League Goals (49): Jones 10, Cramb 7, Parrish 5, Carmichael 4, Darby 4, Schofield 4, Brabin 3, Colcombe 3, Moore 2, Brodie 1, Clark 1, Marquis 1, Maxfield 1, Noteman 1, Williams (P.) 1, Opponent 1.
Coca-Cola Cup Goals (1): Wilcox 1. **F.A. Cup Goals (2)**: Carmichael 1, Jones 1.
Auto Windscreens Shield Goals (3): Clark 1, Colcombe 1, Moore 1.
'Player of Year' 1996: Darren Moore.
Average Home League Attendance 1995-96: 2,090. **Capacity for 1996-97**: 8,608 (seats 1,259, standing 7,349).
Record Attendance: 37,149 v Hull City (Div. 3N) 2 October 1948.

EXETER CITY

Ground: St. James' Park, Wells Street, Exeter, Devon EX4 6PX.
Telephone: 01392-54073. **Clubcall**: 0891 446868. **Club Nickname**: Grecians.
First-choice Colours: Red and white shirts; black shorts; red and white stockings.

Anderson, C .... 5(8)	Braithwaite, L .... 14(9)	Chamberlain, M ... 29(4)
Bailey, D .... 41(1)	Buckle, P 22	Cooper, M .... 26(1)
Blake, N 44	Came, M 38	Coughlin, R .... 6(2)
Bradbury, L 14	Cecere, M .... 5(8)	Foster, A .... 4(3)

Fox, P 46	Morgan, J .... 2(4)	Richardson, J 43
Gavin, M .... 24(4)	Myers, C .... 7(1)	Ross, M 7
Hare, M .... 10(3)	Parsley, N .... 29(3)	Sharpe, J .... 9(4)
Hughes, D .... 25(1)	Pears, R .... 19(3)	Thirlby, A .... –(2)
McConnell, B .... 1(7)	Phillips, M .... 11(2)	Turner, R .... 6(6)
Medlin, N .... 2(4)	Rice, G .... 17(2)	

League Goals (46): Cooper 6, Bradbury 5, Pears 5, Came 4, Braithwaite 3, Phillips 3, Turner 3, Blake 2, Buckle 2, Gavin 2, Ross 2, Bailey 1, Cecere 1, Chamberlain 1, Richardson 1, Sharpe 1, Opponents 4.
Coca-Cola Cup Goals (1): Richardson 1. **F.A. Cup Goals**: None. **Auto Windscreens Shield Goals (1)**: Came 1.
'Player of Year' 1996: Mark Came.
Average Home League Attendance 1995-96: 3,442. **Capacity for 1996-97**: 10,570 (seats 1,690, standing 8,880).
Record Attendance: 20,984 v Sunderland (F.A. Cup 6) 4 March 1931.

FULHAM

Ground: Craven Cottage, Stevenage Road, London SW6 6HH.
Telephone: 0171-736-6561. **Club Line**: 0891 440044. **Club Nickname**: Cottagers. **First-choice Colours**: White shirts; black shorts; white stockings.

Adams, M 5	Cusack, N .... 38(4)	Marshall, J .... 14(2)
Angus, T .... 30(1)	Finnigan, T .... 1(1)	Mison, M .... 16(7)
Barber, P 13	Gray, M 6	Moore, K .... 17(3)
Barkus, L .... 3(6)	Hamill, R .... 6(19)	Morgan, S 41
Blake, M .... 35(3)	Hamsher, J .... –(3)	Scott, R 21
Bolt, D .... 7(3)	Harrison, L 5	Simpson, G .... 5(2)
Bower, D 4	Herrera, R .... 42(1)	Taylor, M 7
Brazil, G .... 17(1)	Jupp, D .... 35(1)	Thomas, M .... 32(4)
Brooker, P .... 9(10)	Lange, T 41	Williams, C .... 2(11)
Conroy, M .... 38(2)	McAree, R .... 16(1)	

League Goals (57): Conroy 9, Morgan 6, Blake 5, Cusack 5, Scott 5, Thomas 5, Mison 4, Adams 2, Angus 2, Bolt 2, Brooker 2, Hamill 2, McAree 2, Barber 1, Barkus 1, Brazil 1, Moore 1, Opponents 2.
Coca-Cola Cup Goals (6): Conroy 2, Barkus 1, Brazil 1, Cusack 1, Mison 1. **F.A. Cup Goals (9)**: Conroy 3, Angus 1, Brooker 1, Cusack 1, Hamill 1, Jupp 1, Thomas 1. **Auto Windscreens Shield Goals (5)**: Jupp 2, Morgan 2, Conroy 1.
'Player of Year' 1996: Nick Cusack.
Average Home League Attendance 1995-96: 4,191. **Capacity for 1996-97**: 14, 969 (seats 5,119, standing 9,850).
Record Attendance: 49,335 v Millwall (Div. 2) 8 October 1938.

GILLINGHAM

Ground: Priestfield Stadium, Redfern Avenue, Gillingham, Kent ME7 4DD.
Telephone: 01634-851854. **Clubcall**: 0891 800676. **Club Nickname**: Gills.
First-choice Colours: Blue shirts; blue shorts; white stockings.

Ansah, A .... –(2)	Foster, A .... 1(10)	O'Connor, M 18
Arnott, A .... –(1)	Freeman, D .... 4(5)	Puttnam, D .... 10(16)
Bailey, D .... 40(5)	Gayle, J 9	Ratcliffe, S 41
Brown, S .... –(1)	Green, R 35	Rattray, K .... 18(8)
Butler, S .... 14(6)	Harris, M 44	Smith, N .... 36(1)
Butler, T .... 34(2)	Manuel, B .... 6(4)	Stannard, J 46
Carpenter, R .... 7(5)	Martin, E .... 27(4)	Thomas, G .... 14(1)
Castle, S .... 5(1)	Micklewhite, G ... 17(14)	Watson, A .... 13(4)
Dunne, J .... 1(1)	Naylor, D .... 30(1)	Watson, P .... –(1)
Fortune-West, L ... 36(4)		

League Goals (49): Fortune-West 12, Bailey 8, Butler (S.) 6, Gayle 3, Ratcliffe 3, Rattray 3, Green 2, Harris 2, Butler (T.) 1, Castle 1, Foster 1, Martin 1, Naylor 1, O'Connor 1, Puttman 1, Smith 1, Watson (A.) 1, Opponent 1.

Coca-Cola Cup Goals (3): Bailey 1, Fortune-West 1, Naylor 1. **F.A. Cup Goals (6)**: Fortune-West 2, Bailey 1, Martin 1, Ratcliffe 1, Opponent 1. **Auto Windscreens Shield Goals (4)**: Foster 2, Butler (S.) 1, Freeman 1.
'Player of Year' 1996: Jim Stannard.
Average Home League Attendance 1995-96: 7,198. **Capacity for 1996-97**: 10,600 (seats 1,090, standing 9,510).
Record Attendance: 23,002 v Q.P.R. (F.A. Cup 3) 10 January 1948.

HARTLEPOOL UNITED

Ground: Victoria Park, Clarence Road, Hartlepool, Cleveland TS24 8BZ.
Telephone: 01429-222077. **Clubcall**: 0891 664447. **Club Nickname**: Pools.
First-choice Colours: Sky blue shirts; blue shorts; blue stockings.

Allinson, J .... 3(1)
Allon, J 22
Billing, P .... 35(1)
Canham, T .... 25(4)
Conlon, P .... 11(4)
Debont, A 1
Dixon, A 3
Ford, G .... 2(1)
Foster, L .... –(1)
Gallagher, I 1
Halliday, S .... 36(3)
Henderson, D ...... 33(3)
Homer, C .... 1(4)
Horne, B 32
Houchen, K .... 36(2)
Howard, S .... 32(7)
Hutt, S .... –(1)
Ingram, D .... 32(1)
Jones, S .... 7(2)
Key, L 1
Lee, G .... 3(3)
Lowe, K 13
Lynch, C .... 13(6)
McAuley, S 46
McGuckin, I 40
O'Connor, P 1
Oliver, K .... 7(5)
Reddish, S .... 18(2)
Roberts, D 4
Slater, D .... –(1)
Sloan, S .... 1(5)
Stokoe, G .... 8(3)
Tait, M .... 38(1)
Walton, P .... 1(2)

League Goals (47): Allon 8, Halliday 7, Howard 7, Houchen 6, Conlon 4, Henderson 3, Lowe 3, Ingram 2, McGuckin 2, Tait 2, Canham 1, Lynch 1, Opponent 1.
Coca-Cola Cup Goals (1): McGuckin 1. **F.A. Cup Goals (2)**: Halliday 1, Sloan 1.
Auto Windscreens Shield Goals (3): Howard 2, Allon 1.
'Player of Year' 1996: Brian Horne.
Average Home League Attendance 1995-96: 2,072. **Capacity for 1996-97**: 7,229 (seats 3,966, standing 3,263).
Record Attendance: 17,426 v Manchester United (F.A. Cup 3) 5 January 1957.

HEREFORD UNITED

Ground: Edgar Street, Hereford HR4 9JU.
Telephone: 01432-276666. **Clubcall**: 0891 555808. **Club Nickname**: United.
First-choice Colours: Black and white shirts; black shorts; black stockings.

Blatherwick, S 10
Brough, J 22
Clarke, D 5
Cross, N .... 32(5)
Debont, A 8
Downing, K 29
Evans, G 24
Fishlock, M .... 26(1)
Hargreaves, C ..... 15(2)
James, T 17
Lloyd, K .... 25(2)
Lyne, N .... 22(10)
Mackenzie, C 38
Pick, G .... 10(4)
Pitman, J .... 12(1)
Pounder, T .... 31(3)
Preedy, P .... 5(7)
Reece, A 6
Smith, D .... 39(1)
Steele, T .... –(7)
Stoker, G .... 28(3)
Stokoe, G 2
Watkiss, S 19
White, S .... 39(1)
Wilkins, R 42

League Goals (65): White 29, Cross 8, Smith 8, Fishlock 3, Stoker 3, Wilkins 3, Hargreaves 2, James 2, Pounder 2, Blatherwick 1, Brough 1, Lyne 1, Mackenzie 1, Preedy 1.
Play-offs – Appearances: Brough –(1), Cross 2, Fishlock 2, Hargreaves 1, James 2, Lyne 1(1), Mackenzie 2, Pitman 2, Pounder –(1), Smith 2, Stoker 2, Watkiss 2, White 2, Wilkins 2. **Goals (2)**: Smith 1, White 1. **Coca-Cola Cup Goals (2)**: Reece 1, Smith 1. **F.A. Cup Goals (6):** White 3, Brough 1, Cross 1, Stoker 1. **Auto Windscreens Shield Goals (8)**: Cross 2, Smith 2, Wilkins 2, Stoker 1, White 1.
'Player of Year' 1996: Steve White.
Average Home League Attendance 1995-96: 2,973. **Capacity for 1996-97**: 8,843 (seats 2,761, standing 6,082).

Record Attendance: 18,114 v Sheffield Wednesday (F.A. Cup 3) 4 January 1958.

LEYTON ORIENT

Ground: Leyton Stadium, Brisbane Road, Leyton, London E10 5NE.
Telephone: 0181-539-2223. **Clubcall**: 0891 121150. **Club Nickname**: O's.
First-choice Colours: Red shirts; black shorts; red stockings.

Arnott, A 19
Austin, K .... 32(9)
Ayorinde, S 1
Baker, J .... 4(16)
Bellamy, G 32
Berry, G .... 4(3)
Brooks, S .... 34(7)
Caldwell, P 28
Chapman, D 38
Cockerill, G 38
Currie, D .... 9(1)
Fearon, R 18
Gray, A .... 3(4)
Hanson, D .... 7(4)
Hendon, I 38
Inglethorpe, A 30
Kelly, A .... 32(2)
Kelly, R .... 5(1)
Lakin, B .... 5(3)
McCarthy, A .... 40(3)
Purse, D .... 9(3)
Shearer, L .... 5(3)
Stanislaus, R .... 20(1)
Warren, M .... 15(7)
Watson, M .... –(1)
West, C 39
Williams, L .... 1(2)

League Goals (44): West 16, Inglethorpe 9, Arnott 3, Kelly (A.) 3, Brooks 2, Chapman 2, Hendon 2, Austin 1, Bellamy 1, Cockerill 1, Hanson 1, Shearer 1, Warren 1, Watson 1.
Coca-Cola Cup Goals (2): Austin 1, West 1. **F.A. Cup Goals**: None. **Auto Windscreens Shield Goals (1)**: Hendon 1.
'Player of Year' 1996: Ian Hendon.
Average Home League Attendance 1995-96: 4,478. **Capacity for 1996-97**: 12,573 (seats 7,145, standing 5,428).
Record Attendance: 34,345 v West Ham United (F.A. Cup 4) 25 January 1964.

LINCOLN CITY

Ground: Sincil Bank, Lincoln LN5 8LD.
Telephone: 01522-522224. **Clubcall**: 0891 664666. **Club Nickname**: Imps.
First-choice Colours: Red and white shirts; black shorts; red stockings.

Ainsworth, G 31
Alcide, C .... 22(5)
Allon, J .... 3(1)
Appleton, M 4
Barnett, J .... 27(5)
Bos, G .... 10(1)
Bound, M .... 3(1)
Brightwell, D 5
Brown, G 35
Brown, S .... 21(4)
Carbon, M 26
Daley, P .... 6(6)
Davis, N 3
Daws, T .... 8(3)
Dixon, B .... 10(2)
Dyer, A 1
Fleming, T .... 17(5)
Greenall, C 4
Holmes, S 23
Huckerby, D 16
Hulme, K .... 4(1)
Johnson, A .... 17(5)
Johnson, D .... 14(10)
Key, L 5
Leaning, A 7
Megson, G 2
Minett, J .... 39(3)
Mudd, P .... 2(2)
Onwere, U .... 33(2)
Puttnam, D .... 4(1)
Richardson, B 34
Robertson, J .... 21(1)
Storey, B .... –(2)
Wanless, P .... 7(1)
West, D .... 7(1)
Westley, S 9
Whitney, J .... 25(1)
Williams, S .... 1(3)

League Goals (57): Ainsworth 12, Alcide 6, Bos 5, Minett 5, Onwere 4, Brown (S.) 3, Carbon 3, Daws 3, Whitney 3, Barnett 2, Holmes 2, Huckerby 2, Daley 1, Johnson (D.) 1, Puttnam 1, Storey 1, West 1, Westley 1, Opponent 1.
Coca-Cola Cup Goals: None. **F.A. Cup Goals**: None. **Auto Windscreens Shield Goals (8)**: Brown (S.) 2, Huckerby 2, Johnson (D.) 2, Ainsworth 1, Onwere 1.
'Player of Year' 1996: Gareth Ainsworth.
Average Home League Attendance 1995-96: 2,870. **Capacity for 1996-97**: 10,918 (seats 9,251, standing 1,667).
Record Attendance: 23,196 v Derby County (League Cup 4) 15 November 1967.

MANSFIELD TOWN

Ground: Field Mill, Quarry Lane, Mansfield, Notts. NG18 5DA.
Telephone: 01623-23567. **Clubcall**: 0891 121311. **Club Nickname**: Stags.
First-choice Colours: Amber and blue shirts; blue shorts; amber and blue stockings.

Alexander, K .... –(1)
Baraclough, I 11
Barber, P 4
Boothroyd, A .... 42(1)
Bowling, I 44
Brien, T 4
Carmichael, M 1
Clarke, D .... 1(2)
Doolan, J 42
Eustace, S .... 25(2)
Hackett, W 32
Hadley, S .... 27(6)
Harper, S 29
Howarth, L 17
Ireland, S .... 38(1)
Kerr, D .... 4(1)
Kilcline, B .... 18(1)
Lampkin, K .... 2(4)
Onuora, I .... 7(7)
Parkin, S .... 25(1)
Peel, N 2
Peters, M 21
Robinson, I .... 4(5)
Sale, M .... 24(3)
Sedgemore, B .... 4(5)
Sherlock, P .... 14(4)
Slawson, S .... 21(8)
Timons, C .... 16(1)
Todd, M .... 10(2)
Trinder, J 1
Varadi, I 1
Weaver, N 1
Williams, R .... 5(5)
Wood, S .... 9(1)

League Goals (54): Hadley 7, Sale 7, Ireland 6, Harper 5, Slawson 5, Hackett 3, Williams 3, Baraclough 2, Boothroyd 2, Doolan 2, Peters 2, Sherlock 2, Barber 1, Carmichael 1, Eustace 1, Onuora 1, Parkin 1, Robinson 1, Timons 1, Woods 1. **Coca-Cola Cup Goals (1)**: Peters 1. **F.A. Cup Goals (4)**: Doolan 1, Harper 1, Parkin 1, Sherlock 1. **Auto Windscreens Shield Goals (2)**: Hadley 1, Doolan 1.
'Player of Year' 1996: Ian Bowling.
Average Home League Attendance 1995-96: 2,415. **Capacity for 1996-97**: 7,033 (seats 3,445, standing 3,578).
Record Attendance: 24,567 v Nottingham Forest (F.A. Cup 3) 10 January 1953.

NORTHAMPTON TOWN

Ground: Sixfields Stadium, Upton Way, Northampton NN5 5QA.
Telephone: 01604-757773. **Clubcall**: 0839 664477. **Club Nickname**: Cobblers.
First-choice Colours: Claret shirts; white shorts; claret stockings.

Armstrong, G 4
Beckford, J .... –(1)
Burns, C .... 40(3)
Cahill, O .... 2(1)
Colkin, L .... 14(10)
Doherty, N .... 3(6)
Gibb, A .... 12(11)
Grayson, N .... 37(5)
Hughes, D .... 7(1)
Hunter, R .... 26(8)
Lee, C .... 1(4)
Maddison, L 21
Mountfield, D 4
Norton, D .... 42(2)
O'Shea, D .... 37(1)
Peer, D .... 37(5)
Sampson, I .... 30(3)
Scott, R 5
Smith, A 2
Taylor, M 1
Taylor, S .... 1(1)
Thompson, G ..... 21(13)
Turley, W 2
Warburton, R 44
White, J .... 40(5)
Williams, G .... 25(9)
Woodman, A 44
Worboys, G .... 4(9)

League Goals (51): White 16, Grayson 11, Burns 7, Sampson 4, Warburton 3, Gibb 2, Thompson 2, Armstrong 1, Colkin 1, Doherty 1, Peer 1, Williams 1, Worboys 1. **Coca-Cola Cup Goals (3)**: Burns 1, Colkin 1, Peer 1. **F.A. Cup Goals (1)**: Warburton 1. **Auto Windscreens Shield Goals (3)**: Burns 1, Grayson 1, Hunter 1.
'Player of Year' 1996: Ray Warburton.
Average Home League Attendance 1995-96: 4,831. **Capacity for 1996-97**: 7,653 (all-seated).
Record Attendance: 24,523 v Fulham (Div. 1) 23 April 1966.

PLYMOUTH ARGYLE

Ground: Home Park, Plymouth, Devon PL2 3DQ.
Telephone: 01752-562561. **Clubcall**: 0839 442270. **Club Nickname**: Pilgrims.
First-choice Colours: Green and white shirts; black shorts; green and white stockings.

Baird, I .... 24(3)
Barlow, M .... 25(3)
Billy, C .... 22(10)
Blackwell, K 20
Burnett, W 6
Cherry, S 16
Clayton, G .... 32(4)
Corazzin, C .... 1(5)
Curran, C .... 6(1)
Evans, M .... 41(4)
Hammond, N 4
Heathcote, M 44
Hill, K .... 21(3)
Hodgson, D .... 3(2)
Leadbitter, C .... 29(5)
Littlejohn, A .... 40(2)
Logan, R .... 25(6)
McCall, S .... 2(2)
Magee, K .... –(4)
Mauge, R .... 36(1)
Nugent, K .... 4(2)
O'Hagan, D .... –(6)
Partridge, S .... 6(1)
Patterson, M .... 42(1)
Petterson, A 6
Saunders, M .... 4(6)
Shilton, S .... –(1)

Twiddy, C .... 1(1)	Williams, P 46	Wotton, P .... –(1)

League Goals (68): Littlejohn 17, Evans 12, Baird 6, Mauge 6, Barlow 5, Billy 4, Heathcote 4, Logan 4, Clayton 2, Partridge 2, Williams 2, Corazzin 1, Leadbitter 1, Saunders 1, Opponent 1.
Play-offs – Appearances: Barlow 3, Billy 1, Cherry 3, Corazzin –(1), Curran 3, Evans 3, Heathcote 3, Leadbitter 3, Littlejohn 3, Logan 3, Mauge 2(1), Patterson 3, Williams 3. **Goals (4)**: Evans 1, Leadbitter 1, Mauge 1, Williams 1. **Coca-Cola Cup Goals (1)**: Heathcote 1. **F.A. Cup Goals (5)**: Baird 1, Heathcote 1, Leadbitter 1, Littlejohn 1, Opponent 1. **Auto Windscreens Shield Goals**: None.
'Player of Year' 1996: Mick Heathcote.
Average Home League Attendance 1995-96: 7,120. **Capacity for 1996-97**: 19,640 (seats 6,788, standing 12,852).
Record Attendance: 43,596 v Aston Villa (Div. 2) 10 October 1936.

PRESTON NORTH END

Ground: Deepdale, Lowthorpe Road, Preston, Lancashire PR1 6RU.
Telephone: 01772-902020. **Clubcall**: 0891 660220. **Club Nickname**: Lilywhites. **First-choice Colours**: White shirts; navy shorts; navy stockings.

Ainsworth, G .... –(2)	Gage, K .... 4(3)	Moyes, D 41
Atkinson, G .... 42(2)	Grant, T .... –(1)	Raynor, P .... 2(1)
Barrick, D .... 39(1)	Holmes, S 8	Richardson, B 3
Bennett, G .... 5(3)	Johnson, A 2	Saville, A 44
Birch, P 11	Kidd, R .... 23(7)	Sharp, R 1
Bishop, C 4	Kilbane, K .... 7(4)	Smart, A .... –(2)
Brown, M .... 6(4)	Lancashire, G .... 2(4)	Sparrow, P 13
Bryson, I 44	Lucas, D 1	Squires, J .... 3(4)
Cartwright, L .... 22(4)	McDonald, N .... 8(3)	Vaughan, J 40
Davey, S .... 37(1)	Magee, K .... 4(1)	Wilcox, R 27
Fensome, A 20	Moilanen, T 2	Wilkinson, S .... 36(6)
Fleming, T 5		

League Goals (78): Saville 29, Davey 10, Wilkinson 10, Bryson 9, Atkinson 5, Cartwright 3, Moyes 3, Birch 2, Lancashire 2, Bennett 1, Brown 1, Kilbane 1, Squires 1, Wilcox 1.
Coca-Cola Cup Goals (3): Bryson 1, Cartwright 1, Kidd 1. **F.A. Cup Goals (3)**: Cartwright 1, Wilcox 1, Wilkinson 1. **Auto Windscreens Shield Goals (3)**: Atkinson 1, Kidd 1, Saville 1.
'Player of Year' 1996: Andy Saville.
Average Home League Attendance 1995-96: 10,012. **Capacity for 1996-97**: 18,700 (seats 9,131, standing 9,569).
Record Attendance: 42,684 v Arsenal (Div. 1) 23 April 1938.

ROCHDALE

Ground: Spotland, Sandy Lane, Rochdale, Lancashire OL11 5DS.
Telephone: 01706-44648. **Clubcall**: 0891 555858. **Club Nickname**: Dale.
First-choice Colours: Blue shirts; white shorts; blue stockings.

Barlow, N .... 1(1)	Lyons, P .... 1(2)	Sharp, R 1
Bayliss, D .... 25(3)	Martin, D .... 33(4)	Shaw, G .... 8(9)
Butler, P 38	Mitchell, N .... 3(1)	Stuart, M .... 32(2)
Clarke, C 6	Moulden, P .... 6(10)	Taylor, J .... 8(8)
Deary, J 36	Peake, J .... 45(1)	Thackeray, A .... 27(2)
Formby, K 18	Pilkington, K 6	Thompson, D 43
Gray, I 20	Powell, F .... –(2)	Thompstone, I .... 11(15)
Hall, D .... 9(5)	Price, J 3	Valentine, P .... 22(1)
Hardy, J .... 5(2)	Proctor, J .... 1(2)	Whitehall, S 46
Key, L 14	Russell, A .... 20(5)	Williams, P .... 1(11)
Lancaster, D .... 13(1)	Ryan, D .... 4(3)	

League Goals (57): Whitehall 20, Stuart 13, Deary 4, Peake 4, Thompson 4, Butler 3, Taylor 3, Lancaster 2, Hall 1, Moulden 1, Thompstone 1, Opponent 1.

Coca-Cola Cup Goals (3): Shaw 1, Thompstone 1, Opponent 1. **F.A. Cup Goals (8)**: Deary 2, Moulden 3, Peake 2, Martin 1, Whitehall 1. **Auto Windscreens Shield Goals (9)**: Moulden 3, Whitehall 3, Deary 1, Peake 1, Opponent 1.
'Player of Year' 1996: Paul Butler.
Average Home League Attendance 1995-96: 2,214. **Capacity for 1996-97**: 6,448 (seats 2,054, standing 4,394).
Record Attendance: 24,231 v Notts County (F.A. Cup 2) 10 December 1949.

SCARBOROUGH

Ground: McCain Stadium, Seamer Road, Scarborough, North Yorkshire YO12 4HF.
Telephone: 01723-375094. **Clubcall**: None. **Club Nickname**: Boro.
First-choice Colours: Red shirts; white shorts; red and white stockings.

Antony, G 2
Boardman, C .... 6(3)
Charles, S 41
Cook, M 2
Curtis, A .... 3(2)
D'Auria, D 18
Fairclough, W 7
Foreman, M .... 1(3)
Gardner, J .... 5(1)
Heald, O .... 2(7)
Hicks, S .... 39(3)
Ironside, I 40
Kelly, G 6
Kinnaird, P 3
Knowles, D 46
Lucas, R 44
McHugh, S .... –(1)
Magee, K .... 26(2)
Midgley, C .... 14(2)
Myers, C .... 8(1)
O'Riordan, D 1
Page, D .... 26(10)
Partridge, S .... 5(2)
Ritchie, A .... 33(4)
Robinson, R 1
Rockett, J 39
Sansom, C .... 5(1)
Sunderland, J .... 3(2)
Thew, L .... 9(5)
Todd, M 23
Toman, A .... 12(4)
Trebble, N .... 24(7)
Wells, M .... 10(4)
Willgrass, A .... 2(5)

League Goals (39): Ritchie 8, Charles 5, Page 5, Trebble 5, Rockett 4, Toman 2, D'Auria 1, Gardner 1, Heald 1, Hicks 1, Knowles 1, Magee 1, Midgley 1, Todd 1, Wells 1, Opponent 1.
Coca-Cola Cup Goals (1): D'Auria 1. **F.A. Cup Goals**: None. **Auto Windscreens Shield Goals (1)**: Heald 1.
'Player of Year' 1996: Stuart Hicks.
Average Home League Attendance 1995-96: 1,714. **Capacity for 1996-97**: 5,608 (seats 3,496, standing 2,112).
Record Attendance: 9,000 v Luton Town (F.A. Cup 3) 8 January 1938.

SCUNTHORPE UNITED

Ground: Glanford Park, Doncaster Road, Scunthorpe, South Humberside DN15 8TD.
Telephone: 01724-848077. **Clubcall**: 0891 121652. **Club Nickname**: Irons.
First-choice Colours: Sky blue and claret shirts; sky blue shorts; sky blue stockings.

Bradley, R .... 36(2)
Bullimore, W .... 11(3)
Butler, L 2
Clarkson, P .... 21(3)
D'Auria, D 27
Eyre, J .... 36(3)
Ford, T .... 35(3)
Germaine, G 11
Graham, D .... 1(2)
Hope, C .... 38(2)
Housham, S .... 21(7)
Jones, R 11
Knill, A 38
McFarlane, A .... 41(5)
Murfin, A 1
Nicholson, M ...... 13(23)
O'Halloran, K .... 6(1)
Paterson, J .... 23(3)
Samways, M 33
Sansam, C .... 2(3)
Thornber, S .... 14(2)
Turnbull, L .... 16(7)
Varadi, I .... –(2)
Walsh, M .... 22(3)
Wilson, P 40
Young, S .... 7(7)

League Goals (67): McFarlane 16, Eyre 10, Ford 7, Clarkson 6, D'Auria 5, Hope 3, Jones 3, Knill 3, Turnbull 3, Bullimore 2, Paterson 2, Bradley 1, Graham 1, Nicholson 1, Sansam 1, Wilson 1, Young 1, Opponent 1.
Coca-Cola Cup Goals (4): Eyre 2, Ford 1, McFarlane 1. **F.A. Cup Goals (5)**: McFarlane 2, Eyre 1, Ford 1, Paterson 1. **Auto Windscreens Shield Goals (5)**: McFarlane 2, Eyre 1, Housham 1, Opponent 1.
'Player of Year' 1996: Tony Ford.
Average Home League Attendance 1995-96: 2,434. **Capacity for 1996-97**: 9,183 (seats 6,410, standing 2,773).

Record Attendance (at previous ground, Old Show Ground): 23,935 v Portsmouth (F.A. Cup 4) 30 January 1954.

TORQUAY UNITED

Ground: Plainmoor, Torquay, Devon TQ1 3PS.
Telephone: 01803-328666. **Clubcall**: 0891 664565. **Club Nickname**: Gulls.
First-choice Colours: Navy and yellow shirts; navy shorts; yellow stockings.

Baker, P 20
Barnes, D –(1)
Barrow, L 35(6)
Bayes, A 28
Bedeau, A 1(3)
Buckle, P 11
Byng, D 4(10)
Canham, S 3
Cooke, J 1
Coughlin, R 22(3)
Croft, B –(1)
Curran, C 17(2)
Garner, S 10(1)
Gore, I 25
Gregg, M 1
Haddaoui, R –(2)
Hall, M 22(7)
Hancox, R 15(10)
Hathaway, I 22(4)
Hawthorne, M 17(5)
Hodges, K 1(1)
Jack, R 12(2)
Kelly, T 26(5)
Laight, E 8(12)
Mateu-Pinto, J 5(5)
Monk, G 4(1)
Moors, G –(1)
Ndah, J 16
Newhouse, A 4
Newland, R 17
Oatway, A 24
O'Riordan, D 6(2)
Partridge, S 3
Povey, N 3
Preston, M 4(3)
Ramsey, P 18
Stamps, S 20(3)
Thomas, W 1(5)
Travis, S 4(4)
Watson, A 29
Williams, P 9
Winter, S 36

League Goals (30): Baker 4, Buckle 4, Ndah 3, Gore 2, Jack 2, Laight 2, Newhouse 2, Partridge 2, Watson 2, Curran 1, Garner 1, Hancox 1, Hathaway 1, Mateu-Pinto 1, Stamps 1, Opponent 1.
Coca-Cola Cup Goals (4): Barrow 2, Hathaway 1, Hawthorne 1. **F.A. Cup Goals (6)**: Barrow 1, Byng 1, Gore 1, Hawthorne 1, Mateu-Pinto 1, Opponent 1. **Auto Windscreens Shield Goals (3)**: Curran 1, Hathaway 1, Stamps 1.
'Player of Year' 1996: Tony Oatway.
Average Home League Attendance 1995-96: 2,454. **Capacity for 1996-97**: 6,000 (seats 2,300, standing 3,700).
Record Attendance: 21,908 v Huddersfield Town (F.A. Cup 4) 29 January 1955.

WIGAN ATHLETIC

Ground: Springfield Park, Wigan, Lancashire WN6 7BA.
Telephone: 01942-244433. **Clubcall**: 0891 121655. **Club Nickname**: Latics.
First-choice Colours: Blue, white and green shirts; blue shorts; blue and white stockings.

Barnwell-Edinboro, J 2(8)
Benjamin, I 1(2)
Biggins, W 15(3)
Black, T 8(13)
Butler, J 33
Carragher, M 22(6)
Diaz, I 31(6)
Doolan, J 2(1)
Farnworth, S 43
Farrell, A 21(2)
Felgate, D 3
Greenall, C 37
Johnson, G 27
Kelly, T 2
Kilford, I 18(7)
Lancashire, G 5
Leonard, M 32(3)
Lightfoot, C 11(3)
Lowe, D 7
Lyons, A 14(8)
Martinez, R 42
Miller, D 4(3)
Mutch, A 7
Ogden, N 10
Pender, J 40(1)
Rimmer, N 27(3)
Robertson, J 14
Seba, J 8(12)
Sharp, K 20

League Goals (62): Diaz 10, Martinez 9, Leonard 7, Sharp 6, Johnson 3, Kilford 3, Lancashire 3, Lowe 3, Seba 3, Biggins 2, Black 2, Greenall 2, Barnwell-Edinboro 1, Butler 1, Farrell 1, Lightfoot 1, Lyons 1, Mutch 1, Pender 1, Robertson 1, Opponent 1.
Coca-Cola Cup Goals (2): Lyons 1, Martinez 1. **F.A. Cup Goals (9):** Martinez 3, Black 2, Diaz 2, Leonard 1, Opponent 1. **Auto Windscreens Shield Goals (1)**: Benjamin 1.
'Player of Year' 1996: Roberto Martinez.
Average Home League Attendance 1995-96: 2,856. **Capacity for 1996-97**: 7,097 (seats 1,109, standing 5,988).
Record Attendance: 27,500 v Hereford United (F.A. Cup 2) 12 December 1953.

SCOTTISH LEAGUE ROLL CALL
APPEARANCES & SCORERS 1995-96
(Figures in brackets = appearances as substitute)

PREMIER DIVISION

ABERDEEN
Ground: Pittodrie Stadium, Aberdeen. **Capacity:** 21,634 (all-seated).
Telephone: 01224-632328. **Colours:** Red and navy blue.

Bernard, P .... 27(4)
Booth, S .... 20(4)
Buchan, M .... 1(3)
Christie, K .... –(2)
Craig, M .... –(1)
Dodds, W .... 28(3)
Glass, S 32
Grant, B .... 22(3)
Hetherston, P .... 9(2)
Inglis, J 24
Irvine, B .... 17(1)
Jess, E 25
Kpedekpo, M .... 1(4)
McKimmie, S 29
McKinnon, R .... –(1)
Miller, J 31
Robertson, H .... 5(6)
Rowson, D .... 7(2)
Shearer, D .... 15(15)
Smith, G 33
Snelders, T .... 6(1)
Thomson, S .... –(4)
Watt, M 30
Windass, D .... 19(1)
Woodthorpe, C 15

League Goals (52): Booth 9, Miller 9, Dodds 7, Windass 6, Glass 3, Irvine 3, Jess 3, Shearer 3, Bernard 1, Buchan 1, Inglis 1, Woodthorpe 1, Opponents 5. **Scottish League Cup Goals (13)**: Dodds 5, Booth 3, Inglis 1, Miller 1, Shearer 1, Woodthorpe 1, Opponent 1. **Scottish Cup Goals (7)**: Shearer 3, Windass 3, Bernard 1.

CELTIC
Ground: Celtic Park, Glasgow. **Capacity:** 44,864.
Telephone: 0141-556-2611. **Colours:** Green and white.

Boyd, T 34
Cadete .... 2(4)
Collins, J .... 26(3)
Donnelly, S 35
Falconer, W .... –(2)
Grant, P .... 30(1)
Gray, S .... 3(2)
Hay, C .... 1(3)
Hughes, J 26
Mackay, M .... 9(2)
McKinlay, T 32
McLaughlin, B .... 11(15)
McNamara, J 26
McQuilken, J .... 3(1)
McStay, P .... 29(1)
Marshall, G 36
O'Donnell, P .... 14(1)
O'Neil, B .... 3(2)
Thom, A .... 31(1)
Van Hooijdonk, P 34
Vata, R .... 5(1)
Walker, A .... 4(12)
Wieghorst, M .... 2(9)

League Goals (74): Van Hooijdonk 26, Collins 11, Donnelly 6, Cadete 5, Thom 5, McLaughlin 4, Grant 3, O'Donnell 3, Walker 3, Hughes 2, McStay 2, Gray 1, Mackay 1, McNamara 1, Wieghorst 1.
Scottish League Cup Goals (5): Van Hooijdonk 2, Collins 1, Donnelly 1, Thom 1. **Scottish Cup Goals (8)**: Van Hooijdonk 4, Donnelly 2, Thom 2. **European Cup-Winners' Cup Goals (7)**: Thom 4, Donnelly 2, Walker.

FALKIRK
Ground: Brockville Park, Falkirk. **Capacity:** 12,066.
Telephone: 01324-624121. **Colours:** Navy blue and sky blue.

Abbott, G .... –(1)
Clark, J .... 14(3)
Craig, A 14
Elliot, D .... 31(1)
Ferguson, D 26
Finnigan, A .... 8(1)
Fulton, S .... 4(1)
Graham, A 8
Gray, A 16
Hagen, D .... 21(4)
Hamilton, G .... –(1)
Henderson, N .... –(9)
Inglis, N 1
Iorfa, D .... 3(1)
James, K .... 10(4)
Johnston, F .... 3(3)
Johnston, M 31
Kirk, S .... 16(4)
Lamont, W 7
Lawrie, A 1
Mackenzie, S .... 27(3)

McDonald, C .... 4(5)
McGowan, J .... 27(2)
McGraw, M .... 2(7)
McGrillen, P .... 24(6)
McLaughlin, J ...... 15(1)
Munro, S 13
Napier, C .... 3(1)
Oliver, N 3
Parks, A 28
Rice, B .... 1(4)
Seaton, A .... –(1)
Weir, D 34
Whiteside, G .... –(2)
Wright, G .... 1(1)

League Goals (31): Johnston 5, McGrillen 5, Kirk 4, Craig 3, Weir 3, Clark 2, James 2, Finnigan 1, Iorfa 1, Mackenzie 1, McDonald 1, McGowan 1, McLaughlin 1, Opponent 1.
Scottish League Cup Goals (3): Johnston 2, Henderson 1. **Scottish Cup Goals**: None.

HEART OF MIDLOTHIAN

Ground: Tynecastle Park, Edinburgh. **Capacity:** 16,613 (all-seated).
Telephone: 0131-337-6132. **Colours:** Maroon.

Berry, N .... 16(3)
Bruno, P 22
Callaghan, S .... –(1)
Cameron, C 4
Colquhoun, J ...... 20(11)
Eskilsson, H .... 8(2)
Fulton, S 26
Hagen, D .... 5(2)
Hamilton, B .... 8(4)
Hogarth, M 1
Jamieson, W .... 2(3)
Johnston, A .... 30(3)
Lawrence, A .... 17(9)
Leitch, D .... 4(2)
Levein, C 1
Locke, G 29
Mackay, G .... 21(5)
McManus, A .... 17(1)
McPherson, D ...... 22(4)
Millar, J .... 16(4)
Miller, C .... 2(1)
Naysmith, G .... –(1)
Nelson, C 4
O'Connor, G 3
Pointon, N .... 21(1)
Ritchie, P 28
Robertson, J .... 28(5)
Rousset, G 25
Smith, H 3
Smith, P .... 4(5)
Thomas, K .... –(3)
Winnie, D 6
Wishart, F 1
Wright, G 2

League Goals (55): Robertson 11, Johnston 8, Colquhoun 5, Lawrence 4, Locke 4, Millar 4, Pointon 3, Cameron 2, Eskillson 2, Fulton 2, Mackay 2, McManus 2, Bruno 1, Hagen 1, McPherson 1, Ritchine 1, Opponents 2.
Scottish League Cup Goals (9): McPherson 3, Colquhoun 1, Hagen 1, Hamilton 1, Lawrence 1, Leitch 1, Robertson 1. **Scottish Cup Goals (8)**: Ritchie 2, Berry 1, Colquhoun 1, Johnston 1, Lawrence 1, McPherson 1, Robertson 1.

HIBERNIAN

Ground: Easter Road Stadium, Edinburgh. **Capacity:** 15,590 (all-seated).
Telephone: 0131-661-2159. **Colours:** Green and white.

Dods, D .... 14(1)
Donald, G .... 2(11)
Dow, A 8
Evans, G .... 12(11)
Farrell, D .... 7(1)
Harper, K .... 14(2)
Hunter, G 22
Jackson, C .... 19(4)
Jackson, D 36
Leighton, J 36
Love, G .... 11(3)
McAllister, K .... 29(2)
McGinlay, P .... 30(1)
McLaughlin, J 9
Millen, A 25
Miller, Graeme .... –(1)
Miller, Greg .... 1(2)
Miller, W 13
Mitchell, G 6
O'Neill, M .... 27(2)
Renwick, M .... 1(1)
Tortolano, J .... 14(1)
Tweed, S 31
Weir, M .... 4(5)
Wright, K .... 25(3)

League Goals (43): Jackson 11, Wright 9, O'Neill 6, McGinlay 5, McAllister 4, Harper 3, Evans 2, Donald 1, Dow 1, Weir 1.
Scottish League Cup Goals (3): Jackson 2, McGinlay 1. **Scottish Cup Goals**: None.

KILMARNOCK

Ground: Rugby Park, Kilmarnock. **Capacity:** 18,128 (all-seated).
Telephone: 01563-525184. **Colours:** Royal blue and white.

Anderson, D 28
Black, T 30
Brown, T .... 19(6)
Connor, R .... 22(1)
Findlay, W .... 2(1)
Geddes, A 2
Henry, J .... 22(7)
Holt, G .... 17(9)
Lauchlan, J 5
Lekovic, D 33
MacPherson, A 35
McIntyre, J 7

McKee, C .... 19(9)	Montgomerie, S ... 12(2)	Skilling, M .... 13(2)
Maskrey, S .... 13(8)	Reilly, M .... 22(6)	Whitworth, N 28
Meldrum, C 1	Roberts, M .... 2(9)	Wright, P .... 35(1)
Mitchell, A .... 29(1)		

League Goals (39): Wright 13, Brown 6, Black 4, McKee 4, Henry 3, Mitchell 3, McIntyre 2, MacPherson 1, Maskrey 1, Skilling 1, Opponent 1. **Scottish League Cup Goals (2)**: Roberts 1, Wright 1. **Scottish Cup Goals (3)**: Wright 2, Anderson 1.

MOTHERWELL

Ground: Fir Park, Motherwell. **Capacity:** 13,742 (all-seated). **Telephone:** 01698-333333. **Colours:** Claret and amber.

Arnott, D .... 23(4)	Hendry, J .... 8(8)	McSkimming, S .... 13(2)
Burns, A .... 14(14)	Howie, S 36	Martin, B 33
Coyne, T .... 9(5)	Krivokapic, M 13	May, E 28
Davies, W .... 26(7)	Lambert, P 35	Philliben, J .... 19(5)
Denham, G .... 11(2)	McCart, C 20	Ritchie, I .... 5(5)
Dolan, J. .... 24(3)	McCulloch, L .... –(1)	Roddie, A .... 12(12)
Essandoh, R .... –(4)	McKinnon, R 27	Ross, I 1
Falconer, W 15	McLeish, A 1	Van der Gaag, M 12
Ferguson, P 1	McMillan, S .... 10(2)	

League Goals (28): Falconer 5, Coyne 4, Arnott 3, Burns 3, Davies 2, Hendry 2, Lambert 2, Martin 2, McSkimming 1, May 1, Van der Gaag 1, Opponents 2. **Scottish League Cup Goals (4)**: Arnott 3, Lambert 1. **Scottish Cup Goals**: None. **UEFA Cup Goals (3)**: Arnott 1, Burna 1, McSkimming 1.

PARTICK THISTLE

Ground: Firhill Stadium, Glasgow. **Capacity:** 20,876. **Telephone:** 0141-945-4811. **Colours:** Red and yellow.

Adams, C .... 1(4)	Henderson, N ...... 12(4)	Pittman, S 14
Ayton, S .... 1(4)	Lyons, A 9	Shepherd, A .... –(1)
Cairns, M 3	MacDonald, W ..... 11(6)	Slavin, J 8
Cameron, I .... 32(3)	MacLeod, M 1	Smith, T .... 24(1)
Craig, A 9	McCue, J .... 2(1)	Stirling, J 2
Curran, H .... 3(5)	McDonald, R .... 12(4)	Tierney, P 1
Dinnie, A 31	McKee, K .... 10(1)	Turner, T .... 20(2)
Docherty, S .... 19(5)	McMahon, S .... –(1)	Walker, J 33
Foster, W 19	McWilliams, D ...... 25(2)	Watson, G 32
Gibson, A .... 8(14)	Milne, C .... 19(3)	Welsh, S 35

League Goals (29): McDonald 6, Lyons 5, McWilliams 4, Docherty 3, Turner 3, Craig 2, Smith 2, Cameron 1, Gibson 1, Henderson 1, Watson 1. **Play-off Goals (2)**: Cameron 1, Lyons 1. **Scottish League Cup Goals (10)**: Craig 4, McWilliams 2, Curran 1, Foster 1, McDonald 1, Pittman 1. **Scottish Cup Goals**: None.

RAITH ROVERS

Ground: Stark's Park, Kirkcaldy. **Capacity:** 11,462. **Telephone:** 01592-263514. **Colours:** Navy blue.

Bonar, P .... 4(1)	Duffield, P 9	Landels, G .... –(1)
Broddle, J .... 23(4)	Forrest, G .... –(1)	Lennon, D .... 30(3)
Buist, M 2	Fridge, L 1	McAnespie, S .... 2(1)
Cameron, C 30	Geddes, A 9	McCulloch, G 7
Coyle, R .... 22(2)	Graham, A .... 18(7)	McInally, J .... 23(2)
Crawford, S .... 21(7)	Humphries, M 9	McKilligan, N .... 1(2)
Dair, J .... 19(1)	Kirk, S .... 6(1)	McMillan, I .... 4(4)
Dargo, C .... –(1)	Kirkwood, D .... 25(3)	Millar, J 3
Dennis, S 25	Krivokapic, M 5	Nicholl, J .... –(1)

Raeside, R .... 6(2)
Rougier, A .... 17(6)
Sellars, N .... –(1)
Sinclair, D .... 31(1)
Taylor, A .... 1(8)
Thomson, S 26
Thomson, S 9
Wilson, B .... 8(5)

League Goals (41): Cameron 9, Duffield 5, Graham 5, Lennon 5, Crawford 3, Dair 3, Kirkwood 3, Sinclair 3, Kirk 1, Millar 1, Raeside 1, Rougier 1, Thomson 1. **Scottish League Cup Goals (3)**: Kirkwood 2, Rougier 1. **Scottish Cup Goals (3)**: Crawford 2, Lennon 1. **UEFA Cup Goals (10)**: Lennon 4, Cameron 1, Crawford 1, Dair 1, McAnespie 1, Rougier 1, Wilson 1.

RANGERS

Ground: Ibrox Stadium, Glasgow. **Capacity:** 50,800 (all-seated).
Telephone: 0141-427-8500. **Colours:** Royal blue.

Andersen, E 6
Bollan, G 4
Brown, J .... 8(6)
Cleland, A .... 21(4)
Durie, G .... 21(6)
Durrant, I .... 6(9)
Ferguson, I .... 16(2)
Gascoigne, P .... 27(1)
Goram, A 30
Gough, C 29
Laudrup, B 22
McCall, S .... 19(2)
McCoist, A .... 18(7)
McGinty, B 2
McInnes, D .... 5(1)
McLaren, A 36
Mikhailichenko, A ... 6(5)
Miller, C .... 17(6)
Moore, C .... 9(2)
Murray, N .... 2(3)
Petric, G .... 32(1)
Robertson, D 25
Salenko, O .... 14(2)
Scott, C 3
Shields, G 1
Snelders, T 2
Steven, T .... 5(1)
Thomson, W 1
Van Vossen, P .... 3(4)
Wright, S 6

League Goals (85): Durie 17, McCoist 16, Gascoigne 14, Salenko 7, Andersen 6, Gough 3, McCall 3, McLaren 3, Miller 3, Robertson 3, Ferguson 2, Laudrup 2, Cleland 1, Moore 1, Petric 1, Opponents 3.
Scottish League Cup Goals (8): McCoist 3, Hateley 2, Gascoigne 1, McCall 1, Salenko 1. **Scottish Cup Goals (24)**: Durie 4, Cleland 3, Ferguson 3, Gascoigne 3, Laudrup 3, Miller 3, McCoist 1, Mikhailichenko 1, Robertson 1, Van Vossen 1, Opponent 1. **European Cup Goals (7)**: Durie 2, Gough 2, Ferguson 1, Gascoigne 1, Laudrup 1.

FIRST DIVISION

AIRDRIEONIANS

Ground: Broadwood Stadium, Cumbernauld. **Capacity:** 8,050 (all-seated).
Telephone: 01236-762067. **Colours:** White and red.

Black, K 33
Bonar, P .... 9(3)
Boyle, J 36
Connelly, G .... –(8)
Connolly, P 6
Cooper, S 24
Davies, J .... 33(2)
Duffield, P .... 19(5)
Harvey, P .... 27(7)
Hetherston, P .... 7(2)
Jack, P .... 9(5)
McClelland, J .... 1(2)
McIntyre, J .... 22(7)
McIntyre, T .... 12(5)
McPeak, A .... –(1)
Martin, J 20
Rhodes, A 16
Sandison, J 30
Smith, A .... 28(3)
Stewart, A 30
Sweeney, S 24
Tait, S .... 2(2)
Wilson, M .... 8(5)

League Goals (43): McIntyre 10, Duffield 7, Connolly 4, Cooper 4, Hetherston 4, Davies 3, Black 2, Boyle 2, Harvey 2, Smith 2, Sandison 1, Opponents 2.
Scottish League Cup Goals (7): Boyle 2, Duffield 2, Cooper 1, McIntyre 1. Opponent 1. **Scottish Cup Goals (6)**: Duffield 3, Bonar 1, Copper 1, Smith 1. **Challenge Cup Goals (2)**: Boyle 1, McIntyre 1.

CLYDEBANK

Ground: Boghead Park, Dumbarton. **Capacity:** 5,007.
Telephone: 0141-955-9048. **Colours:** White, red and black.

Agnew, P .... 4(3)
Bowman, G 33
Brannigan, K 5
Connell, G 34
Connelly, D .... 3(4)
Crawford, D .... –(1)
Currie, T .... 27(1)
Dunn, R .... 3(2)
Eadie, K .... 26(2)
Flannigan, C .... 8(17)
Grady, J .... 35(1)
Hardie, D .... –(1)
Irons, D 8
Jack, S .... 14(4)
Keane, G .... –(1)
Kerrigan, S .... –(1)
Lansdowne, A ...... 10(4)
Lovering, P .... 11(10)
McLaughlin, I 1
Matthews, G 36
Melvin, W .... –(1)
Miller, S .... 3(4)
Murdoch, S .... 27(1)
Nicholls, D 35
Robertson, J .... 25(6)
Sutherland, C .... 25(1)
Teale, G .... 9(7)
Tomlinson, C 14

League Goals (39): Eadie 11, Grady 9, Robertson 5, Flannigan 3, Bowman 2, Connell 2, Nicholls 2, Sutherland 2, Irons 1, Lovering 1, Teale 1.
Scottish League Cup Goals (1): Robertson 1. **Scottish Cup Goals**: None.
Challenge Cup Goals (5): Grady 2, Kerrigan 2, Nicholls 1.

DUMBARTON

Ground: Boghead Park, Dumbarton. **Capacity:** 5,007.
Telephone: 01389-762569 **Colours:** White and yellow.

Burns, H .... 10(1)
Charnley, J .... 16(2)
Dallas, S .... 8(14)
Dennison, P 2
Fabiani, R .... 19(1)
Foster, A .... 10(2)
Gibson, C .... 23(6)
Glancy, M 1
Goldie, J .... 1(1)
Gow, S .... 20(1)
Granger, A .... 20(11)
Hamilton, J 3
King, T .... 27(1)
MacFarlane, I 22
McGarvey, M ...... 14(10)
McGivern, S .... 9(2)
McKinnon, C .... 31(2)
Marsland, J 18
Martin, P 12
Meechan, J .... 31(1)
Meechan, K .... 12(1)
Melvin, M .... 32(1)
Mooney, M .... 31(5)
Sharp, L .... 14(1)
Ward, H .... 10(4)

League Goals (23): Mooney 5, Granger 3, Dallas 2, Gibson 2, McGarvey 2, Ward 2, Burns 1, Charnley 1, Foster 1, McKinnon 1, Martin 1, Sharp 1, Opponent 1.
Scottish League Cup Goals: None. **Scottish Cup Goals (1)**: Mooney 1.
Challenge Cup Goals: None.

DUNDEE

Ground: Dens Park Stadium, Dundee. **Capacity:** 14,481.
Telephone: 01382-826104. **Colours:** Navy blue and white.

Adamczuk, D .... 8(5)
Anderson, I .... 9(8)
Bain, K .... 7(3)
Britton, G .... 15(10)
Cargill, A .... 11(7)
Charnley, J 12
Duffy, C 31
Duffy, J 19
Farningham, R ..... 13(5)
Hamilton, J .... 30(3)
Hutchison, M .... –(1)
McBain, R .... 3(3)
McCann, N 22
McKeown, G .... 13(4)
McQueen, T 21
Magee, D .... –(1)
Manley, R 17
Mathers, P .... 1(1)
O'Driscoll, J .... 1(4)
Pageaud, M 35
Rae, G .... 4(2)
Shaw, G .... 33(3)
Smith, B 20
Teasdale, M 1
Tosh, P .... 29(1)
Tully, C 2
Vrto, D .... 25(2)
Wieghorst, M 14

League Goals (53): Hamilton 14, Tosh 9, Shaw 7, Wieghorst 4, Charnley 3, Duffy 3, Farnigham 3, Britton 2, McCann 2, Bain 1, Cargill 1, McKeown 1, O'Driscoll 1, Opponents 2.
Scottish League Cup Goals (15): McCann 5, Shaw 3, Wieghorst 3, Hamilton 2, Tosh 2. **Scottish Cup Goals (1)**: Duffy 1. **Challenge Cup Goals (8)**: Hamilton 3, Anderson (I.) 1, Anderson (J.) 1, Cargill 2, Shaw 1.

DUNDEE UNITED

Ground: Tannadice Park, Dundee. **Capacity:** 12,608 (all-seated).
Telephone: 01382-833166. **Colours:** Tangerine and black.

Bett, J 23
Bowman, D .... 16(1)
Brewster, C .... 23(7)
Caldwell, N 2
Connolly, P .... 3(3)
Coyle, O .... 20(8)
Crabbe, S .... 1(1)
Dailly, C .... 20(10)
Hannah, D .... 4(3)
Honeyman, B .... –(1)
Johnson, I .... 25(3)
Keith, M .... –(4)
McKinlay, W 5
McKinnon, R .... 5(4)
McLaren, A .... 23(8)
McQuilken, J .... 6(3)
McSwegan, G ...... 19(6)
Malpas, M 30
Maxwell, A 34
O'Hanlon, K 2
Perry, M .... 18(2)
Pressley, S 35
Robertson, A .... 1(3)
Shannon, R 26
Walker, P .... –(2)
Welsh, B .... 21(2)
Winters, R .... 34(1)

League Goals (73): Brewster 17, McSwegan 17, Winters 7, Coyle 5, Johnson 4, McKinlay 4, McLaren 3, Bett 2, Malpas 2, Perry 2, Connolly 1, Dailly 1, Hannah 1, Pressley 1, Shannon 1, Welsh 1, Opponents 4.
Play-off Goals (3): Coyle 1, Dailly 1, Welsh 1. **Scottish League Cup Goals (5)**: Connolly 2, Caldwell 1, McKinlay 1, Winters 1. **Scottish Cup Goals (4)**: Coyle 3, Brewster 1. **Challenge Cup Goals (10)**: Connolly 2, Johnson 2, Winters 2, Brewster 1, Dailly 1, Honeyman 1, McKinlay 1.

DUNFERMLINE ATHLETIC

Ground: East End Park, Dunfermline. **Capacity:** 18,394.
Telephone: 01383-724295. **Colours:** Black and white.

Bingham, D .... 12(3)
Callaghan, T .... –(3)
Clark, J 11
Cooper, N .... 2(2)
Den Bieman, I .... 16(10)
Farrell, G .... 4(2)
Fenwick, P .... –(1)
Ferguson, S .... –(1)
Fleming, D .... 25(8)
French, H .... 21(2)
Hegarty, R .... 3(6)
Ireland, C 10
Kinnaird, P .... 6(3)
McCathie, N 18
McCulloch, M .... 4(6)
McNamara, J 7
Millar, M 25
Miller, C 24
Moore, A 28
Petrie, S .... 31(3)
Rice, B .... 5(1)
Rissannen, K .... 1(1)
Robertson, C .... 27(1)
Shaw, G .... 17(11)
Smith, A .... 17(2)
Smith, P .... 10(1)
Tod, A 36
Van de Kamp, G 26
Westwater, I .... 10(1)

League Goals (73): Petrie 13, Shaw 12, Smith 9, Millar 5, Moore 5, Robertson 5, Tod 5, French 4, Bingham 3, Fleming 3, McCathie 3, Clark 1, Den Bieman 1, Heggarty 1, McNamara 1, Opponents 2.
Scottish League Cup Goals (4): Den Bieman 1, McCathie 1, Moore 1, Petrie 1. **Scottish Cup Goals (3)**: Bingham 1, Petrie 1, Smith 1. **Challenge Cup Goals (6)**: Shaw 2, McNamara 1, Millar 1, Petrie 1, Tod 1.

GREENOCK MORTON

Ground: Cappielow Park, Greenock. **Capacity:** 14,267.
Telephone: 01475-723571. **Colours:** Royal blue and white.

Anderson, J .... 29(1)
Blaikie, A .... –(3)
Blair, P .... 3(15)
Boe, A 3
Collins, D 36
Cormack, P .... 23(2)
Hawke, W .... 34(1)
Hunter, J .... –(1)
Johnstone, D .... 27(2)
Laing, D .... 3(23)
Lilley, D 35
Lindberg, J 26
McArthur, S .... 17(6)
McCahill, S 24
McInnes, D 12
McPherson, C ...... 17(7)
Mahood, A 31
Rajamaki, M .... 34(2)
Reid, B 9
Wylie, D 33

League Goals (57): Lilley 14, Hawke 13, Rajamaki 11, Anderson 4, Mahood 4, Cormack 2, Johnstone 2, Lindberg 2, Collins 1, Laing 1, McCahill 1, McInnes 1, Opponent 1.
Scottish League Cup Goals: None. **Scottish Cup Goals (3)**: Cormack 1, Lilley 1, Rajamaki 1. **Challenge Cup Goals**: None.

HAMILTON ACADEMICAL

Ground: Cliftonhill Stadium, Coatbridge. **Capacity:** 1,238.
Telephone: 01698-286103. **Colours:** White and red.

Baptie, C 31
Chalmers, P 1
Clark, G .... 14(3)
Cormack, D .... 10(1)
Craig, D 17
Diver, D .... 1(3)
Ferguson, A 26
Geraghty, M .... 17(3)
Hartley, P .... 29(2)
Hillcoat, C 31
Lorimer, D .... 5(10)
McCarrison, D .... –(3)
McCloy, S .... 1(4)
McCormick, S .... 5(4)
McCulloch, S .... 4(6)
McEntegart, S ...... 28(1)
McFarlane, D .... –(1)
McIntosh, M 23
McInulty, S .... 17(2)
McKenzie, P .... 11(12)
McParland, J .... –(1)
McQuade, J .... 9(4)
McStay, R .... 16(4)
Paterson, C 9
Quitongo, J .... 18(4)
Renicks, S .... 29(1)
Sherry, J .... 24(1)
Thomson, S .... 19(2)
Tighe, M 1

League Goals (40): Hartley 11, Geraghty 6, McEntegart 4, McStay 4, Quitongo 4, Clark 3, Baptie 1, Craig 1, McCulloch 1, McIntosh 1, McQuade 1, Renicks 1, Sherry 1, Opponent 1.
Scottish League Cup Goals: None. **Scottish Cup Goals**: None. **Challenge Cup Goals (2)**: Clark 2.

ST. JOHNSTONE

Ground: McDiarmid Park, Perth. **Capacity:** 10,673 (all-seated).
Telephone: 01738-626961. **Colours:** Royal blue and white.

Cherry, P .... 13(2)
Davidson, C 2
Donaldson, E 14
English, I .... –(1)
Farquhar, G .... 10(5)
Ferguson, I .... 3(7)
Grant, R .... 19(8)
Griffin, D .... 22(9)
Irons, D .... 9(8)
Jenkinson, L 18
McCluskey, S 2
McGowne, K 23
McLean, S .... 1(5)
McQuillan, J 25
Main, A 34
O'Boyle, G 35
O'Neil, J 34
Preston, A .... 25(2)
Proctor, M .... 2(4)
Robertson, S 2
Scott, P 28
Sekerlioglu, A 17
Tosh, S .... 8(1)
Twaddle, K .... 17(9)
Weir, J 29
Whiteford, A .... 3(1)
Young, S .... 1(3)

League Goals (60): O'Boyle 21, Scott 8, Grant 5, O'Neil 5, Twaddle 4, Jenkinson 2, McGowne 2, McQuillan 2, Preston 2, Sekerlioglu 2, Farquhar 1, Ferguson 1, Tosh 1, Opponents 4.
Scottish League Cup Goals (1): O'Boyle 1. **Scottish Cup Goals (5)**: Scott 3, Grant 1, O'Boyle 1. **Challenge Cup Goals (2)**: O'Neil 1, Scott 1.

ST. MIRREN

Ground: St. Mirren Park, Paisley. **Capacity:** 15,410.
Telephone: 0141-889-2558. **Colours:** White, black and grey.

Archdeacon, P ..... 16(4)
Baker, M 26
Bone, A .... 3(2)
Boyd, J .... 12(2)
Combe, A 21
Dawson, R 8
Dick, J .... 24(2)
Fenwick, P 26
Fullarton, J .... 19(3)
Galloway, G 1
Gillies, R .... 28(5)
Hetherston, B .... 16(7)
Hringsson, H .... –(1)
Inglis, G .... –(1)
Iwelumo, C .... 2(3)
Lavety, B .... 27(2)
Law, R .... 15(5)
Love, F .... –(1)
McGrotty, G .... 3(7)
McIntyre, P .... 19(6)
McLaughlin, B ...... 29(1)
McMillan, J .... –(8)
McWhirter, N 17
Makela, J 1
Milne, D .... 1(4)
Money, I 12
Prentice, A .... –(2)
Scrimgour, D 13
Smith, B .... 6(6)
Taylor, S .... 14(10)
Watson, S .... 18(12)
Yardley, M 29

League Goals (46): Lavety 11, Yardley 8, Boyd 3, Fenwick 3, Gillies 3, Taylor 3, Archdeacon 2, Dick 2, Fullarton 2, Hetherston 2, McLaughlin 2, Bone 1, Iwelumo 1, McMillan 1, Watson 1, Opponent 1.
Scottish League Cup Goals (1): McLaughlin 1. **Scottish Cup Goals**: None. **Challenge Cup Goals (3)**: Laverty 2, Dawson 1.

SECOND DIVISION

AYR UNITED

Ground: Somerset Park, Ayr. **Capacity:** 12,128.
Telephone: 01292-263435. **Colours:** White and black.

Agnew, S .... 2(1)
Balfour, E .... 12(2)
Barnstaple, K .... 2(3)
Bell, R .... 4(1)
Biggart, K .... 9(16)
Bilsland, B .... 15(6)
Boyce, D 4
Burns, G .... –(1)
Byrne, D .... 8(2)
Chalmers, P 5
Clarke, J .... 7(2)
Connie, C .... 10(3)
Connelly, S .... 1(1)
Coyle, R 4
Dalziel, G .... 16(7)
Diver, D 9
Duncan, C 21
English, I 8
George, D .... 24(1)
Henderson, D 11
Hood, G .... 19(1)
Jamieson, W 20
Kinnaird, P .... 16(2)
Lamont, W 4
Law, R 6
MacFarlane, C .... 3(2)
McKilligan, N .... 7(3)
Mooney, S 1
Moore, V 11
Napier, C 10
Nolan, J 1
Paavola, T 3
Rolling, F 2
Scott, M 7
Sharples, J 26
Shepherd, A .... 10(1)
Smith, H 9
Smith, M .... 8(2)
Stainrod, S 2
Steel, T .... 10(5)
Tannock, R .... 12(2)
Traynor, J .... 20(4)
Wilson, S .... 7(1)
Wilson, W .... 9(1)
Yule, R .... 1(1)

League Goals (40): Bilsland 5, English 5, Dalziel 4, Diver 4, Sharples 4, Henderson 3, Hood 2, Kinnaird 2, Moore 2, Paavola 2, Balfour 1, Chalmers 1, George 1, Jamieson 1, Smith 1, Steele 1, Wilson 1.
Scottish League Cup Goals: None. **Scottish Cup Goals**: None. **Challenge Cup Goals (1)**: Bilsland 1.

BERWICK RANGERS

Ground: Shielfield Park, Berwick-upon-Tweed. **Capacity:** 4,131.
Telephone: 01289-307424. **Colours:** Black and gold.

Banks, A .... 26(4)
Chivers, D .... –(1)
Clarke, J .... 3(2)
Clegg, N .... –(6)
Cole, A 8
Coughlin, J 3
Cowan, M .... 25(1)
Forrester, P .... 25(10)
Fraser, G 36
Gallacher, J 4
Govan, M .... –(1)
Graham, T 33
Irvine, W 35
Kane, K .... 22(6)
McGlynn, D .... 15(2)
McQueen, J .... 5(1)
Neil, M .... 33(2)
Reid, A .... 23(1)
Rutherford, P .... 6(3)
Thomson, M 2
Valentine, C 31
Walton, K .... 13(10)
Wilson, M .... 17(8)
Young, N 31

League Goals (64): Irvine 13, Forrester 10, Fraser 7, McGlynn 6, Banks 5, Neil 5, Walton 5, Cowan 3, Graham 3, Reid 2, Rutherford 2, Cole 1, Kane 1, Wilson 1.
Scottish League Cup Goals (1): Clegg 1. **Scottish Cup Goals (6)**: Kane 2, Fraser 1, Irvine 1, Reid 1, Opponent 1. **Challenge Cup Goals (1)**: Cole 1.

CLYDE

Ground: Broadwood Stadium, Cumbernauld. **Capacity:** 8,050 (all-seated).
Telephone: 01236-451511. **Colours:** White, black and red.

Angus, I 33
Annand, E 35
Brown, J 9
Brownlie, P .... 2(2)
Campbell, P .... –(2)
Coleman, S .... –(1)
Dawson, R 8
Dickson, J .... 5(8)
Falconer, M .... 2(7)
Ferguson, G .... 26(1)
Gillies, K 30
Harrison, T .... 21(6)
Hillcoat, J 25
Knox, K .... 28(1)
McCarron, J .... 1(1)
McCheyne, G ..... 11(10)
McCluskey, G .... 5(11)
McConnell, I .... 15(5)
McEwan, C 1
McLay, J .... 9(2)
McQueen, J 11
Muir, J .... –(1)
Nicholas, C 31
Nisbet, I .... 4(12)
O'Neill, M .... 19(4)
Parks, G 1
Patterson, P .... 4(9)
Prunty, J .... 11(8)
Thomson, J 24
Watson, G 25

League Goals (47): Annand 21, Nicholas 5, Harrison 4, McCluskey 3, Angus 2, McConnell 2, O'Neill 2, Thomson 2, Falconer 1, Knox 1, McCarron 1, McCheyne

1, Nisbet 1, Patterson 1.
Scottish League Cup Goals (1): Annand 1. **Scottish Cup Goals (9)**: Annand 3, Nicholas 2, Angus 1, Harrison 1, McCheyne 1, McConnell 1. **Challenge Cup Goals**: None.

EAST FIFE

Ground: Bayview Park, Methil. **Capacity:** 5,433.
Telephone: 01333-426323. **Colours:** Black and gold.

Allan, G 36	Dixon, A .... 17(3)	Hope, D .... 18(7)
Andrew, B .... 10(6)	Donaghy, M 32	Hunter, P .... –(3)
Archibald, S .... 29(2)	Dwarika, A .... 12(10)	Hutcheon, S .... 7(18)
Balmain, K 1	Ferguson, P .... 5(1)	McStay, J 34
Beaton, D .... 32(1)	Gartshore, P .... 6(4)	Robertson, D 1
Broddle, J 6	Gibb, R 24	Scott, R .... 32(2)
Chalmers, P .... 6(2)	Hamill, A .... 12(3)	Sneddon, A .... –(3)
Cusick, J 33	Hamilton, L 35	Struthers, D .... –(2)
Demmin, C 3	Hildersley, R 5	Winiarski, S .... –(1)

League Goals (50): Scott 11, Dwarika 8, Archibald 6, Allan 4, Beaton 4, Chalmers 4, Hutcheon 4, Donaghy 3, Cusick 2, Gartshore 2, Gibb 1, McStay 1.
Scottish League Cup Goals (5): Scott 3, Allan 1, Hutcheon 1. **Scottish Cup Goals (4)**: Allan 1, Dwarika 1, Gibb 1, Scott 1. **Challenge Cup Goals (2)**: Scott 2.

FORFAR ATHLETIC

Ground: Station Park, Forfar. **Capacity:** 8,732.
Telephone: 01307-463576. **Colours:** Sky blue and navy blue.

Allison, J .... 22(4)	Hamilton, J 19	McPhee, I 19
Archibald, E 9	Hannigan, P .... 21(12)	McVicar, D 23
Arthur, G 33	Heddle, I .... 6(2)	Mann, R .... 25(1)
Bingham, D 5	Henderson, D 5	Morgan, A 34
Bowes, M .... 27(2)	Higgins, G .... 24(2)	O'Neill, H .... 4(2)
Christie, S .... –(2)	Inglis, G .... 18(5)	Paterson, A .... 2(6)
Craig, D .... 27(1)	Irvine, N .... 16(3)	Sexton, B .... 5(2)
Donegan, J .... 3(4)	Loney, J .... 2(3)	Strain, J .... 1(2)
Glennie, S .... 24(1)	McKillop, A 22	

League Goals (37): Higgins 12, Hannigan 6, Morgan 6, Bingham 3, Mann 3, Bowes 2, Craig 2, Ingles 2, Allison 1.
Scottish League Cup Goals (1): Loney 1. **Scottish Cup Goals (8)**: Bowes 3, Ingles 2, Morgan 2, Mann 1. **Challenge Cup Goals (2)**: Bingham 1, Mann 1.

MONTROSE

Ground: Links Park Stadium, Montrose. **Capacity:** 4,338.
Telephone: 01674-673200. **Colours:** Royal blue, white and yellow.

Brown, M .... –(1)	Kydd, S .... 4(7)	Masson, C .... 8(1)
Cooper, C .... 19(3)	Larter, D 33	Masson, P .... 19(2)
Craib, M .... 26(1)	MacDonald, I 34	Robertson, I 11
Ferrie, A .... 8(14)	MacRonald, C .... 3(1)	Smith, S .... 25(3)
Garden, M 1	McAvoy, N .... 12(1)	Stephen, L .... 22(3)
Grant, D .... 24(1)	McGlashan, C 33	Taylor, S .... 11(16)
Haro, M 19	Mailer, C .... 32(1)	Tindal, K .... 17(3)
Kennedy, A .... 14(2)	Massie, R 3	Tosh, J .... 18(1)

League Goals (33): McGlashan 16, Taylor 5, Kennedy 4, MacDonald 2, Smith 2, Grant 1, McAvoy 1, Mailer 1, Masson 1.
Scottish League Cup Goals: None. **Scottish Cup Goals (6)**: McGlashan 4, Kennedy 1, Masson 1. **Challenge Cup Goals (3)**: Grant 1, McGlahan 1, Masson 1.

QUEEN OF THE SOUTH

Ground: Palmerston Park, Dumfries. **Capacity:** 8,312.
Telephone: 01387-254853. **Colours:** Royal blue and white.

Alexander, R .... –(1)
Allen, C 1
Brown, J .... 9(6)
Bryce, T .... 35(1)
Burridge, J 6
Butter, J 26
Campbell, C .... 15(1)
Campbell, D .... 11(6)
Cody, S .... 13(3)
Dobie, M .... 17(1)
Graham, C .... –(3)
Harris, C .... 25(8)
Hetherington, K 6
Jackson, D .... 4(1)
Kennedy, D .... 34(1)
Leslie, S .... 10(3)
Lilley, D 23
McAllister, J 2
McColm, R 4
McFarlane, A .... 23(2)
McKeown, B .... 30(1)
McKeown, D .... 30(3)
McLaren, J .... 10(13)
Mallan, S .... 27(5)
Millar, J .... –(1)
Pettit, S .... –(1)
Ramsay, S .... 16(10)
Telfer, G .... –(2)
Wilson, S .... 19(5)

League Goals (54): Mallan 12, Bryce 10, Harris 9, McLaren 7, Dobie 6, Campbell 2, Wilson 2, Cody 1, Jackson 1, Kennedy 1, McFarlane 1, Opponents 2.
Scottish League Cup Goals (3): Campbell 1, Harris 1, Mallan 1. **Scottish Cup Goals (2)**: Bryce 1, Mallan 1. **Challenge Gup Goals**: None.

STENHOUSEMUIR

Ground: Ochilview Park, Stenhousemuir. **Capacity:** 2,700.
Telephone: 01324-562992. **Colours:** Maroon, sky blue and white.

Aitken, N .... 7(15)
Armstrong, G 34
Bannon, E 29
Brannigan, K 11
Christie, M .... 18(1)
Clarke, J .... –(1)
Fisher, J 33
Haddow, L .... 24(2)
Henderson, J .... 6(5)
Hunter, P .... 25(3)
Hutchison, G .... 35(1)
Little, G .... 2(5)
Little, I 33
Logan, P .... 8(6)
McGeachie, G ...... 21(1)
McKenzie, R 36
Mathieson, M .... 30(1)
Roseburgh, D .... 6(4)
Scott, C .... 6(2)
Sprott, A .... 30(1)
Steel, T .... 1(2)
Swanson, D .... 1(3)

League Goals (51): Mathieson 10, Hutchison 9, Little 9, Hunter 8, Sprott 8, Fisher 2, Aitken 1, Bannon 1, Henderson 1, Logan 1, Opponent 1.
Scottish League Cup Goals (1): Fisher 1. **Scottish Cup Goals (6)**: McGeachie 2, Hutchison 1, Little 1, Mathieson 1, Opponent 1. **Challenge Cup Goals (8)**: Hutchison 4, Little 1, Logan 1, Mathieson 1, Opponent 1.

STIRLING ALBION

Ground: Forthbank Stadium, Stirling. **Capacity:** 3,808.
Telephone: 01786-450399. **Colours:** Red and white.

Bennett, J .... 1(7)
Bone, A 27
Deas, P 35
Farquhar, A .... –(3)
Gibson, J .... 18(11)
Kirkham, D .... –(2)
McCormick, S 33
McGeown, M 26
McGrotty, G .... 2(4)
McInnes, I .... 15(1)
McKechnie, M 3
McLeod, J .... 23(3)
McQuilter, R 35
Mitchell, C .... 32(4)
Monaghan, M 10
Paterson, A 33
Paterson, G 26
Roberts, P .... –(3)
Taggart, C .... 33(2)
Tait, T 28
Watson, P .... 5(3)
Watters, W .... –(2)
Wood, D .... 11(3)

League Goals (83): McCormick 24, Bone 19, Taggart 8, Tait 7, Gibson 6, McInnes 4, Paterson (A.) 4, McQuilter 3, McLeod 2, Mitchell 2, Wood 2, Watson 1, Opponent 1.
Scottish League Cup Goals (4): McCormick 1, McLeod 1, Taggart 1, Tait 1.
Scottish Cup Goals (4): McCormick 3, Mitchell 1. **Challenge Cup Goals (9)**: McCormick 3, McLeod 2, Tait 2, Gibson 1, Taggart 1.

STRANRAER

Ground: Stair Park, Stranraer. **Capacity:** 6,100.
Telephone: 01776-703271. **Colours:** Blue and red.

Bilsland. B .... 4(6)
Callaghan, T .... 2(7)
Connelly, D .... 3(2)
Crawford, D .... 12(2)
Duffy, B 9
Duncan, G .... 29(4)
Ferguson, W .... 1(10)
Gallagher, A .... 18(1)
Grant, A .... 18(4)
Henderson, D 20
Howard, N .... 28(2)
Hughes, J 32
Kerrigan, S .... 19(2)
McAulay, I .... 23(2)
McCaffrey, J 7
McGowan, N .... 1(3)
McGuire, D .... 5(10)
McLean, P .... 1(3)
McMillan, J .... 4(2)
Millar, G .... 19(2)
Pickering, M .... –(1)
Reilly, R .... 14(9)
Robertson, J .... 33(1)
Ross, S 27
Shepherd, A 2
Skippen, R .... –(1)
Sloan, T 36
Walker, T .... 29(3)

League Goals (38): Grant 6, Kerrigan 5, Walker 4, Duncan 3, Henderson 3, Sloan 3, Ferguson 2, McGuire 2, McMillan 2, Bilsland 1, Crawford 1, Howard 1, Hughes 1, McAulay 1, Reilly 1, Robertson 1, Opponent 1.
Scottish League Cup Goals: None. **Scottish Cup Goals**: None. **Challenge Cup Goals**: None.

THIRD DIVISION

ALBION ROVERS

Ground: Cliftonhill Stadium, Coatbridge. **Capacity:** 1,238.
Telephone: 01236-606334. **Colours:** Yellow, black and white.

Bell, D .... 17(4)
Brown, M 7
Byrne, D 17
Clark, M 11
Collins, L 8
Crawford, P .... 11(14)
Deeley, B .... 15(5)
Duncan, M .... 1(2)
Friar, J 5
Gallagher, J 33
Henderson, B .... 3(4)
Lavery, J 4
MacFarlane, C 16
McBride, J .... 12(1)
McConville, R 1
McDonald, D .... 24(1)
McEwan, A .... 5(2)
McInally, A 6
Miller, D 2
Moffat, J 21
Moonie, D 4
Moore, V 8
Morrison, A 1
Osborne, M 9
Percy, A 1
Pickering, M .... 8(1)
Quinn, K .... –(1)
Reilly, J .... 7(3)
Reilly, R 3
Richardson, J 1
Riley, D 1
Robertson, S 1
Russell, R .... 5(7)
Ryan, M .... 20(3)
Scott, M 3
Seggie, D .... 2(4)
Shanks, C .... 17(2)
Smith, B .... 3(1)
Speirs, C 9
Strain, B .... 20(7)
Thompson, D 7
Watson, B 1
Willock, A .... 12(5)
Wright, A 1
Young, G 32
Yule, R .... 1(1)

League Goals (37): Young 12, McBride 5, Crawford 2, McFarlane 2, Moore 2, Riley 2, Strain 2, Wilcox 2, Byrne 1, Collins 1, McDonald 1, McEwan 1, McNally 1, Newman 1, Scott 1, Spiers 1.
Scottish League Cup Goals: None. **Scottish Cup Goals**: None. **Challenge Cup Goals (3)**: Crawford 1, McBride 1, Scott 1.

ALLOA

Ground: Recreation Park, Alloa. **Capacity:** 4,111.
Telephone: 01259-722695. **Colours:** Gold and black.

Balfour, R 26
Bennett, J 25
Cadden, S .... 13(3)
Conway, V .... 7(1)
Cully, D .... 4(4)
Cummings, P 1
Diver, D .... 11(1)
Gilmour, J .... 20(5)
Graham, P 9
Hannah, K .... 6(4)
Johnston, N .... 9(7)
Kane, K 4
Kirkham, D .... 2(1)
Lamont, W 1
Lawrie, D 5
Little, T .... 8(6)
McAneny, P 29
McAvoy, N 17
McCardle, R 1
McCormack, J ...... 15(4)
McCulloch, K .... 12(1)
McKay, S .... 16(1)
McKenzie, C .... 3(2)
Moffat, B .... 33(2)
Morrison, S .... 21(5)
Nelson, M .... 16(5)
Newbigging, W ..... 15(1)
Rixon, S .... 17(9)
Smith, G .... 14(2)
Stewart, W 1
Watters, W .... 3(1)
Whyte, M .... 18(7)
Wylie, R .... 14(5)

League Goals (26): Moffat 5, Rixon 5, Gilmour 2, McKay 2, Morrison 2, Whyte 2, Bennett 1, Cadden 1, Hannah 1, Johnstone 1, McAnenay 1, McCulloch 1, Newbigging 1, Watters 1.
Scottish League Cup Goals (2): Moffat 1, Rixon 1. **Scottish Cup Goals (1)**: Rixon 1. **Challenge Cup Goals (4)**: Moffat 3, Diver 1.

ARBROATH

Ground: Gayfield Park, Arbroath. **Capacity:** 6,488.
Telephone: 01241-872157. **Colours:** Maroon and white.

Clark, P .... 13(1)
Crawford, J .... 19(2)
Dunn, G .... 25(1)
Elder, S .... 29(1)
Elliot, D .... 13(11)
Florence, S .... 8(3)
Fowler, J .... 5(9)
Gardner, R .... 15(2)
Hinchcliffe, C 11
Kennedy, A .... 7(3)
Kerr, J .... 4(3)
Kerr, R 1
Lindsay, J .... 7(3)
McAulay, J .... 33(2)
McCabe, G .... 12(7)
McCormick, S ...... 28(3)
McLean, C .... –(1)
McMillan, T .... 5(3)
McVicar, D 8
Middleton, A .... 15(1)
Peters, S .... 31(2)
Pew, D .... 32(4)
Phinn, J 5
Porteous, I .... 10(6)
Roberts, P .... 4(7)
Scott, S .... –(1)
Sexton, B .... 2(5)
Ward, J 18
Waters, M .... 14(3)
Watters, W .... 20(2)
Welsh, B .... 2(4)

League Goals (41): McCormick 8, Pew 8, Elliot 5, Porteous 5, Waters 5, Gardner 3, Elder 2, Kennedy 2, Roberts 2, Ward 1.
Scottish League Cup Goals (3): McCormick 2, Lindsay 1. **Scottish Cup Goals (2)**: McCormick 1, Opponent 1. **Challenge Cup Goals**: None.

BRECHIN CITY

Ground: Glebe Park, Brechin. **Capacity:** 3,960.
Telephone: 01356-622856. **Colours:** Red, blue and white.

Allan, R 33
Baillie, R .... 2(6)
Balfour, D 1
Brand, R .... 9(5)
Brown, B 1
Brown, R 36
Buick, G 12
Cairney, H 33
Christie, G .... 25(2)
Conway, F 30
Farnan, C 35
Ferguson, S .... 20(1)
Garden, S .... 1(1)
Graham, J .... 1(1)
Heddle, I .... 7(1)
Kerrigan, S .... 2(4)
McKellar, J .... 18(4)
McNeill, W .... 28(3)
Marr, S 1
Mearns, G 8
Mitchell, B 36
Price, G 1
Reid, S .... –(1)
Ross, A .... 23(3)
Scott, W 21
Smith, R .... 9(5)
Sorbie, S 3

League Goals (41): Ross 8, McNeill 7, Brand 6, McKellar 3, Brown 2, Buick 2, Cairney 2, Christie 2, Farnan 2, Mitchell 2, Price 2, Ferguson 1, Smith 1, Opponent 1.
Scottish League Cup Goals (2): Brand 2. **Scottish Cup Goals (3)**: Cairney 1, Christie 1, Mitchell 1. **Challenge Cup Goals (4)**: Brand 2, Brown 1, Mearns 1.

CALEDONIAN THISTLE

Ground: Telford Street Park, Inverness. **Capacity:** 5,480.
Telephone: 01463-230274. **Colours:** Royal blue and red.

Bennett, G .... 30(3)
Benson, R 3
Brennan, D .... 11(3)
Calder, J 34
Christie, C .... 24(5)
Green, D .... 4(7)
Hastings, R 28
Hercher, A .... 30(4)
Lisle, M .... 7(5)
MacArthur, I 24
MacKenzie, P .... –(4)
MacMillan, N .... 3(5)
McAllister, M .... 15(5)
McGinlay, D .... 9(13)
McRitchie, M 2
Mitchell, C .... 12(9)
Noble, M 36
Ross, D .... 28(4)
Scott, J .... 28(2)
Stewart, I .... 33(3)
Teasdale, M 19
Thomson, B .... 16(4)

League Goals (64): Stewart 23, Christie 12, Hercher 10, Ross 4, Mitchell 3, Hastings 2, Scott 2, Teasdale 2, Thomson 2, Brennan 1, Green 1, McAllister 1, Opponent 1.

Scottish League Cup Goals (1): Opponent 1. **Scottish Cup Goals (6)**: Hercher 2, Ross 1, Stewart 1, Teasdale 1, Thomson 1. **Challenge Cup Goals (1)**: MacMillan 1.

COWDENBEATH

Ground: Central Park, Cowdenbeath. **Capacity:** 5,258.
Telephone: 01383-610166. **Colours:** Royal blue and white.

Bowmaker, K .... 16(5)
Brock, J .... 4(6)
Brough, G .... 3(4)
Buckley, G .... 6(9)
Chapman, G .... –(1)
Conn, S .... 16(2)
De Melo, A .... 1(3)
Hamilton, A .... 12(3)
Humphreys, M 35
Hutchison, K .... 1(1)
Mackenzie, A 8
McGregor, J 2
McMahon, B 28
Malloy, B 18
Maratea, D .... 13(4)
Meldrum, G 35
Millar, G .... 6(7)
O'Neill, H .... 16(2)
Oliver, S .... 4(1)
Petrie, E .... 3(2)
Russell, N .... 32(1)
Scott, D .... 26(2)
Smith, C .... 2(4)
Soutar, G .... 3(5)
Spence, J .... –(3)
Steven, S 36
Stewart, W .... 3(10)
Wardell, S 1
Winter, C 32
Wood, G .... 30(1)
Yardley, M 4

League Goals (45): Scott 10, Wood 7, Buckley 3, Conn 3, Mackenzie 3, Steven 3, Winter 3, Bowmaker 2, Humphreys 2, Meldrum 2, O'Neill 2, Yardley 2, McMahon 1, Malloy 1, Soutar 1.
Scottish League Cup Goals (1): Sprott 1. **Scottish Cup Goals (1)**: Maratea 1. **Challenge Cup Goals**: None.

EAST STIRLINGSHIRE

Ground: Firs Park, Falkirk. **Capacity:** 1,880.
Telephone: 01324-623583. **Colours:** White and black.

Abercromby, M .... 17(5)
Cameron, D .... –(6)
Cuthbert, L .... –(2)
Docherty, R .... 4(2)
Dodds, J .... –(1)
Dwyer, P 31
Farquhar, A .... 5(3)
Frater, A .... 1(2)
Geraghty, M 11
Hunter, M .... 12(2)
Lamont, P .... 6(7)
Lawrie, D 1
Lee, I .... 31(2)
Lee, R 34
MacLean, S .... 18(8)
McBride, M .... 28(3)
McDougall, G 28
McKenna, T .... 3(1)
Millar, G .... 3(1)
Moffat, J 8
Murray, N .... 3(2)
Neill, A .... 31(2)
Orr, J .... 6(1)
Ross, B .... 20(1)
Russell, G 30
Scott, C 3
Sneddon, S 23
Stirling, D .... 11(15)
Watt, D .... 28(2)

League Goals (58): Dwyer 20, McBride 8, McLean 5, Hunter 4, Lee 4, Geraghty 3, Lamont 3, Watt 3, Abercromby 2, Neill 2, Sneddon 2, Opponents 2.
Scottish League Cup Goals (2): Abercromby 2. **Scottish Cup Goals**: None. **Challenge Cup Goals**: None.

LIVINGSTON

Ground: Almondvale Stadium, Livingston. **Capacity:** 4,000 (all-seated).
Telephone: 01506-417000. **Colours:** Black and amber.

Alleyne, D .... 19(1)
Bailey, L .... 20(7)
Callaghan, W .... 6(17)
Campbell, S 19
Coulston, D .... –(1)
Davidson, G 32
Douglas, R 24
Duthie, M .... 25(4)
Graham, T 15
Harvey, G .... 6(12)
Hislop, T 4
Laidlaw, S 1
McBride, J .... –(2)
McCartney, C 4
McLeod, G 34
McMartin, G 36
Martin, C 1
Sinclair, C .... 17(4)
Smart, C 31
Sorbie, S .... 5(6)
Stoute, H 12
Thorburn, S .... 3(3)
Tierney, P 16
Williamson, S .... 23(3)
Wright, G .... 7(3)
Young, J 36

League Goals (51): Young 18, Bailey 5, Duthie 3, McLeod 3, McMartin 3, Sinclair 3, Alleyne 2, Campbell 2, Harvey 2, Laidlaw 2, Tierney 2, Williamson 2, Hislop 1, Smart 1, Opponents 2.

Scottish League Cup Goals (4): Young 2, Bailey 1, McMartin 1, **Scottish Cup Goals (5)**: Harvey 3, Duthie 2, **Challenge Cup Goals (4)**: Callaghan 1, McLeod 1, Sinclair 1, Young 1.

QUEEN'S PARK

Ground: Hampden Park, Glasgow. **Capacity:** 9,222 (all-seated): Only North Stand and North Stand Gantry will be used.
Telephone: 0141-632-1275. **Colours:** White and black.

Arbuckle, D 35	Ferry, D .... 9(8)	McInally, A .... 4(4)
Brodie, D .... 7(11)	Fraser, R .... 13(3)	McPhee, B .... 20(12)
Bruce, G 8	Graham, D .... 32(1)	Matchett, J .... 3(2)
Callan, D .... 23(7)	Kennedy, K .... –(7)	Maxwell, I 29
Caven, R 31	Kerr, G .... 4(4)	Orr, G .... 11(1)
Chalmers, J 28	McCusker, J .... 3(4)	Porter, C .... 6(10)
Edgar, S .... 28(5)	McGinlay, M .... –(1)	Smith, M 1
Elder, G 26	McGoldrick, K 36	Ward, J .... 1(1)
Ferguson, P 23	McGrath, D .... 5(1)	Wilson, D .... 10(3)

League Goals (40): Edgar 6, Ferry 5, McGoldrick 5, McPhee 5, Caven 3, Arbuckle 2, Fraser 2, Graham 2, McClusker 2, Maxwell 2, Orr 2, Callan 1, Kerr 1, Porter 1, Opponent 1.
Scottish League Cup Goals (1): McPhee 1. **Scottish Cup Goals (4)**: Edgar 3, McGoldrick 1. **Challenge Cup Goals**: None.

ROSS COUNTY

Ground: Victoria Park, Dingwall. **Capacity:** 5,400.
Telephone: 01349-862253. **Colours:** Navy blue and white.

Bellshaw, J 35	Herd, W 36	Milne, C .... 31(3)
Bradshaw, P .... 4(4)	Hutchison, S 32	Robertson, C .... 11(6)
Connelly, G .... 27(4)	Mackay, D 36	Ruickbie, R .... 1(4)
Crainie, D 5	MacLeod, A .... 15(10)	Somerville, C .... 23(1)
Ferries, K .... 31(5)	MacMillan, D 4	Stewart, R .... –(1)
Furphy, W .... 28(3)	MacPherson, J ..... 19(5)	Watt, W .... 2(3)
Golabek, S 22	McFee, R .... –(13)	Williamson, R .... 18(3)
Grant, B .... 16(18)		

League Goals (56): Milne 16, Grant 11, MacPherson 11, Connelly 4, Bellshaw 2, Ferris 2, Golabek 2, MacLeod 2, Somerville 2, Williamson 2, Bradshaw 1, Furphy 1.
Scottish League Cup Goals: None. **Scottish Cup Goals (2)**: Grant 1, Opponent 1. **Challenge Cup Goals (2)**: Connelly 1, Milne 1.

QUOTE-UNQUOTE

BOBBY CHARLTON when England dismissed Sir Alf Ramsey: "How can they sack a Sir?"

ALAN SMITH, his Arsenal career prematurely ended by a knee injury: "Whatever I do as a job in the future, nothing will be as exciting as playing."

RUUD GULLIT to his new Chelsea team-mates last season: "If you have the ball, you command the game. If you kick and rush, it depends on luck."

MIKE BATESON, chairman of Torquay: "The problem with this division is that you are dealing with players who want paying beyond their skills."

TERRY VENABLES: "Practice makes permanent, not perfect. If you are practising the wrong things, you are just going to get good at doing the wrong things."

PLAYING STAFFS 1996-97

(As notified at time of going to press)

F.A. CARLING PREMIERSHIP

ARSENAL

Name	Height ft. in.	Previous Club	Birthplace	Birthdate
Goalkeepers				
Bartram, Vince	6. 2	Bournemouth	Birmingham	7.08.68
Harper, Lee	6. 1	Sittingbourne	Dulwich	30.10.71
Seaman, David	6. 4	Q.P.R.	Rotherham	19.09.63
Defenders				
Adams, Tony	6. 3	–	Romford	10.10.66
Bould, Steve	6. 4	Stoke	Stoke	16.11.62
Dixon, Lee	5. 8	Stoke	Manchester	17.03.64
Keown, Martin	6. 1	Everton	Oxford	24.07.66
Linighan, Andy	6. 4	Norwich	Hartlepool	18.06.62
McGowan, Gavin	5. 8	–	Blackheath	16.01.76
Marshall, Scott	6. 1	–	Edinburgh	1.05.73
Morrow, Steve	5. 11	–	Belfast	2.07.70
Rose, Matthew	5. 11	–	Dartford	24.09.75
Taylor, Ross	5. 10	–	Southend	14.01.77
Winterburn, Nigel	5. 8	Wimbledon	Nuneaton	11.12.63
Woolsey, Jeffrey	5. 11	–	Upminster	8.11.77
Midfield				
Crowe, Jason	5. 7	–	Kent	30.09.78
Hillier, David	5. 10	–	Blackheath	18.12.69
Hughes, Stephen	6. 0	–	Wokingham	18.09.76
McDonald, James	6. 0	–	Inverness	22.02.79
Parlour, Ray	5. 10	–	Romford	7.03.73
Platt, David	5. 10	Sampdoria, Ita.	Chadderton	10.06.66
Selley, Ian	5. 9	–	Chertsey	14.06.74
Forwards				
Bergkamp, Dennis	6. 0	Inter Milan, Ita.	Amsterdam, Hol.	10.05.69
Black, Michael	5. 8	–	Chigwell	6.10.76
Clarke, Adrian	5. 9	–	Suffolk	28.09.74
Dickov, Paul	5. 5	–	Livingston	1.11.72
Hartson, John	6. 2	Luton	Swansea	5.04.75
Helder, Glenn	5. 11	Vitesse Arnhem, Hol.	Leiden, Hol.	28.10.68
Kiwomya, Chris	5. 9	Ipswich	Huddersfield	2.12.69
McGoldrick, Eddie	5. 10	Crystal Palace	London	30.04.65
Merson, Paul	6. 0	–	Northolt	20.03.68
Rankin, Isaiah	5. 10	–	Edmonton	22.05.78
Read, Paul	5. 11	–	Harlow	25.09.73
Shaw, Paul	5. 11	–	Burnham	4.09.73
Wright, Ian	5. 9	Crystal Palace	Woolwich	3.11.63

ASTON VILLA

Name	Height ft. in.	Previous Club	Birthplace	Birthdate
Goalkeepers				
Bosnich, Mark	6. 1	Sydney Croatia, Aust.	Fairfield, Aust.	13.01.72
Brock, Stuart	6. 1	–	Birmingham	26.09.76

Oakes, Michael	6. 1	–	Northwich	30.10.73
Rachel, Adam	5. 11	–	Birmingham	10.12.76
Defenders				
Charles, Gary	5. 9	Derby	London	13.04.70
Ehiogu, Ugo	6. 2	W.B.A.	London	3.11.72
King, Phil	5. 8	Sheff. Wed.	Bristol	28.12.67
McGrath, Paul	6. 2	Man. Utd.	Ealing	4.12.59
Nelson, Fernando	6. 2	Sporting Lisbon, Por.	Lisbon, Por	–
Petty, Ben	6. 0	–	Solihull	22.03.77
Scimeca, Riccardo	6. 1	–	Leamington Spa	13.06.75
Staunton, Steve	6. 0	Liverpool	Drogheda	19.01.69
Tiler, Carl	6. 4	Nott'm. Forest	Sheffield	11.01.70
Wright, Alan	5. 4	Blackburn	Ashton-u-Lyme	28.09.71
Midfield				
Burchell, Lee	5. 7	–	Birmingham	12.11.76
Draper, Mark	5. 10	Leicester City	Nottingham	11.11.70
Farrelly, Gareth	6. 0	Home Farm	Dublin	28.08.75
Hines, Leslie	6. 5	–	Iserlohn, Ger.	7.01.77
Kirby, Alan	5. 7	–	Waterford	8.09.77
Southgate, Gareth	6. 0	Crystal Palace	Watford	3.09.70
Taylor, Ian	6. 1	Sheff. Wed.	Birmingham	4.06.68
Townsend, Andy	5. 11	Chelsea	Maidstone	23.07.63
Forwards				
Byfield, Darren	5. 11	–	Birmingham	29.09.76
Carr, Franz	5. 6	Leicester City	Preston	24.09.66
Davis, Neil	5. 8	Redditch Utd.	Bloxwich	15.08.73
Hendrie, Lee	5. 9	–	Birmingham	18.05.77
Joachim, Julian	5. 7	Leicester City	Peterborough	12.09.74
Johnson, Tommy	5. 11	Derby	Newcastle	15.01.71
Lee, Alan	6. 2	–	Galway	21.08.78
Milosevic, Savo	6. 0	Partizan Bel., Yug.	Bijelina, Yug.	2.09.73
Murray, Scott	5. 10	Fraserburgh	Aberdeen	26.05.74
Yorke, Dwight	5. 11	St. Clair's, Tobago	Tobago	3.11.71

BLACKBURN ROVERS

Name	Height ft. in.	Previous Club	Birthplace	Birthdate
Goalkeepers				
Flowers, Tim	6. 2	Southampton	Kenilworth	3.02.67
Given, Shay	6. 2	Celtic	Lifford	20.04.76
Defenders				
Berg, Henning	6. 0	Lillestrom, Nor.	Eidsvoll, Nor.	1.09.69
Coleman, Chris	6. 2	Crystal Palace	Swansea	10.06.70
Croft, Gary	5. 8	Grimsby	Burton-on-Trent	17.02.74
Hendry, Colin	6. 1	Man. City	Keith	7.12.65
Kenna, Jeff	5. 11	Southampton	Dublin	27.08.70
Le Saux, Graeme	5. 10	Chelsea	Jersey	17.10.68
Marker, Nicky	6. 0	Plymouth	Exeter	3.05.65
Pearce, Ian	6. 3	Chelsea	Bury St. Edmunds	7.05.74
Reed, Adam	6. 0	Darlington	Rotherham	18.02.75
Midfield				
Bohinen, Lars	5. 11	Nott'm. Forest	Vadso, Nor.	8.09.66
Flitcroft, Garry	6. 0	Man. City	Bolton	6.11.72
Gallacher, Kevin	5. 8	Coventry	Clydebank	23.11.66
Holmes, Matt	5. 7	West Ham	Luton	1.08.69
McKinlay, Billy	5. 8	Dundee Utd.	Glasgow	22.04.69
Ripley, Stuart	6. 0	Middlesbrough	Middlesbrough	20.11.67
Sherwood, Tim	6. 1	Norwich	St. Albans	6.02.69
Warhurst, Paul	6. 0	Sheff. Wed.	Stockport	26.09.69

Wilcox, Jason	6. 0	–	Bolton	15.07.71
Forwards				
Donis, Georgios	6. 0	Panathinaikos, Gre.	Greece	29.10.69
Fenton, Graham	5. 10	Aston Villa	Wallsend	22.05.74
Gudmundsson, Niklas	6. 0	Halmstad, Swe.	Halmstad, Swe.	20.02.72
Newell, Mike	6. 0	Everton	Liverpool	27.01.65
Shearer, Alan	5. 11	Southampton	Newcastle	13.08.70
Sutton, Chris	6. 3	Norwich	Nottingham	10.03.73

CHELSEA

Name	Height ft. in.	Previous Club	Birthplace	Birthdate
Goalkeepers				
Hitchcock, Kevin	6. 1	Mansfield	Custom House	5.10.62
Kharine, Dmitri	6. 3	CSKA Moscow, Rus.	Moscow, Rus.	16.08.68
Defenders				
Barness, Anthony	5. 10	Charlton	Lewisham	25.03.72
Clarke, Steve	5. 9	St. Mirren	Saltcoats	29.08.63
Clement, Neil	5. 10	–	Reading	3.10.78
Gullit, Ruud	6. 1	Sampdoria, Ita.	Surinam	1.09.62
Hughes, John	5. 10	–	Hammersmith	19.04.76
Johnsen, Erland	6. 0	Bayern Munich, Ger.	Fredrikstad, Nor.	5.04.67
Kjeldbjerg, Jakob	6. 2	Silkeborg, Den.	Viberg, Den.	21.10.69
LeBoeuf, Franck	6. 1	Strasbourg	Paris, Fra.	22.01.68
Lee, David	6. 3	–	Kingswood	26.11.69
McCann, Christian	5. 8	–	Newham	28.11.76
Minto, Scott	5. 8	Charlton	Cheshire	6.08.71
Myers, Andy	5. 8	–	Hounslow	3.11.73
Petrescu, Dan	5. 9	Sheff. Wed.	Bucharest, Rom.	22.12.67
Phelan, Terry	5. 9	Man. City	Manchester	16.03.67
Sinclair, Frank	5. 8	–	Lambeth	3.12.71
Midfield				
Burley, Craig	6. 1	–	Ayr	24.09.71
Di Matteo, Roberto	5. 10	Lazio, Ita.	Berne, Swi.	29.05.70
Morris, Jody	5. 4	–	London	28.12.78
Newton, Eddie	5. 9	–	Hammersmith	13.12.71
Peacock, Gavin	5. 8	Newcastle	Welling	18.11.67
Rocastle, David	5. 9	Man. City	Lewisham	2.05.67
Wise, Dennis	5. 6	Wimbledon	Kensington	15.12.66
Forwards				
Hughes, Mark	5. 10	Man. Utd.	Wrexham	1.11.63
Nicholls, Mark	5. 10	–	Middlesex	30.05.77
Spencer, John	5. 7	Rangers	Glasgow	11.09.70
Stein, Mark	5. 7	Stoke	Capetown, S.A.	28.01.66
Vialli, Gianluca	5. 11	Juventus, Ita.	Cremona, Ita.	9.07.64

COVENTRY CITY

Name	Height ft. in.	Previous Club	Birthplace	Birthdate
Goalkeepers				
Filan, John	5. 11	Cambridge Utd.	Sydney, Aust.	8.02.70
Ogrizovic, Steve	6. 5	Shrewsbury	Mansfield	12.09.57
Defenders				
Borrows, Brian	5. 10	Bolton	Liverpool	20.12.60
Burrows, David	5. 10	Everton	Dudley	25.10.68
Busst, David	6. 1	Moor Green	Birmingham	30.06.67
Daish, Liam	6. 2	Birmingham	Portsmouth	23.09.68
Gillespie, Gary	6. 2	Celtic	Bonnybridge	5.07.60

Hall, Marcus	6. 1	–	Coventry	24.03.76
Pickering, Ally	5. 11	Rotherham	Manchester	22.06.67
Shaw, Richard	5. 9	Crystal Palace	Brentford	11.09.68
Midfield				
Boland, Willie	5. 9	–	Ennis	6.08.75
Hurst, Lee	6. 0	–	Nuneaton	21.09.70
Isaias, Marques	5. 10	Benfica, Por.	Rio de Janeiro, Bra.	17.11.63
Jess, Eoin	5. 7	Aberdeen	Aberdeen	13.12.70
Richardson, Kevin	5. 7	Aston Villa	Newcastle	4.12.62
Salako, John	5. 9	Crystal Palace	Nigeria	11.02.69
Strachan, Gordon	5. 6	Leeds	Edinburgh	9.02.57
Telfer, Paul	5. 9	Luton	Edinburgh	21.10.71
Williams, Paul	6. 0	Derby	Burton	26.03.71
Forwards				
Christie, Iyseden	6. 0	–	Coventry	14.11.76
Dublin, Dion	6. 1	Man. Utd.	Leicester	22.04.69
Ndlovu, Peter	5. 8	Highlanders, Zim.	Bulawayo, Zim.	25.02.73
Whelan, Noel	6. 2	Leeds	Leeds	30.12.74

DERBY COUNTY

Name	Height ft. in.	Previous Club	Birthplace	Birthdate
Goalkeepers				
Hoult, Russell	6. 4	Leicester City	Leicester	22.11.72
Quy, Andrew	5. 11	Tottenham	Harlow	4.07.76
Sutton, Steve	6. 1	Nott'm. Forest	Hartington	16.04.61
Taylor, Martin	5. 11	Mile Oak Rovers	Tamworth	9.12.66
Defenders				
Ashbee, Ian	6. 0	–	Birmingham	6.09.76
Boden, Chris	5. 9	Aston Villa	Wolverhampton	13.10.73
Carsley, Lee	5. 9	–	Birmingham	28.02.74
Kavanagh, Jason	5. 9	Birmingham	Birmingham	23.11.71
Laursen, Jacob	5. 11	Silkeborg, Den.	Vedle, Den.	6.10.71
Powell, Chris	5. 10	Southend	Lambeth	8.09.69
Rowett, Gary	6. 1	Everton	Bromsgrove	6.03.74
Stimac, Igor	6. 2	Hadjuk Split, Cro.	Methoric	6.09.67
Sutton, Wayne	6. 0	–	Derby	1.10.75
Tretton, Andrew	6. 0	–	Derby	9.10.76
Wassall, Darren	6. 0	Nott'm. Forest	Edgbaston	27.06.68
Yates, Dean	6. 2	Notts County	Leicester	26.10.67
Midfield				
Asanovic, Aljosa	5. 10	Hadjuk Split, Cro.	Split, Cro.	14.12.65
Cooper, Kevin	5. 6	–	Derby	8.02.75
Flynn, Sean	5. 7	Coventry	Birmingham	13.03.68
Powell, Darryl	6. 1	Portsmouth	Lambeth	15.01.71
Trollope, Paul	5. 9	Torquay	Swindon	3.06.72
Van der Laan, Robin	5. 11	Port Vale	Schiedam, Hol.	5.09.68
Wright, Nick	5. 9	–	Derby	15.10.75
Forwards				
Carbon, Matt	6. 3	Lincoln City	Nottingham	8.06.75
Dailly, Christian	5. 10	Dundee Utd.	Dundee	23.10.73
Davies, Will	6. 2	–	Wirkswoth	27.09.75
Gabbiadini, Marco	5. 10	Crystal Palace	Nottingham	20.01.68
Simpson, Paul	5. 6	Oxford Utd.	Carlisle	26.07.66
Smith, Craig	6. 1	–	Mansfield	2.08.76
Sturridge, Dean	5. 7	–	Birmingham	27.07.73
Ward, Ashley	6. 2	Norwich	Manchester	24.11.70
Willems, Ron	6. 0	Grasshoppers, Swi.	Epa, Hol.	20.09.66

EVERTON

Name	Height ft. in.	Previous Club	Birthplace	Birthdate
Goalkeepers				
Kearton, Jason	6. 1	Brisbane Lions, Aust.	Ipswich, Aust.	9.07.69
Moore, Richard	6. 0	–	Scunthorpe	2.09.77
Southall, Neville	6. 1	Bury	Llandudno	16.09.58
Speare, James	5. 11	–	Liverpool	5.11.76
Defenders				
Allen, Graham	6. 1	–	Bolton	8.04.77
Barrett, Earl	5. 11	Aston Villa	Rochdale	28.04.67
Hills, John	5. 10	Blackpool	Blackpool	21.04.78
Hinchcliffe, Andy	5. 10	Man. City	Manchester	5.02.69
Hottiger, Marc	5. 10	Newcastle	Lausanne, Swi.	7.11.67
Hussin, Edward	5. 11	–	Liverpool	13.12.77
Jackson, Matt	6. 1	Luton	Leeds	19.10.71
Moore, Neil	6. 1	–	Liverpool	21.09.72
O'Connor, Jon	5. 10	–	Darlington	19.10.76
Short, Craig	6. 2	Derby	Bridlington	26.06.68
Tynan, Robert	5. 11	–	Birkenhead	13.01.78
Unsworth, David	5. 11	–	Preston	16.10.73
Watson, Dave	6. 0	Norwich	Liverpool	20.11.61
Midfield				
Ebbrell, John	5. 7	–	Bromborough	1.10.69
Grant, Tony	5. 7	–	Liverpool	14.11.74
Grugel, Mark	5. 8	–	Liverpool	9.03.76
Holcroft, Peter	6. 0	–	Liverpool	3.01.76
Kanchelskis, Andrei	5. 10	Man. Utd.	Kirovograd, Ukr.	23.01.69
McCann, Gavin	6. 1	–	Blackpool	10.01.78
Parkinson, Joe	5. 11	Bournemouth	Eccles	11.06.71
Samways, Vinny	5. 8	Tottenham	Bethnal Green	27.10.68
Speed, Gary	5. 9	Leeds	Hawarden	8.09.69
Stuart, Graham	5. 8	Chelsea	Tooting	24.10.70
Forwards				
Amokachi, Daniel	5. 10	Bruges, Bel.	Groko, Nig.	30.12.72
Branch, Paul	5. 11	–	Liverpool	12.02.72
Ferguson, Duncan	6. 2	Rangers	Stirling	27.12.71
Limpar, Anders	5. 8	Arsenal	Solna, Swe.	24.09.65
Quayle, Mark	5. 10	–	Liverpool	2.10.78
Rideout, Paul	5. 11	Rangers	Bournemouth	14.08.64
Townsend, Richard	5. 11	–	Chester	1.07.76

LEEDS UNITED

Name	Height ft. in.	Previous Club	Birthplace	Birthdate
Goalkeepers				
Beeney, Mark	6. 4	Brighton	Pembury	30.12.67
Lukic, John	6. 4	Arsenal	Chesterfield	11.12.60
Defenders				
Beesley, Paul	6. 1	Sheff. Utd.	Wigan	21.07.65
Bowman, Robert	5. 10	–	Durham	21.11.75
Couzens, Andy	5. 9	–	Leeds	4.06.75
Dorigo, Tony	5. 10	Chelsea	Melbourne, Aust.	31.12.65
Jobson, Richard	6. 2	Oldham	Hull	9.05.63
Kelly, Gary	5. 9	Home Farm	Drogheda	9.07.74
Pemberton, John	5. 11	Sheff. Utd.	Oldham	11.11.64
Wetherall, David	6. 3	Sheff. Wed.	Sheffield	14.03.71
Midfield				
Blunt, Jason	5. 8	–	Penzance	16.08.77

Bowyer, Lee	5. 9	Charlton	London	3.01.77
Ford, Mark	5. 7	–	Pontefract	10.10.75
Gray, Andy	5. 10	–	Harrogate	15.11.77
Harte, Ian	5. 7	–	Drogheda	31.08.77
McAllister, Gary	5. 10	Leicester City	Motherwell	25.12.64
Palmer, Carlton	6. 2	Sheff. Wed.	Oldbury	5.12.65
Radebe, Lucas	6. 2	Kaizer Chiefs, S.A.	South Africa	12.04.69
Tinkler, Mark	5. 10	–	Bishop Auckland	24.10.74
Forwards				
Deane, Brian	6. 3	Sheff. Utd.	Leeds	7.02.68
Rush, Ian	6. 0	Liverpool	Flint	20.10.61
Wallace, Rod	5. 7	Southampton	Lewisham	2.10.69
Yeboah, Tony	6. 0	Eint. Frankfurt, Ger.	Kunasi, Ghana	6.06.66

LEICESTER CITY

Name	Height ft. in.	Previous Club	Birthplace	Birthdate
Goalkeepers				
Kalac, Zeljko	6. 7	Sydney United, Aust.	Sydney, Aust.	16.12.72
Poole, Kevin	5. 10	Middlesbrough	Bromsgrove	21.07.63
Defenders				
Dodds, Andrew	6. 0	–	Gateshead	15.10.77
Grayson, Simon	6. 0	Leeds	Ripon	16.12.69
Hill, Colin	6. 0	Sheff. Utd.	Hillingdon	12.11.63
Kaamark, Pontus	5. 10	Gothenburg, Swe.	Vasteras, Swe.	5.04.69
Rolling, Franck	6. 1	Ayr	Colmar, Fra.	23.08.68
Walsh, Steve	6. 3	Wigan	Fulwood	3.11.64
Watts, Julian	6. 3	Sheff. Wed.	Sheffield	17.03.71
Wenlock, Stephen	5. 8	–	Peterborough	11.03.78
Whitlow, Mike	6. 0	Leeds	Northwich	13.01.68
Willis, Jimmy	6. 2	Darlington	Liverpool	12.07.68
Midfield				
Campbell, Stuart	5. 8	–	Corby	9.12.77
Izzet, Mustapha	5. 6	Chelsea	Hackney	31.10.74
Lennon, Neil	5. 10	Crewe	Lurgan	25.06.71
Lewis, Neil	5. 8	–	Wolverhampton	28.06.74
McMahon, Sam	5. 10	–	Newark	10.02.76
Parker, Garry	6. 0	Aston Villa	Oxford	7.09.65
Quinley, Lee	5. 10	–	Leicester	5.10.77
Taylor, Scott	5. 9	Reading	Portsmouth	28.11.70
Forwards				
Claridge, Steve	6. 0	Birmingham	Portsmouth	10.04.66
Hallam, Craig	5. 10	–	Leicester	11.11.76
Heskey, Emile	6. 2	–	Leicester	11.01.78
Lawrence, James	6. 0	Doncaster	Balham	8.03.70
Robins, Mark	5. 8	Norwich	Ashton-u-Lyme	22.12.69
Skeldon, Kevin	5. 11	–	Edinburgh	27.04.78
Wilson, Stuart	5. 6	–	Leicester	16.09.77

LIVERPOOL

Name	Height ft. in.	Previous Club	Birthplace	Birthdate
Goalkeepers				
James, David	6. 5	Watford	Welwyn	1.08.70
Stensgaard, Michael	6. 2	Hvidovre, Den.	Denmark	1.09.74
Warner, Tony	6. 4	–	Liverpool	11.05.74
Defenders				
Babb, Phil	6. 0	Coventry	Lambeth	30.11.70

Bjornebye, Stig	5. 10	Rosenborg, Nor.	Norway	11.12.69
Jones, Rob	5. 8	Crewe	Wrexham	5.11.71
Matteo, Dominic	6. 1	–	Dumfries	24.04.74
Ruddock, Neil	6. 2	Tottenham	Battersea	9.05.68
Scales, John	6. 2	Wimbledon	Harrogate	4.07.66
Wright, Mark	6. 2	Derby	Dorchester	1.08.63
Midfield				
Barnes, John	5. 11	Watford	Kingston, Jam.	7.11.63
Cassidy, Jamie	5. 9	–	Liverpool	21.11.77
Charnock, Phil	5. 11	–	Southport	14.02.75
Harkness, Steve	5. 10	Carlisle	Carlisle	27.08.71
Kennedy, Mark	5. 11	Millwall	Dublin	15.05.76
McAteer, Jason	5. 11	Bolton	Birkenhead	18.06.71
Redknapp, Jamie	6. 0	Bournemouth	Barton-on-Sea	25.06.73
Thomas, Michael	5. 9	Arsenal	Lambeth	24.08.67
Thompson, David	5. 7	–	Liverpool	12.09.77
Forwards				
Collymore, Stan	6. 3	Nott'm. Forest	Stone	22.01.71
Fowler, Robbie	5. 11	–	Liverpool	9.04.75
Jones, Lee	5. 8	Wrexham	Wrexham	29.05.73
McManaman, Steve	6. 0	–	Liverpool	11.02.72

MANCHESTER UNITED

Name	Height ft. in.	Previous Club	Birthplace	Birthdate
Goalkeepers				
Culkin, Nick	6. 2	York	York	6.07.78
Gibson, Paul	6. 2	–	Sheffield	1.11.76
Pilkington, Kevin	6. 0	–	Hitchin	8.03.74
Schmeichel, Peter	6. 4	Brondby, Den.	Gladsaxe, Den.	18.11.63
Van der Gouw, Raimond	6. 3	Vitesse Arnhem, Hol.	Oldenzaal, Hol.	24.03.63
Defenders				
Casper, Chris	6. 0	–	Burnley	28.04.75
Clegg, Michael	5. 8	–	Tameside	3.07.77
Curtis, John	5. 9	–	Nuneaton	3.09.78
Duncan, Andrew	5. 11	–	Hexham	20.10.77
Hilton, David	5. 11	–	Barnsley	10.11.77
Irwin, Denis	5. 8	Oldham	Cork	31.10.65
Johnsen, Ronnie	6. 2	Besiktas, Tur.	Oslo, Nor.	10.06.69
McGibbon, Pat	6. 1	Portadown	Lurgan	6.09.73
May, David	6. 0	Blackburn	Oldham	24.06.70
Murdock, Colin	6. 3	–	Ballymena	2.07.75
Neville, Gary	5. 10	–	Bury	18.02.75
Neville, Philip	5. 10	–	Bury	21.01.77
O'Kane, John	5. 10	–	Nottingham	15.11.74
Pallister, Gary	6. 4	Middlesbrough	Ramsgate	30.06.65
Wallwork, Ronnie	5. 9	–	Manchester	10.09.77
Midfield				
Appleton, Michael	5. 9	–	Salford	4.12.75
Beckham, David	6. 0	–	Leytonstone	2.05.75
Brebner, Grant	5. 9	–	Edinburgh	6.12.77
Butt, Nicky	5. 10	–	Manchester	21.01.75
Davies, Simon	6. 0	–	Winsford	23.04.74
Keane, Roy	5. 10	Nott'm. Forest	Cork	10.08.71
Smith, Tommy	5. 9	–	Northampton	25.11.77
Teather, Paul	5. 11	–	Rotherham	26.12.77
Trees, Robert	5. 10	–	Manchester	18.12.77

Name	Height ft. in.	Previous Club	Birthplace	Birthdate
Forwards				
Brightwell, Stuart	5. 6	–	Easington	31.01.79
Brown, David	5. 9	Oldham	Bolton	2.10.78
Cantona, Eric	6. 2	Leeds	Paris, Fra.	24.05.66
Cole, Andy	5. 11	Newcastle	Nottingham	15.10.71
Cooke, Terry	5. 7	–	Marston Green	5.08.76
Giggs, Ryan	5. 11	–	Cardiff	29.11.73
McClair, Brian	5. 10	Celtic	Airdrie	8.12.63
Macken, Jon	5. 10	–	Manchester	7.09.77
Mulryne, Phil	5. 8	–	Belfast	1.01.78
Mustoe, Neil	5. 8	–	Gloucester	5.11.76
Scholes, Paul	5. 6	–	Salford	16.11.74
Sharpe, Lee	6. 0	Torquay	Halesowen	27.05.71
Solskjar, Ole Gunnar	5. 9	Molde, Nor.	Norway	–
Thornley, Ben	5. 9	–	Bury	21.04.75
Tomlinson, Graeme	5. 9	Bradford City	Keighley	10.12.75
Twiss, Michael	5. 10	–	Salford	26.12.77
Wilson, Mark	5. 11	–	Scunthorpe	9.02.79

MIDDLESBROUGH

Name	Height ft. in.	Previous Club	Birthplace	Birthdate
Goalkeepers				
Miller, Alan	6. 3	Arsenal	Epping	29.03.70
Roberts, Ben	6. 0	–	Bishop Auckland	22.06.75
Walsh, Gary	6. 3	Man. Utd.	Wigan	21.03.68
Defenders				
Anderson, Viv	6. 1	Barnsley	Nottingham	29.08.56
Barron, Michael	5. 10	–	Chester-le-Street	22.12.74
Cox, Neil	6. 0	Aston Villa	Scunthorpe	8.10.71
Fleming, Curtis	5. 10	St. Patrick's Ath.	Manchester	8.10.68
Harrison, Craig	5. 10	–	Gateshead	10.11.77
Liddle, Craig	5. 11	Blyth Spartans	Chester-le-Street	21.10.71
Morris, Chris	5. 11	Celtic	Newquay	24.12.63
Pearson, Nigel	6. 1	Sheff. Wed.	Nottingham	21.08.63
Vickers, Steve	6. 1	Tranmere	Bishop Auckland	13.10.67
Whelan, Phil	6. 4	Ipswich	Stockport	7.08.72
White, Alan	5. 11	–	Darlington	22.03.76
Whyte, Derek	5. 11	Celtic	Glasgow	31.08.68
Midfield				
Blackmore, Clayton	5. 8	Man. Utd.	Neath	23.09.64
Branco	5. 9	Internacional, Bra.	Bage, Bra.	4.04.64
Cummins, Michael	5. 8	–	Dublin	1.06.78
Emerson	5. 7	Porto, Por.	Rio de Janeiro, Bra.	12.04.72
Kavanagh, Graham	5. 10	Home Farm	Dublin	2.12.73
Lee, Paddy	5. 7	Man. Utd.	Dublin	2.08.77
Moore, Alan	5. 10	–	Dublin	25.11.74
Mustoe, Robbie	5. 10	Oxford Utd.	Oxford	28.08.68
O'Halloran, Keith	5. 9	Cherry Orchard	Dublin	10.11.75
Pollock, Jamie	5. 11	–	Stockton	16.02.74
Robson, Bryan	5. 10	Man. Utd.	Chester-le-Street	11.01.57
Stamp, Phil	5. 10	–	Middlesbrough	12.12.75
Summerbell, Mark	5. 10	–	Durham	30.10.76
Forwards				
Bagayoko, Salif	5. 11	–	Manosque, Fra.	9.05.77
Barmby, Nick	5. 7	Tottenham	Hull	11.02.74
Beck, Mikkel	6. 2	Fortuna Cologne, Ger.	Copenhagen, Den.	–
Fjortoft, Jan-Aage	6. 3	Swindon	Aalesund, Nor.	10.01.67

Freestone, Chris	5. 9	Arnold Town	Nottingham	4.09.71
Hendrie, John	5. 7	Leeds	Lennoxtown	24.10.63
Hignett, Craig	5. 9	Crewe	Whiston	12.01.70
Juninho	5. 5	Sao Paulo, Bra.	Sao Paulo, Bra.	22.03.73
McGargle, Steph	5. 9	–	Gateshead	24.10.75
Moreno, Jaime	5. 7	FC Blooming, Bol.	Santa Cruz, Bol.	19.01.74
Ravanelli, Fabrizio	6. 1	Juventus, Ita.	Perugia, Ita.	11.12.68
Richardson, Paul	6. 0	–	Durham	22.07.77
Wilkinson, Paul	6. 1	Watford	Louth	30.10.64

NEWCASTLE UNITED

Name	Height ft. in.	Previous Club	Birthplace	Birthdate
Goalkeepers				
Harper, Stephen	6. 0	–	Easington	14.03.75
Hislop, Shaka	6. 6	Reading	London	22.02.69
Keen, Peter	6. 0	–	Middlesbrough	16.11.76
Srnicek, Pavel	6. 2	Banik Ostrava, Cze.	Ostrava, Cze.	10.03.68
Defenders				
Albert, Philippe	6. 3	Anderlecht, Bel.	Bouillon, Bel.	10.08.67
Arnison, Paul	5. 9	–	Hartlepool	18.09.77
Barton, Warren	5. 11	Wimbledon	Stoke Newington	19.03.69
Beresford, John	5. 5	Portsmouth	Sheffield	4.09.66
Elliott, Rob	5. 10	–	Newcastle	25.12.73
Elliot, Stuart	5. 8	–	Hendon	27.08.77
Howey, Steve	6. 1	–	Sunderland	26.10.71
Peacock, Darren	6. 2	Q.P.R.	Bristol	3.02.68
Watson, Steve	6. 1	–	North Shields	1.04.74
Midfield				
Batty, David	5. 8	Blackburn	Leeds	2.12.68
Clark, Lee	5. 7	–	Wallsend	27.10.72
Crawford, Jimmy	5. 11	Bohemians	Dublin	1.05.73
Holland, Chris	5. 9	Preston	Whalley	11.09.75
Lee, Robert	5. 11	Charlton	West Ham	1.02.66
Forwards				
Asprilla, Faustino	5. 9	Parma, Ita.	Tulua, Col.	10.11.69
Beardsley, Peter	5. 8	Everton	Newcastle	18.01.61
Brayson, Paul	5. 4	–	Newcastle	16.09.77
Eatock, David	5. 4	Chorley	Blackrod	11.11.76
Ferdinand, Les	5. 11	Q.P.R.	Acton	8.12.66
Gillespie, Keith	5. 9	Man. Utd.	Larne	18.02.75
Ginola, David	6. 0	Paris St. Germain, Fra.	Gassin, Fra.	25.01.67
Huckerby, Darren	5. 10	Lincoln City	Nottingham	23.04.76
Kitson, Paul	5. 10	Derby	County Durham	9.01.71

NOTTINGHAM FOREST

Name	Height ft. in.	Previous Club	Birthplace	Birthdate
Goalkeepers				
Clark, Richard	5. 11	–	Nuneaton	6.04.77
Crossley, Mark	6. 0	–	Barnsley	16.06.69
Fettis, Alan	6. 2	Hull	Belfast	1.02.71
Henry, David	6. 3	Crusaders	Belfast	12.11.77
Rigby, Malcolm	6. 1	Notts County	Nottingham	13.03.76
Wright, Tommy	6. 1	Newcastle	Belfast	29.08.63
Defenders				
Blatherwick, Steve	6. 1	Notts County	Nottingham	20.09.73

Chettle, Steve	6. 1	–	Nottingham	27.09.68
Cooper, Colin	5. 9	Millwall	Durham	28.02.67
Haaland, Alf Inge	5. 10	Byrne FK, Nor.	Stavanger, Nor.	23.11.72
Jerkan, Nikola	6. 4	Real Oviedo, Spa.	Zagreb, Cro.	8.12.64
Lyttle, Des	5. 8	Swansea	Wolverhampton	24.09.71
Morgan, Ian	6. 2	–	Birmingham	11.10.77
Pearce, Stuart	5. 10	Coventry	Shepherds Bush	24.04.62
Thom, Stuart	6. 2	–	Dewsbury	27.12.76
Midfield				
Allen, Chris	5. 11	Oxford Utd.	Oxford	18.11.72
Archer, Paul	5. 8	–	Leicester	25.04.78
Armstrong, Craig	5. 11	–	South Shields	23.05.75
Atkinson, Craig	6. 1	–	Rotherham	29.09.77
Bart-Williams, Chris	5. 11	Sheff. Wed.	Sierra Leone	16.06.74
Burns, John	5. 10	–	Dublin	4.12.77
Cowling, Lee	5. 9	–	Doncaster	22.09.77
Finnigan, John	5. 8	–	Wakefield	28.03.76
Gemmill, Scot	5. 11	–	Paisley	2.01.71
Howe, Stephen	5. 7	–	Annitsford	6.11.73
O'Neill, Shane	5. 10	–	Limavady	20.06.78
Phillips, David	5. 9	Norwich	Wegberg, Ger.	29.07.63
Smith, Paul	5. 11	Hastings Town	Hastings	25.01.76
Stone, Steve	5. 8	–	Gateshead	20.08.71
Stratford, Lee	5. 10	–	Barnsley	11.11.75
Walker, Justin	5. 10	–	Nottingham	6.09.75
Warner, Vance	6. 0	–	Leeds	3.09.74
Woan, Ian	5. 10	Runcorn	Wirral	14.12.67
Forwards				
Campbell, Kevin	6. 1	Arsenal	Lambeth	4.02.70
Guinan, Stephen	6. 1	–	Birmingham	24.12.75
Irving, Richard	5. 8	Man. Utd.	Halifax	10.09.75
Lee, Jason	6. 3	Southend	Newham	9.05.71
McGregor, Paul	5. 10	–	Liverpool	17.12.74
Orr, Stephen	5. 9	–	Belper	19.01.78
Roy, Bryan	5. 10	Foggia, Ita.	Amsterdam, Hol.	12.02.70
Saunders, Dean	5. 8	Galatasaray, Tur.	Swansea	21.06.64
Silenzi, Andrea	6. 3	Torino, Ita.	Rome, Ita.	10.02.66
Walley, Mark	5. 10	–	Barnsley	17.09.76

SHEFFIELD WEDNESDAY

Name	Height ft. in.	Previous Club	Birthplace	Birthdate
Goalkeepers				
Clarke, Matthew	6. 3	Rotherham	Sheffield	3.11.73
Pressman, Kevin	6. 2	–	Fareham	6.11.67
Scargill, Jon	6. 1	–	Dewsbury	9.04.77
Defenders				
Atherton, Peter	5. 10	Coventry	Orrell	6. 04.70
Briscoe, Lee	5. 11	–	Pontefract	30.09.75
Linighan, Brian	6. 3	–	Hartlepool	2.11.73
Newsome, Jon	6. 2	Norwich	Sheffield	6.09.70
Nolan, Ian	5. 11	Tranmere	Liverpool	9.07.70
Nicol, Steve	5. 10	Notts County	Irvine	11.12.61
Stefanovic, Dejan	6. 2	R.S. Belgrade, Yug.	Belgrade, Yug.	28.10.74
Walker, Des	5. 11	Sampdoria, Ita.	Hackney	26.11.65
Midfield				
Blinker, Regi	5. 9	Feyenoord, Hol.	Rotterdam, Hol.	2.06.69
Hyde, Graham	5. 8	–	Doncaster	10.11.70
Jones, Ryan	6. 3	–	Sheffield	23.07.73

Pembridge, Mark	5. 7	Derby	Merthyr Tydfil	29.11.70
Sheridan, John	5. 10	Nott'm. Forest	Stretford	1.10.64
Waddle, Chris	6. 1	Marseille, Fra.	Gateshead	14.12.60
Whittingham, Guy	5. 10	Aston Villa	Evesham	10.11.64
Williams, Mike	5. 10	Maltby	Bradford	21.11.69
Forwards				
Barker, Richard	6. 1	–	Sheffield	30.05.75
Booth, Andy	6. 1	Huddersfield	Huddersfield	17.03.73
Bright, Mark	6. 1	Crystal Palace	Stoke	6.06.62
Daly, Matthew	6. 3	–	Dewsbury	8.10.76
Donaldson, O'Neill	5. 11	Doncaster	Birmingham	24.11.69
Hirst, David	6. 0	Barnsley	Barnsley	7.12.67

SOUTHAMPTON

Name	Height ft. in.	Previous Club	Birthplace	Birthdate
Goalkeepers				
Beasant, Dave	6. 4	Chelsea	Willesden	20.03.59
Flahavan, Daryl	5. 10	–	Southampton	9.09.77
Moss, Neil	6. 2	Bournemouth	New Milton	10.05.75
Defenders				
Blamey, Nathan	5. 10	–	Plymouth	10.06.77
Charlton, Simon	5. 7	Huddersfield	Huddersfield	25.10.71
Dodd, Jason	5. 11	–	Bath	2.11.70
Monk, Gary	6. 1	Torquay	Bedford	6.03.79
Monkou, Ken	6. 3	Chelsea	Surinam	29.11.64
Neilson, Alan	5. 11	Newcastle	Wegberg, Ger.	26.09.72
Piper, David	5. 8	–	Bournemouth	31.10.77
Spedding, Duncan	6. 2	–	Camberley	7.09.77
Midfield				
Benali, Francis	5. 10	–	Southampton	30.12.68
Care, Simon	5. 8	–	Newbury	23.12.77
Hughes, David	5. 10	–	St. Albans	30.12.72
Magilton, Jim	6. 1	Oxford Utd.	Belfast	6.05.69
Oakley, Matthew	5. 10	–	Peterborough	17.08.77
Robinson, Matthew	5. 10	–	Exeter	23.12.74
Sheerin, Paul	5. 10	–	Edinburgh	28.08.74
Stockley, Sam	5. 10	–	Tiverton	5.09.77
Tisdale, Paul	5. 9	–	Malta	14.01.73
Venison, Barry	5. 10	Galatasaray, Tur.	Consett	16.08.64
Forwards				
Basham, Stephen	5. 10	–	Southampton	2.12.77
Bennett, Frankie	5. 7	–	Birmingham	3.01.69
Heaney, Neil	5. 9	Arsenal	Middlesbrough	3.11.71
Le Tissier, Matthew	6. 1	Vale Recreation	Guernsey	14.10.68
Shipperley, Neil	6. 1	Chelsea	Chatham	30.10.74
Warren, Christer	5. 10	–	Poole	10.10.74
Watson, Gordon	5. 10	Sheff. Wed.	Sidcup	20.03.71
Williams, Andrew	5. 10	–	Bristol	8.10.77

SUNDERLAND

Name	Height ft. in.	Previous Club	Birthplace	Birthdate
Goalkeepers				
Coton, Tony	6. 2	Man. Utd.	Tamworth	19.05.61
Preece, David	6. 0	–	Sunderland	28.08.76

Defenders				
Ball, Kevin	5. 9	Portsmouth	Hastings	12.11.64
Hall, Gareth	5. 8	Chelsea	Croydon	12.03.69
Holloway, Darren	5. 11	–	Bishop Auckland	3.10.77
Kay, John	5. 10	Wimbledon	Sunderland	29.01.64
Kubicki, Dariusz	5. 10	Aston Villa	Warsaw, Pol.	6.06.63
Melville, Andy	6. 1	Oxford Utd.	Swansea	29.11.68
Ord, Richard	6. 2	–	Easington	3.03.70
Scott, Martin	5. 9	Bristol City	Sheffield	7.01.68
Midfield				
Agnew, Steve	5. 9	Leicester City	Shipley	9.11.65
Aiston, Sam	5. 10	Newcastle	Newcastle	21.11.76
Armstrong, Gordon	6. 0	–	Newcastle	15.07.67
Atkinson, Brian	5. 10	–	Darlington	19.01.71
Bracewell, Paul	5. 8	Newcastle	Heswall	19.07.62
Gray, Michael	5. 9	–	Sunderland	3.08.64
Pickering, Stephen	5. 9	–	Sunderland	25.09.76
Smith, Martin	5. 11	–	Sunderland	13.11.74
Rae, Alex	5. 9	Millwall	Glasgow	30.09.69
Forwards				
Angell, Brett	6. 1	Everton	Marlborough	20.08.68
Bridges, Michael	5. 10	–	Whitley Bay	5.08.78
Brodie, Steve	5. 7	–	Sunderland	14.01.73
Grant, Steve	5. 10	Athlone Town	Birr	14.04.77
Howey, Lee	6. 3	–	Sunderland	1.04.69
Kelly, David	5. 11	Wolves	Birmingham	25.11.65
Mawson, David	5. 11	–	Sunderland	4.03.77
Mullin, John	5. 9	Burnley	Bury	11.08.75
Russell, Craig	5. 11	–	South Shields	4.02.74

TOTTENHAM HOTSPUR

Name	Height ft. in.	Previous Club	Birthplace	Birthdate
Goalkeepers				
Brown, Simon	6. 1	–	Chelmsford	3.12.76
Day, Chris	6. 2	–	Whipps Cross	28.07.75
Walker, Ian	6. 1	–	Watford	31.10.71
Defenders				
Arber, Mark	6. 0	–	South Africa	9.10.77
Austin, Dean	6. 0	Southend	Hemel Hempstead	26.04.70
Calderwood, Colin	6. 0	Swindon	Stranraer	20.01.65
Campbell, Sol	6. 1	–	Newham	18.09.74
Carr, Steve	5. 7	–	Dublin	29.08.76
Cundy, Jason	6. 1	Chelsea	Wimbledon	12.11.69
Darcy, Ross	6. 0	–	Balbriggan	21.03.78
Davies, Darren	5. 10	–	Port Talbot	13.08.78
Edinburgh, Justin	5. 10	Southend	Basildon	18.12.69
Kerslake, David	5. 9	Leeds	Stepney	19.06.66
Mabbutt, Gary	5. 9	Bristol Rovers	Bristol	23.08.61
Maher, Kevin	6. 0	–	Ilford	17.10.76
Nethercott, Stuart	5. 11	–	Chadwell Heath	21.03.73
Scott, Kevin	6. 2	Newcastle	Easington	17.12.66
Townley, Leon	6. 0	–	Loughton	16.02.76
Wilson, Clive	5. 7	Q.P.R.	Manchester	13.11.61
Midfield				
Brady, Garry	5. 8	–	Glasgow	7.09.76
Clapham, Jamie	5. 9	–	Lincoln	7.12.75
Clemence, Stephen	5. 11	–	Liverpool	31.03.78

Dozzell, Jason	6. 1	Ipswich	Ipswich	9.12.67
Gain, Peter	6. 1	–	Hammersmith	11.11.76
Hill, Danny	5. 9	–	Edmonton	1.10.74
Howells, David	5. 11	–	Guildford	15.12.67
McVeigh, Paul	5. 11	–	Belfast	6.12.77
Mannix, Alan	5. 8	–	Castle Knock	23.10.77
Sinton, Andy	5. 8	Sheff. Wed.	Newcastle	19.03.66
Spencer, Simon	5. 10	–	Islington	10.09.76
Turner, Andy	5. 9	–	Woolwich	23.05.75
Webb, Simon	5. 11	–	Castle Bar	19.01.78
Wormull, Simon	5. 10	–	Crawley	1.12.76
Forwards				
Allen, Rory	5. 9	–	Beckenham	17.10.77
Anderton, Darren	6. 1	Portsmouth	Southampton	3.03.72
Armstrong, Chris	6. 0	Crystal Palace	Newcastle	19.06.71
Fenn, Neale	5. 10	–	Edmonton	18.01.77
Fox, Ruel	5. 6	Newcastle	Ipswich	14.01.68
Janney, Mark	5. 10	–	Romford	2.12.77
McMahon, Gerry	5. 11	Glenavon	Belfast	29.12.73
Mahorn, Paul	5. 8	–	Whipps Cross	13.08.73
Rosenthal, Ronny	5. 11	Liverpool	Haifa, Israel	11.10.63
Sheringham, Teddy	6. 0	Nott'm. Forest	Highams Park	2.04.66

WEST HAM UNITED

Name	Height ft. in.	Previous Club	Birthplace	Birthdate
Goalkeepers				
Mautone, Steve	6. 1	Canberra Cosmos, Aust.	Melbourne, Aust.	10.08.70
Miklosko, Ludek	6. 5	Banik Ostrava, Cze.	Ostrava, Cze.	9.12.61
Defenders				
Bilic, Slaven	6. 2	Karlsruhe, Ger.	Croatia	11.09.68
Blaney, Steven	6. 0	–	London	24.03.77
Bowen, Mark	5. 8	Norwich	Neath	7.12.63
Breacker, Tim	5. 11	Luton	Bicester	2.07.65
Brown, Kenny	5. 8	Plymouth	Upminster	11.07.67
Dicks, Julian	5. 10	Liverpool	Bristol	8.08.68
Ferdinand, Rio	6. 2	–	London	7.11.78
Hall, Richard	6. 2	Southampton	Ipswich	14.03.72
Moore, Jason	5. 8	–	Kent	16.02.79
Philson, Graeme	5. 1	Coleraine	Londonderry	24.03.75
Potts, Steve	5. 7	–	Hartford, U.S.A.	7.05.67
Rieper, Marc	6. 4	Brondby, Den.	Rodoure, Den.	5.06.68
Rowland, Keith	5. 10	Bournemouth	Portadown	1.09.71
Whitbread, Adrian	6. 2	Swindon	Epping	22.10.71
Midfield				
Bishop, Ian	5. 9	Man. City	Liverpool	29.05.65
Canham, Scott	5. 8	–	West Ham	5.11.74
Hodges, Lee	5. 5	–	London	2.03.78
Hughes, Michael	5. 7	Strasbourg, Fra.	Belfast	2.08.71
Lampard, Frank	6. 0	–	London	21.06.78
Moncur, John	5. 7	Swindon	Stepney	22.09.66
Omoyinmi, Emmanuel	5. 6	–	Nigeria	28.12.77
Slater, Robbie	5. 11	Blackburn	Ormskirk	22.11.64
Williamson, Daniel	5. 10	–	Newham	5.12.73
Forwards				
Boogers, Marco	6. 1	Sp. Rotterdam, Hol.	Dordrecht, Hol.	12.01.67
Cottee, Tony	5. 7	Everton	West Ham	11.07.65

Dowie, Iain	6. 1	Crystal Palace	Hatfield	9.01.65
Dumitrescu, Ilie	5. 8	Tottenham	Bucharest, Rom.	6.01.69
Futre, Paulo	5. 10	AC Milan, Ita.	Montijo, Por.	28.02.66
Jones, Steve	6. 0	Bournemouth	Cambridge	17.03.70
Lazaridis, Stan	5. 9	West Adelaide, Aust.	Perth, Aust.	16.08.72
Raducioiu, Florin	5. 10	Espanol, Spa.	Bucharest, Rom.	17.03.70
Shipp, Daniel	5. 11	–	London	25.09.76

WIMBLEDON

Name	Height ft. in.	Previous Club	Birthplace	Birthdate
Goalkeepers				
Heald, Paul	6. 2	Leyton Orient	Rotherham	20.09.68
Murphy, Brendan	5. 11	Hull	Wexford	19.08.75
Sullivan, Neil	6. 0	Sutton United	Sutton	24.02.70
Defenders				
Blackwell, Dean	6. 1	–	Camden	5.12.69
Cunningham, Ken	6. 0	Millwall	Dublin	28.06.71
Elkins, Gary	5. 9	Fulham	Wallingford	4.05.66
Fitzgerald, Scott	6. 0	–	Westminster	13.08.69
Futcher, Andy	5. 7	–	Enfield	10.02.78
Hodges, Danny	6. 0	–	Greenwich	14.09.76
Jupp, Duncan	6. 0	Fulham	Guildford	25.01.75
Kimble, Alan	5. 8	Cambridge Utd.	Poole	6.08.66
Laidlaw, Iain	6. 2	–	Newcastle	10.12.76
McAllister, Brian	5. 11	–	Glasgow	30.11.70
Pearce, Andy	6. 4	Sheff. Wed.	Bradford	20.04.66
Perry, Chris	5. 8	–	Carshalton	26.04.73
Reeves, Alan	6. 1	Rochdale	Birkenhead	19.11.67
Thatcher, Ben	5. 10	Millwall	Swindon	30.11.75
Thorn, Andy	6. 0	Crystal Palace	Carshalton	12.11.66
Midfield				
Castledine, Stewart	5. 11	–	Wandsworth	22.01.73
Earle, Robbie	5. 10	Port Vale	Newcastle-u-Lyme	27.01.65
Fear, Peter	5. 10	–	Sutton	10.09.73
Jones, Vinnie	6. 0	Chelsea	Watford	5.01.65
Leonhardsen, Oyvind	5. 10	Rosenborg, Nor.	Kristiansund, Nor.	17.08.70
Piper, Len	5. 6	–	Camberwell	8.08.77
Forwards				
Ardley, Neal	5. 8	–	Epsom	1.09.72
Blissett, Gary	6. 1	Brentford	Manchester	29.06.64
Clarke, Andy	5. 8	Barnet	Islington	22.07.67
Ekoku, Efan	6. 1	Norwich	Manchester	8.06.67
Euell, Jason	6. 2	–	London	6.02.77
Gayle, Marcus	6. 2	Brentford	Hammersmith	27.09.70
Goodman, Jon	5. 11	Millwall	Walthamstow	2.06.71
Harford, Mick	6. 3	Coventry	Sunderland	12.02.59
Holdsworth, Dean	5. 11	Brentford	Walthamstow	8.11.68
Newhouse, Aidan	6. 0	Chester	Wallasey	23.05.72
Payne, Grant	5. 9	–	Woking	25.12.75

NATIONWIDE FOOTBALL LEAGUE

First Division

BARNSLEY

Name	Height ft. in.	Previous Club	Birthplace	Birthdate
Goalkeepers				
Sollitt, Adam	6. 0	–	Sheffield	22.06.77
Watson, David	5. 9	–	Barnsley	10.11.73
Defenders				
Appleby, Matt	5. 10	Darlington	Middlesbrough	16.04.72
Archdeacon, Owen	5. 7	Celtic	Greenock	4.03.66
Bishop, Charlie	5. 9	Bury	Nottingham	16.02.68
Clyde, Darron	6. 1	–	Limavady	26.03.76
Davis, Steve	6. 0	Burnley	Birmingham	26.07.65
De Zeeuw, Arjan	6. 1	Telstar, Hol.	Castricum, Hol.	16.04.70
Eaden, Nick	5. 8	–	Sheffield	12.12.72
Fearon, Dean	6. 0	–	Barnsley	9.01.76
Fleming, Gary	5. 7	Man. City	Londonderry	17.02.67
Hume, Mark	6. 1	–	Barnsley	21.05.78
Jones, Dean	6. 0	–	Barnsley	12.10.77
Jones, Scott	5. 7	–	Sheffield	1.05.75
Morgan, Chris	5. 11	–	Barnsley	13.02.78
Moses, Adrian	5. 8	–	Doncaster	4.05.75
Perry, Jon	6. 0	–	Hamilton, N.Z.	22.11.76
Sheridan, Darren	5. 4	–	Manchester	8.12.67
Shirtliff, Peter	6. 0	Wolves	Sheffield	6.04.61
Thompson, Neil	5. 10	Ipswich	Beverley	2.10.63
Midfield				
Bennett, Troy	5. 9	–	Barnsley	25.12.75
Bullock, Martin	5. 4	–	Derby	5.03.75
Gregory, Andrew	5. 7	–	Barnsley	8.10.76
McClare, Sean	5. 7	–	Rotherham	12.01.78
O'Connell, Brendan	5. 9	Burnley	Waterloo	12.11.66
Redfearn, Neil	5. 8	Oldham	Bradford	20.06.65
Van der Velden, Carel	5. 7	Den Bosch, Hol.	Arnhem, Hol.	3.08.72
Wilson, Danny	5. 4	Sheff. Wed.	Wigan	1.01.60
Forwards				
Beckett, Luke	5. 8	–	Sheffield	25.11.76
Bochenski, Simon	5. 8	–	Worksop	6.12.75
Hurst, Glynn	5. 7	–	Barnsley	17.01.76
Jackson, Chris	5. 9	–	Barnsley	16.01.76
Liddell, Andy	5. 6	–	Leeds	28.06.73
Payton, Andy	5. 7	Celtic	Burnley	23.10.67
Regis, David	6. 0	Southend	Paddington	3.03.64
Rose, Karl	5. 4	–	Barnsley	12.10.78
Ten Heuvel, Laurens	5. 10	Den Bosch, Hol.	Duivendrecht, Hol.	6.06.76

BIRMINGHAM CITY

Name	Height ft. in.	Previous Club	Birthplace	Birthdate
Goalkeepers				
Bennett, Ian	6. 0	Peterborough	Worksop	10.10.70

Griemink, Bart	6. 4	WKE Emmen, Hol.	Oss, Hol.	29.03.72
Defenders				
Ablett, Gary	6. 0	Everton	Liverpool	19.11.65
Barnett, Dave	6. 0	Barnet	Birmingham	16.04.67
Bass, Jonathan	6. 0	–	Weston-s-mare	1.07.76
Breen, Gary	6. 2	Peterborough	London	12.12.73
Bruce, Steve	6. 0	Man. Utd.	Corbridge	31.12.60
Edwards, Andy	6. 3	Southend	Epping	17.09.71
Frain, John	5. 9	–	Birmingham	8.10.68
Grainger, Martin	5. 10	Brentford	Enfield	23.08.72
Hinton, Craig	5. 11	–	Wolverhampton	26.11.77
Johnson, Michael	5. 11	Notts County	Nottingham	4.07.73
Poole, Gary	6. 0	Southend	Stratford	11.09.67
Rea, Simon	6. 1	–	Birmingham	20.09.76
Midfield				
Bowen, Jason	5. 6	Swansea	Methyr Tydfil	24.08.72
Castle, Steve	5. 10	Plymouth	Ilford	17.05.66
Cornforth, John	6. 1	Swansea	Whitley Bay	7.10.67
Donowa, Louie	5. 9	Bristol City	Ipswich	24.09.64
Finnan, Steve	6. 0	Welling United	Limerick	20.04.76
Forsyth, Richard	5. 10	Kidderminster	Dudley	3.10.70
Horne, Barry	5. 10	Everton	St. Asaph	18.05.62
Hunt, Jonathan	5. 10	Southend	London	2.11.71
Legg, Andrew	6. 0	Notts County	Neath	28.07.66
Otto, Ricky	5. 10	Southend	Dartford	9.11.67
Robinson, Steve	5. 8	–	Nottingham	17.01.75
Tait, Paul	6. 1	–	Sutton Coldfield	31.07.71
Webb, Matthew	5. 8	–	Bristol	24.09.76
Forwards				
Barnes, Paul	5. 10	York	Leicester	16.11.67
Barnes, Steve	5. 4	Welling United	Wembley	5.01.76
Devlin, Paul	5. 8	Stafford Rangers	Birmingham	14.04.72
Dyer, Wayne	6. 0	–	Birmingham	24.11.77
Francis, Delton	5. 9	–	Birmingham	12.03.78
Francis, Kevin	6. 7	Stockport	Birmingham	6.12.67
Furlong, Paul	6. 1	Chelsea	Wood Green	1.10.68
Hatton, Paul	6. 0	–	Kidderminster	2.11.78
McKenzie, Chisty	5. 11	–	Birmingham	26.02.78
Martin, Jae	5. 10	Southend	London	5.02.76
Muir, Ian	5. 8	Tranmere	Coventry	5.05.63
Peschisolido, Paul	5. 4	Stoke	Scarborough, Can.	27.05.71

BOLTON WANDERERS

Name	Height ft. in.	Previous Club	Birthplace	Birthdate
Goalkeepers				
Branagan, Keith	6. 0	Millwall	Fulham	10.07.66
Davison, Aidan	6. 1	Millwall	Sedgefield	11.05.68
Ward, Gavin	6. 2	Bradford City	Sutton Coldfield	30.06.70
Defenders				
Bergsson, Gudni	6. 1	Tottenham	Iceland	21.07.65
Coleman, Simon	6. 0	Sheff. Wed.	Worksop	13.06.68
Fairclough, Chris	5. 11	Leeds	Nottingham	12.04.64
Hallows, Marcus	6. 1	Leigh	Bolton	7.07.75
Phillips, Jimmy	6. 0	Middlesbrough	Bolton	8.02.66
Small, Bryan	5. 9	Aston Villa	Birmingham	15.11.71
Spooner, Nicky	5. 10	–	Manchester	5.06.71
Strong, Greg	6. 2	Wigan	Bolton	5.09.75
Taggart, Gerry	6. 1	Barnsley	Belfast	18.10.70

Midfield				
Burnett, Wayne	6. 0	Plymouth	Lambeth	4.09.71
Curcic, Sasa	5. 9	Part. Belgrade, Yug.	Belgrade, Yug.	14.02.72
Frandsen, Per	5. 8	FC Copenhagen, Den.	Copenhagen, Den.	–
Green, Scott	5. 10	Derby	Walsall	15.01.70
Johansen, Michael	5. 10	FC Copenhagen, Den.	Golstrup, Den.	–
Sellars, Scott	5. 8	Newcastle	Sheffield	27.11.65
Taylor, Scott	5. 10	Millwall	Chertsey	5.05.78
Thompson, Alan	6. 0	Newcastle	Newcastle	22.12.73
Todd, Andrew	5. 10	Middlesbrough	Derby	21.09.74
Forwards				
Blake, Nathan	5. 11	Sheff. Utd.	Cardiff	27.01.72
DeFreitas, Fabian	6. 1	Volendam, Hol.	Paramaribo, W.I.	28.07.72
Lee, David	5. 7	Southampton	Whitefield	5.11.67
McAnespie, Steve	5. 9	Raith	Kilmarnock	1.02.72
McGinlay, John	5. 9	Millwall	Inverness	8.04.64
Paatelainen, Mika-Matti	6. 0	Aberdeen	Helsinki, Fin.	3.02.67
Whitehead, Stuart	5. 11	Bromsgrove	Bromsgrove	17.07.76
Whittaker, Stuart	5. 8	Liverpool	Liverpool	2.01.75

BRADFORD CITY

Name	Height ft. in.	Previous Club	Birthplace	Birthdate
Goalkeepers				
Gould, Jonathan	6. 1	Coventry	Paddington	18.07.68
Scott, Colin	6. 2	Rangers	–	–
Defenders				
Ford, John	6. 0	Swansea	Birmingham	12.04.68
Huxford, Richard	5. 11	Birmingham	Scunthorpe	25.07.69
Jacobs, Wayne	5. 8	Rotherham	Sheffield	3.02.69
Liburd, Richard	5. 10	Middlesbrough	Nottingham	26.09.73
Mohan, Nicky	6. 1	Leicester City	Middlesbrough	6.10.70
Sas, Marco	6. 0	NAC Breda, Hol.	–	–
Youds, Eddie	6. 1	Ipswich	Liverpool	3.05.70
Midfield				
Bullimore, Wayne	5. 10	Scunthorpe	Mansfield	12.09.70
Duxberry, Lee	5. 8	Huddersfield	Keighley	7.10.69
Hamilton, Des	5. 11	–	Bradford	15.08.76
Kiwomya, Andy	5. 9	Scunthorpe	Huddersfield	1.10.67
Mitchell, Graham	6. 0	Huddersfield	Shipley	16.02.68
Murray, Shaun	5. 7	Scarborough	Newcastle	7.02.70
Forwards				
Midgley, Craig	5. 11	–	Bradford	24.05.76
Ormondroyd, Ian	6. 5	Leicester City	Bradford	22.09.64
Regtop, Erik	6. 0	Heerenveen, Hol.	–	–
Shutt, Carl	5. 11	Birmingham	Sheffield	10.10.61
Stallard, Mark	6. 0	Derby	Derby	24.10.74

CHARLTON ATHLETIC

Name	Height ft. in.	Previous Club	Birthplace	Birthdate
Goalkeepers				
Petterson, Andy	6. 1	Luton	Freemantle, Aust.	26.09.69
Salmon, Mike	6. 2	Wrexham	Leyland	14.07.64

Defenders				
Balmer, Stuart	6. 1	Celtic	Falkirk	20.06.69
Brown, Steve	6. 1	–	Brighton	13.05.72
Chandler, Dean	6. 0	–	London	6.05.76
Chapple, Phil	6. 2	Cambridge Utd.	Norwich	26.11.66
Rufus, Richard	6. 1	–	Lewisham	12.01.75
Stuart, Jamie	5. 10	–	Southwark	15.10.76
Sturgess, Paul	5. 11	–	Dartford	4.08.75
Midfield				
Curbishley, Alan	5. 11	Brighton	Forest Gate	8.11.57
Jones, Keith	5. 9	Southend	Dulwich	14.10.64
Linger, Paul	5. 8	–	Tower Hamlets	20.12.74
Mortimer, Paul	5. 11	Crystal Palace	London	8.05.68
Newton, Shaun	5. 8	Brighton	Camberwell	20.08.75
Nicholls, Kevin	–	–	–	–
Notley, Jay	–	–	–	–
Robinson, John	5. 10	Brighton	Bulawayo, Zim.	29.08.71
Tindall, Jason	–	–	–	–
Forwards				
Allen, Bradley	5. 7	Q.P.R.	Harold Wood	13.09.71
Leaburn, Carl	6. 3	–	Lewisham	30.03.69
Lisbie, Kevin	–	–	–	–
Robson, Mark	5. 7	West Ham	Newham	22.05.69
Whyte, David	5. 9	Crystal Palace	Greenwich	20.04.71

CRYSTAL PALACE

Name	Height ft. in.	Previous Club	Birthplace	Birthdate
Goalkeepers				
Martyn, Nigel	6. 2	Bristol Rovers	St. Austell	11.08.66
Defenders				
Andersen, Leif	6. 5	Moss FK, Nor.	Oslo, Nor.	19.04.71
Boxall, Danny	5. 8	–	Croydon	24.08.77
Burton, Sagi	6. 2	–	Birmingham	25.11.77
Cyrus, Andrew	5. 8	–	London	30.09.76
Davies, Gareth	6. 1	Hereford	Hereford	11.12.73
Edworthy, Marc	5. 8	Plymouth	Barnstaple	24.12.72
Gordon, Dean	6. 0	–	Thornton Heath	10.02.73
Quinn, Robert	5. 11	–	Sidcup	8.11.76
Tuttle, David	6. 2	Sheff. Utd.	Reading	6.02.72
Vincent, Jamie	5. 10	–	London	18.06.75
Midfield				
Enqvist, Bjorn	5. 10	Malmo, Swe.	Sweden	12.10.77
Folan, Anthony	5. 10	–	Lewisham	18.09.78
Ginty, Rory	5. 9	–	Galway	23.01.77
Hopkin, David	5. 9	Chelsea	Glasgow	21.08.70
Houghton, Ray	5. 7	Aston Villa	Glasgow	9.01.62
Maddison, Neil	5. 11	Southampton	Darlington	2.10.69
Matthew, Damian	5. 11	Chelsea	Islington	23.09.70
Parry, David	5. 10	–	Belfast	12.03.78
Pitcher, Darren	5. 9	Charlton	Mile End	12.10.69
Roberts, Andy	5. 10	Millwall	Dartford	20.03.74
Rodger, Simon	5. 9	–	Shoreham-by-Sea	3.10.71
Scully, Tony	5. 7	–	Dublin	12.06.76
Thomson, Steve	5. 8	–	Glasgow	23.01.78
Wales, Danny	5. 10	–	Southwark	17.11.77
Forwards				
Dyer, Bruce	5. 11	Watford	Ilford	13.04.75
Freedman, Dougie	5. 9	Barnet	Glasgow	21.01.74

Harris, Jason	6. 1	–	Sutton	24.11.76
McKenzie, Leon	5. 10	–	Croydon	17.05.78
Ndah, George	6. 1	–	Camberwell	23.12.74
Veart, Carl	5. 10	Sheff. Utd.	Whyalla, Aust.	21.05.70

GRIMSBY TOWN

Name	Height ft. in.	Previous Club	Birthplace	Birthdate
Goalkeepers				
Crichton, Paul	6. 0	Doncaster	Pontefract	3.10.68
Love, Andrew	6. 2	–	Grimsby	28.03.79
Pearcey, Jason	6. 1	Mansfield	Leamington Spa	23.07.71
Defenders				
Fickling, Ashley	5. 10	Sheff. Utd.	Sheffield	15.11.72
Gallimore, Tony	5. 11	Carlisle	Crewe	21.02.72
Gowshall, Joby	5. 11	–	Louth	7.08.75
Handyside, Peter	6. 1	–	Dumfries	31.07.74
Jobling, Kevin	5. 9	Leicester City	Sunderland	1.01.68
Laws, Brian	5. 8	Nott'm. Forest	Wallsend	14.10.61
Lever, Mark	6. 3	–	Beverley	29.03.70
McDermott, John	5. 7	–	Middlesbrough	3.02.69
Neil, James	5. 9	–	Bury St. Edmunds	28.02.76
Rodger, Graham	6. 2	Luton	Glasgow	1.04.67
Smith, Richard	5. 11	Leicester City	Lutterworth	3.10.70
Midfield				
Clare, Daryl	5. 8	–	Jersey	1.08.78
Harsley, Paul	5. 7	–	Scunthorpe	29.05.78
Oster, John	5. 7	–	Boston	8.12.78
Shakespeare, Craig	5. 10	W.B.A.	Birmingham	26.10.63
Walker, John	5. 6	Rangers	Robroyston	12.12.73
Widdrington, Tommy	5. 10	Southampton	Newcastle	21.11.71
Forwards				
Black, Kingsley	5. 8	Nott'm. Forest	Luton	22.06.68
Childs, Gary	5. 7	Birmingham	Birmingham	19.04.64
Forrester, Jamie	5. 6	Leeds	Bradford	1.11.74
Lester, Jack	5. 10	–	Sheffield	8.10.75
Livingstone, Steve	6. 1	Chelsea	Middlesbrough	8.09.69
Mendonca, Clive	5. 10	Sheff. Utd.	Tullington	9.09.68
Southall, Nicky	5. 10	Hartlepool	Stockton	28.01.72
Woods, Neil	6. 0	Bradford City	York	30.07.66

HUDDERSFIELD TOWN

Name	Height ft. in.	Previous Club	Birthplace	Birthdate
Goalkeepers				
Francis, Steve	6. 1	Reading	Billericay	29.05.64
Norman, Tony	6. 1	Sunderland	Clwyd	24.02.58
O'Connor, Derek	5. 11	–	Dublin	9.03.78
Defenders				
Collins, Sam	6. 2	–	Pontefract	5.06.77
Cowan, Tom	5. 8	Sheff. Utd.	Bellshill	28.08.69
Dyson, Jon	6. 1	–	Mirfield	18.12.71
Gonsalves, Ryan	5. 11	–	Leeds	22.12.77
Gray, Kevin	6. 0	Mansfield	Sheffield	7.01.72
Jenkins, Steve	5. 11	Swansea	Merthyr Tydfill	16.07.72
Morrison, Andy	6. 1	Blackpool	Inverness	30.07.70

Murphy, Stephen	5. 11	–	Dublin	5.04.78
Ryan, Robbie	5. 10	–	Dublin	16.05.77
Sanders, Steven	5. 10	–	Halifax	2.06.78
Sinnott, Lee	6. 1	Bradford City	Walsall	12.07.65
Scully, Pat	6. 1	Southend	Dublin	23.06.70
Midfield				
Bullock, Darren	5. 8	Nuneaton Borough	Worcester	12.02.69
Collins, Simon	6. 0	–	Pontefract	16.12.73
Crosby, Gary	5. 8	Nott'm. Forest	Sleaford	8.05.64
Dalton, Paul	5. 11	Plymouth	Middlesbrough	25.04.67
Heary, Thomas	5. 9	–	Dublin	14.02.79
Illingworth, Jeremy	5. 10	–	Huddersfield	20.05.77
Kelly, Mark	6. 0	–	Gibraltar	15.10.76
Makel, Lee	5. 9	Blackburn	Sunderland	11.01.73
Reid, Paul	5. 8	Bradford City	Oldbury	19.01.68
Stott, Michael	5. 11	–	Huddersfield	26.12.77
Sweet, Ben	6. 0	–	Huddersfield	21.07.78
Forwards				
Baldry, Simon	5. 10	–	Huddersfield	12.02.76
Dunn, Iain	5. 10	Goole Town	Howden	1.04.70
Edwards, Rob	5. 9	Crewe	Manchester	23.02.70
Jepson, Ronnie	6. 0	Exeter	Stoke	12.05.63
Lawson, Ian	5. 11	–	Huddersfield	4.11.77
Payton, Andy	5. 9	Barnsley	Burnley	3.10.67
Rowe, Rodney	5. 9	–	Huddersfield	30.07.75
Stewart, Marcus	5. 10	Bristol Rovers	Bristol	7.11.72

IPSWICH TOWN

Name	Height ft. in.	Previous Club	Birthplace	Birthdate
Goalkeepers				
Forrest, Craig	6. 5	–	Vancouver, Can.	20.09.67
Wright, Richard	6. 2	–	Ipswich	5.11.77
Defenders				
Ellis, Kevin	6. 2	–	Great Yarmouth	12.05.77
Mowbray, Tony	6. 1	Celtic	Saltburn	22.11.63
Swailes, Chris	6. 2	Doncaster	Gateshead	19.10.70
Taricco, Maurico	5. 8	Argentinos Jun., Arg	Buenos Aires, Arg.	10.03.73
Vaughan, Tony	6. 1	–	Manchester	11.10.75
Wark, John	5. 11	Middlesbrough	Glasgow	4.08.57
Midfield				
Mason, Paul	5. 9	Aberdeen	Liverpool	3.09.63
Milton, Simon	5. 10	Bury Town	Fulham	23.08.63
Norfolk, Lee	5. 10	–	New Zealand	17.10.75
Petta, Bobby	5. 9	Feyenoord, Hol.	Rotterdam, Hol.	6.08.74
Sedgley, Steve	6. 1	Tottenham	Enfield	26.05.68
Slater, Stuart	5. 9	Celtic	Sudbury	27.03.69
Sonner, Danny	5. 11	Preussen, Ger.	Wigan	9.01.72
Stockwell, Mick	5. 9	–	Chelmsford	14.02.65
Tanner, Adam	6. 0	–	Maldon	25.10.73
Thomsen, Claus	6. 3	Aarhus, Den.	Aarhus, Den.	31.05.70
Williams, Geraint	5. 7	Derby	Treorchy	5.01.62
Forwards				
Gregory, Neil	5. 11	–	Ndola, Zambia	7.10.72
Marshall, Ian	6. 1	Oldham	Liverpool	20.03.66
Mathie, Alex	5. 10	Newcastle	Bathgate	20.12.68
Naylor, Richard	6. 1	–	Leeds	28.02.77
Scowcroft, James	6. 1	–	Bury St. Edmunds	15.11.75

MANCHESTER CITY

Name	Height ft. in.	Previous Club	Birthplace	Birthdate
Goalkeepers				
Dibble, Andy	6. 2	Luton	Cwmbran	8.06.65
Immel, Eike	6. 2	VfB Stuttgart, Ger.	Marburg-Lahn, Ger.	27.11.60
Margetson, Martyn	6. 0	–	Neath	8.09.71
Defenders				
Brightwell, Ian	5. 10	–	Lutterworth	9.04.68
Curle, Keith	6. 0	Wimbledon	Bristol	14.11.63
Edghill, Richard	5. 9	–	Oldham	23.09.74
Foster, John	5. 10	–	Manchester	19.09.73
Frontzeck, Michael	5. 11	B. M'gladbach, Ger.	Stuttgart, Ger.	26.03.64
Hiley, Scott	5. 9	Birmingham	Plymouth	27.09.68
Ingram, Rae	5. 11	–	Manchester	6.12.74
Kernaghan, Alan	6. 2	Middlesbrough	Otley	25.04.67
Symons, Kit	6. 1	Portsmouth	Basingstoke	8.03.71
Midfield				
Beagrie, Peter	5. 8	Everton	Middlesbrough	28.11.65
Brown, Michael	5. 10	–	Hartlepool	25.01.77
Clough, Nigel	5. 10	Liverpool	Sunderland	19.03.66
Crooks, Lee	5. 11	–	Wakefield	14.01.78
Kerr, David	5. 10	–	Dumfries	6.09.74
Kinkladze, Georgi	5. 8	Dinamo Tbilisi	Tbilisi, Geo.	6.07.73
Lomas, Steve	6. 0	–	Hanover, Ger.	18.01.74
Phillips, Martin	5. 9	Exeter	Exeter	13.03.76
Summerbee, Nick	5. 11	Swindon	Altrincham	26.08.71
Thomas, Scott	5. 9	–	Bury	30.10.74
Forwards				
Creaney, Gerry	5. 11	Portsmouth	Coatbridge	13.04.70
Kavelashvili, Mikhail	5. 11	S. Vladikavkaz, Rus.	Georgia	22.07.71
Quinn, Niall	6. 4	Arsenal	Dublin	6.10.66
Rosler, Uwe	6. 0	Nurnburg, Ger.	Attenburg, Ger.	15.11.68

NORWICH CITY

Name	Height ft. in.	Previous Club	Birthplace	Birthdate
Goalkeepers				
Barber, Paul	6. 3	–	Burnley	30.08.77
Gunn, Bryan	6. 2	Aberdeen	Thurso	22.12.63
Marshall, Andy	6. 2	–	Bury	14.04.75
Defenders				
Bradshaw, Carl	5. 10	Sheff. Utd.	Sheffield	2.10.68
Brownrigg, Andrew	6. 0	Hereford	Sheffield	2.08.76
Mills, Danny	5. 11	–	Norwich	18.05.77
Newman, Rob	6. 2	Bristol City	Bradford-on-Avon	13.12.63
Polston, John	5. 11	Tottenham	Walthamstow	10.06.68
Prior, Spencer	6. 3	Southend	Rochford	22.04.71
Ullathorne, Robert	5. 8	–	Wakefield	11.10.71
Wright, Johnny	5. 9	–	Belfast	24.11.75
Midfield				
Adams, Neil	5. 8	Oldham	Stoke-on-Trent	23.11.65
Carey, Shaun	5. 8	–	Kettering	13.05.76
Johnson, Andy	6. 1	–	Bristol	2.05.74
Milligan, Mike	5. 8	Oldham	Manchester	20.02.67
Rush, Matthew	5. 11	West Ham	Dalston	6.08.71
Simpson, Karl	5. 11	–	Newmarket	12.10.76
Sutch, Daryl	6. 0	–	Lowestoft	11.09.71

Forwards				
Akinbiyi, Ade	6. 1	–	Hackney	10.10.74
Cureton, Jamie	5. 8	–	Bristol	28.08.75
Eadie, Darren	5. 8	–	Chippenham	10.06.75
Fleck, Robert	5. 9	Chelsea	Glasgow	11.08.65
Hilton, Damian	6. 2	–	Norwich	6.09.77
O'Neill, Keith	6. 1	–	Dublin	16.02.76
Scott, Keith	6. 3	Stoke	London	9.06.67

OLDHAM ATHLETIC

Name	Height ft. in.	Previous Club	Birthplace	Birthdate
Goalkeepers				
Darnbourgh, Lee	6. 0	–	Castleton	21.06.77
Gerrard, Paul	6. 2	–	Heywood	22.01.73
Hallworth, Jon	6. 1	Ipswich	Stockport	26.10.65
Defenders				
Fleming, Craig	6. 0	Halifax Town	Halifax	6.10.71
Graham, Richard	6. 3	–	Dewsbury	28.11.74
Lonergan, Darren	5. 11	Waterford	Cork	29.01.74
McNivern, Scott	5. 9	–	Blackpool	27.05.78
Makin, Chris	5. 10	–	Manchester	8.05.73
Redmond, Steve	6. 0	Man. City	Liverpool	2.11.67
Serrant, Carl	5. 11	–	Bradford	16.03.76
Snodin, Ian	5. 7	Everton	Rotherham	15.08.63
Midfield				
Evans, Richard	5. 11	–	Wrexham	16.10.76
Gannon, John	5. 9	Sheff. Utd.	Wimbledon	18.12.66
Halle, Gunnar	5. 11	Lillestrom, Nor.	Larvik, Nor.	11.08.65
Henry, Nick	5. 7	–	Liverpool	21.02.69
Hughes, Andrew	5. 10	–	Stockport	2.01.78
Orlygsson, Toddy	5. 11	Stoke	Odense, Den.	2.08.66
Richardson, Lee	5. 11	Aberdeen	Halifax	12.03.69
Rickers, Paul	5. 8	–	Castleford	9.05.75
Forwards				
Banger, Nicky	5. 9	Southampton	Southampton	25.02.71
Barlow, Stuart	5. 10	Everton	Liverpool	16.07.68
Beckford, Darren	6. 0	Norwich	Manchester	12.05.67
Beresford, David	5. 7	–	Rochdale	11.11.76
McCarthy, Sean	6. 0	Bradford City	Bridgend	12.09.67

OXFORD UNITED

Name	Height ft. in.	Previous Club	Birthplace	Birthdate
Goalkeepers				
Jackson, Elliot	6. 0	–	Swindon	27.08.77
Whitehead, Phil	6. 2	Barnsley	Halifax	17.12.69
Defenders				
Elliott, Matt	6. 3	Scunthorpe	Roehampton	1.11.68
Ford, Mike	6. 0	Cardiff	Bristol	9.02.66
Gilchrist, Phil	6. 0	Hartlepool	Stockton	25.08.73
Marsh, Simon	5. 11	–	Perivale	29.01.77
Robinson, Les	5. 10	Doncaster	Shirebrook	1.03.67
Midfield				
Ford, Bobby	5. 9	–	Bristol	22.09.74
Gray, Martin	5. 10	Sunderland	Stockton	17.08.71
Lewis, Mickey	5. 8	Derby	Birmingham	15.02.65
McGregor, Marc	5. 10	–	Southend	30.04.78

Massey, Stuart	5. 10	Crystal Palace	Crawley	17.11.64
Murphy, Matt	5. 10	Corby Town	Northampton	20.08.71
Smith, David	5. 10	Norwich	Liverpool	26.12.70
Forwards				
Aldridge, Martin	5. 11	Northampton	Northampton	6.12.74
Angel, Mark	5. 9	Sunderland	Sunderland	23.08.75
Beauchamp, Joey	5. 10	Swindon	Oxford	13.03.71
Druce, Mark	5. 11	–	Oxford	3.03.74
Jemson, Nigel	5. 10	Notts County	Hutton	10.08.69
Moody, Paul	6. 2	Southampton	Waterlooville	13.06.67
Powell, Paul	5. 9	–	Wallingford	30.06.78
Rush, David	5. 10	Sunderland	Sunderland	15.05.71
Stevens, Mark	6. 3	–	Swindon	3.12.77

PORTSMOUTH

Name	Height ft. in.	Previous Club	Birthplace	Birthdate
Goalkeepers				
Flahavan, Aaron	6. 1	–	Southampton	15.12.75
Knight, Alan	6. 1	–	Balham	3.07.61
Defenders				
Awford, Andy	5. 9	–	Worcester	14.07.72
Butters, Guy	6. 2	Tottenham	Hillingdon	30.10.69
Dobson, Tony	6. 1	Blackburn	Coventry	5. 02.69
Hinshelwood, Danny	5. 9	Nott'm. Forest	Bromley	12.12.75
Perrett, Russell	6. 2	Lymington	Barton-on-Sea	18.06.73
Pethick, Robbie	5. 10	Weymouth	Tavistock	8.09.70
Russell, Lee	5. 10	–	Southampton	3.09.69
Thomson, Andrew	6. 3	Swindon	Swindon	28.03.74
Waterman, David	5. 10	–	Guernsey	16.05.77
Midfield				
Allen, Martin	5. 10	West Ham	Reading	14.08.65
Igoe, Samuel	5. 6	–	Spelthorne	30.09.75
McGrath, Lloyd	5. 8	Hong Kong	Birmingham	24.02.65
McLoughlin, Alan	5. 8	Southampton	Manchester	20.04.67
Rees, Jason	5. 5	Luton	Aberdare	22.12.69
Simpson, Fitzroy	5. 6	Man. City	Trowbridge	26.02.70
Tilley, Anthony	5. 7	–	Zambia	11.02.77
Forwards				
Bradbury, Lee	6. 0	–	Isle of Wight	3.07.75
Burton, Deon	5. 8	–	Ashford, Kent	25.10.76
Carter, Jimmy	5. 10	Arsenal	London	9.11.65
Durnin, John	5. 10	Oxford Utd.	Liverpool	18.08.65
Hall, Paul	5. 9	Torquay	Manchester	3.07.72
Simpson, Robert	5. 9	Tottenham	Luton	3.03.76
Walsh, Paul	5. 8	Man. City	Plumstead	1.10.62
Wood, Paul	5. 9	Bournemouth	Middlesbrough	1.11.64

PORT VALE

Name	Height ft. in.	Previous Club	Birthplace	Birthdate
Goalkeepers				
Boswell, Matthew	6. 0	–	Shrewsbury	19.08.77
Musselwhite, Paul	6. 1	Scunthorpe	Portsmouth	22.12.68
Van Heusden, Arjan	6. 2	Noordwijk, Hol.	Alphen, Hol.	11.12.72
Defenders				
Aspin, Neil	6. 0	Leeds	Gateshead	12.04.65
Glover, Dean	5. 11	Middlesbrough	Birmingham	29.12.63

Griffiths, Gareth	6. 2	Rhyl	Winsford	10.04.70
Hill, Andy	5. 11	Man. City	Maltby	20.01.65
Holwyn, Jermaine	6. 2	Ajax, Hol.	Amsterdam, Hol.	16.04.73
Stokes, Dean	5. 7	Halesowen Town	Birmingham	23.05.70
Tankard, Allen	5. 10	Wigan	Islington	21.05.69
Midfield				
Bogie, Ian	5. 7	Leyton Orient	Newcastle	6.12.67
Eyre, Richard	5. 8	–	Poynton	15.09.76
Guppy, Steve	5. 11	Newcastle	Winchester	29.03.69
McCarthy, Jon	5. 9	York	Middlesbrough	18.08.70
Porter, Andy	5. 9	–	Congleton	17.09.68
Talbot, Stewart	5. 10	Moor Green	Birmingham	14.06.73
Walker, Ray	5. 10	Aston Villa	North Shields	28.09.63
Forwards				
Corden, Wayne	5. 9	–	Leek	1.11.75
Cunningham, Dean	5. 7	–	Burslem	28.05.77
Foyle, Martin	5. 10	Oxford Utd.	Salisbury	2.05.63
Glover, Lee	5. 10	Nott'm. Forest	Kettering	24.04.70
Mills, Lee	6. 1	Derby	Mexborough	10.07.70
Naylor, Tony	5. 6	Crewe	Manchester	29.03.67
O'Reilly, Justin	6. 0	Gresley Rovers	Derby	29.06.73

QUEENS PARK RANGERS

Name	Height ft. in.	Previous Club	Birthplace	Birthdate
Goalkeepers				
Hurst, Richard	6. 0	–	Hammersmith	23.12.76
Roberts, Tony	6. 0	–	Bangor	4.08.69
Sharp, Lee	6. 2	Lincoln Utd.	Lincoln	18.12.76
Sommer, Juergen	6. 5	Luton	New York, U.S.A.	27.02.64
Defenders				
Bardsley, David	5. 10	Oxford Utd.	Manchester	11.09.64
Brazier, Matthew	5. 9	–	Whipps Cross	2.07.76
Brevett, Rufus	5. 8	Doncaster	Derby	24.09.69
Challis, Trevor	5. 8	–	Paddington	23.10.75
McDermott, Andrew	5. 9	Aust. Inst. of Sport	Sydney, Aust.	24.03.77
McDonald, Alan	6. 2	–	Belfast	12.10.63
Maddix, Danny	5. 11	Tottenham	Ashford, Kent	11.10.67
Perry, Mark	5. 10	–	Perivale	19.10.78
Plummer, Chris	6. 2	–	Isleworth	12.10.76
Ready, Karl	6. 1	–	Neath	14.08.72
Yates, Steve	5. 10	Bristol Rovers	Bristol	29.01.70
Midfield				
Barker, Simon	5. 9	Blackburn	Bolton	4.11.64
Graham, Mark	5. 7	–	Newry	24.10.74
Impey, Andy	5. 8	Yeading	Hammersmith	30.09.71
Murray, Paul	5. 8	Carlisle	Carlisle	31.08.76
Quashie, Nigel	5. 9	–	Nunhead	20.07.78
Forwards				
Bruce, Paul	5. 10	–	London	18.02.78
Charles, Lee	5. 11	Chertsey Town	Hillingdon	20.08.71
Dichio, Daniele	6. 3	–	Hammersmith	19.10.74
Gallen, Kevin	5. 11	–	Hammersmith	21.09.75
Hateley, Mark	6. 4	Rangers	Derby	7.11.61
Mahoney-Johnson, Michael	5. 10	–	Paddington	6.11.76
Sinclair, Trevor	5. 10	Blackpool	Dulwich	2.03.73
Slade, Steven	5. 10	Tottenham	Romford	6.10.75

READING

Name	Height ft. in.	Previous Club	Birthplace	Birthdate
Goalkeepers				
Hammond, Nicky	6. 0	Plymouth	Hornchurch	7.09.67
Mihailov, Borislav	6. 1	Botev Plovdiv, Bul.	Sofia, Bul.	12.02.63
Defenders				
Bernal, Andy	5. 10	Syd. Olympic, Aust.	Canberra, Aust.	16.05.66
Bodin, Paul	6. 0	Swindon	Cardiff	13.09.64
Booty, Martyn	5. 8	Crewe	Leicester	30.05.71
Garrity, James	6. 1	Newcastle	Newcastle	7.05.78
Hopkins, Jeff	6. 0	Bristol Rovers	Swansea	14.04.64
Hunter, Barry	6. 4	Wrexham	Coleraine	18.11.68
Kerr, Dylan	5. 9	Leeds	Valetta, Malta	14.01.67
McPherson, Keith	5. 11	Northampton	Greenwich	11.09.63
Sanders, Guy	5. 11	–	Rugby	18.02.78
Simpson, Derek	5. 10	–	Lanark	23.12.76
Swales, Stephen	5. 8	Scarborough	Whitby	26.12.73
Thorp, Michael	6. 0	–	Wallingford	5.12.75
Wdowczyk, Dariusz	5. 11	Celtic	Warsaw, Pol.	21.09.62
Midfield				
Bass, David	5. 11	–	Frimley	29.11.74
Carey, Alan	5. 7	–	London	21.08.75
Caskey, Darren	5. 8	Tottenham	Basildon	21.08.74
Freeman, Andrew	5. 10	Crystal Palace	Reading	8.09.77
Gilkes, Michael	5. 8	–	Hackney	20.07.65
Gooding, Mick	5. 9	Wolves	Newcastle	12.04.59
Holsgrove, Paul	6. 1	Millwall	Wellington	26.08.69
Parkinson, Phil	6. 0	Bury	Chorley	1.12.67
Robertson, Andrew	5. 10	Oxford Utd.	Wokingham	7.11.77
Forwards				
Lambert, James	5. 7	–	Henley	14.09.73
Lovell, Stuart	5. 10	–	Sydney, Aust.	9.01.72
Meaker, Michael	5. 11	Q.P.R.	Greenford	18.08.71
Morley, Trevor	5. 11	West Ham	Nottingham	20.03.61
Nogan, Lee	5. 10	Watford	Cardiff	21.05.69
Quinn, Jimmy	6. 0	Bournemouth	Belfast	18.11.59
Williams, Martin	5. 9	Luton	Luton	12.07.73

SHEFFIELD UNITED

Name	Height ft. in.	Previous Club	Birthplace	Birthdate
Goalkeepers				
Heritage, Paul	6. 2	–	Sheffield	17.04.79
Kelly, Alan	6. 3	Preston	Preston	11.08.68
Tracey, Simon	6. 0	Wimbledon	Woolwich	9.12.67
Defenders				
Beard, Mark	5. 11	Millwall	Roehampton	8.10.74
Dyer, Liam	5. 11	–	Doncaster	2.05.78
Hocking, Matthew	5. 10	–	Boston	30.01.78
Hodgson, Doug	6. 2	Heidelberg, Aust.	Kingston, Aust.	27.02.69
Nilsen, Roger	5. 11	Viking Stavanger, Nor.	Tromso, Nor.	8.08.69
Sandford, Lee	6. 0	Stoke	Basingstoke	22.04.68
Short, Chris	5. 10	Notts County	Munster, Ger.	9.05.70
Vonk, Michel	6. 3	Man. City	Alkmaar, Hol.	28.10.68
Midfield				
Anthony, Graham	5. 8	–	South Shields	9.08.75
Hartfield, Charlie	6. 0	Arsenal	Lambeth	4.09.71

Hawes, Steven	5. 8	–	High Wycombe	17.07.78
Hutchison, Don	6. 2	West Ham	Gateshead	9.05.71
Patterson, Mark	5. 6	Bolton	Darwen	24.05.65
Quinn, Wayne	5. 10	–	Truro	19.11.76
Reed, John	5. 8	–	Rotherham	27.08.72
Scott, Andy	6. 1	Sutton United	Epsom	2.08.72
Spackman, Nigel	6. 0	Chelsea	Romsey	2.12.60
Ward, Mitch	5. 8	–	Sheffield	18.06.71
Forwards				
Bettney, Chris	5. 10	–	Chesterfield	27.10.77
Kachuro, Peter	5. 11	D. Minsk, Belarus	Belarus	2.08.72
Starbuck Phil	5. 10	Huddersfield	Nottingham	24.11.68
Taylor, Gareth	6. 2	Crystal Palace	Western-s-Mare	25.02.73
Walker, Andy	5. 8	Celtic	Glasgow	6.04.65
White, David	6. 1	Leeds	Manchester	30.10.67
Whitehouse, Dane	5. 9	–	Sheffield	14.10.70
Wood, Paul	5. 7	–	Sheffield	14.10.77

SOUTHEND UNITED

Name	Height ft. in.	Previous Club	Birthplace	Birthdate
Goalkeepers				
Royce, Simon	6. 2	Heybridge Swifts	Forest Gate	9.09.71
Sansome, Paul	6. 0	Millwall	New Addington	6.10.61
Defenders				
Bodley, Mick	6. 1	Barnet	Hayes	14.09.67
Dublin, Keith	5. 11	Watford	Brent	29.01.66
Lapper, Michael	6. 0	U.S.S.F.	U.S.A.	28.08.70
McNally, Mark	5. 10	Celtic	Motherwell	10.03.71
Roget, Leo	6. 1	–	Ilford	1.08.77
Simpson, Mark	5. 10	Portsmouth	London	27.12.67
Midfield				
Byrne, Paul	5. 11	Celtic	Dublin	30.06.72
Gridelet, Phil	6. 1	Barnsley	Edgware	30.04.67
Hails, Julian	5. 10	Fulham	Lincoln	20.11.67
Marsh, Mike	5. 8	Galatasaray, Tur.	Liverpool	21.07.69
Sussex, Andy	6. 3	Crewe	Islington	23.11.64
Tilson, Steve	5. 11	Burnham	Wickford	27.07.66
Whelan, Ronnie	5. 10	Liverpool	Dublin	25.09.61
Forwards				
Boere, Jeroen	6. 3	Crystal Palace	Arnhem, Hol.	18.11.67
Rammell, Andy	6. 2	Barnsley	Nuneaton	10.02.67
Thomson, Andy	5. 10	Queen of the South	Motherwell	1.04.71

STOKE CITY

Name	Height ft. in.	Previous Club	Birthplace	Birthdate
Goalkeepers				
Morgan, Philip	6. 2	Ipswich	Stoke	18.12.74
Muggleton, Carl	6. 1	Celtic	Leicester	13.09.68
Prudhoe, Mark	6. 0	Darlington	Washington	11.11.63
Defenders				
Clarkson, Ian	5. 10	Birmingham	Solihull	4.12.70
Cranson, Ian	5. 10	Sheff. Wed.	Easington	2.07.64
Dreyer, John	6. 1	Luton	Alnwick	11.06.63
Overson, Vince	6. 2	Birmingham	Kettering	15.05.62
Sigurdsson, Larus	6. 0	Thor FC, Ice.	Akuveyni, Ice.	4.06.73
Whittle, Justin	6. 1	Celtic	Derby	18.03.71

Worthington, Nigel	5. 10	Leeds	Ballymena	4.11.61
Midfield				
Beeston, Carl	5. 10	–	Stoke	30.06.67
Devlin, Mark	5. 10	–	Irvine	18.01.73
Gleghorn, Nigel	6. 0	Birmingham	Seaham	12.08.62
Keen, Kevin	5. 7	Wolves	Amersham	25.02.67
Potter, Graham	6. 1	Birmingham	Solihull	20.05.75
Wallace, Ray	5. 7	Leeds	Greenwich	2.10.69
Forwards				
Carruthers, Martin	5. 11	Aston Villa	Nottingham	7.08.72
Gayle, John	6. 3	Burnley	Bromsgrove	30.07.64
Macari, Michael	5. 7	–	Kilwinning	4.02.73
Macari, Paul	5. 8	–	Manchester	23.08.76
Sturridge, Simon	5. 5	Birmingham	Birmingham	9.12.69

SWINDON TOWN

Name	Height ft. in.	Previous Club	Birthplace	Birthdate
Goalkeepers				
Digby, Fraser	6. 1	Man. Utd.	Sheffield	23.04.67
Talia, Frank	6. 1	Blackburn	Melbourne, Aust.	20.07.72
Defenders				
Culverhouse, Ian	5. 10	Norwich	Bishop's Stortford	22.09.64
Drysdale, Jason	5. 10	Newcastle	Bristol	17.11.70
Horlock, Kevin	6. 0	West Ham	Plumstead	1.11.72
Murray, Edwin	5. 11	–	Redbridge	31.08.73
O'Sullivan, Wayne	5. 8	–	Cyprus	25.02.74
Robinson, Mark	5. 9	Newcastle	Rochdale	21.11.68
Seagraves, Mark	6. 0	Bolton	Bootle	22.10.66
Smith, Alex	5. 8	–	Liverpool	15.02.76
Taylor, Shaun	6. 1	Exeter	Plymouth	26.02.63
Midfield				
Allen, Paul	5. 7	Southampton	Aveley	28.08.62
Collins, Lee	5. 8	–	Bellshill	3.02.74
Gooden, Ty	5. 8	Wycombe	Canvey Island	23.10.72
Hooper, Dean	5. 10	Hayes	Harefield	13.04.71
McMahon, Steve	5. 9	Man. City	Liverpool	20.08.61
Watson, Kevin	5. 9	Tottenham	Hackney	3.01.74
Forwards				
Allison, Wayne	6. 1	Bristol City	Huddersfield	16.10.68
Cone, Steve	5. 8	Aston Villa	Gloucester	29.09.74
Finney, Steve	5. 10	Man. City	Hexham	31.10.73
Thorne, Peter	6. 0	Blackburn	Manchester	21.06.73

TRANMERE ROVERS

Name	Height ft. in.	Previous Club	Birthplace	Birthdate
Goalkeepers				
Coyne, Danny	5. 11	–	Prestatyn	27.08.73
Nixon, Eric	6. 4	Man. City	Manchester	4.10.62
Defenders				
Brannan, Ged	6. 0	–	Liverpool	15.01.72
Challinor, Dave	6. 1	–	Chester	2.10.75
Higgins, Dave	6. 0	Caernarfon Town	Liverpool	19.08.61
McGreal, John	5. 11	–	Birkenhead	2.06.72
Mungall, Steve	5. 8	Motherwell	Bellshill	22.05.58
Rogers, Alan	5. 10	–	Liverpool	3.01.77
Stevens, Gary	5. 11	Rangers	Barrow	27.03.63

Teale, Shaun	6. 0	Aston Villa	Southport	10.03.64
Thomas, Tony	5. 11	–	Liverpool	12.07.71
Midfield				
Cook, Paul	5. 11	Coventry	Liverpool	22.02.67
Irons, Kenny	5. 10	–	Liverpool	4.11.70
Mahon, Alan	5. 10	–	Dublin	4.04.78
Morgan, Alan	5. 10	–	Aberystwyth	2.11.73
Morrissey, John	5. 8	Wolves	Liverpool	8.03.65
Nevin, Pat	5. 6	Everton	Glasgow	6.09.63
O'Brien, Liam	6. 1	Newcastle	Dublin	5.09.64
Woods, Billy	6. 0	Cork City	Cork	24.10.73
Forwards				
Aldridge, John	5. 11	Real Sociedad, Spa.	Liverpool	18.09.58
Branch, Graham	6. 2	Heswall	Liverpool	12.02.72
Jones, Gary	6. 3	–	Chester	10.05.75
Kenworthy, Jon	5. 8	–	St. Asaph	18.08.74
Moore, Ian	5. 11	–	Birkenhead	26.08.76

WEST BROMWICH ALBION

Name	Height ft. in.	Previous Club	Birthplace	Birthdate
Goalkeepers				
Adamson, Chris	5. 11	–	Northumberland	4.11.78
Cutler, Neil	6. 1	–	Birmingham	3.09.76
Germaine, Gary	6. 0	–	Birmingham	2.08.76
Reece, Paul	5. 10	Notts County	Nottingham	16.07.68
Spink, Nigel	6. 2	Aston Villa	Chelmsford	8.08.58
Defenders				
Agnew, Paul	5. 9	Grimsby	Lisburn	15.08.65
Brien, Tony	5. 11	Rotherham	Dublin	10.02.69
Burgess, Daryl	5. 11	–	Birmingham	20.04.71
Comyn, Andy	6. 1	Plymouth	Wakefield	2.06.68
Hamner, Gareth	5. 10	Newtown	Shrewsbury	12.10.73
Herbert, Craig	5. 10	Torquay	Coventry	9.11.75
Holmes, Paul	5. 10	Everton	Stockbridge	18.02.68
Mardon, Paul	6. 0	Birmingham	Bristol	14.09.69
Nicholson, Shane	5. 10	Derby	Newark	3.06.70
Raven, Paul	6. 1	Doncaster	Salisbury	28.07.70
Midfield				
Buckley, Simon	5. 9	–	Stoke	29.02.76
Butler, Peter	5. 9	Notts County	Halifax	27.08.66
Coldicott, Stacy	5. 8	–	Redditch	29.04.74
Cunnington, Shaun	5. 9	Sunderland	Bourne	4.01.66
Darby, Julian	6. 0	Coventry	Bolton	3.10.67
Donovan, Kevin	5. 8	Huddersfield	Halifax	17.12.71
Gilbert, David	5. 4	Grimsby	Lincoln	22.06.63
Groves, Paul	5. 11	Grimsby	Derby	28.02.66
Hamilton, Ian	5. 9	Scunthorpe	Stevenage	14.12.67
Smith, David	5. 8	Birmingham	Stonehouse	29.03.68
Sneekes, Richard	5. 11	Bolton	Amsterdam, Hol.	30.10.68
Forwards				
Ashcroft, Lee	5. 10	Preston	Preston	7.09.72
Hargreaves, Chris	5. 11	Hull	Cleethorpes	12.05.72
Hunt, Andy	6. 0	Newcastle	Thurrock	9.06.70
Rodosthenous, Mike	5. 11	–	London	25.08.76
Taylor, Bob	5. 10	Bristol City	Easington	3.02.67

WOLVERHAMPTON WANDERERS

Name	Height ft. in.	Previous Club	Birthplace	Birthdate
Goalkeepers				
Stowell, Mike	6. 2	Everton	Portsmouth	19.04.65
Defenders				
Emblen, Neil	6. 2	Millwall	Bromley	19.06.71
Law, Brian	6. 2	Q.P.R.	Merthyr	1.01.70
Masters, Neil	6. 1	Bournemouth	Lisburn	25.05.72
Pearce, Dennis	5. 9	Aston Villa	Wolverhampton	10.09.74
Richards, Dean	6. 2	Bradford City	Bradford	9.06.74
Smith, James	5. 6	–	Birmingham	17.09.74
Thompson, Andy	5. 4	W.B.A.	Cannock	9.11.67
Williams, Adrian	6. 2	Reading	Reading	16.08.71
Young, Eric	6. 3	Crystal Palace	Singapore	25.03.60
Midfield				
Atkins, Mark	6. 1	Blackburn	Doncaster	14.08.68
Corica, Steve	5. 8	Leicester City	Cairns, Aust.	24.03.73
Daley, Tony	5. 8	Aston Villa	Birmingham	18.10.67
Ferguson, Darren	5. 10	Man. Utd.	Glasgow	9.02.72
Foley, Domonic	6. 1	St. James' Gate	Cork	7.07.76
Froggatt, Steve	5. 10	Aston Villa	Lincoln	9.03.73
Osborn, Simon	5. 10	Q.P.R.	New Addington	19.01.72
Thomas, Geoff	6. 1	Crystal Palace	Manchester	5.08.64
Wright, Jermaine	5. 9	Millwall	Greenwich	15.08.75
Forwards				
Bull, Steve	5. 11	W.B.A.	Tipton	28.03.65
Crowe, Glen	5. 10	–	Dublin	25.12.77
Goodman, Don	5. 10	Sunderland	Leeds	9.05.66
Roberts, Iwan	6. 2	Leicester City	Bangor	26.06.68

Second Division

BLACKPOOL

Name	Height ft. in.	Previous Club	Birthplace	Birthdate
Goalkeepers				
Banks, Steven	6. 0	Gillingham	Hillingdon	9.02.72
Defenders				
Allardyce, Craig	6. 2	Preston	Bolton	9.06.75
Barlow, Andy	5. 9	Oldham	Oldham	24.11.65
Bradshaw, Darren	5. 11	Peterborough	Sheffield	19.03.67
Brown, Phil	5. 11	Bolton	South Shields	30.05.59
Bryns, Marvin	6. 0	Q.P.R.	Paddington	2.08.75
Darton, Scott	5. 11	W.B.A.	Ipswich	27.03.75
Dixon, Ben	6. 1	Lincoln	Lincoln	16.09.74
Hooks, John	5. 8	Southampton	Armagh	10.02.77
Linighan, David	6. 2	Ipswich	Hartlepool	9.01.65
Lydiate, Jason	5. 11	Bolton	Manchester	29.10.71
Midfield				
Beech, Chris	5. 11	–	Blackpool	16.09.74
Bonner, Mark	5. 10	–	Ormskirk	7.06.74
Gouck, Andy	5. 9	–	Blackpool	8.06.72
Mellon, Micky	5. 8	W.B.A.	Paisley	18.03.72

Philpott, Lee	5. 9	Leicester	Barnet	21.02.70
Forwards				
Ellis, Tony	5. 11	Preston	Salford	20.10.64
Preece, Andy	6. 1	Crystal Palace	Evesham	27.03.67
Quinn, James	6. 1	Birmingham	Coventry	15.12.74
Symons, Paul	5. 10	–	Newcastle	20.04.76
Thorpe, Lee	6. 0	–	Wolverhampton	14.12.75
Watson, Andy	5. 9	Carlisle	Huddersfield	1.04.67

BOURNEMOUTH

Name	Height ft. in.	Previous Club	Birthplace	Birthdate
Goalkeepers				
Andrews, Ian	6. 2	Southampton	Nottingham	1.12.64
Glass, Jimmy	6. 1	Crystal Palace	Epsom	1.08.73
Defenders				
McElhatton, Michael	6. 0	–	County Kerry	16.04.75
Morris, Mark	6. 1	Sheff. Utd.	Morden	26.09.62
Pennock, Adrian	5. 11	Norwich	Ipswich	27.03.71
Young, Neil	5. 9	Tottenham	Harlow	31.08.73
Midfield				
Beardsmore, Russell	5. 6	Man. Utd.	Wigan	28.09.68
Brissett, Jason	5. 11	Peterborough	Redbridge	7.09.74
Cotterill, Leo	5. 9	Ipswich	Cambridge	2.09.74
Holland, Matthew	5. 9	West Ham	Bury	11.04.74
Mean, Scott	5. 11	–	Crawley	13.12.73
Murray, Robert	5. 11	–	Hammersmith	31.10.74
Oldbury, Marcus	5. 7	Norwich	Bournemouth	29.03.76
Rawlinson, Mark	5. 8	Man. Utd.	Bolton	9.06.75
Forwards				
Bailey, John	5. 8	Enfield	London	6.05.69
Coll, Owen	6. 0	Tottenham	Donegal	9.04.76
Cox, Ian	6. 0	Crystal Palace	Croydon	25.03.71
Fletcher, Steven	6. 2	Hartlepool	Hartlepool	26.06.72
O'Neill, Jon	5. 11	Celtic	Glasgow	3.01.74
Robinson, Stephen	5. 7	Tottenham	Crumlin	10.12.74
Town, David	5. 9	–	Bournemouth	9.12.76
Watson, Mark	6. 3	West Ham	Birmingham	28.12.73

BRENTFORD

Name	Height ft. in.	Previous Club	Birthplace	Birthdate
Goalkeepers				
Dearden, Kevin	5. 11	Tottenham	Luton	8.03.70
Fernandes, Tamar	6. 3	–	Paddington	7.12.74
Defenders				
Ashby, Barry	6. 2	Watford	Brent	21.11.70
Bates, Jamie	6. 1	–	Croydon	24.02.68
Hurdle, Gus	5. 10	Fulham	London	14.10.73
Hutchings, Carl	6. 0	–	Hammersmith	24.12.72
Statham, Brian	5. 11	Tottenham	Zimbabwe	21.05.69
Midfield				
Abrahams, Paul	5. 9	Colchester	Colchester	31.10.73
Anderson, Ijah	5. 11	Southend	Hackney	30.12.75
Bent, Marcus	6. 0	–	London	19.05.78
Davis, Paul	5. 10	Arsenal	London	9.12.61
Harney, Lee	5. 11	Leyton Orient	Harlow	21.12.66
Myall, Stuart	5. 9	Brighton	Eastbourne	12.11.74

Ravenscroft, Craig	5. 7	–	London	20.12.74
Smith, Paul	5. 11	Southend	Lenham	18.09.71
Forwards				
Asaba, Carl	6. 1	Dulwich Hamlet	London	28.01.73
Forster, Nick	5. 9	Gillingham	Oxted	8.09.73
McGhee, David	5. 10	–	Sussex	19.06.76
McPherson, Malcolm	5. 7	West Ham	Glasgow	19.12.74
Omigie, Joe	6. 2	–	Hammersmith	13.06.72
Taylor, Rob	6. 1	Leyton Orient	Norwich	30.04.71

BRISTOL CITY

Name	Height ft. in.	Previous Club	Birthplace	Birthdate
Goalkeepers				
Dykstra, Sieb	6. 5	Q.P.R.	Kerkrade, Hol.	20.10.66
Welch, Keith	6. 1	Rochdale	Bolton	3.10.68
Defenders				
Bryant, Matt	6. 0	–	Bristol	21.09.70
Carey, Louis	5. 11	–	Bristol	22.01.77
Dryden, Richard	6. 0	Birmingham	Stroud	14.06.69
Hansen, Vegard	6. 1	Stromsgodset, Nor.	Drammen, Nor.	8.08.69
Huggins, Dean	5. 11	–	Cardiff	21.11.76
Langan, Kevin	6. 0	–	Jersey	7.04.78
McLeary, Alan	5. 10	Charlton	Lambeth	6.10.64
Shail, Mark	6. 1	Yeovil	Sandviken, Swe.	15.10.66
Midfield				
Brennan, James	5. 9	Sora Lazio, Can.	Toronto, Can.	8.05.77
Edwards, Rob	6. 0	Carlisle	Kendal	1.01.73
Goodridge, Gregory	5. 6	Q.P.R.	Barbados	10.07.71
Hewlett, Matthew	6. 1	–	Bristol	25.02.76
Kuhl, Martin	5. 11	Derby	Frimley	10.01.65
Loydon, Gareth	5. 10	–	Hereford	23.03.78
Owers, Gary	6. 0	Sunderland	Newcastle	3.10.68
Paterson, Scott	5. 11	Liverpool	Aberdeen	13.05.72
Plummer, Dwayne	5. 10	–	Bristol	12.05.78
Forwards				
Agostini, Paul	5. 10	Young Boys of Berne, Swi.	Adelaide, Aust.	9.06.75
Barclay, Dominic	5. 9	–	Bristol	5.09.76
Barnard, Darren	5. 10	Chelsea	Rintein, Ger.	30.11.71
Bent, Junior	5. 5	Huddersfield	Huddersfield	1.03.70
Goater, Shaun	6. 0	Rotherham	Hamilton, Berm.	25.02.70
Nugent, Kevin	6. 1	Plymouth	Edmonton	10.04.69
Partridge, Scott	5. 9	Bradford City	Leicester	13.10.74
Perry, Richard	6. 0	–	Darlington	24.08.78
Seal, David	5. 11	Eendracht Aalst, Aust.	Sydney, Aust.	26.1.72
Tinnion, Brian	5. 11	Bradford City	Stanley	23.02.68

BRISTOL ROVERS

Name	Height ft. in.	Previous Club	Birthplace	Birthdate
Goalkeepers				
Collett, Andy	6. 0	Middlesbrough	Stockton	28.10.73
Higgs, Shane	6. 2	–	Oxford	13.05.77
Defenders				
Bowey, Steven	5. 8	Army	Durham	10.07.74
Clark, Billy	6. 0	Bournemouth	Christchurch	19.05.67

Harte, Stuart	5. 9	–	Basingstoke	12.12.77
Pritchard, David	5. 7	Telford United	Wolverhampton	27.05.72
Tillson, Andy	6. 2	Q.P.R.	Huntingdon	30.06.66
White, Tom	5. 11	–	Bristol	26.01.76
Midfield				
Browning, Marcus	5. 11	–	Bristol	22.04.71
Gurney, Andy	5. 7	–	Bristol	25.01.74
Hayfield, Matthew	5. 10	–	Bristol	8.08.75
Skinner, Justin	6. 0	Fulham	Chiswick	30.01.69
Holloway, Ian	5. 8	Q.P.R.	Kingswood	12.03.63
Forwards				
Archer, Lee	5. 6	–	Bristol	6.11.72
Beadle, Peter	6. 2	Watford	London	13.05.72
French, John	5. 10	–	Bristol	25.09.76
Miller, Paul	6. 0	Wimbledon	Bisley	31.01.68

BURNLEY

Name	Height ft. in.	Previous Club	Birthplace	Birthdate
Goalkeepers				
Beresford, Marlon	6. 1	Sheff. Wed.	Lincoln	2.09.69
Russell, Wayne	6. 2	Ebbw Vale	Cardiff	29.11.67
Defenders				
Brass, Chris	5. 9	–	Easington	24.07.75
Dowell, Wayne	5. 10	–	County Durham	28.12.73
Helliwell, Ian	6. 4	Stockport	Rotherham	7.11.62
Hoyland, Jamie	6. 0	Sheff. Utd.	Sheffield	23.01.66
Parkinson, Gary	5. 11	Bolton	Thornaby	10.01.68
Swan, Peter	6. 3	Plymouth	Leeds	28.09.66
Vinnicombe, Chris	5. 8	Rangers	Exeter	20.10.70
West, Gareth	6. 2	–	Oldham	1.08.78
Winstanley, Mark	6. 1	Bolton	St. Helens	22.01.68
Midfield				
Adams, Derek	5. 10	Aberdeen	Glasgow	25.06.75
Borland, John	5. 8	–	Lancaster	28.01.77
Harrison, Gerry	5. 9	Huddersfield	Lambeth	15.04.72
Joyce, Warren	5. 9	Plymouth	Oldham	20.01.65
Thompson, Steve	5. 11	Leicester City	Oldham	2.11.64
Webster, James	5. 9	–	Burnley	1.08.78
Weller, Paul	5. 8	–	Brighton	6.03.75
Forwards				
Cooke, Andy	5. 11	Newtown	Stoke	20.01.74
Duerden, Ian	5. 11	–	Burnley	27.03.78
Eastwood, Phil	5. 10	–	Blackburn	6.04.78
Eyres, David	5. 10	Blackpool	Liverpool	26.02.64
Nogan, Kurt	5. 11	Brighton	Cardiff	9.09.70
Robinson, Liam	5. 8	Bristol City	Bradford	20.12.65
Smith, Paul	6. 1	–	Easington	22.01.76

BURY

Name	Height ft. in.	Previous Club	Birthplace	Birthdate
Goalkeepers				
Bracey, Lee	6. 0	Halifax Town	London	11.09.68
Kelly, Gary	5. 10	Newcastle	Fulwood	3.08.66
Defenders				
Bimson, Stuart	5. 11	Macclesfield Town	Liverpool	29.09.69
Jackson, Michael	6. 0	Crewe	Liverpool	4.12.73

Lucketti, Chris	6. 0	Halifax Town	Manchester	28.09.71
Reid, Nicky	5. 9	Woking	Manchester	30.10.60
West, Dean	5. 8	Lincoln City	Wakefield	5.12.72
Woodward, Andrew	6. 0	Crewe	Stockport	23.09.73
Midfield				
Brabin, Gary	5. 11	Doncaster	Liverpool	9.12.70
Davis, Nicky	5. 11	Altrincham	Manchester	15.03.70
Hughes, Ian	5. 11	–	Bangor	2.08.74
Johnrose, Lennie	5. 10	Hartlepool	Preston	29.11.69
Matthews, Rob	5. 11	York	Slough	14.10.70
Reid, Shaun	5. 8	Rochdale	Huyton	13.10.65
Rigby, Tony	5. 10	Barrow	Ormskirk	10.08.72
Steele, Winnie	5. 8	–	Basildon	28.02.77
Forwards				
Carter, Mark	5. 10	Barnet	Liverpool	17.12.60
Johnson, David	5. 6	Man. Utd.	Kingston, Jam.	15.08.76
Pugh, David	6. 2	Chester	Liverpool	19.09.64
Shuttleworth, Barry	5. 8	–	Accrington	9.07.77
Stant, Phil	6. 0	Cardiff	Bolton	13.10.62
Thomson, Peter	6. 3	–	Crumpsall	30.06.77

CHESTERFIELD

Name	Height ft. in.	Previous Club	Birthplace	Birthdate
Goalkeepers				
Beasley, Andrew	6. 1	Doncaster	Sedgley	5.02.64
Mercer, Billy	6. 2	Sheff. Utd.	Liverpool	22.05.69
Defenders				
Carr, Darren	6. 3	Crewe	Bristol	4.09.68
Dyche, Sean	6. 0	Nott'm. Forest	Kettering	28.06.71
Jules, Mark	5. 9	Scarborough	Bradford	5.09.71
Law, Nicky	6. 0	Rotherham	Greenwich	8.09.61
Perkins, Chris	5. 11	Mansfield	Nottingham	9.01.74
Rogers, Lee	5. 11	Doncaster	Doncaster	21.10.66
Williams, Mark	6. 0	Shrewsbury	Cheshire	28.09.70
Midfield				
Curtis, Tom	5. 8	Derby	Exeter	1.03.73
Hewitt, Jamie	5. 10	Doncaster	Chesterfield	17.05.68
Robinson, Philip	5. 9	Huddersfield	Stafford	6.01.67
Forwards				
Davies, Kevin	6. 0	–	Sheffield	26.03.77
Holland, Paul	5. 10	Sheff. Utd.	Lincoln	8.07.73
Howard, Jonathan	5. 10	Rotherham	Sheffield	7.10.71
Lormor, Tony	6. 0	Peterborough	Ashington	29.10.70
Lund, Gary	6. 1	Notts County	Grimsby	13.09.64
Morris, Andrew	6. 4	Rotherham	Sheffield	17.11.67

CREWE ALEXANDRA

Name	Height ft. in.	Previous Club	Birthplace	Birthdate
Goalkeepers				
Gayle, Mark	6. 2	Walsall	Bromsgrove	21.10.69
Defenders				
Collins, Wayne	5. 11	Winsford United	Manchester	4.03.69
Lightfoot, Chris	6. 0	Wigan	Warrington	1.04.70
Macauley, Steve	6. 0	Fleetwood Town	Fleetwood	4.03.69
Pore, Stephen	5. 11	–	Mowlop	–
Smith, Shaun	5. 10	Halifax Town	Leeds	9.04.71

Turpin, Simon	6. 3	–	Blackburn	11.08.75
Unsworth, Lee	6. 0	Ashton United	Eccles	25.02.73
Westwood, Ashley	6. 0	Man. Utd.	Bridgnorth	31.08.76
Midfield				
Murphy, Danny	5. 9	–	Chester	18.03.77
Savage, Rob	5. 10	Man. Utd.	Wrexham	18.10.74
Tierney, Francis	5. 10	–	Liverpool	10.09.75
Whalley, Gareth	5. 9	–	Manchester	19.12.73
Forwards				
Adebola, Dele	6. 3	–	Lagos	23.06.75
Garvey, Steve	5. 9	–	Manchester	22.11.73
Little, Colin	5. 8	Hyde United	Wythemshawe	–
Rivers, Mark	5. 11	–	Crewe	26.11.75

GILLINGHAM

Name	Height ft. in.	Previous Club	Birthplace	Birthdate
Goalkeepers				
Stannard, Jim	6. 2	Fulham	London	6.10.62
Defenders				
Butler, Tony	6. 2	–	Stockport	28.09.72
Green, Richard	6. 1	Swindon	Wolverhampton	22.11.67
Harris, Mark	6. 3	Swansea	Reading	15.02.63
Naylor, Dominic	5. 8	Plymouth	Watford	12.08.70
Thomas, Glen	6. 0	Barnet	Hackney	6.10.67
Watson, Paul	5. 9	–	Hastings	4.01.75
Midfield				
Carpenter, Richard	5. 11	–	Sheppey	30.09.72
O'Connor, Mark	5. 9	Bournemouth	Essex	10.03.63
Ratcliffe, Simon	6. 0	Brentford	Davyhulme	8.02.67
Rattray, Kevin	5. 11	–	London	6.10.68
Smith, Neil	5. 9	Tottenham	Lambeth	30.09.71
Forwards				
Bailey, Dennis	5. 10	Q.P.R.	Lambeth	30.11.65
Butler, Steve	6. 1	Cambridge Utd.	Birmingham	27.01.62
Fortune-West, Leo	6. 3	Stevenage Borough	Stratford	9.04.71
Puttnam, Dave	5. 11	Lincoln City	Leicester	3.09.67

LUTON TOWN

Name	Height ft. in.	Previous Club	Birthplace	Birthdate
Goalkeepers				
Abbey, Nathan	6. 1	–	London	11.07.78
Davis, Kelvin	6. 1	–	Bedford	29.06.76
Feuer, Ian	6. 7	West Ham	Las Vegas, U.S.A.	20.05.71
Defenders				
Chenery, Ben	6. 0	–	Ipswich	28.01.77
Davis, Steve	6. 2	Burnley	Hexham	30.10.68
Harvey, Richard	5. 10	–	Letchworth	17.04.69
James, Julian	5. 10	–	Tring	22.03.70
Johnson, Marvin	6. 0	–	Wembley	29.10.68
Linton, Des	6. 1	Leicester City	Birmingham	5.09.71
Patterson, Darren	6. 2	Crystal Palace	Belfast	15.10.69
Peake, Trevor	6. 0	Coventry	Nuneaton	10.02.57
Simpson, Gary	6. 2	–	Ashford, Kent	14.02.76
Skelton, Aaron	5. 10	–	Welwyn	22.11.74
Thomas, Mitchell	6. 2	West Ham	Luton	2.10.64
Upson, Matthew	6. 1	–	Eye	18.04.79

Willmott, Chris	6. 1	–	Bedford	30.09.77
Midfield				
Alexander, Graham	5. 10	Scunthorpe	Coventry	10.10.71
Evers, Sean	5. 8	–	Hitchin	10.10.77
Hughes, Ceri	5. 10	–	Rhonda	26.02.71
Kean, Robert	5. 7	–	Luton	3.06.78
McLaren, Paul	6. 0	–	High Wycombe	17.11.76
Oakes, Scott	5. 11	Leicester City	Leicester	5.08.72
Oldfield, David	6. 0	Leicester City	Perth, Aust.	30.05.68
Waddock, Gary	5. 10	Bristol Rovers	Kingsbury	17.03.62
Forwards				
Douglas, Stuart	5. 10	–	London	9.04.78
Grant, Kim	5. 10	Charlton	Ghana	25.09.72
Guentchev, Bontcho	5. 10	Ipswich	Bulgaria	7.07.64
Marshall, Dwight	5. 7	Plymouth	Jamaica	3.10.65
Riseth, Vidar	6. 0	Kongsvinger, Nor.	Levanger, Nor.	21.04.62
Taylor, John	6. 3	Bradford City	Norwich	24.10.64
Thorpe, Tony	5. 9	Leicester City	Leicester	10.04.74
Woodsford, Jamie	5. 9	–	Ipswich	9.11.76

MILLWALL

Name	Height ft. in.	Previous Club	Birthplace	Birthdate
Goalkeepers				
Carter, Tim	6. 2	Oxford Utd.	Bristol	5.10.67
Keller, Kasey	6. 1	Portland Univ., U.S.A.	Washington, U.S.A.	27.11.69
Nurse, David	6. 4	Man. City	Kings Lynn	12.10.76
Defenders				
Connor, James	6. 0	–	Twickenham	22.08.74
Lavin, Gerard	5. 10	Watford	Corby	5.02.74
Rogan, Anton	5. 11	Oxford Utd.	Belfast	25.03.66
Sinclair, David	5. 11	Raith	Dunfermline	6.10.69
Stevens, Keith	6. 0	–	Merton	21.06.64
Van Blerk, Jason	6. 1	Go Ahead Eagles, Hol.	Sydney, Aust.	16.03.68
Webber, Damian	6. 4	Bognor Regis	Rustington	8.10.68
Witter, Tony	6. 1	Q.P.R.	London	12.08.65
Midfield				
Bowry, Bobby	5. 8	Crystal Palace	Croydon	19.05.71
Dair, Jason	5. 11	Raith	Dunfermline	15.06.74
Dolby, Tony	5. 11	–	Greenwich	16.04.74
Doyle, Maurice	5. 8	Q.P.R.	Ellesmere Port	17.10.69
Forbes, Steven	6. 2	Sittingbourne	London	24.12.75
Hartley, Paul	5. 9	Hamilton	Baillieston	19.10.76
Neill, Lucas	6. 1	–	Sydney, Aust.	9.03.78
Newman, Ricky	5. 10	Crystal Palace	Guildford	5.08.70
Savage, Dave	6. 2	Longford Town	Dublin	30.07.73
Forwards				
Crawford, Steve	5. 10	Raith	Dunfermline	9.01.74
Fuchs, Uwe	6. 1	Kaiserslautern, Ger.	Kaiserslautern, Ger.	23.07.66
Malkin, Chris	6. 3	Tranmere	Bebington	4.06.67

NOTTS COUNTY

Name	Height ft. in.	Previous Club	Birthplace	Birthdate
Goalkeepers				
Pollitt, Michael	6. 4	Darlington	Bolton	29.02.72
Ward, Darren	5. 11	Mansfield	Worksop	11.05.74

Defenders				
Baraclough, Ian	6. 1	Mansfield	Leicester	4.12.70
Derry, Shaun	5. 11	–	Nottingham	6.12.77
Forsyth, Michael	5. 11	Derby	Liverpool	20.03.66
Gallagher, Tommy	5. 10	–	Nottingham	25.08.74
Hogg, Graeme	6. 1	Hearts	Aberdeen	17.06.64
Hoyle, Colin	5. 11	Bradford City	Derby	15.01.72
Murphy, Shaun	6. 0	Perth Italia, Aust.	Sydney, Aust.	5.11.70
Redmile, Matthew	6. 3	–	Nottingham	12.11.76
Strodder, Gary	6. 1	W.B.A.	Mirfield	1.04.65
Walker, Richard	6. 0	–	Derby	9.11.71
Wilder, Chris	5. 11	Rotherham	Wortley	23.09.67
Midfield				
Butler, Peter	5. 9	West Ham	Halifax	27.08.66
Galloway, Mick	5. 11	–	Nottingham	13.10.74
Hunt, James	5. 11	–	Nottingham	17.12.76
Richardson, Ian	6. 0	Birmingham	Barking	22.10.70
Ridgway, Ian	5. 8	–	Nottingham	28.12.75
Rogers, Paul	6. 0	Sheff. Utd.	Portsmouth	21.03.65
Simpson, Michael	5. 9	–	Nottingham	28.02.74
Forwards				
Agana, Tony	6. 0	Sheff. Utd.	London	2.10.63
Arkins, Vincent	6. 1	Shelbourne	Dublin	18.09.70
Battersby, Tony	6. 0	Sheff. Utd.	Doncaster	30.08.75
Jones, Gary	6. 0	Southend	Huddersfield	6.04.69
Martindale, Gary	5. 11	Peterborough	Liverpool	24.06.71

PETERBOROUGH UNITED

Name	Height ft. in.	Previous Club	Birthplace	Birthdate
Goalkeepers				
Sheffield, Jon	6. 0	Cambridge Utd.	Bedworth	1.02.69
Tyler, Mark	5. 11	–	Norwich	2.04.77
Defenders				
Basham, Michael	6. 2	Swansea	Barking	27.09.73
Boothroyd, Adrian	5. 10	Mansfield	Bradford	8.02.71
Clark, Simon	6. 0	–	Boston	12.03.67
Drury, Adam	5. 10	–	Cottenham	29.08.78
Foran, Mark	6. 4	Sheff. Utd.	Aldershot	30.10.73
Heald, Gregory	6. 2	Enfield	London	26.09.71
Meredith, Thomas	5. 10	–	London	27.10.77
Spearing, Tony	5. 7	Plymouth	Romford	7.10.64
Welsh, Steve	6. 1	Partick	Glasgow	19.04.68
Midfield				
Ebdon, Marcus	5. 10	Everton	Pontypool	17.10.70
Houghton, Scott	5. 5	Walsall	Hitchin	22.10.71
Le Bihan, Neil	6. 0	Tottenham	Croydon	14.03.76
Payne, Derek	5. 7	Watford	Watford	26.04.67
Rowe, Zeke	5. 6	Chelsea	Stoke Newington	30.10.73
Sedgemore, Ben	6. 0	Birmingham	Wolverhampton	5.08.75
Willis, Roger	6. 1	Southend	Sheffield	17.06.67
Forwards				
Carter, Danny	5. 9	Leyton Orient	Hackney	29.06.69
Farrell, Sean	6. 1	Fulham	Watford	28.02.69
Grazioli, Giuliano	5. 11	Wembley	London	23.03.75
Griffiths, Carl	6. 0	Portsmouth	Oswestry	15.07.71
Inman, Niall	5. 9	–	Wakefield	6.02.78
McGleish, Scott	5. 9	Charlton	St. Pancras	10.02.74
Morrison, David	5. 11	Chelmsford City	Waltham Forest	30.11.74

O'Connor, Martyn	5. 8	Walsall	Walsall	10.12.67
Power, Lee	5. 10	Bradford City	London	30.06.72

PLYMOUTH ARGYLE

Name	Height ft. in.	Previous Club	Birthplace	Birthdate
Goalkeepers				
Blackwell, Kevin	5. 11	Huddersfield	Luton	21.12.58
Dungey, James	5. 10	–	Plymouth	7.02.78
Defenders				
Curran, Chris	5. 11	Torquay	Birmingham	17.09.71
Heathcote, Mick	6. 2	Cambridge Utd.	Durham	10.09.65
Logan, Richard	6. 0	Huddersfield	Barnsley	24.05.69
Patterson, Mark	5. 10	Derby	Leeds	13.09.68
Williams, Paul	5. 6	Huddersfield	Leicester	11.09.69
Wotton, Paul	5. 10	–	Plymouth	17.08.77
Midfield				
Barlow, Martin	5. 7	–	Barnstaple	25.06.71
Billy, Chris	6. 0	Huddersfield	Huddersfield	2.01.73
Leadbitter, Chris	5. 9	Bournemouth	Middlesbrough	17.10.67
Mauge, Ronnie	5. 10	Bury	Islington	10.03.69
Saunders, Mark	5. 9	Tiverton	–	–
Forwards				
Corazzin, Carlo	5. 9	Cambridge Utd.	Canada	25.12.71
Evans, Michael	6. 0	–	Plymouth	1.01.73
Littlejohn, Adrian	5. 9	Sheff. Utd.	Wolverhampton	26.09.70

PRESTON NORTH END

Name	Height ft. in.	Previous Club	Birthplace	Birthdate
Goalkeepers				
Lucas, David	6. 0	–	Preston	23.11.77
Moilanen, Teuvo	6. 2	FF Jaro, Fin.	Oulu, Fin.	12.12.73
Defenders				
Barrick, Dean	5. 7	Cambridge Utd.	Hemsworth	30.09.69
Gage, Kevin	5. 10	Sheff. Utd.	Chiswick	21.04.64
Kidd, Ryan	6. 0	Port Vale	Radcliffe	6.10.71
Moyes, David	6. 1	Hamilton	Glasgow	25.04.63
Sharp, Ray	5. 11	Dunfermline	Stirling	16.11.69
Sparrow, Paul	6. 0	Crystal Palace	London	24.03.75
Squires, Jamie	6. 1	–	Preston	15.11.75
Wilcox, Russell	6. 0	Doncaster	Hemsworth	25.03.64
Midfield				
Atkinson, Graeme	5. 8	Hull	Hull	11.11.71
Brown, Michael	5. 9	Shrewsbury	Birmingham	8.02.68
Bryson, Ian	5. 11	Barnsley	Kilmarnock	26.11.62
Cartwright, Lee	5. 8	–	Rossendale	19.09.72
Davey, Simon	5. 10	Carlisle	Swansea	1.10.70
Kilbane, Kevin	5. 7	–	Preston	21.10.74
McDonald, Neil	5. 11	Bolton	Wallsend	2.11.65
McKenna, Paul	5. 10	–	Chorley	20.10.77
Forwards				
Bennett, Gary	5. 11	Tranmere	Liverpool	20.09.63
Grant, Tony	5. 10	Leeds	Louth	20.08.76
Saville, Andy	6. 0	Birmingham	Hull	12.12.64
Smart, Allan	5. 10	Caledonian Th.	Perth	8.07.74
Wilkinson, Steve	6. 0	Mansfield	Lincoln	1.09.68

ROTHERHAM UNITED

Name	Height ft. in.	Previous Club	Birthplace	Birthdate
Goalkeepers				
Farrelly, Steve	6. 5	Macclesfield Town	Liverpool	27.03.65
Defenders				
Blades, Paul	6. 0	Wolves	Peterborough	5.01.65
Breckin, Ian	5. 11	–	Rotherham	24.02.75
Hurst, Paul	5. 4	–	Sheffield	25.09.74
Monington, Mark	6. 1	Burnley	Mansfield	21.10.70
Richardson, Neil	6. 0	–	Sunderland	3.03.68
Sandeman, Bradley	5. 11	Port Vale	Northampton	24.02.70
Smith, Scott	5. 8	–	Christchurch, N.Z.	6.03.75
Midfield				
Bowyer, Gary	6. 1	Hereford	Manchester	22.06.71
Garner, Darren	5. 9	Dorchester Town	Plymouth	10.12.71
Goodwin, Shaun	5. 8	–	Rotherham	14.06.69
Hayward, Andy	6. 0	Frickley Athletic	Barnsley	21.06.70
McGlashan, John	6. 2	Peterborough	Dundee	3.06.67
Roscoe, Andy	5. 10	Bolton	Liverpool	4.06.73
Forwards				
Peel, Nathan	6. 1	Burnley	Blackburn	17.05.72
Slawson, Steve	6. 0	Notts County	Nottingham	13.11.72

SHREWSBURY TOWN

Name	Height ft. in.	Previous Club	Birthplace	Birthdate
Goalkeepers				
Edwards, Paul	6. 2	Crewe	Liverpool	22.02.65
Defenders				
Lynch, Thomas	6. 0	Sunderland	Limerick	10.10.64
Scott, Richard	5. 9	Birmingham	Dudley	29.09.74
Seabury, Kevin	5. 9	–	Shrewsbury	24.11.73
Simkin, Darren	6. 0	Wolves	Walsall	24.03.70
Walton, David	6. 2	Sheff. Utd.	Bedlingham	10.04.73
Whiston, Peter	6. 0	Southampton	Widnes	4.01.68
Midfield				
Cope, James	5. 11	–	Birmingham	4.10.77
Dempsey, Mark	5. 8	Leyton Orient	Dublin	10.12.72
Evans, Paul	5. 8	–	Oswestry	1.09.74
Reed, Ian	5. 8	–	Lichfield	4.09.75
Rowbotham, Darren	5. 10	Crewe	Cardiff	22.10.66
Taylor, Mark	5. 9	Sheff. Wed.	Walsall	22.02.66
Forwards				
Anthrobus, Steven	6. 1	Wimbledon	Lewisham	10.11.68
Berkley, Austin	5. 9	Swindon	Gravesend	28.01.73
Currie, Darren	5. 9	West Ham	Hampstead	29.11.74
Spink, Dean	5. 11	Aston Villa	Birmingham	22.01.67
Stevens, Ian	5. 10	Bury	Malta	21.10.66
Ward, Nicholas	5. 10	–	Wrexham	30.11.77
Wray, Shaun	6. 1	–	Dudley	14.03.78

STOCKPORT COUNTY

Name	Height ft. in.	Previous Club	Birthplace	Birthdate
Goalkeepers				
Edwards, Neil	5. 8	Leeds	Aberdare	5.12.70

Jones, Paul	6. 3	Wolves	Chirk	18.04.67
Defenders				
Bound, Matthew	6. 2	Southampton	Bradford-on-Avon	9.11.72
Connelly, Sean	5. 10	–	Sheffield	26.06.70
Dinning, Tony	5. 11	Newcastle	Wallsend	12.04.75
Flynn, Mike	6. 0	Preston	Oldham	23.02.69
Gannon, Jim	6. 2	Sheff. Utd.	London	7.09.68
Searle, Damon	5. 11	Cardiff	Cardiff	26.10.71
Todd, Lee	5. 5	Hartlepool	Hartlepool	7.03.72
Midfield				
Beaumont, Chris	5. 11	Rochdale	Sheffield	5.12.65
Bennett, Tom	5. 11	Wolves	Falkirk	12.12.69
Durkan, Kieron	5. 10	Wrexham	Chester	1.12.73
Eckhardt, Jeff	6. 0	Fulham	Sheffield	7.10.65
Jeffers, John	5. 10	Port Vale	Liverpool	5.10.68
Lloyd-Williams, Marc	5. 11	Bangor	Bangor	8.02.73
Marsden, Chris	5. 11	Notts County	Sheffield	3.01.69
Ware, Paul	5. 9	Stoke	Congleton	7.11.70
Forwards				
Armstrong, Alun	6. 0	Newcastle	Gateshead	22.02.75
Landon, Richard	6. 3	Plymouth	Barnsley	22.03.70
Mike, Adie	6. 0	Man. City	Manchester	16.11.73
Mutch, Andy	5. 10	Swindon	Liverpool	28.12.63

WALSALL

Name	Height ft. in.	Previous Club	Birthplace	Birthdate
Goalkeepers				
Walker, Jim	5. 11	Notts County	Sutton-in-Ashfield	9.07.73
Wood, Trevor	6. 0	Port Vale	Jersey	3.11.68
Defenders				
Daniel, Ray	5. 10	Portsmouth	Luton	10.12.64
Evans, Wayne	5. 10	Welshpool	Welshpool	25.08.71
Mountfield, Derek	6. 1	Carlisle	Liverpool	2.11.62
Mountford, Paul	5. 9	–	Stourbridge	26.04.78
Ntamark, Charlie	5. 8	–	Paddington	22.07.64
Rogers, Darren	5. 9	Wycombe	Birmingham	9.04.70
Roper, Ian	6. 3	–	Nuneaton	20.06.77
Rowland, Stephen	5. 10	–	Birmingham	11.02.78
Ryder, Stuart	6. 1	–	Sutton Coldfield	6.11.73
Viveash, Adrian	6. 1	Swindon	Swindon	30.09.69
Midfield				
Bradley, Darren	5. 7	W.B.A.	Birmingham	24.11.65
Keates, Dean	5. 4	–	Walsall	30.06.78
Keister, John	5. 8	–	Manchester	11.11.70
Marsh, Chris	6. 0	–	Dudley	14.01.70
Thomas, Wayne	–	–	–	–
Forwards				
Butler, Martin	5. 7	–	Wordsley	15.09.74
Lightbourne, Kyle	6. 2	Scarborough	Bermuda	29.09.68
Platt, Clive	6. 3	–	London	27.10.77
Wilson, Kevin	5. 7	Notts County	Banbury	18.04.61

WATFORD

Name	Height ft. in.	Previous Club	Birthplace	Birthdate
Goalkeepers				
Chamberlain, Alec	6. 2	Sunderland	Ely	20.06.64

Miller, Kevin	6. 1	Birmingham	Falmouth	15.03.69
Defenders				
Bazeley, Darren	5. 10	–	Northampton	5.10.72
Belgrave, Kevin	5. 10	–	Bedford	20.04.78
Foster, Colin	6. 4	West Ham	Chislehurst	16.07.64
Holdsworth, David	6. 1	–	Walthamstow	8.11.68
Ludden, Dominic	5. 7	Leyton Orient	Basildon	30.03.74
Millen, Keith	6. 2	Brentford	Croydon	26.09.66
Page, Robert	6. 0	–	Llwynypia	3.09.74
Rooney, Mark	6. 0	–	London	19.05.78
Midfield				
Easton, Clint	5. 10	–	Barking	1.10.77
Hessenthaler, Andy	5. 7	Redbridge Forest	Gravesend	17.08.65
Johnson, Richard	5. 10	–	Kurri Kurri, Aust.	27.04.74
Palmer, Steve	6. 1	Ipswich	Brighton	31.03.68
Porter, Gary	5. 6	–	Sunderland	6.03.66
Ramage, Craig	5. 9	Derby	Derby	30.03.70
Talboys, Steve	5. 10	Wimbledon	Bristol	18.09.66
Forwards				
Andrews, Wayne	5. 10	–	London	25.11.77
Connolly, David	5. 8	–	Willesden	6.06.77
Dixon, Kerry	6. 0	Millwall	Luton	24.07.61
Lowndes, Nathan	5. 11	Leeds	Salford	2.06.77
Mooney, Tommy	5. 11	Southend	Middlesbrough	11.08.71
Penrice, Gary	5. 8	Q.P.R.	Bristol	23.03.64
Phillips, Kevin	5. 7	Baldock Town	Hitchin	25.07.73
Simpson, Colin	6. 1	–	Oxford	30.04.76
White, Devon	6. 3	Notts County	Nottingham	2.03.64

WREXHAM

Name	Height ft. in.	Previous Club	Birthplace	Birthdate
Goalkeepers				
Cartwright, Mark	6. 2	York	Chester	13.01.73
Marriott, Andy	6. 1	Nott'm. Forest	Sutton-in-Ashfield	11.10.70
Defenders				
Carey, Brian	6. 3	Leicester City	Cork	31.05.68
Brace, Deryn	5. 7	Norwich	Haverfordwest	15.03.75
Hardy, Phil	5. 7	–	Chester	9.04.73
Humes, Tony	6. 0	Ipswich	Blyth	19.03.66
Jones, Barry	5. 11	Liverpool	Prescot	20.06.70
Jones, Paul	5. 11	–	Birkenhead	2.10.76
McGregor, Mark	5. 10	–	Chester	16.02.77
David Ridler	5. 8	–	Liverpool	12.03.76
Midfield				
Brammer, David	5. 9	–	Bromborough	28.02.75
Cross, Jonathan	5. 10	–	Wallasey	2.03.75
Chalk, Martyn	5. 6	Stockport	Louth	30.08.69
Coady, Lewis	6. 0	–	Lancashire	20.09.76
Futcher, Stephen	5. 11	–	Chester	24.10.76
Hughes, Bryan	5. 11	–	Liverpool	19.06.76
Owen, Gareth	5. 7	–	Chester	21.10.71
Phillips, Wayne	5. 10	–	Bangor	15.12.70
Skinner, Craig	5. 9	Plymouth	Bury	21.10.70
Ward, Peter	5. 10	Stockport	County Durham	15.10.64
Williams, Scott	6. 0	–	Bangor	7.08.74
Forwards				
Connolly, Karl	5. 9	–	Prescot	9.02.70
Morris, Steve	5. 10	Liverpool	Liverpool	13.05.76

Russell, Kevin	5. 8	Notts County	Portsmouth	6.12.66
Watkin, Steve	5. 10	–	Wrexham	16.06.71

WYCOMBE WANDERERS

Name	Height ft. in.	Previous Club	Birthplace	Birthdate
Goalkeepers				
Cheesewright, John	5. 11	Hong Kong	Harold Wood	12.01.73
Defenders				
Bell, Micky	5. 10	Northampton	Newcastle	15.11.71
Cousins, Jason	5. 10	Brentford	Hayes	4.10.70
Crossley, Matthew	6. 1	Basingstoke	Basingstoke	18.03.68
Evans, Terry	6. 4	Brentford	Hammersmith	12.04.65
McCarthy, Paul	6. 0	Brighton	Cork	4.08.71
Rowbotham, Jason	5. 8	Raith	Cardiff	3.01.69
Skiverton, Terry	5. 11	Chelsea	Mile End	29.06.75
Midfield				
Brown, Steve	6. 0	Northampton	Northampton	6.07.66
Carroll, David	6. 0	Ruislip Manor	Paisley	20.09.66
McGorry, Brian	5. 10	Peterborough	Liverpool	16.04.70
Matthew, Lawrence	5. 10	Grays Athletic	Northampton	19.06.74
Patterson, Gary	6. 0	Shrewsbury	Newcastle	27.11.72
Ryan, Keith	5. 11	Berkhamsted Town	Northampton	25.06.70
Forwards				
Clark, Anthony	5. 7	–	Camberwell	7.04.77
De Souza, Miguel	5. 11	Birmingham	Newham	11.02.70
Farrell, David	5. 10	Aston Villa	Marston Green	11.11.71
McGavin, Steve	5. 9	Birmingham	North Walsham	24.01.69
Williams, John	6. 0	Coventry	Birmingham	11.05.68

YORK CITY

Name	Height ft. in.	Previous Club	Birthplace	Birthdate
Goalkeepers				
Kiely, Dean	6. 0	Coventry	Salford	10.10.70
Warrington, Andy	6. 3	–	Sheffield	10.06.76
Defenders				
Atkin, Paul	6. 0	Bury	Nottingham	3.09.69
Atkinson, Paddy	5. 9	Newcastle	Singapore	22.05.70
Barras, Tony	6. 0	Stockport	Stockton-on-Tees	29.03.71
Hall, Wayne	5. 9	Hatfield Main	Rotherham	25.10.68
McMillan, Andy	5. 10	–	South Africa	22.06.68
Sharples, John	6. 0	Ayr	Bury	26.01.73
Tutill, Steve	5. 11	–	Derwent	1.10.69
Midfield				
Bushell, Steve	5. 9	–	Manchester	28.12.72
Jordan, Scott	5. 9	–	Newcastle	19.07.75
Murty, Graeme	5. 10	–	Middlesbrough	13.11.74
Osborne, Wayne	5. 10	–	Stockton-on-Tees	14.01.77
Pepper, Nigel	5. 10	Rotherham	Rotherham	25.04.68
Pouton, Alan	6. 0	Newcastle	Newcastle	1.02.77
Randall, Adrian	5. 10	Burnley	Amesbury	10.11.68
Williams, Darren	5. 8	–	Middlesbrough	28.04.77
Forwards				
Bull, Gary	5. 10	Birmingham	Tipton	12.06.66
Campbell, Neil	5. 10	–	Middlesbrough	26.01.77
Cresswell, Richard	5. 11	–	Bridlington	20.09.77
Himsworth, Gary	5. 7	Darlington	Appleton	19.12.69

Naylor, Glenn	5. 9	–	York	11.08.72
Reed, Martin	6. 1	–	Scarborough	10.01.78
Stephenson, Paul	5. 9	Brentford	Newcastle	2.01.68
Tolson, Neil	6. 1	Bradford City	Wordley	25.10.73

Third Division

BARNET

Name	Height ft. in.	Previous Club	Birthplace	Birthdate
Goalkeepers				
Pearce, Lee	6. 0	–	Hammersmith	22.11.77
Taylor, Maik	6. 5	Farnborough	Germany	4.09.71
Defenders				
Campbell, Jamie	6. 2	Luton	Birmingham	21.10.72
Gale, Shaun	6. 1	Portsmouth	Reading	8.10.69
Goodhind, Warren	5. 11	–	South Africa	16.08.77
Hamlet, Alan	6. 0	–	Walthamstow	13.09.77
Howarth, Lee	6. 2	Mansfield	Bolton	3.01.68
McDonald, David	5. 10	Peterborough	Dublin	2.01.71
Pardew, Alan	6. 1	Charlton	Wimbledon	18.07.61
Primus, Linvoy	6. 0	Charlton	Stratford	14.09.73
Thompson, Neil	5. 11	–	Clapton	13.04.78
Midfield				
Adams, Keiran	5. 11	–	St. Ives	20.10.77
Brady, Matt	5. 10	–	London	27.10.77
Codner, Robert	5. 11	Wycombe	Walthamstow	23.01.65
Gallagher, Kierran	5. 9	–	Barnet	23.12.76
Mills, Danny	5. 11	Charlton	Sidcup	13.02.75
Simpson, Phillip	5. 8	Stevenage Borough	London	18.10.69
Tomlinson, Michael	5. 8	Leyton Orient	Lambeth	15.09.72
Wilson, Paul	5. 9	Barking	Forest Gate	26.09.64
Forwards				
Devine, Shaun	6. 0	Omonia Nicosia, Cyp.	London	6.09.72
Dunwell, Richard	6. 1	Collier Row	London	17.06.71
Hodges, Lee	5. 11	Tottenham	Epping	4.09.73

BRIGHTON & HOVE ALBION

Name	Height ft. in.	Previous Club	Birthplace	Birthdate
Goalkeepers				
Ormerod, Mark	6. 0	–	Bournemouth	5.02.76
Rust, Nicky	6. 0	Arsenal	Cambridge	25.09.74
Defenders				
Allan, Derek	6. 0	Southampton	Irvine	24.12.74
Hobson, Gary	6. 1	Hull	Hull	12.11.72
McGarrigle, Kevin	5. 11	–	Newcastle-u-Tyne	9.04.77
Smith, Peter	6. 1	Alma Swanley	Stone	12.07.69
Tuck, Stuart	5. 11	–	Brighton	1.10.74
Virgo, James	5. 10	–	Brighton	21.12.76
Yorke-Johnson, Ross	6. 0	–	Brighton	2.01.76
Midfield				
Fox, Mark	5. 11	–	Basingstoke	17.11.75

Mundee, Denny	5. 10	Brentford	Swindon	10.10.68
Parris, George	5. 9	Birmingham	Barking	11.09.64
Storer, Stuart	5. 11	Exeter	Rugby	16.01.67
Thompson-Minton, Jeff	5. 6	Tottenham	Hackney	28.12.73
Forwards				
Andrews, Phillip	5. 11	–	Andover	14.09.76
Fox, Simon	5. 10	–	Basingstoke	28.08.77
McDonald, Paul	5. 6	Southampton	Motherwell	20.04.68
McDougald, Junior	5. 11	Tottenham	Texas, U.S.A.	12.01.75
Maskell, Craig	5. 10	Southampton	Aldershot	10.04.68

CAMBRIDGE UNITED

Name	Height ft. in.	Previous Club	Birthplace	Birthdate
Goalkeepers				
Barrett, Scott	5. 11	Gillingham	Derby	2.04.63
Davies, Martin	6. 2	Coventry	Swansea	28.06.74
Defenders				
Craddock, Jody	6. 0	Christchurch	Redditch	25.07.75
Granville, Daniel	5. 11	–	Islington	19.01.75
Howes, Shaun	5. 10	–	Norwich	7.11.77
Joseph, Marc	6. 0	–	Leicester	10.11.76
Palmer, Lee	5. 11	Gillingham	Gillingham	19.09.70
Thompson, David	6. 2	Blackpool	Ashington	20.11.68
Vowden, Colin	6. 0	Cambridge City	Newmarket	13.09.71
Midfield				
Beall, Billy	5. 7	–	Enfield	4.12.77
Hayes, Adi	6. 2	–	Norwich	22.05.78
Hyde, Micah	5. 9	–	Newham	10.11.74
Joseph, Matthew	5. 7	Arsenal	Bethnal Green	30.09.72
Pack, Lenny	5. 10	–	Salisbury	27.09.76
Raynor, Paul	5. 9	Preston	Nottingham	29.04.66
Wanless, Paul	6. 1	Lincoln City	Banbury	14.12.73
Forwards				
Barnwell-Edinboro, Jamie	5. 9	Coventry	Hull	26.12.75
Kyd, Michael	5. 8	–	Hackney	21.05.77
Richards, Tony	6. 2	Sudbury	Newham	17.09.73
Turner, Robbie	6. 3	Exeter	Ripon	18.09.66

CARDIFF CITY

Name	Height ft. in.	Previous Club	Birthplace	Birthdate
Goalkeepers				
Williams, Steven	6. 3	Coventry	Aberystwyth	16.10.74
Defenders				
Baddeley, Lee	6. 1	–	Cardiff	12.07.74
Fleming, Hayden	5. 6	–	London	14.03.78
Jarman, Lee	6. 2	–	Cardiff	16.12.77
Perry, Jason	5. 11	–	Newport	2.04.70
Rodgerson, Ian	5. 8	Sunderland	Hereford	9.04.66
Scott, Andrew	6. 0	Blackburn	Manchester	27.06.75
Young, Scott	6. 1	–	Tonypandy	14.01.76
Midfield				
Fowler, Jason	6. 1	Bristol City	Bristol	20.08.74
Harding, Paul	5. 9	Birmingham	Mitcham	6.03.64

Wigg, Nathan	5. 9	–	Newport	27.09.74
Forwards				
Adams, Darren	5. 7	Danson	Newham	12.01.74
Clark, Allan	5. 7	–	London	11.09.77
Dale, Carl	5. 8	Chester	Colwyn Bay	29.04.66
Flack, Steven	6. 2	Cambridge City	Cambridge	29.05.71
Gardner, James	5. 11	Scarborough	Dunfermline	29.09.67
Haworth, Simon	6. 2	–	Cardiff	30.03.77
Johnson, Glenn	5. 11	–	Sydney, Aust.	16.07.72
Philliskirk, Tony	6. 1	Burnley	Sunderland	10.02.65
Vick, Leigh	5. 10	–	Cardiff	8.01.78
White, Steve	5. 11	Hereford	Chipping Sodbury	2.01.59

CARLISLE UNITED

Name	Height ft. in.	Previous Club	Birthplace	Birthdate
Goalkeepers				
Caig, Anthony	6. 1	–	Whitehaven	11.04.74
Defenders				
Edmondson, Darren	6. 0	–	Coniston	4.11.71
Joyce, Joseph	5. 10	Scunthorpe	Consett	18.03.61
Robinson, Jamie	6. 0	Barnsley	Liverpool	22.02.72
Varty, William	6. 2	–	Workington	1.10.76
Walling, Dean	6. 0	Rochdale	Leeds	17.04.69
Midfield				
Aspinall, Warren	5. 8	Bournemouth	Wigan	13.09.67
Conway, Paul	6. 1	Oldham	London	17.04.70
Hayward, Steve	5. 10	Derby	Walsall	8.09.71
Hopper, Tony	5. 11	–	Carlisle	31.05.76
Prokas, Richard	5. 10	–	Penrith	22.01.76
Forwards				
Currie, David	5. 11	Barnsley	Stockton	27.11.62
Delap, Rory	6. 0	–	Birmingham	6.07.76
Jansen, Matthew	5. 10	–	Carlisle	20.10.77
McAlindon, Gareth	5. 10	Newcastle	Hexham	6.04.77
Reeves, David	6. 0	Notts County	Birkenhead	19.11.67
Thomas, Rod	5. 7	Watford	London	10.10.70
Thorpe, Jeff	5. 11	–	Whitehaven	17.11.72

CHESTER CITY

Name	Height ft. in.	Previous Club	Birthplace	Birthdate
Goalkeepers				
Stewart, Billy	5. 11	Northampton	Liverpool	1.01.65
Defenders				
Alsford, Julian	6. 2	Watford	Poole	24.12.72
Brown, Greg	5. 10	–	Manchester	31.07.78
Davidson, Ross	5. 8	Sheff. Utd.	Chertsey	13.11.73
Jackson, Peter	6. 0	Huddersfield	Bradford	6.04.61
Jenkins, Iain	5. 9	Everton	Prescot	24.11.72
Rogers, Dave	6. 1	Tranmere	Liverpool	25.08.75
Whelan, Spencer	6. 2	Liverpool	Liverpool	17.09.71
Woods, Matthew	6. 1	Everton	Gosport	9.09.76
Midfield				
Bishop, Eddie	5. 10	Tranmere	Liverpool	28.11.62
Fisher, Neil	5. 10	Bolton	St. Helens	7.11.70

Flitcroft, David	5. 11	Preston	Bolton	14.01.74
Noteman, Kevin	5. 10	Doncaster	Preston	15.10.69
Preece, Roger	5. 8	Wrexham	Much Wenlock	9.06.69
Priest, Chris	5. 10	Everton	Leigh	18.10.73
Richardson, Nick	6. 1	Bury	Halifax	11.04.67
Shelton, Gary	5. 7	Bristol City	Nottingham	21.03.58
Forwards				
Milner, Andy	6. 0	Rochdale	Kendal	10.02.67
Murphy, John	6. 1	–	Whiston	18.10.76
Regis, Cyrille	6. 0	Wycombe	French Guyana	9.02.58
Rimmer, Stuart	5. 7	Barnsley	Southport	12.10.64

COLCHESTER UNITED

Name	Height ft. in.	Previous Club	Birthplace	Birthdate
Goalkeepers				
Emberson, Carl	6. 1	Millwall	Epsom	13.07.73
Defenders				
Barnes, David	5. 10	Watford	London	16.11.61
Betts, Simon	5. 7	Scarborough	Middlesbrough	3.03.73
Cawley, Peter	6. 3	Barnet	London	15.09.65
Dunne, Joe	5. 10	Gillingham	Dublin	25.05.73
English, Tony	6. 1	Coventry	Luton	19.10.66
Gibbs, Paul	5. 9	Diss Town	Gorleston	26.10.72
Greene, David	6. 2	Luton	Luton	26.10.73
McCarthy, Tony	6. 1	Millwall	Dublin	9.11.69
Midfield				
Gregory, David	5. 11	Ipswich	Colcester	23.01.70
Locke, Adam	5. 10	Southend	Croydon	20.08.70
Whitton, Steve	6. 0	Ipswich	East Ham	4.12.60
Wilkins, Richard	6. 0	Hereford	Streatham	28.05.65
Forwards				
Adcock, Tony	5. 10	Luton	Bethnal Green	27.02.63
Fry, Chris	5. 8	Hereford	Cardiff	23.10.69
Lock, Tony	5. 8	–	Harlow	3.09.76
Reinelt, Rob	5. 11	Gillingham	Epping	11.03.74

DARLINGTON

Name	Height ft. in.	Previous Club	Birthplace	Birthdate
Goalkeepers				
Johnson, Frank	6. 2	–	South Shields	–
Newell, Paul	6. 1	Barnet	Greenwich	23.02.69
Defenders				
Bernard, Mark	6. 0	Rotherham	Sheffield	31.09.73
Crosby, Andy	6. 2	Wrexham	Rotherham	3.03.73
Gregan, Sean	6. 2	–	Middlesbrough	29.03.74
Shaw, Simon	5. 11	–	Middlesbrough	21.09.73
Midfield				
Gaughan, Steve	5. 11	Sunderland	Doncaster	14.04.70
Jones, Gary	5. 9	–	Fulham	22.05.76
Olsson, Paul	6. 0	Hartlepool	Hull	24.12.65
Twynham, Gary	6. 0	Man. Utd.	Manchester	8.02.76
Forwards				
Blake, Robert	5. 10	–	Middlesbrough	4.05.76
Painter, Robbie	5. 10	Burnley	Wigan	26.01.71
Roberts, Darren	6. 0	Chesterfield	Birmingham	12.10.69

DONCASTER ROVERS

Name	Height ft. in.	Previous Club	Birthplace	Birthdate
Goalkeepers				
Leach, Gavin	6. 1	Stockton	Middlesbrough	9.08.77
O'Connor, Gary	6. 3	Hearts	Edinburgh	7.04.77
Williams, Dean	6. 1	Brentford	Lichfield	5.01.72
Defenders				
Gore, Ian	5. 11	Blackpool	Liverpool	10.01.68
Marquis, Paul	6. 2	West Ham	Enfield	29.08.72
Moore, Darren	6. 2	Torquay	Birmingham	22.04.74
Murphy, Jamie	6. 1	Blackpool	Manchester	25.02.73
Parrish, Sean	5. 10	Telford United	Wrexham	14.03.72
Robertson, Paul	5. 8	Runcorn	Liverpool	5.02.72
Robinson, Earl	6. 1	–	Birmingham	8.10.78
Utley, Darren	6. 0	–	Barnsley	28.09.77
Midfield				
Clark, Ian	5. 11	Stockton	Stockton	23.10.74
Colcombe, Scott	5. 6	Torquay	West Bromwich	15.12.71
Doling, Stuart	5. 8	Portsmouth	Newport, I.O.W.	28.10.72
Hayrettin, Hakan	5. 9	Cambridge Utd.	London	4.02.70
Schofield, Jon	5. 11	Lincoln City	Barnsley	16.05.65
Smith, Mike	5. 11	Runcorn	Liverpool	28.09.73
Speight, Martyn	5. 9	–	Stockton	26.07.78
Walker, Steve	5. 10	Blyth Spartans	Ashington	2.11.73
Warren, Lee	6. 0	Hull	Manchester	28.02.69
Forwards				
Byng, David	6. 2	Torquay	Coventry	9.07.77
Cramb, Colin	6. 0	Hearts	Lanark	23.06.74
Paul, Martin	6. 0	Bristol Rovers	Lancashire	2.02.75

EXETER CITY

Name	Height ft. in.	Previous Club	Birthplace	Birthdate
Goalkeepers				
Bayes, Ashley	6. 1	Torquay	Lincoln	19.04.72
Fox, Peter	5. 10	Stoke	Scunthorpe	5.07.57
Defenders				
Blake, Noel	6. 4	Dundee	Jamaica	31.02.62
Chamberlain, Mark	5. 9	Brighton	Stoke	19.11.61
Hare, Mathew	6. 0	–	Barnstaple	26.12.76
Hughes, Darren	5. 10	Nothampton	Prescot	6.10.65
Myers, Chris	5. 11	Scarborough	Yeovil	1.04.69
Rice, Gary	6. 0	–	Zambia	25.09.75
Midfield				
Bailey, Danny	5. 9	Reading	Leyton	21.05.64
Medlin, Nicky	5. 9	–	Camborne	23.11.76
Forwards				
Braithwaite, Leon	6. 0	Bishop's Stortford	Hackney	13.12.72
Gnazgnazi, Suryan	5. 7	–	Honiton	24.08.77
McConnell, Barry	5. 9	–	Exeter	1.01.77
Pears, Richard	5. 11	–	Exeter	16.07.76

FULHAM

Name	Height ft. in.	Previous Club	Birthplace	Birthdate
Goalkeepers				
Lange, Tony	6. 0	W.B.A.	West Ham	10.12.64
Defenders				
Angus, Terry	6. 0	Northampton	Coventry	14.01.66
Blake, Mark	6. 0	Shrewsbury	Portsmouth	17.12.67
Hamsher, John	5. 10	–	London	14.01.78
Herrera, Robbie	5. 6	Q.P.R.	Torquay	12.06.70
Stewart, Simon	6. 1	Sheff. Wed.	Leeds	1.11.73
Midfield				
Adams, Micky	5. 8	Stoke	Sheffield	8.11.61
Barkus, Lea	5. 6	Reading	Reading	7.12.74
Brooker, Paul	5. 8	–	London	25.11.76
Cockerill, Glenn	5. 10	Leyton Orient	Grimsby	25.08.59
Cusack, Nick	6. 0	Oxford Utd.	Rotherham	24.12.65
McAree, Rod	5. 7	Dungannon	Dungannon	10.08.74
Misom, Michael	6. 3	–	London	8.11.75
Morgan, Simon	5. 10	Leicester City	Birmingham	5.09.66
Forwards				
Conroy, Mike	6. 0	Preston	Glasgow	31.12.65
Freeman, Darren	5. 11	Gillingham	Brighton	22.08.73
Hamill, Rory	5. 10	Port Stewart	Coleraine	4.05.76
Scott, Rob	6. 1	Sheff. Utd.	Epsom	15.08.73
Thomas, Martin	5. 8	Leyton Orient	Lyndhurst	12.09.73

HARTLEPOOL UNITED

Name	Height ft. in.	Previous Club	Birthplace	Birthdate
Goalkeepers				
Pears, Stephen	6. 0	Liverpool	Brandon	22.01.62
Defenders				
Davies, Glen	6. 2	Burnley	Brighton	20.07.76
Ingram, Denny	5. 10	–	Sunderland	27.06.76
Lee, Graeme	6. 2	–	Middlesbrough	31.05.78
McAuley, Sean	5. 10	–	Sheffield	23.06.72
McGuckin, Ian	6. 2	–	Middlesbrough	24.04.73
Tait, Mick	5. 11	Gretna	Wallsend	30.09.56
Midfield				
Allinson, Jamie	6. 1	–	Stockton	15.06.78
Clegg, David	5. 10	Liverpool	Liverpool	23.10.76
Cooper, Mark	5. 8	Exeter	Wakefield	18.12.68
Gallagher, Ian	5. 10	–	Hartlepool	30.05.78
Homer, Chris	5. 9	–	Stockton	16.04.77
Howard, Stephen	6. 1	–	Durham	10.05.76
Forwards				
Allon, Joe	5. 11	Port Vale	Gateshead	12.11.66
Halliday, Stephen	5. 10	Charlton	Sunderland	3.05.76
Houchen, Keith	6. 1	Port Vale	Middlesbrough	27.07.60

HEREFORD UNITED

Name	Height ft. in.	Previous Club	Birthplace	Birthdate
Goalkeepers				
Mackenzie, Chris	6. 0	Corby Town	Northampton	14.05.72

Defenders				
Brough, John	6. 0	Telford United	Ilkeston	8.01.73
James, Tony	6. 3	Leicester City	Sheffield	27.06.67
Smith, Dean	6. 0	Walsall	West Bromwich	19.03.71
Stoker, Gareth	5. 10	Shrewsbury	Bishop Auckland	22.02.73
Townsend, Quentin	5. 8	Wolves	Worcester	13.02.77
Midfield				
Downing, Keith	5. 9	Cardiff	Birmingham	23.07.65
Fishlock, Murray	5. 8	Trowbridge Town	Marlborough	23.09.73
Hibbard, Mark	5. 8	–	Hereford	12.08.77
Mahon, Gavin	6. 0	Wolves	Birmingham	2.01.77
Preedy, Phil	5. 10	–	Hereford	20.11.75
Warner, Robert	5. 10	–	Stratford-on-Avon	20.04.77
Forwards				
Foster, Ian	6. 0	Liverpool	Liverpool	11.11.76
Pitman, Jamie	5. 8	Swindon	Warminster	6.01.76

HULL CITY

Name	**Height ft. in.**	**Previous Club**	**Birthplace**	**Birthdate**
Goalkeepers				
Carroll, Roy	6. 2	–	Co. Fermanagh	30.09.77
Wilson, Steve	5. 10	–	Hull	24.04.74
Defenders				
Allison, Neil	6. 2	–	Hull	20.10.73
Brien, Tony	6. 0	W.B.A.	Dublin	10.02.69
Dewhurst, Robert	6. 3	Blackburn	Keighley	10.09.71
Greaves, Mark	6. 1	Brigg Town	Hull	22.01.75
Lowthorpe, Adam	5. 7	–	Hull	7.08.75
Marks, Jamie	5. 9	Leeds	Belfast	18.03.77
Rioch, Gregor	5. 11	Peterborough	Sutton Coldfield	24.06.75
Trevitt, Simon	5. 11	Huddersfield	Dewsbury	20.12.67
Wilkinson, Ian	6. 2	–	Hull	19.09.77
Wright, Ian	6. 1	Bristol Rovers	Lichfield	10.03.72
Midfield				
Gilbert, Kenny	5. 8	Aberdeen	Aberdeen	8.03.75
Joyce, Warren	5. 9	Burnley	Oldham	20.01.65
Mann, Neil	5. 10	Grimsby	Nottingham	19.11.72
Maxfield, Scott	5. 8	Doncaster	Thorne	13.07.76
Quigley, Michael	5. 7	Man. City	Manchester	2.10.70
Wharton, Paul	5. 4	Leeds	Newcastle	26.06.77
Forwards				
Brown, Andy	6. 3	Leeds	Edinburgh	11.10.76
Darby, Duane	5. 11	Doncaster	Birmingham	17.10.73
Fewings, Paul	5. 11	–	Hull	18.02.78
Gordon, Gavin	6. 1	–	Manchester	24.06.79
Mason, Andrew	5. 11	Bolton	Bolton	22.11.74
Peacock, Richard	5. 10	–	Sheffield	29.10.72

LEYTON ORIENT

Name	**Height ft. in.**	**Previous Club**	**Birthplace**	**Birthdate**
Goalkeepers				
Sealey, Les	6. 1	West Ham	Bethnal Green	29.09.57
Defenders				
Austin, Kevin	5. 9	Saffron Walden T.	London	12.02.73
Caldwell, Peter	6. 1	Q.P.R.	Dorchester	5.06.72
Channing, Justin	5. 11	Bristol Rovers	Reading	19.11.68

Hendon, Ian	6. 0	Tottenham	Ilford	5.12.71
McCarthy, Alan	5. 11	Q.P.R.	Tooting	11.01.72
Martin, Alvin	6. 1	West Ham	Bootle	29.07.58
Shearer, Lee	5. 10	–	Southend	23.10.77
Midfield				
Ayorinde, Sam	–	–	–	–
Baker, Joe	5. 10	Charlton	London	19.04.77
Garland, Peter	5. 10	Charlton	Croydon	20.01.71
Hanson, David	5. 9	–	Huddersfield	19.11.68
Ling, Martin	5. 7	Swindon	West Ham	15.07.66
Martin, David	6. 1	Gillingham	East Ham	25.04.63
Warren, Mark	6. 1	–	Clapton	12.11.74
Forwards				
Arnott, Andy	6. 1	Gillingham	Chatham	18.10.73
Inglethorpe, Alex	5. 11	Watford	Epsom	14.11.71
Kelly, Tony	5. 11	Bury	Coventry	14.02.66
West, Colin	6. 2	Swansea	Walsall	13.11.62

LINCOLN CITY

Name	Height ft. in.	Previous Club	Birthplace	Birthdate
Goalkeepers				
Richardson, Barry	6. 1	Preston	Wallsend	5.08.69
Defenders				
Brown, Grant	6. 0	Leicester City	Sunderland	19.11.69
Davies, Neil	6. 1	Fleetwood Town	Liverpool	9.11.76
Fleming, Terry	5. 9	Preston	Marston Green	5.01.73
Holmes, Steve	6. 2	Preston	Middlesbrough	13.01.71
Robertson, John	6. 2	Wigan	Liverpool	8.01.74
Westley, Shane	6. 2	Cambridge Utd.	Canterbury	16.06.65
Whitney, Jon	5. 10	Huddersfield	Nantwich	23.12.70
Midfield				
Barnett, Jason	5. 8	Wolves	Shrewsbury	21.04.76
Minett, Jason	5. 9	Exeter	Peterborough	12.08.71
Forwards				
Ainsworth, Gareth	5. 9	Preston	Blackburn	10.05.73
Alcide, Colin	6. 2	Emley	Huddersfield	14.04.72
Bos, Gijesbert	6. 0	Ijsselmeervogels, Hol.	Spackenburg, Hol.	22.02.73
Brown, Steve	6. 0	Gillingham	Southend	6.12.73

MANSFIELD TOWN

Name	Height ft. in.	Previous Club	Birthplace	Birthdate
Goalkeepers				
Bowling, Ian	6. 4	Bradford City	Sheffield	27.07.65
Defenders				
Clark, Darrell	5. 11	–	Mansfield	16.12.77
Doolan, John	6. 1	Everton	Liverpool	7.05.74
Hackett, Warren	6. 0	Doncaster	Newham	16.12.71
Kilcline, Brian	6. 2	Swindon	Nottingham	7.05.62
Peters, Mark	6. 0	Peterborough	St. Asaph	6.07.72
Robinson, Ian	5. 9	–	Nottingham	25.08.78
Midfield				
Ireland, Simon	5. 10	Blackburn	Barnstaple	23.11.71
Onuora, Iffy	6. 2	Huddersfield	Glasgow	28.07.67
Parkin, Steve	5. 6	W.B.A.	Mansfield	7.11.65
Sherlock, Paul	5. 11	Notts County	Wigan	17.11.73

Watkiss, Stuart	6. 2	Hereford	Wolverhampton	8.05.66
Wood, Simon	5. 9	–	Hull	24.09.76
Forwards				
Clifford, Mark	6. 0	–	Nottingham	11.09.77
Eustace, Scott	6. 0	Leicester City	Leicester	13.06.75
Hadley, Stewart	6. 1	Derby	Derby	30.12.73
Harper, Steve	5. 10	Doncaster	Stoke	3.02.69
Sale, Mark	6. 5	Preston	Burton-on-Trent	27.02.72

NORTHAMPTON TOWN

Name	Height ft. in.	Previous Club	Birthplace	Birthdate
Goalkeepers				
Turley, Billy	6. 3	Evesham	Wolverhampton	15.07.73
Woodman, Andy	6. 3	Exeter	Denmark Hill	11.08.71
Defenders				
Colkin, Lee	5. 11	–	Nuneaton	15.07.74
Maddison, Lee	5. 11	Bristol Rovers	Bristol	5.10.72
O'Shea, Danny	6. 0	Cambridge Utd.	Kennington	26.03.63
Sampson, Ian	6. 2	Sunderland	Wakefield	14.11.68
Warburton, Ray	6. 0	York	Rotherham	7.10.67
Midfield				
Burns, Chris	6. 1	Swansea	Manchester	9.11.67
Grayson, Neil	5. 10	Boston Utd.	York	1.11.64
Hunter, Roy	5. 10	W.B.A.	Saltburn	29.10.73
Peer, Dean	6. 2	Walsall	Dudley	8.08.69
Warner, Michael	5. 9	Tamworth	Harrogate	17.01.74
Forwards				
Cahill, Ollie	5. 10	Clonmel	Clonmel	29.09.75
Gibb, Alistair	5. 9	Norwich	Salisbury	17.02.76
Lee, Christian	6. 1	Doncaster	Aylesbury	8.10.76
Thompson, Garry	6. 1	Cardiff	Birmingham	7.10.59
White, Jason	6. 0	Scarborough	Meriden	19.10.71

ROCHDALE

Name	Height ft. in.	Previous Club	Birthplace	Birthdate
Goalkeepers				
Gray, Ian	6. 2	Oldham	Manchester	25.02.75
Defenders				
Barlow, Neil	6. 0	–	Bury	24.03.78
Bayliss, Dave	6. 0	–	Liverpool	8.06.76
Farrell, Andy	5. 11	Wigan	Colchester	7.10.65
Formby, Kevin	5. 11	Burscough	Ormskirk	22.07.71
Hill, Keith	6. 0	Plymouth	Bolton	17.05.69
Lyons, Paul	5. 10	Man. Utd.	Leigh	24.06.77
Price, James	5. 11	–	Preston	1.02.78
Thackeray, Andy	5. 9	Wrexham	Huddersfield	13.02.68
Midfield				
Deary, John	5. 10	Burnley	Ormskirk	18.10.62
Fensome, Andy	5. 7	Preston	Northampton	18.02.69
Martin, Dean	5. 10	Scunthorpe	Huddersfield	9.09.67
Russell, Alex	5. 11	Burscough	Crosby	17.03.73
Thompson, Dave	5. 9	Chester	Manchester	27.05.62
Forwards				
Lancaster, Dave	6. 3	Bury	Preston	8.09.61
Leonard, Mark	6. 0	Wigan	St. Helens	27.09.62
Stuart, Mark	5. 10	Huddersfield	Chiswick	15.12.66

Taylor, Jamie	5. 6	–	Bury	11.01.77
Whitehall, Steve	5. 9	Southport	Bromborough	8.12.66

SCARBOROUGH

Name	Height ft. in.	Previous Club	Birthplace	Birthdate
Goalkeepers				
Ironside, Ian	6. 2	Stockport	Sheffield	8.03.64
Martin, Kevin	6. 1	–	Bromsgrove	22.06.76
Defenders				
Bennett, Gary	6. 0	Sunderland	Manchester	4.12.61
Hanby, Robert	5. 10	Barnsley	Pontefract	24.12.74
Hicks, Stuart	6. 1	Preston	Peterborough	30.05.67
Knowles, Darren	5. 6	Stockport	Sheffield	8.10.70
Rockett, Jason	6. 1	Rotherham	London	26.09.69
Midfield				
Sunderland, Jon	5. 9	Blackpool	Newcastle	2.11.75
Wells, Mark	5. 8	Huddersfield	Leicester	17.10.71
Willgrass, Alexandre	6. 3	–	Scarborough	8.04.76
Forwards				
Daws, Tony	5. 8	Lincoln City	Sheffield	10.09.66
Ritchie, Andy	5. 11	Oldham	Oldham	28.11.60
Williams, Gareth	5. 10	Northampton	Isle of Wight	12.03.67

SCUNTHORPE UNITED

Name	Height ft. in.	Previous Club	Birthplace	Birthdate
Goalkeepers				
Samways, Mark	6. 1	Doncaster	Doncaster	11.11.68
Defenders				
Bradley, Russell	6. 0	Halifax Town	Birmingham	28.03.66
Hope, Chris	6. 0	Nott'm. Forest	Sheffield	14.11.72
Knill, Alan	6. 4	Bury	Slough	8.10.64
Murfin, Andrew	5. 9	–	–	–
Walsh, Michael	5. 11	–	Rotherham	5.08.77
Wilson, Paul	5. 10	York	Bradford	2.08.68
Midfield				
Clarkson, Phil	5. 10	Crewe	Hambleton	13.11.68
D'Auria, David	5. 9	Scarborough	Swansea	26.03.70
Housham, Steve	5. 10	–	Gainsborough	24.02.76
Turnbull, Lee	6. 0	Doncaster	Stockton	27.09.67
Forwards				
Eyre, John	5. 10	Oldham	Hull	9.10.74
McFarlane, Andy	6. 3	Swansea	Wolverhampton	30.11.66
Paterson, Jamie	5. 5	Falkirk	Dumfries	26.04.73
Sertori, Mark	6. 1	Bury	Manchester	1.09.67

SWANSEA CITY

Name	Height ft. in.	Previous Club	Birthplace	Birthdate
Goalkeepers				
Freestone, Roger	6. 3	Chelsea	Newport, Gwent	19.08.68
Jones, Lee	6. 3	AFC Porth	Pontypridd	9.08.70
Miles, Ben	6. 1	Southall	Middlesex	13.04.76
Defenders				
Clode, Mark	5. 10	Plymouth	Plymouth	24.02.73

Cook, Andy	5. 9	Exeter	Southampton	10.08.69
Edwards, Christian	6. 2	–	Caerphilly	23.11.75
Garnett, Shaun	6. 2	Tranmere	Liverpool	22.11.69
Jones, Steve	5. 10	Cheltenham	Bristol	25.12.70
King, Robert	5. 8	Torquay	Merthyr	2.09.77
Molby, Jan	6. 2	Liverpool	Kolding, Den.	4.07.63
Moreira, Joao	6. 2	Benfica, Por.	Portugal	30.06.70
O'Leary, Kristian	6. 0	–	Port Talbot	30.08.77
Walker, Keith	6. 0	St. Mirren	Edinburgh	17.04.66
Midfield				
Ampadu, Kwame	5. 10	W.B.A.	Bradford	20.12.70
Chapple, Shaun	5. 11	–	Swansea	14.02.73
Grey, Jonathan	5. 11	–	Swansea	2.09.77
Hodge, John	5. 7	Exeter	Ormskirk	1.04.69
Lacy, Damian	5. 9	–	Bridgend	3.08.77
Penney, David	5. 10	Oxford Utd.	Wakefield	17.08.64
Price, Jason	6. 2	Aberaman	Aberdare	12.04.77
Forwards				
Brown, Linton	5. 10	Hull	Hull	12.04.68
Coates, Jonathan	5. 8	–	Swansea	27.06.75
Heggs, Carl	6. 1	W.B.A.	Leicester	11.10.70
McDonald, Colin	5. 7	Falkirk	Edinburgh	10.04.74
Thomas, David	5. 10	–	Caerphilly	26.09.75
Torpey, Steve	6. 3	Bradford City	Islington	8.12.70

TORQUAY UNITED

Name	Height ft. in.	Previous Club	Birthplace	Birthdate
Goalkeepers				
Newland, Ray	6. 2	Chester	Liverpool	19.07.71
Wilmot, Rhys	6. 1	Crystal Palace	Newport, Gwent	21.02.62
Defenders				
Barrow, Lee	5. 11	Scarborough	Worksworth	1.05.73
Stamps, Scott	5. 10	–	Birmingham	20.03.75
Watson, Alex	6. 2	Bournemouth	Liverpool	5.04.68
Winter, Steve	5. 8	Taunton Town	Bristol	26.10.73
Midfield				
Hathaway, Ian	5. 6	Rotherham	Wordsley	22.08.68
Hodges, Kevin	5. 8	Plymouth	Bridport	12.06.60
McCall, Steve	5. 11	Pymouth	Carlisle	15.10.60
Oatway, Charlie	5. 6	Cardiff	Hammersmith	28.11.73
Preston, Michael	5. 8	–	Plymouth	22.11.77
Forwards				
Baker, Paul	6. 1	York	Newcastle	5.01.63
Hancox, Richard	5. 10	Stourbridge	Stourbridge	4.10.70
Jack, Rodney	5. 6	St. Vincent, Bar.	Kingstown, Bar.	28.09.72
Ndah, Jamie	6. 2	Kingstonian	East Dulwich	5.08.71
Nelson, Garry	5. 10	Charlton	Braintree	16.01.61

WIGAN ATHLETIC

Name	Height ft. in.	Previous Club	Birthplace	Birthdate
Goalkeepers				
Butler, Lee	6. 2	Barnsley	Sheffield	30.05.66
Farnworth, Simon	5. 11	Preston	Chorley	28.10.63
Statham, Mark	6. 2	Nott'm. Forest	Barnsley	11.11.75
Defenders				
Butler, John	5. 11	Stoke	Liverpool	7.02.62

Carragher, Matthew	5. 9	–	Liverpool	14.01.76
Greenall, Colin	5. 11	Lincoln City	Billinge	30.12.63
Johnson, Gavin	5. 11	Luton	Stowmarket	10.10.70
Moore, Andy	5. 9	–	Liverpool	2.05.78
Pender, John	6. 0	Burnley	Luton	19.11.63
Salt, Daniel	5. 10	–	Warrington	17.11.77
Midfield				
Diaz, Isidro	5. 7	CF Balaguer, Spa.	Valencia, Spa.	15.05.72
Fearns, Terry	5. 11	–	Liverpool	24.10.77
Kilford, Ian	5. 10	Nott'm. Forest	Bristol	6.10.73
Love, Michael	5. 11	Hinckley Athletic	Stockport	27.11.73
Martinez, Roberto	5. 11	CF Balaguer, Spa.	Balaguer, Spa.	13.07.73
Sharp, Kevin	5. 9	Leeds	Ontario, Can.	19.09.74
Forwards				
Biggins, Wayne	5. 11	Oxford Utd.	Sheffield	20.11.61
Black, Tony	5. 8	Bamber Bridge	Barrow-in-Furness	15.07.69
Jones, Graeme	6. 0	Doncaster	Gateshead	13.03.70
Lancashire, Graham	5. 10	Preston	Blackpool	19.10.72
Lowe, David	5. 10	Leicester City	Liverpool	30.08.65
Seba, Jesus	5. 6	Real Zaragoza, Spa.	Zaragoza, Spa.	11.04.74
Tyrell, Kevin	5. 10	–	Warrington	5.10.77

SCOTTISH LEAGUE SQUADS 1996-97

PREMIER DIVISION

ABERDEEN: Paul Bernard; Scott Booth; Robert Brown; Martin Buchan; Kevin Christie; Neil Cooper; David Craig; Michael Craig; William Dodds; Stephen Glass; Iain Good; Brian Grant; John Inglis; Brian Irvine; Paul Kane; Ilian Kiriakov; Malcolm Kpedekpo; Stewart McKimmie; Joseph Miller; Kevin Morgan; Michael Newlands; Hugh Robertson; David Rowson; Duncan Shearer; Gary Smith; Derek Stillie; Michael Watt; Dean Windass; Colin Woodthorpe; Dennis Wyness; Darren Young. **Player-Manager:** Roy Aitken.

CELTIC: Marc Anthony; Patrick Bonner; Paul Borland; Thomas Boyd; Charles Boyle; Jorge Cadete; Martin Coughlin; Craig Culkin; Paul Dalglish; Peter Davis; Simon Donnelly; Paulo Di Canio; Barry Elliot; Patrick Fitzpatrick; Kevin Gilligan; Peter Grant; Stuart Gray; Christopher Hay; John Hughes; Patrick Kelly; James Kerr; Gerard Lyttle; Peter MacDonald; Malcolm MacKay; John McBride; Andrew McCondichie; Timothy McGrath; Charles McGuinness; Thomas McKinlay; Brian McLaughlin; Jackie McNamara; Paul McStay; Gordon Marshall; Graeme Morrison; Andrew O'Brien; Philip O'Donnell; Brian O'Neil; William Stark; Alan Stubbs; Andreas Thom; Pierre Van Hooijdonk; Rudi Vata; Brian Vaugh; Morten Wieghorst. **Player-Manager:** Tommy Burns.

DUNDEE UNITED: Paul Black; David Bowman; Craig Brewster; Owen Coyle; Scott Crabbe; Christopher Devine; Craig Easton; Steven Fallon; Juan Ferreri; Stuart Gilmour; Dale Gray; David Hannah; John Hughes; Ian Johnson; Marino Keith; Grahame Kennedy; Raymond McKinnon; Andrew McLaren; James

McQuilken; Gary McSwegan; Maurice Malpas; Alastair Maxwell; David Mitchell; Kelham O'Hanlon; Mark Perry; Steven Pressley; Alexander Robertson; Robert Shannon; Andrew Stewart; Anthony Stirling; Richard Thomson; Paul Walker; Brian Welsh; Robert Winters. **Manager:** Billy Kirkwood.

DUNFERMLINE ATHLETIC: Damien Alexander; David Bingham; John Clark; Henry Curran; Ivo Den Bieman; John Dickson; Gerard Farrell; Steven Ferguson; Derek Fleming; John Fraser; Hamish French; Ryan Hegarty; Craig Ireland; Mark McCulloch; Marc Millar; Allan Moore; Stewart Petrie; Craig Reynolds; Brian Rice; Craig Robertson; Robert Ryan; Gregory Shaw; Andrew Smith; Andrew Tod; Guido Van de Kamp; Kenneth Ward; Ian Westwater. **Manager:** Robert Paton.

HEART OF MIDLOTHIAN: Anthony Barr; Neil Berry; Mark Bradley; Pasquale Bruno; John Burns; Stuart Callaghan; Colin Cameron; John Colquhoun; Stephen Frail; Stephen Fulton; Brian Hamilton; Myles Hogarth; Derek Holmes; Robert Horn; Allan Johnston; Alan Lawrence; Donald Leitch; Craig Levein; Gary Locke; Gary MacKay; Allan McManus; Grant McNichol; David McPherson; David Murie; Grant Murray; Gary Naysmith; Craig Nelson; Neil Pointon; Paul Ritchie; John Robertson; Gilles Rousset; Paul Smith; Andrew Storrar; Kevin Thomas; David Winnie. **Manager:** Jim Jefferies.

HIBERNIAN: Steven Anderson; Scott Bannerman; Graeme Bryson; Paul Cook; Darren Dods; Graeme Donald; Andrew Dow; Gareth Evans; David Farrell; Jason Gardiner; Kevin Harper; Gordon Hunter; Christopher Jackson; Darren Jackson; James Leighton; Graeme Love; Kevin McAllister; Stuart McCaffrey; Ian McDonald; Patrick McGinlay; Joseph McLaughlin; Ross McNab; John Martin; Andrew Millen; Greg Miller; Kenneth Miller; William Miller; Andrew Newman; Michael O'Neill; Eric Paton; Christopher Reid; Michael Renwick; Paul Riley; Joseph Tortolano; Steven Tweed; Michael Weir; Craig Wight; Keith Wright. **Manager:** Alex Miller.

KILMARNOCK: Damiano Agostini; Derek Anderson; David Bagen; Thomas Brown; Alexander Burke; Stuart Davidson; John Dillon; Kevin Doig; William Findlay; Iain Fitzpatrick; Martin Graham; Steven Hamilton; Gary Hay; John Henry; Gary Holt; Alan Kerr; James Laughlan; Dragoje Lekovic; Rodney Lennox; Angus MacPherson; Gary McCutcheon; James McIntyre; Colin McKee; Stephen Maskrey; Colin Meldrum; Alistair Mitchell; Samuel Montgomerie; Mark Reilly; Mark Roberts; Alexander Ryan; Mark Skilling; Gerrit Tallon; Robert Vincent; Scott Walker; Neil Whitworth; Robert Williamson; Paul Wright. **Manager:** Alex Totten.

MOTHERWELL: Douglas Arnott; Alexander Burns; Thomas Coyne; Stephen Craigan; William Davies; Greig Denham; James Dolan; Roy Essandoh; William Falconer; Garry Gow; John Hendry; Scott Howie; Paul Lambert; Christopher McCart; Lee McCulloch; Robert McKinnon; Stephen McMillan; Shaun McSkimming; Brian Martin; Edward May; John Philliben; Innes Ritchie; Andrew Roddie; Ian Ross; Mitchell Van der Gaag; Stephen Woods. **Player-manager:** Alex McLeish.

RAITH ROVERS: Graeme Bogie; Paul Bonar; David Craig; Craig Dargo; Shaun Dennis; Peter Duffield; Christopher Francis; Alexander Geddes; Mark Humphries; Alistair Hynd; Stephen Kirk; David Kirkwood; Miodrag Krivokapic; Graeme Landels; Daniel Lennon; Greg Logan; Greig McCulloch; James McInally; Dean McPherson; Iain Mauchlen; John Millar; Anthony Rougier; Neil Sellars; David Sinclair; Craig Smart; Jay Stein; Alexander Taylor; Scott (M) Thomson; Scott (Y) Thomson. **Manager:** Jim Thomson.

RANGERS: Erik Bo Andersen; Jonas Bjorklund; Gary Bollan; Steven Boyack; John Brown; Alexander Cleland; Lee Dair; Gordon Durie; Ian Durrant; Barry Ferguson; Ian Ferguson; Darren Fitzgerald; Paul Gascoigne; James Gibson; Andrew Goram; Charles Gough; David Graham; Francis Haggarty; Christopher Jardine; Jaswinder Juttla; Brian Laudrup; Stuart McCall; Alistair McCoist; Brian McGinty; Derek McInnes; Paul McKnight; Alan McLaren; Paul McShane; Charles Miller; Ross Milligan; Craig Moore; John Morrow; Neil Murray; Barry Nicholson; Iain Nicolson; Gordan Petric; Michael Rae; David Robertson; Barry Robson; Greg Shields; Theodorus Snelders; Trevor Steven; Michael Stone; Peter Van Vossen; James Watt; Scott Wilson; Stephen Wright; David Young. **Manager:** Walter Smith.

FIRST DIVISION

AIRDRIEONIANS: Kenneth Black; James Boyle; Gordon Connelly; Patrick Connolly; Stephen Cooper; John Davies; Paul Harvey; Graham Hay; Peter Hetherston; Paul Jack; John Lamb; John McClelland; Thomas McIntyre; Gerard McKenna; Anthony McPeak; John Martin; Andrew Rhodes; James Sandison; Anthony Smith; Alexander Stewart; Sean Sweeny; Stephen Tait; Marvyn Wilson. **Manager:** Alex MacDonald.

CLYDEBANK: Paul Agnew; Gary Bowman; Kenneth Brannigan; Graham Connell; Thomas Currie; Kenneth Eadie; James Grady; David Irons; Paul Lovering; Gary Matthews; William Melvin; Scott Miller; Scott Murdoch; David Nicholls; Joseph Robertson; Colin Sutherland; Gary Teale. **Player-coach:** Brian Wright.

DUNDEE: Dariusz Adamczuk; Iain Anderson; Kevin Bain; Gerrard Britton; Andrew Cargill; James Charnley; Cornelius Duffy; Raymond Farningham; David Fisher; James Hamilton; Andrew Matheson; Roy McBain; Neil McCann; Gary McGlynn; Gary McKeown; Thomas McQueen; Gary Miller; Jerry O'Driscoll; Michel Pageaud; Gavin Rae; George Shaw; Barry Smith; Paul Tosh; Craig Tully; Dusan Vrto; Lee Wilkie. **Player-manager:** James Duffy.

EAST FIFE: Gilbert Allan; Benjamin Andrew; David Beaton; Graham Bell; William Burns; John Cusick; Craig Demmin; Alan Dixon; Mark Donaghy; Mark Dunnett; Arnold Dwarika; Philip Gartshore; Richard Gibb; Alexander Hamill; Lindsay Hamilton; David Henderson; Ronald Hildersley; Douglas Hope; Stephen Hutcheon; Derek Long; Darren McLeod; John McStay; Ian Mair; Gordon Rae; Dean Robertson; Robert Scott; Alan Sneddon; Stefan Winiarski;. **Player-manager:** Steve Archibald.

FALKIRK: Martyn Corrigan; Albert Craig; David Elliot; Derek Ferguson; Alastair Graham; Bruce Graham; Andrew Gray; David Hagen; Neil Inglis; Kevin James; Andrew Lawrie; Jamie McGowan; Mark McGraw; Paul McGrillen; Scott McKenzie; Neil Oliver; Anthony Parks; Andrew Seaton; David Weir; Garry Whiteside. **Manager:** Eamonn Bannon.

GREENOCK MORTON: Stephen Aitken; John Anderson; Alan Blaikie; Paul Blair; Derek Collins; Peter Cormack; Ross Fanning; Patrick Flannery; Warren Hawke; Douglas Johnstone; Derek Lilley; Janne Lindberg; Scott McArthur; Stephen McCahill; Craig McPherson; Alan Mahood; Barry Mason; Ross Matheson; Marko Rajamaki; Derek Reeley; Brian Reid; Bryan Salvin; David Wylie. **Manager:** Allan McGraw.

PARTICK THISTLE: Charles Adams; Alan Archibald; Stuart Ayton; Kevin Budinauckas; Mark Cairns; Ian Cameron; Alan Dinnie; Stephen Docherty; Nicholas Henderson; Andrew Lyons; William MacDonald; James McCue; Derek McWilliams; Callum Milne; James Slavin; Thomas Smith; Jered Stirling; Thomas Turner; Joseph Walker; Gregg Watson. **Player-Manager:** Murdo MacLeod.

ST. JOHNSTONE: Gordon Brown; Callum Davidson; Euan Donaldson; Gary Farquhar; Ian Ferguson; Gordon Freedman; Roderick Grant; Robert Greenock; Danny Griffin; Leigh Jenkinson; Charles King; Kieran McAnespie; Stuart McCluskey; Kevin McGowne; John McQuillan; Alan Main; George O'Boyle; John O'Neil; Allan Preston; Stephen Robertson; Philip Scott; Attila Sekerlioglu; Steven Tosh; Kevin Twaddle; James Weir; Andrew Whiteford. **Player-manager:** Paul Sturrock.

ST. MIRREN: Paul Archdeacon; Martin Baker; John Boyd; Alan Combe; James Dick; Paul Fenwick; James Fullarton; Richard Gillies; Brian Hetherston; Barry Lavety; Fraser Love; Barry McLaughlin; Norman McWhirter; Junior Mendes; Christopher Pollock; Alan Prentice; Derek Scrimgour; Brian Smith; Stuart Taylor; Stephen Watson; Mark Yardley. **Manager:** Jimmy Bone.

STIRLING ALBION: Paul Armstrong; John Bennett; Alexander Bone; Paul Deas; John Gibson; David Kirkham; Stephen McCormick; Mark McGeown; Gary McGrotty; Ian McInnes; Joseph McLeod; Ronald McQuilter; Colin Mitchell; Michael Monaghan; Andrew Paterson; Garry Paterson; Raymond Stewart; Craig Taggart; Thomas Tait; Paul Watson; David Wood. **Player-manager:** Kevin Drinkell.

SECOND DIVISION

AYR UNITED: Evan Balfour; Robert Bell; Kevin Biggart; Gordon Burns; Stuart Connolly; Ronald Coyle; Isaac English; Duncan George; Darren Henderson; Scott Hewitt; Gregg Hood; William Jamieson; John Kerr; Steven Kerrigan; Paul Kinnaird; Robert Law; Henry Smith; David Stewart; Philip Taylor; John Traynor; William Wilson. **Player-manager:** Gordon Dalziel.

BERWICK RANGERS: Neil Clegg; John Coughlin; Paul Forrester; Graeme Fraser; John Gallacher; Thomas Graham; Thomas Hendrie; Thomas King; David McGlynn; James McQueen; Martin Neil; Alastair Reid; Greig Robertson; Paul Rutherford; Craig Valentine; Kevin Walton; Barry Ward; Mark Wilson; Neil Young. **Manager:** Ian Ross.

BRECHIN CITY: Raymond Allan; Richard Baillie; Roddy Black; Ralph Brand; Robert Brown; Garry Buick; Henry Cairney; Harry Cargill; Graeme Christie; Francis Conway; Graham Davidson; Neil Ewen; Craig Farnan; Scott Ferguson; Craig Feroz; Stuart Garden; Ian Heddle; Steve Kerrigan; James McKellar; William McNeill; Brian Mitchell; Scott Reid; Alexander Ross; Walter Scott; Greig Smith; Raymond Smith; Ronnie Smollet; Stuart Sorbie. **Manager:** John Young.

CLYDE: Edward Annand; James Brown; Paul Brownlie; Paul Campbell; Graeme Ferguson; Kenneth Gillies; Thomas Harrison; Keith Knox; Graeme McCheyne; Ian McConnell; John McLay; Steve McNulty; Miller Mathieson; Charles Nicholas; Martin O'Neill; Gordon Parks; James Prunty; Donald Shanks. **Manager:** Alex Smith.

DUMBARTON: Hugh Burns; Callum Campbell; Alan Foster; Charles Gibson; Martin Glancy; Stephen Gow; Alan Granger; Thomas King; Ian MacFarlane; Martin McGarvey; Samuel McGivern; Colin McKinnon; James Marsland; Paul Martin; James Meechan; Kenneth Meechan; Martin Melvin; Martin Mooney; Lee Sharp; Hugh Ward. **Manager:** Jim Fallon.

HAMILTON ACADEMICAL: Crawford Baptie; Jamie Bruce; Gary Clark; David Cormack; Allan Ferguson; Michael Geraghty; Christopher Hillcoat; David Laird; David Lorimer; Steven McCormick; Scott McCulloch; Sean McEntegart; Martin McIntosh; Paul McKenzie; John McQuade; Jose Quitongo; Steven Renicks; James Sherry; Steven Thomson. **Manager:** Iain Munro.

LIVINGSTON: David Alleyne; Lee Bailey; Colin Bowsher; William Callaghan; Stephen Campbell; Graeme Davidson; Robert Douglas; Mark Duthie; Thomas Graham; Graham Harvey; Stephen Higgins; Michael Korotrich; Craig McCartney; Gordon McLeod; Grant McMartin; Craig Martin; Christopher Sinclair; Craig Smart; Horace Stoute; Stuart Thorburn; Peter Tierney; Stewart Williamson; Barry Wood; Jason Young. **Manager:** Jim Leishman.

QUEEN OF THE SOUTH: James Brown; Thomas Bryce; James Butter; Colin Campbell; Gary Cochrane; Stephen Cody; Mark Dobie; Neil Johnstone; David Kennedy; Steven Leslie; David Lilley; Robert McColm; Andrew McFarlane; Brian McKeown; Desmond McKeown; Stephen Mallan; Kevin Proudfoot; Steven Ramsay; John Rowe. **Managers:** Rowan Alexander (player-manager) and Mark Shanks.

STENHOUSEMUIR: Neil Aitken; Graeme Armstrong; Alan Banks; Gordon Buchanan; Martin Christie; Steven Ellison; James Fisher; Lloyd Haddow; James Henderson; Paul Hunter; Gareth Hutchison; Ian Little; Paul Logan; George McGeachie; Roderick McKenzie; David Roseburgh; Colin Scott; Adrian Sprott; Iain Stewart; James Thomson. **Manager:** Terry Christie.

STRANRAER: Brian Bilsland; Derek Crawford; Bernard Duffy; Graham Duncan; Anthony Gallagher; Alexander Grant; Nigel Howard; James Hughes; Alan Lansdowne; Ian McAulay; John McCaffrey; Neil McGowan; John McMillan; Graham Millar; Campbell Money; John Robertson; Thomas Sloan; Gordon Young. **Player-manager:** Campbell Money.

THIRD DIVISION

ALBION ROVERS: Martin Brown; David Byrne; Martin Clark; John Dickson; John Gallagher; Colin MacFarlane; Douglas McGuire; Anthony McInally; James Moffat; Marc Osborne; Mark Pickering; Robert Reilly; Stephen Ross; Robert Russell; Martin Ryan; Barry Strain; Thomas Walker. **Player-manager:** Vince Moore.

ALLOA: Robert Balfour; Stephen Cadden; Mark Cowan; Peter Dwyer; James Gilmour; Paul Graham; William Irvine; Neil Johnston; Kevin Kane; Thomas Little; Stuart Mackay; Paul McAneny; Neil McAvoy; John McCormack; Keith McCulloch; Barrie Moffat; Mark Nelson; Mark Whyte; Robert Wilson; Roderick Wylie. **Manager:** Tom Hendrie.

ARBROATH: Gary Balfour; Patrick Clark; Jonathan Crawford; Stuart Elder; David Elliott; Steven Florence; John Fowler; Robert Gardner; Craig Hinchcliffe; James Kerr; John McAulay; Stephen McCormick; Thomas McMillan; Donald McVicar; Brian Mackie; Alan Middleton; Scott Peters; David Pew; James Phinn; Paul Roberts; John Thomson; John Ward; Michael Waters; William Watters; Brian Welsh. **Manager:** John Brogan.

COWDENBEATH: Kevin Bowmaker; Grant Brough; Samuel Conn; Armando De Melo; Ross Godfrey; Alistair Hamilton; Martin Humphreys; Kevin Hutchison; James McGregor; Barry McMahon; Brian Malloy; Domenico Maratea; Graham Meldrum; Hugh O'Neill; Steven Oliver; Alan Ritchie; Neil Russell; David Scott; Craig Sinclair; Graeme Soutar; James Spence; Shaun Steven; William Stewart; Craig Winter; Garry Wood. **Manager:** Tommy Steven.

EAST STIRLINGSHIRE: Mark Abercromby; Alastair Farquhar; Murray Hunter; Iain Lee; Robert Lee; Martin McBride; Mungo McCallum; Gordon McDougall; Alan Neill; Brian Ross; Gordon Russell; Scott Sneddon; David Watt; Ewan Wilson. **Manager:** Willie Little.

FORFAR ATHLETIC: John Allison; Eric Archibald; Gordon Arthur; Mark Bowes; Douglas Craig; John Donegan; Barry Gardiner; Stuart Glennie; Derek Guthrie; James Hamilton; Paul Hannigan; Gary Higgins; Grant Inglis; Neil Irvine; James Loney; Ian Lowe; Alan McKillop; Ian McPhee; Robert Mann; Andrew Morgan; Brian Sexton. **Manager:** Tom Campbell.

INVERNESS CALEDONIAN THISTLE: Graeme Bennett; Robert Benson; David Brennan; James Calder; Charles Christie; Richard Hastings; Alan Hercher; Iain MacArthur; Donald MacDonald; Mark McAllister; David McGinlay; Paul McKenzie; Mark McRitchie; Michael Noble; David Ross; John Scott; Iain Stewart; Michael Teasdale; Brian Thomson; Ross Tokely. **Manager**: Steve Paterson.

MONTROSE: Scott Brady; Justin Brown; Ryan Constable; Craig Cooper; Mark Craib; Alistair Ferrie; Derek Grant; Mark Haro; Allan Kennedy; Stephen Kydd; David Larter; Mark Lavelle; Graham Lawrie; Innes MacDonald; Colin McGlashan; Craig Mailer; Ronald Massie; Christopher Masson; Paul Masson; Mark Robb; Ian Robertson; Michael Ross; Shaun Smith; Levi Stephen; Scott Taylor; Kevin Tindal; James Tosh; Kevin Walker; Robert Wood. **Manager:** David Smith.

QUEEN'S PARK: David Arbuckle; Gordon Bruce; Dominic Callan; Ross Caven; Scott Edgar; Graeme Elder; Paul Ferguson; Daniel Ferry; Robert Fraser; David Graham; Kenneth Kennedy; Kevin McGoldrick; Ian Maxwell; Garry Orr; James Ward; Derek Wilson. **Player-coach:** Hugh McCann.

ROSS COUNTY: Johnston Bellshaw; Paul Bradshaw; Gordon Connelly; Keith Ferries; William Furphy; Stuart Golabek; Brian Grant; William Herd; Stephen Hutchison; David MacKay; Alexander MacLeod; Andrew MacLeod; Jamie MacPherson; Colin Milne; Christopher Somerville; Robert Stewart; William Watt; Robert Williamson. **Manager:** Neale Cooper.

GASCOIGNE BANNED

Paul Gascoigne will miss the start of Rangers' European Cup campaign this season, through a 2-match suspension after being sent off away to Borussia Dortmund in the Champions' League last December.

LEAGUE FIXTURES 1996-97

F.A. Premier League: F.A. Carling Premiership.
Football League: Nationwide Football League.

Friday, August 16th

First Division
Manchester City v Ipswich Town

Saturday, August 17th

Premiership
Arsenal v West Ham United
Blackburn Rovers v Tottenham H.
Coventry City v Nott'm. Forest
Derby County v Leeds United
Everton v Newcastle United
Middlesbrough v Liverpool
Sheffield Wed. v Aston Villa
Sunderland v Leicester City
Wimbledon v Manchester Utd.

First Division
Bradford City v Portsmouth
Grimsby Town v Wolves
Huddersfield T. v Charlton Athletic
Norwich City v Swindon Town
Oldham Athletic v Stoke City
Port Vale v Bolton Wand.
Q.P.R. v Oxford United
Reading v Sheffield United
Southend United v Tranmere Rovers
W.B.A. v Barnsley

Second Division
Bournemouth v Watford
Blackpool v Chesterfield
Bristol Rovers v Peterborough Utd.
Bury v Brentford
Crewe Alexandra v Stockport Co.
Gillingham v Bristol City
Luton Town v Burnley
Millwall v Wrexham
Notts County v Preston N.E.
Plymouth Argyle v York City
Walsall v Rotherham United

Third Division
Brighton & H.A. v Chester City
Cambridge United v Barnet
Colchester Utd. v Hartlepool United
Doncaster Rov. v Carlisle United
Fulham v Hereford United
Hull City v Darlington
Leyton Orient v Scunthorpe Utd.
Mansfield Town v Exeter City
Scarborough v Cardiff City
Swansea City v Rochdale
Torquay United v Lincoln City
Wigan Athletic v Northampton T.

Sunday, August 18th

Premiership
Southampton v Chelsea

First Division
Birmingham City v Crystal Palace

Second Division
Shrewsbury Town v Wycombe Wand.

Monday, August 19th

Premiership
Liverpool v Arsenal

Tuesday, August 20th

Premiership
Leeds United v Sheffield Wed.

First Division
Bolton Wand. v Manchester City

Wednesday, August 21st

Premiership
Aston Villa v Blackburn Rovers
Chelsea v Middlesbrough
Leicester City v Southampton
Manchester Utd. v Everton
Newcastle United v Wimbledon
Nott'm. Forest v Sunderland
Tottenham H. v Derby County
West Ham United v Coventry City

Friday, August 23rd

First Division
Portsmouth v Q.P.R.
Tranmere Rovers v Grimsby Town

Saturday, August 24th

Premiership
Aston Villa v Derby County
Chelsea v Coventry City
Leicester City v Arsenal
Liverpool v Sunderland
Newcastle United v Sheffield Wed.
Nott'm. Forest v Middlesbrough
Tottenham H. v Everton
West Ham United v Southampton

First Division
Bolton Wand. v Norwich City
Charlton Athletic v W.B.A.
Crystal Palace v Oldham Athletic
Ipswich Town v Reading
Oxford United v Southend United
Sheffield United v Birmingham City
Stoke City v Manchester City
Swindon Town v Port Vale
Wolves v Bradford City

Second Division
Brentford v Luton Town
Bristol City v Blackpool
Burnley v Walsall
Chesterfield v Bury
Peterborough Utd. v Crewe Alexandra
Preston N.E. v Bristol Rovers
Rotherham United v Shrewsbury Town
Stockport Co. v Notts County
Watford v Millwall
Wrexham v Plymouth Argyle
Wycombe Wand. v Gillingham
York City v Bournemouth

Third Division
Barnet v Wigan Athletic
Cardiff City v Brighton & H.A.
Carlisle United v Hull City
Chester City v Cambridge United
Darlington v Swansea City
Exeter City v Scarborough
Hartlepool United v Fulham
Hereford United v Doncaster Rov.
Lincoln City v Leyton Orient
Northampton T. v Mansfield Town
Rochdale v Colchester Utd.
Scunthorpe Utd. v Torquay United

Sunday, August 25th

Premiership
Manchester Utd. v Blackburn Rovers

First Division
Barnsley v Huddersfield T.

Monday, August 26th

Premiership
Leeds United v Wimbledon

Tuesday, August 27th

First Division
Charlton Athletic v Birmingham City
Crystal Palace v W.B.A.
Ipswich Town v Grimsby Town
Oxford United v Norwich City
Portsmouth v Southend United
Sheffield United v Huddersfield T.
Tranmere Rovers v Port Vale

Second Division
Brentford v Gillingham
Bristol City v Luton Town
Burnley v Shrewsbury Town
Chesterfield v Walsall
Peterborough Utd. v Notts County
Preston N.E. v Crewe Alexandra
Rotherham United v Blackpool
Stockport Co. v Bournemouth
Watford v Plymouth Argyle
Wrexham v Bristol Rovers
Wycombe Wand. v Bury
York City v Millwall

Third Division
Barnet v Brighton & H.A.
Cardiff City v Wigan Athletic
Carlisle United v Leyton Orient
Chester City v Swansea City
Darlington v Colchester Utd.
Exeter City v Doncaster Rov.
Hartlepool United v Mansfield Town
Hereford United v Hull City
Lincoln City v Cambridge United
Northampton T. v Torquay United
Rochdale v Fulham
Scunthorpe Utd. v Scarborough

Wednesday, August 28th

First Division
Barnsley v Reading
Stoke City v Bradford City
Swindon Town v Oldham Athletic
Wolves v Q.P.R.

Friday, August 30th

First Division
W.B.A. v Sheffield United

Third Division
Swansea City v Lincoln City

Saturday, August 31st

First Division
Birmingham City v Barnsley
Bradford City v Tranmere Rovers
Grimsby Town v Portsmouth
Huddersfield T. v Crystal Palace
Manchester City v Charlton Athletic
Norwich City v Wolves
Oldham Athletic v Ipswich Town
Port Vale v Oxford United
Reading v Stoke City
Southend United v Swindon Town

Second Division
Bournemouth v Peterborough Utd.
Blackpool v Wycombe Wand.
Bristol Rovers v Stockport Co.
Bury v Bristol City
Crewe Alexandra v Watford

Gillingham v Chesterfield
Luton Town v Rotherham United
Millwall v Burnley
Notts County v York City
Plymouth Argyle v Preston N.E.
Shrewsbury Town v Brentford
Walsall v Wrexham

Third Division
Brighton & H.A. v Scunthorpe Utd.
Cambridge United v Cardiff City
Colchester Utd. v Hereford United
Doncaster Rov. v Darlington
Fulham v Carlisle United
Hull City v Barnet
Leyton Orient v Hartlepool United
Mansfield Town v Rochdale
Scarborough v Northampton T.
Torquay United v Exeter City
Wigan Athletic v Chester City

Sunday, September 1st
First Division
Q.P.R. v Bolton Wand.

Monday, September 2nd
Premiership
Sheffield Wed. v Leicester City

Tuesday, September 3rd
Premiership
Wimbledon v Tottenham H.

Wednesday, September 4th
Premiership
Arsenal v Chelsea
Blackburn Rovers v Leeds United
Coventry City v Liverpool
Derby County v Manchester Utd.
Everton v Aston Villa
Middlesbrough v West Ham United
Southampton v Nott'm. Forest
Sunderland v Newcastle United

Friday, September 6th
First Division
Wolves v Charlton Athletic

Saturday, September 7th
Premiership
Aston Villa v Arsenal
Leeds United v Manchester Utd.
Liverpool v Southampton
Middlesbrough v Coventry City
Nott'm. Forest v Leicester City
Sheffield Wed. v Chelsea
Tottenham H. v Newcastle United
Wimbledon v Everton

First Division
Bradford City v Norwich City
Grimsby Town v Swindon Town
Ipswich Town v Huddersfield T.
Manchester City v Barnsley
Oldham Athletic v Sheffield United
Portsmouth v Port Vale
Q.P.R. v W.B.A.
Southend United v Bolton Wand.
Stoke City v Crystal Palace
Tranmere Rovers v Birmingham City

Second Division
Bournemouth v Crewe Alexandra
Blackpool v Walsall
Bristol City v Preston N.E.
Bury v Rotherham United
Chesterfield v Brentford
Gillingham v Burnley
Millwall v Bristol Rovers
Plymouth Argyle v Notts County
Watford v Stockport Co.
Wrexham v Peterborough Utd.
Wycombe Wand. v Luton Town
York City v Shrewsbury Town

Third Division
Barnet v Northampton T.
Brighton & H.A. v Scarborough
Cambridge United v Torquay United
Cardiff City v Exeter City
Carlisle United v Swansea City
Chester City v Lincoln City
Doncaster Rov. v Mansfield Town
Fulham v Colchester Utd.
Hereford United v Hartlepool United
Hull City v Rochdale
Leyton Orient v Darlington
Wigan Athletic v Scunthorpe Utd.

Sunday, September 8th
Premiership
Sunderland v West Ham United

First Division
Reading v Oxford United

Monday, September 9th
Premiership
Blackburn Rovers v Derby County

Tuesday, September 10th
First Division
Barnsley v Stoke City
Birmingham City v Oldham Athletic
Bolton Wand. v Grimsby Town
Charlton Athletic v Southend United
Crystal Palace v Ipswich Town
Huddersfield T. v Tranmere Rovers
Oxford United v Wolves
Port Vale v Manchester City

Sheffield United v Bradford City
W.B.A. v Reading

Second Division
Brentford v Plymouth Argyle
Bristol Rovers v Bournemouth
Burnley v Blackpool
Crewe Alexandra v Bury
Luton Town v Gillingham
Notts County v Watford
Peterborough Utd. v Millwall
Preston N.E. v York City
Rotherham United v Chesterfield
Shrewsbury Town v Bristol City
Stockport Co. v Wrexham
Walsall v Wycombe Wand.

Third Division
Colchester Utd. v Brighton & H.A.
Darlington v Wigan Athletic
Exeter City v Fulham
Hartlepool United v Carlisle United
Lincoln City v Hull City
Mansfield Town v Barnet
Northampton T. v Leyton Orient
Rochdale v Chester City
Scarborough v Doncaster Rov.
Scunthorpe Utd. v Cambridge United
Swansea City v Hereford United
Torquay United v Cardiff City

Wednesday, September 11th

First Division
Norwich City v Q.P.R.
Swindon Town v Portsmouth

Friday, September 13th

First Division
Huddersfield T. v Oldham Athletic

Saturday, September 14th

Premiership
Coventry City v Leeds United
Derby County v Sunderland
Everton v Middlesbrough
Manchester Utd. v Nott'm. Forest
Newcastle United v Blackburn Rovers
Southampton v Tottenham H.
West Ham United v Wimbledon

First Division
Barnsley v Q.P.R.
Birmingham City v Stoke City
Bolton Wand. v Portsmouth
Charlton Athletic v Reading
Crystal Palace v Manchester City
Norwich City v Southend United
Oxford United v Bradford City
Port Vale v Grimsby Town
Sheffield United v Ipswich Town
Swindon Town v Tranmere Rovers

Second Division
Brentford v Blackpool
Bristol Rovers v Watford
Burnley v Wycombe Wand.
Crewe Alexandra v Wrexham
Luton Town v Chesterfield
Notts County v Millwall
Peterborough Utd. v York City
Preston N.E. v Bournemouth
Rotherham United v Bristol City
Shrewsbury Town v Bury
Stockport Co. v Plymouth Argyle
Walsall v Gillingham

Third Division
Colchester Utd. v Hull City
Darlington v Hereford United
Exeter City v Brighton & H.A.
Hartlepool United v Wigan Athletic
Lincoln City v Barnet
Mansfield Town v Leyton Orient
Northampton T. v Cambridge United
Rochdale v Doncaster Rov.
Scarborough v Carlisle United
Scunthorpe Utd. v Cardiff City
Swansea City v Fulham
Torquay United v Chester City

Sunday, September 15th

Premiership
Chelsea v Aston Villa
Leicester City v Liverpool

First Division
W.B.A. v Wolves

Monday, September 16th

Premiership
Arsenal v Sheffield Wed.

Friday, September 20th

First Division
Ipswich Town v Charlton Athletic

Saturday, September 21st

Premiership
Aston Villa v Manchester Utd.
Blackburn Rovers v Everton
Leeds United v Newcastle United
Liverpool v Chelsea
Middlesbrough v Arsenal
Nott'm. Forest v West Ham United
Sheffield Wed. v Derby County
Sunderland v Coventry City

First Division
Bradford City v Bolton Wand.
Grimsby Town v Oxford United
Manchester City v Birmingham City
Oldham Athletic v Barnsley

Portsmouth v Norwich City
Q.P.R. v Swindon Town
Reading v Crystal Palace
Southend United v Port Vale
Tranmere Rovers v W.B.A.
Wolves v Sheffield United

Second Division
Bournemouth v Notts County
Blackpool v Shrewsbury Town
Bristol City v Walsall
Bury v Luton Town
Chesterfield v Burnley
Gillingham v Rotherham United
Millwall v Crewe Alexandra
Plymouth Argyle v Bristol Rovers
Watford v Peterborough Utd.
Wrexham v Preston N.E.
Wycombe Wand. v Brentford
York City v Stockport Co.

Third Division
Barnet v Exeter City
Brighton & H.A. v Torquay United
Cambridge United v Scarborough
Cardiff City v Northampton T.
Carlisle United v Darlington
Chester City v Scunthorpe Utd.
Doncaster Rov. v Swansea City
Fulham v Mansfield Town
Hereford United v Rochdale
Hull City v Hartlepool United
Leyton Orient v Colchester Utd.
Wigan Athletic v Lincoln City

Sunday, September 22nd

Premiership
Tottenham H. v Leicester City

First Division
Stoke City v Huddersfield T.

Monday, September 23rd

Premiership
Wimbledon v Southampton

Friday, September 27th

First Division
Swindon Town v Wolves

Saturday, September 28th

Premiership
Arsenal v Sunderland
Chelsea v Nott'm. Forest
Coventry City v Blackburn Rovers
Derby County v Wimbledon
Everton v Sheffield Wed.
Leicester City v Leeds United
Southampton v Middlesbrough

First Division
Barnsley v Grimsby Town
Birmingham City v Q.P.R.
Bolton Wand. v Stoke City
Charlton Athletic v Oldham Athletic
Crystal Palace v Southend United
Huddersfield T. v Reading
Norwich City v Tranmere Rovers
Oxford United v Portsmouth
Sheffield United v Manchester City
W.B.A. v Ipswich Town

Second Division
Brentford v York City
Bristol Rovers v Chesterfield
Burnley v Bristol City
Crewe Alexandra v Plymouth Argyle
Luton Town v Blackpool
Notts County v Wrexham
Peterborough Utd. v Wycombe Wand.
Preston N.E. v Millwall
Rotherham United v Bournemouth
Shrewsbury Town v Watford
Stockport Co. v Gillingham
Walsall v Bury

Third Division
Colchester Utd. v Doncaster Rov.
Darlington v Fulham
Exeter City v Cambridge United
Hartlepool United v Chester City
Lincoln City v Cardiff City
Mansfield Town v Hereford United
Northampton T. v Brighton & H.A.
Rochdale v Leyton orient
Scarborough v Wigan Athletic
Scunthorpe Utd. v Barnet
Swansea City v Hull City
Torquay United v Carlisle United

Sunday, September 29th

Premiership
Manchester Utd. v Tottenham H.
West Ham United v Liverpool

First Division
Port Vale v Bradford City

Monday, September 30th

Premiership
Newcastle United v Aston Villa

Tuesday, October 1st

First Division
Bradford City v Swindon Town
Grimsby Town v Norwich City
Ipswich Town v Barnsley
Oldham Athletic v W.B.A.
Portsmouth v Crystal Palace
Reading v Birmingham City
Southend United v Sheffield United

Stoke City v Charlton Athletic
Tranmere Rovers v Oxford United

Second Division
Bournemouth v Walsall
Bristol City v Brentford
Bury v Burnley
Chesterfield v Shrewsbury Town
Crewe Alexandra v Blackpool
Gillingham v Notts County
Plymouth Argyle v Peterborough Utd.
Watford v Preston N.E.
Wrexham v Luton Town
Wycombe Wand. v Rotherham United
York City v Bristol Rovers

Third Division
Barnet v Scarborough
Brighton & H.A. v Lincoln City
Cambridge United v Darlington
Cardiff City v Rochdale
Carlisle United v Colchester Utd.
Chester City v Northampton T.
Doncaster Rov. v Hartlepool United
Fulham v Torquay United
Hereford United v Scunthorpe Utd.
Hull City v Mansfield Town
Leyton Orient v Swansea City
Wigan Athletic v Exeter City

Wednesday, October 2nd

First Division
Q.P.R. v Port Vale
Wolves v Bolton Wand.

Second Division
Millwall v Stockport Co.

Friday, October 4th

First Division
Stoke City v Norwich City

Second Division
Wrexham v Shrewsbury Town

Third Division
Swansea City v Colchester Utd.

Saturday, October 5th

First Division
Bradford City v Southend United
Charlton Athletic v Barnsley
Grimsby Town v Q.P.R.
Huddersfield T. v Birmingham City
Ipswich Town v Swindon Town
Manchester City v W.B.A.
Oldham Athletic v Port Vale
Oxford United v Bolton Wand.
Tranmere Rovers v Portsmouth
Wolves v Reading

Second Division
Brentford v Rotherham United
Bristol Rovers v Crewe Alexandra
Burnley v Stockport Co.
Bury v Blackpool
Chesterfield v Bristol City
Gillingham v Bournemouth
Luton Town v Walsall
Plymouth Argyle v Millwall
Preston N.E. v Peterborough Utd.
Wycombe Wand. v Notts County
York City v Watford

Third Division
Barnet v Torquay United
Cambridge United v Hartlepool United
Carlisle United v Mansfield Town
Chester City v Cardiff City
Darlington v Rochdale
Doncaster Rov. v Leyton Orient
Hereford United v Scarborough
Hull City v Scunthorpe Utd.
Lincoln City v Exeter City
Northampton T. v Fulham
Wigan Athletic v Brighton & H.A.

Sunday, October 6th

First Division
Crystal Palace v Sheffield United

Friday, October 11th

First Division
Norwich City v Ipswich Town

Second Division
Bristol City v York City

Saturday, October 12th

Premiership
Blackburn Rovers v Arsenal
Derby County v Newcastle United
Everton v West Ham United
Leeds United v Nott'm. Forest
Leicester City v Chelsea
Manchester Utd. v Liverpool
Tottenham H. v Aston Villa
Wimbledon v Sheffield Wed.

First Division
Barnsley v Crystal Palace
Birmingham City v Bradford City
Bolton Wand. v Oldham Athletic
Port Vale v Stoke City
Portsmouth v Charlton Athletic
Q.P.R. v Manchester City
Reading v Grimsby Town
Sheffield United v Tranmere Rovers
Swindon Town v Oxford United
W.B.A. v Huddersfield T.

Second Division
Bournemouth v Wycombe Wand.
Blackpool v Gillingham
Crewe Alexandra v Brentford
Millwall v Chesterfield
Notts County v Bristol Rovers
Peterborough Utd. v Bury
Rotherham United v Burnley
Shrewsbury Town v Luton Town
Stockport Co. v Preston N.E.
Walsall v Plymouth Argyle
Watford v Wrexham

Third Division
Brighton & H.A. v Cambridge United
Cardiff City v Barnet
Colchester Utd. v Wigan Athletic
Exeter City v Northampton T.
Fulham v Doncaster Rov.
Hartlepool United v Darlington
Leyton Orient v Hull City
Mansfield Town v Swansea City
Rochdale v Carlisle United
Scarborough v Chester City
Scunthorpe Utd. v Lincoln City
Torquay United v Hereford United

Sunday, October 13th

Premiership
Coventry City v Southampton

First Division
Southend United v Wolves

Monday, October 14th

Premiership
Sunderland v Middlesbrough

Tuesday, October 15th

First Division
Barnsley v Oxford United
Birmingham City v Ipswich Town
Bolton Wand. v Tranmere Rovers
Port Vale v Crystal Palace
Portsmouth v Wolves
Reading v Manchester City
Sheffield United v Charlton Athletic
Southend United v Grimsby Town

Second Division
Bournemouth v Plymouth Argyle
Blackpool v Wrexham
Bristol City v Wycombe Wand.
Crewe Alexandra v York City
Notts County v Chesterfield
Peterborough Utd. v Brentford
Rotherham United v Bristol Rovers
Shrewsbury Town v Gillingham
Stockport Co. v Luton Town
Walsall v Preston N.E.
Watford v Burnley

Third Division
Brighton & H.A. v Hereford United
Cardiff City v Darlington
Colchester Utd. v Barnet
Exeter City v Carlisle United
Fulham v Cambridge United
Hartlepool United v Swansea City
Leyton Orient v Chester City
Mansfield Town v Wigan Athletic
Rochdale v Lincoln City
Scarborough v Hull City
Scunthorpe Utd. v Northampton T.
Torquay United v Doncaster Rov.

Wednesday, October 16th

First Division
Norwich City v Oldham Athletic
Q.P.R. v Bradford City
Swindon Town v Huddersfield T.
W.B.A. v Stoke City

Second Division
Millwall v Bury

Friday, October 18th

First Division
Oxford United v Birmingham City

Saturday, October 19th

Premiership
Arsenal v Coventry City
Aston Villa v Leeds United
Chelsea v Wimbledon
Middlesbrough v Tottenham H.
Nott'm. Forest v Derby County
Sheffield Wed. v Blackburn Rovers
Southampton v Sunderland
West Ham United v Leicester City

First Division
Bradford City v Barnsley
Charlton Athletic v Bolton Wand.
Crystal Palace v Swindon Town
Grimsby Town v W.B.A.
Huddersfield T. v Southend United
Ipswich Town v Portsmouth
Manchester City v Norwich City
Oldham Athletic v Reading
Stoke City v Sheffield United
Wolves v Port Vale

Second Division
Brentford v Walsall
Bristol Rovers v Blackpool
Burnley v Notts County
Bury v Watford
Chesterfield v Crewe Alexandra
Gillingham v Millwall
Luton Town v Peterborough Utd.
Plymouth Argyle v Bristol City
Preston N.E. v Shrewsbury Town

Wrexham v Bournemouth
Wycombe Wand. v Stockport Co.
York City v Rotherham United

Third Division
Barnet v Hartlepool United
Cambridge United v Rochdale
Carlisle United v Cardiff City
Chester City v Exeter City
Darlington v Mansfield Town
Doncaster Rov. v Brighton & H.A.
Hereford United v Leyton Orient
Hull City v Fulham
Lincoln City v Scarborough
Northampton T. v Colchester Utd.
Swansea City v Scunthorpe Utd.
Wigan Athletic v Torquay United

Sunday, October 20th

Premiership
Liverpool v Everton
Newcastle United v Manchester Utd.

First Division
Tranmere Rovers v Q.P.R.

Friday, October 25th

First Division
Barnsley v Bolton Wand.

Third Division
Cambridge United v Doncaster Rov.

Saturday, October 26th

Premiership
Arsenal v Leeds United
Chelsea v Tottenham H.
Coventry City v Sheffield Wed.
Leicester City v Newcastle United
Middlesbrough v Wimbledon
Southampton v Manchester Utd.
Sunderland v Aston Villa
West Ham United v Blackburn Rovers

First Division
Birmingham City v Norwich City
Charlton Athletic v Oxford United
Crystal Palace v Grimsby Town
Huddersfield T. v Port Vale
Ipswich Town v Tranmere Rovers
Oldham Athletic v Southend United
Reading v Swindon Town
Sheffield United v Q.P.R.
Stoke City v Portsmouth
W.B.A. v Bradford City

Second Division
Blackpool v Watford
Brentford v Millwall
Bristol City v Notts County
Burnley v Plymouth Argyle
Bury v Bristol Rovers
Chesterfield v York City
Gillingham v Preston N.E.
Luton Town v Bournemouth
Rotherham Utd. v Peterborough Utd.
Shrewsbury Town v Crewe Alexandra
Walsall v Stockport Co.
Wycombe Wand. v Wrexham

Third Division
Barnet v Carlisle United
Brighton & H.A. v Fulham
Cardiff City v Leyton Orient
Chester City v Hereford United
Exeter City v Hartlepool United
Lincoln City v Colchester Utd.
Northampton T. v Darlington
Scarborough v Mansfield Town
Scunthorpe Utd. v Rochdale
Torquay United v Swansea City
Wigan Athletic v Hull City

Sunday, October 27th

Premiership
Liverpool v Derby County

First Division
Manchester City v Wolves

Monday, October 28th

Premiership
Nott'm. Forest v Everton

Tuesday, October 29th

First Division
Bolton Wand. v Reading
Bradford City v Crystal Palace
Grimsby Town v Oldham Athletic
Oxford United v Stoke City
Port Vale v Barnsley
Portsmouth v Birmingham City
Southend United v Manchester City
Tranmere Rovers v Charlton Athletic

Second Division
Bournemouth v Bristol City
Bristol Rovers v Brentford
Crewe Alexandra v Rotherham United
Notts County v Walsall
Peterborough Utd. v Shrewsbury Town
Plymouth Argyle v Gillingham
Preston N.E. v Burnley
Stockport Co. v Chesterfield
Watford v Luton Town
Wrexham v Bury
York City v Wycombe Wand.

Third Division
Carlisle United v Chester City
Colchester Utd. v Exeter City
Darlington v Barnet

Doncaster Rov. v Lincoln City
Fulham v Scunthorpe Utd.
Hartlepool United v Northampton T.
Hereford United v Cambridge United
Hull City v Cardiff City
Leyton Orient v Scarborough
Mansfield Town v Torquay United
Rochdale v Brighton & H.A.
Swansea City v Wigan Athletic

Wednesday, October 30th

First Division
Norwich City v Sheffield United
Q.P.R. v Ipswich Town
Swindon Town v W.B.A.
Wolves v Huddersfield T.

Second Division
Millwall v Blackpool

Saturday, November 2nd

Premiership
Aston Villa v Nott'm. Forest
Derby County v Leicester City
Leeds United v Sunderland
Manchester Utd. v Chelsea
Sheffield Wed. v Southampton
Tottenham H. v West Ham United
Wimbledon v Arsenal

First Division
Bolton Wand. v Huddersfield T.
Bradford City v Oldham Athletic
Norwich City v Charlton Athletic
Oxford United v Ipswich Town
Port Vale v Birmingham City
Portsmouth v W.B.A.
Q.P.R. v Stoke City
Southend United v Reading
Swindon Town v Manchester City
Tranmere Rovers v Crystal Palace
Wolves v Barnsley

Second Division
Bournemouth v Bury
Bristol Rovers v Gillingham
Crewe Alexandra v Wycombe Wand.
Millwall v Walsall
Notts County v Shrewsbury Town
Peterborough Utd. v Blackpool
Plymouth Argyle v Luton Town
Preston N.E. v Rotherham United
Stockport Co. v Bristol City
Watford v Brentford
Wrexham v Chesterfield
York City v Burnley

Third Division
Carlisle United v Wigan Athletic
Colchester Utd. v Cardiff City
Darlington v Scarborough

Doncaster Rov. v Chester City
Fulham v Lincoln City
Hartlepool United v Brighton & H.A.
Hereford United v Barnet
Hull City v Cambridge United
Leyton Orient v Torquay United
Mansfield Town v Scunthorpe Utd.
Rochdale v Exeter City
Swansea City v Northampton T.

Sunday, November 3rd

Premiership
Blackburn Rovers v Liverpool
Newcastle United v Middlesbrough

First Division
Grimsby Town v Sheffield United

Monday, November 4th

Premiership
Everton v Coventry City

Friday, November 8th

First Division
Huddersfield T. v Bradford City

Saturday, November 9th

First Division
Barnsley v Norwich City
Birmingham City v Bolton Wand.
Charlton Athletic v Grimsby Town
Ipswich Town v Southend United
Manchester City v Oxford United
Oldham Athletic v Portsmouth
Reading v Tranmere Rovers
Sheffield United v Swindon Town
Stoke City v Wolves
W.B.A. v Port Vale

Second Division
Blackpool v Bournemouth
Brentford v Stockport Co.
Bristol City v Millwall
Burnley v Crewe Alexandra
Bury v York City
Chesterfield v Preston N.E.
Gillingham v Wrexham
Luton Town v Notts County
Rotherham United v Watford
Shrewsbury Town v Bristol Rovers
Walsall v Peterborough Utd.
Wycombe Wand. v Plymouth Argyle

Third Division
Barnet v Rochdale
Brighton & H.A. v Mansfield Town
Cambridge United v Swansea City
Cardiff City v Fulham
Chester City v Hull City
Exeter City v Leyton Orient

Lincoln City v Darlington
Northampton T. v Carlisle United
Scarborough v Hartlepool United
Scunthorpe Utd. v Doncaster Rov.
Torquay United v Colchester Utd.
Wigan Athletic v Hereford United

Sunday, November 10th

First Division
Crystal Palace v Q.P.R.

Friday, November 15th

First Division
Tranmere Rovers v Oldham Athletic

Saturday, November 16th

Premiership
Aston Villa v Leicester City
Blackburn Rovers v Chelsea
Everton v Southampton
Leeds United v Liverpool
Manchester Utd. v Arsenal
Newcastle United v West Ham United
Tottenham H. v Sunderland
Wimbledon v Coventry City

First Division
Bolton Wand. v Crystal Palace
Bradford City v Ipswich Town
Grimsby Town v Stoke City
Norwich City v Reading
Oxford United v Huddersfield T.
Port Vale v Sheffield United
Portsmouth v Manchester City
Q.P.R. v Charlton Athletic
Southend United v W.B.A.
Swindon Town v Barnsley
Wolves v Birmingham City

Sunday, November 17th

Premiership
Derby County v Middlesbrough

Monday, November 18th

Premiership
Sheffield Wed. v Nott'm. Forest

Tuesday, November 19th

Second Division
Bournemouth v Brentford
Bristol Rovers v Burnley
Crewe Alexandra v Bristol City
Notts County v Bury
Peterborough Utd. v Gillingham
Plymouth Argyle v Chesterfield
Preston N.E. v Luton Town
Stockport v Blackpool
Watford v Wycombe Wand.
Wrexham v Rotherham United
York City v Walsall

Third Division
Carlisle United v Cambridge United
Colchester Utd. v Scunthorpe Utd.
Darlington v Exeter City
Doncaster Rov. v Northampton T.
Fulham v Barnet
Hartlepool United v Cardiff City
Hereford United v Lincoln City
Hull City v Torquay United
Leyton orient v Wigan Athletic
Mansfield Town v Chester City
Rochdale v Scarborough
Swansea City v Brighton & H.A.

Wednesday, November 20th

First Division
Manchester City v Huddersfield T.

Second Division
Millwall v Shrewsbury Town

Friday, November 22nd

Third Division
Chester City v Colchester Utd.

Saturday, November 23rd

Premiership
Chelsea v Newcastle United
Coventry City v Aston Villa
Leicester City v Everton
Liverpool v Wimbledon
Middlesbrough v Manchester Utd.
Nott'm. Forest v Blackburn Rovers
Southampton v Leeds United
Sunderland v Sheffield Wed.
West Ham United v Derby County

First Division
Barnsley v Portsmouth
Birmingham City v Swindon Town
Charlton Athletic v Bradford City
Crystal Palace v Wolves
Huddersfield T. v Grimsby Town
Ipswich Town v Port Vale
Manchester City v Tranmere Rovers
Oldham Athletic v Oxford United
Reading v Q.P.R.
Sheffield United v Bolton Wand.
Stoke City v Southend United
W.B.A. v Norwich City

Second Division
Blackpool v Notts County
Brentford v Wrexham
Bristol City v Peterborough Utd.
Burnley v Bournemouth
Bury v Plymouth Argyle
Chesterfield v Watford
Gillingham v York City

Luton Town v Bristol Rovers
Rotherham United v Millwall
Shrewsbury Town v Stockport Co.
Walsall v Crewe Alexandra
Wycombe Wand. v Preston N.E.

Third Division
Barnet v Doncaster Rov.
Brighton & H.A. v Carlisle United
Cambridge United v Leyton Orient
Cardiff City v Hereford United
Exeter City v Hull City
Lincoln City v Mansfield Town
Northampton T. v Rochdale
Scarborough v Swansea City
Scunthorpe Utd. v Darlington
Torquay United v Hartlepool United
Wigan Athletic v Fulham

Sunday, November 24th
Premiership
Arsenal v Tottenham H.

Saturday, November 30th
Premiership
Aston Villa v Middlesbrough
Blackburn Rovers v Southampton
Derby County v Coventry City
Everton v Sunderland
Manchester Utd. v Leicester City
Newcastle United v Arsenal
Sheffield Wed. v West Ham United
Wimbledon v Nott'm. Forest

First Division
Bolton Wand. v Barnsley
Bradford City v W.B.A.
Grimsby Town v Crystal Palace
Norwich City v Birmingham City
Oxford United v Charlton Athletic
Port Vale v Huddersfield T.
Portsmouth v Stoke City
Q.P.R. v Sheffield United
Southend United v Oldham Athletic
Swindon Town v Reading
Tranmere Rovers v Ipswich Town
Wolves v Manchester City

Second Division
Bournemouth v Luton Town
Bristol Rovers v Bury
Millwall v Brentford
Notts County v Bristol City
Peterborough Utd. v Rotherham Utd.
Plymouth Argyle v Burnley
Preston N.E. v Gillingham
Stockport Co. v Walsall
Watford v Blackpool
Wrexham v Wycombe Wand.
York City v Chesterfield

Third Division
Carlisle United v Barnet
Colchester Utd. v Lincoln City
Darlington v Northampton T.
Doncaster Rov. v Cambridge United
Fulham v Brighton & H.A.
Hartlepool United v Exeter City
Hereford United v Chester City
Hull City v Wigan Athletic
Leyton Orient v Cardiff City
Mansfield Town v Scarborough
Rochdale v Scunthorpe Utd.
Swansea City v Torquay United

Sunday, December 1st
Premiership
Leeds United v Chelsea

Monday, December 2nd
Premiership
Tottenham H. v Liverpool

Tuesday, December 3rd
Second Division
Blackpool v Plymouth Argyle
Brentford v Notts County
Bristol City v Watford
Burnley v Wrexham
Bury v Preston N.E.
Chesterfield v Peterborough Utd.
Gillingham v Crewe Alexandra
Luton Town v York City
Rotherham United v Stockport Co.
Shrewsbury Town v Bournemouth
Walsall v Bristol Rovers
Wycombe Wand. v Millwall

Third Division
Barnet v Leyton Orient
Brighton & H.A. v Darlington
Cambridge United v Mansfield Town
Cardiff City v Swansea City
Chester City v Fulham
Exeter City v Hereford United
Lincoln City v Carlisle United
Northampton T. v Hull City
Scarborough v Colchester Utd.
Scunthorpe Utd. v Hartlepool United
Torquay United v Rochdale
Wigan Athletic v Doncaster Rov.

Saturday, December 7th
Premiership
Arsenal v Derby County
Chelsea v Everton
Coventry City v Tottenham H.
Leicester City v Blackburn Rovers
Liverpool v Sheffield Wed.
Middlesbrough v Leeds United
Southampton v Aston Villa

Sunderland v Wimbledon

First Division
Barnsley v Southend United
Birmingham City v Grimsby Town
Charlton Athletic v Swindon Town
Crystal Palace v Oxford United
Huddersfield T. v Norwich City
Ipswich Town v Wolves
Manchester City v Bradford City
Oldham Athletic v Q.P.R.
Reading v Port Vale
Sheffield United v Portsmouth
Stoke City v Tranmere Rovers
W.B.A. v Bolton Wand.

Sunday, December 8th

Premiership
West Ham United v Manchester Utd.

Monday, December 9th

Premiership
Nott'm. Forest v Newcastle United

Friday, December 13th

Second Division
Preston N.E. v Blackpool

Third Division
Doncaster Rov. v Cardiff City
Swansea City v Barnet

Saturday, December 14th

Premiership
Arsenal v Southampton
Coventry City v Newcastle United
Derby County v Everton
Leeds United v Tottenham H.
Liverpool v Nott'm. Forest
Middlesbrough v Leicester City
Sheffield Wed. v Manchester Utd.
West Ham United v Aston Villa
Wimbledon v Blackburn Rovers

First Division
Barnsley v Tranmere Rovers
Birmingham City v W.B.A.
Bolton Wand. v Ipswich Town
Bradford City v Reading
Charlton Athletic v Port Vale
Manchester City v Grimsby Town
Norwich City v Crystal Palace
Oxford United v Sheffield United
Portsmouth v Huddersfield T.
Q.P.R. v Southend United
Stoke City v Swindon Town
Wolves v Oldham Athletic

Second Division
Bournemouth v Millwall
Burnley v Brentford
Gillingham v Bury
Luton Town v Crewe Alexandra
Notts County v Rotherham United
Plymouth Argyle v Shrewsbury Town
Stockport Co. v Peterborough Utd.
Walsall v Watford
Wycombe Wand. v Chesterfield
York City v Wrexham

Third Division
Brighton & H.A. v Hull City
Cambridge United v Wigan Athletic
Chester City v Darlington
Fulham v Leyton Orient
Hereford United v Carlisle United
Lincoln City v Northampton T.
Mansfield Town v Colchester Utd.
Rochdale v Hartlepool United
Scunthorpe Utd. v Exeter City
Torquay United v Scarborough

Sunday, December 15th

Premiership
Sunderland v Chelsea

Second Division
Bristol City v Bristol Rovers

Wednesday, December 18th

Second Division
Millwall v Luton Town

Friday, December 20th

Second Division
Crewe Alexandra v Notts County
Peterborough Utd. v Burnley

Third Division
Colchester Utd. v Cambridge United
Northampton T. v Hereford United

Saturday, December 21st

Premiership
Blackburn Rovers v Middlesbrough
Chelsea v West Ham United
Everton v Leeds United
Leicester City v Coventry City
Manchester Utd. v Sunderland
Nott'm. Forest v Arsenal
Southampton v Derby County
Tottenham H. v Sheffield Wed.

First Division
Crystal Palace v Charlton Athletic
Grimsby Town v Bradford City
Huddersfield T. v Q.P.R.
Ipswich Town v Stoke City
Oldham Athletic v Manchester City
Port Vale v Norwich City
Reading v Portsmouth
Sheffield United v Barnsley

Southend United v Birmingham City
Swindon Town v Bolton Wand.
Tranmere Rovers v Wolves
W.B.A. v Oxford United

Second Division
Blackpool v York City
Brentford v Preston N.E.
Bristol Rovers v Wycombe Wand.
Bury v Stockport Co.
Chesterfield v Bournemouth
Rotherham United v Plymouth Argyle
Shrewsbury Town v Walsall
Watford v Gillingham
Wrexham v Bristol City

Third Division
Barnet v Chester City
Cardiff City v Mansfield Town
Carlisle United v Scunthorpe Utd.
Darlington v Torquay United
Exeter City v Swansea City
Hartlepool United v Lincoln City
Hull City v Doncaster Rov.
Scarborough v Fulham
Wigan Athletic v Rochdale

Sunday, December 22nd

Premiership
Aston Villa v Wimbledon

Third Division
Leyton Orient v Brighton & H.A.

Monday, December 23rd

Premiership
Newcastle United v Liverpool

Thursday, December 26th

Premiership
Aston Villa v Chelsea
Blackburn Rovers v Newcastle United
Leeds United v Coventry City
Liverpool v Leicester City
Middlesbrough v Everton
Nott'm. Forest v Manchester Utd.
Sheffield Wed. v Arsenal
Sunderland v Derby County
Tottenham H. v Southampton
Wimbledon v West Ham United

First Division
Bradford City v Sheffield United
Grimsby Town v Bolton Wand.
Ipswich Town v Crystal Palace
Manchester City v Port Vale
Oldham Athletic v Birmingham City
Portsmouth v Swindon Town
Q.P.R. v Norwich City
Reading v W.B.A.
Southend United v Charlton Athletic
Stoke City v Barnsley
Tranmere Rovers v Huddersfield T.
Wolves v Oxford United

Second Division
Bournemouth v Bristol Rovers
Blackpool v Burnley
Bristol City v Shrewsbury Town
Bury v Crewe Alexandra
Chesterfield v Rotherham United
Gillingham v Luton Town
Millwall v Peterborough Utd.
Plymouth Argyle v Brentford
Watford v Notts County
Wrexham v Stockport Co.
Wycombe Wand. v Walsall
York City v Preston N.E.

Third Division
Barnet v Mansfield Town
Brighton & H.A. v Colchester Utd.
Cambridge United v Scunthorpe Utd.
Cardiff City v Torquay United
Carlisle United v Hartlepool United
Chester City v Rochdale
Doncaster Rov. v Scarborough
Fulham v Exeter City
Hereford United v Swansea City
Hull City v Lincoln City
Leyton Orient v Northampton T.
Wigan Athletic v Darlington

Saturday, December 28th

Premiership
Arsenal v Aston Villa
Chelsea v Sheffield Wed.
Coventry City v Middlesbrough
Derby County v Blackburn Rovers
Everton v Wimbledon
Leicester City v Nott'm. Forest
Manchester Utd. v Leeds United
Newcastle United v Tottenham H.
Southampton v Liverpool
West Ham United v Sunderland

First Division
Barnsley v Manchester City
Birmingham City v Tranmere Rovers
Bolton Wand. v Southend United
Charlton Athletic v Wolves
Crystal Palace v Stoke City
Huddersfield T. v Ipswich Town
Norwich City v Bradford City
Oxford United v Reading
Port Vale v Portsmouth
Sheffield United v Oldham Athletic
Swindon Town v Grimsby Town
W.B.A. v Q.P.R.

Second Division
Brentford v Chesterfield
Bristol Rovers v Millwall

Burnley v Gillingham
Crewe Alexandra v Bournemouth
Luton Town v Wycombe Wand.
Notts County v Plymouth Argyle
Peterborough Utd. v Wrexham
Preston N.E. v Bristol City
Rotherham United v Bury
Shrewsbury Town v York City
Stockport Co. v Watford
Walsall v Blackpool

Third Division
Colchester Utd. v Fulham
Darlington v Leyton Orient
Exeter City v Cardiff City
Hartlepool United v Hereford United
Lincoln City v Chester City
Mansfield Town v Doncaster Rov.
Northampton T. v Barnet
Rochdale v Hull City
Scarborough v Brighton & H.A.
Scunthorpe Utd. v Wigan Athletic
Swansea City v Carlisle United
Torquay United v Cambridge United

Wednesday, January 1st, 1997

Premiership
Arsenal v Middlesbrough
Chelsea v Liverpool
Coventry City v Sunderland
Derby County v Sheffield Wed.
Everton v Blackburn Rovers
Leicester City v Tottenham H.
Manchester Utd. v Aston Villa
Newcastle United v Leeds United
Southampton v Wimbledon
West Ham United v Nott'm. Forest

First Division
Barnsley v Oldham Athletic
Birmingham City v Manchester City
Bolton Wand. v Bradford City
Charlton Athletic v Ipswich Town
Crystal Palace v Reading
Huddersfield T. v Stoke City
Norwich City v Portsmouth
Oxford United v Grimsby Town
Port Vale v Southend United
Sheffield United v Wolves
Swindon Town v Q.P.R.
W.B.A. v Tranmere Rovers

Second Division
Brentford v Wycombe Wand.
Bristol Rovers v Plymouth Argyle
Burnley v Chesterfield
Crewe Alexandra v Millwall
Luton Town v Bury
Notts County v Bournemouth
Peterborough Utd. v Watford
Preston N.E. v Wrexham
Rotherham United v Gillingham
Shrewsbury Town v Blackpool
Stockport Co. v York City
Walsall v Bristol City

Third Division
Colchester Utd. v Leyton Orient
Darlington v Carlisle United
Exeter City v Barnet
Hartlepool United v Hull City
Lincoln City v Wigan Athletic
Mansfield Town v Fulham
Northampton T. v Cardiff City
Rochdale v Hereford United
Scarborough v Cambridge United
Scunthorpe Utd. v Chester City
Swansea City v Doncaster Rov.
Torquay United v Brighton & H.A.

Saturday, January 4th

Second Division
Bournemouth v Preston N.E.
Blackpool v Brentford
Bristol City v Rotherham United
Bury v Shrewsbury Town
Chesterfield v Luton Town
Gillingham v Walsall
Millwall v Notts County
Plymouth Argyle v Stockport Co.
Watford v Bristol Rovers
Wrexham v Crewe Alexandra
Wycombe Wand. v Burnley
York City v Peterborough Utd.

Third Division
Barnet v Lincoln City
Brighton & H.A. v Exeter City
Cambridge United v Northampton T.
Cardiff City v Scunthorpe Utd.
Carlisle United v Scarborough
Chester City v Torquay United
Doncaster Rov. v Rochdale
Fulham v Swansea City
Hereford United v Darlington
Hull City v Colchester Utd.
Leyton Orient v Mansfield Town
Wigan Athletic v Hartlepool United

Friday, January 10th

First Division
Tranmere Rovers v Swindon Town

Saturday, January 11th

Premiership
Aston Villa v Newcastle United
Blackburn Rovers v Coventry City
Leeds United v Leicester City
Liverpool v West Ham United
Middlesbrough v Southampton
Nott'm. Forest v Chelsea

Sheffield Wed. v Everton
Sunderland v Arsenal
Tottenham H. v Manchester Utd.
Wimbledon v Derby County

First Division
Bradford City v Oxford United
Grimsby Town v Port Vale
Ipswich Town v Sheffield United
Manchester City v Crystal Palace
Oldham Athletic v Huddersfield T.
Portsmouth v Bolton Wand.
Q.P.R. v Barnsley
Reading v Charlton Athletic
Southend United v Norwich City
Stoke City v Birmingham City
Wolves v W.B.A.

Second Division
Bournemouth v Rotherham United
Blackpool v Luton Town
Bristol City v Burnley
Bury v Walsall
Chesterfield v Bristol Rovers
Gillingham v Stockport Co.
Millwall v Preston N.E.
Plymouth Argyle v Crewe Alexandra
Watford v Shrewsbury Town
Wrexham v Notts County
Wycombe Wand. v Peterborough Utd.
York City v Brentford

Third Division
Barnet v Scunthorpe Utd.
Brighton & H.A. v Northampton T.
Cambridge United v Exeter City
Cardiff City v Lincoln City
Carlisle United v Torquay United
Chester City v Hartlepool United
Doncaster Rov. v Colchester Utd.
Fulham v Darlington
Hereford United v Mansfield Town
Hull City v Swansea City
Leyton Orient v Rochdale
Wigan Athletic v Scarborough

Saturday, January 18th

Premiership
Arsenal v Everton
Chelsea v Derby County
Coventry City v Manchester Utd.
Leicester City v Wimbledon
Liverpool v Aston Villa
Middlesbrough v Sheffield Wed.
Nott'm. Forest v Tottenham H.
Southampton v Newcastle United
Sunderland v Blackburn Rovers
West Ham United v Leeds United

First Division
Barnsley v Ipswich Town
Birmingham City v Reading
Bolton Wand. v Wolves
Charlton Athletic v Stoke City
Crystal Palace v Portsmouth
Huddersfield T. v Manchester City
Norwich City v Grimsby Town
Oxford United v Tranmere Rovers
Port Vale v Q.P.R.
Sheffield United v Southend United
Swindon Town v Bradford City
W.B.A. v Oldham Athletic

Second Division
Blackpool v Crewe Alexandra
Brentford v Bristol City
Bristol Rovers v York City
Burnley v Bury
Luton Town v Wrexham
Notts County v Gillingham
Peterborough Utd. v Plymouth Argyle
Preston N.E. v Watford
Rotherham United v Wycombe Wand.
Shrewsbury Town v Chesterfield
Stockport Co. v Millwall
Walsall v Bournemouth

Third Division
Colchester Utd. v Carlisle United
Darlington v Cambridge United
Exeter City v Wigan Athletic
Hartlepool United v Doncaster Rov.
Lincoln City v Brighton & H.A.
Mansfield Town v Hull City
Northampton T. v Chester City
Rochdale v Cardiff City
Scarborough v Barnet
Scunthorpe Utd. v Hereford United
Swansea City v Leyton Orient
Torquay United v Fulham

Saturday, January 25th

Second Division
Blackpool v Millwall
Brentford v Bristol Rovers
Bristol City v Bournemouth
Burnley v Preston N.E.
Bury v Wrexham
Chesterfield v Stockport Co.
Gillingham v Plymouth Argyle
Luton Town v Watford
Rotherham United v Crewe Alexandra
Shrewsbury Town v Peterborough Utd.
Walsall v Notts County
Wycombe Wand. v York City

Third Division
Barnet v Darlington
Brighton & H.A. v Rochdale
Cambridge United v Hereford United
Cardiff City v Hull City
Chester City v Carlisle United
Exeter City v Colchester Utd.

Lincoln City v Doncaster Rov.
Northampton T. v Hartlepool United
Scarborough v Leyton Orient
Scunthorpe Utd. v Fulham
Torquay United v Mansfield Town
Wigan Athletic v Swansea City

Tuesday, January 28th

First Division
Bradford City v Port Vale
Grimsby Town v Barnsley
Ipswich Town v W.B.A.
Oldham Athletic v Charlton Athletic
Portsmouth v Oxford United
Reading v Huddersfield T.
Southend United v Crystal Palace
Tranmere Rovers v Norwich City

Wednesday, January 29th

First Division
Manchester City v Sheffield United
Q.P.R. v Birmingham City
Stoke City v Bolton Wand.
Wolves v Swindon Town

Friday, January 31st

Third Division
Colchester Utd. v Torquay United
Swansea City v Cambridge United

Saturday, February 1st

Premiership
Aston Villa v Sunderland
Blackburn Rovers v West Ham United
Derby County v Liverpool
Everton v Nott'm. Forest
Leeds United v Arsenal
Manchester Utd. v Southampton
Newcastle United v Leicester City
Sheffield Wed. v Coventry City
Tottenham H. v Chelsea
Wimbledon v Middlesbrough

First Division
Bolton Wand. v Birmingham City
Bradford City v Huddersfield T.
Grimsby Town v Charlton Athletic
Norwich City v Barnsley
Oxford United v Manchester City
Port Vale v W.B.A.
Portsmouth v Oldham Athletic
Q.P.R. v Crystal Palace
Southend United v Ipswich Town
Swindon Town v Sheffield United
Tranmere Rovers v Reading
Wolves v Stoke City

Second Division
Bournemouth v Blackpool
Bristol Rovers v Shrewsbury Town
Crewe Alexandra v Burnley
Millwall v Bristol City
Notts County v Luton Town
Peterborough Utd. v Walsall
Plymouth Argyle v Wycombe Wand.
Preston N.E. v Chesterfield
Stockport Co. v Brentford
Watford v Rotherham United
Wrexham v Gillingham
York City v Bury

Third Division
Carlisle United v Northampton T.
Darlington v Lincoln City
Doncaster Rov. v Scunthorpe Utd.
Fulham v Cardiff City
Hartlepool United v Scarborough
Hereford United v Wigan Athletic
Hull City v Chester City
Leyton Orient v Exeter City
Mansfield Town v Brighton & H.A.
Rochdale v Barnet

Saturday, February 8th

First Division
Barnsley v Port Vale
Birmingham City v Portsmouth
Charlton Athletic v Tranmere Rovers
Crystal Palace v Bradford City
Huddersfield T. v Wolves
Ipswich Town v Q.P.R.
Manchester City v Southend United
Oldham Athletic v Grimsby Town
Reading v Bolton Wand.
Sheffield United v Norwich City
Stoke City v Oxford United
W.B.A. v Swindon Town

Second Division
Blackpool v Peterborough Utd.
Brentford v Watford
Bristol City v Stockport Co.
Burnley v York City
Bury v Bournemouth
Chesterfield v Wrexham
Gillingham v Bristol Rovers
Luton Town v Plymouth Argyle
Rotherham United v Preston N.E.
Shrewsbury Town v Notts County
Walsall v Millwall
Wycombe Wand. v Crewe Alexandra

Third Division
Barnet v Hereford United
Brighton & H.A. v Hartlepool United
Cambridge United v Hull City
Cardiff City v Colchester Utd.
Chester City v Doncaster Rov.
Exeter City v Rochdale
Lincoln City v Fulham
Northampton T. v Swansea City

Scarborough v Darlington
Scunthorpe Utd. v Mansfield Town
Torquay United v Leyton Orient
Wigan Athletic v Carlisle United

Friday, February 14th

Third Division
Colchester Utd. v Chester City

Saturday, February 15th

Premiership
Aston Villa v Coventry City
Blackburn Rovers v Nott'm. Forest
Derby County v West Ham United
Everton v Leicester City
Leeds United v Southampton
Manchester Utd. v Middlesbrough
Newcastle United v Chelsea
Sheffield Wed. v Sunderland
Tottenham H. v Arsenal
Wimbledon v Liverpool

First Division
Bolton Wand. v Sheffield United
Bradford City v Charlton Athletic
Grimsby Town v Huddersfield T.
Norwich City v W.B.A.
Oxford United v Oldham Athletic
Port Vale v Ipswich Town
Portsmouth v Barnsley
Q.P.R. v Reading
Southend United v Stoke City
Swindon Town v Birmingham City
Tranmere Rovers v Manchester City
Wolves v Crystal Palace

Second Division
Bournemouth v Burnley
Bristol Rovers v Luton Town
Crewe Alexandra v Walsall
Millwall v Rotherham United
Notts County v Blackpool
Peterborough Utd. v Bristol City
Plymouth Argyle v Bury
Preston N.E. v Wycombe Wand.
Stockport Co. v Shrewsbury Town
Watford v Chesterfield
Wrexham v Brentford
York City v Gillingham

Third Division
Carlisle United v Brighton & H.A.
Darlington v Scunthorpe Utd.
Doncaster Rov. v Barnet
Fulham v Wigan Athletic
Hartlepool United v Torquay United
Hereford United v Cardiff City
Hull City v Exeter City
Leyton Orient v Cambridge United
Mansfield Town v Lincoln City
Rochdale v Northampton T.

Swansea City v Scarborough

Saturday, February 22nd

Premiership
Arsenal v Wimbledon
Chelsea v Manchester Utd.
Coventry City v Everton
Leicester City v Derby County
Liverpool v Blackburn Rovers
Middlesbrough v Newcastle United
Nott'm. Forest v Aston Villa
Southampton v Sheffield Wed.
Sunderland v Leeds United
West Ham United v Tottenham H.

First Division
Barnsley v Wolves
Birmingham City v Port Vale
Charlton Athletic v Norwich City
Crystal Palace v Tranmere Rovers
Huddersfield T. v Bolton Wand.
Ipswich Town v Oxford United
Manchester City v Swindon Town
Oldham Athletic v Bradford City
Reading v Southend United
Sheffield United v Grimsby Town
Stoke City v Q.P.R.
W.B.A. v Portsmouth

Second Division
Blackpool v Stockport Co.
Brentford v Bournemouth
Bristol City v Crewe Alexandra
Burnley v Bristol Rovers
Bury v Notts County
Chesterfield v Plymouth Argyle
Gillingham v Peterborough Utd.
Luton Town v Preston N.E.
Rotherham United v Wrexham
Shrewsbury Town v Millwall
Walsall v York City
Wycombe Wand. v Watford

Third Division
Barnet v Fulham
Brighton & H.A. v Swansea City
Cambridge United v Carlisle United
Cardiff City v Hartlepool United
Chester City v Mansfield Town
Exeter City v Darlington
Lincoln City v Hereford United
Northampton T. v Doncaster Rov.
Scarborough v Rochdale
Scunthorpe Utd. v Colchester Utd.
Torquay United v Hull City
Wigan Athletic v Leyton Orient

Friday, February 28th

First Division
Tranmere Rovers v Stoke City

Third Division
Colchester Utd. v Scarborough
Doncaster Rov. v Wigan Athletic

Saturday, March 1st

Premiership
Aston Villa v Liverpool
Blackburn Rovers v Sunderland
Derby County v Chelsea
Everton v Arsenal
Leeds United v West Ham United
Manchester Utd. v Coventry City
Newcastle United v Southampton
Sheffield Wed. v Middlesbrough
Tottenham H. v Nott'm. Forest
Wimbledon v Leicester City

First Division
Bolton Wand. v W.B.A.
Bradford City v Manchester City
Grimsby Town v Birmingham City
Norwich City v Huddersfield T.
Oxford United v Crystal Palace
Port Vale v Reading
Portsmouth v Sheffield United
Q.P.R. v Oldham Athletic
Southend United v Barnsley
Swindon Town v Charlton Athletic
Wolves v Ipswich Town

Second Division
Bournemouth v Shrewsbury Town
Bristol Rovers v Walsall
Crewe Alexandra v Gillingham
Millwall v Wycombe Wand.
Notts County v Brentford
Peterborough Utd. v Chesterfield
Plymouth Argyle v Blackpool
Preston N.E. v Bury
Stockport Co. v Rotherham United
Watford v Bristol City
Wrexham v Burnley
York City v Luton Town

Third Division
Carlisle United v Lincoln City
Darlington v Brighton & H.A.
Fulham v Chester City
Hartlepool United v Scunthorpe Utd.
Hereford United v Exeter City
Hull City v Northampton T.
Leyton Orient v Barnet
Mansfield Town v Cambridge United
Rochdale v Torquay United
Swansea City v Cardiff City

Tuesday, March 4th

Premiership
Arsenal v Manchester Utd.
Sunderland v Tottenham H.

First Division
Barnsley v Swindon Town
Birmingham City v Wolves
Charlton Athletic v Q.P.R.
Crystal Palace v Bolton Wand.
Huddersfield T. v Oxford United
Ipswich Town v Bradford City
Oldham Athletic v Tranmere Rovers
Reading v Norwich City
Sheffield United v Port Vale
W.B.A. v Southend United

Wednesday, March 5th

Premiership
Chelsea v Blackburn Rovers
Coventry City v Wimbledon
Leicester City v Aston Villa
Liverpool v Leeds United
Middlesbrough v Derby County
Nott'm. Forest v Sheffield Wed.
Southampton v Everton
West Ham United v Newcastle United

First Division
Manchester City v Portsmouth
Stoke City v Grimsby Town

Friday, March 7th

Third Division
Cambridge United v Colchester Utd.

Saturday, March 8th

Premiership
Arsenal v Nott'm. Forest
Coventry City v Leicester City
Derby County v Southampton
Leeds United v Everton
Liverpool v Newcastle United
Middlesbrough v Blackburn Rovers
Sheffield Wed. v Tottenham H.
Sunderland v Manchester Utd.
West Ham United v Chelsea
Wimbledon v Aston Villa

First Division
Barnsley v Sheffield United
Birmingham City v Southend United
Bolton Wand. v Swindon Town
Bradford City v Grimsby Town
Charlton Athletic v Crystal Palace
Manchester City v Oldham Athletic
Norwich City v Port Vale
Oxford United v W.B.A.
Portsmouth v Reading
Q.P.R. v Huddersfield T.
Stoke City v Ipswich Town
Wolves v Tranmere Rovers

Second Division
Bournemouth v Chesterfield
Bristol City v Wrexham

Burnley v Peterborough Utd.
Gillingham v Watford
Luton Town v Millwall
Notts County v Crewe Alexandra
Plymouth Argyle v Rotherham United
Preston N.E. v Brentford
Stockport Co. v Bury
Walsall v Shrewsbury Town
Wycombe Wand. v Bristol Rovers
York City v Blackpool

Third Division
Brighton & H.A. v Leyton Orient
Chester City v Barnet
Doncaster Rov. v Hull City
Fulham v Scarborough
Hereford United v Northampton T.
Lincoln City v Hartlepool United
Mansfield Town v Cardiff City
Rochdale v Wigan Athletic
Scunthorpe Utd. v Carlisle United
Swansea City v Exeter City
Torquay United v Darlington

Friday, March 14th
Third Division
Cardiff City v Doncaster Rov.
Colchester Utd. v Mansfield Town

Saturday, March 15th
Premiership
Aston Villa v West Ham United
Blackburn Rovers v Wimbledon
Chelsea v Sunderland
Everton v Derby County
Leicester City v Middlesbrough
Manchester Utd. v Sheffield Wed.
Newcastle United v Coventry City
Nott'm. Forest v Liverpool
Southampton v Arsenal
Tottenham H. v Leeds United

First Division
Crystal Palace v Norwich City
Grimsby Town v Manchester City
Huddersfield T. v Portsmouth
Ipswich Town v Bolton Wand.
Oldham Athletic v Wolves
Port Vale v Charlton Athletic
Reading v Bradford City
Sheffield United v Oxford United
Southend United v Q.P.R.
Swindon Town v Stoke City
Tranmere Rovers v Barnsley
W.B.A. v Birmingham City

Second Division
Blackpool v Preston N.E.
Brentford v Burnley
Bristol Rovers v Bristol City
Bury v Gillingham

Chesterfield v Wycombe Wand.
Crewe Alexandra v Luton Town
Millwall v Bournemouth
Peterborough Utd. v Stockport Co.
Rotherham United v Notts County
Shrewsbury Town v Plymouth Argyle
Watford v Walsall
Wrexham v York City

Third Division
Barnet v Swansea City
Carlisle United v Hereford United
Darlington v Chester City
Exeter City v Scunthorpe Utd.
Hartlepool United v Rochdale
Hull City v Brighton & H.A.
Northampton T. v Lincoln City
Scarborough v Torquay United
Wigan Athletic v Cambridge United

Sunday, March 16th
Third Division
Leyton Orient v Fulham

Friday, March 21st
Third Division
Colchester Utd. v Rochdale
Doncaster Rov. v Hereford United

Saturday, March 22nd
Premiership
Arsenal v Liverpool
Blackburn Rovers v Aston Villa
Coventry City v West Ham United
Derby County v Tottenham H.
Everton v Manchester Utd.
Middlesbrough v Chelsea
Sheffield Wed. v Leeds United
Southampton v Leicester City
Sunderland v Nott'm. Forest
Wimbledon v Newcastle United

First Division
Birmingham City v Sheffield United
Bradford City v Wolves
Grimsby Town v Tranmere Rovers
Huddersfield T. v Barnsley
Manchester City v Stoke City
Norwich City v Bolton Wand.
Oldham Athletic v Crystal Palace
Port Vale v Swindon Town
Q.P.R. v Portsmouth
Reading v Ipswich Town
Southend United v Oxford United
W.B.A. v Charlton Athletic

Second Division
Bournemouth v York City
Blackpool v Bristol City
Bury v Chesterfield
Crewe Alexandra v Peterborough Utd.

Gillingham v Wycombe Wand.
Luton Town v Brentford
Millwall v Watford
Notts County v Stockport Co.
Plymouth Argyle v Wrexham
Shrewsbury Town v Rotherham United
Walsall v Burnley

Third Division
Brighton & H.A. v Cardiff City
Cambridge United v Chester City
Fulham v Hartlepool United
Hull City v Carlisle United
Leyton Orient v Lincoln City
Mansfield Town v Northampton T.
Scarborough v Exeter City
Swansea City v Darlington
Torquay United v Scunthorpe Utd.
Wigan Athletic v Barnet

Sunday, March 23rd

Second Division
Bristol Rovers v Preston N.E.

Friday, March 28th

First Division
Ipswich Town v Manchester City

Second Division
Wrexham v Millwall

Third Division
Cardiff City v Scarborough

Saturday, March 29th

Premiership
Aston Villa v Sheffield Wed.
Chelsea v Southampton
Leeds United v Derby County
Leicester City v Sunderland
Liverpool v Middlesbrough
Manchester Utd. v Wimbledon
Newcastle United v Everton
Nott'm. Forest v Coventry City
Tottenham H. v Blackburn Rovers
West Ham United v Arsenal

First Division
Barnsley v W.B.A.
Bolton Wand. v Port Vale
Charlton Athletic v Huddersfield T.
Crystal Palace v Birmingham City
Oxford United v Q.P.R.
Portsmouth v Bradford City
Sheffield United v Reading
Stoke City v Oldham Athletic
Swindon Town v Norwich City
Tranmere Rovers v Southend United
Wolves v Grimsby Town

Second Division
Brentford v Bury
Bristol City v Gillingham
Burnley v Luton Town
Chesterfield v Blackpool
Peterborough Utd. v Bristol Rovers
Preston N.E. v Notts County
Rotherham United v Walsall
Stockport Co. v Crewe Alexandra
Watford v Bournemouth
Wycombe Wand. v Shrewsbury Town
York City v Plymouth Argyle

Third Division
Barnet v Cambridge United
Carlisle United v Doncaster Rov.
Chester City v Brighton & H.A.
Darlington v Hull City
Exeter City v Mansfield Town
Hartlepool United v Colchester Utd.
Hereford United v Fulham
Lincoln City v Torquay United
Northampton T. v Wigan Athletic
Rochdale v Swansea City
Scunthorpe Utd. v Leyton Orient

Monday, March 31st

First Division
Birmingham City v Charlton Athletic
Bradford City v Stoke City
Grimsby Town v Ipswich Town
Huddersfield T. v Sheffield United
Norwich City v Oxford United
Oldham Athletic v Swindon Town
Port Vale v Tranmere Rovers
Q.P.R. v Wolves
Reading v Barnsley
Southend United v Portsmouth
W.B.A. v Crystal Palace

Second Division
Blackpool v Rotherham United
Bristol Rovers v Wrexham
Bury v Wycombe Wand.
Crewe Alexandra v Preston N.E.
Gillingham v Brentford
Notts County v Peterborough Utd.
Plymouth Argyle v Watford

Third Division
Brighton & H.A. v Barnet
Cambridge United v Lincoln City
Colchester Utd. v Darlington
Doncaster Rov. v Exeter City
Fulham v Rochdale
Hull City v Hereford United
Leyton Orient v Carlisle United
Mansfield Town v Hartlepool United
Scarborough v Scunthorpe Utd.
Swansea City v Chester City
Torquay United v Northampton T.

Wigan Athletic v Cardiff City

Tuesday, April 1st

Second Division
Bournemouth v Stockport Co.
Luton Town v Bristol City
Shrewsbury Town v Burnley
Walsall v Chesterfield

Wednesday, April 2nd

Second Division
Millwall v York City

Friday, April 4th

First Division
Tranmere Rovers v Bradford City

Saturday, April 5th

Premiership
Aston Villa v Arsenal
Leeds United v Blackburn Rovers
Leicester City v Sheffield Wed.
Liverpool v Coventry City
Manchester Utd. v Derby County
Newcastle United v Sunderland
Nott'm. Forest v Southampton
Tottenham H. v Wimbledon
West Ham United v Middlesbrough

First Division
Barnsley v Birmingham City
Bolton Wand. v Q.P.R.
Charlton Athletic v Manchester City
Crystal Palace v Huddersfield T.
Ipswich Town v Oldham Athletic
Oxford United v Port Vale
Portsmouth v Grimsby Town
Sheffield United v W.B.A.
Stoke City v Reading
Swindon Town v Southend United
Wolves v Norwich City

Second Division
Brentford v Shrewsbury Town
Bristol City v Bury
Burnley v Millwall
Chesterfield v Gillingham
Peterborough Utd. v Bournemouth
Preston N.E. v Plymouth Argyle
Rotherham United v Luton Town
Stockport Co. v Bristol Rovers
Watford v Crewe Alexandra
Wrexham v Walsall
Wycombe Wand. v Blackpool
York City v Notts County

Third Division
Barnet v Hull City
Cardiff City v Cambridge United
Carlisle United v Fulham
Chester City v Wigan Athletic
Darlington v Doncaster Rov.
Exeter City v Torquay United
Hartlepool United v Leyton Orient
Hereford United v Colchester Utd.
Lincoln City v Swansea City
Northampton T. v Scarborough
Rochdale v Mansfield Town
Scunthorpe Utd. v Brighton & H.A.

Wednesday, April 9th

First Division
Manchester City v Bolton Wand.

Friday, April 11th

Second Division
Rotherham United v Brentford

Third Division
Colchester Utd. v Swansea City

Saturday, April 12th

Premiership
Arsenal v Leicester City
Blackburn Rovers v Manchester Utd.
Coventry City v Chelsea
Derby County v Aston Villa
Everton v Tottenham H.
Middlesbrough v Nott'm. Forest
Sheffield Wed. v Newcastle United
Southampton v West Ham United
Sunderland v Liverpool
Wimbledon v Leeds United

First Division
Barnsley v Charlton Athletic
Birmingham City v Huddersfield T.
Bolton Wand. v Oxford United
Norwich City v Stoke City
Port Vale v Oldham Athletic
Portsmouth v Tranmere Rovers
Q.P.R. v Grimsby Town
Reading v Wolves
Sheffield United v Crystal Palace
Southend United v Bradford City
Swindon Town v Ipswich Town
W.B.A. v Manchester City

Second Division
Bournemouth v Gillingham
Blackpool v Bury
Bristol City v Chesterfield
Crewe Alexandra v Bristol Rovers
Millwall v Plymouth Argyle
Notts County v Wycombe Wand.
Peterborough Utd. v Preston N.E.
Shrewsbury Town v Wrexham
Stockport Co. v Burnley
Walsall v Luton Town
Watford v York City

Third Division
Brighton & H.A. v Wigan Athletic
Cardiff City v Chester City
Exeter City v Lincoln City
Fulham v Northampton T.
Hartlepool United v Cambridge United
Leyton Orient v Doncaster Rov.
Mansfield Town v Carlisle United
Rochdale v Darlington
Scarborough v Hereford United
Scunthorpe Utd. v Hull City
Torquay United v Barnet

Saturday, April 19th

Premiership
Arsenal v Blackburn Rovers
Aston Villa v Tottenham H.
Chelsea v Leicester City
Liverpool v Manchester Utd.
Middlesbrough v Sunderland
Newcastle United v Derby County
Nott'm. Forest v Leeds United
Sheffield Wed. v Wimbledon
Southampton v Coventry City
West Ham United v Everton

First Division
Bradford City v Birmingham City
Charlton Athletic v Portsmouth
Crystal Palace v Barnsley
Grimsby Town v Reading
Huddersfield T. v W.B.A.
Ipswich Town v Norwich City
Manchester City v Q.P.R.
Oldham Athletic v Bolton Wand.
Oxford United v Swindon Town
Stoke City v Port Vale
Tranmere Rovers v Sheffield United
Wolves v Southend United

Second Division
Brentford v Crewe Alexandra
Burnley v Rotherham United
Bury v Peterborough Utd.
Chesterfield v Millwall
Gillingham v Blackpool
Luton Town v Shrewsbury Town
Plymouth Argyle v Walsall
Preston N.E. v Stockport Co.
Wrexham v Watford
Wycombe Wand. v Bournemouth
York City v Bristol City

Third Division
Barnet v Cardiff City
Cambridge United v Brighton & H.A.
Carlisle United v Rochdale
Chester City v Scarborough
Darlington v Hartlepool United
Doncaster Rov. v Fulham
Hereford United v Torquay United
Hull City v Leyton Orient
Lincoln City v Scunthorpe Utd.
Northampton T. v Exeter City
Swansea City v Mansfield Town
Wigan Athletic v Colchester Utd.

Sunday, April 20th

Second Division
Bristol Rovers v Notts County

Tuesday, April 22nd

Premiership
Blackburn Rovers v Sheffield Wed.
Leeds United v Aston Villa
Sunderland v Southampton
Wimbledon v Chelsea

Wednesday, April 23rd

Premiership
Coventry City v Arsenal
Derby County v Nott'm. Forest
Everton v Liverpool
Leicester City v West Ham United
Manchester Utd. v Newcastle United
Tottenham H. v Middlesbrough

Saturday, April 26th

First Division
Barnsley v Bradford City
Birmingham City v Oxford United
Bolton Wand. v Charlton Athletic
Norwich City v Manchester City
Port Vale v Wolves
Portsmouth v Ipswich Town
Q.P.R. v Tranmere Rovers
Reading v Oldham Athletic
Sheffield United v Stoke City
Southend United v Huddersfield T.
Swindon Town v Crystal Palace
W.B.A. v Grimsby Town

Second Division
Bournemouth v Wrexham
Blackpool v Bristol Rovers
Bristol City v Plymouth Argyle
Crewe Alexandra v Chesterfield
Millwall v Gillingham
Notts County v Burnley
Peterborough Utd. v Luton Town
Rotherham United v York City
Shrewsbury Town v Preston N.E.
Stockport Co. v Wycombe Wand.
Walsall v Brentford
Watford v Bury

Third Division
Brighton & H.A. v Doncaster Rov.
Cardiff City v Carlisle United
Colchester Utd. v Northampton T.
Exeter City v Chester City

Fulham v Hull City
Hartlepool United v Barnet
Leyton Orient v Hereford United
Mansfield Town v Darlington
Rochdale v Cambridge United
Scarborough v Lincoln City
Scunthorpe Utd. v Swansea City
Torquay United v Wigan Athletic

Saturday, May 3rd

Premiership
Arsenal v Newcastle United
Chelsea v Leeds United
Coventry City v Derby County
Leicester City v Manchester Utd.
Liverpool v Tottenham H.
Middlesbrough v Aston Villa
Nott'm. Forest v Wimbledon
Southampton v Blackburn Rovers
Sunderland v Everton
West Ham United v Sheffield Wed.

Second Division
Brentford v Peterborough Utd.
Bristol Rovers v Rotherham United
Burnley v Watford
Bury v Millwall
Chesterfield v Notts County
Gillingham v Shrewsbury Town
Luton Town v Stockport Co.
Plymouth Argyle v Bournemouth
Preston N.E. v Walsall
Wrexham v Blackpool
Wycombe Wand. v Bristol City
York City v Crewe Alexandra

Third Division
Barnet v Colchester Utd.
Cambridge United v Fulham
Carlisle United v Exeter City
Chester City v Leyton Orient
Darlington v Cardiff City
Doncaster Rov. v Torquay United
Hereford United v Brighton & H.A.
Hull City v Scarborough
Lincoln City v Rochdale
Northampton T. v Scunthorpe Utd.
Swansea City v Hartlepool United
Wigan Athletic v Mansfield Town

Sunday, May 4th

First Division
Bradford City v Q.P.R.
Charlton Athletic v Sheffield United
Crystal Palace v Port Vale
Grimsby Town v Southend United
Huddersfield T. v Swindon Town
Ipswich Town v Birmingham City
Manchester City v Reading
Oldham Athletic v Norwich City
Oxford United v Barnsley
Stoke City v W.B.A.
Tranmere Rovers v Bolton Wand.
Wolves v Portsmouth

Sunday, May 11th

Premiership
Aston Villa v Southampton
Blackburn Rovers v Leicester
Derby County v Arsenal
Everton v Chelsea
Leeds United v Middlesbrough
Manchester Utd. v West Ham United
Newcastle United v Nott'm. Forest
Sheffield Wed. v Liverpool
Tottenham H. v Coventry City
Wimbledon v Sunderland

SCOTTISH LEAGUE FIXTURES 1996-97

Saturday, August 10th

Premier Division
Aberdeen v Celtic
Dundee United v Motherwell
Dunfermline A. v Heart of Midlothian
Hibernian v Kilmarnock
Rangers v Raith Rovers

Saturday, August 17th

Premier Division
Celtic v Raith Rovers
Dundee United v Hibernian
Dunfermline Athletic v Rangers
Heart of Midlothian v Kilmarnock
Motherwell v Aberdeen

First Division
East Fife v St. Mirren
Greenock Morton v Clydebank
Partick Thistle v Dundee
St. Johnstone v Falkirk
Stirling Albion v Airdrieonians

Second Division
Ayr United v Hamilton Academical

Clyde v Berwick Rangers
Dumbarton v Stranraer
Livingston v Queen of the South
Stenhousemuir v Brechin City

Third Division
Albion Rovers v Forfar Athletic
Arbroath v Ross County
Caledonian Thistle v Cowdenbeath
Montrose v Alloa
Queen's Park v East Stirlingshire

Saturday, August 24th

Premier Division
Hibernian v Dunfermline Athletic
Kilmarnock v Celtic
Raith Rovers v Motherwell
Rangers v Dundee United

First Division
Airdrieonians v East Fife
Clydebank v Stirling Albion
Dundee v Greenock Morton
Falkirk v Partick Thistle
St. Mirren v St. Johnstone

Second Division
Berwick Rangers v Stenhousemuir
Brechin City v Ayr United
Hamilton Academical v Clyde
Queen of the South v Dumbarton
Stranraer v Livingston

Third Division
Alloa v Arbroath
Cowdenbeath v Montrose
East Stirlingshire v Albion Rovers
Forfar Athletic v Caledonian Thistle
Ross County v Queen's Park

Sunday, August 25th

Premier Division
Aberdeen v Heart of Midlothian

Saturday, August 31st

First Division
East Fife v Clydebank
Greenock Morton v Falkirk
Partick Thistle v St. Mirren
St. Johnstone v Airdrieonians
Stirling Albion v Dundee

Second Division
Ayr United v Berwick Rangers
Clyde v Queen of the South
Dumbarton v Brechin City
Livingston v Hamilton Academical
Stenhousemuir v Stranraer

Third Division
Albion Rovers v Cowdenbeath
Arbroath v East Stirlingshire
Caledonian Thistle v Alloa
Montrose v Ross County
Queen's Park v Forfar Athletic

Saturday, September 7th

Premier Division
Celtic v Hibernian
Heart of Midlothian v Dundee United
Kilmarnock v Dunfermline Athletic
Motherwell v Rangers
Raith Rovers v Aberdeen

First Division
Clydebank v St. Mirren
Dundee v Airdrieonians
Greenock Morton v East Fife
St. Johnstone v Partick Thistle
Stirling Albion v Falkirk

Second Division
Berwick Rangers v Queen of South
Clyde v Dumbarton
Livingston v Brechin City
Stenhousemuir v Ayr United
Stranraer v Hamilton Academical

Third Division
Albion Rovers v Caledonian Thistle
Cowdenbeath v Queen's Park
East Stirlingshire v Forfar Athletic
Montrose v Arbroath
Ross County v Alloa

Saturday, September 14th

Premier Division
Aberdeen v Kilmarnock
Dundee United v Celtic
Dunfermline Athletic v Motherwell
Hibernian v Raith Rovers
Rangers v Heart of Midlothian

First Division
Airdrieonians v Greenock Morton
East Fife v St. Johnstone
Falkirk v Clydebank
Partick Thistle v Stirling Albion
St. Mirren v Dundee

Second Division
Ayr United v Clyde
Brechin City v Stranraer
Dumbarton v Livingston
Hamilton Acad. v Berwick Rangers
Queen of the South v Stenhousemuir

Third Division
Alloa v Cowdenbeath

Arbroath v Albion Rovers
Caledonian Thist. v East Stirlingshire
Forfar Athletic v Ross County
Queen's Park v Montrose

Saturday, September 21st

Premier Division
Aberdeen v Hibernian
Celtic v Dunfermline Athletic
Heart of Midlothian v Motherwell
Kilmarnock v Rangers
Raith Rovers v Dundee United

First Division
Airdrieonians v Partick Thistle
Clydebank v St. Johnstone
Dundee v East Fife
St. Mirren v Falkirk
Stirling Albion v Greenock Morton

Second Division
Berwick Rangers v Dumbarton
Brechin City v Hamilton Academical
Queen of the South v Ayr United
Stenhousemuir v Livingston
Stranraer v Clyde

Third Division
Albion Rovers v Alloa
Caledonian Thistle v Queen's Park
Cowdenbeath v Ross County
East Stirlingshire v Montrose
Forfar Athletic v Arbroath

Saturday, September 28th

Premier Division
Dundee United v Aberdeen
Dunfermline Athletic v Raith Rovers
Hibernian v Heart of Midlothian
Motherwell v Kilmarnock
Rangers v Celtic

First Division
East Fife v Stirling Albion
Falkirk v Airdrieonians
Greenock Morton v St. Mirren
Partick Thistle v Clydebank
St. Johnstone v Dundee

Second Division
Ayr United v Stranraer
Clyde v Brechin City
Dumbarton v Stenhousemuir
Hamilton Acad. v Queen of the South
Livingston v Berwick Rangers

Third Division
Alloa v East Stirlingshire
Arbroath v Cowdenbeath
Montrose v Forfar Athletic
Queen's Park v Albion Rovers
Ross County v Caledonian Thistle

Saturday, October 5th

First Division
Airdrieonians v St. Mirren
Dundee v Clydebank
East Fife v Falkirk
Greenock Morton v Partick Thistle
Stirling Albion v St. Johnstone

Second Division
Brechin City v Berwick Rangers
Dumbarton v Ayr United
Livingston v Clyde
Stenhousemuir v Hamilton Acad.
Stranraer v Queen of the South

Third Division
Albion Rovers v Montrose
Caledonian Thistle v Arbroath
East Stirlingshire v Ross County
Forfar Athletic v Cowdenbeath
Queen's Park v Alloa

Saturday, October 12th

Premier Division
Aberdeen v Dunfermline Athletic
Celtic v Motherwell
Dundee United v Kilmarnock
Hibernian v Rangers
Raith Rovers v Heart of Midlothian

First Division
Clydebank v Airdrieonians
Falkirk v Dundee
Partick Thistle v East Fife
St. Johnstone v Greenock Morton
St. Mirren v Stirling Albion

Second Division
Ayr United v Livingston
Berwick Rangers v Stranraer
Clyde v Stenhousemuir
Hamilton Academical v Dumbarton
Queen of the South v Brechin City

Third Division
Alloa v Forfar Athletic
Arbroath v Queen's Park
Cowdenbeath v East Stirlingshire
Montrose v Caledonian Thistle
Ross County v Albion Rovers

Saturday, October 19th

Premier Division
Dunfermline Athletic v Dundee United
Kilmarnock v Raith Rovers
Motherwell v Hibernian
Rangers v Aberdeen

First Division
Airdrieonians v Stirling Albion
Clydebank v Greenock Morton
Dundee v Partick Thistle
Falkirk v St. Johnstone
St. Mirren v East Fife

Second Division
Berwick Rangers v Clyde
Brechin City v Stenhousemuir
Hamilton Academical v Ayr United
Queen of the South v Livingston
Stranraer v Dumbarton

Third Division
Alloa v Montrose
Cowdenbeath v Caledonian Thistle
East Stirlingshire v Queen's Park
Forfar Athletic v Albion Rovers
Ross County v Arbroath

Sunday, October 20th

Premier Division
Heart of Midlothian v Celtic

Saturday, October 26th

Premier Division
Aberdeen v Raith Rovers
Dundee United v Heart of Midlothian
Dunfermline Athletic v Kilmarnock
Hibernian v Celtic
Rangers v Motherwell

First Division
East Fife v Airdrieonians
Greenock Morton v Dundee
Partick Thistle v Falkirk
St. Johnstone v St. Mirren
Stirling Albion v Clydebank

Second Division
Ayr United v Brechin City
Clyde v Hamilton Academical
Dumbarton v Queen of the South
Livingston v Stranraer
Stenhousemuir v Berwick Rangers

Third Division
Albion Rovers v East Stirlingshire
Arbroath v Alloa
Caledonian Thistle v Forfar Athletic
Montrose v Cowdenbeath
Queen's Park v Ross County

Saturday, November 2nd

Premier Division
Celtic v Aberdeen
Heart of Mid. v Dunfermline Ath.
Kilmarnock v Hibernian
Motherwell v Dundee United
Raith Rovers v Rangers

First Division
Clydebank v Falkirk
Dundee v St. Mirren
Greenock Morton v Airdrieonians
St. Johnstone v East Fife
Stirling Albion v Partick Thistle

Second Division
Berwick Rangers v Hamilton Acad.
Clyde v Ayr United
Livingston v Dumbarton
Stenhousemuir v Queen of the South
Stranraer v Brechin City

Third Division
Albion Rovers v Arbroath
Cowdenbeath v Alloa
East Stirling. v Caledonian Thistle
Montrose v Queen's Park
Ross County v Forfar Athletic

Saturday, November 9th

First Division
Airdrieonians v Dundee
East Fife v Greenock Morton
Falkirk v Stirling Albion
Partick Thistle v St. Johnstone
St. Mirren v Clydebank

Second Division
Ayr United v Stenhousemuir
Brechin City v Livingston
Dumbarton v Clyde
Hamilton Academical v Stranraer
Queen of South v Berwick Rangers

Third Division
Alloa v Ross County
Arbroath v Montrose
Caledonian Thistle v Albion Rovers
Forfar Athletic v East Stirlingshire
Queen's Park v Cowdenbeath

Thursday, November 14th

Premier Division
Celtic v Rangers

Saturday, November 16th

Premier Division
Aberdeen v Dundee United
Heart of Midlothian v Hibernian
Kilmarnock v Motherwell
Raith Rovers v Dunfermline Athletic

First Division
Airdrieonians v Falkirk
Clydebank v Partick Thistle
Dundee v St. Johnstone

St. Mirren v Greenock Morton
Stirling Albion v East Fife

Second Division
Berwick Rangers v Livingston
Brechin City v Clyde
Queen of the South v Hamilton Acad.
Stenhousemuir v Dumbarton
Stranraer v Ayr United

Third Division
Albion Rovers v Queen's Park
Caledonian Thistle v Ross County
Cowdenbeath v Arbroath
East Stirlingshire v Alloa
Forfar Athletic v Montrose

Saturday, November 23rd

Premier Division
Dundee United v Raith Rovers
Dunfermline Athletic v Celtic
Hibernian v Aberdeen
Motherwell v Heart of Midlothian
Rangers v Kilmarnock

First Division
East Fife v Dundee
Falkirk v St. Mirren
Greenock Morton v Stirling Albion
Partick Thistle v Airdrieonians
St. Johnstone v Clydebank

Second Division
Ayr United v Queen of the South
Clyde v Stranraer
Dumbarton v Berwick Rangers
Hamilton Academical v Brechin City
Livingston v Stenhousemuir

Third Division
Alloa v Albion Rovers
Arbroath v Forfar Athletic
Montrose v East Stirlingshire
Queen's Park v Caledonian Thistle
Ross County v Cowdenbeath

Saturday, November 30th

Premier Division
Celtic v Heart of Midlothian
Dundee United v Dunfermline Athletic
Hibernian v Motherwell
Raith Rovers v Kilmarnock

First Division
Clydebank v Dundee
Falkirk v East Fife
Partick Thistle v Greenock Morton
St. Johnstone v Stirling Albion
St. Mirren v Airdrieonians

Second Division
Ayr United v Dumbarton
Berwick Rangers v Brechin City
Clyde v Livingston
Hamilton Acad. v Stenhousemuir
Queen of the South v Stranraer

Third Division
Alloa v Queen's Park
Arbroath v Caledonian Thistle
Cowdenbeath v Forfar Athletic
Montrose v Albion Rovers
Ross County v East Stirlingshire

Sunday, December 1st

Premier Division
Aberdeen v Rangers

Saturday, December 7th

Premier Division
Dunfermline Athletic v Aberdeen
Heart of Midlothian v Raith Rovers
Kilmarnock v Dundee United
Motherwell v Celtic
Rangers v Hibernian

First Division
Airdrieonians v Clydebank
Dundee v Falkirk
East Fife v Partick Thistle
Greenock Morton v St. Johnstone
Stirling Albion v St. Mirren

Tuesday, December 10th

Premier Division
Dundee United v Rangers

Wednesday, December 11th

Premier Division
Celtic v Kilmarnock
Dunfermline Athletic v Hibernian
Heart of Midlothian v Aberdeen
Motherwell v Raith Rovers

Saturday, December 14th

Premier Division
Aberdeen v Motherwell
Hibernian v Dundee United
Kilmarnock v Heart of Midlothian
Raith Rovers v Celtic
Rangers v Dunfermline Athletic

First Division
Airdrieonians v St. Johnstone
Dundee v Stirling Albion
Falkirk v Greenock Morton
St. Mirren v Partick Thistle

Second Division
Brechin City v Queen of the South
Dumbarton v Hamilton Academical
Livingston v Ayr United
Stenhousemuir v Clyde
Stranraer v Berwick Rangers

Third Division
Albion Rovers v Ross County
Caledonian Thistle v Montrose
East Stirlingshire v Cowdenbeath
Forfar Athletic v Alloa
Queen's Park v Arbroath

Saturday, December 21st

Premier Division
Celtic v Dundee United
Heart of Midlothian v Rangers
Kilmarnock v Aberdeen
Motherwell v Dunfermline Athletic
Raith Rovers v Hibernian

First Division
Clydebank v East Fife
Stirling Albion v Airdrieonians

Second Division
Clyde v Berwick Rangers
Stenhousemuir v Brechin City

Third Division
Caledonian Thistle v Cowdenbeath
Montrose v Alloa
Queen's Park v East Stirlingshire

Thursday, December 26th

Premier Division
Aberdeen v Celtic
Dundee United v Motherwell
Dunfermline A. v Heart of Midlothian
Hibernian v Kilmarnock
Rangers v Raith Rovers

First Division
East Fife v St. Mirren
Greenock Morton v Clydebank
Partick Thistle v Dundee
St. Johnstone v Falkirk

Second Division
Ayr United v Hamilton Academical
Dumbarton v Stranraer
Livingston v Queen of the South

Third Division
Albion Rovers v Forfar Athletic
Arbroath v Ross County

Saturday, December 28th

Premier Division
Aberdeen v Hibernian
Celtic v Dunfermline Athletic
Heart of Midlothian v Motherwell
Kilmarnock v Rangers
Raith Rovers v Dundee United

First Division
Airdrieonians v Partick Thistle
Clydebank v St. Johnstone
Dundee v East Fife
St. Mirren v Falkirk
Stirling Albion v Greenock Morton

Second Division
Berwick Rangers v Ayr United
Brechin City v Dumbarton
Hamilton Academical v Livingston
Queen of the South v Clyde
Stranraer v Stenhousemuir

Third Division
Alloa v Caledonian Thistle
Cowdenbeath v Albion Rovers
East Stirlingshire v Arbroath
Forfar Athletic v Queen's Park
Ross County v Montrose

Wednesday, January 1st, 1997

Premier Division
Dundee United v Aberdeen
Dunfermline Athletic v Raith Rovers
Hibernian v Heart of Midlothian
Motherwell v Kilmarnock

First Division
East Fife v Stirling Albion
Falkirk v Airdrieonians
Greenock Morton v St. Mirren
Partick Thistle v Clydebank
St. Johnstone v Dundee

Second Division
Ayr United v Stranraer
Clyde v Brechin City
Dumbarton v Stenhousemuir
Hamilton Acad. v Queen of South
Livingston v Berwick Rangers

Third Division
Alloa v East Stirlingshire
Arbroath v Cowdenbeath
Montrose v Forfar Athletic
Queen's Park v Albion Rovers
Ross County v Caledonian Thistle

Thursday, January 2nd

Premier Division
Rangers v Celtic

Saturday, January 4th
Premier Division
Aberdeen v Dunfermline Athletic
Celtic v Motherwell
Dundee United v Kilmarnock
Hibernian v Rangers
Raith Rovers v Heart of Midlothian

First Division
Airdrieonians v Greenock Morton
East Fife v St. Johnstone
Falkirk v Clydebank
Partick Thistle v Stirling Albion
St. Mirren v Dundee

Saturday, January 11th
Premier Division
Dunfermline Athletic v Dundee United
Heart of Midlothian v Celtic
Kilmarnock v Raith Rovers
Motherwell v Hibernian

First Division
Clydebank v St. Mirren
Dundee v Airdrieonians
Greenock Morton v East Fife
St. Johnstone v Partick Thistle
Stirling Albion v Falkirk

Second Division
Berwick Rangers v Dumbarton
Brechin City v Hamilton Academical
Queen of the South v Ayr United
Stenhousemuir v Livingston
Stranraer v Clyde

Third Division
Albion Rovers v Alloa
Caledonian Thistle v Queen's Park
Cowdenbeath v Ross County
East Stirlingshire v Montrose
Forfar Athletic v Arbroath

Sunday, January 12th
Premier Division
Rangers v Aberdeen

Saturday, January 18th
Premier Division
Celtic v Hibernian
Heart of Midlothian v Dundee United
Kilmarnock v Dunfermline Athletic
Motherwell v Rangers
Raith Rovers v Aberdeen

First Division
Airdrieonians v St. Mirren
Dundee v Clydebank
East Fife v Falkirk
Greenock Morton v Partick Thistle
Stirling Albion v St. Johnstone

Second Division
Brechin City v Berwick Rangers
Dumbarton v Ayr United
Livingston v Clyde
Stenhousemuir v Hamilton Acad.
Stranraer v Queen of the South

Third Division
Albion Rovers v Montrose
Caledonian Thistle v Arbroath
East Stirlingshire v Ross County
Forfar Athletic v Cowdenbeath
Queen's Park v Alloa

Saturday, February 1st
Premier Division
Aberdeen v Kilmarnock
Dundee United v Celtic
Dunfermline Athletic v Motherwell
Hibernian v Raith Rovers
Rangers v Heart of Midlothian

First Division
Clydebank v Airdrieonians
Falkirk v Dundee
Partick Thistle v East Fife
St. Johnstone v Greenock Morton
St. Mirren v Stirling Albion

Second Division
Ayr United v Livingston
Berwick Rangers v Stranraer
Clyde v Stenhousemuir
Hamilton Academical v Dumbarton
Queen of the South v Brechin City

Third Division
Alloa v Forfar Athletic
Arbroath v Queen's Park
Cowdenbeath v East Stirlingshire
Montrose v Caledonian Thistle
Ross County v Albion Rovers

Saturday, February 8th
Premier Division
Celtic v Raith Rovers
Dundee United v Hibernian
Dunfermline Athletic v Rangers
Heart of Midlothian v Kilmarnock
Motherwell v Aberdeen

First Division
East Fife v Clydebank
Greenock Morton v Falkirk
Partick Thistle v St. Mirren
St. Johnstone v Airdrieonians
Stirling Albion v Dundee

Second Division
Ayr United v Clyde
Brechin City v Stranraer
Dumbarton v Livingston
Hamilton Acad. v Berwick Rangers
Queen of the South v Stenhousemuir

Third Division
Alloa v Cowdenbeath
Arbroath v Albion Rovers
Caledonian Th. v East Stirlingshire
Forfar Athletic v Ross County
Queen's Park v Montrose

Tuesday, February 11th

Premier Division
Hibernian v Dunfermline Athletic
Kilmarnock v Celtic
Raith Rovers v Motherwell

Wednesday, February 12th

Premier Division
Aberdeen v Heart of Midlothian
Rangers v Dundee United

Saturday, February 15th

Second Division
Berwick Rangers v Queen of South
Clyde v Dumbarton
Livingston v Brechin City
Stenhousemuir v Ayr United
Stranraer v Hamilton Academical

Third Division
Albion Rovers v Caledonian Thistle
Cowdenbeath v Queen's Park
East Stirlingshire v Forfar Athletic
Montrose v Arbroath
Ross County v Alloa

Saturday, February 22nd

Premier Division
Dunfermline Athletic v Aberdeen
Heart of Midlothian v Raith Rovers
Kilmarnock v Dundee United
Motherwell v Celtic
Rangers v Hibernian

First Division
Airdrieonians v East Fife
Clydebank v Stirling Albion
Dundee v Greenock Morton
Falkirk v Partick Thistle
St. Mirren v St. Johnstone

Second Division
Berwick Rangers v Stenhousemuir
Brechin City v Ayr United
Hamilton Academical v Clyde
Queen of the South v Dumbarton
Stranraer v Livingston

Third Division
Alloa v Arbroath
Cowdenbeath v Montrose
East Stirlingshire v Albion Rovers
Forfar Athletic v Caledonian Thistle
Ross County v Queen's Park

Saturday, March 1st

Premier Division
Aberdeen v Rangers
Celtic v Heart of Midlothian
Dundee United v Dunfermline Athletic
Hibernian v Motherwell
Raith Rovers v Kilmarnock

First Division
East Fife v Dundee
Falkirk v St. Mirren
Greenock Morton v Stirling Albion
Partick Thistle v Airdrieonians
St. Johnstone v Clydebank

Second Division
Ayr United v Berwick Rangers
Clyde v Queen of the South
Dumbarton v Brechin City
Livingston v Hamilton Academical
Stenhousemuir v Stranraer

Third Division
Albion Rovers v Cowdenbeath
Arbroath v East Stirlingshire
Caledonian Thistle v Alloa
Montrose v Ross County
Queen's Park v Forfar Athletic

Saturday, March 8th

Second Division
Ayr United v Queen of the South
Clyde v Stranraer
Dumbarton v Berwick Rangers
Hamilton Academical v Brechin City
Livingston v Stenhousemuir

Third Division
Alloa v Albion Rovers
Arbroath v Forfar Athletic
Montrose v East Stirlingshire
Queen's Park v Caledonian Thistle
Ross County v Cowdenbeath

Saturday, March 15th

Premier Division
Aberdeen v Dundee United
Heart of Midlothian v Hibernian
Kilmarnock v Motherwell
Raith Rovers v Dunfermline Athletic

First Division
Airdrieonians v Falkirk
Clydebank v Partick Thistle
Dundee v St. Johnstone
St. Mirren v Greenock Morton
Stirling Albion v East Fife

Second Division
Berwick Rangers v Livingston
Brechin City v Clyde
Queen of South v Hamilton Acad.
Stenhousemuir v Dumbarton
Stranraer v Ayr United

Third Division
Albion Rovers v Queen's Park
Caledonian Thistle v Ross County
Cowdenbeath v Arbroath
East Stirlingshire v Alloa
Forfar Athletic v Montrose

Sunday, March 16th

Premier Division
Celtic v Rangers

Saturday, March 22nd

Premier Division
Dundee United v Raith Rovers
Dunfermline Athletic v Celtic
Hibernian v Aberdeen
Motherwell v Heart of Midlothian
Rangers v Kilmarnock

First Division
Clydebank v Dundee
Falkirk v East Fife
Partick Thistle v Greenock Morton
St. Johnstone v Stirling Albion
St. Mirren v Airdrieonians

Second Division
Ayr United v Dumbarton
Berwick Rangers v Brechin City
Clyde v Livingston
Hamilton Acad. v Stenhousemuir
Queen of the South v Stranraer

Third Division
Alloa v Queen's Park
Arbroath v Caledonian Thistle
Cowdenbeath v Forfar Athletic
Montrose v Albion Rovers
Ross County v East Stirlingshire

Saturday, April 5th

Premier Division
Aberdeen v Motherwell
Hibernian v Dundee United
Kilmarnock v Heart of Midlothian
Raith Rovers v Celtic
Rangers v Dunfermline Athletic

First Division
Airdrieonians v Clydebank
Dundee v Falkirk
East Fife v Partick Thistle
Greenock Morton v St. Johnstone
Stirling Albion v St. Mirren

Second Division
Brechin City v Queen of the South
Dumbarton v Hamilton Academical
Livingston v Ayr United
Stenhousemuir v Clyde
Stranraer v Berwick Rangers

Third Division
Albion Rovers v Ross County
Caledonian Thistle v Montrose
East Stirlingshire v Cowdenbeath
Forfar Athletic v Alloa
Queen's Park v Arbroath

Saturday, April 12th

Premier Division
Celtic v Kilmarnock
Dundee United v Rangers
Dunfermline Athletic v Hibernian
Heart of Midlothian v Aberdeen
Motherwell v Raith Rovers

First Division
Airdrieonians v Dundee
East Fife v Greenock Morton
Falkirk v Stirling Albion
Partick Thistle v St. Johnstone
St. Mirren v Clydebank

Second Division
Ayr United v Stenhousemuir
Brechin City v Livingston
Dumbarton v Clyde
Hamilton Academical v Stranraer
Queen of South v Berwick Rangers

Third Division
Alloa v Ross County
Arbroath v Montrose
Caledonian Thistle v Albion Rovers
Forfar Athletic v East Stirlingshire
Queen's Park v Cowdenbeath

Saturday, April 19th

Premier Division
Celtic v Aberdeen
Heart of Mid. v Dunfermline Ath.
Kilmarnock v Hibernian
Motherwell v Dundee United
Raith Rovers v Rangers

First Division
Clydebank v Falkirk
Dundee v St. Mirren
Greenock Morton v Airdrieonians
St. Johnstone v East Fife
Stirling Albion v Partick Thistle

Second Division
Berwick Rangers v Hamilton Acad.
Clyde v Ayr United
Livingston v Dumbarton
Stenhousemuir v Queen of the South
Stranraer v Brechin City

Third Division
Albion Rovers v Arbroath
Cowdenbeath v Alloa
East Stirlingshire v Caledonian Th.
Montrose v Queen's Park
Ross County v Forfar Athletic

Saturday, April 26th

First Division
Airdrieonians v Stirling Albion
Clydebank v Greenock Morton
Dundee v Partick Thistle
Falkirk v St. Johnstone
St. Mirren v East Fife

Second Division
Berwick Rangers v Clyde
Brechin City v Stenhousemuir
Hamilton Academical v Ayr United
Queen of the South v Livingston
Stranraer v Dumbarton

Third Division
Alloa v Montrose
Cowdenbeath v Caledonian Thistle
East Stirlingshire v Queen's Park
Forfar Athletic v Albion Rovers
Ross County v Arbroath

Saturday, May 3rd

Premier Division
Aberdeen v Raith Rovers
Dundee United v Heart of Midlothian
Dunfermline Athletic v Kilmarnock
Hibernian v Celtic
Rangers v Motherwell

First Division
East Fife v Airdrieonians
Greenock Morton v Dundee
Partick Thistle v Falkirk
St. Johnstone v St. Mirren
Stirling Albion v Clydebank

Second Division
Ayr United v Brechin City
Clyde v Hamilton Academical
Dumbarton v Queen of the South
Livingston v Stranraer
Stenhousemuir v Berwick Rangers

Third Division
Albion Rovers v East Stirlingshire
Arbroath v Alloa
Caledonian Thistle v Forfar Athletic
Montrose v Cowdenbeath
Queen's Park v Ross County

Saturday, May 10th

Premier Division
Celtic v Dundee United
Heart of Midlothian v Rangers
Kilmarnock v Aberdeen
Motherwell v Dunfermline Athletic
Raith Rovers v Hibernian

First Division
Airdrieonians v St. Johnstone
Clydebank v East Fife
Dundee v Stirling Albion
Falkirk v Greenock Morton
St. Mirren v Partick Thistle

Second Division
Berwick Rangers v Ayr United
Brechin City v Dumbarton
Hamilton Academical v Livingston
Queen of the South v Clyde
Stranraer v Stenhousemuir

Third Division
Alloa v Caledonian Thistle
Cowdenbeath v Albion Rovers
East Stirlingshire v Arbroath
Forfar Athletic v Queen's Park
Ross County v Montrose

SCOTTISH CROWDS UP AGAIN

Scottish League attendances exceeded four million in aggregate last season – an increase of 6.2 per cent.

Rangers topped the list with an average of 43,342, and **Celtic's** gate increased to 33,925 with the opening of their new stand.

Top average crowd in Div. 1 was **Dundee United's** 7,701. Lowest average in Scotland was **Cowdenbeath**'s 332.

GM VAUXHALL CONFERENCE FIXTURES 1996-97

Saturday 17th August

Altrincham v Rushden & Diamonds
Hayes v Southport
Hednesford Town v Dover Athletic
Kidderminster Harriers v Gateshead
Macclesfield Town v Kettering Town
Morecambe v Woking
Northwich Victoria v Bath City
Slough Town v Stalybridge Celtic
Stevenage Borough v Halifax Town
Telford United v Farnborough Town
Welling United v Bromsgrove Rovers

Monday 19th August

Hednesford T. v Stevenage Borough

Tuesday 20th August

Bromsgrove Rovers v Telford United
Dover Athletic v Hayes
Farnborough T. v Kidderminster Har.
Halifax Town v Altrincham
Kettering Town v Welling United
Slough Town v Rushden & Diamonds
Southport v Stalybridge Celtic
Woking v Bath City

Wednesday 21st August

Gateshead v Northwich Victoria
Morecambe v Macclesfield Town

Saturday 24th August

Altrincham v Welling United
Bath City v Kettering Town
Bromsgrove Rovers v Southport
Dover Athletic v Kidderminster Har.
Farnborough T. v Macclesfield T.
Halifax Town v Slough Town
Rushden & Dia'ds v Northwich Vic.
Stalybridge Celtic v Hayes
Stevenage Borough v Morecambe
Telford United v Gateshead
Woking v Hednesford Town

Monday 26th August

Bath City v Dover Athletic
Gateshead v Altrincham
Hayes v Rushden & Diamonds
Kettering Town v Woking
Kidderminster Harriers v Slough Town
Macclesfield T. v Stevenage Borough
Morecambe v Telford United
Northwich Victoria v Bromsgrove Rov.
Southport v Halifax Town
Stalybridge Celtic v Hednesford Town
Welling United v Farnborough Town

Saturday 31st August

Farnborough Town v Gateshead
Hayes v Bromsgrove Rovers
Hednesford Town v Bath City
Kettering Town v Halifax Town
Macclesfield Town v Dover Athletic
Northwich Vic. v Stevenage Borough
Rushden & Dia'ds v Stalybridge Celtic
Slough Town v Altrincham
Southport v Kidderminster Harriers
Welling United v Morecambe
Woking v Telford United

Monday 2nd September

Hednesford Town v Northwich Victoria
Kidderminster Harr. v Stalybridge C.
Stevenage Borough v Welling United

Tuesday 3rd September

Altrincham v Morecambe
Bromsgrove Rovers v Kettering Town
Dover Athletic v Woking
Farnborough Town v Hayes
Halifax Town v Gateshead
Rushden & Diamonds v Macclesfield T.
Slough Town v Bath City
Telford United v Southport

Saturday 7th September

Bath City v Gateshead
Bromsgrove Rovers v Macclesfield T.
Dover Athletic v Altrincham
Halifax Town v Rushden & Diamonds
Kettering Town v Hayes
Kidderminster Har. v Welling United
Morecambe v Hednesford Town
Southport v Slough Town
Stalybridge Celtic v Woking
Telford United v Stevenage Borough

Monday 9th September

Hednesford T. v Bromsgrove Rovers
Northwich Vic. v Rushden & Diamonds
Stevenage Borough v Bath City

Tuesday 10th September

Altrincham v Halifax Town
Hayes v Kidderminster Harriers
Kettering Town v Dover Athletic
Macclesfield Town v Morecambe

Stalybridge Celtic v Telford United
Welling United v Slough Town
Woking v Farnborough Town

Wednesday 11th September

Gateshead v Southport

Saturday 14th September

Altrincham v Woking
Kidderminster Har. v Macclesfield T.
Northwich Victoria v Telford United
Slough Town v Bromsgrove Rovers

Monday 16th September

Kidderminster Har. v Stevenage B.

Tuesday 17th September

Bath City v Hayes
Bromsgrove Rovers v Altrincham
Dover Athletic v Slough Town
Halifax Town v Stalybridge Celtic
Rushden & Dia'ds v Farnborough T.
Southport v Northwich Victoria
Telford United v Kettering Town

Wednesday 18th September

Morecambe v Gateshead

Saturday 21st September

Altrincham v Kidderminster Harriers
Farnborough Town v Morecambe
Gateshead v Dover Athletic
Hayes v Halifax Town
Kettering Town v Southport
Macclesfield Town v Bath City
Slough Town v Hednesford Town
Stalybridge Celtic v Northwich Victoria
Stevenage Boro. v Bromsgrove Rov.
Welling United v Telford United
Woking v Rushden & Diamonds

Monday 23rd September

Northwich Victoria v Hednesford Town

Tuesday 24th September

Altrincham v Southport
Bath City v Kidderminster Harriers
Farnborough T. v Bromsgrove Rovers
Halifax Town v Telford United
Hayes v Welling United
Rushden & Dia'ds v Stevenage B.
Slough Town v Kettering Town
Stalybridge Celtic v Morecambe
Woking v Dover Athletic

Wednesday 25th September

Gateshead v Macclesfield Town

Saturday 28th September

Bromsgrove Rovers v Slough Town
Northwich Victoria v Macclesfield Town
Telford United v Altrincham

Monday 30th September

Hednesford T. v Rushden & Diamonds
Kidderminster Harriers v Hayes

Tuesday 1st October

Altrincham v Stalybridge Celtic
Dover Athletic v Bath City
Kettering Town v Farnborough Town
Macclesfield Town v Halifax Town
Slough Town v Woking
Southport v Gateshead
Telford United v Bromsgrove Rovers
Welling United v Stevenage Borough

Wednesday 2nd October

Morecambe v Northwich Victoria

Saturday 5th October

Bath City v Altrincham
Bromsgrove Rovers v Gateshead
Halifax Town v Kidderminster Harriers
Hayes v Telford United
Hednesford Town v Farnborough Town
Northwich Victoria v Dover Athletic
Rushden & Diamonds v Welling United
Slough Town v Morecambe
Stalybridge Celtic v Kettering Town
Stevenage Borough v Southport
Woking v Macclesfield Town

Monday 7th October

Bath City v Welling United
Dover Athletic v Rushden & Diamonds
Farnborough Town v Hayes
Halifax Town v Altrincham
Kettering Town v Slough Town
Stalybridge Celtic v Telford United

Saturday 12th October

Altrincham v Northwich Victoria
Dover Athletic v Farnborough Town
Gateshead v Morecambe
Kettering Town v Hednesford Town
Kidderminster Har. v Rushden & Dia'ds
Macclesfield Town v Stalybridge Celtic
Telford United v Bath City
Welling United v Hayes
Woking v Stevenage Borough

Saturday 19th October

Bath City v Stalybridge Celtic
Bromsgrove Rovers v Dover Athletic
Farnborough T. v Stevenage Borough
Halifax Town v Woking
Hayes v Altrincham
Hednesford Town v Southport
Macclesfield Town v Welling United
Morecambe v Kettering Town
Northwich Vic. v Kidderminster Har.
Rushden & Diamonds v Gateshead
Slough Town v Telford United

Saturday 26th October

Farnborough T. v Northwich Victoria

Saturday 2nd November

Altrincham v Slough Town
Dover Athletic v Halifax Town
Kettering Town v Gateshead
Kidderminster Har. v Farnborough T.
Morecambe v Bath City
Northwich Victoria v Hayes
Southport v Rushden & Diamonds
Stalybridge Celtic v Bromsgrove Rov.
Stevenage Borough v Woking
Telford United v Macclesfield Town
Welling United v Hednesford Town

Saturday 9th November

Bath City v Halifax Town
Bromsgrove Rov. v Stevenage Borough
Farnborough Town v Kettering Town
Gateshead v Welling United
Hayes v Stalybridge Celtic
Hednesford Town v Altrincham
Rushden & Diamonds v Dover Athletic
Slough Town v Kidderminster Harriers
Southport v Macclesfield Town
Telford United v Morecambe
Woking v Northwich Victoria

Saturday 16th November

Hayes v Farnborough Town
Morecambe v Slough Town
Welling United v Bath City

Tuesday 19th November

Macclesfield Town v Hednesford Town

Saturday 23rd November

Altrincham v Farnborough Town
Bath City v Woking
Dover Athletic v Telford United
Halifax Town v Welling United
Kettering Town v Bromsgrove Rovers
Kidderminster Har. v Hednesford T.
Macclesfield Town v Hayes
Morecambe v Rushden & Diamonds
Northwich Victoria v Slough Town
Stalybridge Celtic v Southport
Stevenage Borough v Gateshead

Saturday 30th November

Bromsgrove Rovers v Morecambe
Farnborough Town v Southport
Halifax Town v Kettering Town
Hayes v Gateshead
Hednesford Town v Stalybridge Celtic
Rushden & Diamonds v Bath City
Slough Town v Macclesfield Town
Stevenage Borough v Dover Athletic
Telford United v Kidderminster Har.
Welling United v Northwich Victoria
Woking v Altrincham

Saturday 7th December

Altrincham v Stevenage Borough
Bath City v Hednesford Town
Gateshead v Woking
Kettering Town v Slough Town
Kidderminster Har. v Dover Athletic
Morecambe v Hayes
Northwich Victoria v Farnborough T.
Southport v Bromsgrove Rovers
Stalybridge Celtic v Halifax Town
Telford United v Rushden & Diamonds

Tuesday 10th December

Macclesfield T. v Kidderminster Har.

Saturday 14th December

Dover Athletic v Northwich Victoria
Farnborough Town v Slough Town
Gateshead v Bath City
Halifax Town v Morecambe
Hednesford Town v Hayes
Kidderminster Harriers v Kettering T.
Rushden & Dia'ds v Bromsgrove Rov.
Southport v Altrincham
Stalybridge Celtic v Macclesfield Town
Stevenage Borough v Telford United
Welling United v Woking

Saturday 21st December

Bath City v Stevenage Borough
Bromsgrove Rovers v Farnborough T.
Dover Athletic v Stalybridge Celtic
Hayes v Kettering Town
Hednesford Town v Gateshead
Macclesfield Town v Telford United
Morecambe v Altrincham
Northwich Victoria v Southport
Rushden & Dia'ds v Kidderminster Har.
Slough Town v Welling United
Woking v Halifax Town

Thursday 26th December

Altrincham v Macclesfield Town
Farnborough Town v Bath City
Gateshead v Stalybridge Celtic
Halifax Town v Northwich Victoria
Hayes v Woking
Kettering T. v Rushden & Diamonds
Kidderminster Har. v Bromsgrove Rov.
Southport v Morecambe
Stevenage Borough v Slough Town
Telford United v Hednesford Town
Welling United v Dover Athletic

Saturday 28th December

Altrincham v Bromsgrove Rovers
Farnborough Town v Dover Athletic
Gateshead v Halifax Town
Kidderminster Harriers v Bath City

Northwich Victoria v Morecambe
Southport v Hednesford Town
Stalybridge Celtic v Rushden & Dia'ds
Stevenage Borough v Hayes
Telford United v Welling United
Woking v Slough Town

Wednesday 1st January 1997

Bath City v Farnborough Town
Bromsgrove Rov. v Kidderminster Har.
Dover Athletic v Welling United
Hednesford Town v Telford United
Macclesfield Town v Altrincham
Morecambe v Southport
Northwich Victoria v Halifax Town
Rushden & Diamonds v Kettering T.
Slough Town v Stevenage Borough
Stalybridge Celtic v Gateshead
Woking v Hayes

Saturday 4th January

Altrincham v Hednesford Town
Farnborough Town v Woking
Gateshead v Slough Town
Halifax Town v Bromsgrove Rovers
Hayes v Dover Athletic
Kettering Town v Morecambe
Kidderminster Har. v Northwich Vic.
Southport v Bath City
Stevenage Borough v Macclesfield T.
Telford United v Stalybridge Celtic
Welling United v Rushden & Diamonds

Saturday 11th January

Bath City v Morecambe
Bromsgrove Rov. v Stalybridge Celtic
Dover Athletic v Southport
Gateshead v Telford United
Hayes v Stevenage Borough
Hednesford T. v Kidderminster Har.
Macclesfield Town v Woking
Northwich Victoria v Kettering Town
Rushden & Diamonds v Halifax Town
Slough Town v Farnborough Town
Welling United v Altrincham

Saturday 25th January

Altrincham v Hayes
Farnborough T. v Rushden & Dia'ds
Halifax Town v Hednesford Town
Kettering Town v Bath City
Macclesfield Town v Slough Town
Morecambe v Bromsgrove Rovers
Southport v Welling United
Stalybridge Celtic v Dover Athletic
Stevenage B. v Kidderminster Har.
Telford United v Northwich Victoria
Woking v Gateshead

Saturday 1st February

Bath City v Southport
Bromsgrove Rovers v Halifax Town
Dover Athletic v Kettering Town
Hayes v Macclesfield Town
Hednesford Town v Woking
Kidderminster Har. v Telford United
Northwich Victoria v Altrincham
Rushden & Diamonds v Morecambe
Slough Town v Gateshead
Stalybridge Celtic v Farnborough Town

Saturday 8th February

Southport v Stevenage Borough
Welling United v Stalybridge Celtic

Saturday 15th February

Dover Athletic v Bromsgrove Rovers
Farnborough Town v Stalybridge Celtic
Gateshead v Hednesford Town
Halifax Town v Bath City
Kidderminster Harriers v Altrincham
Macclesfield T. v Rushden & Dia'ds
Morecambe v Welling United
Slough Town v Northwich Victoria
Stevenage Borough v Kettering Town
Telford United v Hayes
Woking v Southport

Monday 17th February

Hednesford Town v Halifax Town

Saturday 22nd February

Altrincham v Telford United
Bath City v Macclesfield Town
Bromsgrove Rovers v Woking
Gateshead v Rushden & Diamonds
Halifax Town v Farnborough Town
Hayes v Slough Town
Hednesford Town v Morecambe
Kettering T. v Kidderminster Harriers
Northwich Victoria v Welling United
Southport v Dover Athletic
Stalybridge Celtic v Stevenage B.

Saturday 1st March

Bromsgrove Rovers v Hayes
Dover Athletic v Stevenage Borough
Farnborough Town v Altrincham
Kettering Town v Stalybridge Celtic
Macclesfield Town v Gateshead
Morecambe v Halifax Town
Rushden & Diamonds v Woking
Welling United v Southport

Saturday 8th March

Bath City v Bromsgrove Rovers
Dover Athletic v Macclesfield Town
Gateshead v Kettering Town
Hayes v Morecambe
Kidderminster Harriers v Halifax Town

Rushden & Diamonds v Hednesford T.
Southport v Farnborough Town
Stalybridge Celtic v Altrincham
Stevenage Borough v Northwich Vic.
Telford United v Slough Town
Woking v Welling United

Saturday 15th March

Altrincham v Bath City
Bromsgrove Rov. v Rushden & Dia'ds
Halifax Town v Dover Athletic
Kettering Town v Telford United
Macclesfield Town v Southport
Morecambe v Farnborough Town
Northwich Victoria v Gateshead
Slough Town v Hayes
Stevenage Borough v Hednesford T.
Welling United v Kidderminster Har.
Woking v Stalybridge Celtic

Saturday 22nd March

Bath City v Telford United
Bromsgrove Rov. v Northwich Victoria
Gateshead v Hayes
Hednesford Town v Kettering Town
Morecambe v Dover Athletic
Rushden & Diamonds v Slough Town
Southport v Woking
Stalybridge Celtic v Kidderminster Har.
Welling United v Halifax Town

Tuesday 25th March

Farnborough Town v Welling United
Halifax Town v Macclesfield Town
Kettering Town v Stevenage Borough

Saturday 29th March

Bath City v Slough Town
Dover Athletic v Rushden & Diamonds
Gateshead v Bromsgrove Rovers
Halifax Town v Southport
Hayes v Hednesford Town
Kettering Town v Altrincham
Kidderminster Harriers v Morecambe
Macclesfield Town v Northwich Victoria
Stalybridge Celtic v Welling United
Stevenage Borough v Farnborough T.
Telford United v Woking

Monday 31st March

Altrincham v Gateshead
Bromsgrove Rovers v Bath City
Farnborough Town v Halifax Town
Hednesford Town v Macclesfield Town
Morecambe v Stevenage Borough
Northwich Victoria v Stalybridge Celtic
Rushden & Diamonds v Hayes
Slough Town v Dover Athletic
Southport v Telford United
Welling United v Kettering Town

Woking v Kidderminster Harriers

Saturday 5th April

Bromsgrove Rovers v Hednesford T.
Dover Athletic v Morecambe
Gateshead v Farnborough Town
Hayes v Northwich Victoria
Rushden & Diamonds v Southport
Stalybridge Celtic v Bath City
Stevenage Borough v Altrincham
Welling United v Macclesfield Town
Woking v Kettering Town

Saturday 12th April

Altrincham v Dover Athletic
Bath City v Rushden & Diamonds
Gateshead v Stevenage Borough
Hednesford Town v Welling United
Kettering Town v Northwich Victoria
Kidderminster Town v Woking
Macclesfield v Farnborough
Southport v Slough Town
Telford United v Halifax Town

Saturday 19th April

Bath City v Welling United
Dover Athletic v Gateshead
Halifax Town v Hayes
Hednesford Town v Slough Town
Morecambe v Kidderminster Harriers
Rushden & Diamonds v Telford United
Southport v Kettering Town
Stevenage B. v Stalybridge Celtic
Woking v Bromsgrove Rovers

Saturday 26th April

Altrincham v Kettering Town
Farnborough Town v Hednesford Town
Hayes v Bath City
Kidderminster Harriers v Southport
Macclesfield T. v Bromsgrove Rovers
Morecambe v Stalybridge Celtic
Northwich Victoria v Woking
Slough Town v Halifax Town
Stevenage B. v Rushden & Diamonds
Telford United v Dover Athletic
Welling United v Gateshead

Saturday 3rd May

Bath City v Northwich Victoria
Bromsgrove Rovers v Welling United
Dover Athletic v Hednesford Town
Farnborough Town v Telford United
Gateshead v Kidderminster Harriers
Halifax Town v Stevenage Borough
Kettering Town v Macclesfield Town
Rushden & Diamonds v Altrincham
Southport v Hayes
Stalybridge Celtic v Slough Town
Woking v Morecambe